The Routledge Handbook of Discourse Processes

The second edition of *The Routledge Handbook of Discourse Processes* provides a state-of-the-art overview of the field of discourse processes, highlighting the subject's interdisciplinary foundations and bringing together established and emergent scholars to provide a dynamic roadmap of the evolution of work in these areas.

This new edition reflects several of the enormous changes in the world since the publication of the first edition—changes in modes of communication and an increased urgency to understand how people comprehend and trust information. The contents of this volume attempt to address fundamental questions about what we should now be thinking about reading, listening, talking, and writing. The chapters collected here represent a wide range of empirical methods currently available: lab or field experiments, with a range of measures, from quantitative to qualitative; observational studies, including classrooms or organizational communication; corpus analyses; conversation analysis; computational modeling; and linguistic analyses. The chapters also draw attention to the explosion of contextually rich and computationally intensive data analysis tools which have changed the research landscape, along with more contemporary measures of people's discourse use, from eye-tracking to video analysis tools to brain scans. *The Routledge Handbook of Discourse Processes, Second edition* is the ideal resource for graduate students, researchers, and practitioners in a variety of disciplines, including discourse analysis, conversation analysis, cognitive psychology, and cognitive science.

Michael F. Schober is Professor of Psychology and Vice Provost for Research at The New School, USA. He served as Editor of *Discourse Processes* from 2005–15.

David N. Rapp is Professor of Psychology and Learning Sciences and a Charles Deering McCormick Professor of Teaching Excellence at Northwestern University, USA. He is the current Editor of *Discourse Processes*.

M. Anne Britt is Distinguished Teaching and Research Professor of Psychology at Northern Illinois University, USA. She recently was Co-PI on the IES-funded Project READI, which focused on evidence-based argumentation for disciplinary learning.

Routledge Handbooks in Linguistics

Routledge Handbooks in Linguistics provide overviews of a whole subject area or sub-discipline in linguistics, and survey the state of the discipline including emerging and cutting-edge areas. Edited by leading scholars, these volumes include contributions from key academics from around the world and are essential reading for both advanced undergraduate and postgraduate students.

Further titles in this series can be found online at www.routledge.com/series/RHIL

The Routledge Handbook of Heritage Language Education
Edited by Olga E. Kagan, Maria M. Carreira, and Claire Hitchins Chik

The Routledge Handbook of Language and Humor
Edited by Salvatore Attardo

The Routledge Handbook of Language and Dialogue
Edited by Edda Weigand

The Routledge Handbook of Language and Politics
Edited by Ruth Wodak and Bernhard Forchtner

The Routledge Handbook of Language and Media
Edited by Daniel Perrin and Colleen Cotter

The Routledge Handbook of Ecolinguistics
Edited by Alwin F. Fill and Hermine Penz

The Routledge Handbook of Lexicography
Edited by Pedro A. Fuertes-Olivera

The Routledge Handbook of Discourse Processes, Second Edition
Edited by Michael F. Schober, David N. Rapp, and M. Anne Britt

The Routledge Handbook of Discourse Processes

Second Edition

Edited by Michael F. Schober, David N. Rapp, and M. Anne Britt

NEW YORK AND LONDON

Second edition published 2018
by Routledge
605 Third Avenue, New York, NY 10017

and by Routledge
2 Park Square, Milton Park, Abingdon, Oxon, OX14 4RN

First issued in paperback 2022

Routledge is an imprint of the Taylor & Francis Group, an informa business

© 2018 Taylor & Francis

The right of Michael F. Schober, David N. Rapp, and M. Anne Britt to be
identified as the authors of the editorial material, and of the authors for their
individual chapters, has been asserted in accordance with sections 77 and 78
of the Copyright, Designs and Patents Act 1988.

All rights reserved. No part of this book may be reprinted or reproduced or
utilised in any form or by any electronic, mechanical, or other means, now
known or hereafter invented, including photocopying and recording, or in
any information storage or retrieval system, without permission in writing
from the publishers.

Every effort has been made to contact copyright-holders. Please advise
the publisher of any errors or omissions, and these will be corrected in
subsequent editions.

Trademark notice: Product or corporate names may be trademarks or
registered trademarks, and are used only for identification and explanation
without intent to infringe.

Publisher's Note
The publisher has gone to great lengths to ensure the quality of this reprint
but points out that some imperfections in the original copies may be apparent.

First edition published by Routledge 2003

Library of Congress Cataloging-in-Publication Data
A catalog record for this book has been requested

ISBN 13: 978-1-03-240206-2 (pbk)
ISBN 13: 978-1-138-92009-5 (hbk)
ISBN 13: 978-1-315-68738-4 (ebk)

DOI: 10.4324/9781315687384

Typeset in Times New Roman
by Swales & Willis Ltd, Exeter, Devon, UK

Contents

List of Figures	*viii*
List of Contributors	*ix*

Introduction: Discourse Processes Evolving   1
Michael F. Schober, David N. Rapp, and M. Anne Britt

PART I
Overviews   **5**

1 Reading Comprehension Theories: A View from the Top Down   7
Panayiota Kendeou and Edward J. O'Brien

2 Theories and Approaches to the Study of Conversation and
Interactive Discourse   22
William S. Horton

3 Studying Discourse Processes in Institutional Contexts   69
Adrian Bangerter and Joep Cornelissen

PART II
Research Methods for Studying Discourse Processes:
State of the Art and Challenges   **97**

4 Research Methods: Conversation Analysis   99
Saul Albert

5 Research Methods: The Study of Language Processing in
Human Conversation   109
Sarah Brown-Schmidt

Contents

6 Research Methods: Big Data Approaches to Studying Discourse
Processes 117
Michael N. Jones and Melody W. Dye

7 Research Methods: Online Measures of Text Processing 125
Johanna K. Kaakinen

8 Research Methods: Neuroscientific Methods to Study Discourse
Processes 131
Christopher A. Kurby

PART III
Topical Reviews **139**

9 The Role of Sourcing in Discourse Comprehension 141
Ivar Bråten, Marc Stadtler, and Ladislao Salmerón

10 Discourse Updating: Acquiring and Revising Knowledge through
Discourse 167
Tobias Richter and Murray Singer

11 Discourse Processing in Technology-Mediated Environments 191
Darren Gergle

12 Discourse and Expertise: The Challenge of Mutual Understanding
between Experts and Laypeople 222
Rainer Bromme and Regina Jucks

13 Discourse Processing and Development through the Adult Lifespan 247
Elizabeth A. L. Stine-Morrow and Gabriel A. Radvansky

14 The Cognitive Neuroscience of Discourse: Covered Ground and
New Directions 269
Jeffrey M. Zacks, Raymond A. Mar, and Navona Calarco

15 Beliefs and Discourse Processing 295
Michael B. Wolfe and Thomas D. Griffin

16 Classroom Discourse: What Do We Need to Know for Research
and for Practice? 315
Catherine O'Connor and Catherine Snow

Contents

17 The Modern Reader: Should Changes to How We Read Affect
    Research and Theory?   343
    Joseph P. Magliano, Matthew T. McCrudden, Jean-Francois Rouet,
    and John Sabatini

18 Toward an Integrated Perspective of Writing as a Discourse Process   362
    Danielle S. McNamara and Laura K. Allen

    Afterword: World-Wide Changes in Discourse and the Changing
    Field of Discourse Processes   390
    Arthur C. Graesser, Morton Ann Gernsbacher, and
    Susan R. Goldman

Index   397

Figures

3.1	Three grand traditions of research on discourse and their relative explanatory foci	72
4.1	Paul and Anne's pattern of gaze orientation in Extract 4.1	102
5.1	Example tangram figures	110
11.1	Example chat interfaces from Gergle et al. (2004) that manipulate the degree of text persistence	196
11.2	The hardware prototype developed and used by Yatani and colleagues (2012)	200
11.3	The panel on the left illustrates that when Player 1 touches a piece the relevant tactile feedback is provided to Player 2. When Player 2 touches the screen, Player 1 receives tactile feedback on the same area of the device	201
11.4	Work by Mutlu and colleagues uses a robotic agent, Robovie, to explore computational and generative models of role-signaling, turn-taking, and topic-signaling in multi-party environments	203
14.1	Meta-analytic results from Mar (2011) visualizing brain regions associated with narrative comprehension	276
18.1 a–b	Together these two figures illustrate that the three writing stages (planning, translating, and reviewing) were no longer specified in Hayes' *stage theory* model, and the primary additions were the addition of working memory, motivation, and affect	365

Contributors

Saul Albert, Postdoctoral Associate in Psychology, Tufts University, Massachusetts, USA.

Laura K. Allen, Assistant Professor of Psychology, Department of Psychology, Mississippi State University, Mississippi, USA.

Adrian Bangerter, Professor of Work Psychology, Institute of Work and Organizational Psychology, University of Neuchâtel, Switzerland.

Ivar Bråten, Professor of Educational Psychology, University of Oslo, Oslo, Norway.

M. Anne Britt, Professor of Psychology, Northern Illinois University, DeKalb, Illinois, USA.

Rainer Bromme, Senior Professor of Science Communication, University of Muenster, Muenster, Germany.

Sarah Brown-Schmidt, Associate Professor of Psychology and Human Development, Vanderbilt University, Nashville, Tennessee, USA.

Navona Calarco, Research Analyst at the Research Imaging Centre, Campbell Family Mental Health Institute, Centre for Addiction and Mental Health, Toronto, Canada.

Joep Cornelissen, Professor of Corporate Communication and Management, Rotterdam School of Management, Erasmus University, The Netherlands.

Melody W. Dye, PhD Candidate, Cognitive Science Program, Indiana University, Bloomington, Indiana, USA.

Darren Gergle, Professor of Communication Studies and Electrical Engineering and Computer Science (by courtesy), Northwestern University, Evanston, Illinois, USA.

Morton Ann Gernsbacher, Vilas Research Professor and Sir Frederic Bartlett Professor of Psychology, University of Wisconsin-Madison, Madison, Wisconsin, USA.

Susan R. Goldman, Distinguished Professor of Liberal Arts & Sciences, Psychology and Education; Co-Director Learning Sciences Research Institute, University of Illinois at Chicago, Illinois, USA.

ix

Contributors

Arthur C. Graesser, Distinguished University Professor of Interdisciplinary Research, Department of Psychology and Institute for Intelligent Systems, University of Memphis, Memphis, Tennessee, USA.

Thomas D. Griffin, Assistant Professor, Department of Psychology, University of Illinois at Chicago, Illinois, USA.

William S. Horton, Associate Professor of Psychology, Northwestern University, Evanston, Illinois, USA.

Michael N. Jones, W. K. Estes Professor of Psychology and Cognitive Science, Indiana University, Bloomington, Indiana, USA.

Regina Jucks, Professor, Institute of Psychology for Education, University of Muenster, Muenster, Germany.

Johanna K. Kaakinen, PhD, University lecturer, University of Turku, Finland.

Panayiota Kendeou, Associate Professor of Educational Psychology and Guy Bond Chair in Reading, University of Minnesota, Twin Cities, Minnesota, USA.

Christopher A. Kurby, Associate Professor of Psychology, Department of Psychology, Grand Valley State University, Allendale, Michigan, USA.

Joseph P. Magliano, Professor of Psychology and Director of the Center for the Interdisciplinary Study of Language and Literacy, Northern Illinois University, DeKalb, Illinois, USA.

Raymond A. Mar, Associate Professor of Psychology, York University, Toronto, Ontario, Canada.

Matthew T. McCrudden, Associate Professor of the Faculty of Education, Victoria University of Wellington, Wellington, New Zealand.

Danielle S. McNamara, Professor of Psychology, Department of Psychology, Institute for the Science of Teaching and Learning, Arizona State University, Tempe, Arizona, USA.

Edward J. O'Brien, Professor of Psychology, University of New Hampshire, Durham, New Hampshire, USA.

Catherine O'Connor, Professor of Education and Linguistics, School of Education, Boston University, Boston, Massachusetts, USA.

Gabriel A. Radvansky, Professor of Psychology, University of Notre Dame, Notre Dame, Indiana, USA.

David N. Rapp, Professor of Learning Sciences and Professor of Psychology, Northwestern University, Evanston, Illinois, USA.

Contributors

Tobias Richter, Professor of Psychology, University of Würzburg, Germany.

Jean-Francois Rouet, Senior Researcher with the French National Center for Scientific Research (CNRS), University of Poitiers, Poitiers, France.

John Sabatini, Senior Researcher at Educational Testing Services, Princeton, New Jersey, USA.

Ladislao Salmerón, Associate Professor of Psychology, University of Valencia, Valencia, Spain.

Michael F. Schober, Professor of Psychology, New School for Social Research; Vice Provost for Research, The New School, New York, USA.

Murray Singer, PhD, Professor Emeritus, University of Manitoba, Winnipeg, Manitoba, Canada.

Catherine Snow, Patricia Albjerg Graham Professor, Harvard University Graduate School of Education, Cambridge, Massachusetts, USA.

Marc Stadtler, Associate Professor of Psychology, University of Muenster, Muenster, Germany.

Elizabeth A. L. Stine-Morrow, Professor of Educational Psychology, Psychology, the Beckman Institute, University of Illinois at Urbana-Champaign, Illinois, USA.

Michael B. Wolfe, Professor of Psychology, Grand Valley State University, Allendale, Michigan, USA.

Jeffrey M. Zacks, Professor of Psychological & Brain Sciences and of Radiology, and Associate Chair of Psychological & Brain Sciences, Washington University in Saint Louis, Saint Louis, Missouri, USA.

Introduction
Discourse Processes Evolving

Michael F. Schober, David N. Rapp, and M. Anne Britt

Many of us now routinely engage in new modes of discourse that would have been unimaginable in even the relatively recent past: texting on sophisticated mobile devices with emoji and audio attachments—maybe even dictating the text message rather than typing it; posting visual images on social media networks for friends that may well be seen by strangers; providing information to an automated telephone agent on the way to talking to a live human employee; writing a quick response to an online newspaper article that is immediately available to be seen by millions; or chatting with family members across the world via video, from our living rooms or while we are walking on a city street, while also seeing ourselves in a "self view" window. We respond to voice messages with an email, switch to talking face to face in the middle of a text interchange, and forward news items to individuals and groups with breathtaking ease. And we communicate across the globe in unprecedented ways, seeing immediate live news feeds from places we may know little about, posting messages that go viral and cause unanticipated effects in sectors we hadn't imagined they would. We have access to more and more different kinds of information, and to the means of delivering anything we might be thinking about to others, than have ever been available or might even have been anticipated in the recent past.

At the same time, we continue to talk face to face and on the phone, read novels and newspapers (though perhaps not only on paper), and even occasionally write letters or shopping lists by hand. Traditional spoken and written forms of discourse—the kinds that discourse process researchers have been focusing on for years—have not yet disappeared, and are not going anywhere soon, even among the most enthusiastic adopters of new modes and technologies for interaction. And of course not everyone is part of the communication revolution, whether through lack of access or by choice. For many in the world, the infrastructure supporting access to complex communication technologies has yet to be built (and may never be built), and the expense of adopting new technologies can be prohibitive. And even among those who have access, some people prefer familiar modes—talking face to face rather than talking with an automated system, reading a newspaper in print rather than online, or telling a story in person rather than leaving traces of thoughts and actions online that could have unintended consequences with unimagined audiences.

So we are in a time of intense transition, in which daily discourse continues to be transformed by the introduction of new communication options, some of which will take hold and spread, and some that will fade away. At least in some modes of discourse, the boundaries between reading, listening, writing, and talking have become more porous. Or at least the opportunities to participate and create new streams of discourse have expanded: People can read knowing that as they read, they can make their thoughts immediately available if they want to, and that the author and other readers might respond. Listeners can be aware that a video record of speech that in the past would have been evanescent is now reviewable in a way that can hold speakers newly accountable—and that might change the care with which speakers speak and the longer-term consequences of what they say.

We have also entered a period of intense questioning about the basis of facts and information, struggling with which sources of information can be trusted, and considering how divergent narratives and world views can—or can't—be reconciled. There is a new need to understand how beliefs and understandings proliferate in "echo chambers" and "filter bubbles" of subcommunities of communication, what kinds of communication persuade people, and how communication dynamics and flow, in both old and new media, connect with individual understandings, expectations, and attitudes.

All this makes it an exciting time for researchers interested in understanding the mental and interactive processes underlying discourse empirically—for seasoned researchers and for those entering the multidisciplinary study of discourse processes. This second edition of the *Handbook of Discourse Processes* is intended as an update to the earlier 2003 edition that presents new reviews of the scientific state of the art in various domains of discourse processing. It also reflects at least some of the enormous changes in the world since the publication of the first edition—changes in modes of communication and an increased urgency to understand how people comprehend and trust information. The contents of this volume attempt to address fundamental questions about how differently—if at all—we should now be thinking about reading, listening, talking, and writing. Have the mental processes involved in reading (for example) changed in an important way, for some or all readers? Or is the difference really in *what* we are reading, and in what way we are engaging with content, and with what kind of interactivity and multi-modal task-switching? Are the mental processes required for planning spoken discourse that considers potential unintended audiences new ones that need to be documented and catalogued, or can current theories and accounts accommodate new kinds of speaking?

As in the first edition, the chapters collected here represent a wide range of empirical methods currently available: lab or field experiments (with a range of measures, from quantitative to qualitative), observational studies (e.g., of classrooms or organizational communication), corpus analyses, conversation analysis, computational modeling, and linguistic analyses. The chapters also draw attention to the explosion of contextually rich and computationally intensive data analysis tools which have changed the research landscape, along with more contemporary measures of people's discourse use, from eye-tracking to video analysis tools to brain scans.

Organizing Strategy

This edition of the handbook differs from the first in a few ways that are designed to address how the world and how discourse research have changed since the first edition. First, a number of the chapters were commissioned from pairs or teams of researchers who represent different strands of expertise within a topic area (sometimes even holding contradictory views), and who

Introduction

in several cases had never written together before. Our intention was for these contributions to represent a greater breadth of perspectives and background knowledge than the individual researchers would be likely to incorporate, and we hoped that this interaction between researchers might articulate new and useful framings and understandings. Many thanks to the contributors who were willing to take a chance on working in this way; we think the results bring new insights that demonstrate how important cross-field fertilization is in addressing the complexity of discourse.

Second, the opening chapters that present overviews of theories and challenges that cross many areas of discourse processing include not only chapters about reading (Kendeou and O'Brien) and interactive conversation (Horton), but also a chapter that articulates and adds into the theoretical mix an additional set of approaches from organizational communication (Bangerter and Cornelissen). As we see it, contextualizing where and how different streams of research that don't always connect as communities of practice might fit together is particularly important as modes and forms of discourse change. These chapters present useful syntheses from perspectives that have been central to the empirical study of discourse but that haven't always connected with each other.

Third, this edition includes a set of chapters that focus specifically on methods of empirical discourse research. Given the proliferation of available methods and the range of approaches, it seemed important—and, we hope, useful—for a handbook to highlight methodological advances, catalog their successes and challenges, and clarify which kinds of questions can be addressed through which different methods. As a multidisciplinary enterprise that examines complex phenomena, the study of discourse processes requires a willingness to attend to and make use of multiple methods, and these chapters in the handbook make this explicit.

The chapters that make up the remainder of the handbook encompass a set of problem areas of practical significance that also represent critical areas of research focus in the scientific study of discourse processing. The range of topics by necessity covers only a sampling of possible areas, but it ranges widely, from sourcing in discourse comprehension (Bråten, Stadtler, and Salmerón) to acquiring and revising knowledge through discourse (Richter and Singer), discourse processing in technology-mediated environments (Gergle), mutual understanding between experts and laypeople (Bromme and Jucks), discourse development through the adult lifespan (Stine-Morrow and Radvansky), the cognitive neuroscience of discourse (Zacks, Mar, and Calarco), beliefs and discourse processing (Wolfe and Griffin), classroom discourse (O'Connor and Snow), how modern reading should or shouldn't change our theoretical accounts (Magliano, McCrudden, Rouet, and Sabatini), and writing as a discourse process (McNamara and Allen).

Finally, the handbook includes an Afterword by the editors of the first edition (Graesser, Gernsbacher, and Goldman). We are grateful that they approached us about the project of creating an updated handbook, and we believe their take on the changes in the field since that edition and on the material in this edition should be invaluable to the reader.

Many questions not addressed in this handbook, of course, remain. There is a need for critical work on, for example, multilingual and cross-community discourse in a globalizing world, and cultural influences on different kinds of discourse. Much remains to be explored about the interplay between individual-level mental processes and larger networked social processes, and about the specific cumulative effects of individual moments of learning and interaction. We hope that the material in this handbook—the syntheses of research and theorizing, the presentation of methods, and the framing of new questions—encourages current and next generations of researchers to build on what is known thus far to investigate the continuing evolution of discourse and the processes underlying it.

Part I
Overviews

1

Reading Comprehension Theories

A View from the Top Down

Panayiota Kendeou
UNIVERSITY OF MINNESOTA

Edward J. O'Brien
UNIVERSITY OF NEW HAMPSHIRE

The Nature of Reading Comprehension

Comprehension is complex and multidimensional. It depends on the execution and integration of many processes (for reviews, see Alexander & The Disciplined Reading and Learning Research Laboratory, 2012; Kendeou & Trevors, 2012; McNamara & Magliano, 2009; RAND, 2002). To understand a sentence, for example, one must visually process the words, identify their phonological, orthographic, and semantic representations, and connect words using rules of syntax to form an understanding of the underlying meaning. In this chapter, we do not focus on any of the factors that help readers at these lower levels of the comprehension process (Perfetti & Stafura, 2014). Instead, we focus on comprehension processes beyond individual words and sentences. These comprehension processes help readers understand and integrate meaning across sentences, make use of relevant background knowledge, generate inferences, identify the discourse structure, and take into consideration the authors' goals and motives (Graesser, 2015). The end product is a mental representation that reflects an overall meaning of the extended written discourse. For all of these comprehension processes to be successful, many interacting factors play a role, such as reader characteristics, text properties, and the demands of the task at hand (Kintsch, 1998; RAND, 2002; Rapp & van den Broek, 2005). These factors individually and jointly influence reading processes and products. Achieving a basic level of comprehension that reflects the intended meaning of a simple text, however, is not sufficient. Individuals must also be able to analyze, synthesize, and evaluate information within and across texts (Alexander & DRLRL, 2012; NAEP, 2013). These even higher-level processes result in *deeper comprehension* (Graesser, 2015) and learning from texts (Goldman & Pellegrino, 2015).

Discourse scientists have recently called for a focus on these sorts of higher-level processes (Kendeou, McMaster, & Christ, 2016; McNamara, Jacovina, & Allen, 2016) that support deeper comprehension of the texts we read (Graesser, 2015), and thus deep learning (Goldman & Pellegrino, 2015). These calls have implications for shifting the focus of the discourse processes field from the investigation of passive to strategic processes and from simple to complex products. In this chapter, we discuss the implications for embracing this shift in focus in the context of theories and models of reading comprehension. We also provide an overview of the main challenges this shift in focus poses for our existing theoretical frameworks, methods, and definitions.

Embracing Complexity: A Theory of Reading Comprehension?

The complexity of reading comprehension demands a theory that describes the cognitive and linguistic processes involved, as well as their respective interactions across development. Recently, Perfetti and Stafura (2014) argued that "There is no theory of reading, because reading has too many components for a single theory" (p. 22). This statement begs the question: Does the complexity of reading truly limit the development of a comprehensive theory of reading comprehension? We agree with Perfetti and Stafura that for a phenomenon as complex as reading comprehension it is unlikely to develop a single, comprehensive theory in a traditional sense. But if we cannot develop a comprehensive theory of reading comprehension, what is the alternative? One alternative is the development of multiple theories, each focusing on a separate component of reading. This approach has been fruitful for the development of theories for lower-level processes, such as the reading and learning of words (see Ehri, 2014 for a review). A second alternative is the development of a 'good-enough' approximation of a theory of reading comprehension. In fact, discourse scientists have put forth several models and frameworks that have attempted to do just that. These models and frameworks are concerned with the mental representation the reader constructs in the process of understanding entire texts. As such, collectively they consist of a good theoretical approximation of many component processes that would be needed to develop a comprehensive model of reading comprehension.

Reviewing current models of reading comprehension processes is beyond the scope of this chapter, and excellent reviews can be found elsewhere (e.g., McNamara & Magliano, 2009). We would like, however, to highlight the focus and main claims of several of these models. To this end, we will briefly review the prominent models in the extant literature that deal with the comprehension of single texts, because the comprehension of multiple texts will be touched upon in other sections in this volume. These single-text models include the Construction-Integration model (Kintsch & van Dijk, 1978; Kintsch, 1988), the Structure Building model (Gernsbacher, 1990), the Resonance model (Myers & O'Brien, 1998; O'Brien & Myers, 1999), the Event-Indexing model (Zwaan, Magliano, & Graesser, 1995), the Causal Network model (Trabasso, van den Broek, & Suh, 1989), the Constructionist model (Graesser, Singer, & Trabasso, 1994), and the Landscape model (van den Broek, Young, Tzeng, & Linderholm, 1999). Each of these models taps into different aspects of reading comprehension processes and, collectively, they provide a complete view of reading comprehension processes.

The Construction-Integration model (Kintsch, 1988) posits that comprehension involves two phases – construction and integration. Construction is the activation of information in the text along with the reader's related prior knowledge, whereas integration is the spreading of the activation. The result of these two phases is the construction of a mental representation of what the text is about (i.e., a situation model). In the Structure Building model

(Gernsbacher, 1990) comprehension involves laying a foundation structure at the beginning of reading a text that serves to map subsequent text information. When subsequent text information maps well on this structure, it gets integrated into the evolving mental representation, and when it does not the reader shifts and lays a foundation for another structure. Importantly, Gernsbacher proposed that these processes (i.e., laying the foundation, mapping, and shifting) are common across modalities (text, discourse, picture, video). The Resonance model (Myers & O'Brien, 1998; O'Brien & Myers, 1999) describes factors that influence the activation of information from the text and the reader's prior knowledge during reading. The model has been employed to show that memory-based retrieval mechanisms are sufficient to explain much of what is involved in the activation of information that is used to construct inferences during reading. It has also provided an excellent account of how readers gain access to earlier portions of a text (e.g., Albrecht & O'Brien, 1995; O'Brien, 1995; Peracchi & O'Brien, 2004). The Event-Indexing model (Zwaan et al., 1995) specifies five dimensions of coherence during situation model construction that readers are sensitive to and monitor during reading: time, space, causality, motivation, and agents. The Causal Network model (Trabasso et al., 1989) describes situation model construction through the lens of causal reasoning, and outlines four types of causal relations (enabling, psychological, motivational, and physical) that facilitate the construction of causal networks during reading. The Constructionist model (Graesser et al., 1994) focuses on the deliberate, strategic processes that can result in deep comprehension. The Landscape model (van den Broek et al., 1999) posits comprehension as the fluctuation of concept activation that is driven by text factors as well as the reader's criteria for comprehension or standards of coherence.

To date, we contend that the best approximation to a theory of reading comprehension is the Construction-Integration (CI) model. The CI model (Kintsch & van Dijk, 1978; Kintsch, 1988; van Dijk & Kintsch, 1983) describes the iterative processes in mapping current discourse input to the prior discourse context and background knowledge. *Construction* refers to the activation of the information in the text and background knowledge. There are four potential sources of activation during the construction phase: the current text input (e.g., a proposition), the prior sentence, background knowledge, and prior text. As this information is activated, it is connected into a network of propositions and concepts. *Integration* refers to the continuous spread of activation within this network with the level of activation of individual propositions fluctuating until activation settles. Eventually, over iterations, the level of activation of individual propositions within the network stabilizes. Activation sources from the construction process are iteratively integrated within the limits set by working memory. This iterative process prunes the network so that only those concepts and ideas that are connected to many others stay in the network; less connected concepts lose activation and drop from the model. This pruning process tends to maintain concepts and ideas that are relevant to the current situation model while reducing activation of irrelevant concepts and ideas. With every new cycle this process repeats and, at the completion of reading, the result is a situation model, namely a mental representation of what the text is about.

The notion of a *situation model* proposed in the context of the CI model is central in the discourse literature because it is considered the final product of reading comprehension, whereas its construction involves the processes of reading comprehension. Despite its sophistication and status as the best approximation of what the reader takes away from a completed comprehension process, situation models are insufficient to account for what is described as *deeper comprehension* (Graesser, 2015). Deeper comprehension also involves *higher-order thinking* (McNamara et al., 2016) such as analyzing, synthesizing, and evaluating information. No current model, including the CI model, can sufficiently explain this level of comprehension. An excellent example of the distinction between understanding at the level of the situation model and understanding what goes beyond the situation model is demonstrated in Goldman's recent work on the comprehension of literary texts (e.g., narratives, folk tales, poems, science fiction), as exemplified by the differences between a 'literal stance' and an 'interpretive stance' (Goldman, McCarthy, & Burkett, 2015). Specifically, in the context of a literal stance, namely an orientation toward what the text 'says,' readers develop an understanding of what the text is about akin to the situation model level. However, in the context of an interpretive stance, namely an orientation toward what the text 'means' (e.g., comprehending the intended meaning of a fable or parable), readers develop an understanding abstracted from the specific situation. For example, an interpretive understanding of the fable about "the tortoise and the hare" requires far more than the development of a situation model of a race between a tortoise and a hare; it requires a much deeper interpretive understanding (i.e., slow and steady wins the race). This level of understanding constitutes deeper comprehension.

Greater precision in the conceptualization and prediction of deeper comprehension is, in our view, a reasonable target for the development of a comprehensive theory of reading comprehension. Engaging in further theory development in the field of discourse processes is important not only for the field itself, but also for its position in current and future policy initiatives aimed at increasing reading proficiency and learning (Goldman & Pellegrino, 2015; Graesser, 2015; Kendeou et al., 2016). McNamara and Magliano (2009) noted that such a comprehensive theory can only be viable if it can generate testable predictions and be computationally implemented. In doing so, there needs to be a greater specification of reading comprehension processes and products across a range of situations, readers, and tasks. We turn to this issue next.

From Passive to Strategic Processes

Given the increased focus on deeper comprehension, we believe that the field of discourse processes needs to move toward *greater specification and approximation* of deeper comprehension as a product and the processes involved in it. Inevitably, this also means moving toward greater specification and approximation of *strategic processing*, as strategic processing and deeper comprehension are closely intertwined. That is, strategic processing is often necessary for deeper comprehension to occur (Graesser, 2007). We do not deny, however, that in situations in which we are dealing with a highly-skilled reader with expertise in a particular domain, deeper comprehension could also occur with relatively few, if any, strategic processes (Ericsson & Kintsch, 1995). But, in general, we contend that as we increase the focus on deeper comprehension, it requires that we increasingly shift our focus away from passive processes and more toward strategic processes.

Strategic processes are intentional, voluntary, and generally fully conscious; they are also more amenable to self-regulation and tend to rely more on serial processing (Schneider & Shiffrin, 1977; Sternberg, 1999). These characteristics make strategic processes more dependent on attentional resources and subject to voluntary control. In contrast, passive processes are effortless, unintentional, and generally outside conscious awareness; they are also difficult to stop or regulate and typically rely on a parallel type of processing (Schneider & Shiffrin, 1977; Sternberg, 1999). These characteristics make passive processes relatively independent of attentional resources and not subject to voluntary control.

Despite these definitions, trying to define with any degree of precision exactly what constitutes passive and strategic processing during reading comprehension is an almost impossible task because the line that divides passive from strategic processes is thin. Not only is it thin, but it is always fluctuating and shifting as a function of the reader, the text, and the task at hand. For example, the process of generating inferences that can be strategic for some individuals (mediated by expertise; Ericsson & Kintsch, 1995), texts (mediated by background knowledge demands; McNamara & Kintsch, 1996), tasks (Cerdán, Gilabert, & Vidal-Abarca, 2011; Rouet, Vidal-Abarca, Erboul, & Millogo, 2001), instructions (McCrudden, Magliano, & Schraw, 2010; McCrudden & Schraw, 2007), or goals (Kendeou, Bohn-Gettler, & Fulton, 2011; van den Broek, Lorch, Linderholm, & Gustafson, 2001) can at other times be passive. During these fluctuations from strategic to passive processes, comprehension is a fluid, dynamic mixture of processes that cannot be meaningfully distinguished on the passive–strategic continuum. For this reason, it makes sense to examine strategic processes in situations in which we are not operating near that elusive thin line or boundary with passive processes. In fact, to the extent that we try to examine processes that operate close to that elusive line, we simply open up unhelpful arguments about which side of the line the specific process is actually operating.

Avoiding this thin elusive line that divides passive from strategic comprehension processes makes sense when the goal is to examine comprehension processes that are primarily either passive or strategic. Note, however, that we do not deny that trying to estimate where that line lands in specific situations is important, so that we can understand better the conditions that enable a shift from passive to strategic comprehension. For example, Long and Lea (2005) argued that such a shift will likely take place during the integration phase of comprehension when a convergence-like passive process is deemed inadequate. Van den Broek, Rapp, and Kendeou (2005) argued that such a shift is determined by a reader's standards of coherence and the extent to which those are met. To the extent that identifying the conditions that influence the position of the line and predict its fluctuations has merit, and we believe that it does, more systematic research is needed to do so.

Relatedly, there has been a healthy debate in the field of discourse processes about the role of passive and strategic processes during reading comprehension. This is also reflected in the relative emphasis on the importance of passive (or memory-based) and strategic (goal-directed) processes that varies across different models (McNamara & Magliano, 2009). For example, the Resonance model heavily emphasizes passive processes, whereas the Constructionist model emphasizes strategic ones. Importantly, however, neither view denies that comprehension is driven by both passive and strategic processes.

Overall, in the field's current understanding of comprehension, we have learned a great deal about the *passive processes* involved in comprehension and much less about the *strategic processes*. Thus, future research on passive processes is likely only to refine much of what we already know (see O'Brien & Cook, 2015). Future research on strategic processes, however, has the potential to advance the field in ways that can approximate with ever-increasing precision a theory of reading comprehension that can also account for deeper comprehension – and we contend that understanding deeper comprehension is a crucial next step in the evolution of theories of reading comprehension.

Examining Complexity: A Cluster Approach

Moving toward a greater understanding of *the mechanisms and limitations* of strategic processing in the service of deeper comprehension (e.g., Goldman et al., 2015; Graesser, 2015; McNamara et al., 2016) begs for identifying a paradigm that will allow for the programmatic and systematic investigation of these challenging questions. In this context, a paradigm in which one tries to isolate and examine individual processes will not work because by definition strategic processes are driven by the reader. Once we bring in the reader *as a factor*, we have a minimum of two factors that interact (i.e., the reader and the text) in ways that cannot be easily partialled out. And it is extremely challenging to derive a set of clear rules that predict, *a priori*, how these factors interact to impact strategic comprehension processes.

This challenge raises yet another question: If by default we have multiple factors interacting and driving strategic processes, then how can we examine strategic processes systematically? It makes more sense to accept that we are dealing with multiple factors; that is, *a cluster* of factors at play. One way to address this challenge is a *cluster approach*, which involves considering a *cluster* of factors that tend to co-occur. These factors may be the result of manipulations at the level of the instructional context in which reading takes place (such as reading instructions), text properties (such as the structure of a text, genre), and reader characteristics (such as reading skill, working memory, prior knowledge) in various permutations. Previous work that has identified specific interactions and co-variation among these factors can serve as the foundation for the cluster approach proposed here.

To be clear, what we are proposing is not a traditional reader-by-text-by-task-components interaction approach, even though it may lead to such an investigation. Instead, we conceptualize clusters as a group of processes that maximize the similarity of observations within the same group and minimize the similarity of observations across different groups. Within such an approach it is likely that initially clusters may have a relatively large size, which weakens our ability to predict comprehension. But successively they can get smaller, which will allow for better approximation and prediction. Thus, even though initially these clusters may be large and unwieldy, with continuous experimentation intending to identify processes that continuously co-occur, these clusters should begin to break down to smaller clusters, which increases the potential of being directly manipulated and tested. Just as important, as the size of a cluster decreases, the number of identified clusters ought to increase; and this creates greater precision. From a methodological point of view, the identification of clusters involves a shift from a variable-oriented approach (that assumes data are drawn from a homogeneous population) to a person-oriented approach (that assumes data are drawn from more than one population) and back again (von Eye & Bogat, 2006). A person-oriented approach employs methods that decompose data into groups (e.g., cluster analysis and latent class analysis), establishes the external validity of the groups, and interprets them based on theory.

Consider, for example, work in the field of reading disabilities where a cluster of factors has been identified at the reader level. Specifically, following the influential Simple View of Reading (SVR; Gough & Tunmer, 1986; Hoover & Gough, 1990), researchers examined the co-variation of two key components, decoding and comprehension, and identified groups of readers with low comprehension and high decoding performance (often labeled 'poor comprehenders'), who exhibit specific patterns of reading behavior. It has been estimated that approximately 10% of students in Grades 2–4 are classified as 'poor comprehenders' (for reviews, see Hogan, Adlof, & Alonzo, 2014; Hulme & Snowling, 2011; Spencer, Quinn, & Wagner, 2014) who struggle with reading comprehension even though their decoding skills are intact. This group is the result of considering only two factors that tend to co-occur, but its identification with precision allowed researchers to better understand poor comprehenders' strategic reading behavior, or lack thereof, through direct experimentation. Another example comes from the work of expertise and working memory. Ericsson and Kintsch (1995) proposed the notion of 'long-term working memory' as an expanded working memory capacity to account for the ability of experts within a domain to access reliably and quickly relevant background knowledge. They supported their claims from work in text comprehension and expert performance. In this context, prior knowledge and working memory are the two factors involved, and the specific cluster identified is 'high prior knowledge-high working memory.' This cluster allowed Ericsson and Kintsch to study more systematically the conditions under which a process shifts from passive to strategic status and vice versa. A final example comes from the work of McNamara and colleagues (McNamara, 2001; McNamara & Kintsch, 1996; McNamara, Kintsch, Songer, & Kintsch, 1996) on the reverse cohesion effect, namely the interaction between reader prior knowledge and text cohesion, such that high-knowledge readers show better comprehension when they read a low-cohesion than when they read a high-cohesion version of a text. Importantly, using this cluster as the starting point, O'Reilly and McNamara (2007) examined the role of reading skill and showed that less-skilled, high-knowledge readers benefit from low-cohesion texts, whereas skilled, high-knowledge readers benefit from high-cohesion texts (the reverse 'reverse cohesion effect').

It is important to understand and appreciate that much of the early work following such a bottom-up, descriptive approach would be unlikely to uncover novel and exciting new findings; but it will serve to identify clusters of factors that already have some intuitive appeal – that is, they tend to co-occur as a function of specific situations, readers, and text types. This is part of the challenge and we cannot stress enough how difficult this challenge may be. Upon the identification of robust clusters, however, we can apply traditional experimental paradigms to investigate strategic comprehension in a systematic way.

Prior Knowledge: An Integral Component

As we increase the focus on strategic processes and deeper comprehension, the focus also shifts to the role of prior knowledge during discourse experiences (e.g., Albrecht & O'Brien, 1991; Myers, Cook, Kambe, Mason, & O'Brien, 2000). However, existing models and theories have yet to adequately incorporate prior knowledge as an integral component of reading comprehension (Kendeou et al., 2016). Perhaps the most impressive influence of prior knowledge during reading is that it can both facilitate and interfere with the acquisition of new knowledge from text (Kendeou & O'Brien, 2015). Knowledge acquisition in this context involves the process of encoding new information in memory, the success of which is often gauged by how well the information can later be retrieved from memory. Equally important is knowledge revision; that is, the modification of pre-existing, often incorrect knowledge in memory that must be revised to accommodate newly acquired information. There is renewed interest in various literatures in both of these comprehension products, knowledge acquisition and knowledge revision, and the processes associated with them (Cervetti & Hiebert, 2015; Common Core State Standards Initiative, 2010; Goldman & Pellegrino, 2015; Rapp & Braasch, 2014).

Knowledge acquisition during reading is currently the focus in the context of the Common Core State Standards/English Language Arts and Literacy in the United States (CCSS/ELA, 2010). Among the significant changes brought by the CCSS/ELA is a focus on knowledge development in different domains or disciplines (Cervetti & Hiebert, 2015), defined as situated reading practices within specific disciplines (Lee & Spratley, 2010). Knowledge revision during reading is also currently the focus in the context of investigations of the misinformation effect (Ecker, Lewandowsky, Cheung, & Maybery, 2015; Rapp, Hinze, Kohlhepp, & Ryskin, 2014), revising misconceptions (Braasch, Goldman, & Wiley, 2013; Kendeou & O'Brien, 2014; Sinatra & Broughton, 2011), and updating

(Kendeou, Smith, & O'Brien, 2013; O'Brien, Cook, & Guéraud, 2010; O'Brien, Cook, & Peracchi, 2004; O'Brien, Rizzella, Albrecht, & Halleran, 1998; Pérez, Cain, Castellanos, & Bajo, 2015; Rapp & Kendeou, 2007, 2009).

Kendeou and O'Brien (2014) suggested that knowledge acquisition and knowledge revision during reading are closely intertwined. Specifically, by definition, in the early stage of the knowledge revision process, the knowledge base will be dominated by pre-existing knowledge; evidence that any sort of knowledge revision has occurred will be subtle and difficult to measure. It is only after the amount, and quality, of new information integrated into the knowledge base (i.e., knowledge acquisition) crosses some threshold that overt evidence of knowledge revision will be detected. Thus, knowledge acquisition and knowledge revision during reading involve the same underlying processes; the main distinction is that revision has the added burden to overcome previously acquired information, whereas knowledge acquisition takes advantage of previously acquired information.

Does the added burden of knowledge revision to overcome previously acquired information necessitate strategic processes? We contend that the answer depends on the level at which the knowledge is misconceived. Specifically, Chi (2008) specifies three levels of misconceived knowledge: (a) false beliefs, (b) flawed mental models, and (c) incorrect ontological categories. A false belief is a single incorrect idea – often equated with incorrect factual information; a mental model is an organized system of ideas or beliefs that are interrelated; finally, ontological categories are organizational systems designed to categorize concepts. As Kendeou, Walsh, Smith, and O'Brien (2014) have demonstrated, strategic comprehension is not always required for the revision of knowledge misconceived at the individual belief level – the presentation of an explicit causal explanation that refutes the incorrect belief and provides the correct information creates a well-integrated network of information that is sufficient to eliminate activation of the misconceived prior knowledge. However, for misconceived knowledge at higher levels, it would be difficult to achieve revision without recruiting strategic processes.

Just as important, if we start to bring in specific reader factors to the knowledge revision process, then we enter a level of processing that requires strategic processes. For example, consider what happens when the to-be-revised information implicates the self or is personally relevant to the reader. Prasad et al. (2009) found that self-identified Republicans strengthened their original belief in a connection between the events of 9/11 and the Iraqi government *after* that connection was explicitly refuted and challenged. The phenomenon of intensified original beliefs as a consequence of an attempted correction is often referred to as the 'backfire effect' (Nyhan & Reifler, 2010). Other researchers have observed similar effects for a range of issues including climate change (Hart & Nisbet, 2012), genetically modified foods (Trevors, Muis, Pekrun, Sinatra, & Winne, 2016), and vaccinations (Nyhan & Reifler, 2015; Nyhan, Reifler, Richey, & Freed, 2014). These findings suggest that the recruitment of strategic processes to justify one's knowledge and beliefs can also impede knowledge revision and highlight the need to understand better the relation and interdependencies between strategic processes and comprehension in various contexts (see Richter & Singer, this volume).

Implications of Embracing and Examining Complexity

Increased focus on the examination of strategic processes and deeper comprehension has several implications. One implication pertains to the actual texts used to examine such processes. Specifically, investigating the complexity of strategic processes requires using naturalistic texts. Such texts can account for a large number of text factors, many of which have been partially uncovered through the systematic manipulations of 'textoids' in typical lab settings. Textoids are texts in which a particular process of interest can be isolated and examined. These texts have been used extensively when examining passive processes because they allow for control and isolation of specific processes. However, when examining strategic processes, which are by definition more complex, it becomes increasingly difficult to observe them in the content of textoids. Consider, for example, a study by McNerney, Goodwin, and Radvansky (2011) that examined comprehension of an extended, real-world novel. These researchers assessed whether text factors that have been identified in textoids would also influence comprehension of the longer narrative. The study demonstrated that even though many of the 'text-based' factors identified in previous research clearly impacted comprehension, there were also important differences between findings obtained with textoids and this naturalistic text. For example, even though reading times increased – reflecting increased processing – during the introduction of new characters in the extended text (consistent with findings from textoids), reading times did not increase during the introduction of a new setting in the extended text (inconsistent with findings from textoids).

A second implication pertains to the ways in which deeper comprehension as a construct by itself is assessed in standardized settings. In fact, recent approaches to assessment fit well within the 'top-down' view of reading comprehension that embraces its complexity and contextual nature (Magliano & Graesser, 2012). For example, the Global Integrated Scenario-Based Assessment (GISA; O'Reilly & Sabatini, 2013; Sabatini & O'Reilly, 2013) views reading comprehension as a complex, goal-directed activity, and as such, it draws on the extant literature to assess deep comprehension in authentic environments that focus on the synergy of several factors rather than on individual factors or components. On the other hand, the Reading Inventory and Scholastic Evaluation (RISE; Sabatini & O'Reilly, 2013) assesses specific factors that have been identified in the extant literature, such as vocabulary and fluency. Most important, when relations between GISA and RISE were explored, Sabatini, O'Reilly, Halderman, and Bruce (2014) reported that the RISE subtests accounted for approximately 65% of the variance in GISA. Part of the residual variance unaccounted for presumably comprises the complex, deep comprehension required in GISA that cannot be captured by the individual factors themselves. Motivation and strategy knowledge have to be part of this unaccounted variance as well (McNamara et al., 2016).

A third implication pertains to the 'transformation' of strategic processes to trainable reading comprehension strategies. Specifically, as we identify with greater precision the factors that influence strategic processes during reading, we can use that information to develop and teach effective reading comprehension strategies tailored for specific types of readers, texts, and tasks. Graesser (2007) defined a reading strategy as "a cognitive or behavioral action that is enacted under a particular contextual condition, with the goal of improving some aspect of comprehension" (p. 7). Alexander and DRLRL (2012) defined strategies as "intentional, purposeful, and effortful procedures" to solve problems during reading (p. 264). As we initiate work to understand better the nuances of strategic processes, we will be able to also identify when, and under what conditions, specific reading strategies are likely to be the most effective.

A fourth implication pertains to factors that have received little attention to date in discourse processes but have documented influences on higher-order processes. One such factor is emotions. Emotions influence intrinsic motivation (Kang et al., 2009), attention allocation (Scrimin & Mason, 2015), and learning (D'Mello, Lehman, Pekrun, & Graesser, 2014; Muis et al., 2015). In their comprehensive review, Fiedler and Beier (2014) note that negative emotions may facilitate conscientiousness, the avoidance of surface-level errors, selective attention on task-relevant stimuli, and detailed representations, whereas positive emotions facilitate constructive inferences, creative problem-solving, and higher-order organization and integration of complex stimuli. In the context of reading comprehension, Bohn-Gettler and Rapp (2011) found that participants who were induced into positive or negative moods engaged in a greater proportion of paraphrasing and a lower proportion of non-coherence building processes during comprehension (e.g., associations, opinions) than were participants who received a neutral induction (see also Bohn-Gettler & Rapp, 2014). Recent work also highlights the relations between emotions and knowledge and attitude revision (Broughton, Sinatra, & Nussbaum, 2013; Sinatra & Seyranian, 2016; Trevors et al., 2016).

Finally, as we shift our focus to strategic processes and deep comprehension, there may be more opportunities for the integration of different modes of communication. Discourse scientists investigate not only reading, but also writing, oral conversation, and other forms of communication (Graesser, 2015). Both reading and writing are considered aspects of written language, whereas conversation is considered an aspect of oral language. Further, reading comprehension is a receptive use of language, whereas oral conversation and writing are productive uses of language. Even though the integration of reading, writing, and oral conversation is important, the complexity of these discourse processes has given rise to the development of distinct lines of disciplinary inquiry in each (e.g., Horton & Gerrig, 2005; Schober & Clark, 1989). These lines have the potential to converge in the study of strategic processes. For example, work on argumentation emphasizes both comprehension of arguments during reading and production of arguments during writing in a single paradigm (Iordanou, Kendeou, & Beker, 2016) and across disciplines (Lee & Spratley, 2010) in the service of learning.

Conclusions

Comprehension of discourse requires the cooperative completion of many component processes. Some of these processes are passive in nature; others are more strategic. Passive processes are typically categorized as lower-level processes (e.g., activation, integration), whereas strategic processes are typically categorized as higher-order processes (e.g., analyzing, synthesizing, and evaluating information). Overall, in our current understanding of comprehension, we have learned a great deal about the passive processes involved, and much less about the strategic processes. Future research on passive processes is likely to only refine much of what we already know (see O'Brien & Cook, 2015). However, future research on strategic processes has the potential to advance the field of discourse processes in ways that can approximate with ever-increasing precision a theory of reading comprehension that can also account for deeper comprehension – and we contend that understanding deeper comprehension is an important next step in the evolution of theories of reading comprehension. In concert with theoretical developments within the field, recent policy initiatives in the United States (CCSS/ELA, 2010) have also resulted in a greater focus on higher-level processes that support deeper comprehension. This increased focus has implications for the direction of the discourse processes field in the future. As we shift our attention from passive to strategic processes and from simple to complex products, we need to embrace the complexity of reading comprehension in a way that preserves scientific rigor while approximating a theory of reading comprehension with increased precision. Doing so is not only challenging, but also requires revisiting and revising our definitions, methods, and theoretical models and frameworks. In this context, we offer one potential approach (i.e., the cluster approach), not with the goal of advocating it as the correct approach, but rather as one of many potential approaches with the goal of stimulating our thinking, and ultimately to reach a more complete understanding of the comprehension process.

Acknowledgments

The authors would like to thank David N. Rapp, Brooke R. Lea, Andrew Elfenbein, Gregory Trevors, Sashank Varma, Reese Butterfuss, and the UMN Textgroup for their comments on earlier versions of this chapter.

Suggested Reading

Alexander, P. A., & The Disciplined Reading and Learning Research Laboratory (DRLRL). (2012). Reading into the future: Competence for the 21st century. *Educational Psychology, 47*(4), 259–280.
Graesser, A. C. (2015). Deeper learning with advances in discourse science and technology. *Policy Insights from the Behavioral and Brain Sciences, 2*(1), 42–50.
Kendeou, P., McMaster, K. L., & Christ, T. J. (2016). Reading comprehension: Core components and processes. *Policy Insights from the Behavioral and Brain Sciences, 3*, 62–69.
McNamara, D. S., & Magliano, J. (2009). Toward a comprehensive model of comprehension. *Psychology of Learning and Motivation, 51*, 297–384.
O'Brien, E. J., & Cook, A. E. (2015). Models of discourse comprehension. In A. Pollatsek & R. Treiman (Eds), *The Oxford handbook of reading* (pp. 217–231). London: Oxford University Press.

References

Albrecht, J. E., & O'Brien, E. J. (1991). Effects of centrality on retrieval of text-based concepts. *Journal of Experimental Psychology: Learning, Memory, and Cognition, 17*, 932–939.
Albrecht, J. E., & O'Brien, E. J. (1995). Goal processing and the maintenance of global coherence. In R. F. Lorch & E. J. O'Brien (Eds), *Sources of coherence in reading* (pp. 159–176). Hillsdale, NJ: Erlbaum.
Alexander, P. A., & The Disciplined Reading and Learning Research Laboratory (DRLRL). (2012). Reading into the future: Competence for the 21st century. *Educational Psychology, 47*(4), 259–280.
Bohn-Gettler, C. M., & Rapp, D. N. (2011). Depending on my mood: Mood-driven influences on text comprehension. *Journal of Educational Psychology, 103*(3), 562–577.
Bohn-Gettler, C. M., & Rapp, D. N. (2014). Emotions in reading and writing. In R. Pekrun & L. Linnenbrink-Garcia (Eds), *Handbook of emotions in education* (pp. 437–457). London: Taylor and Francis.
Braasch, J. L., Goldman, S. R., & Wiley, J. (2013). The influences of text and reader characteristics on learning from refutations in science texts. *Journal of Educational Psychology, 105*(3), 561–578.
Broughton, S. H., Sinatra, G. M., & Nussbaum, E. M. (2013). "Pluto has been a planet my whole life!" Emotions, attitudes, and conceptual change in elementary students' learning about Pluto's reclassification. *Research in Science Education, 43*, 529–550. doi:10.1007/s11165-011-9274-x.
Cerdán, R., Gilabert, R., & Vidal-Abarca, E. (2011). Selecting information to answer questions: Strategic individual differences when searching texts. *Learning and Individual Differences, 21*(2), 201–205.
Cervetti, G. N., & Hiebert, E. H. (2015). The sixth pillar of reading instruction. *The Reading Teacher, 68*, 548–551.
Chi, M. T. H. (2008). Three types of conceptual change: Belief revision, mental model transformation, and categorical shift. In S. Vosniadou (Ed.), *Handbook of research on conceptual change* (pp. 61–82). Hillsdale, NJ: Erlbaum.
Common Core State Standards Initiative (CCSS). (2010). *Common core state standards for English language arts and literacy in history/social studies, science, and technical subjects.* Washington, DC: CCSSO & National Governors Association.

D'Mello, S., Lehman, B., Pekrun, R., & Graesser, A. (2014). Confusion can be beneficial for learning. *Learning and Instruction, 29*, 153–170.

Ecker, U. K., Lewandowsky, S., Cheung, C. S., & Maybery, M. T. (2015). He did it! She did it! No, she did not! Multiple causal explanations and the continued influence of misinformation. *Journal of Memory and Language, 85*, 101–115.

Ehri, L. C. (2014). Orthographic mapping in the acquisition of reading, spelling memory, and vocabulary learning. *Scientific Studies of Reading, 18*, 5–12.

Ericsson, K. A., & Kintsch, W. (1995). Long-term working memory. *Psychological Review, 102*(2), 211–245.

Fiedler, K., & Beier, S. (2014). Affect and cognitive processes. In R. Pekrun & L. Linnenbrink-Garcia (Eds), *Handbook of emotions in education* (pp. 36–55). New York, NY: Routledge.

Gernsbacher, M. A. (1990). *Language comprehension as structure building*. Hillsdale, NJ: Lawrence Erlbaum.

Goldman, S. R., McCarthy, K. S., & Burkett, C. (2015). 17 interpretive inferences in literature. In E. J. O'Brien, A. E. Cook, & R. F. Lorch (Eds), *Inferences during reading* (pp. 386–410). Cambridge, UK: Cambridge University Press.

Goldman, S. R., & Pellegrino, J. W. (2015). Research on learning and instruction implications for curriculum, instruction, and assessment. *Policy Insights from the Behavioral and Brain Sciences, 2*(1), 33–41.

Gough, P. B., & Tunmer, W. E. (1986). Decoding, reading, and reading disability. *Remedial and Special Education, 7*(1), 6–10.

Graesser, A. C. (2007). An introduction to strategic reading comprehension. In D. S. McNamara (Ed.), *Reading comprehension strategies: Theories, interventions, and technologies* (pp. 3–26). Mahwah, NJ: Lawrence Erlbaum.

Graesser, A. C. (2015). Deeper learning with advances in discourse science and technology. *Policy Insights from the Behavioral and Brain Sciences, 2*(1), 42–50.

Graesser, A. C., Singer, M., & Trabasso, T. (1994). Constructing inferences during narrative text comprehension. *Psychological Review, 101*(3), 371–395.

Hart, P. S., & Nisbet, E. C. (2012). Boomerang effects in science communication: How motivated reasoning and identity cues amplify opinion polarization about climate mitigation policies. *Communication Research, 39*, 701–723. doi:10.1177/0093650211416646.

Hogan, T. P., Adlof, S. M., & Alonzo, C. N. (2014). On the importance of listening comprehension. *International Journal of Speech-Language Pathology, 16*(3), 199–207.

Hoover, W. A., & Gough, P. B. (1990). The simple view of reading. *Reading and Writing, 2*(2), 127–160.

Horton, W. S., & Gerrig, R. J. (2005). The impact of memory demands on audience design during language production. *Cognition, 96*(2), 127–142.

Hulme, C., & Snowling, M. J. (2011). Children's reading comprehension difficulties nature, causes, and treatments. *Current Directions in Psychological Science, 20*, 139–142.

Iordanou, K., Kendeou, P., & Beker, K. (2016). Argumentative reasoning. In J. A. Greene, W. A. Sandoval, & I. Bråten (Eds), *Handbook of epistemic cognition*. New York, NY: Routledge.

Kang, M. J., Hsu, M., Krajbich, I. M., Loewenstein, G., McClure, S. M., Wang, J. T., & Camerer, C. F. (2009). The wick in the candle of learning: Epistemic curiosity activates reward circuitry and enhances memory. *Psychological Science, 20*, 963–973.

Kendeou, P., Bohn-Gettler, C., & Fulton, S. (2011). What we have been missing: The role of goals in reading comprehension. In M. T. McCrudden, J. Magliano, & G. Schraw (Eds), *Text relevance and learning from text* (pp. 375–394). Charlotte, NC: Information Age Publishing.

Kendeou, P., McMaster, K. L., & Christ, T. J. (2016). Reading comprehension: Core components and processes. *Policy Insights from the Behavioral and Brain Sciences, 3*, 62–69.

Kendeou, P., & O'Brien, E. J. (2014). The knowledge revision components (KReC) framework: Processes and mechanisms. In D. N. Rapp & J. L. G. Braasch (Eds), *Processing inaccurate information: Theoretical and applied perspectives from cognitive science and the educational sciences* (pp. 353–377). Cambridge, MA: MIT Press.

Kendeou, P., & O'Brien, E. J. (2015). Prior knowledge: Acquisition and revision. In P. Afflerbach (Ed.), *Handbook of individual differences in reading: Text and context* (pp. 151–163). New York, NY: Routledge Publishing.

Kendeou, P., Smith, E. R., & O'Brien, E. J. (2013). Updating during reading comprehension: Why causality matters. *Journal of Experimental Psychology: Learning, Memory, & Cognition, 39*, 854–865.

Kendeou, P., & Trevors, G. (2012). Learning from texts we read: What does it take? In M. J. Lawson & J. R. Kirby (Eds), *The quality of learning* (pp. 251–275). Cambridge, UK: Cambridge University Press.

Kendeou, P., Walsh, E. K., Smith, E. R., & O'Brien, E. J. (2014). Knowledge revision processes in refutation texts. *Discourse Processes, 51*(5–6), 374–397.

Kintsch, W. (1988). The role of knowledge in discourse comprehension: A construction-integration model. *Psychological Review, 95*(2), 163–182.

Kintsch, W. (1998). *Comprehension: A paradigm for cognition.* New York, NY: Cambridge University Press.

Kintsch, W., & Van Dijk, T. A. (1978). Toward a model of text comprehension and production. *Psychological Review, 85*(5), 363–394.

Lee, C. D., & Spratley, A. (2010). *Reading in the disciplines: The challenges of adolescent literacy.* New York, NY: Carnegie Corporation.

Long, D. L., & Lea, R. B. (2005). Have we been searching for meaning in all the wrong places? Defining the "search after meaning" principle in comprehension. *Discourse Processes, 39*, 279–298.

Magliano, J. P., & Graesser, A. C. (2012). Computer-based assessment of student-constructed responses. *Behavior Research Methods, 44*(3), 608–621.

McCrudden, M. T., Magliano, J. P., & Schraw, G. (2010). Exploring how relevance instructions affect personal reading intentions, reading goals and text processing: A mixed methods study. *Contemporary Educational Psychology, 35*(4), 229–241.

McCrudden, M. T., & Schraw, G. (2007). Relevance and goal-focusing in text processing. *Educational Psychology Review, 19*(2), 113–139.

McNamara, D. S. (2001). Reading both high-coherence and low-coherence texts: Effects of text sequence and prior knowledge. *Canadian Journal of Experimental Psychology/Revue canadienne de psychologie expérimentale, 55*, 51–62.

McNamara, D. S., Jacovina, M. E., & Allen, L. K. (2016). Higher order thinking in comprehension. In P. Afflerbach (Ed.), *Handbook of individual differences in reading: Text and context* (pp. 164–176). New York, NY: Routledge.

McNamara, D. S., & Kintsch, W. (1996). Learning from texts: Effects of prior knowledge and text coherence. *Discourse Processes, 22*(3), 247–288.

McNamara, D. S., Kintsch, E., Songer, N. B., & Kintsch, W. (1996). Are good texts always better? Interactions of text coherence, background knowledge, and levels of understanding in learning from text. *Cognition and Instruction, 14*, 1–43.

McNamara, D. S., & Magliano, J. (2009). Toward a comprehensive model of comprehension. *Psychology of Learning and Motivation, 51*, 297–384.

McNerney, M. W., Goodwin, K. A., & Radvansky, G. A. (2011). A novel study: A situation model analysis of reading times. *Discourse Processes, 48*(7), 453–474.

Muis, K. R., Pekrun, R., Sinatra, G. M., Azevedo, R., Trevors, G., Meier, E., & Heddy, B. C. (2015). The curious case of climate change: Testing a theoretical model of epistemic beliefs, epistemic emotions, and complex learning. *Learning and Instruction, 39*, 168–183.

Myers, J. L., Cook, A. E., Kambe, G., Mason, R. A., & O'Brien, E. S. (2000). Semantic and episodic effects on bridging inferences. *Discourse Processes, 29*, 179–199.

Myers, J. L., & O'Brien, E. J. (1998). Accessing the discourse representation during reading. *Discourse Processes, 26*(2–3), 131–157.

National Assessment of Educational Progress (NAEP). (2013). *The nation's report card.* Retrieved from http://nces.ed.gov/nationsreportcard/subject/publications/main2013/pdf/2014451.pdf.

Nyhan, B., & Reifler, J. (2010). When corrections fail: The persistence of political misperceptions. *Political Behavior, 32*(2), 303–330.

Nyhan, B., & Reifler, J. (2015). Does correcting myths about the flu vaccine work? An experimental evaluation of the effects of corrective information. *Vaccine, 33*(3), 459–464.

Nyhan, B., Reifler, J., Richey, S., & Freed, G. L. (2014). Effective messages in vaccine promotion: A randomized trial. *Pediatrics, 133*(4), e835–e842.

O'Brien, E. J. (1995). Automatic components of discourse comprehension. In R. F. Lorch & E. J. O'Brien (Eds), *Sources of coherence in reading* (pp. 159–176). Hillsdale, NJ: Erlbaum.

O'Brien, E. J., & Cook, A. E. (2015). Models of discourse comprehension. In A. Pollatsek & R. Treiman (Eds), *The Oxford handbook of reading* (pp. 217–231). London: Oxford University Press.

O'Brien, E. J., Cook, A. E., & Guéraud, S. (2010). Accessibility of outdated information. *Journal of Experimental Psychology: Learning, Memory, and Cognition, 36*, 979–991.

O'Brien, E. J., Cook, A. E., & Peracchi, K. A. (2004). Updating situation models: A reply to Zwaan and Madden. *Journal of Experimental Psychology: Learning, Memory, and Cognition, 30*, 289–291.

O'Brien, E. J., & Myers, J. L. (1999). Text comprehension: A view from the bottom up. In S. R. Goldman, A. C. Graesser, & P. van den Broek (Eds), *Narrative comprehension, causality, and coherence: Essays in honor of Tom Trabasso* (pp. 35–53). Mahwah, NJ: LEA.

O'Brien, E. J., Rizzella, M. L., Albrecht, J. E., & Halleran, J. G. (1998). Updating a situation model: A memory-based text processing view. *Journal of Experimental Psychology: Learning, Memory, and Cognition, 24*(5), 1200–1210.

O'Reilly, T., & McNamara, D. S. (2007). Reversing the reverse cohesion effect: Good texts can be better for strategic, high-knowledge readers. *Discourse Processes, 43*(2), 121–152.

O'Reilly, T., & Sabatini, J. (2013). Reading for understanding: How performance moderators and scenarios impact assessment design. *ETS Research Report Series, 2013*(2), i–47.

Peracchi, K. A., & O'Brien, E. J. (2004). Character profiles and the activation of predictive inferences. *Memory & Cognition, 32*, 1044–1052.

Pérez, A., Cain, K., Castellanos, M. C., & Bajo, T. (2015). Inferential revision in narrative texts: An ERP study. *Memory & Cognition, 43*(8), 1105–1135.

Perfetti, C., & Stafura, J. (2014). Word knowledge in a theory of reading comprehension. *Scientific Studies of Reading, 18*(1), 22–37.

Prasad, M., Perrin, A. J., Bezila, K., Hoffman, S. G., Kindleberger, K., Manturuk, K., & Smith Powers, A. (2009). "There must be a reason": Osama, Saddam, and inferred justification. *Sociological Inquiry, 79*, 142–162.

RAND. (2002). *Reading for understanding: Toward an R&D program in reading comprehension.* Santa Monica, CA: RAND.

Rapp, D. N., & Braasch, J. L. G. (Eds) (2014). *Processing inaccurate information: Theoretical and applied perspectives from cognitive science and the educational sciences.* Cambridge, MA: MIT Press.

Rapp, D. N., Hinze, S. R., Kohlhepp, K., & Ryskin, R. A. (2014). Reducing reliance on inaccurate information. *Memory & Cognition, 42*, 11–26.

Rapp, D. N., & Kendeou, P. (2007). Revising what readers know: The effectiveness of refutations as a function of task and content. *Memory & Cognition, 35*, 2019–2032.

Rapp, D. N., & Kendeou, P. (2009). Noticing and revising discrepancies as texts unfold. *Discourse Processes, 46*, 1–24.

Rapp, D. N., & van den Broek, P. (2005). Dynamic text comprehension: An integrative view of reading. *Current Directions in Psychological Science, 14*, 276–279.

Rouet, J. F., Vidal-Abarca, E., Erboul, A. B., & Millogo, V. (2001). Effects of information search tasks on the comprehension of instructional text. *Discourse Processes, 31*(2), 163–186.

Sabatini, J., & O'Reilly, T. (2013). Rationale for a new generation of reading comprehension assessments. In B. Miller, L. E. Cutting, & P. McCardle (Eds), *Unraveling the behavioral, neurobiological, and genetic components of reading comprehension* (pp. 100–111). Baltimore, MD: Brooks Publishing.

Sabatini, J., O'Reilly, T., Halderman, L., & Bruce, K. (2014). Integrating scenario-based and component reading skill measures to understand the reading behavior of struggling readers. *Learning Disabilities Research & Practice, 29*(1), 36–43.

Schneider, W., & Shiffrin, R. M. (1977). Controlled and automatic human information processing: Detection, search, and attention. *Psychological Review, 84*(1), 1–66.

Schober, M. F., & Clark, H. H. (1989). Understanding by addressees and overhearers. *Cognitive Psychology, 21*(2), 211–232.

Scrimin, S., & Mason, L. (2015). Does mood influence text processing and comprehension? Evidence from an eye-movement study. *British Journal of Educational Psychology.* doi:10.1111/bjep.12080.

Sinatra, G. M., & Broughton, S. H. (2011). Bridging reading comprehension and conceptual change in science education: The promise of refutation text. *Reading Research Quarterly, 46*(4), 374–393.

Sinatra, G. M., & Seyranian, V. (2016). Warm change about hot topics: The role of motivation and emotion in attitude and conceptual change about controversial science topics. In L. Corno & E. Anderman (Eds), *APA handbook of educational psychology* (3rd ed.) (pp. 245–256). New York, NY: Routledge.

Spencer, M., Quinn, J. M., & Wagner, R. K. (2014). Specific reading comprehension disability: Major problem, myth, or misnomer? *Learning Disabilities Research & Practice, 29*(1), 3–9.

Sternberg, R. J. (1999). Intelligence as developing expertise. *Contemporary Educational Psychology, 24*(4), 359–375.

Trabasso, T., van den Broek, P., & Suh, S. Y. (1989). Logical necessity and transitivity of causal relations in stories. *Discourse Processes, 12*(1), 1–25.

Trevors, G., Muis, K. R., Pekrun, R., Sinatra, G., & Winne, P. H. (2016). Identity and epistemic emotions during knowledge revision: A potential account for the backfire effect. *Discourse Processes, 53*, 339–370. doi:10.1080/0163853X.2015.1136507.

van den Broek, P., Lorch, R. F. Jr, Linderholm, T., & Gustafson, M. (2001). The effects of readers' goals on inference generation and memory for texts. *Memory & Cognition, 29*, 1081–1087.

van den Broek, P., Rapp, D. N., & Kendeou, P. (2005). Integrating memory-based and constructionist processes in accounts of reading comprehension. *Discourse Processes, 39*(2–3), 299–316.

van den Broek, P., Young, M., Tzeng, Y., & Linderholm, T. (1999). The landscape model of reading: Inferences and the online construction of a memory representation. In H. van Oostendorp & S. R. Goldman (Eds), *The construction of mental representations during reading* (pp. 71–98). Mahwah, NJ: Erlbaum.

Van Dijk, T. A., & Kintsch, W. (1983). *Strategies of discourse comprehension.* New York, NY: Academic Press.

Von Eye, A., & Bogat, G. A. (2006). Person-oriented and variable-oriented research: Concepts, results, and development. *Merrill-Palmer Quarterly, 52*, 390–420.

Zwaan, R. A., Magliano, J. P., & Graesser, A. C. (1995). Dimensions of situation model construction in narrative comprehension. *Journal of Experimental Psychology: Learning, Memory, and Cognition, 21*(2), 386–397.

2

Theories and Approaches to the Study of Conversation and Interactive Discourse

William S. Horton

NORTHWESTERN UNIVERSITY

Introduction

Conversation is arguably the most fundamental means we have of interacting with others. Through conversation, people share information, form relationships, solve problems, and accomplish a multitude of everyday goals. From the time we acquire our first words in infancy, we spend much of our lives conversing—not only in person, but also via telephone, via email, and increasingly, via newer media online. Unsurprisingly, given its central importance as the primary setting for communication and social interaction, conversation in all its forms has been the focus of a great deal of scholarly work, as researchers from a variety of fields have sought to describe how people interact during conversation as well as the socio-cognitive mechanisms that shape these interactions.

In this chapter, I provide a highly selective overview of this work, focusing primarily upon several major strands of research that have had—and continue to have—a strong influence upon our understanding of the interpersonal and psychological determinants of spoken discourse. The chapter begins by describing some of the major contributions of Conversation Analysis concerning the structures and routines through which people engage in talk-in-interaction. Then, I turn to psycholinguistic research on conversational interaction, considering approaches that emphasize how interlocutors collaborate to accomplish particular communicative goals as well as approaches that focus primarily upon the underlying linguistic and cognitive processes that facilitate successful interactions. Work from these viewpoints illustrates quite vividly the extent to which language in interaction is a function of both individual processes and collaborative social action. Then, in the final section, I briefly describe several other areas of research that have the potential to provide a more complete picture of conversation and social interaction. While existing accounts have successfully identified a number of features and processes associated with canonical instances of face-to-face dialogue, it remains to be seen if and how these might translate to other forms and modes of social interaction.

The Nature of Conversation

The term *conversation* can refer to a variety of communicative situations, including 3:00am dorm room chats, workplace discussions, ordering food at a restaurant, or even text messages sent via smartphone. What most conversations have in common is the fact that they involve interactive, communicative exchanges between two or more people. Crucially, conversations involve more than just the autonomous encoding and decoding of linguistic messages—that is, utterances are not simply a "conduit" for information transmission between independent speakers and listeners (Cherry, 1956; Reddy, 1979). In the vast majority of conversational situations, the communicative actions of interlocutors are tightly coupled (Clark, 1996; Garrod, 1999); one person's contributions are shaped by what has been said previously in the discourse and in turn strongly shape what follows next. As a result, the meanings expressed in conversation emerge through the coordinated verbal and nonverbal contributions of speakers acting interdependently (what Krauss & Fussell, 1996, label the *dialogic* view of communication).

As an example of this interdependence in action, consider this time-stamped transcript of a portion of a telephone conversation, taken from the CallHome American English Corpus (Kingsbury, Strassel, McLemore, & McIntyre, 1997; original transcript notations left intact).

[EN_5388]

> 1692.84 1694.80 B: %um, have you talked to ((ever)), %um
>
> 1694.88 1696.00 B: what's her name &Sheila?
>
> 1696.73 1697.35 A: &Sheila who?
>
> 1697.62 1698.76 B: &Sheila %um
>
> 1699.30 1702.00 B: ne- %um what's her name &Nadine and them's sister.
>
> 1700.67 1701.07 A: ((&White))
>
> 1702.00 1702.93 A: (( ))
>
> 1703.11 1704.23 B: You see her still?
>
> 1703.94 1705.90 A: the twins getting ready to graduate girl.
>
> 1705.89 1706.62 B: Really?
>
> 1706.44 1706.92 A: Yes.
>
> 1707.16 1707.35 A: [baby crying]
>
> 1708.11 1709.28 A: I know we getting old.
>
> 1710.00 1711.17 B: [noise] whoa.
>
> 1711.10 1712.88 A: They in the b- (( )) this year.
>
> 1712.99 1714.83 A: {sniff} [baby making noise]
>
> 1714.04 1715.29 B: Golly.
>
> 1715.13 1716.36 A: &Nadine and &Sheila both a-

1716.52 1718.34 A: w- &Nadine with one and sh-

1718.50 1719.42 A: &Sheila's with the other one.

1719.45 1720.18 B: Really?

1720.03 1721.12 A: Doing the dance, yeah.

1722.17 1722.34 A: [baby]

1722.44 1723.31 B: %mm %mm %mm.

1723.77 1725.98 B: {breath} No &Sheila getting old. {laugh}

1723.99 1724.43 A: yeah.

1725.63 1726.51 A: {laugh}

1726.23 1728.01 B: She got some kids graduating.

1727.14 1727.58 A: (( )) [distortion]

1727.83 1728.58 A: uh-huh.

1728.91 1730.16 B: After all this time.

This conversation involves two friends (A and B) who have not spoken to each other in some time. In this excerpt, A is catching B up on news about their mutual acquaintance "Sheila." What is notable is how closely A and B work together throughout this interaction, first to identify Sheila and then to discuss her now-grown children. Yet, even though many of the utterances are seemingly incomplete or leave much unsaid (e.g., "*with one . . . with the other one*"), the speakers appear to have only momentary difficulties ("*Sheila who?*") as the interaction unfolds. They tease each other ("*I know we getting old*") and even share in a joke ("*No Sheila getting old*"). Ordinary conversations such as this are rarely like the idealized interactions found in screenplays written for the stage or screen (Linell, 1998, 2005). As even the most cursory examination of transcripts or recordings of real interactions quickly makes clear, a simple encoding/decoding perspective is unlikely to ever be sufficient to account for what people actually do in conversation.

Communicative Constraints

How, then, have researchers attempted to understand what is going on in such conversational situations? As one might imagine, scholarly work on conversation and spoken dialogue is broad, ranging from explorations of millisecond-level processes to macro-level descriptions of discourse phenomena spanning minutes, hours, or even days. Moreover, important insights about interactive language use have come from numerous sources, including qualitative descriptions of spontaneous discourse, close readings of carefully selected dialogic excerpts, quantitative explorations of large-scale corpora, as well as through carefully constructed laboratory investigations.

For much of this work, the universal or default setting for conversation (and language use in general) has generally been taken to be face-to-face dialogue (Bavelas, Hutchinson, Kenwood, & Matheson, 1997; Clark, 1996; Fillmore, 1981; Linell, 2005). Conversations, though, take place through many communicative media, including not only older technologies such as written messages and telephone calls but also more recent innovations such as videoconferencing, electronic mail, and online "micro-blogging" sites such as Twitter (Gernsbacher, 2014). Importantly, many communicative situations shape interactions in ways that often depart from the norms associated with face-to-face dialogue. Clark and Brennan (1991) highlighted a number of features of conversational contexts that constrain how people communicate in particular situations. Although Clark and Brennan did not intend their list to be exhaustive, it provides a useful starting point for appreciating the diversity of communicative circumstances that any comprehensive theory of conversation should consider.

Several of the constraints identified by Clark and Brennan (1991)—*co-presence, visibility,* and *audibility*—stem from the conversational modality. Whereas face-to-face conversation typically involves two or more speakers who are co-present—i.e., at the same location—and who can see and hear each other, many situations involve physically distant speakers or restricted channels of transmission. For example, traditional telephone conversations and voice mail are typically strictly auditory, while video chat technologies like Skype allow both auditory and visual information. However, both telephone calls and video chat limit the degree of co-presence experienced between individuals (Olson & Olson, 2000), and, in video chat at least, the perceptual salience of one's interlocutor can vary greatly depending on how zoomed-in the camera is. All else being equal, certain conversational activities— such as pointing or referring to other persons or objects in the immediate environment—are likely to be facilitated in settings that permit co-present multimodal interaction (Bangerter, 2004; Boyle, Anderson, & Newlands, 1994; Clark & Krych, 2004; Doherty-Sneddon et al., 1997; Gergle, Kraut, & Fussell, 2004).

A second set of constraints, *cotemporality, simultaneity,* and *sequentiality,* concerns the relative timing of speakers' conversational contributions. Interaction in face-to-face dialogue is typically immediate and synchronous; utterances are received at the same time as they are produced, and feedback and other listener responses (verbal and nonverbal) can occur in parallel with a speaker's utterances. In telecommunication terms, face-to-face dialogues are "full-duplex," with information flowing freely between interlocutors in real time. Face-to-face conversations also generally involve closely timed sequences of turns across speakers (Sacks, Schegloff, & Jefferson, 1974). In contrast, other media permit different degrees of flexibility regarding when and how individuals receive and respond to each other's messages. Email conversations, for example, involve communicative exchanges widely separated in time, and can involve disjointed sequences of messages interrupted by other events (Severinson Eklundh, 1994). Across many communicative circumstances, the opportunity (or lack thereof) for real-time interaction is likely to be tremendously important. For example, in educational contexts the advent of new online technologies has prompted explorations into the benefits of synchronous versus asynchronous forms of teacher–student interaction (e.g., Garrison & Kanuka, 2004; Giesbers, Rienties, Tempelaar, & Gijselaers, 2014; Li, Finley, Pitts, & Guo, 2011; Simonidesová & Hlavňová, 2013).

The final constraints in Clark and Brennan's (1991) list, *reviewability* and *revisability,* capture the extent to which particular communicative contributions are ephemeral and changeable. These constraints generally interact with conversation modality, given that opportunities to edit one's spoken utterances are typically limited compared to written forms of communication. On the comprehension side, signals conveyed through speech or signed languages are fleeting, whereas written messages are more enduring and can be saved by recipients and even re-read as needed. On the production side, people can generally consider and modify what they say in written media more thoroughly than they can in spoken discourse. As a result, speakers may be held less accountable for what they say compared to writers.

The kinds of effort involved in successful communication are likely to be drastically different when messages can be planned, reviewed, and revised (Biber, 1986; Chafe, 1982; Chafe & Tannen, 1987; Redeker, 1984).

Participant Roles

In addition to the possibilities for interaction afforded by different settings, individuals can also take on various roles within a given conversation. While some version of the "speaker" and "listener" roles—one on the production side and the other on the comprehension side—are minimally necessary for any given interaction to be called a conversation, these labels are generally insufficient for capturing the range of available roles across conversational contexts (Hymes, 1972; Levinson, 1988). The term "listener," in particular, is problematic because it typically doesn't distinguish an individual who is simply attending to an utterance from the intended recipient of that utterance. For this reason, researchers often use "addressee" to specify the individual (or individuals) to whom a given utterance is directed (Bavelas & Gerwing, 2011; Clark & Carlson, 1982).

Further distinctions are possible. Goffman (1976, 1981) offered the useful observation that only some individuals in a communicative context may be "ratified" for the purposes of the current conversation. That is, these individuals are considered to have the status of *participants* in the interaction, with the concomitant right to contribute to the conversation as necessary. In addition, multiparty situations can have one or more *side-participants* who are considered part of the conversation but do not act as either speaker or addressee during particular exchanges (Clark & Carlson, 1982). Imagine, for example, that Amy, Bob, and Chris are college friends catching up over dinner. When Amy asks Bob about his current job, Amy is the speaker and Bob the addressee, but when Bob answers Amy's question, he takes on the role of speaker and she becomes the addressee; throughout this exchange, Chris remains a side-participant. But, as a ratified participant, Chris would be expected, at other points in the conversation, to adopt the role of speaker or addressee. As even this simple example makes clear, conversational roles are constantly shifting. This fact has important implications for models of interactive dialogue, which must strive to account for how participants rapidly and smoothly transition between roles. Indeed, as we shall see later, some researchers have proposed that, much of the time, individuals are engaged in both production and comprehension simultaneously, blurring the boundaries between conversational roles further (Pickering & Garrod, 2013).

Finally, the immediate conversational context may also include one or more *non-participants* (Clark & Carlson, 1982; Clark & Schaefer, 1987b). For example, if Diane were at an adjacent table while Amy and company are having dinner, Diane would serve as an "overhearer" from their perspective. Lacking the status of ratified participants, overhearers have access to what is said without being considered part of the conversation. In some circumstances, though, conversational participants may not be aware of possible overhearers. Clark (1996; Clark & Schaefer, 1987b) distinguished, in particular, "bystanders" (cf. Goffman, 1981), who are openly present in the conversational context (e.g., if Diane's table were close by and visible), from "eavesdroppers," whose presence is unknown (e.g., if Diane were listening from a neighboring booth). This distinction is important not only for speakers, who may be confronted with the task of designing utterances for fellow participants knowing that they will also be heard by overhearers (Clark & Schaefer, 1987b, 1992; Wilkes-Gibbs & Clark, 1992), but also for listeners, who may come away with different understandings depending on whether they believe that particular utterances were produced with them in mind (Schober & Clark, 1989).

With these general features of conversations we can begin to consider some of the most important theoretical and methodological approaches that have contributed to our understanding of dialogue and talk-in-interaction. Traditionally, work on conversation has been marked by a tension between two distinct levels of analysis. First, there is a rich history of scholarship focusing on the *interactive* nature of conversation, often in naturalistic or spontaneous contexts.[1] Within this focus, the minimal unit of analysis is the dyad, and the forms and content of particular conversational contributions are understood as being shaped by high-level communicative goals that play out over time. Other perspectives, however, emphasize the fact that conversational behavior is also a product of *individual* cognitive processes. Within this focus, the unit of analysis is the individual speaker or addressee, and the emphasis is on understanding the mental activities that give rise to the production or interpretation of discrete utterances, often based on evidence from tightly controlled settings. Historically, these perspectives have been quite separate (Clark, 1992). The past couple of decades, though, have seen the rapid development of integrative approaches to studying dialogue that have sought to combine the insights of both perspectives (Brennan, Galati, & Kuhlen, 2010; Trueswell & Tanenhaus, 2005). As we shall see, all of these viewpoints generally share a commitment to the idea that conversation involves the coordinated contributions of speakers and addressees working together to achieve particular communicative goals. Where they differ, typically, is in the degree to which they emphasize interactive versus individual mechanisms.

Conversation Analysis

Some of the most important insights about conversation and spoken interaction have come from work carried out under the umbrella of Conversation Analysis (CA). CA first emerged as a distinct field of study in the 1960s and 1970s, led by the groundbreaking efforts of Sacks, together with Schegloff and Jefferson (see Sidnell, 2010, and Heritage & Clayman, 2010, for useful background on the origins of CA). In developing this approach, Sacks, Schegloff, Jefferson, and their colleagues were deeply influenced by two strands of thought within sociology: Goffman's work on "situations" and especially his emphasis on ordinary face-to-face dialogue as the primary locus of social interactions (Goffman, 1959), and Garfinkel's development of ethnomethodology as a way of describing how commonsense knowledge and expectations shape people's understandings of actions within particular settings (Garfinkel, 1967). Sacks distilled these influences through a specific interest in the forms and structures of social interaction—viewing "talk," in particular, as the paradigmatic case of interaction. Together with Schegloff and Jefferson, the work by Sacks laid the foundation of an analytic approach calling upon researchers to engage in the close and detailed examination of the patterns that constitute natural episodes of talk.

In its classic form, CA shares a specific set of theoretical and methodological assumptions (Sacks, 1984). Above all, talk is seen as "orderly." That is, despite all appearances to the contrary, even the most casual of conversations is assumed to be organized along principles that not only can be identified by the analyst through careful observation, but which are also used by the conversational participants themselves as a basis for understanding what is being accomplished through the interaction (Schegloff & Sacks, 1973). Conversational organization is seen as, fundamentally, *social* organization, in the sense that the relevant structures are considered part of the sociocultural knowledge of individuals within communities of interaction. By following or failing to follow particular patterns of organization in talk, participants display their orientations to the interaction at hand. For this reason, even the smallest of interactive behaviors are potentially important for the conversation analyst attempting to identify these patterns.

More than most other approaches to social and linguistic interaction, CA relies almost exclusively upon recordings and transcripts of natural talk in spontaneous interactive contexts (Jefferson, 2004; Sacks, 1984). This emphasis upon spontaneous interaction is based on the belief that invented or experimentally derived examples of talk are necessarily filtered through the theoretical perspectives and judgments of the researchers responsible for their creation. Spontaneous conversations, in contrast, allow participants to freely exhibit a wide range of behaviors at will—often in ways that are not predictable beforehand. From the perspective of CA, this is critically important because it is the participants themselves who are in the best position to reveal, through how they choose to act and to respond to others, what particular contributions "mean" for them within the context of the interaction (Schegloff, 1968, 1987).

Perhaps the most distinctive aspect of CA, relative to other approaches to the study of conversation, is the fact that the researcher's task is seen as one of *discovery*, rather than being driven by a priori questions or expectations. That is, research in CA is typically not concerned with testing particular hypotheses through controlled experimental manipulation. Instead, through close and repeated examination of natural interactive behaviors as captured in recordings and transcripts, the goal of the conversation analyst is to inductively extract information about how particular interactions are organized and about the means through which participants orient themselves to the task of achieving this organization. As a consequence of this focus on the regularities of interactive behaviors in conversation, CA tends to emphasize the public character of talk and what is being accomplished in interaction, rather than trying to develop accounts of the mental processes of individual speakers.

One of the particular strengths of CA is the sheer diversity of interactive settings considered by its researchers, such as chats between friends at pubs, patient–doctor interactions, encounters with police while being arrested, or business negotiations. This is vastly different from the types of constrained, laboratory-based interactions that have generally been the bread and butter of psycholinguistic investigations of language and discourse. Also notable is the diversity of topics addressed by work in CA—including, but not limited to, the role of silence, epistemic status, acquisition of conversational routines in childhood, apologies, laughter and emotion, storytelling, and various forms of requests. A common goal of this work has been to situate these and other topics within more general descriptions of conversational structures that crosscut particular areas of focus. Here, I highlight two of the most important aspects of conversational structure uncovered by research in CA: *organization of sequences* and *turn-taking*. The insights from CA on both these topics have had a tremendous impact on our understanding of conversation more broadly.

Organization of Sequences

Within CA, the basic conversational unit is not the individual utterance but the *adjacency pair* (Schegloff, 1968; Schegloff & Sacks, 1973). Adjacency pairs consist of two utterances, spoken by different participants, organized such that when one speaker produces the first pair part, the other speaker subsequently completes the sequence through production of the second part of the pair. Perhaps the most familiar type of adjacency pair is the *question-answer* sequence, as shown in the following excerpt from the CallHome corpus. Immediately prior to this excerpt, B has been describing a teaching job that she is about to start at a private school:

Conversation and Interactive Discourse

[EN_4665]

933.53 934.71 A: And what grade is it again?

934.71 935.08 B: Third.

935.25 935.67 A: okay.

A's utterance "*And what grade is it again?*" is immediately followed by B's response "*Third,*" comprising a question-answer pair. Conversation analysts have identified many types of adjacency pairs, including *offer-acceptance, greeting-greeting, invitation-acceptance, inform-acknowledge*, and even *blame-denial* (Stivers, 2013). By treating the adjacency pair as a central unit of analysis, CA further emphasizes the fact that contributions from individual speakers do not stand alone; utterances are generally produced in response to other utterances, often with the effect of eliciting particular utterances in response.

The analytic importance of adjacency pairs stems in part from the fact that they are seen as the basic means through which participants display and coordinate their understandings of the purpose of the current exchange. The nature of the second pair part, such as "*Third*" in response to "*And what grade is it again?*", reveals the second speaker's interpretation of the meaning of the first pair part (e.g., that speaker A was asking a question). The production of a first pair part also makes the second pair part *conditionally relevant* (Schegloff, 1968)— that is, the first part of an adjacency pair leads to the strong expectation that the second speaker will complete the pair by producing an appropriate response, known as a *preferred second* (Levinson, 1983; see Traum & Allen, 1994, for the related notion of "discourse obligations"). If the second speaker responds in a different way (e.g., by refusing an invitation), the production of such *dispreferred seconds* is often accompanied by additional signals of conversational effort, such as a delay before responding (Kendrick & Torreira, 2015; Stivers et al., 2009), discourse markers such as "well" or "oh" (Schegloff & Lerner, 2009), or hedging or forms of self-explanation (Holtgraves, 1997).

Most conversations consist of sequences of interleaved adjacency pairs, such that the second part of a given pair simultaneously functions as the first part of a subsequent pair. In the previous excerpt, for example, B's response "*Third*" also functions as the first part of an inform-acknowledge pair, which is completed with A's "*okay.*" However, a given response need not follow immediately upon the first pair part; adjacency pairs can be embedded within longer stretches of talk, separated by one or more *insertion sequences* (Schegloff, 1972) as speakers carry out other actions before popping back "up" and completing the original pair. Consider once again this portion of the conversational excerpt presented at the beginning of this chapter:

1692.84 1694.80 B: %um, have you talked to ((ever)), %um

1694.88 1696.00 B: what's her name &Sheila?

1696.73 1697.35 A: &Sheila who?

1697.62 1698.76 B: &Sheila %um

1699.30 1702.00 B: ne- %um what's her name &Nadine and them's sister.

1700.67 1701.07 A: ((&White))

1702.00 1702.93 A: (( ))

1703.11 1704.23 B: You see her still?

1703.94 1705.90 A: the twins getting ready to graduate girl.

Here, speaker B initiates a question-answer sequence by asking if A has talked to *"what's her name Sheila?"* However, rather than immediately completing this sequence by answering the question, speaker A initiates a second question-answer sequence by asking for clarification: *"Sheila who?"* This prompts speaker B to provide additional information, *"Nadine and them's sister,"* which also serves as the first part of an inform-acknowledge pair, leading speaker A to indicate (by answering *"White"* to her own question *"Sheila who?"*) that she understands who they are talking about. With this established, speaker B returns to her original question (*"You see her still?"*), allowing A to finally complete this sequence by providing evidence that she does, in fact, have recent knowledge about Sheila (*"the twins getting ready to graduate girl"*).

Work in CA has also identified how conversational sequences can be expanded through the addition of one or more *pre-sequences* at the beginning of particular conversational exchanges (Schegloff, 1980). Pre-sequences consist of additional adjacency pairs that function to elicit the addressee's tacit cooperation with the main purpose of the coming exchange. For example, a speaker may initiate a *pre-invitation* sequence (*"Hey, are you doing anything tonight?"*) to probe the addressee's availability before continuing with the main invitation. Other kinds of pre-sequences identified by CA researchers include *pre-announcements* (*"Have you heard the news?"*), *pre-requests* (*"Do you have a moment?"*), and *pre-narratives* (*"Did I tell you what happened?"*). Pre-sequences are also common at the beginnings of conversations because it usually isn't socially desirable for speakers to approach someone and launch directly into the heart of what they might want to talk about. Instead, they often find some way to signal their interest in initiating an interaction, and then wait for the other person to indicate a willingness to enter into conversation. In the case of telephone conversations, for example, the ringing of the phone functions as a signal of the caller's desire to talk. In Schegloff's (1968, 2007) terms, this initiates a *summons-answer* pre-sequence, which, depending on the nature of the call, may be followed by an *identification-recognition* sequence (*"It's Mary" "Oh, hi!"*) plus one or more "personal state inquiries" (*"How are you?" "I'm fine, how are you?"*). Only once these preliminaries are taken care of does the primary purpose of the conversation emerge (*"So, I'm calling because . . ."*).

This may seem like a lot of work just to start talking, yet openings and other pre-sequences occur routinely across many different interaction contexts (closings as well; Schegloff & Sacks, 1973). In general, these structures appear to fulfill specific socio-communicative needs, giving speakers a way of implicitly "agreeing" to participate in an upcoming exchange (as well as a way of opting out, if they wish). From the perspective of CA, by observing the patterns that participants follow as they work through particular conversational activities, and by collecting together numerous instances of such observations across multiple contexts, the analyst is able to provide a characterization of how such activities are organized and strung together in sequences in response to these and other interactive demands.

Turn-Taking

Another topic of central importance within CA concerns how and when individuals take turns speaking in natural conversation (Clayman, 2013). Turn-taking is a fundamental aspect of most forms of human social interaction, being present even in pre-linguistic infants (Gratier et al., 2015). Evidence of vocal alternation is also present in many primate species (e.g., Chow, Mitchell, & Miller, 2015; Takahashi, Narayanan, & Ghazanfar, 2013), suggesting that the capacity for turn-taking may be phylogenetically older than our capacity for language (Levinson, 2016). In addition, many of the features of turn-taking in human conversations are highly similar across even very diverse languages (Stivers et al., 2009), rounding out the picture of turn-taking as a universal aspect of interpersonal coordination.

In conversational contexts, a turn can be thought of as a single, distinct contribution to the discourse from a single speaker. Although one might be tempted to equate a turn with a complete sentence, in practice a meaningful turn can consist of as little as a simple shake of the head or backchannel response (*"mhm"* or *"oh?"*; Yngve, 1970), or as much as an uninterrupted minutes-long narrative. Moreover, a complete turn does not necessarily have to be syntactically well formed; in naturalistic dialogue a large proportion of conversational turns consists entirely of partial or ungrammatical sentences (as seen in the earlier excerpts), or may even be purely visual or gestural.

From the CA perspective, the absolute length or well-formedness of a given turn is generally less important as a feature of orderliness in dialogue than the fact that individuals alternate speaking in a systematic fashion. That is, after one speaker talks, the next speaker responds, and then the first speaker may respond in kind, and so forth. A common assumption is that successive conversational turns are timed so as to minimize, insofar as possible, both the duration of gaps where no one is talking as well as moments where more than one person talks at once (the "no-gap-no-overlap" principle; Sacks et al., 1974). This is probably more of an ideal than an absolute goal, however. Heldner and Edlund (2010) measured occurrences of gaps and overlaps in several dialogue corpora and found that slightly over 40% of speaker transitions involved noticeable gaps (i.e., longer than 200 ms, the estimated threshold for detection), while another 40% of transitions involved some degree of overlap. In a similar corpus analysis, Levinson and Torreira (2015) found that overlapping speech was relatively common (30% of speaker transitions consisted of "between-overlaps" in which one speaker started speaking during the other's turn, and continued after the previous speaker stopped). These moments were fleeting, though, with 75% of such overlaps lasting less than 375 ms. Likewise, looking cross-linguistically, Stivers et al. (2009) found an average "response offset" between speakers of approximately 200 ms across the languages they examined. Thus, even if perfectly smooth transitions are the exception rather than the rule, these observations still suggest that turn-taking in conversation happens with impressive efficiency.

A fundamental area of interest within CA concerns how speakers manage these transitions between turns. Sacks et al. (1974) provided the first and still most influential model of the regularities underlying conversational turn-taking. On their model, the organization of turn-taking is governed by two complementary principles: *turn-construction*, or knowing when one speaker has completed his or her turn, and *turn-allocation*, the implicit procedures for determining what happens once a turn is considered complete.

How do interlocutors know when a turn is completed? Listeners could, of course, simply wait for unambiguous evidence that the speaker has finished talking before jumping in with their own utterance. Some communication systems have such evidence built in; for example, the conventional use of "Over" when talking via two-way radio or the mere act of hitting SEND when texting via smartphone. Consistent with this idea, several early descriptions of turn-taking in dialogue (e.g., Duncan, 1972, 1974; Yngve, 1970) suggested that speakers manage the transition between turns by displaying particular types of *turn-yielding signals*, most often instantiated through combinations of prosody, gesture, or eye gaze, to indicate their willingness to hand over the conversational "floor" to someone else. A problem, however, is that in many circumstances this procedure would inevitably lead to sizeable gaps between turns, given that listeners would first have to recognize that a particular turn-yielding signal has occurred before speaking (Riest, Jorschick, & De Ruiter, 2015). Nevertheless, the work of Duncan (1972) and others (e.g., Argyle, Lefebvre, & Cook, 1974; Duncan & Fiske, 1977;

Goodwin, 1981; Kendon, 1967) established the relevance of speaker gaze and other non-verbal behaviors for shaping face-to-face interaction. Building on these early insights, work on the role of multimodal resources such as eye gaze and manual gestures for coordinating meaning and action continues to be important for our understanding of social interaction more generally (e.g., Bavelas, Coates, & Johnson, 2002; Bolden, 2003; Kendon, 1997; Mondada, 2007; Rossano, 2013; Rossano, Brown, & Levinson, 2009; Seyfeddinipur & Gullberg, 2014; Sidnell & Stivers, 2005).

Unlike the signaling view, which places most of the burden for successful turn-taking on the shoulders of the current speaker, work in CA strongly emphasizes the *interactive* organization of turn-taking (Goodwin, 1981; Levinson & Torreira, 2015). On the model proposed by Sacks et al. (1974), transitions between speakers in natural dialogue are managed entirely locally, in ways determined primarily by the actions of the participants themselves—unlike other settings where speaker turns are determined by external factors, such as political debates or courtroom testimony (Levinson, 1983). In particular, individuals are thought to use the syntactic and intonational properties of an utterance, together with pragmatic information based on the discourse context, to "project" when the current turn will likely be completed (Ford & Thompson, 1996; Gravano & Hirschberg, 2011). This involves identification of what Sacks et al. (1974) called the *turn constructional unit (TCU)*. By identifying the current TCU, listeners are better able to anticipate the points at which an instance of this type of unit is likely to end. These points are known as *transition-relevance places*, and represent moments of potential transition from one speaker to the next. Through the projection of upcoming transition-relevance places, listeners can be ready to contribute a next turn without having to wait for evidence that the current speaker is done.

As described by Sacks et al. (1974), speakers and listeners share the responsibility of navigating potential points of transition by adhering to a small set of ordered turn-allocation principles that govern "who speaks next." Essentially, the current speaker is seen as having priority for selecting the next speaker (e.g., by addressing someone by name [Lerner, 2003] or by producing the first part of an adjacency pair prompting a particular response [Schegloff, 2007]). But, if this does not occur, an addressee may take the opportunity at a particular transition-relevance place to "self-select" and start speaking. Alternatively, the addressee may choose not to self-select, or may produce a *continuer* (Schegloff, 1982) like "*mhm*" to indicate the speaker should go on. In such cases, the current speaker can continue talking until the next transition-relevance place is reached, at which point the same principles come into play again.

This simple system for allocating turns among speakers was intended, in the view of Sacks et al. (1974), to transcend particular variations in turn order, turn length, and numbers of participants, providing a highly general account for how turn-taking is organized across various situations. Combined with the related work on sequence organization and other fundamental topics such as conversational repair (Kitzinger, 2013; Hayashi, Raymond, & Sidnell, 2013; Schegloff, Jefferson, & Sacks, 1977), research within CA has been quite successful in capturing how the actions of conversational participants are patterned and organized in systematic ways across a myriad of interactive contexts.

Quantification in CA

An important starting assumption for research in CA is that behaviors are contextually situated, occurring for specific reasons at particular times and places in the discourse. If particular actions are taken out of a meaningful context, or if classes of behaviors are aggregated across instances for analysis purposes, the nuances of why and how people interact in the ways they do are potentially lost. For these reasons, researchers in CA have typically eschewed quantitative investigations of conversational phenomena, preferring instead to describe how interlocutors exhibit particular behaviors in spontaneous interactions. As argued by Schegloff (1996), a full characterization of conversational practices requires knowledge about both the *forms* of particular actions (e.g., uses of *"Oh"* to preface responses; Heritage, 1998) as well as the *positions* at which these forms appear conversationally (e.g., the distribution of *"Oh"* in second position following initial questions). Quantification of behavior, which necessarily abstracts away from the specifics of particular instances, is problematic under these criteria because conversational actions are always "positioned"—that is, they occur (or fail to occur) for specific reasons at specific moments in the interaction (Schegloff, 1993). On this view, seemingly objective characterizations of behavior such as "laughter per minute" are at best misleading, because conversational actions like laughter are inherently responsive, becoming relevant at particular places in the interaction where they serve particular functions.

However, some scholars working within the CA tradition have begun to add forms of quantitative measurement to their analytic toolbox, undertaking systematic investigations of topics such as turn-taking as a way of shedding light on the mechanisms that facilitate orderly interactions (e.g., Casillas & Frank, 2013; de Ruiter, Mitterer, & Enfield, 2006; Riest et al., 2015). Stivers (2015), for example, has argued for the validity of mixed-methods approaches that combine traditional CA concerns with the application of quantitative techniques (see also de Ruiter, 2013). While acknowledging several limitations of quantitative approaches (i.e., formal coding schemes can be reductive by imposing categorical boundaries on continuous phenomena; such codes are inflexible in the face of new observations that don't fall within their analytic frame; quantitative methods may not be appropriate for low-frequency phenomena), Stivers suggests that, when firmly situated within CA analytic principles (especially the thorough consideration of both the forms and positions of interactive phenomena), a "top-down CA-grounded formal coding approach" can be beneficial for answering certain questions not possible to address through CA alone, such as how interaction practices vary along with more general characteristics of participants, including their attitudes, age, gender, race, or language.

As an example of such an approach, Stivers (2015) highlights Stivers and Majid (2007), who examined turn-taking in interactions between pediatricians and children with their parents during routine medical visits. In considering the factors that influenced next-speaker-selection in question-answer sequences during these visits, Stivers and Majid found that pediatricians were less likely to "select" Black children to answer medical questions compared to White or Asian children. Reaching this conclusion involved the quantitative coding of sequence types and their distributions across interactions involving different racial identities; even so, this work is rooted in an understanding of the principles that govern turn-taking (Sacks et al., 1974). This would seem to satisfy Schegloff's (1993) caution: "quantification is no substitute for analysis. We need to know what the phenomena are, how they are organized, and how they are related to each other *as a precondition* for cogently bringing quantitative analysis to bear" (p. 114; emphasis in original).

Conversation as Collaboration

As we have seen, CA has been focused on capturing the intricacies of how people spontaneously talk to one another in naturalistic settings. As a general rule, though, work in CA has been mostly agnostic about the cognitive states of conversational participants, preferring instead to consider "talk-in-interaction" itself as the primary object of study. This is in sharp contrast, of course, to other approaches that take how people produce and respond to utterances as direct evidence for particular communicative intentions (the so-called *intentional stance*; Dennett, 1987). Even so, the insights about conversation organization and structure provided by CA have been tremendously influential on many other fields, including empirical research on discourse.

One of the most significant examples of this influence can be found in the work of Clark and colleagues (Clark, 1996; Clark & Brennan, 1991; Clark & Schaefer, 1987a, 1989; Clark & Wilkes-Gibbs, 1986), who have articulated a theoretical perspective that, like CA, emphasizes the deeply collaborative nature of language use in characterizing the organization and structure of spoken interactions. Unlike CA, though, this approach embraces empirical investigation as a way of identifying patterns of conversational coordination and how these patterns change in response to different conversational constraints. However, the experimental methods commonly used in many areas of psycholinguistics (e.g., chronometric button-press procedures) have traditionally required research participants to engage with decontextualized linguistic stimuli, usually without the guidance of genuine communicative goals (Clark, 1992). This is problematic, of course, from the perspective of wanting to understand how utterances are produced and understood in interaction. Thus, experimental research on collaborative dialogue has generally turned to methods that permit quantitative behavioral measurement while still allowing some degree of naturalistic communicative interaction with a partner.

Clark's (1992, 1996) model rests on the fundamental assumption that conversations are not reducible to the products of the autonomous actions of individual speakers. Instead, conversations are seen as a special kind of *joint activity* that, like playing a duet or shaking hands, requires two or more people to closely coordinate their individual behaviors for some common purpose (Clark, 1996; see also Grosz & Sidner, 1990, and Cohen & Levesque, 1994, for more formal accounts of discourse as joint action). From this perspective, the products of joint actions are more than just the sum of the actions taken by individual participants. Instead, the kinds of activities that we recognize as "conversation" are thought to represent the emergent products of intersubjective coordination. Crucially, this coordination takes place not only at the level of utterance content, as interlocutors work out the meanings they intend to communicate, but also at the level of process, as interlocutors synchronize how and when to interact to realize these intentions (Clark, 1994, 2004). As we shall see, empirical research in this area has mostly focused on how interlocutors coordinate on meaning (usually in terms of establishing reference), but utterances contain numerous features relevant for the "management" of talk. These so-called *collateral signals* (Clark, 1996) include discourse markers like "*well*" and "*oh*" (Fox Tree, 2010; Schiffrin, 1987), editing expressions like "*no, I mean . . .*" (Levelt, 1989), repair initiators like "*huh?*" or "*sorry?*" (Drew, 1997), as well as various backchannel responses like "*uh-huh*" or "*gosh*" (Goodwin, 1986; Schegloff, 1982). Bangerter and Clark (2003) described the role of these and similar *project markers* as helping interlocutors navigate between different levels of the ongoing discourse—both horizontally (topic-to-topic transitions) and vertically (e.g., openings/ closings, repairs). In general, such devices express speakers' meta-communicative orientations toward what is being said.

From the perspective of Clark's collaborative model, communicative actions of all kinds are inherently oriented toward other participants in the conversation. That is, just as playing a successful duet requires that musicians attend to what their duet partners are doing, and that they make continuous adjustments (e.g., in timing or amplitude) to their own performance in response, successful conversational coordination requires that individuals attend to the verbal and nonverbal actions of other participants and plan their own contributions in accordance with current conversational purposes (Clark, 1996). Moreover, speakers and addressees, like musicians in a duet, are expected to be mutually aware that these adjustments are reciprocal—i.e., that you are adjusting to me at the same time that I am adjusting to you.

Common Ground

On this view, achieving such close collaboration requires that speakers and addressees take into account the knowledge and intentions of other conversational participants, while also assuming that other participants are doing the same thing in return (Grice, 1975). In other words, successful coordination involves attending to *common ground*, which refers to the knowledge and beliefs taken as shared within a particular conversational context (Stalnaker, 1978). For a simple joint action like shaking hands, the relevant common ground might include our beliefs that we each have the intention of greeting one another, our concurrent awareness of the physical location and movements of one another's hands and bodies, and assumptions about the sociocultural context that prompt us to shake hands rather than, say, bump fists (Clark, 1996; Clark & Marshall, 1981). Failing to consider this information at the right time can lead to moments of difficulty, as anyone who has experienced an awkward part-handshake/part-fistbump can attest.

Clark's (1992, 1996) collaborative model, then, suggests that the consideration of common ground is an integral part of language use in dialogue. Such consideration, however, poses a challenge for psychological theories of conversation, given that this requires an account of how speakers and addressees come to represent the commonality of particular knowledge. Clark and Marshall (1981) proposed a specific solution to this challenge by suggesting that speakers and addressees rely on particular kinds of inferences about the knowledge that can be taken as part of common ground. Clark and Marshall described these inferences as being based on evidence for *co-presence* (linguistic, physical, or sociocultural) between speakers and addressees. In the case of linguistic co-presence, for example, a speaker may recall previous instances in which certain information was mentioned in conversation with a particular addressee. Given such evidence, the speaker is justified in treating this information as part of the common ground she shares with that addressee without having to independently represent the full mutuality of this knowledge (i.e., bypassing the need to consider a regress of statements such as: *I know X; You know that I know X; I know that you know that I know X; You know that I know that you know X;* [ad infinitum]; Schiffer, 1972).

As part of this view, inferences concerning common ground involve searching appropriate knowledge representations for evidence of co-presence. The products of these inferential processes are understood as specifying the relevant context for language use (Clark & Carlson, 1981). That is, speakers and addressees are assumed to restrict processing, insofar as possible, to just the set of information inferred to be in common ground. For example, if an addressee knows two possible individuals named *Jane*, but has reason to believe that only one of these individuals is also known to the current speaker, then any reference by that speaker to "*Jane*" should be taken as referring *only* to the individual in common ground. In language production, the analogous idea was expressed by Clark, Schreuder, and Buttrick (1983) as the *principle of optimal design*: "The speaker designs his utterance in such a way that he has good reason to believe that the addressee can readily compute what he meant on the basis of the utterance along with the rest of their common ground" (p. 246). In a very different context, Sacks et al. (1974) referred to this feature of discourse as *recipient design*, whereas psycholinguists have tended to prefer the term *audience design* to describe how speakers tailor utterances for particular addressees (Clark & Murphy, 1982; Gann & Barr, 2014; Horton & Gerrig, 2002).

Under optimal design, inferences concerning common ground are an intrinsic part of conversational actions. Even so, it is important to appreciate the heuristic nature of these inferences. Approximations of what others know may suffice much of the time, given that opportunities for collaboration should provide relatively inexpensive ways to recover if and when interlocutors get something wrong; optimality is seen as a *goal* of communication rather than an absolute requirement. Still, the general supposition of this account is that individuals strive to interact on the basis of beliefs about mutual knowledge.

Grounding

Another important aspect of the collaborative model is that common ground is seen as inherently dynamic. Interlocutors may start out with certain assumptions about the information they are likely to have in common (based on memories of past interactions or salient cues related to language, gender, or sociocultural identities, for example), but new or more specific beliefs about shared knowledge will inevitably emerge over time, as speakers introduce concepts into the discourse and elaborate on existing ideas. The most thorough account of this process comes from the work on *grounding* by Clark and colleagues (Clark, 1996; Clark & Brennan, 1991; Clark & Schaefer, 1989; Clark & Wilkes-Gibbs, 1986; Fox Tree, 2000; Isaacs & Clark, 1987; Schober & Clark, 1989; see also Kashima, Klein, & A. E. Clark, 2007, and Smith & Jucker, 1998, for similar accounts). Grounding refers to the means through which interlocutors work together to establish mutual beliefs that particular utterances have been understood as intended. Once such beliefs have been established, the information being communicated by the speaker (along with the belief that this information has been understood as intended) can be taken to be in common ground.

As shown in the opening conversational excerpt where two speakers work together to establish the identity of "Sheila," grounding necessarily involves coordinated contributions from both individuals (Clark & Schaefer, 1989). Echoing the CA notion of an adjacency pair, this involves, at a minimum, two phases. First, in a *presentation* phase, the speaker presents some information for consideration by an addressee. Then, in an *acceptance* phase, the addressee indicates his or her understanding of the previously presented utterance. All else being equal, it is only when the addressee displays acceptance of the initially presented information that the communicative intention behind that utterance can be considered to have been recognized and the relevant information added to common ground. This acceptance can happen either explicitly or implicitly. Consider, for example, a statement like "*I spoke to Mary the other day.*" Here, the speaker presents the referent "Mary" for consideration, after which the addressee may accept this reference explicitly ("*Oh yes, Mary!*") or may accept this information implicitly, with a response that tacitly acknowledges Mary but also moves the conversation forward ("*Oh, how is she?*"). Presentation and acceptance can also be carried out through nonverbal means. In the context of a joint Lego construction task, for example, Clark and Krych (2004) found that model builders often sought confirmation for their next move by simply picking up and wordlessly "hovering" a potential piece in place until acknowledgment was received (see also Brennan, 2005).

On the collaborative model, an addressee's acceptance of a statement like *"I spoke to Mary"* gives the interlocutors reason to believe that the referent Mary (plus the newly introduced fact of the speaker's recent interaction with Mary) is part of their current common ground—although more explicit forms of acceptance may lead to stronger assumptions about commonality (Brown-Schmidt, 2012; Clark, 1996; see also Knutsen & Le Bigot, 2012). Addressees may also, of course, fail to accept the information presented by the speaker— either because they weren't playing close attention to what the speaker was saying (*"What did you say?"*) or because they didn't understand some aspect of what the speaker was talking about (*"Mary who?"*). In such cases, a lack of immediate acceptance is likely to trigger additional multi-turn sequences as speakers try to identify and resolve the issue. Such grounding sequences can be nested multiple times as interlocutors work out the necessary information that will allow them to move forward. The similarity of these ideas to descriptions of the organization of conversational sequences offered by CA is not accidental—for Clark (1996, 2012), adjacency pairs and similar phenomena are a primary means through which interlocutors carry out a wide variety of joint conversational actions for purposes of grounding.

A crucial feature of conversational grounding is that interlocutors work at establishing these mutual understandings to the degree necessary to satisfy their current communicative goals. Clark and Schaefer (1989) referred to this as the *grounding criterion*: "the contributor and the partners mutually believe that the partners have understood what the contributor meant, to a criterion sufficient for current purposes" (p. 262). In circumstances where the need for mutual understanding is relatively high, such as giving directions to a specific location, this criterion will be more stringent and individuals will work harder to make sure that each contribution has been understood (Clark, 1996). When the need for mutual understanding is relatively low, not every contribution may need to be fully grounded to the same extent. For example, for a query like *"When is our meeting?"* the response *"Before noon"* would be inadequate if the speaker's intention is to know the specific time, but would likely be sufficient if the goal is merely to establish whether the meeting in question will happen relatively early or late in the day (or at all). The grounding criterion determines, in part, the likelihood that any given contribution will be accepted as adequate evidence for mutual beliefs.

Clark and Wilkes-Gibbs (1986) documented these processes of conversational grounding in detail by examining the interactions of individuals as they repeatedly engaged in a so-called referential communication task involving matching sets of abstract geometric figures known as Tangrams (Elffers, 1976). Originally developed to examine the acquisition of communicative competence in children (Piaget, 1959; Piaget & Inhelder, 1956) and adopted as a way to examine differences between "social" and "non-social" language in both children and adults (Glucksberg & Krauss, 1967; Krauss & Weinheimer, 1964, 1966), referential communication paradigms typically involve pairs of participants carrying out a joint activity (sorting, matching, route navigation, puzzle assembly) that requires that they communicate about a set of concrete items to achieve some final goal (Yule, 1997). The version used by Clark and Wilkes-Gibbs (and many others since) assigns one participant, the Director, the task of instructing the other participant, the Matcher, how to arrange a set of Tangrams in a specific sequence. By having participants carry out this same procedure multiple times, it is possible to observe not only how speakers and addressees work together to establish particular conceptualizations for the task referents, but also how, once established, these conceptualizations are reused and further refined over time. Tangrams and similar novel and/or abstract stimuli are especially useful in this context because interlocutors generally must engage in more extended forms of grounding to uniquely identify each item.

As shown by Clark and Wilkes-Gibbs (1986), initial referring expressions for such stimuli are frequently long and detailed, as speakers seek to provide enough information to allow their partners to accurately identify the correct referent. In addition, speakers' early descriptions are often marked as provisional, either through the use of "hedges" (e.g., *kinda big*) or with distinct intonational contours (e.g., rising final tone) that indicate uncertainty (Sacks & Schegloff, 1979). For example, a speaker might say something like *"It's kind of like the tree?"* when attempting to describe a particular figure. The tentative nature of such presentational utterances invites further interaction, through which particular conceptualizations may be refined further through extended clarification sequences.

However, once particular referring expressions have been accepted, these conceptualizations may then be taken as being part of common ground. Brennan and Clark (1996) used the term *conceptual pact* to refer to the tacit agreements established between conversational partners for how to refer to particular referents. Importantly, these conceptual pacts allow pairs to be more efficient during subsequent interactions about the same figures. Later expressions for particular items are generally anchored in the conceptualizations previously established as acceptable, often becoming shorter over time. For example, Clark and Wilkes-Gibbs (1986) described how a speaker, after initially identifying a particular Tangram by saying that it *"looks like a person who's ice skating, except they're sticking two arms out in front,"* on subsequent occasions referred to the same figure as *"the person ice skating, with two arms"* and eventually just *"the ice skater."* Conceptual pacts also allow subsequent referring expressions to become less provisional; hedges and similar markers of uncertainty often fall away as agreements for how to refer to particular figures become more firmly established. Clark and Wilkes-Gibbs accounted for these processes by proposing that interlocutors adhere to a *principle of least collaborative effort*, under which they work together to minimize their joint effort. Given this notion of collaborative effort, speakers are often justified in producing less-than-ideal references on the expectation that their contributions will be refashioned through processes of negotiation in ways that ultimately facilitate shared conversational perspectives.

Evidence concerning the interactive nature of these tacit agreements was obtained by Brennan and Clark (1996), who asked pairs of individuals to engage in a referential communication task in which target objects were initially presented together with other pictures of the same kind (e.g., several shoes or several cars). This required pairs to negotiate relatively specific ways of referring to critical objects (e.g., *pennyloafer* or *blue convertible*). Then, Brennan and Clark asked speakers to carry out additional trials with either the same addressee or with a new addressee. At this point, though, the picture displays changed as well, such that each object was now unique (e.g., a single shoe). With a new addressee, speakers quickly reverted to basic-level terms for these now-unique objects. With the same addressee, however, speakers often continued to use referring expressions that had been established previously, even though labels such as *pennyloafer* were now overly specific (see also Koolen, Gatt, Goudbeek, & Krahmer, 2011). The persistence of these previously negotiated perspectives was attributed to the availability of conceptual pacts in the interlocutors' common ground. Similar evidence for the communicative relevance of conceptual pacts has since been demonstrated in a wide variety of contexts, including children's communication (Branigan, Bell, & McLean, 2016), in interactions with adults with autistic spectrum disorders (Nadig, Seth, & Sasson, 2015), and even human–robot interactions (Iio et al., 2015).

Cognitive Processes in Conversation

On the whole, the studies carried out by Clark and colleagues illustrate how speakers and addressees modify and build upon their initial discourse representations by collaborating on shared understandings of relevant conversational topics. The results of this approach have been immensely important for informing psychologically oriented models of spoken discourse (Trueswell & Tanenhaus, 2005). However, similar to work within CA, studies examining the collaborative aspects of communication have frequently been focused on the macro-level dynamics of dialogue management and the activities used to realize particular forms of collaboration. As such, they are often less directly informative about the moment-by-moment cognitive processes involved in utterance production and interpretation.

Interactive Alignment

In contrast, other empirical approaches to the study of conversation are very much oriented around explicating the real-time mechanisms and mental representations of individual speakers and hearers in interaction. In this context, one of the most influential ideas to emerge in the last decade is the *interactive alignment model* proposed by Pickering and Garrod (2004, 2013; Garrod & Pickering, 2009). Like CA and like Clark's (1996) collaborative model, Pickering and Garrod view speaking and listening as tightly integrated. Indeed, the interactive alignment account was explicitly intended to contrast with traditional theoretical and empirical approaches to language processing that focus on the autonomous comprehension and/or production of decontextualized sentences (Garrod & Pickering, 2004). However, unlike Clark and colleagues, who regard utterance production and interpretation as being strongly shaped by collaborative goals, Pickering and Garrod see conversational coordination as being mediated in large part via domain-general cognitive mechanisms. Specifically, Pickering and Garrod (2004) proposed that, given assumptions of representational "parity" between comprehension and production, the bottom-up activation of representations during comprehension can directly shape the form and content of that individual's subsequent production, resulting in similar utterances across individuals. Levelt and Kelter (1982) provided an early demonstration of such alignment as part of a study in which they simply called up shopkeepers and asked either *"What time do you close?"* or *"At what time do you close?"* In general, the form of the response closely matched the form used to ask the question: when asked *"What time do you close?"* shopkeepers were more likely to respond *"5pm,"* but if asked *"At what time do you close?"* they were more likely to respond *"At 5pm."* The processes responsible for formulating the answer appear to have been influenced by the lexical and syntactic information present in the question.

On Pickering and Garrod's (2004) account, linguistic coordination emerges through the low-level co-activation of representations across individuals in dialogue. Such interactive alignment is thought to be akin to other types of perception–behavior links (Chartrand & Bargh, 1999; Dijksterhuis & Bargh, 2001) that have been observed in a variety of interactive settings, including mimicry of nonverbal behaviors (Bailenson & Yee, 2005; Bavelas, 2007; Chartrand & van Baaren, 2009), synchrony of postural sway and other motor movements (Richardson, Marsh, Isenhower, Goodman, & Schmidt, 2007; Shockley, Richardson, & Dale, 2009; Shockley, Santana, & Fowler, 2003), and various types of coordination in language and action (Louwerse, Dale, Bard, & Jeuniaux, 2012;

Sebanz, Bekkering, & Knoblich, 2006; Semin, 2007). Common to many of these phenomena is the idea that particular forms of interpersonal coordination can emerge on the basis of relatively local (individual) processes.

With respect to conversational alignment in particular, a large body of research has established that interlocutors readily display various forms of alignment, at practically all levels of language use (Wachsmuth, de Ruiter, Jaecks, & Kopp, 2013). Going under various labels—e.g., "accommodation" (Giles, Coupland, & Coupland, 1991), "convergence" (Garrod & Doherty, 1994; Pardo, 2006), or "entrainment" (Brennan & Clark, 1996)—this work has found robust evidence for cross-speaker alignment in acoustic-phonetic (Kim, Horton, & Bradlow, 2011; Levitan & Hirschberg, 2011; Pardo, 2006, 2013), lexical (Brennan & Clark, 1996; Foltz, Gaspers, Thiele, Stenneken, & Cimiano, 2015; Jucks, Becker, & Bromme, 2008), syntactic (Branigan, Pickering, & Cleland, 2000; Carbary, Frohning, & Tanenhaus, 2010; Jaeger & Snider, 2013; Reitter, Moore, & Keller, 2006; Schoot, Menenti, Hagoort, & Segaert, 2014 [although see Healey, Purver, & Howes, 2014]), gestural (Holler & Wilkin, 2011; Kopp & Bergmann, 2013), and conceptual (Garrod & Anderson, 1987; Garrod & Doherty, 1994; van Lierop, Goudbeek, & Krahmer, 2012; Markman & Makin, 1998; Schober, 2005) aspects of utterances, across a wide variety of discourse contexts.

In general, Pickering and Garrod (2004) view the mechanisms responsible for interactive alignment and imitation as exerting their effects directly, in an effortless and automatic fashion (Garrod & Pickering, 2009). These mechanisms include both short-term priming, based on the transient co-activation of relevant linguistic representations following exposure to particular input, as well as longer-term processes of "routinization" arising through the repeated co-activation of representations over time (Garrod & Anderson, 1987; Pickering & Garrod, 2005). In either form, though, alignment is understood as happening independent of intention; speakers generally are not *trying* to align their verbal and nonverbal actions to those of their partners.

An interesting puzzle, though, arises from the fact that evidence for alignment in dialogue can appear stronger (or weaker) across different communicative contexts. On a "pure" automatic account, speakers who are exposed to particular behaviors should show a tendency toward linguistic imitation regardless of other factors. However, many forms of low-level alignment appear to be subject to influence from higher-level considerations. In some cases, this may be intentional on the part of speakers. For example, Giles and colleagues (1991) have noted that particular forms of communication accommodation—like adopting the word choice or accent of a conversational partner—can occur for explicitly strategic reasons, as when speakers wish to facilitate particular interpersonal goals by becoming, in a sense, more similar to a partner. Specific social contexts (such as a minority group member in a majority group context) may even prompt speakers to show evidence of linguistic *divergence* instead (Borhuis & Giles, 1977). Sociolinguists have sometimes used the term "style matching" to describe instances in which speakers selectively modify particular linguistic and paralinguistic features (such as vocabulary, speaking rate, or pitch) to manage the social distance between themselves and their interlocutors (Bell, 1984; Bell & Johnson, 1997; Niederhoffer & Pennebaker, 2002).

But even in cases where speakers' overt intentions to align are not at issue, variation in alignment can still be observed. For example, work on spontaneous behavioral mimicry has shown that, despite occurring below the threshold of awareness, the implicit tendency to imitate the behaviors of others is often enhanced when individuals hold positive attitudes toward their partner or have the goal to affiliate (Chartrand & Lakin, 2013; Kavanagh & Winkielman, 2016). Likewise, phonetic imitation appears to be selective as well, being influenced under some conditions by social factors such as gender (Pardo, 2006; Namy, Nygaard, & Sauerteig, 2002), liking (Babel, 2010), speaker attractiveness (Babel, 2012), and dialogue role (Pardo, Cajori Jay, & Krauss, 2010). Similar socially mediated effects have also been shown for syntactic alignment (Balcetis & Dale, 2005; Branigan, Pickering, Pearson, McLean, & Brown, 2011; Weatherholz, Campbell-Kibler, & Jaeger, 2014). Branigan et al. (2011) frame this general issue as involving a distinction between "unmediated" and "mediated" forms of alignment. Whereas unmediated alignment occurs entirely via bottom-up, linguistic processes, mediated forms of alignment are shaped by non-linguistic factors such as beliefs and goals. As yet, there is no general account that can explain these patterns of variation. While it is possible to imagine that the relevant mechanisms could remain essentially cognitive (e.g., top-down factors may prompt closer attention to particular verbal or nonverbal behaviors in select partners, leading to more distinct discourse representations that can facilitate priming), it seems clear that these mechanisms are likely to interact with social and interpersonal considerations in complex ways.

On Pickering and Garrod's (2004) view, though, the significance of interactive alignment for conversation goes beyond the simple repetition of words, syntax, or speech sounds. As interlocutors alternate between the roles of speaker and listener, this cross-speaker co-activation of relevant representations at one level of language use is thought to spread to other levels of representation, facilitating additional forms of alignment over time. For example, Cleland and Pickering (2003) showed that, after hearing a complex noun phrase like *the car that's blue*, speakers were more likely to produce similar syntactic constructions (*the sheep that's red*) than alternative constructions (*the red sheep*). However, the likelihood of producing *the sheep that's red* was also greater after hearing *the goat that's red* than after hearing *the car that's red*. In this case, semantic alignment led to greater alignment at the syntactic level. The importance of this process is that these forms of alignment can percolate upwards, driving convergence beyond individual words or structures. Through such "output/input co-ordination" (Garrod & Anderson, 1987) across multiple levels of representation, interlocutors' situation models—i.e., their high-level representations of what the discourse is about (Zwaan & Radvansky, 1998)—are ultimately brought into closer alignment as conversations proceed.

Prediction-by-Simulation

More recently, Pickering and Garrod (2013) have proposed an extension of their model that places an even greater emphasis upon the tightly interwoven nature of comprehension and production processes in dialogue. In doing so, they address how interlocutors manage to coordinate relevant contributions at the level of timing as well as content, dealing with some of the same complexities of conversational turn-taking discussed previously in the context of CA (Sacks et al., 1974). Inspired by the notion of *forward models* in work on motor control (e.g., Wolpert, 1997), Pickering and Garrod (2013) propose that both speakers and addressees rely on processes of covert imitation to "predict" one another's upcoming contributions. During comprehension, for example, an addressee may covertly imitate the speaker, effectively projecting a forward model of the speaker's most likely utterance as it is being produced (Garrod, Gambi, & Pickering, 2014; Pickering & Garrod, 2007). Such *prediction-by-simulation* can then allow the addressee to implicitly anticipate what the speaker will say and to prepare a response accordingly. Similar forward projection is thought to occur during production as well, as speakers engage comprehension processes to anticipate how an utterance will likely be understood. These ideas are consistent with a wide range of findings showing that individuals can successfully anticipate upcoming linguistic input (e.g., Kutas, Delong, & Smith, 2011; Pickering & Garrod, 2007; van Berkum, Brown, Zwitserlood, Kooijman, & Hagoort, 2005). As Pickering and Garrod (2013) argue, not only can such prediction-by-simulation provide a mechanistic account of the kinds of "projection" required to explain the kinds of finely attuned turn-taking present in many conversations (Levinson & Torreira, 2015; Stivers et al., 2009), but in the limit, it can also readily explain how interlocutors are routinely able to finish each other's sentences ("collaborative completions," Lerner, 2004; see also Bolden, 2003; Clark & Wilkes-Gibbs, 1986; Howes, Purver, Healey, Mills, & Gregoromichelaki, 2011; Poesio & Reiser, 2010).

Whither Alignment?

Part of the appeal of Pickering and Garrod's (2004, 2013) proposals is that they preserve the fundamental idea of conversation as a joint activity, yet make a very specific set of claims about the nature of the individual processes involved in both the production and comprehension of utterances during interaction. Some researchers, though, have questioned the degree to which alignment—and behavior matching more broadly—is likely to be the primary driver of coordination in dialogue. One set of concerns emerge from the observation that, taken to the extreme, the very notion of alignment would seem to predict that individuals in conversations should come to speak similarly to one another over time in a variety of contexts (Howes, Healey, & Purver, 2010). In real-world interactions, however, the reciprocal mirroring of the recent speech and actions of one's interlocutor may more likely be the exception rather than the rule, and the idiosyncratic experiences and knowledge of different individuals would seem to preclude complete representational convergence (Brennan et al., 2010).

In addition, general broad-based alignment—what some researchers have called "indiscriminate" alignment (Fusaroli et al., 2012)—may not be directly beneficial for all aspects of conversational coordination. For example, Reitter and Moore (2014) examined dialogues taken from the HCRC Map Task corpus (Anderson et al., 1991), as well as the Switchboard corpus of telephone conversations (Marcus et al., 1994), and found that, while forms of syntactic alignment were present in both corpora, evidence for alignment was generally stronger in the task-oriented interactions. However, success at the map task (as measured by accuracy in following the route) was predicted *not* by local repetition but rather by slower syntactic adaptation across speakers over time. Taking task success as an indication of the kind of high-level convergence of situation models posited by Pickering and Garrod (2004) to be the end result of interactive alignment, Reitter and Moore suggest that forms of long-term syntactic adaptation between partners may be more important for successful coordination in this task context than immediate repetition (see also Fusaroli et al., 2012, for a similar conclusion). This complicates the more generalist view of alignment found in Pickering and Garrod (2004).

Another potential concern about interactive alignment is the fact that the priming mechanisms assumed by Pickering and Garrod (2004), taken on their own, account most readily for instances of cross-interlocutor similarity. But, as we have already seen in the patterns of conversational organization considered under CA, as well as in the kinds of collaborative joint actions highlighted by Clark and colleagues (e.g., Clark & Schaefer, 1989), a central feature of conversational coordination is the fact that speakers routinely produce systematically *different* actions from their partners. That is, conversations unfold through the move-by-move sequencing of distinct contributions across interlocutors (Enfield & Sidnell, 2014). The CA notion of adjacency pair, for example, is based on the observation that each speaker makes a unique contribution to particular exchanges for particular purposes (Schegloff, 2007). If one person offers an invitation, for example, the other person may accept, thus completing the exchange, but these actions will necessarily be different. Although some exchanges can involve repetition (e.g., greeting-greeting pairs like "*Hi!*" "*Hi!*"), most adjacency pairs—and coordinated conversational actions more broadly—seem to be driven more by complementarity than by similarity.

Indeed, the complementary nature of utterances across speakers is what helps drive conversations forward—what Mills (2014) has called conversational "progressivity." While some forms of repetition or identity of expression are undoubtedly important for conversational coherence (e.g., lexical entrainment may allow interlocutors to believe they are talking about the same things on different occasions; Brennan & Clark, 1996), or for managing particular conversational problems (e.g., requests for clarification often involve repeating back part of a partner's previous utterance; Benjamin & Walker, 2014; Schegloff, 1992; Wu, 2009), such similarity of conversational action is likely to occur against a background of difference, as speakers produce and respond to utterances in distinct but complementary ways.

Based on these and similar observations, some researchers have proposed that cross-speaker repetition and other forms of reciprocal convergence may be merely one type of conversational synchrony among a much wider range of interdependent behaviors. Fusaroli and Tylén (2016) use the term *interpersonal synergies* to refer to those context-sensitive aspects of conversational organization that emerge at the level of the interaction rather than the individual speaker. As part of a broader dynamical systems account of human interaction, Dale, Fusaroli, Duran, and Richardson (2014) propose that these kinds of interpersonal synergies may emerge through processes of "self-organization" among multiple interdependent mechanisms, subject to modulation by social variables. On this account, particular social contexts may "afford" certain types of communicative behaviors in response to another's verbal and nonverbal actions. Dale et al. suggest that patterns of complementarity, as especially stable forms of interpersonal synergy, are likely to be a powerful means through which interlocutors flexibly and incrementally adapt to one another for purposes of conversational coordination.

Debates on Conversational Coordination

One topic that has garnered the lion's share of attention in work on language processing and conversation is the question of *when* information about a conversational partner—including inferences about common ground—is likely to influence what people do in interaction. Although the collaborative view described by Clark and colleagues was not intended as a fine-grained description of the mechanisms governing conversational coordination, this account readily supports the idea that attention to the perspectives and knowledge of others can influence the form and content of language use from the earliest moments of processing. In contrast, we have seen that a central aspect of Pickering and Garrod's (2004) interactive alignment model is the claim that domain-general mechanisms enable forms of conversational coordination independent of higher-level collaborative concerns. This contrast, between assumptions about the pervasive and immediate consideration of common ground on one hand, and the secondary (and perhaps absent) consideration of such knowledge on the other, has been the focus of a substantial amount of work, as researchers have proposed different accounts of the potential time course with which knowledge of one's conversational partner may be incorporated into the production and comprehension of utterances—and the nature of the cognitive mechanisms that could make this possible (for overviews, see Barr & Keysar, 2006; Brennan & Hanna, 2009; Brown-Schmidt & Hanna, 2011; Galati & Brennan, 2010; Horton, 2012; Schober & Brennan, 2003).

Perspective Adjustment

One model that has been especially important in this respect is the *perspective adjustment* account proposed by Keysar, Barr, and colleagues (Barr & Keysar, 2006; Keysar, Barr, & Horton, 1998; Keysar, Barr, Balin, & Paek, 1998). This model presents a view of the time course of language processing in dialogue in which one's *own* knowledge, rather than what believes about one's partner, forms the starting point for utterance planning and interpretation (Keysar et al., 1998; Keysar, Lin, & Barr, 2003). Although positing an egocentric basis for language use might seem to fly in the face of evidence for the tight interpersonal coordination of knowledge and action during conversation, the general logic is that considering the knowledge and perspectives of others is an effortful process that requires time and cognitive resources beyond what is necessary for routine aspects of utterance planning and interpretation, and that anchoring processing in one's own perspective will suffice under most circumstances (Epley, Keysar, Van Boven, & Gilovich, 2004; Nickerson, 1999). Similar to interactive alignment, this model holds that consideration of common ground will generally occur late in language processing, if adjustment is needed, or through mechanisms of interactive repair.

One of the most significant aspects of the perspective adjustment view is that it provides a clear processing account of the time course with which one may expect information relevant to common ground to exert an impact upon language use during conversation. To examine this issue, Keysar and other psycholinguists have frequently relied on versions of the so-called *visual world paradigm* (Huettig, Rommers, & Meyer, 2011; Spivey & Huette, 2016; Tanenhaus, Spivey-Knowlton, Eberhard, & Sedivy, 1995; see also Brown-Schmidt, this volume), which involves recording (at relatively fine-grained temporal and spatial resolutions) when and where people look to a visual display they engage in a concurrent linguistic task. Originally developed as a way of demonstrating that comprehenders readily integrate visual scene information during incremental language comprehension (Tanenhaus et al., 1995), visual world eyetracking has been readily adapted to referential communication contexts as a way of (relatively) unobtrusively measuring the moment-by-moment focus of attention of individuals in naturalistic interactive dialogue (Brown-Schmidt, Campana, & Tanenhaus, 2005; Brown-Schmidt & Tanenhaus, 2008; Hanna & Tanenhaus, 2004; Keysar, Barr, Balin, & Brauner, 2000; Richardson, Dale, & Kirkham, 2007). Using eyetracking with carefully controlled visual displays allows researchers to explore questions about the time course with which individuals consider interpretations of particular utterances in interaction, something that is not possible when examining written transcripts or when measuring responses to isolated sentences (for examples of other work using this paradigm, see the chapters in Knoeferle, Pyykkönen-Klauck, & Crocker, 2016).

In their seminal study using visual world eyetracking to examine perspective adjustment in utterance comprehension, Keysar et al. (2000) examined whether addressees in a referential communication task would initially rely on their own perspective when considering which object in a display is the intended referent for expressions like "*the bottom block*." Because assigning distinct perspectives across interlocutors is critical for testing hypotheses about the role of common ground in conversation ("unconfounding" common ground; Keysar, 2007), this task used displays in which select objects were *privileged* from the participants' point of view—that is, they were visible to participants but not to the confederate speaker. When the display contained a plausible referent for critical expressions (i.e., a block below the other blocks in the display) at these privileged locations, analyses of addressees' eye fixations to the display revealed that the presence of this privileged distractor momentarily interfered with successful identification of the intended referent, suggesting that utterance interpretation was initially anchored in the addressees' own perspective. Similar visual world eyetracking studies by Keysar, Barr, and colleagues have provided further evidence for the claim that inferences about others' perspective can have relatively late effects during language processing (Barr, 2008; Epley, Morewedge, & Keysar, 2004; Keysar et al., 2003; Kronmüller & Barr, 2007; Wu & Keysar, 2007; see also Horton & Keysar, 1996; Keysar et al., 1998, for non-eyetracking evidence).

Constraint-Based Models

Other studies using similar paradigms, however, have obtained evidence indicating that common ground can also have more immediate effects upon utterance interpretation (Brown-Schmidt, 2009; Brown-Schmidt, Gunlogson, & Tanenhaus, 2008; Hanna & Tanenhaus, 2004; Hanna, Tanenhaus, & Trueswell, 2003; Heller, Grodner, & Tanenhaus, 2008; Metzing & Brennan, 2003). These findings are generally in line with the idea that speakers and addressees strive to be sensitive to the communicative needs of others in conversation. Despite the intense interest focused on this issue from all sides, there is no clear consensus why studies may only sometimes reveal evidence for the rapid consideration of common ground. A variety of reasons for these discrepancies has been suggested, though, with many of these suggestions focusing on factors related to specific aspects of the paradigms used in this domain, such as the presence or absence of a live communicative partner (Brown-Schmidt & Hanna, 2011) or confederate partner (Kuhlen & Brennan, 2013), the goodness of fit between visually available objects and the linguistic expressions used by speakers in particular experimental contexts (Hanna et al., 2003; Heller et al., 2008; Keysar et al., 2003; Nadig & Sedivy, 2002), and the potential availability of salient contextual cues concerning simple "one-bit" differences in perspectives (Galati & Brennan, 2010).

A more general conclusion from this body of work, though, may also be that the nature of evidence in favor (or not) of early consideration of common ground is likely to be strongly influenced by the types of cues present in the conversational situation (including those derived from methodological choices imposed by researchers; Rubio-Fernández, 2008), as well as by the ability of particular speakers and addressees to attend to these cues and use them in a timely fashion. In line with this idea, a number of researchers have proposed that common ground may best be treated as one of many possible contextual constraints on language use in dialogue (Brown-Schmidt & Hanna, 2011). This proposal is inspired by more general *constraint-based* models within psycholinguistics that view language processing as a constraint-satisfaction procedure aimed at finding the "best" interpretation given multiple probabilistic cues (e.g., MacDonald, Pearlmutter, & Seidenberg, 1994; McRae, Spivey-Knowlton, & Tanenhaus, 1998). On this idea, evidence for or against the timely sensitivity to another's perspective in conversation will depend in large part on the salience and strength of relevant cues to common ground, weighted against other cues present within the communicative context (e.g., Brown-Schmidt, 2012; Brown-Schmidt et al., 2008; Hanna et al., 2003; Heller et al., 2008).

Evidence supporting the notion of common ground as a probabilistic constraint on dialogue comes from studies that demonstrate early but partial effects of perspective on utterance interpretation. For example, Hanna et al. (2003) conducted a visual world eyetracking study in which addressees followed instructions to move objects around displays with both privileged and shared locations, similar to Keysar et al. (2000). Unlike Keysar et al., Hanna et al. examined situations in which critical referring expressions like "*the red triangle*" could apply equally to *both* a mutually visible referent as well as a hidden referent (i.e., there were red triangles in both locations). Hanna et al. found that addressees, upon hearing the critical reference, were more likely to look at the mutually visible object, indicating that listeners could indeed restrict attention to shared referents. Importantly, though, this effect was not absolute; addressees still looked to the privileged object at least some of the time, and did so more compared to a control condition in which the privileged location contained an unrelated object. In line with the constraint-based perspective, the speed of referent identification was seemingly influenced by the availability of other objects that could serve as a match for the referring expression. Hanna et al. suggested that addressees may regularly strive to consider common ground, but their success at doing will be subject to influence from other factors relevant to the communicative situation (see also Nadig & Sedivy, 2002).[2]

Other Cognitive Constraints

Most of the work just discussed has focused, in one way or another, on how salient features of conversational contexts may facilitate consideration of perspective-relevant information. At the same time, other work has explored how characteristics of particular speakers or addressees, such as their age (Horton & Spieler, 2007), culture (Wu & Keysar, 2007), spatial abilities (Schober, 2009), or language background (Ryskin, Brown-Schmidt, Canseco-Gonzalez, Yiu, & Nguyen, 2014), may influence perspective-taking as well. Moreover, a further implication of the constraint-based approach is that domain-general cognitive capacities are likely to be yet another source of constraint upon when and how individuals attend to perspective-relevant information in dialogue. Wardlow-Lane and Ferreira (2008), for example, demonstrated the importance of general mechanisms of attention allocation for perspective-taking, showing that speakers' utterances in a referential communication task were more likely to be influenced by privileged information when that information had been rendered especially salient in context, and thus harder to ignore. Likewise, Brown-Schmidt (2009) and Wardlow (2013) have shown that individual differences in executive control and working memory can impact when and how individuals in conversation attend to common ground (although these effects may be unreliable; cf. Ryskin et al., 2014). In a similar vein, cognitive load has been shown to impact perspective-taking as well (Kronmüller & Barr, 2007; Lin, Keysar, & Epley, 2010).

Another proposal along these lines is Horton and Gerrig's (2005a, 2016) *memory-based* account, which highlights the importance of ordinary memory mechanisms for shaping conversational behavior. Memory clearly has a significant role to play in conversational interaction, given that speakers regularly make reference to people and places in ways that require some form of memory retrieval. Many discourse phenomena are "historical," in the sense that interlocutors draw upon memories of previous utterances and earlier interactions (either implicitly or explicitly) to know what to say at the present moment. Indeed, Clark and Marshall (1981) incorporated this idea into their account of co-presence heuristics, proposing that speakers and addressees routinely examine appropriate person-centered memory representations for evidence to support particular inferences about common ground. Clark and Marshall's proposal, though, was predicated on the idea that these inferences are driven by high-level collaborative goals. In contrast, the memory-based view, similar to Pickering and Garrod's (2004) interactive alignment account, seeks to explain how individuals may produce conversationally appropriate utterances (most of the time, at least) without necessitating effortful or time-consuming consideration of detailed "models of the partner."

This account is based on the assumption that people habitually encode episodic memories of the encounters they have with others, including contextual details relevant to the nature of those interactions. Importantly, these memory representations are *not* specifically dedicated to the task of encoding co-presence; rather, they are seen as capturing the kinds of information ordinarily associated with routine experiences of life events. Given the availability of these episodic traces in long-term memory, Horton and Gerrig (2005a) propose that other people may then serve as salient cues for the automatic retrieval of this information through a passive process known as *resonance* (Gillund & Schiffrin, 1984; Hintzman, 1986; Ratcliff, 1978), facilitating automatic access to memories of past interactions in ways that can inform language production and comprehension. Importantly, because this memory reactivation has a time course associated with it, determined in part by the recency or frequency with which particular memories have been accessed and the strength of available retrieval cues, this account can readily explain why individuals sometimes make egocentric errors in conversational reference. However, this account also predicts that individuals' conversational contributions can appear to be in accord with assumptions about common ground if salient partner-relevant cues in a particular conversational context support the retrieval of appropriate knowledge, in line with constraint-based views (see also Brown-Schmidt, Yoon, & Ryskin, 2015; Horton & Brennan, 2016). Consistent with this idea, Horton and Gerrig (2005b) used a picture-matching task to demonstrate that giving speakers the opportunity to encode relatively distinct partner-specific memory representations with each of two addressees (by manipulating the correspondences between types of picture cards and each addressee) allowed them to exhibit stronger evidence of audience design when referring to pictures the current addressee was familiar with or not (see also Gorman, Gegg-Harrison, Marsh, & Tanenhaus, 2013).

Integrative Challenges

As this brief survey of psycholinguistic work on conversation and language use makes clear, a pressing issue for scholars interested in interactive discourse is determining the extent to which particular collaborative behaviors are (in larger or smaller part) simultaneously the product of lower-level linguistic and cognitive processes. Contributing to the complexity of this issue is the fact that different approaches have tended to emphasize different aspects of what it means to "use" language in dialogue. While investigations into the dynamics of conversational coordination have provided valuable descriptions of how talk is organized and of the interpersonal concerns that motivate particular forms of joint action at a macro-level, other work within psycholinguistics has tended to focus on when and how socially relevant knowledge makes contact with micro-level processes of incremental utterance planning and interpretation. Integrating these levels of analysis remains a substantial challenge. From this perspective, it is promising to see the development of comprehensive theories explicitly oriented around trying to bridge this gap, such as Pickering and Garrod's (2004, 2013) interactive alignment model and the more recent dynamical systems account proposed by Dale et al. (2014; see also Duran, Dale, & Galati, 2016). Continued progress in this area will almost certainly require a better understanding of how complex interactive behaviors emerge through individual psychological mechanisms.

Current and Future Directions

The preceding sections have highlighted several of the most influential approaches to conversation and spoken discourse, including work from both descriptive and experimental perspectives. Of course, many important questions remain, not only about the mechanisms underlying communicative interactions but also about the extent to which these mechanisms apply across different communicative contexts. In this final section, I briefly consider three additional topics that are likely to be especially important for addressing some of these issues: cognitive neuroscience of interactive dialogue, multiparty interaction, and forms of computer-mediated communication online. Work in each of these areas has the potential to push existing models of conversation and social interaction in new directions.

Neurocognitive Correlates of Communicative Interaction

To date, most experimental research on conversation and social interaction has focused on behavioral measures. But, while work in cognitive neuroscience has led to a number of essential discoveries concerning the intricacies of language processing in individual brains (for some relevant reviews, see Hagoort & Indefrey, 2014; Hickok & Poeppel, 2007; Kutas, van Petten, & Kluender, 2006; Mason & Just, 2006), equivalent advances in our understanding of the neural markers of *interactive* language use have lagged. Not only do neuroimaging and electrophysiological recording have difficulties with signal artifacts caused by movements of the head and mouth associated with speaking (Ganushchak, Christoffels, & Schiller, 2011; Zeffiro & Frymiare, 2006), but more fundamentally, there are significant challenges associated with obtaining meaningful neurocognitive data in tightly controlled settings involving multiple interacting brains (Kuhlen, Allefeld, Anders, & Haynes, 2015).

One tactic used by researchers interested in the neural mechanisms associated with social interaction has been to record brain activity from single participants in pseudo-social contexts, such as while listening to prerecorded stimuli or interpreting the actions of others in fictional narratives (e.g., Dumontheil, Küster, Apperly, & Blakemore, 2010; Mar, 2011; Saxe & Kanwisher, 2003). Work of this nature has led to important findings about the neural circuits associated with the perception and interpretation of social information, including brain regions implicated in our capacity to reason about the mental states of other individuals, or *theory of mind* (Ciaramidaro et al., 2007; Saxe, Carey, & Kanwisher, 2004; Vogeley et al., 2001), and about the possible relationships between theory of mind and brain systems responsible for more general language processes (e.g., Ferstl & von Cramon, 2002).

Neuroscientists have also used noninteractive "single-brain" paradigms to examine potential interrelationships between language production and language comprehension across individuals. For example, Stephens, Silbert, and Hasson (2010) used fMRI to record the brain activity of a speaker as she recounted a personal narrative, and then subsequently recorded the brain activity of a separate group of individuals as they listened to an audiorecording of this same narrative. Interestingly, comparisons of the original speaker's brain activity over time to that of the listeners revealed evidence for substantial speaker-to-listener "neural coupling"—i.e., spatial and temporal correspondences in patterns of brain activity across the speaker and listeners over the course of the narrative. Subsequent research using similar methodologies has since obtained further evidence for these types of cross-brain correspondences (Dumas, Nadel, Soussignan, Martinerie, & Garnero, 2010; Kuhlen, Allefeld, & Haynes, 2012). The relative timing of these patterns across individuals may provide an important clue to what they could mean. In their study, for instance, Stephens et al. (2010)

found that the degree to which listeners' brain activity systematically *preceded* equivalent activity in the speaker correlated with successful comprehension of the narrative. This would seem consistent with models such as Pickering and Garrod (2013) that posit an important role for anticipatory processes in dialogue.

A running theme of this chapter, though, is that interactive dialogue has particular properties that emerge most strongly through the contributions of two or more individuals working in concert. For this reason, there is growing recognition of the need to examine neural activity in the context of genuine interactive settings, rather than via paradigms where communication is essentially "one-way" (Schoot, Hagoort, & Segaert, 2016). Although some studies have examined the brain activity of individuals interacting in real time with a partner whose brain activity is not recorded (Noordzij et al., 2009; Schoot et al., 2014), or while listening to prerecorded utterances presented *after* a real interaction with a confederate (Bögels, Barr, Garrod, & Kessler, 2015), a more complete understanding of the neural correlates of social communication requires methodologies that permit the measurement of brain activity of *multiple* participants in situated, interactive contexts (Hari & Kujala, 2009; Hasson et al., 2012; Montague et al., 2002; Schilbach et al., 2013). Social and cognitive neuroscientists have only recently begun to identify ways to address the challenges associated with such "two-person neuroscience," most commonly via the simultaneous recording of brain activation from multiple individuals, or *hyperscanning* (Montague et al., 2002; see also Koike, Tanabe, & Sadato, 2015; Konvalinka & Roepstorff, 2012).

Similar to the findings from Stephens et al. (2010) and others noted above, studies employing simultaneous hyperscanning with non-linguistic interactive tasks (e.g. Dumas et al., 2010; Saito et al., 2010) have found consistent evidence for neural synchronization across interacting individuals, often localized to brain regions associated with mentalizing and related forms of social coordination. Intriguingly, one study that used a hyperscanning procedure (with functional near-infrared spectroscopy (fNIRS)) in a verbal communication context (Jiang et al., 2012; see also Jiang et al., 2015) found an increase in cross-speaker neural synchrony (localized to the left inferior frontal cortex) in face-to-face dialogue compared to a monologue condition where one person spoke and the other stayed silent. Further research in this vein is clearly needed, but reliable evidence of brain-to-brain neural coupling in interactive dialogue would certainly be a provocative source of data consistent with dynamic models of interpersonal alignment and social action (Hasson et al., 2012; Menenti, Pickering, & Garrod, 2012; Schoot et al., 2016; Stolk, Verhagen, & Toni, 2016). Conversational coordination may emerge not only at the behavioral level, but at the neural level as well. An important question, of course, is whether one of these forms of coordination is more likely to be the cause versus the effect of the other.

Multiparty Interaction

As mentioned in the introduction, dyadic face-to-face interactions have typically been taken to be the default conversational setting. A salient question for research in dialogue, though, is the extent to which the interactive mechanisms found to be important for shaping speaker–addressee interactions might scale successfully to explain the behaviors of individuals in triads and beyond (Branigan, 2006; Traum, 2004). While much of the experimental work on conversation has focused on dyads, conversations between groups of individuals are certainly not rare, and multiparty conversations have long been an important focus within CA (Schegloff, 1996). Recall, for example, the rules governing "next speaker selection" described by Sacks et al. (1974) in their model of conversational turn-taking, which was explicitly intended to apply to conversational groups of varying sizes. On this model, two-party dialogues, with their relatively straightforward alternation of speakers, may represent the "special" case in that speaker transitions are mostly about determining *when* a speaker change occurs (Schegloff, 1996). In multiparty interactions, though, there is the additional consideration of *who* should speak next. At transition-relevant places where the current speaker does not select the next speaker directly, instances of simultaneous "self-selection" by more than one co-participant may lead to multiple people starting to speak at the same time, requiring additional repair work before one person has the conversational floor (Hayashi, 2013). In a similar vein, Sacks and Schegloff's (1979) original notion of *recipient design* was used to describe how, in multi-party situations, speakers may produce referring expressions that effectively function to select the intended next speaker based on what that particular individual would be expected to know (versus others present in the situation).

One complexity introduced by multiparty conversations is the fact that not all individuals may have the same status with respect to the current interaction. As highlighted in the introduction, speakers and addressees often interact in situations where additional individuals are present as side-participants or overhearers (Clark & Carlson, 1982; Clark & Schaefer, 1992). This fact has clear implications for processes of conversational grounding, which is generally understood as involving *direct* collaboration between interlocutors. Side-participants, though, "collaborate" only indirectly. Even so, speakers still seem to assume side-participants have access to the same kinds of information as direct addressees. For example, Wilkes-Gibbs and Clark (1992) showed that, when referring to entities from a previous dialogue, speakers' expressions directed at individuals who had been side-participants for that previous dialogue were similar to those directed at addressees. Eshghi and Healey (2016) have even argued that certain circumstances may allow groups of individuals (e.g., spouses) to function as a "coalition" in conversation, such that even if some members of a group act mostly as side-participants, interlocutors presume *grounding by proxy*, in which information established with an active participant is extended to the coalition as a whole. The same doesn't appear to be true, however, for non-participants (who, you may recall, are not considered "ratified" with respect to the current conversation). In the same study by Wilkes-Gibbs and Clark (1992) described above, speakers' utterances for partners who had been bystanders to the earlier dialogue, relative to expressions for previous side-participants, tended to be longer and contain fewer definite descriptions—and, in fact, were similar to those directed at truly naïve addressees.

On the comprehension side, listeners who do not fully participate in an interaction may have discourse representations that are qualitatively or quantitatively different from actual addressees. Schober and Clark (1989) showed, for example, that overhearers were less efficient and less accurate following the speakers' instructions in a Tangram-matching task than addressees, as predicted by Clark's collaborative model. In another study, Branigan, Pickering, and Cleland (2000) examined syntactic priming in a triadic picture description task, and found that priming was weaker when the current speaker had been a side-participant for the previous trial than when the current speaker had been the previous addressee, indicating that differences in discourse representations may exist between side-participants and addressees as well. Consistent with Pickering and Garrod's (2013) prediction-by-simulation account, attending to a speaker's utterance with the expectation of responding may evoke different sorts of processing compared to merely listening to the same utterance as a side-participant (or overhearer, for that matter; Behnel et al., 2013).

What about situations containing multiple "ratified" participants? Although studies on interpersonal dynamics and group interactions have long been central to social psychology

Conversation and Interactive Discourse

(e.g., Nye & Brower, 1996; Pennington, 2002; Semin & Fiedler, 1992), psycholinguistic work on full-fledged multiparty dialogues is relatively scant. However, speakers do appear sensitive to the presence of multiple addressees. Yoon and Brown-Schmidt (2014) showed that, following several rounds of working with one addressee to establish referring expressions for a set of Tangrams, speakers tended to produce longer and more disfluent expressions for the same Tangrams after an additional naïve person joined the task as a second addressee, suggesting that speakers were trying accommodate this new individual. Interestingly, eyetracking evidence indicated that the original addressees *also* adjusted their expectations for the kinds of expressions the speaker would produce in this new, triadic configuration. All else being equal, speakers and addressees may be able to flexibly adjust to the varying communicative demands of multiparty interactions, at least when circumstances make it fairly straightforward to keep track of the different knowledge states of multiple conversational partners (or potential partners; see also Horton & Gerrig, 2005b). When differences across addressees are more ambiguous or challenging to identify, however, speakers may elect to act more heuristically. For example, in a follow-up to their previous study, Yoon and Brown-Schmidt (2016) obtained evidence suggesting that, when confronted with multiple addressees with heterogenous knowledge states, speakers preferentially adopted the relatively conservative strategy of tailoring utterances toward the needs of the *least* knowledgeable addressee.

Another salient issue concerns the effects of group size on multiparty interactions. As pointed out by Branigan (2006), larger groups are likely to make it difficult to engage in collaborative behaviors with each fellow participant to the same degree, which should have implications for the kinds of discourse representations that emerge from large-group interactions. For example, Fay, Garrod, and Carletta (2000) examined discussions between 5- and 10-person groups and found that, while the smaller 5-person groups were similar to traditional dialogues in that people's post-discussion responses were mostly influenced by those other members of the group with whom they had directly interacted, people in the larger 10-person groups were influenced more by the most dominant speaker within the group—whether or not they had interacted with that individual directly. Similar to the findings on multiparty dialogue from Yoon and Brown-Schmidt (2016), Fay et al. (2000) suggest that, in larger groups, individuals may formulate what they say to be understood by the broadest audience within the group. Interestingly, communicating to larger groups may also cause speakers to avoid sharing information that makes them look bad and to remain relatively focused on their own concerns (Barasch & Berger, 2014). Thus, interacting in larger groups may not only pose challenges for considering a multiplicity of perspectives, but may also be accompanied by shifts in speakers' social goals.

Conversation Through and With Online Technologies

Increasingly, people (in certain cultural communities, at least) are spending a substantial portion of their waking hours on the Internet, including time spent communicating with others via online media, and the social implications of this shift toward digital communications are significant (DiMaggio, Hargittai, Neuman, & Robinson, 2001; Gernsbacher, 2014; Sparrow & Chatman, 2013; see also Gergle, this volume). It is impossible to list all of the (relatively) recent technologies that facilitate conversations online, but these include not only "everyday" technologies like email and text messaging via smartphone, but also multimodal conversation tools like Skype, social networking sites like Twitter, Facebook, and LinkedIn, community forums such as Reddit and Slashdot, mobile messaging platforms like WhatsApp and Snapchat, and even massively multiplayer online games such as World of Warcraft (and, of course, newer types of Internet-based media are created every day, rendering such lists quickly obsolete). Right now it is very much an open question how existing models of conversation and verbal interaction might translate to diverse types of online media, and how these newer modes of conversation may influence some of the interactive phenomena considered throughout this chapter, such as grounding, turn-taking, audience design, accommodation, or alignment—or if one should even expect people to converse in familiar ways when interacting via these newer technologies (Crystal, 2001).

To date, much of the existing work on these issues has focused on how properties of particular digital media shape how people interact in these settings (e.g., see the chapters in Herring, Stein, & Virtanen, 2013), often along the lines of the communicative constraints identified by Clark and Brennan (1991), described previously. For example, as one of the oldest forms of computer-mediated communication, there is already a substantial literature on electronic mail, and how the lack of co-presence between interlocutors communicating asynchronously via email may attenuate particular kinds of social or emotional cues (e.g., Severinson Eklundh, 1994; Sproull & Kiesler, 1986; Walther, 1996). Similarly, the lack of paralinguistic information (like intonation or gesture) in email may cause people to overestimate their communicative effectiveness (Kruger, Epley, Parker, & Ng, 2005).

Other work has explored the nature of conversations via SMS text messaging and instant messaging (IM) chat (e.g., Ling & Baron, 2007). For example, Hancock and Dunham (2001) showed that performance on a referential communication task carried out via IM improved when participants explicitly marked turn completions, while Fox Tree, Mayer, and Betts (2011) asked pairs of participants to engage in brief conversations via IM chat and found that participants with greater instant messaging experience were more likely to use emoticons (e.g., a "smiley-face") to convey information that would ordinarily be expressed via paralinguistic cues. These experienced IM chatters also produced more discourse markers and backchannel responses. Consistent with Clark's (1996) collaborative model, familiarity with the norms and expectations of IM chat seemed to allow these "digital natives" to present their messages in ways that could facilitate conversational grounding within this particular medium.

Certain types of newer communicative media, though, may offer different sorts of challenges for researchers interested in exploring how people interact in online settings. While it may be comparatively straightforward to bring participants into the lab and ask them to use a video- or text-chat interface to interact with a real or virtual partner in particular ways, controlled studies of interactions via certain media like Twitter or Facebook would seem harder to implement, given that people typically use these sites to communicate with their personal social networks for highly specific reasons (boyd & Ellison, 2008). The unique nature of these media, though, provides researchers with other sorts of opportunities to examine questions about the nature of interactions within these settings.

For example, one significant feature of social networking sites is that they have large, highly active user bases, giving researchers access to sizeable collections of online postings (e.g., the Edinburgh Twitter FSD Corpus; Petrović, Osborne, & Lavrenko, 2012) that can be mined in a variety of ways. In one study, Ritter, Cherry, and Dolan (2010) generated a large (1.3 million conversations) corpus of Twitter postings, and used an unsupervised learning technique to construct a model of "dialogue act" sequences on Twitter, examining how certain types of tweets prompt responses from others. They found that Twitter exchanges are frequently initiated through three types of acts: a "Status" act in which a user broadcasts information about what they are currently doing, a "Reference" act in which a user broadcasts links to other content, and a "Question to Follower" act in which the users ask an open question of their followers. Similarly, Danescu-Niculescu-Mizil, Gamon, and Dumais (2011) used the Twitter API (application programming interface) to reconstruct over 215,000 complete conversations (~840k tweets) between 2,200 pairs of users on Twitter. Examining these conversations for a variety of features, they obtained broad evidence of linguistic convergence across communicators, suggesting that forms of communication accommodation (Giles et al., 1991) and alignment may extend to online contexts as well. And intriguingly, Purohit et al. (2013) leveraged Clark's (1996; Clark & Wilkes-Gibbs, 1986) collaborative model of conversation, as well as work in CA (Goodwin & Heritage, 1990), to identify potential markers of social and linguistic coordination within a large collection of tweets related to salient world events (such as the 2011 Japanese earthquake and Hurricane Irene). Using these markers, they were able to highlight how researchers and government officials might be able to mine social media for evidence of "citizen coordination" in times of emergency.

Of course, certain aspects of interactions occurring online may be quite different from other forms of interpersonal communication. Consider, for example, Clark's (1996) suggestion that a necessary precondition for conversational coordination is an awareness that both you and your interlocutor are co-present and attentive in the current context. In face-to-face conversation or small-group discussions, one generally has a sense of who is paying attention (Kuhlen & Brennan, 2010; Rosa, Finch, Bergeson, & Arnold, 2015) and speakers can take certain measures (such as coughing loudly or calling someone by name to get their attention) to ensure that intended addressees know they are being addressed. Moreover, in such settings one typically knows something about the other people present, and utterances are intended for one or a few addressees at most. Many types of online communication, though, involve "one-to-many" interactions (i.e., "broadcasting," Barasch & Berger, 2014) that lack some or all of these features, often prompting users to take advantage of quirks of the interface to get around some of these challenges (such as using the @ sign on Twitter to address or respond to specific others; Honeycutt & Herring, 2009). In particular, the nature of commonality—or what can be taken as common—may change radically in online settings. Not only do one-to-many media like Facebook or Twitter involve asynchronous interactions, but it can be nearly impossible to know who is attending to one's message at any given point in time. As a result, users may not even know which of their friends or followers has read what they wrote, reducing the likelihood that particular information will be taken as "grounded," absent an explicit response.

What are the implications of these types of public online interactions for familiar conversational phenomena like audience design, given that these media often blur the lines between addressee, side-participant, and observer? And, are online communicators and their message recipients aware of these distinctions, and what kinds of adjustments do they make in response? For now, possible answers to these questions are suggestive at best. For example, Marwick and boyd (2011) interviewed a group of active Twitter users and found that these users reported having a clear sense of their "audience" and that they were confident in their ability to tailor tweets for particular subsets of their followers. The accuracy of these assessments was not independently evaluated, however, and other work suggests that people may find it difficult to consider their audience in any detail when communicating with groups of people online. Recall the work showing that communicating to large groups can cause speakers to remain relatively self-focused (Barasch & Berger, 2014). A similar finding was obtained by Chiou and Lee (2013), who asked undergraduate participants (all active Facebook users) to post messages on Facebook for the public at large or for just their

Facebook "friends" (or they did not post anything at all). Results from two perspective-taking tasks (one verbal, one nonverbal) revealed greater egocentrism following the public Facebook posting. Like Barasch and Berger (2014), Chiou and Lee suggest that indiscriminate forms of one-to-many communication may result in a greater focus on the self and thus greater egocentrism. Whether this holds up remains to be seen, but one hallmark of "broadcast" modes of online communication does seem to be that opportunities for reciprocal coordination and joint action are limited at best. From the viewpoint of the kinds of models considered in this chapter, it would not be surprising if these sorts of online-only interactions lead to impoverished forms of mutual understanding.

Conclusion

Because conversation is something that we engage in so regularly and with such ease, it is easy to overlook how complex it really is. Interacting successfully with others requires a multitude of activities: navigating flexibly between talking and listening (or their equivalents in other modalities), attending to the content of what is being said as well as how and when it is said, ensuring that contributions are appropriate for the current conversational context, integrating paralinguistic, gestural, and bodily cues (as the medium allows) together with the linguistic meanings of utterances, and doing all of this within a particular set of social constraints and expectations. Any comprehensive model of conversation would not only need to have an account of relevant processes in multimodal language production and comprehension, but also be able to incorporate interpersonal factors such as theory of mind, politeness, and sociocultural variation—*and* potentially provide a description of how these components come together in particular discourse contexts.

Progress toward these objectives requires, at the very least, that researchers be willing to examine a variety of communicative situations involving different purposes and types of settings. Work within CA has been successful in this regard, considering a diversity of communicative situations as a way of identifying the boundary conditions for descriptions of the constitutive principles governing the orderly organization of talk. Importantly, these principles are seen as both "context-sensitive," in that they are adaptive to local circumstances, and "context-free," in that they apply to a variety of settings and participants (Sacks et al., 1974). In general, CA adopts a synthetic approach to the study of spontaneous dialogue, believing that specific conversational behaviors, such as mutual gaze or forms of requests, cannot be considered in isolation from other aspects of the interaction.

Traditionally, work from a psycholinguistic perspective has been more analytic, examining discrete processes of language comprehension and production separately. One of the most significant shifts prompted by work on dialogue, though, has been greater recognition of the extent to which language use between speakers and addresses is tightly integrated and highly contextualized. Although current theories differ in the extent to which this integration is driven by top-down or bottom-up concerns, exploring these issues has inspired the development of communicative paradigms that allow various forms of naturalistic joint action. Using these paradigms, investigators have been able to systematically explore the potential constraints on interactive coordination—both as characteristics of individual participants and as features of communicative situations—within a variety of experimental tasks.

An important question, of course, is whether conclusions based on evidence from experimental contexts can be meaningfully extended to other types of communicative settings. Conversational actions outside the lab are likely to be motivated for a diversity of reasons that go beyond success or failure on a particular task, and given the very real challenges of balancing realism with experimental control in this domain, it is not always evident how findings from particular types of task-oriented dialogues (like object-matching or route-finding) may generalize to situations that emphasize different sorts of interpersonal or social goals. When a situation allows people to engage with each other more socially, not only will the nature of the interaction inevitably change, but how people experience that situation is likely to change as well (Bickmore & Cassell, 2005; Conrad et al., 2015). Developing general theories of conversation that can capture these differences will undoubtedly require that researchers identify ways to examine relevant issues in the context of "casual" chat and other forms of social interaction, which in turn is likely to involve the further integration of relevant methods and concerns from both CA and cognitive psychology (Potter & Edwards, 2013). At the same time, close examination of spontaneous interactions in a variety of novel contexts will continue to be valuable for suggesting new avenues for systematic investigation. Given the importance of dialogue for nearly every facet of human activity, the challenge for researchers in this area is to develop accounts of the fundamental properties and mechanisms of collaboration that are flexible enough to apply to diverse contexts and agendas.

Suggested Reading

Brennan, S. E., Galati, A., & Kuhlen, A. K. (2010). Two minds, one dialog: Coordinating speaking and understanding. *Psychology of Learning and Motivation, 53*, 301–344.

Clark, H. H. (1996). *Using language*. Cambridge, UK: Cambridge University Press.

Pickering, M. J., & Garrod, S. (2013). An integrated theory of language production and comprehension [and associated commentary]. *Behavioral and Brain Sciences, 36*, 329–392.

Potter, J., & Edwards, D. (2013). Conversation analysis and psychology. In J. Sidnell & T. Stivers (Eds), *The handbook of conversation analysis* (pp. 726–740). Chichester, UK: Wiley-Blackwell.

Sidnell, J. (2010). *Conversation analysis: An introduction*. Chichester, UK: Wiley-Blackwell.

Wachsmuth, I., de Ruiter, J., Jaecks, P., & Kopp, S. (Eds). (2013). *Alignment in communication: Towards a new theory of communication*. Amsterdam: John Benjamins.

Notes

1 When describing conversations, *naturalistic* often refers to the fact that the interaction is unscripted and people can interact freely, while *spontaneous* refers to the fact that speakers choose when to talk and what to talk about. Experimental paradigms involving linguistic interaction may be naturalistic to a greater or lesser degree, but are rarely truly spontaneous.

2 It should be noted, though, that Barr (2008, 2016) has suggested that evidence from experiments like Hanna et al. (2003) may demonstrate early sensitivity to common ground without shedding light on *how* this information is actually used in utterance interpretation. Based on data from several eyetracking experiments showing early anticipatory looks toward objects in common ground but little to no sensitivity to perspective during referent identification in the context of lexical ambiguities, Barr (2008) argues that processes responsible for rapid *access* to common ground-relevant information are distinct from processes involved in the *integration* of this information into a discourse representation. Thus, rather than assuming fully interactive constraints on interpretation, this proposal holds that important aspects of linguistic processing may still be encapsulated from consideration of common ground.

References

Anderson, A., Bader, M., Bard, E., Boyle, E., Doherty, G., Garrod, S., Isard, S., Kowtko, J., MacAllister, J., Miller, J., Sotillo, C., Thompson, H., & Weinert, R. (1991). The HCRC map task corpus. *Language and Speech, 34*, 351–366.

Argyle, M., Lefebvre, L., & Cook, M. (1974). The meaning of five patterns of gaze. *European Journal of Social Psychology, 4*, 125–136.

Babel, M. (2010). Dialect divergence and convergence in New Zealand English. *Language in Society*, *39*, 437–456.

Babel, M. (2012). Evidence for phonetic and social selectivity in spontaneous phonetic imitation. *Journal of Phonetics*, *40*, 177–189.

Bailenson, J. N., & Yee, N. (2005). Digital chameleons: Automatic assimilation of nonverbal gestures in immersive virtual environments. *Psychological Science*, *16*, 814–819.

Balcetis, E., & Dale, R. (2005). An exploration of social modulation of syntactic priming. In B. Bara, L. Barsalou, & M. Bucciarelli (Eds), *Proceedings of the 27th Annual Meeting of the Cognitive Science Society* (pp. 184–189). Mahwah, NJ: Erlbaum.

Bangerter, A. (2004). Using pointing and describing to achieve joint focus of attention in dialogue. *Psychological Science*, *15*, 415–419.

Bangerter, A., & Clark, H. H. (2003). Navigating joint projects with dialogue. *Cognitive Science*, *27*, 195–225.

Barasch, A., & Berger, J. (2014). Broadcasting and narrowcasting: How audience size affects what people share. *Journal of Marketing Research*, *51*, 286–299.

Barr, D. J. (2008). Pragmatic expectations and linguistic evidence: Listeners anticipate but do not integrate common ground. *Cognition*, *109*, 457–474.

Barr, D. J. (2016). Visual world studies of conversational perspective taking: Similar findings, diverging interpretations. In P. Knoeferle, P. Pyykkönen-Klauck, & M. W. Crocker (Eds), *Visually situated language comprehension* (pp. 261–289). Amsterdam: John Benjamins.

Barr, D. J., & Keysar, B. (2006). Perspective taking and the coordination of meaning in language use. In M. J. Traxler & M. A. Gernsbacher (Eds), *Handbook of psycholinguistics, 2nd edition* (pp. 901–938). Amsterdam: Academic Press.

Bavelas, J. B. (2007). Face-to-face dialogue as a micro-social context. In S. D. Duncan, J. Cassell, & E. T. Levy (Eds), *Gesture and the dynamic dimension of language: Essays in honor of David McNeill* (pp. 127–146). Amsterdam: John Benjamins.

Bavelas, J. B., Coates, L., & Johnson, T. (2002). Listener responses as a collaborative process: The role of gaze. *Journal of Communication*, *52*, 566–580.

Bavelas, J. B., & Gerwing, J. (2011). The listener as addressee in face-to-face dialogue. *International Journal of Listening*, *25*, 178–198.

Bavelas, J. B., Hutchinson, S., Kenwood, C., & Matheson, D. H. (1997). Using face-to-face dialogue as a standard for other communication systems. *Canadian Journal of Communication*, *22*, 5–24.

Behnel, M., Cummins, C., Sichelschmidt, L., & de Ruiter, J. (2013). Priming and conceptual pacts in overhearers' adoption of referring expressions. In M. Knauff, M. Pauen, N. Sebanz, & I. Wachsmuth (Eds), *Proceedings of the 35th Annual Conference of the Cognitive Science Society* (pp. 1869–1874). Austin, TX: Cognitive Science Society.

Bell, A. (1984). Language style as audience design. *Language in Society*, *13*, 145–204.

Bell, A., & Johnson, G. (1997). Toward a sociolinguistics of style. *University of Pennsylvania Working Papers in Linguistics*, *4*(1), 2.

Benjamin, T., & Walker, T. (2014). Managing problems of acceptability through high rise-fall repetitions. *Discourse Processes*, *50*, 107–138.

Biber, D. (1986). On the investigation of spoken/written differences. *Studia Linguistica*, *40*, 1–21.

Bickmore, T., & Cassell, J. (2005). Social dialogue with embodied conversational agents. In J. van Kuppevelt, L. Dybkjaer, & N. Bernsen (Eds), *Advances in natural, multimodal dialogue systems* (pp. 1–32). New York, NY: Kluwer Academic.

Bock, K. (1996). Language production: Methods and methodologies. *Psychological Bulletin & Review*, *3*, 395–421.

Bögels, S., Barr, D. J., Garrod, S., & Kessler, K. (2015). Conversational interaction in the scanner: Mentalizing during language processing as revealed by MEG. *Cerebral Cortex*, *25*, 3219–3234.

Bolden, G. B. (2003). Multiple modalities in collaborative turn sequences. *Gesture*, *3*, 187–212.

Borhuis, R. Y., & Giles, H. (1977). The language of intergroup distinctiveness. In H. Giles (Ed.), *Language, ethnicity and intergroup relations* (pp. 119–135). London: Academic Press.

boyd, d. m., & Ellison, N. B. (2008). Social network sites: Definition, history, and scholarship. *Journal of Computer-Mediated Communication*, *13*, 210–230.

Boyle, E. A., Anderson, A. H., & Newlands, A. (1994). The effects of visibility on dialogue and performance in a cooperative problem solving task. *Language and Speech*, *37*, 1–20.

Branigan, H. (2006). Perspectives on multi-party dialogue. *Research on Language and Computation*, *4*, 153–177.

Branigan, H. P., Bell, J., & McLean, J. F. (2016). Do you know what I know? The impact of participant role in children's referential communication. *Frontiers in Psychology*, 7, 213. doi:10.3389/fpsyg.2016.00213.

Branigan, H. P., Pickering, M. J., & Cleland. A. A. (2000). Syntactic co-ordination in dialogue. *Cognition*, *75*, B13–25.

Branigan, H. P., Pickering, M. J., McLean, J. F., & Cleland, A. A. (2007). Syntactic alignment and participant role in dialogue. *Cognition*, *104*, 163–197.

Branigan, H. P., Pickering, M. J., Pearson, J., McLean, J. F., & Brown, A. (2011). The role of beliefs in lexical alignment: Evidence from dialogs with humans and computers. *Cognition*, *121*, 41–57.

Brennan, S. E. (2005). How conversation is shaped by visual and spoken evidence. In J. C. Trueswell & M. K. Tanenhaus (Eds), *Approaches to studying world-situated language use: Bridging the language-as-product and language-as-action traditions* (pp. 95–129). Cambridge, MA: MIT Press.

Brennan, S. E., & Clark, H. H. (1996). Conceptual pacts and lexical choice in conversation. *Journal of Experimental Psychology: Learning, Memory, and Cognition*, *22*, 1482–1493.

Brennan, S. E., Galati, A., & Kuhlen, A. K. (2010). Two minds, one dialog: Coordinating speaking and understanding. *Psychology of Learning and Motivation*, *53*, 301–344.

Brennan, S. E., & Hanna, J. E. (2009). Partner-specific adaptation in dialogue. *Topics in Cognitive Science*, *1*, 274–291.

Brown-Schmidt, S. (2009). The role of executive function in perspective taking during online language comprehension. *Psychonomic Bulletin & Review*, *16*, 893–900.

Brown-Schmidt, S. (2012). Beyond common and privileged: Gradient representations of common ground in real-time language use. *Language and Cognitive Processes*, *27*, 62–89.

Brown-Schmidt, S., Campana, E., & Tanenhaus, M. K. (2005). Real-time reference resolution by naïve participants during a task-based unscripted conversation. In J. C. Trueswell & M. K. Tanenhaus (Eds), *Approaches to studying world-situated language use: Bridging the language-as-product and language-as-action traditions* (pp. 153–171). Cambridge, MA: MIT Press.

Brown-Schmidt, S., Gunlogson, C., & Tanenhaus, M. K. (2008). Addressees distinguish shared from private information when interpreting questions during interactive conversation. *Cognition*, *107*, 1122–1134.

Brown-Schmidt, S., & Hanna, J. E. (2011). Talking in another person's shoes: Incremental perspective-taking in language processing. *Dialogue & Discourse*, 2, 11–33.

Brown-Schmidt, S., & Tanenhaus, M. K. (2008). Real-time investigation of referential domains in unscripted conversation: A targeted language game approach. *Cognitive Science*, *32*, 643–684.

Brown-Schmidt, S., Yoon, S. O., & Ryskin, R. A. (2015). People as contexts in conversation. *Psychology of Learning and Motivation*, *62*, 59–99.

Carbary, K. M., Frohning, E. E., & Tanenhaus, M. K. (2010). Context, syntactic priming, and referential form in an interactive dialogue task: Implications for models of alignment. In S. Ohlsson & R. Catrambone (Eds), *Proceedings of the 32nd Annual Conference of the Cognitive Science Society* (pp. 109–114). Austin, TX. Cognitive Science Society.

Casillas, M., & Frank, M. C. (2013). The development of predictive processes in children's discourse understanding. In M. Knauff, M. Pauen, N. Sebanz, & I. Wachsmuth (Eds), *Proceedings of the 35th Annual Meeting of the Cognitive Science Society* (pp. 299–304). Austin, TX: Cognitive Science Society.

Chafe, W. (1982). Integration and involvement in speaking, writing, and oral literature. In D. Tannen (Ed.), *Spoken and written language: Exploring orality and literacy* (pp. 35–53). Norwood, NJ: Ablex.

Chafe, W., & Tannen, D. (1987). The relation between written and spoken language. *Annual Review of Anthropology*, *16*, 383–407.

Chartrand, T. L., & Bargh, J. A. (1999). The chameleon effect: The perception-behavior link and social interaction. *Journal of Personality and Social Psychology*, *76*, 893–910.

Chartrand, T. L., & Lakin, J. L. (2013). The antecedents and consequences of human behavioral mimicry. *Annual Review of Psychology*, *64*, 285–308.

Chartrand, T. L., & van Baaren, R. (2009). Human mimicry. *Advances in Experimental Social Psychology*, *41*, 219–274.

Cherry, E. C. (1956). *On human communication*. Cambridge, MA: MIT Press.

Chiou, W.-B., & Lee, C.-C. (2013). Enactment of one-to-many communication may induce self-focused attention that leads to diminished perspective taking: The case of Facebook. *Judgment and Decision Making, 8*, 372–380.

Chow, C. P., Mitchell, J. F., & Miller, C. T. (2015). Vocal turn-taking in a non-human primate is learned during ontogeny. *Proceedings of the Royal Society B: Biological Sciences, 282*, 20150069. doi:10.1098/rspb.2015.0069.

Ciaramidaro, A., Adenzato, M., Enrici, I., Erk, S., Pia, L., Bara, B. G., & Walter, H. (2007). The intentional network: How the brain reads varieties of intentions. *Neuropsychologia, 45*, 3105–3113.

Clark, H. H. (1992). *Arenas of language use.* Chicago, IL: University of Chicago Press.

Clark, H. H. (1994). Managing problems in speaking. *Speech Communication, 15*, 243–250.

Clark, H. H. (1996). *Using language.* Cambridge, UK: Cambridge University Press.

Clark, H. H. (2004). Pragmatics of language performance. In L. R. Horn & G. Ward (Eds), *The handbook of pragmatics* (pp. 365–382). Oxford, UK: Blackwell.

Clark, H. H. (2012). Spoken discourse and its emergence. In M. J. Spivey, K. McRae, & M. F. Joanisse (Eds), *Cambridge handbook of psycholinguistics* (pp. 541–557). Cambridge, UK: Cambridge University Press.

Clark, H. H., & Brennan, S. E. (1991). Grounding in communication. In L. B. Resnick, J. M. Levine, & S. D. Teasley (Eds), *Perspectives on socially shared cognition* (pp. 127–149). Washington, DC: APA Books.

Clark, H. H., & Carlson, T. B. (1981). Context for comprehension. In J. Long & A. Baddeley (Eds), *Attention and performance IX* (pp. 313–330). Hillsdale, NJ: Lawrence Erlbaum.

Clark, H. H., & Carlson, T. B. (1982). Hearers and speech acts. *Language, 58*, 332–372.

Clark, H. H., & Krych, M. A. (2004). Speaking while monitoring addressees for understanding. *Journal of Memory and Language, 50*, 62–81.

Clark, H. H., & Marshall, C. R. (1981). Definite reference and mutual knowledge. In A. K. Joshi, B. L. Webber, & I. A. Sag (Eds), *Elements of discourse understanding* (pp. 10–63). Cambridge, UK: Cambridge University Press.

Clark, H. H., & Murphy, G. L. (1982). Audience design in meaning and reference. In J.-F. Le Ny & W. Kintsch (Eds), *Language and comprehension* (pp. 287–299). Amsterdam: North-Holland.

Clark, H. H., & Schaefer, E. F. (1987a). Collaborating on contributions to conversation. *Language and Cognitive Processes, 2*, 1–23.

Clark, H. H., & Schaefer, E. F. (1987b). Concealing one's meaning from overhearers. *Journal of Memory and Language, 26*, 209–225.

Clark, H. H., & Schaefer, E. F. (1989). Contributing to discourse. *Cognitive Science, 13*, 259–294.

Clark, H. H., & Schaefer, E. F. (1992). Dealing with overhearers. In H. H. Clark (Ed.), *Arenas of language use* (pp. 248–274). Chicago, IL: University of Chicago Press.

Clark, H. H., Schreuder, R., & Buttrick, S. (1983). Common ground and the understanding of demonstrative reference. *Journal of Verbal Learning and Verbal Behavior, 22*, 245–258.

Clark, H. H., & Wilkes-Gibbs, D. (1986). Referring as a collaborative process. *Cognition, 22*, 1–39.

Clayman, S. E. (2013). Turn-constructional units and the transition-relevance place. In J. Sidnell & T. Stivers (Eds), *The handbook of conversation analysis* (pp. 151–166). Chichester, UK: Wiley-Blackwell.

Cleland, A. A., & Pickering, M. J. (2003). The use of lexical and syntactic information in language production: Evidence from the priming of noun phrase structure. *Journal of Memory and Language, 49*, 214–230.

Cohen, P. R., & Levesque, H. J. (1994). Preliminaries to a collaborative model of dialogue. *Speech Communication, 15*, 265–274.

Conrad, F. G., Schober, M. F., Jans, M., Orlowski, R. A., Nielsen, D., & Levenstein, R. (2015). Comprehension and engagement in survey interviews with virtual agents. *Frontiers in Psychology, 6*, 1578. doi:10.3389/fpsyg.2015.01578.

Crystal, D. (2001). *Language and the Internet.* Cambridge, UK: Cambridge University Press.

Dale, R., Fusaroli, R., Duran, N. D., & Richardson, D. C. (2014). The self-organization of human interaction. *Psychology of Learning and Motivation, 59*, 43–96.

Danescu-Niculescu-Mizil, C., Gamon, M., & Dumais, S. (2011). Mark my words! Linguistic style accommodation in social media. In *Proceedings of the 20th International Conference on World Wide Web* (pp. 745–754). New York, NY: Association for Computing Machinery.

Dennett, D. C. (1987). *The intentional stance.* Cambridge, MA: MIT Press.

De Ruiter, J. (2013). Methodological paradigms in interaction research. In I. Wachsmuth, J. de Ruiter, P. Jaecks, & S. Kopp (Eds), *Alignment in communication: Towards a new theory of communication* (pp. 11–31). Amsterdam: John Benjamins.

De Ruiter, J. P., Mitterer, H., & Enfield, N. J. (2006). Predicting the end of a speaker's turn: A cognitive cornerstone of conversation. *Language, 82*, 515–535.

Dijksterhuis, A., & Bargh, J. A. (2001). The perception-behavior expressway: Automatic effects of social perception on social behavior. *Advances in Experimental Social Psychology, 33*, 1–40.

DiMaggio, P., Hargittai, E., Neuman, W. R., & Robinson, J. P. (2001). Social implications of the Internet. *Annual Review of Sociology, 27*, 307–336.

Doherty-Sneddon, G., Anderson, A. H., O'Malley, C., Langton, S., Garrod, S., & Bruce, V. (1997). Face-to-face and video-mediated communication: A comparison of dialogue structure and task performance. *Journal of Experimental Psychology: Applied, 3*, 105–125.

Drew, P. (1997). "Open" class repair initiators in response to sequential sources of trouble in conversation. *Journal of Pragmatics, 28*, 69–101.

Dumas, G., Nadel, J., Soussignan, R., Martinerie, J., & Garnero, L. (2010). Inter-brain synchronization during social interaction. *PLoS ONE, 5*(8), e12166. doi:10.1371/journal.pone.0012166.

Dumontheil, I., Küster, O., Apperly, I. A., & Blakemore, S.-J. (2010). Taking perspective into account in a communicative task. *NeuroImage, 52*, 1574–1583.

Duncan, S. J. (1972). Some signals and rules for taking speaking turns in conversation. *Journal of Personality and Social Psychology, 23*, 283–292.

Duncan, S. J. (1974). On the structure of speaker-auditor interaction during speaking turns. *Language in Society, 3*, 161–180.

Duncan, S. J., & Fiske, D. W. (1977). *Face-to-face interaction research: Methods and theory.* New York: Erlbaum.

Duran, N., Dale, R., & Galati, A. (2016). Toward integrative dynamic models for adaptive perspective taking. *Topics in Cognitive Science.* doi:10.1111/tops.12219.

Elffers, J. (1976). *Tangram: The ancient Chinese shapes game.* New York, NY: McGraw-Hill.

Enfield, N. J., & Sidnell, J. (2014). Language presupposes an enchronic infrastructure for social interaction. In D. Dor, C. Knight, & J. Lewis (Eds), *The social origins of language* (pp. 92–104). Oxford, UK: Oxford University Press.

Epley, N., Keysar, B., Van Boven, L., & Gilovich, T. (2004). Perspective taking as egocentric anchoring and adjustment. *Journal of Personality and Social Psychology, 87*, 327–339.

Epley, N., Morewedge, C. K., & Keysar, B. (2004). Perspective taking in children and adults: Equivalent egocentrism but differential correction. *Journal of Experimental Social Psychology, 40*, 760–768.

Eshghi, A., & Healey, P. G. T. (2016). Collective contexts in conversation: Grounding by proxy. *Cognitive Science, 40*, 299–324.

Fay, N., Garrod, S., & Carletta, J. (2000). Group discussion as interactive dialogue or as serial monologue: The influence of group size. *Psychological Science, 11*, 481–486.

Ferstl, E. C., & von Cramon, D. Y. (2002). What does frontomedian cortex contribute to language processing: Coherence or theory of mind? *NeuroImage, 17*, 1599–1612.

Fillmore, C. (1981). Pragmatics and the description of discourse. In P. Cole (Ed.), *Radical pragmatics* (pp. 143–166). New York, NY: Academic Press.

Foltz, A., Gaspers, J., Thiele, K., Stenneken, P., & Cimiano, P. (2015). Lexical alignment in triadic communication. *Frontiers in Psychology, 6*, 127. doi:10.3389/fpsyg.2015.00127.

Ford, C. E., & Thompson, S. A. (1996). Interactional units in conversation: Syntactic, intonational, and pragmatic resources for the projection of turn completion. In E. Ochs, E. A. Schegloff, & S. A. Thompson (Eds), *Interaction and grammar* (pp. 135–184). Cambridge, UK: Cambridge University Press.

Fox Tree, J. E. (2000). Coordinating spontaneous talk. In L. R. Wheeldon (Ed.), *Aspects of language production* (pp. 375–406). Hove, UK: Psychology Press.

Fox Tree, J. E. (2010). Discourse markers across speakers and settings. *Language and Linguistics Compass, 3*, 1–13.

Fox Tree, J. E., Mayer, S. A., & Betts, T. E. (2011). Grounding in instant messaging. *Journal of Educational Computing Research, 45*, 455–475.

Fusaroli, R., Bahrami, B., Olson, K., Roepstorff, A., Rees, G., Frith, C., & Tylén, K. (2012). Coming to terms: Quantifying the benefits of linguistic coordination. *Psychological Science, 23*, 931–939.

Fusaroli, R., & Tylén, K. (2016). Investigating conversational dynamics: Interactive alignment, interpersonal synergy, and collective task performance. *Cognitive Science, 40*, 145–171.

Galati, A., & Brennan, S. E. (2010). Attenuating information in spoken discourse: For the speaker, or for the addressee? *Journal of Memory and Language, 62*, 35–51.

Gann, T. M., & Barr, D. J. (2014). Speaking from experience: Audience design as expert performance. *Language, Cognition, and Neuroscience, 29*, 744–760.

Ganushchak, L. Y., Christoffels, I. K., & Schiller, N. O. (2011). The use of electroencephalography in language production research: A review. *Frontiers in Psychology, 2*, 208. doi:10.3389/fpsyg.2011.00208.

Garfinkel, H. (1967). *Studies in ethnomethodology*. Englewood Cliffs, NJ: Prentice-Hall.

Garrison, D. R., & Kanuka, H. (2004). Blended learning: Uncovering its transformative potential in higher education. *Internet and Higher Education, 7*, 95–105.

Garrod, S. (1999). The challenge of dialogue for theories of language processing. In S. Garrod & M. Pickering (Eds), *Language processing* (pp. 389–415). Hove, UK: Psychology Press.

Garrod, S., & Anderson, A. (1987). Saying what you mean in dialogue: A study in conceptual and semantic co-ordination. *Cognition, 27*, 737–767.

Garrod, S., & Doherty, G. (1994). Conversation, co-ordination and convention: An empirical investigation of how groups establish linguistic conventions. *Cognition, 53*, 181–215.

Garrod, S., Gambi, C., & Pickering, M. J. (2014). Prediction at all levels: Forward model predictions can enhance comprehension. *Language, Cognition and Neuroscience, 29*, 46–48.

Garrod, S., & Pickering, M. J. (2004). Why is conversation so easy? *Trends in Cognitive Sciences, 8*, 8–11.

Garrod, S., & Pickering, M. J. (2009). Joint action, interactive alignment, and dialog. *Topics in Cognitive Science, 1*, 292–304.

Gergle, D., Kraut, R. E., & Fussell, S. R. (2004). Using visual information for grounding and awareness in collaborative tasks. *Human-Computer Interaction, 28*, 1–39.

Gernsbacher, M. A. (2014). Internet-based communication. *Discourse Processes, 51*, 359–373.

Giesbers, B., Rienties, B., Tempelaar, D., & Gijselaers, W. (2014). A dynamic analysis of the interplay between asynchronous and synchronous communication in online learning: The impact of motivation. *Journal of Computer Assisted Learning, 30*, 30–50.

Giles, H., Coupland, J., & Coupland, N. (1991). *Contexts of accommodation: Developments in applied sociolinguistics*. Cambridge, UK: Cambridge University Press.

Gillund, G., & Schiffrin, R. M. (1984). A retrieval model for both recognition and recall. *Psychological Review, 91*, 1–67.

Glucksberg, S., & Krauss, R. (1967). What do people say after they have learned how to talk? Studies in the development of referential communication. *Merrill-Palmer Quarterly, 13*, 309–316.

Goffman, E. (1959). *The presentation of self in everyday life*. New York, NY: Anchor Books.

Goffman, E. (1976). Replies and responses. *Language in Society, 5*, 257–313.

Goffman, E. (1981). *Forms of talk*. Philadelphia, PA: University of Pennsylvania Press.

Goodwin, C. (1981). *Conversational organization: Interaction between speakers and hearers*. New York, NY: Academic Press.

Goodwin, C. (1986). Between and within: Alternative sequential treatments of continuers and assessments. *Human Studies, 9*, 205–217.

Goodwin, C., & Heritage, J. (1990). Conversation analysis. *Annual Review of Anthropology, 19*, 283–307.

Gorman, K. S., Gegg-Harrison, W., Marsh, C. R., & Tanenhaus, M. K. (2013). What's learned together stays together: Speakers' choice of referring expression reflects shared experience. *Journal of Experimental Psychology: Learning, Memory, and Cognition, 39*, 843–853.

Gratier, M., Devouche, E., Guellai, B., Infanti, R., Yilmaz, E., & Parlato-Oliveira, E. (2015). Early development of turn-taking in vocal interaction between mothers and infants. *Frontiers in Psychology, 6*, 1167. doi:10.3389/fpsyg.2015.01167.

Gravano, A., & Hirschberg, J. (2011). Turn-taking cues in task-oriented dialogue. *Computer Speech & Language, 25*, 601–634.

Grice, H. P. (1975). Logic and conversation. In P. Cole & J. L. Morgan (Eds), *Syntax and semantics: Speech acts, Vol. 3* (pp. 41–58). New York, NY: Academic Press.

Grosz, B., & Sidner, C. (1990). Plans for discourse. In P. R. Cohen, J. Morgan, & M. E. Pollack (Eds), *Intentions in communication* (pp. 417–444). Cambridge, MA: MIT Press.

Hagoort, P., & Indefrey, P. (2014). The neurobiology of language beyond single words. *Annual Review of Neuroscience, 37*, 347–362.

Hancock, J. T., & Dunham, P. J. (2001). Language use in computer-mediated communication: The role of coordination devices. *Discourse Processes, 31*, 91–110.

Hanna, J. E., & Tanenhaus, M. K. (2004). Pragmatic effects on reference resolution in a collaborative task: Evidence from eye movements. *Cognitive Science, 28*, 105–115.

Hanna, J. E., Tanenhaus, M. K., & Trueswell, J. C. (2003). The effects of common ground and perspective on domains of referential interpretation. *Journal of Memory and Language, 49*, 43–61.

Hari, R., & Kujala, M. V. (2009). Brain basis of human social interaction: From concepts to brain imaging. *Physiological Reviews, 89*, 453–479.

Hasson, U., Ghazanafar, A. A., Galantucci, B., Garrod, S., & Keysers, C. (2012). Brain-to-brain coupling: A mechanism for creating and sharing a social world. *Trends in Cognitive Sciences, 16*, 114–121.

Hayashi, M. (2013). Turn allocation and turn sharing. In J. Sidnell & T. Stivers (Eds), *The handbook of conversation analysis* (pp. 167–190). Chichester, UK: Wiley-Blackwell.

Hayashi, M., Raymond, G., & Sidnell, J. (Eds). (2013). *Conversational repair and human understanding.* Cambridge, UK: Cambridge University Press.

Healey, P. G. T., Purver, M., & Howes, C. (2014). Divergence in dialogue. *PLoS ONE, 9*, e98598. doi:10.1371/journal.pone.0098598.

Heldner, M., & Edlund, J. (2010). Pauses, gaps and overlaps in conversations. *Journal of Phonetics, 38*, 555–568.

Heller, D., Grodner, D., & Tanenhaus, M. K. (2008). The role of perspective in identifying domains of reference. *Cognition, 108*, 105–115.

Heritage, J. (1998). Oh-prefaced responses to inquiry. *Language in Society, 27*, 291–334.

Heritage, J., & Clayman, S. (Eds). (2010). *Talk in action: Interactions, identities, and institutions.* Chichester, UK: Wiley-Blackwell.

Herring, S. C., Stein, D., & Virtanen, T. (Eds). (2013). *Pragmatics of computer-mediated communication.* Berlin: Walter de Gruyter GmbH.

Hickok, G., & Poeppel, D. (2007). The cortical organization of speech processing. *Nature Reviews Neuroscience, 8*, 393–402.

Hintzman, D. L. (1986). 'Schema abstraction' in a multiple-trace memory model. *Psychological Review, 93*, 411–428.

Holler, J., & Wilkin, K. (2011). Co-speech gesture mimicry in the process of collaborative referring during face-to-face dialogue. *Journal of Nonverbal Behavior, 35*, 133–153.

Holtgraves, T. M. (1997). Yes, but . . . Positive politeness in conversation arguments. *Journal of Language and Social Psychology, 16*, 222–239.

Honeycutt, C., & Herring, S. C. (2009). Beyond microblogging: Conversation and collaboration via Twitter. In *Proceedings of the 42nd Hawaii International Conference on System Sciences* (pp. 1–10). Piscataway, NJ: IEEE.

Horton, W. S. (2012). Shared knowledge, mutual understanding, and meaning negotiation. In H.-J. Schmid (Ed.), *Cognitive pragmatics [Handbook of pragmatics, Vol. 4]* (pp. 375–404). Berlin/New York, NY: Mouton de Gruyter.

Horton, W. S., & Brennan, S. E. (2016). The role of metarepresentation in the production and resolution of referring expressions. *Frontiers in Psychology, 7*, 1111. doi:10.3389/fpsyg.2016.01111.

Horton, W. S., & Gerrig, R. J. (2002). Speakers' experiences and audience design: Knowing *when* and knowing *how* to adjust utterances to addressees. *Journal of Memory and Language, 47*, 589–606.

Horton, W. S., & Gerrig, R. J. (2005a). Conversational common ground and memory processes in language production. *Discourse Processes, 40*, 1–35.

Horton, W. S., & Gerrig, R. J. (2005b). The impact of memory demands on audience design during language production. *Cognition, 96*, 127–142.

Horton, W. S., & Gerrig, R. J. (2016). Revisiting the memory-based processing approach to common ground. *Topics in Cognitive Science.* doi:10.1111/tops.12216.

Horton, W. S., & Keysar, B. (1996). When do speakers take into account common ground? *Cognition, 59*, 91–117.

Horton, W. S., & Spieler, D. H. (2007). Age-related effects in communication and audience design. *Psychology and Aging, 22*, 281–290.

Howes, C., Healey, P. G. T., & Purver, M. (2010). Tracking lexical and syntactic alignment in conversation. In S. Ohlsson & R. Catrambone (Eds), *Proceedings of the 32nd Annual Conference of the Cognitive Science Society* (pp. 2004–2009). Austin, TX: Cognitive Science Society.

Howes, C., Purver, M., Healey, P. G. T., Mills, G., & Gregoromichelaki, E. (2011). On incrementality in dialogue: Evidence from compound contributions. *Dialogue & Discourse*, 2, 279–311.

Huettig, F., Rommers, J., & Meyer, A. S. (2011). Using the visual world paradigm to study language processing: A review and critical evaluation. *Acta Psychologica*, *137*, 151–171.

Hymes, D. (1972). Models of the interaction of language and social life. In J. Gumperz & D. Hymes (Eds), *Directions in sociolinguistics: The ethnography of communication* (pp. 35–71). New York, NY: Holt, Rinehart and Winston.

Iio, T., Shiomi, M., Shinozawa, K., Shimohara, K., Miki, M., & Hagita, N. (2015). Lexical entrainment in human robot interaction: Do humans use their vocabulary to robots? *International Journal of Social Robotics*, *7*, 253–263.

Isaacs, E. A., & Clark, H. H. (1987). References in conversation between experts and novices. *Journal of Experimental Psychology: General*, *116*, 26–37.

Jaeger, T. F., & Snider, N. E. (2013). Alignment as a consequence of expectation adaptation: Syntactic priming is affected by the prime's prediction error given both prior and recent experience. *Cognition*, *127*, 57–83.

Jefferson, G. (2004). Glossary of transcript symbols with an introduction. In G. H. Lerner (Ed.), *Conversation analysis: Studies from the first generation* (pp. 13–31). Amsterdam: John Benjamins.

Jiang, J., Chen, C., Dai, B., Shi, G., Ding, G., Liu, L., & Lu, C. (2015). Leader emergence through interpersonal neural synchronization. *Proceedings of the Natural Academy of Sciences*, *112*, 4274–4279.

Jiang, J., Dai, B., Peng, D., Zhu, C., Liu, L., & Lu, C. (2012). Neural synchronization during face-to-face communication. *The Journal of Neuroscience*, *32*, 16064–16069.

Jucks, R., Becker, B.-M., & Bromme, R. (2008). Lexical entrainment in written discourse: Is experts' word use adapted to the addressee? *Discourse Processes*, *45*, 497–518.

Kashima, Y., Klein, O., & Clark, A. E. (2007). Grounding: Sharing information in social interaction. In K. Fiedler (Ed.), *Social communication* (pp. 27–77). New York, NY: Psychology Press.

Kavanagh, L. C., & Winkielman, P. (2016). The functionality of spontaneous mimicry and its influences on affiliation: An implicit socialization account. *Frontiers in Psychology*, *7*, 458. doi:10.3389/fpsyg.2016.00458.

Kendon, A. (1967). Some functions of gaze-direction in social interaction. *Acta Psychologica*, *26*, 22–63.

Kendon, A. (1997). Gesture. *Annual Review of Anthropology*, *26*, 109–128.

Kendrick, K. H., & Torreira, F. (2015). The timing and construction of preference: A quantitative study. *Discourse Processes*, *52*, 255–289.

Keysar, B. (2007). Unconfounding common ground. *Discourse Processes*, *24*, 253–270.

Keysar, B., Barr, D. J., Balin, J. A., & Brauner, J. S. (2000). Taking perspective in conversation: The role of mutual knowledge in comprehension. *Psychological Science*, *11*, 32–39.

Keysar, B., Barr, D. J., Balin, J. A., & Paek, T. S. (1998). Definite reference and mutual knowledge: Process models of common ground in comprehension. *Journal of Memory and Language*, *39*, 1–20.

Keysar, B., Barr, D. J., & Horton, W. S. (1998). The egocentric bias of language use: Insights from a processing approach. *Current Directions in Psychological Science*, *7*, 46–50.

Keysar, B., Lin, S., & Barr, D. J. (2003). Limits on theory of mind use in adults. *Cognition*, *89*, 25–41.

Kim, M., Horton, W. S., & Bradlow, A. R. (2011). Phonetic convergence in spontaneous conversations as a function of interlocutor language distance. *Laboratory Phonology*, *2*, 125–156.

Kingsbury, P., Strassel, S., McLemore, C., & McIntyre, R. (1997). CALLHOME American English transcripts, LDC97T14. Philadelphia, PA: Linguistic Data Consortium.

Kitzinger, C. (2013). Repair. In J. Sidnell & T. Stivers (Eds), *The handbook of conversation analysis* (pp. 229–256). Chichester, UK: Wiley-Blackwell.

Knoeferle, P., Pyykkönen-Klauck, P., & Crocker, M. W. (Eds). (2016). *Visually situated language comprehension*. Amsterdam: John Benjamins.

Knutsen, D., & Le Bigot, L. (2012). Managing dialogue: How information availability affects collaborative reference production. *Journal of Memory and Language*, *67*, 326–341.

Koike, T., Tanabe, H. C., & Sadato, N. (2015). Hyperscanning neuroimaging technique to reveal the "two-in-one" system in social interactions. *Neuroscience Research*, *90*, 25–32.

Konvalinka, I., & Roepstorff, A. (2012). The two-brain approach: How can mutually interacting brains teach us something about social interaction? *Frontiers in Human Neuroscience, 6*, 215. doi:10.3389/fnhum.2012.00215.

Koolen, R. M. F., Gatt, A., Goudbeek, M. B., & Krahmer, E. J. (2011). Factors causing referential overspecification in definite descriptions. *Journal of Pragmatics, 43*, 3231–3250.

Kopp, S., & Bergmann, K. (2013). Automatic and strategic alignment of co-verbal gestures in dialogue. In I. Wachsmuth, J. de Ruiter, P. Jaecks, & S. Kopp (Eds), *Alignment in communication: Towards a new theory of communication* (pp. 87–107). Amsterdam: John Benjamins.

Krauss, R. M., & Fussell, S. R. (1996). Social psychological models of interpersonal communication. In E. T. Higgins & A. Kruglanski (Eds), *Social psychology: Handbook of basic principles* (pp. 655–701). New York, NY: Guilford Press.

Krauss, R. M., & Weinheimer, S. (1964). Changes in reference phrases as a function of frequency of usage in social interaction: A preliminary study. *Psychonomic Science, 1*, 113–114.

Krauss, R. M., & Weinheimer, S. (1966). Concurrent feedback, confirmation, and the encoding of referents in verbal communication. *Journal of Personality and Social Psychology, 4*, 343–346.

Kronmüller, E., & Barr, D. J. (2007). Perspective-free pragmatics: Broken precedents and the recovery-from-preemption hypothesis. *Journal of Memory and Language, 56*, 436–455.

Kruger, J., Epley, N., Parker, J., & Ng, Z.-W. (2005). Egocentrism over e-mail: Can we communicate as well as we think? *Journal of Personality and Social Psychology, 89*, 925–936.

Kuhlen, A. K., Allefeld, C., Anders, S., & Haynes, J.-D. (2015). Toward a multi-brain perspective on communication in dialogue. In R. M. Willems (Ed.), *Cognitive neuroscience of natural language use* (pp. 182–200). Cambridge, UK: Cambridge University Press.

Kuhlen, A. K., Allefeld, C., & Haynes, J.-D. (2012). Content-specific coordination of listeners' to speakers' EEG during communication. *Frontiers in Human Neuroscience, 6*, 266. doi:10.3389/fnhum.2012.0266.

Kuhlen, A. K., & Brennan, S. E. (2010). Anticipating distracted addressees: How speakers' expectations and addressees' feedback influence storytelling. *Discourse Processes, 47*, 567–587.

Kuhlen, A. K., & Brennan, S. E. (2013). Language in dialogue: When confederates might be hazardous to your data. *Psychonomic Bulletin & Review, 20*, 54–72.

Kutas, M., DeLong, K. A., & Smith, N. J. (2011). A look around at what lies ahead: Prediction and predictability in language processing. In M. Bar (Ed.), *Predictions in the brain: Using our past to generate a future* (pp. 190–207). Oxford, UK: Oxford University Press.

Kutas, M., Van Petten, C. K., & Kluender, R. (2006). Psycholinguistics electrified II (1994–2005). In M. J. Traxler & M. A. Gernsbacher (Eds), *Handbook of psycholinguistics, 2nd edition* (pp. 659–724). Amsterdam: Academic Press.

Lerner, G. H. (2003). Selecting next speaker: The context-sensitive organization of a context-free organization. *Language in Society, 32*, 177–201.

Lerner, G. H. (2004). Collaborative turn sequences. In G. H. Lerner (Ed.), *Conversation analysis: Studies from the first generation* (pp. 225–256). Amsterdam: John Benjamins.

Levelt, W. J. M. (1989). *Speaking: From intention to articulation*. Cambridge, MA: MIT Press.

Levelt, W. J. M., & Kelter, S. (1982). Surface form and memory in question answering. *Cognitive Psychology, 14*, 78–106.

Levinson, S. C. (1983). *Pragmatics*. Cambridge, UK: Cambridge University Press.

Levinson, S. C. (1988). Putting linguistics on a proper footing: Explorations in Goffman's participation framework. In P. Drew & A. Wootton (Eds), *Goffman: Exploring the interaction order* (pp. 161–227). Oxford, UK: Polity Press.

Levinson, S. C. (2016). Turn-taking in human communication: Origins and implications for language processing. *Trends in Cognitive Sciences, 20*, 6–14.

Levinson, S. C., & Torreira, F. (2015). Timing of turn-taking and its implications for processing models of language. *Frontiers in Psychology, 6*, 731. doi:10.3389/fpsyg.2015.00731.

Levitan, R., & Hirschberg, J. (2011). Measuring acoustic-prosodic entrainment with respect to multiple levels and dimensions. In P. Cosi, R. De Mori, G. Di Fabbrizio, & R. Pieraccini (Eds), *INTERSPEECH 2011, 12th Annual Conference of the International Speech Communication Association* (pp. 3081–3084). Florence, Italy: ISCA.

Li, L., Finley, J., Pitts, J., & Guo, R. (2011). Which is a better choice for faculty-student interaction: Synchronous or asynchronous communication? *Journal of Technology Research, 3*, 1–12.

Lin, S., Keysar, B., & Epley, N. (2010). Reflexively mindblind: Using theory of mind to interpret behavior requires effortful attention. *Journal of Experimental Social Psychology, 46*, 551–556.

Linell, P. (1998). *Approaching dialogue: Talk, interaction and contexts in dialogical perspectives.* Amsterdam: John Benjamins.

Linell, P. (2005). *The written language bias in linguistics: Its nature, origins, and transformations.* London: Routledge.

Ling., R., & Baron, N. S. (2007). Text messaging and IM: Linguistic comparison of American college data. *Journal of Language and Social Psychology, 26*, 291–298.

Louwerse, M. M., Dale, R., Bard, E. G., & Jeuniaux, P. (2012). Behavior matching in multimodal communication is synchronized. *Cognitive Science, 36*, 1404–1426.

MacDonald, M. C., Pearlmutter, N. J., & Seidenberg, M. S. (1994). The lexical nature of syntactic ambiguity resolution. *Psychological Review, 101*, 676–703.

Mar, R. A. (2011). The neural bases of social cognition and story comprehension. *Annual Review of Psychology, 62*, 103–134.

Marcus, M. P., Kim, G., Marcinkiewicz, M. A., MacIntyre, R., Bies, A., Ferguson, M., Katz, K., & Schasberger, B. (1994). The Penn Treebank: Annotating predicate argument structure. In C. J. Weinstein (Ed.), *Proceedings of the ARPA Human Language Technology Workshop* (pp. 114–119). Stroudsburg, PA: Association for Computational Linguistics.

Markman, A. B., & Makin, V. A. (1998). Referential communication and category acquisition. *Journal of Experimental Psychology: General, 127*, 331–354.

Marwick, A. E., & boyd, d. (2011). I tweet honestly, I tweet passionately: Twitter users, context collapse, and the imagined audience. *New Media & Society, 13*, 114–133.

Mason, R. A., & Just, M. A. (2006). Neuroimaging contributions to the understanding of discourse processes. In M. J. Traxler & M. A. Gernsbacher (Eds). *Handbook of psycholinguistics, 2nd edition* (pp. 765–799). Amsterdam: Academic Press.

Menenti, L., Pickering, M. J., & Garrod, S. C. (2012). Toward a neural basis of interactive alignment in conversation. *Frontiers in Human Neuroscience, 6*, 185. doi:10.3389/fnhum.2012.00185.

Metzing, C., & Brennan, S. E. (2003). When conceptual pacts are broken: Partner-specific effects in the comprehension of referring expressions. *Journal of Memory and Language, 49*, 201–213.

McRae, K., Spivey-Knowlton, M. J., & Tanenhaus, M. K. (1998). Modeling the influence of thematic fit (and other constraints) in on-line sentence comprehension. *Journal of Memory and Language, 38*, 283–312.

Mills, G. (2014). Dialogue in joint activity: Complementarity, convergence and conventionalization. *New Ideas in Psychology, 32*, 158–173.

Mondada, L. (2007). Multimodal resources for turn-taking: Pointing and the emergence of possible next speakers. *Discourse Studies, 9*, 195–226.

Montague, P. R., Berns, G. S., Cohen, J. D., McClure, S. M., Pagnoni, G., Dhamala, M., Wiest, M. C., Karpov, I., King, R. D., Apple, N., & Fisher, R. E. (2002). Hyperscanning: Simultaneous fMRI during linked social interactions. *NeuroImage, 16*, 1159–1164.

Nadig, A. S., & Sedivy, J. C. (2002). Evidence of perspective-taking constraints in children's on-line reference resolution. *Psychological Science, 13*, 329–336.

Nadig, A., Seth, S., & Sasson, M. (2015). Global similarities and multifaceted differences in the production of partner-specific referential pacts by adults with autism spectrum disorders. *Frontiers in Psychology, 6*, 1888. doi:10.3389/fpsyg.2015.01888.

Namy, L. L., Nygaard, L. C., & Sauerteig, D. (2002). Gender differences in vocal accommodation: The role of perception. *Journal of Language and Social Psychology, 21*, 422–432.

Nickerson, R. S. (1999). How we know—and sometimes misjudge—what others know: Imputing one's own knowledge to others. *Psychological Bulletin, 125*, 737–759.

Niederhoffer, K. G., & Pennebaker, J. W. (2002). Linguistic style matching in social interaction. *Journal of Language and Social Psychology, 21*, 337–360.

Noordzij, M. L., Newmun-Norlund, S. E., de Ruiter, J. P., Hagoort, P., Levinson, S. C., & Toni, I. (2009). Brain mechanisms underlying human communication. *Frontiers in Human Neuroscience, 3*, 14. doi:10.3389/neuro.09.014.2009.

Nye, J. L., & Brower, A. M. (Eds). (1996). *What's social about social cognition? Research on social shared cognition in small groups.* Thousand Oaks, CA: Sage.

Olson, G. M., & Olson, J. S. (2000). Distance matters. *Human-Computer Interaction, 15*, 139–178.

Pardo, J. S. (2006). On phonetic convergence during conversational interaction. *Journal of the Acoustical Society of America, 119*, 2382–2393.

Pardo, J. S. (2013). Measuring phonetic convergence in speech production. *Frontiers in Psychology, 4*, 559. doi:10.3389/fpsyg.2013.00559.

Pardo, J. S., Cajori Jay, I., & Krauss, R. M. (2010). Conversational role influences speech imitation. *Attention, Perception, and Psychophysics, 72*, 2254–2264.

Pennington, D. C. (2002). *The social psychology of behavior in small groups*. Hove, UK: Psychology Press.

Petrović, S., Osborne, M., & Lavrenko, V. (2012). Using paraphrases for improving first story detection in news and Twitter. In *Proceedings of the 2012 Conference of the North American Chapter of the Association for Computational Linguistics: Human Language Technologies (NAACL HLT '12)* (pp. 338–346). Stroudsburg, PA: Association for Computational Linguistics.

Piaget, J. (1959). *The language and thought of the child*. London: Routledge & Kegan Paul.

Piaget, J., & Inhelder, B. (1956). *The child's conception of space*. London: Routledge & Kegan Paul.

Pickering, M. J., & Garrod, S. (2004). Toward a mechanistic psychology of dialogue. *Behavioral and Brain Sciences, 27*, 169–226.

Pickering, M. J., & Garrod, S. (2005). Establishing and using routines during dialogue: Implications for psychology and linguistics. In A. Cutler (Ed.), *Twenty-first century psycholinguistics: Four cornerstones* (pp. 85–101). Mahwah, NJ: Erlbaum.

Pickering, M. J., & Garrod, S. (2007). Do people use language production to make predictions during comprehension? *Trends in Cognitive Sciences, 11*, 105–110.

Pickering, M. J., & Garrod, S. (2013). An integrated theory of language production and comprehension. *Behavioral and Brain Sciences, 36*, 329–392.

Poesio, M., & Reiser, H. (2010). Completions, coordination, and alignment in dialogue. *Dialogue and Discourse, 1*, 1–89.

Potter, J., & Edwards, D. (2013). Conversation analysis and psychology. In J. Sidnell & T. Stivers (Eds), *The handbook of conversation analysis* (pp. 726–740). Chichester, UK: Wiley-Blackwell.

Purohit, H., Hampton, A., Shalin, V. L., Sheth, A. P., Flach, J., & Bhatt, S. (2013). What kind of #conversation is Twitter? Mining #psycholinguistic cues for emergency coordination. *Computers in Human Behavior, 29*, 2438–2447.

Ratcliff, R. (1978). A theory of memory retrieval. *Psychological Review, 85*, 59–108.

Reddy, M. J. (1979). The conduit metaphor: A case of frame conflict in our language about language. In A. Ortony (Ed.), *Metaphor and thought* (pp. 284–297). Cambridge, UK: Cambridge University Press.

Redeker, G. (1984). On differences between spoken and written language. *Discourse Processes, 7*, 43–55.

Reitter, D., & Moore, J. D. (2014). Alignment and task success in spoken dialogue. *Journal of Memory and Language, 76*, 29–46.

Reitter, D., Moore, J. D., & Keller, F. (2006). Priming of syntactic rules in task-oriented dialogue and spontaneous conversation. In R. Sun & N. Miyake (Eds), *Proceedings of the 28th Annual Conference of the Cognitive Science Society* (pp. 685–690). Mahwah, NJ: Erlbaum.

Richardson, D. C., Dale, R., & Kirkham, N. Z. (2007). The art of conversation is coordination: Common ground and the coupling of eye movements during dialogue. *Psychological Science, 18*, 407–413.

Richardson, M. J., Marsh, K. L., Isenhower, R. W., Goodman, J. R. L., & Schmidt, R. C. (2007). Rocking together: Dynamics of intentional and unintentional interpersonal coordination. *Human Movement Science, 26*, 867–891.

Riest, C., Jorschick, A. B., & de Ruiter, J. P. (2015). Anticipation in turn-taking: Mechanisms and information sources. *Frontiers in Psychology, 6*, 89. doi:10.3389/fpsyg.2015.00089.

Ritter, A., Cherry, C., & Dolan, B. (2010). Unsupervised modeling of Twitter conversations. In *Human Language Technologies: The 11th Annual Conference of the North American Chapter of the ACL* (pp. 172–180). Stroudsberg, PA: Association for Computational Linguistics.

Rosa, E. C., Finch, K. H., Bergeson, M., & Arnold, J. E. (2015). The effects of addressee attention on prosodic prominence. *Language, Cognition and Neuroscience, 30*, 48–56.

Rossano, F. (2013). Gaze in conversation. In J. Sidnell & T. Stivers (Eds), *The handbook of conversation analysis* (pp. 308–328). Chichester, UK: Wiley-Blackwell.

Rossano, F., Brown, P., & Levinson, S. C. (2009). Gaze, questioning, and culture. In J. Sidnell (Ed.), *Conversation analysis: Comparative perspectives* (pp. 187–249). Cambridge UK: Cambridge University Press.

Rubio-Fernández, P. (2008). On the automaticity of egocentricity: A review of the egocentric anchoring and adjustment model of perspective-taking. *UCL Working Papers in Linguistics, 20,* 247–274.

Ryskin, R. A., Brown-Schmidt, S., Canseco-Gonzalez, E., Yiu, L. K., & Nguyen, E. T. (2014). Visuospatial perspective-taking in conversation and the role of bilingual experience. *Journal of Memory and Language, 74,* 46–76.

Sacks, H. (1984). Notes on methodology (edited by Gail Jefferson from various lectures). In J. M. Atkinson & J. Heritage (Eds), *Structures of social action* (pp. 21–27). Cambridge, UK: Cambridge University Press.

Sacks, H., & Schegloff, E. A. (1979). Two preferences in the organization of reference to persons and their interaction. In G. Psathas (Ed.), *Everyday language: Studies in ethnomethodology* (pp. 15–21). New York, NY: Irvington Press.

Sacks, H., Schegloff, E. A., & Jefferson, G. A. (1974). A simplest systematics for the organization of turn-taking in conversation. *Language, 50,* 696–735.

Saito, D. N., Tanabe, H. C., Izuma, K., Hayashi, M. J., Morito, Y., Komeda, H., Uchiyama, H., Kosaka, H., Okazawa, H., Fujibayashi, Y., & Sadato, N. (2010). "Stay tuned": Inter-individual synchronization during mutual gaze and joint attention. *Frontiers in Integrative Neuroscience, 3,* 127. doi:10.3389/fnint.2010.00127.

Saxe, R., Carey, S., & Kanwisher, N. (2004). Understanding other minds: Linking developmental psychology and functional neuroimaging. *Annual Review of Psychology, 55,* 87–124.

Saxe, R., & Kanwisher, N. (2003). People thinking about people: The role of the temporo-parietal junction in "theory of mind." *NeuroImage, 19,* 1835–1842.

Schegloff, E. A. (1968). Sequencing in conversational openings. *American Anthropologist, 70,* 1075–1095.

Schegloff, E. A. (1972). Notes on a conversational practice: Formulating place. In D. Sudnow (Ed.), *Studies in social interaction* (pp. 75–119). New York, NY: Free Press.

Schegloff, E. A. (1980). Preliminaries to preliminaries: "Can I ask you a question?" *Sociological Inquiry, 50,* 104–152.

Schegloff, E. A. (1982). Discourse as an interactional achievement: Some uses of "uh huh" and other things that come between sentences. In D. Tannen (Ed.), *Analyzing discourse: Text and talk. Georgetown University Roundtable on Languages and Linguistics 1981* (pp. 71–93). Washington, DC: Georgetown University Press.

Schegloff, E. A. (1987). Some sources of misunderstanding in talk-in-interaction. *Linguistics, 25,* 201–218.

Schegloff, E. A. (1992). Repair after next turn: The last structurally provided defense of intersubjectivity in conversation. *American Journal of Sociology, 97,* 1295–1345.

Schegloff, E. A. (1993). Reflections on quantification in the study of conversation. *Research on Language and Social Interaction, 26,* 99–128.

Schegloff, E. A. (1996). Issues of relevance for discourse analysis: Contingency in action, interaction and co-participant context. In E. H. Hovy & D. Scott (Eds), *Computational and conversational discourse: Burning issues. An interdisciplinary account* (pp. 3–38). Heidelberg, Germany: Springer-Verlag.

Schegloff, E. A. (2007). *Sequence organization in interaction: A primer in conversation analysis (Volume 1).* Cambridge, UK: Cambridge University Press.

Schegloff, E. A., Jefferson, G., & Sacks, H. (1977). The preference for self-correction in the organization of repair in conversation. *Language, 53,* 361–382.

Schegloff, E. A., & Lerner, G. H. (2009). Beginning to respond: *Well*-prefaced responses to *Wh*-questions. *Research on Language and Social Interaction, 42,* 91–115.

Schegloff, E. A., & Sacks, H. (1973). Opening up closings. *Semiotica, 8,* 289–327.

Schiffer, S. R. (1972). *Meaning.* Oxford, UK: Oxford University Press.

Schiffrin, D. (1987). *Discourse markers.* Cambridge, UK: Cambridge University Press.

Schilbach, L., Timmermans, B., Reddy, V., Costall, A., Bente, G., Schlicht, T., & Vogeley, K. (2013). Toward a second-person neuroscience. *Behavioral and Brain Sciences, 36,* 393–462.

Schober, M. F. (2005). Conceptual alignment in conversation. In B. F. Malle & S. D. Hodges (Eds), *Other minds: How humans bridge the divide between self and others* (pp. 239–252). New York, NY: Guilford Press.

Schober, M. F. (2009). Spatial dialogue between partners with mismatched abilities. In K. R. Coventry, T. Tenbrink, & J. A. Bateman (Eds), *Spatial language and dialogue* (pp. 23–39). Oxford, UK: Oxford University Press.

Schober, M. F., & Brennan, S. E. (2003). Processes of interactive spoken discourse: The role of the partner. In A. C. Graesser, M. A. Gernsbacher, & S. R. Goldman (Eds), *Handbook of discourse processes* (pp. 123–164). Mahwah, NJ: Erlbaum.

Schober, M. F., & Clark, H. H. (1989). Understanding by addressees and overhearers. *Cognitive Psychology, 21*, 211–232.

Schoot, L., Hagoort, P., & Segaert, K. (2016). What can we learn from a two-brain approach to verbal interaction? *Neuroscience and Biobehavioral Reviews, 68*, 454–459.

Schoot, L., Menenti, L., Hagoort, P., & Segaert, K. (2014). A little more conversation: The influence of communicative context on syntactic priming in brain and behavior. *Frontiers in Psychology, 5*, 208. doi:10.3389/fpsyg.2014.00208.

Sebanz, N., Bekkering, H., & Knoblich, G. (2006). Joint action: Bodies and minds moving together. *Trends in Cognitive Sciences, 10*, 70–76.

Semin, G. R. (2007). Grounding communication: Synchrony. In A. W. Kruglanski & E. T. Higgins (Eds), *Social psychology: Handbook of basic principles, 2nd edition.* (pp. 630–649). New York, NY: Guilford Press.

Semin, G. R., & Fiedler, K. (Eds). (1992). *Language, interaction and social cognition.* London: Sage.

Severinson Eklundh, K. (1994). Electronic mail as a medium for dialogue. In L. van Waes, E. Woudstra, & P. van den Hoven (Eds), *Functional communication quality (Utrecht studies in language and communication)* (pp. 162–173). Amsterdam: Rodopi Publishers.

Seyfeddinipur, M., & Gullberg, M. (Eds). (2014). *From gesture in conversation to visible action as utterance: Essays in honor of Adam Kendon.* Amsterdam: John Benjamins.

Shockley, K., Richardson, D. C., & Dale, R. (2009). Conversation and coordinative structures. *Topics in Cognitive Science, 1*, 305–319.

Shockley, K., Santana, M.-V., & Fowler, C. A. (2003). Mutual interpersonal postural constraints are involved in cooperative conversation. *Journal of Experimental Psychology: Human Perception and Performance, 29*, 326–332.

Sidnell, J. (2010). *Conversation analysis: An introduction.* Chichester, UK: Wiley-Blackwell.

Sidnell, J., & Stivers, T. (2005). Introduction: Multimodal interaction. *Semotica, 156*, 1–20.

Simonidesová, J., & Hlavňová, B. (2013). The use of Internet communication forms and their quality in the educational process in higher education. In *Proceedings of the International Academic Workshop on Social Science (IAW-SC-2013)* (pp. 786–788). Amsterdam: Atlantis Press.

Smith, S. W., & Jucker, A. H. (1998). Interactive aspects of reference assignment in conversations. *Pragmatics & Cognition, 6*, 153–187.

Sparrow, B., & Chatman, L. (2013). Social cognition in the Internet age: Same as it ever was? *Psychological Inquiry, 24*(4), 273–292.

Spivey, M. J., & Huette, S. (2016). Toward a situated view of language. In P. Knoeferle, P. Pyykkönen-Klauck, & M. W. Crocker (Eds), *Visually situated language comprehension* (pp. 1–30). Amsterdam: John Benjamins.

Sproull, L. S. & Kiesler, S. (1986) Reducing social context cues: Electronic mail in organizational communication. *Management Science, 32*, 1492–1512.

Stalnaker, R. C. (1978). Assertion. In P. Cole (Ed.), *Syntax and semantics Vol. 9, Pragmatics* (pp. 315–332). New York, NY: Academic Press.

Stephens, G. J., Silbert, L. J., & Hasson, U. (2010). Speaker-listener neural coupling underlies successful communication. *Proceedings of the Natural Academy of Sciences, 107*, 14425–14430.

Stivers, T. (2013). Sequence organization. In J. Sidnell & T. Stivers (Eds), *The handbook of conversation analysis* (pp. 191–209). Chichester, UK: Wiley-Blackwell.

Stivers, T. (2015). Coding social interaction: A heretical approach in conversation analysis? *Research on Language and Social Interaction, 48*, 1–19.

Stivers, T., Enfield, N. J., Brown, P., Englert, C., Hayashi, M., Heinemann, T., Hoymann, G., Rossano, F., de Ruiter, J. P., Yoon, K.-E., & Levinson, S. C. (2009). Universals and cultural variation in turn-taking in conversation. *Proceedings of the National Academy of Sciences, 106*, 10587–10592.

Stivers, T., & Majid, A. (2007). Questioning children: Interactional evidence of implicit bias in medical interviews. *Social Psychology Quarterly, 70*, 424–441.

Stolk, A., Verhagen, L., & Toni, I. (2016). Conceptual alignment: How brains achieve mutual understanding. *Trends in Cognitive Sciences, 20*, 180–191.

Takahashi, D. Y., Narayanan, D. Z., & Ghazanfar, A. A. (2013). Coupled oscillator dynamics of vocal turn-taking in monkeys. *Current Biology*, *23*, 2162–2168.

Tanenhaus, M. K., Spivey-Knowlton, M., Eberhard, K., & Sedivy, J. (1995). Integration of visual and linguistic information during spoken language comprehension. *Science*, *268*, 1632–1634.

Tanenhaus, M. K., & Trueswell, J. C. (2005). Eye movements as a tool for bridging the language-as-product and language-as-action traditions. In J. C. Trueswell & M. K. Tanenhaus (Eds), *Approaches to studying world-situated language use: Bridging the language-as-product and language-as-action traditions* (pp. 3–37). Cambridge, MA: MIT Press.

Traum, D. (2004). Issues in multi-party dialogues. In F. Dignum (Ed.), *Advances in agent communication* (pp. 201–211). Berlin: Springer-Verlag.

Traum, D. R., & Allen, J. F. (1994). Discourse obligations in dialogue processing. In *Proceedings of the 32nd Annual Meeting of the Association for Computational Linguistics* (ACL-94) (pp. 1–8). Stroudsberg, PA: Association for Computational Linguistics.

Trueswell, J. C., & Tanenhaus, M. K. (Eds). (2005). *Approaches to studying world-situated language use: Bridging the language-as-product and language-as-action traditions*. Cambridge, MA: MIT Press.

van Berkum, J. J., Brown, C. M., Zwitserlood, P., Kooijman, V., & Hagoort, P. (2005). Anticipating upcoming words in discourse: Evidence from ERPs and reading times. *Journal of Experimental Psychology: Learning, Memory and Cognition*, *31*, 443–467.

van Lierop, K., Goudbeek, M., & Krahmer, E. (2012). Conceptual alignment in reference with artificial and human dialogue partners. In N. Miyake, D. Peebles, & R. P. Cooper (Eds), *Proceedings of the 34th Annual Meeting of the Cognitive Science Society* (pp. 1066–1071). Austin, TX: Cognitive Science Society.

Vogeley, K., Bussfeld, P., Newen, A., Herrmann, S., Happé, F., Falkai, P., Maier, W., Shah, N. J., Fink, G. R., & Zilles, K. (2001). Mind reading: Neural mechanisms of theory of mind and self-perspective. *NeuroImage*, *14*, 170–181.

Wachsmuth, I., de Ruiter, J., Jaecks, P., & Kopp, S. (Eds). (2013). *Alignment in communication: Towards a new theory of communication*. Amsterdam: John Benjamins.

Walther, J. B. (1996). Computer-mediated communication: Impersonal, interpersonal, and hyperpersonal interaction. *Communication Research*, *23*, 3–43.

Wardlow, L. (2013). Individual differences in speakers' perspective-taking: The roles of executive control and working memory. *Psychonomic Bulletin and Review*, *20*, 766–772.

Wardlow-Lane, L., & Ferreira, V. S. (2008). Speaker-external versus speaker-internal forces on utterance form: Do cognitive demands override threats to referential success? *Journal of Experimental Psychology: Learning, Memory, and Cognition*, *34*, 1466–1481.

Weatherholz, K., Campbell-Kibler, K., & Jaeger, T. F. (2014). Socially-mediated syntactic alignment. *Language Variation and Change*, *26*, 387–420.

Wilkes-Gibbs, D., & Clark, H. H. (1992). Coordinating beliefs in conversation. *Journal of Memory and Language*, *31*, 183–194.

Wolpert, D. M. (1997). Computational approaches to motor control. *Trends in Cognitive Sciences*, *1*, 209–216.

Wu, R.-J. R. (2009). Repetition in the initiation of repair. In J. Sidnell (Ed.), *Conversation analysis: Comparative perspectives* (pp. 31–59). Cambridge, UK: Cambridge University Press.

Wu, S., & Keysar, B. (2007). The effect of culture on perspective-taking. *Psychological Science*, *18*, 600–606.

Yngve, V. H. (1970). On getting a word in edgewise. In *Papers from the 6th Regional Meeting of the Chicago Linguistic Society* (pp. 567–578). Chicago, IL: Chicago Linguistic Institute.

Yoon, S. O., & Brown-Schmidt, S. (2014). Adjusting conceptual pacts in three-party conversation. *Journal of Experimental Psychology: Learning, Memory, and Cognition*, *40*, 919–937.

Yoon, S. O., & Brown-Schmidt, S. (2016). *Aim low: Mechanisms of audience design in multiparty conversation*. Manuscript submitted for publication.

Yule, G. (1997). *Referential communication tasks*. Mahwah, NJ: Erlbaum.

Zeffiro, T. A., & Frymiare, J. L. (2006). Functional neuroimaging of speech production. In M. J. Traxler and M. A. Gernsbacher (Eds), *Handbook of psycholinguistics*, *2nd edition* (pp. 125–150). Amsterdam: Academic Press.

Zwaan, R. A., & Radvansky, G. A. (1998). Situation models in language comprehension and memory. *Psychological Bulletin*, *123*, 162–185.

3

Studying Discourse Processes in Institutional Contexts

Adrian Bangerter

UNIVERSITY OF NEUCHÂTEL

Joep Cornelissen

ERASMUS UNIVERSITY

Introduction

Institutions are structures or regularities in social behavior that are self-perpetuating or self-policing. They are a central element of human social life. Examples include organizations (like corporations, small or medium enterprises, churches, armies, and the like), professions (which regulate behavior of their members through ethical codes), and markets (which regulate behavior of actors through supply and demand or conventional means of exchange like currencies). Institutional reality expresses itself through cognitive (taken-for-granted shared beliefs), normative (binding social obligations), and regulative (e.g. legal sanctions) aspects (Scott, 2003). It is now widely recognized that discourse is a central and constitutive element of institutions. It is through discourse that the daily business of institutions is conducted, and so it is through discourse that institutions are enacted and reproduced in everyday life (Phillips, Lawrence, & Hardy, 2004; Cornelissen, Durand, Fiss, Lammers, & Vaara, 2015). As a result, research on discourse processes in institutions can reveal much about how institutions function. At the same time, such research can also lead to a better understanding of the nature of discourse processes, not least because even activities like everyday conversation are constituted by regularities like rules, norms, and conventions, all of which imply some degree of institutionalization.

In particular, given the many kinds of social change occurring in recent years, it is important to understand processes by which institutions emerge and decline, and discourse plays an important role in such processes (Fiol, 2002). It is via discursive processes that institutions lose the taken-for granted status that legitimizes them (Werner & Cornelissen, 2014), and, conversely, it is also through discursive processes that the possibility and desirability of change gets legitimized. The ever-increasing spread of new technologies for communication has enabled discursive processes across multiple institutional contexts as never before, thus changing both the nature of discourse and of institutions. Discourse processes in institutions have become more interactive, faster paced, more informal, more flexible, and more intertwined with other activities. It is important to understand the implications of these changes for institutional functioning and for the study of discourse and communication.

In keeping with the overall framework of this handbook, one can thus ask how discourse processes in institutional contexts have changed in the past years. The scope of such a question is very broad. "Institutional contexts" potentially encompasses any kind of situation where individuals interact in institutionalized roles or about institutional topics. Examples range from doctor-patient communication (Roter & Hall, 2006), humor during team meetings (Lehmann-Willenbrock & Allen, 2014), the multimodal conduct of auctions (Heath & Luff, 2013), or metaphors produced by employees to describe a merger between two banks (Vaara, Tienari, & Säntti, 2003). As these examples suggest, "discourse" is also a notoriously polysemous concept (Alvesson & Karreman, 2000; Van Dijk, 1997a). In the work represented in this *Handbook*, "discourse" refers to two main research traditions. One tradition studies cognitive processes of comprehension and production of various kinds of spoken and written discourse. Researchers in this tradition typically stem from cognitive psychology, educational psychology, psycholinguistics, computer science, and neuroscience and employ mainly experimental and quantitative methods. An alternative tradition studies social and cognitive processes involved in conversational interaction. Researchers typically also stem from psycholinguistics, but also from pragmatics, sociolinguistics, conversation analysis, and ethnomethodology. Clark (1992) refers to these traditions in the study of language as the *product* versus *action* traditions. In a similar vein, Van Dijk has edited two classic volumes on each of these traditions (1997a, b). For the purposes of this chapter, we call them the *discourse-production-and-comprehension* and the *discourse-and-social-action* traditions. These traditions are of course interrelated. Discourse production and comprehension processes are part and parcel of everyday social interaction. For example, characteristics of the language production and comprehension system may affect the coordination of turn-taking in conversation (De Ruiter, Mitterer, & Enfield, 2006).

On the whole, the discourse-production-and-comprehension and the discourse-and-social-action traditions are not primarily concerned with understanding discourse in institutional settings. However, everyday social interactions overwhelmingly take place in the context of institutions of various kinds. As such, they are influenced by the specific aspects of the institutional context. At the same time their very performance contributes to creating and reproducing such institutional realities. This reciprocal link between discourse and institutions has attracted much scholarly attention in organization studies, the interdisciplinary field dedicated to understanding the processes inherent in organizing or coordinating collective human activities. Scholars in this area typically come from management science, organizational behavior, and organizational sociology. We refer to this area of research as the *discourse-and-institutions* tradition.

It would seem obvious that these three "grand" traditions would have much to learn from each other, and indeed there has been some cross-fertilization between them. However, it is no easy task to gain an overview of their potential interactions because they are studied by researchers from different disciplines, who often work from different methodological and epistemological premises. Levinson (2006a, p. 39) writes that the study of social interaction is spread out over an interdisciplinary "no-man's land." For example, experimental psycholinguistics (a prominent representative of the discourse-production-and-comprehension tradition) relies on rigorous experimental control, sophisticated technologies (measurement, brain imaging), and complex statistical analyses to investigate production and comprehension. At the same time, conversation analysis (a prominent representative of the discourse-and-social-action tradition) eschews experimental research and statistics (Schegloff, 1993), preferring to study naturally occurring interactions and situations and focusing on detailed transcription and analysis of examples of real conversations (but see De Ruiter & Albert, 2017). This state of affairs is unfortunate, because researchers in these traditions often are interested in similar phenomena (Levinson, 2006b). Research in the discourse-and-institutions tradition could learn much from more basic research and methodological innovations in both the discourse-production-and-comprehension tradition and the discourse-and-social-action tradition. At the same time, research in the discourse-production-and-comprehension tradition and the discourse-and-social-action tradition could be informed by a more sophisticated understanding of the complex and often subtle nature of institutional realities and their effects on discourse – indeed, research focusing on individuals communicating in interaction has often neglected the effects of macro-level, structural phenomena that are the mainstay of the discourse-and-institutions tradition (Lammers & Barbour, 2006).

The purpose of this chapter is to begin to remedy this state of affairs by charting these three traditions, as well as the specific research paradigms they have engendered, in order to create a background upon which new developments in the study of institutional discourse can be mapped. To our knowledge, there currently exists no review which relates these three traditions. We undertake this task by proceeding in three steps, organized around the central map that is depicted in Figure 3.1. First, in the second section, we describe the three grand traditions of research on discourse: the discourse-production-and-comprehension tradition (Figure 3.1, left) the discourse-and-social-action tradition (Figure 3.1, middle), and the discourse-and-institutions tradition (Figure 3.1, right). We also selectively describe specific research paradigms that have been emerging within these grand traditions, in a variety of blended approaches, since the 1980s. These approaches correspond to some of the boxes in Figure 3.1. Upon this backdrop, in the third section we describe examples of concrete topics where pioneering interdisciplinary encounters between these traditions are occurring (these do not appear in Figure 3.1). These topics exemplify how new research developments that typically come from one of the grand traditions can shed new light on classical topics from another tradition. In the fourth section, we conclude by briefly discussing the benefits of connecting these grand traditions for future interdisciplinary research.

The particular framing of this chapter allows for a "big-picture" map of an overall terrain that is often unknown to researchers working in their own specialized traditions, but where various bilateral connections are possible and indeed, as we will show, growing. We try to make as many of these connections as possible in this chapter. The framing also allows for a view of where the future is going. We anticipate this framing to be useful to scholars in all three grand traditions who are interested in looking beyond their own doorsteps, and young researchers who will benefit from having a comprehensive source to hand that can help them forge innovative new research projects. But a caveat is also in order. Throughout this chapter, and especially in the next section, we will use large brush strokes to paint this big picture. This necessarily entails some simplifications, as well as choices about which aspects of a particular research tradition to present and which to exclude. Our aim is to be representative rather than exhaustive. Moreover, because we are interested in links between the grand traditions, we mainly depict approaches that we deem potentially relevant for connections between these traditions. Moreover, we only represent approaches that have made important contributions to the study of discourse itself. Some approaches analyze discourse as a part of overall investigative activities or use discourse to illuminate social processes, but are not specifically dedicated to furthering scientific understanding of discourse *per se*. We have excluded such approaches from our depiction. An example would be the tradition of computer-supported cooperative work (Olson &

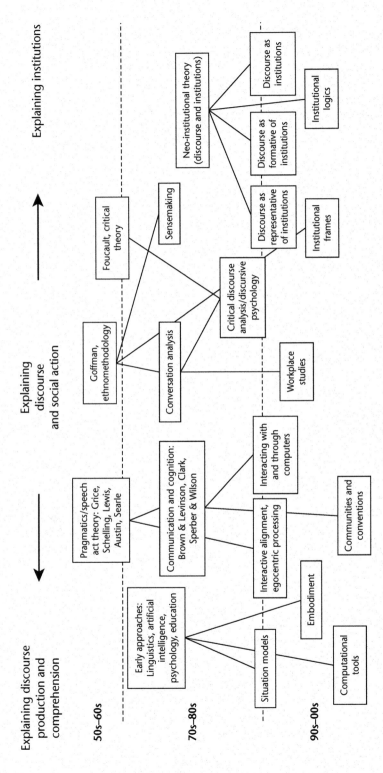

Figure 3.1 Three grand traditions of research on discourse and their relative explanatory foci. Left: The discourse-production-and-comprehension tradition. Middle: The discourse-and-social-action tradition. Right: The discourse-and-institutions tradition

Olson, 2007), which is concerned with studying how collaborative activities can be supported by technology, but which does not primarily focus on advancing understanding of discourse processes.

Three Grand Traditions in the Study of Discourse

Discourse Production and Comprehension

The discourse-production-and-comprehension tradition focuses on explaining the production and comprehension of discourse, typically by investigating the cognitive representations constructed during production and comprehension as well as the processes that give rise to them (Graesser, Gernsbacher, & Goldman, 1997). It emerged in the 1970s from work in fields like text linguistics, cognitive psychology, pragmatics, education, and artificial intelligence (Graesser, Gernsbacher, & Goldman, 2003). A key issue in discourse comprehension is how prior knowledge and current linguistic input interact, in other words, how knowledge is activated. Classic models emphasized the role of memory processes (Myers, O'Brien, Albrecht, & Mason, 1994) or strategic, goal-driven construction (Graesser, Singer, & Trabasso, 1994). More recent models have integrated these approaches (for a review see, e.g., Sparks & Rapp, 2010). In Figure 3.1, we highlight three aspects of the discourse-production-and-comprehension tradition we find particularly relevant for the study of discourse in institutional settings (without claiming that these are necessarily the most representative research trends in this tradition): situation models, embodied cognition, and computational tools.

Situation Models

Discourse comprehension involves constructing representations of a state of affairs depicted in a text. These representations go far beyond the information given as comprehenders build inferences about key dimensions like space, time, causality, intentionality, or protagonists. These representations have variously been termed situation models (Zwaan & Radvansky, 1998) or mental models (Johnson-Laird, 1983). In organizational settings, team mental models, or the extent to which members of a team share ideas about how to perform a task and each other's role in those tasks, are important determinants of team processes and performance (DeChurch & Mesmer-Magnus, 2010). Just as individual-level situation models enable inferences and predictions about a text that go beyond the information given, team mental models enable predictions about what other team members are likely to do without the need for overt communication and thus constitute an important element of successful team coordination. Team mental models can be elicited from discourse of individual team members which is then aggregated. An important future direction in this research field is the extent to which team members are actually aware of the extent and limits of what they share with each other and whether this impacts team performance (Mohammed, Ferzandi, & Hamilton, 2010). This seems especially interesting to link with research from the discourse-as-social-action tradition on perspective-taking (Schober, 1993) and the potentially egocentric nature of language production, especially given that team members may tend to overestimate the effectiveness of communication (Chang, Arora, Lev-Ari, D'Arcy, & Keysar, 2010). Related to these developments, recent theoretical approaches tend to conceptualize team cognition less as an aggregate knowledge structure shared by team members, but rather as an interactive activity (Cooke, Gorman, Meyers, & Duran, 2013).

Embodied Cognition

The notion that cognitive processes are grounded in bodily experience is gaining traction in many areas of cognitive science (Gibbs, 2005; Glenberg, 2010). Early work on this notion comes from various origins, but a prominent source relevant for discourse processing is Lakoff and Johnson's (1980) work on metaphors which suggest that they are not just figures of speech, but fundamental influences on thinking. Metaphors rooted in everyday experience are used to understand abstract concepts. For example, time is understood in spatial terms, as in expressions like "the worst is behind us" or "Thursday is before Saturday" (Boroditsky, 2000, p. 5). Our experiences of temporal duration are affected by concurrently presented but irrelevant spatial information (e.g., distance) (Casasanto & Boroditsky, 2008). Another case for the embodied nature of discourse processing is multimodal communication. Gesture and speech are tightly linked, both in production (De Ruiter, 1998) and comprehension (Kelly, Barr, Church, & Lynch, 1999; Kelly, Özyürek, & Maris, 2010). More generally, comprehenders rapidly and incrementally integrate visual and linguistic information from the earliest stages of comprehension (Tanenhaus, Spivey-Knowlton, Eberhard, & Sedivy, 1995), or mentally simulate sentences to derive their meaning (Glenberg & Kaschak, 2002, p. 562). Embodied cognition has a number of potential applications in applied and other institutional contexts (Davis et al., 2012) and the approach resonates with a rich tradition of research on metaphor (Morgan, 1986) and sensemaking in organizational research which has recently started to investigate the material and embodied nature of sensemaking in real-time and natural contexts of decision-making. For example, Cornelissen, Mantere, and Vaara (2014) analyzed the case of a police operation where an innocent civilian was mistaken for a terrorist and shot. They showed how the gesturing between police officers as well as the material cues encountered and artifacts used during the high-risk operation reinforced a framing of the suspect as a terrorist, thereby inhibiting cues that would have potentially favored alternative accounts and led to another course of action.

Computational Tools

Alongside advances in computational linguistics and corpus linguistics, research in the discourse-production-and-comprehension tradition has led to the development of several computational tools to automatically analyze relevant characteristics (e.g., cohesion) of a large corpus of texts. A relatively well-known package is LIWC (Linguistic Inquiry and Word Count) (Pennebaker, Francis, & Booth, 2001). Latent Semantic Analysis is both a theory and an automated method for analyzing knowledge representation in texts (Landauer, Foltz, & Laham, 1998). More recently developed, Coh-Metrix (McNamara, Graesser, McCarthy, & Cai, 2014) computes a range of metrics in written text, including cohesion indices. These metrics can be used flexibly to study high-level features of text that capture aspects like rhetoric or discourse strategies. Computational tools have great promise for investigating discourse in institutional contexts. For example, there is a vibrant research tradition in organizational research on the discourse of leaders, especially using speech transcripts (Bligh, Kohles, & Meindl, 2004; Fiol, Harris, & House, 1999; Klein & Licata, 2003). A recent study using LIWC and Coh-Metrix to analyze speeches of three autocratic leaders (Mao Tse-Tung, Fidel Castro, and Hosni Mubarak) after natural disasters (Windsor, Dowell, & Graesser, 2014) revealed the strategies those leaders used to apportion blame and claim credit to ultimately further their own interests. In the future, the further development of data science technologies will enable flexible and automatic analyses of large bodies of institutional texts for evidence of higher-level discourse processes. This in turn may even lead to the possibility of tracking processes of institutionalization and de-institutionalization as social movements unfold in real time.

Discourse and Social Action

This tradition investigates the production of discourse as a form of coordinated social action, as a means to perform social actions, or as a vehicle for expressing power relations in society. A primary site of investigation is the use of language in naturally occurring, every-day conversation. Seminal work in the 1950s and 1960s was conducted in the philosophy of language in the form of speech act theory. The main proponents of this approach took issue with a positivist view of language according to which its essential function is to produce true or false statements. Austin (1962) developed the notion of a performative utterance, the meaning of which is neither true nor false, but a means by which one can perform an action, such as naming something, promising, apologizing, or agreeing to marry someone. Austin further noted that utterances often perform several actions at once, distinguishing between locutionary (the ostensible meaning), illocutionary (intended meaning), and perlocutionary (the obtained effect) aspects of utterances. Philosophers of language have tackled the problem of how it is possible to recover the intended meaning of an utterance, which is often only loosely related to the linguistic meaning. Grice (1975) proposed that conversational participants adhere to a cooperative principle, according to which utterances produced in a conversation are presumed to be intended to further the conversation. Grice decomposed the cooperative principle into conversational maxims of quality, quantity, relevance, and manner. Using these maxims, participants are able to infer intended meaning from what is actually said, arriving at various kinds of implicatures. Searle (1975) further developed this issue in his theory of indirect speech acts.

Taylor and Cooren (1997) used Searle (1975) to argue that there is a certain class of speech acts that, when used by individuals, may have a formative role and effect in attributing agency and actorhood to a collective reality, i.e., an organization or institution, and with such an organization or institution in turn being recognized by the individuals involved as a legitimate expression of such agency – with the utterance of the speech act and its acceptance constituting the "organization" or "institution." Specifically, Taylor and Cooren (1997) draw on Searle's notion of declaratives, as speech acts, that are not only self-referential (in declaring that an organizational figure or institution exists and is attributed with agency) but the act itself also executes the very reality that it promotes to exist. Declarations are "speech acts where the illocutionary point of the speech act is to change the world in such a way that the propositional content matches the world, because the world has been changed to match the propositional content" (Searle, 1989, p. 541). Declarations thus have simultaneously what Searle (2010) calls "world-to-word" and "word-to-world" directions of fit: i.e. the world changes to match the word, and the word is a faithful representation of the world. This double link is, as Searle (2010) claims, essential to a joint commitment to a socially created world or reality, such as an organization or institution.

An example of the force of declaratives in creating social reality and instigating collective action is illustrated in a study by Quinn and Worline (2008) into the events aboard United Airlines Flight 93 (one of the planes hijacked in the September 11th attacks). A passenger aboard the plane had realized the hijacking was a terrorist suicide attack and declared (to others) "it is a suicide mission." In this way, he marked the reality that they were in as being different from a "normal" plane hijacking and hostage negotiation. At first, people aboard the plane struggled to accept his declaration in part because they had no precedent for "airplane hijackings being used for suicide missions" (Quinn & Worline, 2008, p. 506). Yet, gradually the declaration became legitimized and accepted, as "by sifting through data, seeking confirmation, questioning and debating, people could become increasingly certain about the accuracy of Tom's narrative for the duress" (p. 507). Accepting the common reality, people then collectively declared themselves an organizational "actor," or force, to counterattack the hijackers.

At the same time as the developments in speech act theory, sociologists were discovering face-to-face interaction. Erving Goffman made pioneering contributions to the understanding of self-presentation and facework (1955), conversation and talk (1961), and the interactional management of negative identity (1963). Goffman's work revealed how everyday talk constitutes a social institution along the lines of other kinds of institutions (organizations, markets, and the like) and described the practices by which this so-called *interaction order* operates (Heritage, 2001). Moreover, his work on frame analysis (1974) has been seminal in organization studies and sociology (e.g., Benford & Snow, 2000). Another pioneer in sociology, Garfinkel (1967) developed the project of ethnomethodology, which advocated investigating the shared understandings and everyday practices members of social groups use to make sense of their experience and create social order.

These seminal developments in the philosophy of language and sociology impacted a number of prominent scholars in the 1970s and 1980s. For example, Grice's (1975) work has influenced Levinson's important textbook on pragmatics (1983), and was reinterpreted by Sperber and Wilson (1986). Goffman and ethnomethodology paved the way for the development of conversation analysis from the late 1960s onward (Sacks, Schegloff, & Jefferson, 1974). And influences from Goffman, Grice, and conversation analysis are clearly identifiable in Clark's theory of grounding and language use (1996), which focuses both on social and cognitive processes in everyday conversation.

Communication and Cognition

Under this label we group landmark works in the fields of pragmatics and the psychology of language. A common denominator of these works is the link between cognition and social interaction, in other words, how cognitive processes enable everyday social interaction. As such, they are heavily influenced by Grice's work, and deal with the implications of the cooperative principle, especially the assumption that mutual knowledge is a prerequisite and result of successful communication. Many of these works are also close to the discourse-production-and-comprehension tradition, insofar as they focus on comprehension and production with little emphasis on the study of real conversation (or insofar as they attempt to explain conversational phenomena by appealing to cognition). For this reason, in Figure 3.1, the communication-and-cognition box is near to the left side of the figure. A first example is Brown and Levinson (1987), who, building on the work of Goffman on face, offer an account of indirect communication by which indirectness results from the use of politeness strategies in order to mitigate the face threats associated with performing various interactional moves. A second example is Sperber and Wilson (1986), who flesh out what they call an inferential model of communication (building on the work of Grice in particular), by which communication involves "producing and interpreting evidence" (p. 2), with such evidence being primarily about recognizing the intentions of the speaker. Their work proposes that intentional communication "carries a guarantee of relevance" (p. 50), i.e., that the very act of communication is an indication to the audience that what is being said is intended to be relevant. Relevance is a powerful principle that organizes the search for speaker meaning that is crucial to comprehending discourse. Sperber and Wilson's (1986) work is notable in its rejection of the mutual knowledge assumption. Another prominent work in the communication-and-cognition label is Clark's (1996) book, which summarizes important aspects of his and his colleagues' work on mutual knowledge or common ground as an important aspect of conversation. Unlike many other cognitive approaches, Clark's (1996) theory of language use is somewhat of a "cross-over" in that it is heavily influenced by conversation analysis.

Interactive Alignment and Egocentric Processing

In the 1990s and 2000s, the question of mutual knowledge in conversation became more controversial. Keysar (1997) proposed that much research on common ground is flawed because experiments do not take into account a potential confound between the common ground and the speaker's egocentric perspective. By designing experiments which separate these two components, it should however be possible to show that speakers' initial utterance design is essentially egocentric (i.e., does not take into account audience design; Horton & Keysar, 1996). These findings have also been criticized (Metzing & Brennan, 2003). The debate has since then increasingly focused on exploring the processes that influence whether communicative utterances are designed by speakers with the audience's perspective in mind (Horton & Gerrig, 2005; Knutsen & Le Bigot, 2012). A recent product of this debate is the constraint-based model (Hanna & Tanenhaus, 2004), which proposes that participants in dialogue rapidly interpret information from different sources as it becomes available (information on a conversational partner's perspective being one such source) and use this information to generate probabilistic evidence for competing interpretations. Pickering and Garrod's (2004) interactive alignment model is a mechanistic approach to explain the interactive phenomena inherent in dialogue. These researchers propose that much of coordination in everyday dialogue is achieved by the alignment of participants' situation models and other levels of dialogue processing (syntactic, lexical) via an automatic priming mechanism.

Conversation Analysis (CA)

CA emerged from initial work between Harvey Sacks, Emmanuel Schegloff, and Gail Jefferson in the 1960s. Via qualitative micro-analyses of detailed transcripts of naturally occurring conversation, CA seeks to account for the procedures by which participants in conversation co-construct organized social action (Goodwin & Heritage, 1990). A seminal paper was Sacks, Schegloff, and Jefferson's (1974) treatment of how participants in conversation allocate turns at talk among themselves. CA has systematically described a range of other fundamental conversational phenomena, like the adjacency pair as a basic element of conversational structure (Schegloff & Sacks, 1973), how problems are repaired (Schegloff, Jefferson, & Sacks, 1977), or how preferences are organized, notably the preference for agreement or acceptance (e.g., Pomerantz, 1984). More recent developments in CA have included a move toward investigating talk in institutional settings, using the CA approach to illuminate how institutions function. This program was outlined in a landmark volume in 1992 (Drew & Heritage, 1992). Since then, CA has been used to explore many institutional processes. In a recently edited handbook (Sidnell & Stivers 2012), chapters focus on psychotherapy, medicine, classroom talk, courtroom talk, and news interviews.

Critical Discourse Analysis and Discursive Psychology

Critical discourse analysis (CDA) is a wide-ranging approach to the study of relations between discourse and social power. It emerged from a range of intellectual precursors, including Marxism, the Frankfurt school of critical theory, and Foucault's works (van Dijk, 2015; see Figure 3.1). CDA tries to address social problems related to power relations, dominance or inequality by exposing the discourses by which such relations are enacted, for example through the analysis of right-wing political discourse (Wodak, 2015) or discourse about gender relations (Wodak, 1997). As such, it is close to the concerns of the discourse-and-institutions tradition and thus appears near the right side of Figure 3.1. Discursive psychology was originally developed at the University of Loughborough (Edwards & Potter, 1992; Potter & Wetherell, 1987). This movement is influenced by conversation analysis and ethnomethodology, but also rhetoric and the sociology of science. It is sharply critical of mainstream cognitive psychology, advocating a redefinition of the classic phenomena of psychology (e.g., memory, attributions, emotions) as social actions accomplished in and through discourse when people try to construct accounts to justify actions or project a particular identity.

Interacting With and Through Computers

This domain of research concerns two areas of human-computer interaction that we refer to as *interacting through computers*, i.e., interacting with other human beings via technological interfaces (e.g., computer programs, videoconference facilities) and *interacting with computers* designed to mimic human interactional partners. In both areas, investigations have benefited from advances made in models of discourse processing and communication and cognition. For example, in interacting with other humans through computers, researchers have analyzed the differences between real-time, face-to-face conversation and various media on the grounding process (Clark & Brennan, 1991). This in turn has led to efforts to mimic informational and interactional affordances available to physically co-present partners (Nardi & Whittaker, 2002) that are not available to remotely communicating partners, such as the sense of perspective conveyed by visual information (e.g., Gergle, Kraut, & Fussell, 2013). The potential gains of interacting with computers that mimic human interactional partners are large. Animated agents that are able to engage humans in reasonably realistic conversations can potentially attain outcomes comparable to those attainable via interactions with human representatives (at a much lower cost) in many institutional situations like learning and instruction (Graesser, Jeon, & Dufty, 2008), survey interviewing (Conrad & Schober, 2008), or health care interventions (Bickmore, Pfeifer, & Jack, 2009). This potential can be realized in part due to the natural tendency for humans to interact with computers in an anthropomorphic fashion (Epley, Waytz, & Cacioppo, 2007). Given the increase in computing power in recent years, it has become possible to endow animated agents with quite advanced adaptive capacities. Accordingly, research efforts have focused on potential benefits of increasing the naturalism of interactions with such agents, for example by investigating whether spoken versus written dialogues lead to better learning (D'Mello, Graesser, & King, 2010). In the future, many more social interactions between individuals and institutional representatives will be either mediated by technology or replace the human representatives themselves.

Workplace Studies

This is an approach within the sociology of work. It is concerned with the investigation of how "tools and artefacts feature in the accomplishment of practical organizational conduct"

(Heath, Knoblauch, & Luff, 2000, p. 308). Workplace studies draw on ethnomethodology and conversation analysis to describe how social interactions in the workplace are situated and contingent, and how material tools and technology are interwoven with those interactions. Workplace studies are typically critical of the assumptions of mainstream cognitive science and human-computer interaction and seek, like conversation analysis, to investigate naturally occurring situations. Many of the investigations in workplace studies are based on fine-grained multimodal analyses using video-recording (Heath, Hindmarsh, & Luff, 2010) with the goal of accessing details of the social organization of work that normally escape analytical focus. For example, a classic study (Hindmarsh & Heath, 2000) investigated the multimodal referential practices of operators in a telecommunications control room, showing how referential practices like precision-timed pointing gestures enabled mutual orientation to relevant information in the course of work activities, and how the referential activity was only intelligible in the context of those activities.

Communities and Conventions

This body of research goes beyond the implicit focus on dyadic conversational situations typical of the communication and cognition approach. The goal is to investigate how repeated interaction among members of a community leads to the emergence of linguistic conventions that are more robust than the conceptual pacts (Brennan & Clark, 1996) elaborated by dyads. Seminal research by Garrod and Doherty (1994) used a task that required participants to coordinate movement through a maze in a series of repeated games. Participants either always played the game with the same partner or repeatedly switched partners within a "community." In the community condition, participants initially took longer to converge on a conventional scheme for describing positions in the maze, but by the end of the experiment, convergence rates were higher than for isolated pairs. This finding suggests that conventions can evolve through repeated interactions among members of a community of language users and has important implications for the study of language emergence and change. Focus has since shifted to studying how abstract symbolic systems can emerge from communication that is initially iconic (e.g., highly idiosyncratic and detailed line drawings of referents) via social collaboration, as opposed to simple linear transmission (Fay, Garrod, Roberts, & Swoboda, 2010) or showing independent effects of cognitive change and collaboration on the emergence of symbol systems (Healey, Swoboda, Umata, & King, 2007). In a recent review, Garrod and Galantucci (2011) described progress in this field, now known as *experimental semiotics*. Research on communities and conventions has much potential for application to understanding initial moments in the development of conventions, and thus for elucidating the foundations of institutional emergence.

Discourse and Institutions

Within the field of organization studies, the subject of institutions and institutionalization has since the 1970s led to a vast and growing stream of research. This stream of research consists of studies that are wedded to various theoretical traditions and camps – or "institutionalisms" – ranging from work on institutional myths, frames, and logics to research in the tradition of institutional work. At the same time, these studies are all part of a broader neo-institutional turn which, in its entirety, holds a central position within the social sciences today (Davis, 2010; Scott, 2003), and is prominent in academic fields such as sociology, and management and organization studies.

Whilst neo-institutionalism may be a broad church encompassing various theoretical traditions, these traditions have traditionally primarily focused on individual and collective cognition as an explanation of the macro-level features of institutions (DiMaggio, 1997). This cognitive focus distinguishes the new institutionalism from the "old" institutionalism (Hirsch & Lounsbury, 1997), and has since the 1970s led to a considerable body of work exploring shared thought structures, or cognitive representations (labeled as frames, categories, templates, schemas, mental models, logics, myths, or scripts), that constitute the legitimate ways of talking and acting socially in particular social or organizational settings (Schneiberg & Clemens, 2006). A core assumption is that identifying such individual and collective representations gets at the heart of institutional reality where "the psychology of mental structures provides a micro-foundation to the sociology of institutions" (DiMaggio, 1997, p. 271).

Representational Approaches to Institutional Discourse

Because of its primary focus on individual and collective cognition, research on institutions has traditionally considered discourse as a "window" into cognition as it exists in a social setting or field at a particular point in time. Schneiberg and Clemens (2006, p. 211) suggest that the common measurement strategy among neo-institutional researchers has been "to use actors' discursive output as topics for analysis, that is, as documentation of cognitive frames, principles, or institutional logics." For example, Jones et al. (2012) recently analyzed the vocabularies of keywords used by movements of architects as they started to frame and define the emerging field of modern architecture. "Modern functional" and "modern organic" architects pronounced and underscored different conceptions of modern architecture and between each other started to promote their own vocabularies, as a code for their design practices. Loewenstein et al. (2012) similarly developed a theory of institutions as captured in, and represented by, vocabularies: collections of words and expressions that coherently interrelate, designate common categories of thinking, and refer to standard practices and conventions in a social setting. Thus, the focus in these works is on socially shared linguistic repertoires of keywords and idioms with institutional change being cast as a variation on, or combination of, existing words and expressions from within that domain (Jones et al., 2012; Loewenstein et al., 2012; Weber et al., 2008). Schneiberg and Clemens (2006) critique this strategy by emphasizing that actors may be working from different cognitive principles and schemes than what they communicate in public and may also not "'mean what they say' in the sense that discursive output does not flow directly from cognition" (Schneiberg & Clemens, 2006, p. 211). In other words, it is based on a rather strict, and to some extent naïve, assumption of discourse processes, one that considers discourse (or public texts) and cognition as isomorphic and thus merely casts discourse as a representation of the cognitive contents that are exchanged between communicating actors. Discourse, in other words, has a "representational" role and is not assigned any formative, dynamic, or constitutive role of itself in shaping the social reality that actors inhabit.

Performative Approaches to Institutional Discourse

These criticisms to some extent present a fork in the road for research on discourse and institutions, in that they have led to different research streams, each of which clearly positions itself against the other. Research has first of all taken a more performative turn to discourse and institutions. This approach, which emerged in the early 2000s, can be

Discourse in Institutional Contexts

labeled as *discourse-as-formative-of-institutions*, and is also sometimes described as rhetorical institutionalism (Green & Li, 2011). It includes theory and research on framing (Kennedy & Fiss, 2009), tropes (Etzion & Ferraro, 2010), discourse (Phillips et al., 2004), and rhetoric (Green, 2004) within institutional settings and fields. A key assumption of this overall approach is that any collective cognition or joint understanding that forms the basis for institutions is not simply pre-existing and accessed or shared by individuals but is in effect constantly *produced*, or *reproduced*, in the use and exchange of discourse, as a central part of social interaction and communication (e.g., Phillips et al., 2004; Green, 2004). Discourse (including all kinds of symbolic expressions such as gestures and bodily signals) has a performative role in that its use pragmatically affects actors in their thoughts and behaviors, and thus has the ability to initiate broader cognitive change at the level of an institutional field. Studies of the role of rhetoric and discourse in the context of taken-for-granted institutionalized realities such as organizational forms, common routines and practices, and the establishment of market categories, for example, focus on the structure and characteristics of discourse used (including a focus on keywords, idioms, or rhetorical arguments) by actors, as ways of (re)producing institutions, and explore how linguistic choices or alterations to a linguistic repertoire may in turn initiate processes of institutional change (e.g., Green & Li, 2011; Maguire et al., 2004). In this tradition, Green et al. (2009) examine the changing rhetoric around total quality management, a business philosophy that they show gradually started to engulf US corporate organizations and became a taken-for-granted argument (enthymeme) that no serious manager could no longer do without. As in this instance, most institutional studies in the organizational domain are quite macro in focus in that the overall aim is to show, through the lens of discourse, changes in broader macro-level organizational or institutional fields.

The contribution of these performative approaches is that, compared to the representational model, they consider language not as a neutral, external window into cognition, but as performative and thus formative of the cognitive basis of institutions, as well as of any changes to such institutions. The assumption is that language use, akin to a physical force (Talmy, 2000), may produce or engender cognitive reactions. This pragmatic force of discourse involves its capacity to effectuate cognitive change, with the choice of certain words (such as slogans, metaphors, and idioms) and grammatical or stylistic features having a direct impact on individuals and collective groups within an institutional setting or field. In addition, performative approaches are often heavily theory-driven, in the sense that they already start with strong theoretical assumptions about this pragmatic force and about the effects of discourse, ranging from a rhetorical to Foucauldian tradition.

Discourse as Constitutive of Institutions

This approach is, compared to the performative approach, far less theory-driven, and to some extent collapses the distinction between discourse and (cognitive) institution as separately distinguishable entities (when discourse is cast as either a window into or force affecting institutions). Discourse is instead seen as the very process through which collective forms such as institutions are constructed in and through local interactions, rather than being merely a conduit for cognition or a means to effect collective thoughts (Ashcraft & Mumby, 2004). In this sense, discourse, in the form of continuous interactions at multiple levels and with multiple potential outcomes, is seen to directly constitute institutions. This view does not negate the performative character of discourse, but is theoretically more agnostic about the actual "force" and effects that discourse may have in changing or maintaining the implied institutional status quo. It is also far less neat as a result, in that ambiguity and indeterminacy are expected and even assumed as an empirical commitment, as opposed to the more linear theory-driven accounts around hegemonic discourses, effective rhetoric, and institutional entrepreneurship typical of the performative approach. In fact, institutions, as common cognitive understandings, are an emergent effect, or outcome, that is tied into ongoing processes of discourse between diverse actors, rather than effectively casting institutions as separate entities at a different level of analysis and divorced from their "micro-foundations" in discourse and communication (see, e.g., Thornton et al., 2012).

The latter point challenges the common sociological tendency to oppose structure and action and macro and micro levels of analysis. The key suggestion here however is not to do away with such dualisms, but to recognize that institutions are first and foremost, as Fairhurst and Putnam (2004, p. 6) put it, "grounded in action" and thus "inhabited" (Hallett, 2010). Institutions, in other words, are constructed and negotiated on the *terra firma* of local, situated interactions in and through discourse (Zietsma & Lawrence, 2010). The resulting emergent outcomes – in terms of maintaining or changing an institution – may be confined to a specific set of interacting actors, but may also spread across a group of actors and organizations in an institutional field (Loewenstein et al., 2012). Importantly, such spread is itself contingent on discourse – consistent with the process of building up common ground and the abovementioned field of experimental semiotics.

This notion of discourse *as* institutions has not yet been fully explored in current research. There are some early papers that are starting to study and analyze institutions from this perspective (Ansari et al., 2013; Cornelissen et al., 2015; Loewenstein et al., 2012), but the overall perspective is still far from mainstream. A recent exception is the study by McPherson and Sauder (2013) on institutional logics in the context of negotiations in drug courts. McPherson and Sauder (2013) conceptualize logics as discourse-specific organizing principles, figures of speech, and arguments that are employed in interactions "on the ground" (as opposed to casting them as abstract macro-level belief systems) and that allow various actors to coordinate and manage their work and to reach consensus in an institutionally complex environment. In shifting to a discourse-as-institutions approach, they in turn argue that

> in order to fully comprehend institutional maintenance and change, organizational scholars must pay careful attention to the ways in which institutions are negotiated, interpreted and enacted by individuals *as they interact*. Thus it is through dynamic local processes that institutional logics are attached to organizational activity in symbolic and substantive ways as actors *constitute and shape* their meaning and relevance.
>
> *(McPherson & Sauder, 2013, p. 168; emphasis added)*

With this approach, discourse becomes constitutive of institutions, as it is primarily in and through the use of discourse in social interactions and communication that institutions exist and are performed and given shape. The metaphor of constitution suggests that in and through discourse use as part of social interaction, actors themselves construct a common base of understanding regulating their thoughts and behaviors. Such understanding may be contingent on prior interactions and may make use of available communal conventions, but may also be affected by the dynamics of the interaction itself (McPherson & Sauder, 2013).

Sensemaking and Institutions

In a parallel development in the field of organization studies, sensemaking emerged as a fundamental concept within organizational research in the late 1970s on the back of a growing interest among scholars in various streams of research that challenged notions of an objective reality in organizational behavior (Weick et al., 2005). As Maitlis and Christianson (2014) recently show, the historical roots of the sensemaking concept are quite diverse, emerging as it were from a confluence of streams of research that were salient at the time. These streams of research included fundamental work on ethnomethodology (see Figure 3.1), cognitive dissonance and speech functions, as well as organizational research on resource dependencies of organizations and studies of managerial attributions for success and failure. The very concept of sensemaking describes how in and through discourse individuals and groups in organizations pragmatically produce intelligible accounts of their environment, which are the "feedstock for institutionalization" (Weick, 1995, p. 35). Despite this link with institutions, sensemaking research has sometimes been criticized for neglecting the role of contexts in explaining cognition (Weber & Glynn, 2006), which is why sensemaking is positioned between the discourse-as-social-action and the discourse-and-institutions traditions in Figure 3.1.

The already mentioned study by Quinn and Worline (2008) of the hijacking of United Airlines Flight 93 on September 11th, 2001 illustrates the central role of discourse as part of sensemaking. People aboard the plane experienced a "shocking and incomprehensible" event that "tend[ed] to strip people of identity, leaving them no sensible narrative to enact" (Quinn & Worline, 2008, p. 501). Prior personal narratives or standard hijacking frames simply broke down in these circumstances. Individuals instead were forced to construct, whilst speaking to each other, a sensible narrative that reestablished an identity for themselves and allowed them to deliberate a novel action pattern of counterattacking the hijackers (Quinn & Worline, 2008). Importantly, this narrative of a counterattack in the context of the hijacking as a suicide mission had no institutional parallel (that is, in traditional hijacking scenarios, passengers and the crew remain seated or try to regain control of the airplane). One key insight of this study is that a novel form of sense, counterattacking the hijackers, had to be constructed from scratch.

In essence, the questions that a sensemaking researcher asks is how people in various organizational and institutional settings make sense of their circumstances in terms of their identity, activities, and relationship to others. Their sensemaking may be habitual and even largely unconscious for most routine activities, which then simply reaffirms the institutional scripts that they use. However, when individuals are faced with changing or unprecedented circumstances such as a crisis (as in Quinn & Worline, 2008) they have to make sense anew, and the sensemaking researcher in those settings looks at various data sources (real-time communication, transcripts, etc.) to reconstruct how individuals variably managed to do this and with what outcomes.

Discourse and Institutional Logics

Another recent analytic framework that links discourse to processes of institutional maintenance and change comes from theory on the micro-foundations of institutional logics (Thornton et al., 2012). Thornton and Ocasio (2008) define an institutional logic as the socially constructed, historical patterns of cultural symbols and material practices, including assumptions, values, and beliefs, through which actors provide meaning to their daily activity, organize time and space, and reproduce their lives and experiences. As such, institutional logics, once established, also "prime" the activation of salient and culturally available knowledge structures, or schemas, in a social context (Thornton et al., 2012, pp. 83–84) and which then guide perceptions, actions, and decision-making in habitual ways. Thornton et al. (2012) ground their more recent model on the emergence and transformation of institutional logics in what they describe as a dynamic constructivist notion of culture, which suggests that whilst actors are situated, embedded, and constrained by institutional logics in their actions, they do have a reflective capacity as well as the ability to associate a particular setting with different logics. Consistent with Sewell (1992), actors can call or act into existence a change to an existing logic, supplant it with another logic or even blend or combine logics such as, for example, combining provincial Indian and modern art (Khaire & Wadhwani, 2010), micro-credit and finance (Battilana & Dorado, 2010), or environmental auditing and financial reporting (Etzion & Ferraro, 2010).

The key question however is how such singular discursive or symbolic acts of individual actors translate into more broad-based cultural change in the form of establishing or revising macro-level institutional logics and the cognitive schemas and practices associated with them. The key mediating processes here, Thornton et al. (2012) suggest, are what they label as the "symbolic representations," or discourse that actors use to articulate institutional logics.

In their model, Thornton et al. (2012) distinguish three forms of discourse that actors use to express an institutional logic: theories, frames, and narratives. They define theories as abstract cause-effect explanations and rationalizations that provide general templates for action. Frames are the symbolic analogue, in Thornton et al. (2012), of cognitive schemas, consistent with Goffman (1974). And finally narratives are discursive accounts that arrange events and activities in a time-based storyline. It is at this level that actors can in and through symbolic expressions imply or directly present a revision or replacement of an institutional logic, and which then through further interaction and communication may spread across an institutional field and may lead to "common ground" among various individuals and groups (Thornton et al., 2012, p. 159) – again, in a very similar way to the grounding process discussed above in the communication and cognition tradition. A key contribution of the Thornton et al. (2012) framework is its focus on tracing how symbolic representations such as frames or narratives evolve, through further interaction and communication, into common category labels and conventionalized knowledge schemas.

Discourse and Institutional Frames

Diehl and McFarland (2010) developed an analytical framework for frame analysis within a social and institutional context by directly drawing on Goffman (1974). They follow Goffman in conceptualizing experience and actions in social situations as grounded in multilayered cognitive frames, which Goffman defined as "principles of organization which govern the subjective meanings we assign to social events" (1974, p. 11). In any given social situation, multiple frames may apply and are hierarchically layered and laminated on one another. Diehl and McFarland (2010) also consider frames, similar to Sewell (1992), as dualistic. This dualistic notion is a key tenet of Goffman's (1974) work. "The difference, then, is between frames operating as the background structure of shared reality on the one hand and as tools for strategic and creative behavior on the other" (Diehl & McFarland, 2010, p. 1719).

Diehl and McFarland (2010) extend this dualistic nature of frames and place it in the context of a broader analytical framework that distinguishes between different layers of frames and that can be used to analyze social situations. They first of all distinguish a "natural frame," which involves researchers understanding events before these are scripted and understood in social terms. From this perspective situations involve actors and their embodied experiences but without any intentional or socially prescribed forms of actions. The second layer involves the "person frame," defined as the "base layer of social interpretation" (p. 1721). Situations are analyzed in terms of understanding conscious and morally responsible actors, but without any further social roles being imposed on them, which is the next layer. The "institutionalized role frame" refers to the culturally legitimate frame for a given strip of activity, which is rooted in the conventions and rules for a given interaction order and thus prescribes certain social roles to actors such as that of a doctor interacting with a patient. The final layer is the "character" frame, which recognizes that "social situations are incomplete and require individuals to negotiate how to proceed in ill-defined spaces, to smooth over interactional rough patches, and to reinforce the underlying order by transforming it in various ways" (Diehl & McFarland, 2010, p. 1721). A doctor may when consulting a patient find it hard to deliver bad news and may adopt a different character (of, say, a sympathetic listener or parent) than the one that may have been institutionally prescribed (Tannen, 1985).

Of particular interest are the links between these different frames, especially between the institutionalized role and character frames. Goffman (1974) saw the seeds for cultural and social change in this linkage but also recognized that the institutionalized frame prefigures and constrains any deviating gestures and behaviors. For example, he argued that given that the institutionalized role frame anchors behavior in a given situated activity it also dictates who can extend or alter roles and in what manner. Diehl and McFarland (2010) capture this prefiguring role of the institutionalized role frame with the idea that the character frame, as an alternative framing in context, is a "lamination" on the straight role frame, meaning something that researchers can detect, although the lamination itself may not always be consciously experienced by the individuals that are being studied. As such, they also suggest that conceptualizing and in turn coordinating experience through the character frame is "Janus-faced" (Diehl & McFarland, 2010, p. 1725). On the one hand it "serves to reinforce the underlying institutionalized role frame upon which it is laminated" (p. 1725). They refer to instances where role performances require improvisation in action in the service of reinforcing or repairing a shared orientation toward the institutionalized role frame. On the other hand, the character frame "allows for actors to project out-of-frame roles and identities" (p. 1725). Roles may provide latitude in terms of behaviors, and thus allow for creative displays that reconfigure rewrite the script for a role altogether. Thus, for Diehl and McFarland (2010), the seeds of institutional change can be found in those moments and occasions when social situations involve clear shifts in "frame formulas" that link role and character frames, and that establish and in turn conventionalize a new interaction order between actors.

Encounters Between Traditions

In this section, we describe examples of concrete topics where pioneering interdisciplinary encounters between these traditions are occurring, blending complex phenomena like embodiment, sensemaking, and storytelling. The examples illustrate how research concepts, methods, and phenomena from fine-grained analytical traditions can be used to address and materialize institutional-theoretical phenomena that have typically been studied at a higher level of abstraction.

Embodiment, Sensemaking, and Institutions

One potential area of cross-fertilization is the recent work on embodiment and ongoing sensemaking in institutionalized settings. Sensemaking challenges the traditional assumption that discourse simply triggers or prompts the retrieval of frames and frame-based meaning and expectations from memory, and proposes instead that words and expressions in context may *construct* the very nature of such frames and expectations as an interaction unfolds (e.g., Quinn & Worline, 2008). Furthermore, one of the main insights that emerges from recent sensemaking studies is that more generally the bodily actions of individuals, including speech, do not simply express previously formed mental concepts or broader cognitive frames (Cornelissen & Clarke, 2010). Instead, bodily practices, including the use of language, bodily gesturing and social interaction, are part and parcel of the very activity in which concepts and conceptualizations are formed (Stigliani & Ravasi, 2012; Whiteman & Cooper, 2011). Recent studies have for example highlighted how designers form conceptualizations through physically grasping, holding, or manipulating material objects such as prototype designs and drawings (Stigliani & Ravasi, 2012; Whiteman & Cooper, 2011). Such conceptualizations are then in effect constructed, rather than accessed, in the interaction with material objects and based on the sensations and ideas that such interactions afford (Whiteman & Cooper, 2011).

When such embodied acts are furthermore taking place in a social context, the physical manipulation of objects may be exploited to cue meaning to others and in essence provides a "scaffolding" around which new meanings are collectively constructed. Stigliani and Ravasi (2012), for example, demonstrate how designers shared visuals and artifacts that grounded common imagery for new products, and that allowed them to collectively elaborate and build up new emergent ideas. In this process, individuals, whilst communicating and interacting with one another, do not need to share or even have access to the same knowledge (Whiteman & Cooper, 2011). Instead, in such ongoing processes of communication, individuals generally exploit the built-up "common ground" between them, say in the form of a redrawn visual diagram (Bechky, 2011), as a resource for constructing collective understanding and for deriving pragmatic inferences (Clark, 1996). This emerging line of sensemaking research is still consistent with the notion of sensemaking as frame-based meaning construction, but draws heavily on ideas of embodied cognition and experimental semiotics. We believe that these connections are worth elaborating further, as these would give a much more rounded, multimodal view of how instances of sensemaking on the ground may maintain or change institutions.

Bodily Gestures and Institutionalizing Communication

Another fruitful area where various research traditions can be combined is investigating "institutionalizing communication": communication that is used by actors to intentionally institutionalize a new entity, like a venture or organization, product, practice, or basic idea. One arena for potential study in which such forms of communication are central is entrepreneurship, as entrepreneurs who are developing new businesses typically have to gain institutional legitimacy for their burgeoning ventures in order to gain broad-based support and access final and social resources. In the absence of prior indicators of success or a clear track record, entrepreneurs must rely on their abilities and skills to communicate and persuade investors of the legitimacy and feasibility of their entrepreneurial venture to gain early stage investment (Cornelissen & Clarke, 2010). Most work focusing on communication and persuasion in entrepreneurial contexts has taken a traditional view of communication which assumes that understanding language requires "breaking down the physical information (e.g. speech sounds) into a language-independent medium" that constitutes a disembodied "language of thought" (Gibbs, 2005, p. 158). This approach is increasingly being challenged by recent work that demonstrates the importance of bodily communication and cues of an entrepreneur alongside speech as essential toward convincing investors of the legitimacy of a venture. Chen et al. (2009), for example, find that the display of an entrepreneur's passion through frequent gesturing and animated facial expressions in business plan presentations or pitches influenced assessments of legitimacy as well as investment decisions. Because entrepreneurs have to sell their venture plans to potential investors, displays of passion are critical to convince targeted individuals to invest, because they indicate that the entrepreneur will be highly motivated to build a venture and pursue goals even when confronted with difficulties.

Gesturing in particular may be an important ingredient of institutionalizing communication. In field and lab experiments, Cornelissen et al. (2015) find that both the frequency and type of gesturing help to institutionalize a novel understanding of a venture or influence the decision to invest. Specifically, symbolic or metaphorical gestures helped frame a novel venture, and led it to be understood by investors seen as taken for granted by them, considerably more so than other more pragmatic and speech-structuring gestures (so-called beats, cohesive and deictic gestures). This effect, however, was only evident when such gestures aligned with metaphors or figurative language in speech (McNeill, 1992), and together produced a singular image that familiarized and in turn institutionalized the new venture. Whilst these findings are tied to the setting of entrepreneurship, we believe that they are nonetheless suggestive for other areas as well (see for example Mondada, 2013, on the embodied nature of turn-taking in town hall meetings as a factor of the construction of participatory democracy).

Framing and Institutional Change

A further set of linkages involves the relationship between an individual's framing in context and interactively established group or collective action frames. In *Frame Analysis*, Goffman's (1974) primary focus is on the experience of interaction and the shared frames that are constructed and agreed upon, and that make such constructions inter-subjectively meaningful and understandable (1974, p. 127). Tannen (1985) refers to these as "interactive frames." In her study of pediatric examinations and consultations, she shows how such frames are not only constructed in interaction, but also reflect principles of interaction that are associated with the social identities of the participants and the institutional setting. A pediatrician in this study talks fluently to her peers about the medical condition of a child, but struggles in her language (with frequent hesitations and circumlocutions) when she decides to bridge between "examination," "consultation," and "mother" frames in an attempt to reassure the mother. Besides Tannen's work, there has been little frame-based research that explores detailed social interactions of this kind, and how they lead to the establishment of joint interactive frames. A closer focus on social interactions – and, specifically, on the discursive alignment between interactants – provides a base for more fine-grained conceptualizations of frame-alignment processes and of the establishment of common ground (Loewenstein et al., 2012), or the settlement of joint meaning, as the basis for new practices, organizational forms, and markets. Yet, surprisingly, very little research exists on how common ground is established in and through repeated interactions, with most research focusing simply on the institutional consequences of its emergence (Barley, 1986; Schneiberg & Clemens, 2006).

Further research might therefore heedfully use the distinction between two basic kinds of common ground – personal and communal common ground (Clark, 1996) – which map onto the concepts of interactive and field frames. Personal common ground is built up by interacting actors in the course of communication or joint activity. When actors in an interaction need to make sense anew or need to bridge understanding, they have to build up personal common ground in a step-by-step manner, akin to interactive frames (Barley, 1986; Bechky, 2011). The conventions created as part of personal common ground during small-scale interactions (e.g., between pairs of actors, or between actors within small movements or groups) can in turn spread from one interaction to the next, leading to the emergence of cultural conventions in the form of field frames, or communal common ground, across actors in an institutional field (Garrod & Doherty, 1994; Fay et al., 2010). Here, then, is yet another example of the rich potential of cross-fertilization between the discourse-and-social-action tradition and the discourse-and-institutions tradition.

Organizational Storytelling

Storytelling has been repeatedly recognized as an important window into organizational processes like culture, politics, or change (Gabriel, 2000). However, research has often focused on the story itself as a decontextualized product (e.g., stories as abstract "types," Martin, Feldman, Hatch, & Sitkin, 1983) as opposed to the storytelling as a situated, collaborative performance. Pioneering studies of storytelling performance were conducted by Orr (1996) and Boje (1991). Orr's (1996) classic ethnography of Xerox photocopy repair technicians revealed the central function of "war stories" in their everyday work activities. The technicians often had to face difficult working conditions in diagnosing and repairing the photocopy machines based on incomplete information and counterproductive rules and procedures. Extensive informal communication is an essential part of their sensemaking about these challenges, of which stories are an important part. Stories are told and retold, and can be re-used in particular to illuminate problematic situations. Storytelling also serves as a marker of community (often being elliptic in nature, and thus relatively opaque to outsiders), a demonstration of professional competence, and a celebration of the technicians' self-views as "lone heroes." Boje (1991) documented stories told in everyday conversations between managers, customers, and workers of an office supply firm. He analyzed both the details of storytelling performance, including their embeddedness in other forms of discourse and their often fragmented nature, and the sensemaking purposes they were used for. Aspects of performance were sometimes linked to strategic purposes (for example, tersely told stories used to obfuscate particular audiences), illustrating the potential link between storytelling performance and the accomplishment of informal organizational activities.

More recent work on storytelling performance has integrated the multimodal, embodied turn (Gylfe et al., 2016) apparent in later developments in the discourse-and-social-action tradition (see Figure 3.1). Sharma and Grant (2011) built on a dramaturgical approach to charismatic leadership to show how charismatic leaders use both discursive and material elements of stage management to perform visionary stories. Bangerter, Mayor, and Pekarek Doehler (2011) studied multimodal reenactments produced during storytelling episodes in nursing shift handover meetings. They showed how the performance of reenactments enabled shared sensemaking about non-routine events (e.g., complaining about difficult patients) or depictions of the narrator as a rational actor (e.g., in justifying a deviation from medical protocol). Küpers, Mantere, and Statler (2013) showed how organizational strategy can constitute an embodied experience by analyzing narrative practices in a workshop during which organizational actors redefined the strategy of the corporation. Storytelling can also affect how individuals gain entry to organizations, with storytelling skills of job candidates playing an increasingly important role in hiring (Bangerter, Corvalan, and Cavin, 2014; Ralston, Kirkwood, & Burant, 2003).

This body of work is strikingly eclectic. There is a mix of researchers from the discourse-and-social-action tradition and the discourse-and-institutions tradition, with both groups interested in understanding the multimodal, embodied performance of stories and how they are used in institutional settings. Despite this shared interest, there is a wide range of research strategies and methods in use, and little cross-fertilization. For example, experimental research on storytelling has the potential to tease apart the effects of different factors like dialogue or media (Bavelas, Gerwing, & Healing, 2014) or audience participation (Kuhlen & Brennan, 2010) on storytelling performance, but this work has been little cited in institutional storytelling research, despite the potential relevance of such factors for institutional processes. Future studies should therefore investigate how detailed storytelling processes may affect institutional phenomena. One potentially promising strand of future research would be to document what kind of social actions are performed through storytelling and how these actions relate to the institutional situation (formative, constitutive, and so on). Another would be how particular features of the telling activity contribute to constitute a situation as an institutional one (Mandelbaum, 2012) or how the activity contributes to enact institutional roles or logics.

Conclusions

In this chapter, we have tried to characterize the deep and reciprocal links between discourse processes and institutional functioning. Because research relevant to this question is spread out over many disciplines, subfields and schools of thought, we have started by describing three grand traditions of research on discourse and their main contributions to understanding discourse processes in institutions. The discourse-production-and-comprehension tradition is dedicated to understanding the cognitive processes in the production and comprehension of discourse, and has led to important advances in situation models, embodied cognition, and computational approaches for the automatic measurement and analysis of discourse. The discourse-and-social-action tradition has investigated the cognitive and social processes involved in coordinating conversations and the use of discourse in society, improving our understanding of how shared knowledge enables social interaction and how social interaction leads to the establishment of precedents and conventions. The discourse-and-institutions tradition approaches these phenomena from the opposite angle, looking at how discourse is constitutive of institutions, for example how discourse processes contribute to creating institutional realities or, on the contrary, to destabilizing them. It should be clear by now that these traditions have much to learn from each other, and we have tried to draw out some concrete examples of work on the ground that is already under way. We also hope to have shown how much potential there is for cross-fertilization.

In conclusion, we would like to revisit the issue of social change touched upon in the introduction. Social change is an excellent case for illustrating the link between discourse and institutions, because it is through discursive processes that seemingly rock-solid institutions or institutional arrangements can become vulnerable to change. Social change puts in perspective both the power that institutions normally have over collective thought and behavior, as well as the sometimes surprisingly sudden nature of their demise. A recent example is the role of social media in the "Arab Spring" popular uprisings that spread over several countries of the Middle East in 2011. Social media enabled the rapid diffusion of discursive content to create shared values and commitment that proved essential to the coordination of social movements instrumental in the uprisings (Howard & Parks, 2012). In an analysis of over a million tweets produced during protests in Egypt in 2011 that led to the resignation of president Hosni Mubarak, Papacharissi and de Fatima Oliveira (2012) used both computerized and qualitative discourse analysis to document a hybridization of traditional and emerging news values. For example, the instantaneous character of tweets conflicts with the traditional news value of fact-checking. On the other hand, phenomena like "crowdsourcing of elites" enabled the rise to prominence of previously unknown activists. This collaboratively constructed stream of "affective news" may have played a role in generating a sense of community among various publics and possibly furthering the uprising.

This kind of case poses a number of challenges. Reducing large-scale and fast-paced technology-mediated phenomena to an interpretable set of phenomena requires the prowess of computational analyses. But an adequate construal of the data also requires insightful analyses of the linkage between discourse and power, and ultimately, the nature of institutional functioning. More generally, the emerging potential for using automated analyses of large sets of existing discourse data (e.g., on social media) will require more dialogue between data scientists and discourse researchers, whether in the case of sudden social change or in related cases like the measurement of social trends (Schober, Pasek, Guggenheim, Lampe, & Conrad, 2016). In other words, understanding important real-world phenomena like in the current example will require harnessing different theoretical and methodological perspectives from each of the three grand traditions we have reviewed in this chapter (Schober et al., 2016).

Thus, whilst such a case is empirically challenging for any team of researchers, it also demonstrates the real value of an interdisciplinary, phenomenon-based approach to discourse and institutions. In the conclusion of their introduction to the first edition of this handbook, Graesser at al. (2003) proposed some future directions research on discourse processes should take to thrive. One of these was indeed a shift from "multidisciplinary" to "interdisciplinary" research. True interdisciplinary research involves joint collaboration on research projects by researchers from two or more disciplines. Those researchers are forced to coordinate their perspectives to solve the concrete problems posed by the project, which typically leads to a deeper understanding of the phenomena studied. Whilst pockets of truly interdisciplinary research have since emerged in the study of discourse processes, we believe that much potential remains with respect to the study of discourse processes in institutions, and we hope this chapter may help some individuals to engage in such joint projects.

Suggested Reading

Alvesson, M., & Karreman, D. (2000). Varieties of discourse: On the study of organizations through discourse analysis. *Human Relations*, *53*, 1125–1149.

Cornelissen, J. P., Durand, R., Fiss, P. C., Lammers, J. C., & Vaara, E. (2015). Putting communication front and center in institutional theory and analysis. *Academy of Management Review*, *40*(1), 10–27.

Drew, P., & Heritage, J. (Eds) (1992). *Talk at work: Language use in institutional and work-place settings*. Cambridge: Cambridge University Press.

Putnam, L. L., & Mumby, D.K. (Eds) (2014). *The SAGE handbook of organizational communication: Advances in theory, research, and methods* (3rd ed.). Los Angeles, CA: Sage.

Schneiberg, M., & Clemens, E. S. (2006). The typical tools for the job: Research strategies in institutional analysis. *Sociological Theory*, *24*, 195–227.

References

Alvesson, M., & Karreman, D. (2000). Varieties of discourse: On the study of organizations through discourse analysis. *Human Relations, 53*, 1125–1149.

Ansari, S. M., Wijen, F. H., & Gray, B. (2013). Constructing a climate change logic: An institutional perspective on the "Tragedy of the commons". *Organization Science, 24*(4), 1014–1040.

Ashcraft, K. L., & Mumby, D. K. (2004). *Reworking gender: A feminist communicology of organization.* Thousand Oaks, CA: Sage.

Austin, J. L. (1962). *How to do things with words.* Oxford: Oxford University Press.

Bangerter, A., Corvalan, P., & Cavin, C. (2014). Storytelling in the selection interview? How applicants respond to past behavior questions. *Journal of Business and Psychology, 29*, 593–604.

Bangerter, A., Mayor, E., & Pekarek Doehler, S. (2011). Reported speech in conversational narratives during nursing shift handover meetings. *Discourse Processes, 48*, 183–213.

Barley, S. R. (1986). Technology as an occasion for structuring: Evidence from observations of CT scanners and the social order of radiology departments. *Administrative Science Quarterly, 31*, 78–108.

Battilana, J., & Dorado, S. (2010). Building sustainable hybrid organizations: The case of commercial microfinance organizations. *Academy of Management Journal, 53*(6), 1419–1440.

Bavelas, J. B., Gerwing, J., & Healing, S. (2014). The effect of dialogue on demonstrations: Direct quotations, facial portrayals, hand gestures, and figurative references. *Discourse Processes, 51*, 619–655.

Bechky, B. (2011). Making organizational theory work: Institutions, occupations, and negotiated orders. *Organization Science, 22*(5), 1157–1167.

Benford, R. D., & Snow, D. A. (2000). Framing processes and social movements: An overview and assessment. *Annual Review of Sociology, 26*, 611–639.

Bickmore, T., Pfeifer, L., & Jack, B. (2009). Taking the time to care: Empowering low health literacy hospital patients with virtual nurse agents. *Proceedings of the ACM SIGCHI Conference on Human Factors in Computing Systems* (CHI), Boston, MA.

Bligh, M. C., Kohles, J. C., & Meindl, J. R. (2004). Charisma under crisis: Presidential leadership, rhetoric, and media responses before and after the September 11th terrorist attacks. *Leadership Quarterly, 15*(2), 211–239.

Boje, D. M. (1991). Organizations as storytelling networks: A study of story performance in an office-supply firm. *Administrative Science Quarterly, 36*, 106–126.

Boroditsky, L. (2000). Metaphoric structuring: Understanding time through spatial metaphors. *Cognition, 75*, 1–28.

Brennan, S. E., & Clark, H. H. (1996). Conceptual pacts and lexical choice in conversation. *Journal of Experimental Psychology: Learning, Memory and Cognition, 22*, 1482–1493.

Brown, P., & Levinson, S. (1987). *Politeness: Some universals in language use.* Cambridge: Cambridge University Press.

Casasanto, D., & Boroditsky, L. (2008). Time in the mind: Using space to think about time. *Cognition, 106*, 579–593. doi:10.1016/j.cognition.2007.03.004.

Chang, V. Y., Arora, V. M., Lev-Ari, S., D'Arcy, M., & Keysar, B. (2010). Interns overestimate the effectiveness of their hand-off communication. *Pediatrics, 125*, 491–496.

Chen, X., Yao, X., & Kotha, S. B. (2009). Passion and preparedness in entrepreneurs' business plan presentations: A persuasion analysis of venture capitalists' funding decisions. *Academy of Management Journal, 52*(1), 199–214.

Clark, H. H. (1992). *Arenas of language use.* Chicago, IL: University of Chicago Press.

Clark, H. H. (1996). *Using language.* Cambridge: Cambridge University Press.

Clark, H. H., & Brennan, S. E. 1991. Grounding in communication. In L. B. Resnick, J. M. Levine, & S. D. Teasley (Eds), *Perspectives on socially shared cognition* (pp. 127–149). Washington: APA Books.

Conrad, F.G., & Schober, M. F. (Eds) (2008). *Envisioning the survey interview of the future.* New York, NY: Wiley.

Cooke, N. J., Gorman, J. C., Meyers, C. W., & Duran, J. L. (2013). Interactive team cognition. *Cognitive Science, 37*, 255–285.

Cornelissen, J. P., & Clarke, J. S. 2010. Imagining and rationalizing opportunities: Inductive reasoning, and the creation and justification of new ventures. *Academy of Management Review, 35*(4), 539–557.

Cornelissen, J. P., Durand, R., Fiss, P. C., Lammers, J. C., & Vaara, E. (2015). Putting communication front and center in institutional theory and analysis. *Academy of Management Review, 40*(1), 10–27. doi:http://dx.doi.org/10.5465/amr.2014.0381.

Cornelissen, J., Mantere, S., & Vaara, E. (2014). The contraction of meaning: The combined effect of communication, emotion and materiality on sensemaking in the Stockwell shooting. *Journal of Management Studies, 51*(5), 699–736.

Davis, G. F. (2010). Do theories of organizations progress? *Organizational Research Methods, 13*, 690–709.

Davis, J. I., Benforado, A., Esrock, E., Turner, A., Dalton, R. C., van Noorden, L., & Leman, M. (2012). Four applications of embodied cognition. *Topics in Cognitive Science, 4*, 786–793.

DeChurch, L. A., & Mesmer-Magnus, J. R. (2010). The cognitive underpinnings of team effectiveness: A meta-analysis. *Journal of Applied Psychology, 95*(1), 32–53.

De Ruiter, J. (1998). *Gesture and speech production.* Nijmegen: Catholic University of Nijmegen, Netherlands.

De Ruiter, J., & Albert, S. (2017). An appeal for a methodological fusion of conversation analysis and experimental psychology. *Research on Language and Social Interaction, 50*, 90–107.

De Ruiter, J., Mitterer, H., & Enfield, N. (2006). Projecting the end of a speaker's turn: A cognitive cornerstone of conversation. *Language, 82*(3), 515–535.

D'Mello, S. K., Graesser, A. C., & King, B. (2010). Toward spoken human-computer tutorial dialogues. *Human Computer Interaction, 25*(4), 289–323.

Diehl, D., & McFarland, D. A. (2010). Towards a historical sociology of situations. *American Journal of Sociology, 115*(6), 1713–1752.

DiMaggio, P. (1997). Culture and cognition. *Annual Review of Sociology, 23*, 263–287.

Drew, P., & Heritage, J. (Eds) (1992). *Talk at work: Language use in institutional and work-place settings.* Cambridge: Cambridge University Press.

Edwards, D., & Potter, J. (1992). *Discursive psychology.* London: Sage.

Epley, N., Waytz, A., & Cacioppo, J. T. (2007). On seeing human: A three-factor theory of anthropomorphism. *Psychological Review, 114*, 864–886.

Etzion, D., & Ferraro, F. (2010). The role of analogy in the institutionalization of sustainability reporting. *Organization Science, 21*(5), 1092–1107.

Fairhurst, G. T., & Putnam, L. L. (2004). Organizations as discursive constructions. *Communication Theory, 14*(1), 5–26.

Fay, N., Garrod, S., Roberts, L., & Swoboda, N. (2010). The interactive evolution of human communication systems. *Cognitive Science, 34*, 351–386.

Fiol, C. M. (2002). Capitalizing on paradox: The role of language in transforming organizational identities. *Organization Science, 13*, 653–666.

Fiol, C. M., Harris, D., & House, R. (1999). Charismatic leadership: Strategies for effecting social change. *Leadership Quarterly, 10*, 449–482.

Gabriel, Y. (2000). *Storytelling in organizations: Facts, fictions, and fantasies.* Oxford: Oxford University Press.

Garfinkel, H. (1967). *Studies in ethnomethodology.* Englewood Cliffs, NJ: Prentice-Hall.

Garrod, S., & Doherty, G. M. (1994). Conversation, co-ordination and convention: An empirical investigation of how groups establish linguistic conventions. *Cognition, 53*, 181–215.

Garrod, S., & Galantucci, B. (2011). Experimental semiotics: A review. *Frontiers in Human Neuroscience, 168*, 161. doi:10.3389/fnhum.2011.00011.

Gergle, D., Kraut, R. E., & Fussell, S.R. (2013). Using visual information for grounding and awareness in collaborative tasks. *Human-Computer Interaction, 28*(1), 1–39.

Gibbs, R. (2005). *Embodiment and cognitive science.* Cambridge: Cambridge University Press.

Glenberg, A. M. (2010). Embodiment as a unifying perspective for psychology. *Wiley Interdisciplinary Reviews: Cognitive Science, 1*, 586–596.

Glenberg, A. M., & Kaschak, M. P. (2002). Grounding language in action. *Psychonomic Bulletin and Review, 9*, 558–565.

Goffman, E. (1955). On face-work: An analysis of ritual elements in social interaction. *Psychiatry, 18*, 213–231.

Goffman, E. (1961). *Encounters: Two studies in the sociology of interaction.* Oxford: Bobbs-Merrill.

Goffman, E. (1963). *Stigma: Notes on the management of spoiled identity.* Englewood Cliffs, NJ: Prentice-Hall.

Goffman, E. (1974). *Frame analysis: An essay on the organization of experience*. Boston, MA: Northeastern University Press.

Goodwin, C., & Heritage, J. (1990). Conversation analysis. *Annual Review of Anthropology, 19*, 283–307.

Graesser, A. C., Gernsbacher, M. A., & Goldman, S. R. (1997). Cognition. In T. Van Dijk (Ed.), *Discourse as structure and process: Discourse studies: A multidisciplinary introduction* (pp. 292–319). Thousand Oaks, CA: Sage.

Graesser, A. C., Gernsbacher, M. A., & Goldman, S. R. (2003). Introduction to the *Handbook of discourse processes*. In A. C. Graesser, M. A. Gernsbacher, & S. R. Goldman (Eds), *Handbook of discourse processes* (pp. 1–24). Mahwah, NJ: Erlbaum.

Graesser, A. C., Jeon, M., & Dufty, D. (2008). Agent technologies designed to facilitate interactive knowledge construction. *Discourse Processes, 45*(4), 298–322.

Graesser, A. C., Singer, M., & Trabasso, T. (1994). Constructing inferences during narrative text comprehension. *Psychological Review, 101*(3), 371–395.

Green, S. E. (2004). A rhetorical theory of diffusion. *Academy of Management Review, 29*(4), 653–669.

Green, S. E., & Li, Y. (2011). Rhetorical institutionalism: Language, agency, and structure in institutional theory since Alvesson 1993. *Journal of Management Studies, 48*(7), 1662–1697.

Green, S., Li, Y., & Nohria, N. (2009). Suspended in self-spun webs of significance: A rhetorical model of institutionalization and institutionally embedded agency. *Academy of Management Journal, 52*(1), 11–36.

Grice, H. P. (1975). Logic and conversation. In P. Cole & J. L. Morgan (Eds), *Syntax and semantics*, Vol. 3. New York, NY: Academic Press.

Gylfe, P., Franck, H., Lebaron, C., & Mantere, S. (2016). Video methods in strategy research: Focusing on embodied cognition. *Strategic Management Journal, 37*(1), 133–148.

Hallett, T. (2010). The myth incarnate: Recoupling processes, turmoil, and inhabited institutions in an urban elementary school. *American Sociological Review, 75*(1), 52–74.

Hanna, J. E., & Tanenhaus, M. K. (2004). Pragmatic effects on reference resolution in a collaborative task: Evidence from eye movements. *Cognitive Science, 28*, 105–115.

Healey, P. G. T., Swoboda, N., Umata, I., & King, J. (2007). Graphical language games: Interactional constraints on representational form. *Cognitive Science, 31*, 285–309.

Heath, C., Hindmarsh, J., & Luff, P. (2010). *Video in qualitative research: Analysing social interaction in everyday life*. London: Sage.

Heath, C., Knoblauch, H., & Luff, P. (2000). Technology and social interaction: The emergence of "workplace studies". *British Journal of Sociology, 51*, 299–320.

Heath, C., & Luff, P. (2013). Embodied action and organisational interaction: Establishing contract on the strike of a hammer. *Journal of Pragmatics, 46*, 24–38.

Heritage, J. (2001). Goffman, Garfinkel, conversation analysis. In M. Wetherell, S. J. Taylor, & S. J. Yates (Eds), *Discourse theory and practice* (pp. 47–57). London: Sage.

Hindmarsh, J., & Heath, C. (2000). Embodied reference: A study of deixis in workplace interaction. *Journal of Pragmatics, 32*(12), 1855–1878.

Hirsch, P. M., & Lounsbury, M. (1997). Ending the family quarrel: Toward a reconciliation of "old" and "new" institutionalism. *American Behavioral Scientist, 40*, 406–418.

Horton, W. S., & Gerrig, R. J. (2005). Conversational common ground and memory processes in language production. *Discourse Processes, 40*, 1–35.

Horton, W. S., & Keysar, B. (1996). When do speakers take into account common ground? *Cognition, 59*, 91–117.

Howard, P. N., & Parks, M. R. (2012). Social media and political change. *Journal of Communication, 62*, 359–362.

Johnson-Laird, P. N. (1983). *Mental models: Towards a cognitive science of language, inference, and consciousness*. Cambridge: Cambridge University Press.

Jones, C., Maoret, M., Massa, F. G., & Svejenova, S. (2012). Rebels with a cause: The formation, contestation and expansion of the de novo category Modern Architecture, 1870–1975. *Organization Science, 23*(6), 1523–1545.

Kelly, S. D., Barr, D., Church, R. B., & Lynch, K. (1999). Offering a hand to pragmatic understanding: The role of speech and gesture in comprehension and memory. *Journal of Memory and Language, 40*, 577–592.

Kelly, S. D., Özyürek, A., & Maris, E. (2010). Two sides of the same coin: Speech and gesture mutually interact to enhance comprehension. *Psychological Science, 21*, 260–267.

Kennedy, M. T., & Fiss, P. C. (2009). Institutionalization, framing, and diffusion: The logic of TQM adoption and implementation decisions among U.S. hospitals. *Academy of Management Journal, 52*(5), 897–918.

Keysar, B. (1997). Unconfounding common ground. *Discourse Processes, 24*, 253–270.

Khaire, M., & Wadhwani, R. D. (2010). Changing landscapes: The construction of meaning and value in a new market category—Modern Indian art. *Academy of Management Journal, 53*(6), 1281–1304.

Klein, O., & Licata, L. (2003). When group representations serve social change: The speeches of Patrice Lumumba during the decolonization of Congo. *British Journal of Social Psychology, 42*, 571–594.

Knutsen, D., & Le Bigot, L. (2012). Managing dialogue: How information availability affects collaborative reference production. *Journal of Memory and Language, 67*, 326–341. doi:10.1016/j.jml.2012.06.001.

Kuhlen, A. K., & Brennan, S. E. (2010). Anticipating distracted addressees: How speakers' expectations and addressees' feedback influence storytelling. *Discourse Processes, 47*, 567–587.

Küpers, W., Mantere, S., & Statler, M. (2013). Strategy as storytelling: A phenomenological exploration of embodied narrative practice. *Journal of Management Inquiry, 22*(1), 83–100.

Lakoff, G., & Johnson, M. (1980). *Metaphors we live by*. Chicago, IL: University of Chicago Press.

Lammers, J. C., & Barbour, J. B. (2006). An institutional theory of organizational communication. *Communication Theory, 16*, 356–377.

Landauer, T. K, Foltz, P. W., & Laham, D. (1998). An introduction to Latent Semantic Analysis. *Discourse Processes, 25*(2&3), 259–284.

Lehmann-Willenbrock, N., & Allen, J. A. (2014). How fun are your meetings? Investigating the relationship between humor patterns in team interactions and team performance. *Journal of Applied Psychology, 99*(6), 1278–1287.

Levinson, S. C. (1983) *Pragmatics*. Cambridge: Cambridge University Press.

Levinson, S. C. (2006a). On the human "interaction engine". In N. J. Enfield & S. C. Levinson (Eds), *Roots of human sociality: Culture, cognition and interaction* (pp. 39–69). Oxford: Berg.

Levinson, S. C. (2006b). Cognition at the heart of human interaction. *Discourse Studies, 8*(1), 85–93. doi:10.1177/1461445606059557.

Loewenstein, J., Ocasio, W., & Jones, C. (2012). Vocabularies and vocabulary structure: A new approach linking categories, practices, and institutions. *Academy of Management Annals, 6*, 41–86.

McNamara, D. S., Graesser, A. C., McCarthy, P. M., & Cai, Z. (2014). *Automated evaluation of text and discourse with Coh-Metrix*. Cambridge: Cambridge University Press.

McNeill, D. (1992). *Hand and mind: What gestures reveal about thought*. Chicago, IL: University of Chicago Press.

McPherson, C. M., & Sauder, M. (2013). Logics in action: Managing institutional complexity in a drug court. *Administrative Science Quarterly, 58*, 165–196.

Maguire, S., Hardy, C., & Lawrence, T. (2004). Institutional entrepreneurship in emerging fields: HIV/AIDS treatment advocacy in Canada. *Academy of Management Journal, 47*(5), 657–679.

Maitlis, S., & Christianson, M. (2014). Sensemaking in organizations: Taking stock and moving forward. *Academy of Management Annals, 8*, 57–125.

Mandelbaum, J. (2012). Storytelling in conversation. In J. Sidnell & T. Stivers (Eds), *The handbook of conversation analysis* (pp. 492–507). Chichester: John Wiley & Sons.

Martin, J., Feldman, M. S., Hatch, M. J., & Sitkin, S. B. (1983). The uniqueness paradox in organizational stories. *Administrative Science Quarterly, 28*, 438–453.

Metzing, C., & Brennan, S. E. (2003). When conceptual pacts are broken: Partner-specific effects in the comprehension of referring expressions. *Journal of Memory and Language, 49*, 201–213.

Mohammed, S., Ferzandi, L., & Hamilton, K. (2010). Metaphor no more: A 15-year review of the team mental model construct. *Journal of Management, 36*(4), 876–910.

Mondada, L. (2013). Embodied and spatial resources for turn-taking in institutional multi-party interactions: The example of participatory democracy debates. *Journal of Pragmatics, 46*, 39–68.

Morgan, G. (1986). *Images of organization*. Newbury Park, CA: Sage.

Myers, J. L., O'Brien, E. J., Albrecht, J. E., & Mason, R. A. (1994). Maintaining global coherence during reading. *Journal of Experimental Psychology: Learning, Memory, and Cognition, 20*, 876–886.

Nardi, B. A., & Whittaker, S. (2002). The place of face-to-face communication in distributed work. In P. Hinds & S. Kiesler (Eds), *Distributed work* (pp. 83–110). Cambridge, MA: MIT Press.

Olson, G. M., & Olson, J. S. (2007). Computer supported cooperative work. In F. Durso, R. Nickerson, S. Dumais, S. Lewandowsky, & T. Perfect (Eds), *Handbook of applied cognition* (pp. 497–526). New York, NY: Wiley.

Orr, J. E. (1996). *Talking about machines: An ethnography of a modern job.* Ithaca, NY: Cornell University Press.

Papacharissi, Z., & de Fatima Oliveira, M. (2012). Affective news and networked publics: The rhythms of news storytelling on #Egypt. *Journal of Communication, 62,* 266–282.

Pennebaker, J. W., Francis, M. E., & Booth, R. J. (2001). *Linguistic inquiry and word count: LIWC 2001.* Mahwah, NJ: Erlbaum Publishers.

Phillips, N., Lawrence, T. B., & Hardy, C. (2004). Discourse and institutions. *Academy of Management Review, 29*(4), 635–652.

Pickering, M. J., & Garrod, S. (2004). Toward a mechanistic psychology of dialogue. *Behavioral and Brain Sciences, 27,* 169–225.

Pomerantz, A. (1984). Agreeing and disagreeing with assessments: Some features of preferred/dispreferred turn shapes. In J. M. Atkinson & J. Heritage (Eds), *Structures of social action* (pp. 57–101). Cambridge: Cambridge University Press.

Potter, J., & Wetherell, M. (1987). *Discourse and social psychology: Beyond attitudes and behaviour.* London: Sage.

Quinn, R., & Worline, M. C. (2008). Enabling courageous collective action: Conversations from United Airlines flight 93. *Organization Science, 19,* 497–516.

Ralston, S. M., Kirkwood, W. G., & Burant, P. A. (2003). Helping interviewees tell their stories. *Business Communication Quarterly, 66,* 8–22.

Roter, D. L., & Hall, J. A. (2006). *Doctors talking with patients/patients talking with doctors: Improving communication in medical visits* (2nd edition). Westport, CT: Praeger.

Sacks, H., Schegloff, E. A., & Jefferson, G. (1974). A simplest systematics for the organization of turn-taking in conversation. *Language, 50,* 696–735.

Schegloff, E. A. (1993). Reflections on quantification in the study of conversation. *Research on Language and Social Interaction, 26,* 99–128.

Schegloff, E. A., Jefferson, G., & Sacks, H. (1977). The preference for self-correction in the organisation of repair in conversation. *Language, 53,* 361–382.

Schegloff, E. A., & Sacks, H. (1973). Opening up closings. *Semiotica, 8,* 289–327.

Schneiberg, M., & Clemens, E. S. (2006). The typical tools for the job: Research strategies in institutional analysis. *Sociological Theory, 3,* 195–227.

Schober, M. F. (1993). Spatial perspective-taking in conversation. *Cognition, 47*(1), 1–24. doi:10.1016/0010-0277(93)90060-9.

Schober, M. F., Pasek, J., Guggenheim, L., Lampe, C., & Conrad, F. G. (2016). Social media analyses for social measurement. *Public Opinion Quarterly, 80,* 180–211.

Scott, W. R. (2003). *Organizations: Rational, natural, and open systems* (5th ed.). Englewood Cliffs, NJ: Prentice-Hall.

Searle, J. (1975). Indirect speech acts. In P. Cole & J. L. Morgan (Eds), *Syntax and semantics, 3: Speech Acts* (pp. 59–82). New York, NY: Academic Press.

Searle, J. R. (1989). How performatives work. *Linguistics and Philosophy, 12,* 535–558.

Searle, J. R. (2010). *Making the social world: The structure of human civilization.* New York, NY: Oxford University Press.

Sewell, W. F. (1992). A theory of structure: Duality, agency, and transformation. *American Journal of Sociology, 98*(1), 1–29.

Sharma, A., & Grant, D. (2011) Narrative, drama and charismatic leadership: The case of Apple's Steve Jobs. *Leadership, 7*(1), 3–26.

Sidnell, J., & Stivers, T. (Eds) (2012). *The handbook of conversation analysis.* Oxford: Wiley-Blackwell.

Sparks, J. R., & Rapp, D. N. (2010). Discourse processing: Examining our everyday language experiences. *Wiley Interdisciplinary Reviews: Cognitive Science, 1*(3), 371–381.

Sperber, D., & Wilson, D. (1986). *Relevance: Communication and cognition.* Oxford: Blackwell.

Stigliani, I., & Ravasi, D. (2012). Organizing thoughts and connecting brains: Material practices and the transition from individual to group-level prospective sensemaking. *Academy of Management Journal, 55,* 1232–1259.

Talmy, L. (2000). *Toward a cognitive semantics*. Cambridge, MA: MIT Press.

Tanenhaus, M. K., Spivey-Knowlton, M. J., Eberhard, K. M., & Sedivy, J. E. (1995). Integration of visual and linguistic information in spoken language comprehension. *Science, 268*, 1632–1634.

Tannen, D. (1985). Frames and schemas in interaction. *Quaderni di Semantica, 6*(2), 326–335.

Taylor, J. R., & Cooren, F. (1997). What makes communication "organizational"? How the many voices of the organization become the one voice of an organization. *Journal of Pragmatics, 27*, 409–438.

Thornton, P. H., & Ocasio, W. (2008). Institutional logics. In R. Greenwood, C. Oliver, R. Suddaby, & K. Sahlin-Andersson (Eds), *The Sage handbook of organizational institutionalism* (pp. 99–129). Thousand Oaks, CA: Sage.

Thornton, P. H., Ocasio, W., & Lounsbury, M. (2012). *The institutional logics perspective: A new approach to culture, structure, and process*. Oxford: Oxford University Press.

Vaara, E., Tienari, J., & Säntti, R. (2003). The international match: Metaphors as vehicles of social identity-building in cross-border mergers. *Human Relations, 56*, 419–451.

van Dijk, T. A. (Ed.) (1997a). *Discourse as structure and process*. London: Sage.

van Dijk, T. A. (Ed.) (1997b). *Discourse as social interaction*. London: Sage.

van Dijk, T. A. (2015). *Critical discourse analysis*. In D. Schiffrin, D. Tannen, & H. E. Hamilton (Eds), *The handbook of discourse analysis* (2nd ed.) (pp. 466–485). Malden, MA: Blackwell.

Weber, K., & Glynn, M. A. (2006). Making sense with institutions: Context, thought and action in Karl Weick's theory. *Organization Studies, 27*, 1639–1660.

Weber, K., Heinze, K., & DeSoucey, M. (2008). Forage for thought: Mobilizing codes in the movement for grass-fed meat and dairy products. *Administrative Science Quarterly, 53*, 529–567.

Weick, K. E. (1995). *Sensemaking in organizations*. Thousand Oaks, CA: Sage.

Weick, K. E., Sutcliffe, K. M., & Obstfeld, D. (2005). Organizing and the process of sensemaking. *Organization Science, 16*, 409–421.

Werner, M. D., & Cornelissen, J. P. (2014). Framing the change: Switching and blending frames and their role in instigating institutional change. *Organization Studies, 35*(10), 1449–1472. doi:http://dx.doi.org/10.1177/0170840614539314.

Whiteman, G., & Cooper, W. H. (2011). Ecological sensemaking. *Academy of Management Journal, 54*, 889–911.

Windsor, L., Dowell, N., & Graesser, A. (2014). The language of autocrats: Leaders' language in natural crises. *Risk, Hazards and Crisis in Public Policy, 5*(4), 446–467. doi:10.1002/rhc3.12068.

Wodak, R. (Ed.) (1997). *Gender and discourse*. London: Sage.

Wodak, R. (2015). *The politics of fear: What right-wing populist discourses mean*. London: Sage.

Zietsma, C., & Lawrence, T. B. (2010). Institutional work in the transformation of an organizational field: The interplay of boundary work and practice work. *Administrative Science Quarterly, 55*, 189–221.

Zwaan, R. A., & Radvansky, G.A. (1998). Situation models in language comprehension and memory. *Psychological Bulletin, 123*, 162–185.

Part II
Research Methods for Studying Discourse Processes
State of the Art and Challenges

4

Research Methods
Conversation Analysis

Saul Albert

TUFTS UNIVERSITY

This section introduces Conversation Analysis (CA) as a method of gathering data involving naturalistic conversational interaction, analyzing it systematically, and reporting on features of its structural organization. There are several recent primers (Sidnell, 2011; Heath, Hindmarsh, & Luff, 2010; Schegloff, 2007a) and a handbook dealing with current issues in CA (Sidnell & Stivers, 2012). This section will provide an overview of both canonical and more recent research, highlighting the aspects of CA and its background that may be unfamiliar to those not using it in their own research. CA is distinctive because it is not only a method for analysis, but it also constitutes an active sub-discipline within many research areas that involve the empirical study of human interaction. CA has its own standards of evidence, some unusual collaborative research practices, and a rich literature spanning sociology, linguistics, anthropology, psychology, and communications. The outline of CA provided here should be used as a guide to contextualize the kinds of claims, arguments, and evidence readers may encounter in the CA literature. First, a straightforward description of how CA is used and what its key findings look like will provide enough background to introduce a practical example. Second, transcription and analysis of a fragment of video data will demonstrate the process of applying CA, along with some open-ended suggestions as to how that analysis might offer evidence for a research argument or hypothesis. Finally, the latter half of this section will provide a snapshot of current issues in CA and how these relate to its development both as a methodology and as a growing field of study. Because CA has not developed within a 'home discipline' as such, it is widely dispersed between many fields, so it is likely that any researcher interested in spoken discourse will find a wealth of CA research within their area of specialism. The intention here is to encourage researchers to draw on core CA findings in their work, to find the CA research and researchers in their own field, and to learn to work with interaction data using these methods

So what is CA useful for? What kinds of questions can one ask with it? And what kinds of answers can be gleaned at different points in the research cycle? CA is especially useful for empirical research on interaction in naturalistic settings where established theories may be lacking or under revision. This is because CA looks for detailed qualitative evidence of how participants work to organize their interactions endogenously within each specific situation. CA relies on a recorded event, utterance, or gesture as analytic evidence only when the participants demonstrably use that event to organize their subsequent actions. On the one hand, this forces analysts to limit the generality of the questions they can ask and the claims they can make. For example, studies of interaction in doctor's offices, courtrooms, or at dinner parties tend to ask questions about how a specific action or utterance is produced in a particular social situation by specific participants. On the other hand, CA's evidential constraints have maintained it as a methodologically coherent field. By focusing analysis on the methods and events demonstrably used by participants to make sense of their own interactions, CA studies tend to be readily comparable with one another. Although individual studies are situationally specific, analysts can develop and test general findings cumulatively working in diverse settings and fields. Over the last 40 years the most robust and broadly tested finding that has provided a basis for many subsequent studies is the turn-taking system described by Sacks, Schegloff, and Jefferson (1974). Without the extended discussion these warrant, the rules of the turn-taking system can be summarized briefly to explain the kind of answers CA can offer.

1   For any turn at talk, at the first possible completion,

    a   current speaker may select next,
    b   next speaker may self-select,
    c   current speaker may continue.

2   If 1c occurs, the rules are re-applied at the next possible completion.

This describes the normative patterns observed in natural conversational turn-taking across contexts in the first decade of CA research. As a finding it provides a framework for further exploratory work in CA, and a strong empirical basis for theory formation experimentation. As a research outcome, this exemplifies how CA can produce detailed, systematic descriptions from cumulative observations.

Alongside these longer-term results, the CA research cycle involves structured observation throughout the process of data gathering, presentation, and collaborative analysis of data within the scope of a single study. Current best practices for CA data gathering involve examining video of an interactional situation from multiple angles where all participants' gaze directions, gestures, body orientation, and talk are – ideally – available for analysis. Within relevant practical and ethical constraints, it is useful to record whatever participants are evidently paying attention to within the setting including objects, tools, documents, and screen captures from any smartphones or computers they may be using. Interaction mediated via text, audio, and video also constitutes viable data; however, for a sequential analysis, CA researchers should be aware that their analysis must take into account the same evidential and temporal contingencies and constraints experienced by the participants in the research setting. For example, phone calls provide ideal data for CA studies because participants and researchers alike can analyze the same audio events in the same order. In face-to-face interactions, however, analysts must be careful not to make assumptions about anything which occurs outside the frame of the video. In either case, analysts must be careful to recognize that since participants cannot pause, rewind, or replay a live interaction, they should not base their analyses on their analyst-oriented methods of accessing and processing the interaction as a data source. Because a CA study may focus on very intricate details, a few seconds of a recording can yield data for a 'single-case analysis', contributing to or questioning cumulative findings. Researchers also re-analyze data from previous studies, using examples from audiovisual corpora and data fragments from the CA literature, often as a foil for discussion.

Transcription is central to CA research as it involves repeatedly reviewing the data to build up an initial description that can be checked by others from an early stage. Variations on Gail Jefferson's transcription conventions[1] provide a level of detail that can be adjusted for the specific phenomena in question. Verbal interaction is typed out turn-by-turn, then symbols are added and arranged spatially to indicate temporal and production features of talk. For example, Extract 4.1 (below) depicts Paul and Anne's talk as their teacher sings a count of eight during a partner dance class. Links to online data are also provided where possible.

```
1   Paul:   N↑o[t ba::d, >°°not ba:d.°°<]
2   Anne:      [ It's like be[ing GENuinely >able °to do it?°<]
3   Tchr:                     [      F    I    v    e        ], (.)
4           s[ix? ( . ) ] ↓five
5   Paul:   [Ye::[p.   ]
6   Anne:          [·hh [aHhh ·Hhh
7   Tchr:               [six se::ven eight?
```

Extract 4.1 CADA_SP01 (video data available at http://bit.ly/CADA_SP01)

Reading while listening to the audio should show how Jefferson's conventions are roughly intuitive: left and right braces show points of overlap, carats show talk speeding up, while colons indicate sound stretches. Because these conventions compromise between precision, detail, and readability there are also some inevitable ambiguities, for example punctuation indicates intonation rather than grammar, and turn-initial capitals mark transcriber hearings of turn-beginnings, but elsewhere they indicate loud talk. The purpose, however, is not analysis of the transcript. Rather transcripts provide a useful sketch to aid more formal description, and a convenient way for analysts to refer to specific moments of the original video when pointing out and describing observable phenomena for instant informal peer review during a CA data session presentation.

In a CA data session, a researcher presents new data and transcripts for repeated viewings and extended analytical discussion amongst a small group of colleagues. Since CA relies on the linguistic and interactional aptitude of the analyst as an inductive guide for recognizing and collecting examples of naturally occurring patterns in interaction, regular data sessions provide an essential opportunity to revise transcripts and test candidate analyses amongst peers. Details of the present data are discussed in relation to cumulative findings, and the implications of, or alternatives to, each analysis are proposed and challenged. Ideally, data sessions are opportunities to teach, learn, and discuss analytical ideas, where experienced and student analysts refine their observations and descriptions by picking out specific fragments of data, and contextualizing findings within the literature. Over time, researchers build 'collections' of data fragments such as Extract 4.1, which forms part of a collection of 'count-ins' where people count up or down to coordinate joint actions – in this case during a partner dance class. A rough collection is a starting point for identifying a distinct social practice as a specifiable analytic phenomenon. Analysis then refines a collection in terms of how participants orient to the sequential organization of an action, and to its lexical, grammatical, and other structural features of composition, design growing and embodiment (Schegloff, 1993, p. 121). For example, before the video clip of Extract 4.1 starts, Paul and Anne have been evaluating their previous attempt at a dance move. The teacher's count starts with a loud, stretched "F I v e", a short pause then a rising "six?", before both pitch and count re-sets to five and moves back up to a final, rising "eight?". At the onset of the count, Paul turns his head to the teachers and back to Anne, hushing his second "°°not ba:d.°°". Anne also speeds up and softens her talk, turning her head toward the teachers then back to Paul as the count reaches its first "F I v e". Paul's minimal "Ye::p" receipts Anne's assessment just as he briefly turns his head away from her again. Her laugh closes the sequence, and they re-establish mutual gaze as the count enters its final phase.

Foregoing any more detailed description of the broader sequential context around Extract 4.1, this fragment provides a simple example of how talk-in-interaction can be transcribed and presented. The embodied turn (Nevile, 2015) in the CA literature has led researchers to add more detail to transcripts of talk, often using illustrations (Laurier, 2014) to describe gesture and gaze direction as well as diagrammatic representations of, for example, pitch tracks and phonological details. Figure 4.1 illustrates the temporal structure of talk and patterns of other-directed mutual gaze just before Paul and Anne start dancing.

In terms of cumulative CA findings, these details could be analyzed alongside generalized CA work on how assessments implicate sequence closure in everyday conversation, and how patterns of mutual gaze work toward topic, focus, and activity shifts (Heath, 1986, pp. 128–148; Mondada, 2006; Rossano, 2012, pp. 227–308). In a more applied project, the way the dancers' turns at talk and gaze shifts match the phase structure of the teacher's count could be analyzed in relation to ongoing research into how bodily-vocal group activities are organized in dance instruction (Keevallik 2014). This fragment may be added to multiple generalized collections including 'embodied closings' or 'countings' as well as specialized sub-collections such as 'dance closings' and 'count-ins'. CA findings are thus developed incrementally by documenting the detail of people's interactional practices in specific settings while contributing to a general understanding of everyday talk-in-interaction. This body of work in CA constitutes a super-set of clearly described co-present interactional practices and provides a baseline for researchers studying interaction in more specialized settings where institutional or practical contingencies may constrain everyday interactional practices in clearly recognizable ways such as in courtroom interaction, doctor-patient interactions, or service encounters (Drew & Heritage, 1992). Identifying and fully describing a new phenomenon in relation to the existing body of CA work on everyday talk may therefore require collection and analysis of hundreds of cases, but a CA single-case analysis can still test an established finding, both within CA or in another field, by demonstrating variations in how a particular interactional practice is conducted in a specific context.

CA can also be used in mixed-methods research, and is especially useful in theory formation, experimental design, and evaluation processes. CA researchers may discover a systematic variation in patterns of situated interaction, which are sometimes as simple as an issue of lexical choice. For example, Heritage et al. (2007) observed that doctors vary the ways they ask about patients' unmet concerns during consultations. Their experiment asked doctors to request whether their patients had 'anything else' or 'something else' to talk about, and discovered that 78% fewer unmet concerns were reported in the latter condition. This example shows how CA's focus on interactional practices in natural settings can provide systematic observations that contribute to ecologically valid experimental variables and guide the formulation of falsifiable theories (Robinson & Heritage, 2014). In conjunction with more conventional social science

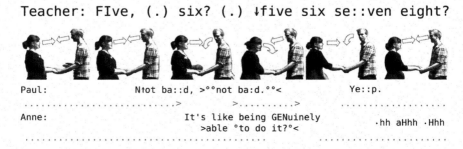

Figure 4.1 Paul and Anne's pattern of gaze orientation in Extract 4.1

methods, CA is useful in similar ways when it foregrounds the participants' orientations to the demand characteristics of the research setting itself. For example, CA studies of interviewing practices reveal how participants treat interviews as interactional situations (Potter & Hepburn, 2012), and these studies can contribute to methodological developments in survey research that are starting to incorporate the pragmatics of talk and the practicalities of survey technologies into a multi-method approach that takes into account an interactional analysis of the survey-taking procedure (Conrad, Schober, & Schwarz, 2013). Similarly, CA studies of methods that rely primarily on introspective self-report (Wooffitt & Holt, 2011) or CA's own practices of video recording (Hazel, 2015) are opening up new opportunities to address long-standing theoretical issues in psychology, sociology, and linguistics as practical, observable issues that are observably managed via the endogenous organization of situated interaction. CA's early focus on talk-in-interaction has both influenced and drawn on the interactional respecification of core questions in linguistics and pragmatics (Ochs, Schegloff, & Thompson, 1996; Levinson, 1983), and psychology (Edwards & Potter 2001; Tileagă & Stokoe, 2015), along with a wider shift in the social sciences toward posing empirical questions in terms of practical action (Button, 1991; Lynch, 1997). To use CA within a broader scientific context, however, it is necessary to clarify how its findings are primarily inductive and descriptive rather than predictive or prescriptive, and how CA must first be combined with experimental and deductive methods in order to develop and test formal hypotheses (Lynch, 2000, p. 522).

Recent studies in this vein based on corpus and experimental data use CA's turn-taking system as an observationally grounded model for exploring psycholinguistic phenomena such as turn-projection in relation to cognition (De Ruiter, Mitterer, & Enfield, 2006; Levinson & Torreira, 2015). These studies address phenomena that are central to neighboring fields, and have also led to significant new research that tests CA's most established findings in large scale cross-linguistic studies using quantitative methods (Stivers et al., 2009; Kendrick, 2015). Although the formal coding of interaction data is only recently becoming an established part of the CA literature (Schegloff, 1993; Stivers, 2015), it opens up opportunities for applying CA findings in research areas that primarily use hypothetico-deductive models of investigation. For instance, the rich tradition of detailed, descriptive CA work on interaction in healthcare (Heritage & Maynard, 2006) is having a significant impact in parts of the medical literature where explanatory conventions and standards of clinical evidence are typified by the randomized controlled trial (Robinson & Heritage, 2014), and this impact has been achieved over decades of work and through careful use of basic CA in specific phases of the research process (Heritage et al., 2007). Most applied uses of CA (Antaki, 2011), however, take an exploratory approach, where the qualitative, ethnomethodological focus on participants' orientations is used to ask fundamental questions that respecify the phenomena and methods of established theory and research practices (Garfinkel, 1967). For example, the earliest basic research in CA used recordings of telephone calls to explore how episodes of talk were opened and closed. As many of these recordings included calls to police lines or other services, these studies opened up new questions about how 'institutional talk' is organized in relation to more everyday talk, and this research inspired a respecification of the kinds of data and methods that are available for the sociological study of institutions like the police, the courts, and the medical profession (Drew & Heritage, 1992). Contemporary applications of CA have also built on these findings to intervene in service delivery and training (Hepburn, Wilkinson, & Butler, 2014; Stokoe, 2014). Similarly, early studies of interaction in specialized settings contributed to the use of CA to respecify the study of practices with large, theory-oriented literatures such as education and language learning (Seedhouse, 2005), courtroom interaction (Drew & Atkinson, 1979), and psychotherapy (Peräkylä et al., 2008) from an interactional standpoint.

These studies also feed cumulative, descriptive findings back to 'basic CA', and can even challenge CA's basic assumptions and methods. For example, classic studies of interaction and communication impairments (Goodwin, 1995) built on pioneering work in CA focused on gesture, gaze, and bodily participation in talk (Goodwin, 1979). This work has not only informed a huge proliferation of CA research and applications in speech and language therapy (Wilkinson, 2014), but has also opened up new methodological challenges for CA. The 'embodied turn' in interaction analysis (Nevile, 2015) has emphasized the many interconnected systems involved in co-producing the organization of turns at talk (Rossano, 2012), contributing to calls for more a detailed understanding of CA's treatment of 'turns' as analytically viable units in face-to-face interaction (Ford, Fox, & Thompson, 2013). This points to some of the key challenges facing CA in building and expanding on its established body of research. The expansion of CA's focus from talk-in-interaction to the analysis of many more combinations of interactional resources threatens the coherence of its cumulative findings and methods. CA's primary focus on talk was initially a matter of convenience: of having access to data from telephone calls. Much of the more recent research that draws on CA refers to itself instead as 'qualitative video analysis' of 'embodied interaction' (Heath, Hindmarsh, & Luff, 2010) to signal a move away from 'just talk'. This 'multimodal' development in CA has been very influential in exploring workplace settings and how people's interactions can reveal their methods for making sense of complex technologies and technologically mediated environments (Heath & Luff, 2000). Studies in this vein emphasize the interactional organization of a far broader range of communicative resources including gesture, gaze, and body orientation, and incorporate broader spatial relationships and material objects (Haddington, Mondada, & Nevile, 2013) into the analysis. On the one hand, this achieves far greater levels of detailed description. On the other, the multifariousness of these systems makes cumulative, systemic findings far more challenging as an immediate analytic goal.

Because CA's detailed descriptions of the organization of everyday talk are becoming increasingly established as reliable research findings, they provide a cumulative basis for various forms of abstraction. This is both promising and a significant challenge for future CA research. Long-standing descriptions such as the turn-taking system can underpin formal coding schemes (Stivers, 2015) and using these data for hypothesis formation and deductive analysis can provide experimental evidence that may expand the field. However, this approach may also underplay the relevance and detail of single cases, and more generally elide CA's traditional role as a talk-centric approach to the ethnomethodological respecification of theoretical questions in interaction research (Steensig & Heinemann, 2015). Even within CA's inductive, qualitative traditions, a highly influential program of CA work on 'epistemics' (Heritage, 2012a) is leading a new approach to long-held questions about how social actions like questions, requests, and invitations are formulated and recognized (Levinson, 2012), and how asymmetries of mutual knowledge are managed in interaction (Stivers, Mondada, & Steensig, 2011). CA research into epistemics approaches relatively abstract issues of knowledge and information in terms of CA's relatively concrete descriptions of how participants deal with the practical organization of everyday talk (Heritage, 2012b). While this approach may facilitate CA's contribution to the larger body of research in psycholinguistics that addresses questions of shared knowledge or "common ground" head on, as experimentally testable cognitive phenomena (Clark & Brennan, 1991), epistemics may also yield an overly abstract explanation for events that would otherwise prompt further detailed analysis (Drew, 2012). These methodological questions and challenges arise from the many new opportunities that have arisen in the last few decades of CA research to generate hypothetical abstractions based on CA's technical findings, and to use these to pursue questions that are

Research Methods: Conversation Analysis

more central within CA's more conventional 'host' disciplines of sociology, psychology, and linguistics. For example, recent CA research on member categorization analysis (Stokoe, 2012; Fitzgerald & Housley, 2015) addresses issues of broad sociological interest such as gender (Speer & Stokoe, 2009), race (Whitehead & Lerner, 2009), and the family by analyzing how participants themselves use and make an issue of these categories in everyday interaction, while being careful not to simply ascribe analyst-oriented meanings to these categories based on their apparent relation to research topics in the social sciences (Schegloff, 2007b).

Long-standing tensions between attention to qualitative detail and analytic abstraction have always been central to CA's development. These tensions between contributing to other social sciences, or fundamentally respecifying social science have remained apparent within CA because of its success in maintaining a balance and continuing to do both. The ongoing methodological debates about the problems and opportunities of coding and quantification in CA (Schegloff, 1993; Stivers, 2015), and the threat of schism between CA and less talk-centric ethnomethodological approaches are a sign of a healthy field, and point to the growing scope, scale, and maturity of CA and its core methods and findings.

Suggested Reading

Sacks, H. (1984). On doing "being ordinary." In J. Heritage & J.M. Atkinson (Eds), *Structures of Social Action: Studies in Conversation Analysis* (pp. 413–429). Cambridge: Cambridge University Press.
Sacks, H., Schegloff, E.A., & Jefferson, G. (1974). A simplest systematics for the organization of turn-taking for conversation. *Language, 50*, 696–735.
Schegloff, E.A. (1992). Repair after next turn: The last structurally provided defense of intersubjectivity in conversation. *American Journal of Sociology, 97*, 1295–1345.
Schegloff, E.A. (2007). *Sequent Organization in Interaction: Volume 1: A primer in CONVERSATION analysis.* Cambridge: Cambridge University Press.
Sidnell, J., & Stivers, T. (2012). *The Handbook of Conversation Analysis.* New York, NY: John Wiley & Sons.

Note

1 See the basic transcription conventions on Prof. Charles Antaki's CA tutorial website: http://ca-tutorials.lboro.ac.uk/notation.htm or the comprehensive account in Atkinson and Heritage (1984, pp. ix–xvi).

References

Antaki, Charles. 2011. "Six Kinds of Applied Conversation Analysis." In *Applied Conversation Analysis: Intervention and Change in Institutional Talk*, edited by Charles Antaki, 1–14. Basingstoke: Palgrave Macmillan.
Atkinson, J.M., & John Heritage. 1984. *Structures of Social Action: Studies in Conversation Analysis.* Edited by J. Maxwell Atkinson and John Heritage. Cambridge: Cambridge University Press.
Button, Graham. 1991. "Introduction: Ethnomethodology and the Foundational Respecification of the Human Sciences." In *Ethnomethodology and the Human Sciences*, edited by Graham Button, 1–9. Cambridge: Cambridge University Press.
Clark, Herbert H., & S.E. Brennan. 1991. "Grounding in Communication." *Perspectives on Socially Shared Cognition* 13: 127–149.
Conrad, Frederick G., Michael F. Schober, & Norbert Schwarz. 2013. "Pragmatic Processes in Survey Interviewing." *Oxford Handbooks Online* (Dec). doi:10.1093/oxfordhb/9780199838639.013.005. http://dx.doi.org/10.1093/oxfordhb/9780199838639.013.005.

De Ruiter, Jan Peter, Holger Mitterer, & Nick J. Enfield. 2006. "Projecting the End of a Speaker's Turn: A Cognitive Cornerstone of Conversation." *Language*: 515–535.

Drew, Paul. 2012. "What Drives Sequences?" *Research on Language and Social Interaction* 45(1): 61–68.

Drew, Paul, & J. Maxwell Atkinson. 1979. *Order in Court: Verbal Interaction in Judicial Settings*. London: Macmillan.

Drew, Paul, & John Heritage. 1992. *Talk at Work: Interaction in Institutional Settings*. Cambridge: Cambridge University Press.

Edwards, Derek, & Jonathan Potter. 2001. "Discursive Social Psychology." In *The New Handbook of Language and Social Psychology*, edited by P. Robinson and H. Giles, 103–118. London: John Wiley & Sons Ltd.

Fitzgerald, Richard, & William Housley. 2015. *Advances in Membership Categorisation Analysis*. Thousand Oaks, CA: SAGE.

Ford, Cecilia E., Barbara A. Fox, & Sandra A. Thompson. 2013. "Units and/or Action Trajectories? The Language of Grammatical Categories and the Language of Social Action." In *Units of Talk – Units of Action*, edited by Geoffrey Raymond and Beatrice Szczepek-Reed. Amsterdam: John Benjamins Publishing Company. doi:10.1075/slsi.25.02for.

Garfinkel, Harold. 1967. *Studies in Ethnomethodology*. Englewood Cliffs, NJ: Prentice-Hall.

Goodwin, Charles. 1979. "The Interactive Construction of a Sentence in Natural Conversation." In *Everyday Language: Studies in Ethnomethodology*, edited by George Psathas, 97–121. New York, NY: Halsted Press.

———. 1995. "Co-Constructing Meaning in Conversations with an Aphasic Man." *Research on Language and Social Interaction* 28(3): 233–260.

Haddington, Pentti, Lorenza Mondada, & Maurice Nevile. 2013. *Being Mobile: Interaction on the Move*. Edited by Pentti Haddington, Lorenza Mondada, & Maurice Nevile. Boston, MA: De Gruyter.

Hazel, S. 2015. "The Paradox from Within: Research Participants Doing-Being-Observed." *Qualitative Research* (Sep). doi:10.1177/1468794115596216. http://dx.doi.org/10.1177/1468794115596216.

Heath, Christian. 1986. *Body Movement and Speech in Medical Interaction*. Cambridge: Cambridge University Press. doi:10.1017/cbo9780511628221. http://dx.doi.org/10.1017/CBO9780511628221.

Heath, Christian, & Paul Luff. 2000. *Technology in Action*. Edited by Christian Heath & Paul Luff. Cambridge: Cambridge University Press. doi:10.1017/cbo9780511489839. http://dx.doi.org/10.1017/CBO9780511489839.

Heath, Christian, Jon Hindmarsh, & Paul Luff. 2010. *Video in Qualitative Research: Analysing Social Interaction in Everyday Life*. London: Sage Publications.

Hepburn, Alexa, Sue Wilkinson, & Carly W. Butler. 2014. "Intervening With Conversation Analysis in Telephone Helpline Services: Strategies to Improve Effectiveness." *Research on Language and Social Interaction* 47(3): 239–254. doi:10.1080/08351813.2014.925661. www.tandfonline.com/doi/abs/10.1080/08351813.2014.925661.

Heritage, John. 2012a. "Epistemics in Action: Action Formation and Territories of Knowledge." *Research on Language & Social Interaction* 45(1): 1–29.

———. 2012b. "The Epistemic Engine: Sequence Organization and Territories of Knowledge." *Research on Language & Social Interaction* 45(1): 30–52.

Heritage, John, & Douglas W. Maynard. 2006. *Communication in Medical Care: Interaction Between Primary Care Physicians and Patients*. Studies in Interactional Sociolinguistics. Cambridge: Cambridge University Press.

Heritage, John, Jeffrey D. Robinson, Marc N. Elliott, Megan Beckett, & Michael Wilkes. 2007. "Reducing Patients' Unmet Concerns in Primary Care: the Difference One Word Can Make." *Journal of General Internal Medicine* 22(10): 1429–1433.

Keevallik, Leelo. 2014. "Turn Organization and Bodily-Vocal Demonstrations." *Journal of Pragmatics* 65: 103–120. doi:10.1016/j.pragma.2014.01.008.

Kendrick, Kobin H. 2015. "The Intersection of Turn-Taking and Repair: The Timing of Other-Initiations of Repair in Conversation." *Name: Frontiers in Psychology* 6: 250.

Laurier, Eric. 2014. "The Graphic Transcript: Poaching Comic Book Grammar for Inscribing the Visual, Spatial and Temporal Aspects of Action." *Geography Compass* 8(4): 235–248. doi:10.1111/gec3.12123.

Levinson, Stephen C. 1983. *Pragmatics*. Cambridge: Cambridge University Press.

——. 2012. "Action Formation and Ascription." In *The Handbook of Conversation Analysis*, edited by Jack Sidnell & Tanya Stivers, 101–130. Cambridge: Cambridge University Press.

Levinson, Stephen C., & Francisco Torreira. 2015. "Timing in Turn-Taking and Its Implications for Processing Models of Language." *Frontiers in Psychology* 6: 731.

Lynch, Michael. 1997. *Scientific Practice and Ordinary Action: Ethnomethodology and Social Studies of Science*. Cambridge: Cambridge University Press.

——. 2000. "The Ethnomethodological Foundations of Conversation Analysis." *Text – Interdisciplinary Journal for the Study of Discourse* 20(4): 517–532. doi:10.1515/text.1.2000.20.4.517. www. degruyter.com/view/j/text.1.2000.20.issue-4/text.1.2000.20.4.517/text.1.2000.20.4.517.xml.

Mondada, Lorenza. 2006. "Participants' Online Analysis and Multimodal Practices: Projecting the End of the Turn and the Closing of the Sequence." *Discourse Studies* 8(1): 117–129. doi:10.1177/1461445606059561.

Nevile, Maurice. 2015. "The Embodied Turn in Research on Language and Social Interaction." *Research on Language and Social Interaction* 48(2): 121–151. doi:10.1080/08351813.2015.10254 99. http://dx.doi.org/10.1080/08351813.2015.1025499 .

Ochs, E., Emanuel A. Schegloff, & Sandra A. Thompson. 1996. *Interaction and Grammar*. Edited by Elinor Ochs, Emanuel A Schegloff, & Sandra A Thompson, 13. Cambridge: Cambridge University Press.

Peräkylä, Anssi, Charles Antaki, Sanna Vehviläinen, & Ivan Leudar. 2008. *Conversation Analysis and Psychotherapy*. Edited by Anssi Peräkylä, Charles Antaki, Sanna Vehviläinen, & Ivan Leudar. Cambridge: Cambridge University Press. doi:10.1017/cbo9780511490002. http://dx.doi. org/10.1017/CBO9780511490002.

Pomerantz, Anita, & John Heritage. 2013. "Preference." In *The Handbook of Conversation Analysis*, edited by Jack Sidnell & Tanya Stivers. Cambridge: Cambridge University Press.

Potter, Jonathan, & Alexa Hepburn. 2012. "Eight Challenges for Interview Researchers." In *The SAGE Handbook of Interview Research: The Complexity of the Craft*, edited by Jaber F. Gubrium, James A. Holstein, Amir B. Marvasti, & Karyn D. McKinney, 555–571. Thousand Oaks, CA: SAGE Publications, Inc. doi:10.4135/9781452218403. http://dx.doi.org/10.4135/9781452218403.

Robinson, Jeffrey D., & John Heritage. 2014. "Intervening With Conversation Analysis: The Case of Medicine." *Research on Language and Social Interaction* 47(3): 201–218.

Rossano, Federico. 2012. "Gaze Behavior in Face-to-Face Interaction." PhD thesis, Radboud Universitet Nijmegen.

Sacks, Harvey, Emanuel A. Schegloff, & Gail Jefferson. 1974. "A Simplest Systematics for the Organization of Turn-Taking for Conversation." *Language* 50(4): 696–735.

Schegloff, Emanuel A. 1993. "Reflections on Quantification in the Study of Conversation." *Research on Language & Social Interaction* 26(1): 99–128. doi:10.1207/s15327973rlsi2601_5.

——. 1995. "Introduction to Lectures on Conversation, Volume I, II." In *Lectures on Conversation, Volume I, II*, edited by Gail Jefferson. Vol. I. Oxford: Blackwell.

——. 2007a. *Sequence Organization in Interaction: Volume 1: A Primer in Conversation Analysis*. Cambridge: Cambridge University Press.

——. 2007b. "A Tutorial on Membership Categorization." *Journal of Pragmatics* 39(3): 462–482. doi:10.1016/j.pragma.2006.07.007. http://linkinghub.elsevier.com/retrieve/pii/S0378216606001640.

Seedhouse, Paul. 2005. "Conversation Analysis and Language Learning." *LTA* 38(4): 165. doi:10.1017/ s0261444805003010. http://dx.doi.org/10.1017/S0261444805003010.

Sidnell, Jack. 2011. *Conversation Analysis: An Introduction*. London: Wiley-Blackwell.

Sidnell, Jack, & Tanya Stivers. 2012. *The Handbook of Conversation Analysis*. Edited by Jack Sidnell and Tanya Stivers. London: Wiley-Blackwell.

Speer, Susan A., & Elizabeth Stokoe. 2009. *Conversation and Gender*. Edited by Susan A. Speer and Elizabeth Stokoe. Cambridge: Cambridge University Press. doi:10.1017/cbo9780511781032. http://dx.doi.org/10.1017/CBO9780511781032.

Steensig, Jakob, & Trine Heinemann. 2015. "Opening up Codings?" *Research on Language and Social Interaction* 48(1): 20–25. doi:10.1080/08351813.2015.993838. http://dx.doi.org/10.1080/0 8351813.2015.993838.

Stivers, Tanya. 2015. "Coding Social Interaction: A Heretical Approach in Conversation Analysis?" *Research on Language and Social Interaction* 48(1): 1–19. doi:10.1080/08351813.2015.993837. http://dx.doi.org/10.1080/08351813.2015.993837.

Stivers, Tanya, Nick J. Enfield, Penelope Brown, Christina Englert, Makoto Hayashi, Trine Heinemann et al. 2009. "Universals and Cultural Variation in Turn-Taking in Conversation." *Proceedings of the National Academy of Sciences of the United States of America* 106(26): 10587–10592.

Stivers, Tanya, Lorenza Mondada, & Jakob Steensig. 2011. *The Morality of Knowledge in Conversation.* Edited by Tanya Stivers, Lorenza Mondada, & Jakob Steensig. Cambridge: Cambridge University Press.

Stokoe, Elizabeth. 2012. "Moving Forward with Membership Categorization Analysis: Methods for Systematic Analysis." *Discourse Studies* 14(3): 277–303. doi:10.1177/1461445612441534. http://dis.sagepub.com/cgi/doi/10.1177/1461445612441534.

———. 2014. "The Conversation Analytic Role-Play Method (CARM): A Method for Training Communication Skills as an Alternative to Simulated Role-Play." *Research on Language and Social Interaction* 47(3): 255–265. doi:10.1080/08351813.2014.925663. www.tandfonline.com/doi/abs/10.1080/08351813.2014.925663.

Tileagă, Cristian, & Elizabeth Stokoe. 2015. *Discursive Psychology: Classic and Contemporary Issues.* London: Routledge.

Whitehead, K. A., & Gene H. Lerner. 2009. "When Are Persons 'White'? On Some Practical Asymmetries of Racial Reference in Talk-in-Interaction." *Discourse & Society* 20(5): 613–641. doi:10.1177/0957926509106413. http://das.sagepub.com/cgi/doi/10.1177/0957926509106413.

Wilkinson, Ray. 2014. "Intervening With Conversation Analysis in Speech and Language Therapy: Improving Aphasic Conversation." *Research on Language and Social Interaction* 47(3): 219–238. doi:10.1080/08351813.2014.925659. www.tandfonline.com/doi/abs/10.1080/08351813.2014.925659.

Wooffitt, Robin, & Nicola Holt. 2011. *Looking In and Speaking Out.* Exeter: Imprint Academic.

5

Research Methods
The Study of Language Processing in Human Conversation

Sarah Brown-Schmidt

VANDERBILT UNIVERSITY

Many standard approaches to the study of language processing employ methodologies that examine the production and comprehension of language in isolation, where an experimental participant functions only in the role of speaker or listener, and the linguistic stimuli are highly controlled. This emphasis on experimental control has afforded the detailed study of processes such as how speakers plan words and phrases (e.g., Konopka, 2012; Meyer, 1996), and the processes by which listeners segment sounds into words and combine those words into meaningful sentences (e.g., Saffran, Newport, & Aslin, 1996; Knoeferle & Crocker, 2006). While much traction has been gained by studying real-time language processing using these methods, this approach does not easily translate to the study of conversation.

Studying the mechanisms of language processing in conversation will allow us to test whether theories developed on the basis of findings from standard paradigms extend to natural conversation. Doing so is critical given that face-to-face conversation is arguably the most basic form of language use. Some processes, such as coordination of linguistic form (Pickering & Garrod, 2004), turn-taking (Sacks, Schegloff, & Jefferson, 1974), and perspective-taking (Brown-Schmidt & Fraundorf, 2015), are firmly rooted in interactive processes. Methods that allow for face-to-face interaction provide a useful tool for studying these behaviors. In addition, unscripted conversation often contains features such as disfluent speech, interruptions, and gesture which communicate information above and beyond the sequence of words a speaker might produce (e.g., Fox Tree, 2001; Fraundorf & Watson, 2014; de Ruiter, Bangerter, & Dings, 2012).

A potentially fruitful research strategy is the pairing of experimentally well-controlled studies with less constrained, conversationally situated ones. For example, in their first two experiments, Levelt and Kelter (1982) examined the relationship between the surface form of a question and its answer in a paradigm where participants were "tested individually in a soundproof and dimly illuminated room," and responded to a series of scripted questions. The results indicated that the answer to a question tends to mimic the form of the question itself. In their third study, the researchers phoned shopkeepers to ask about their store hours, systematically varying the form of the question, and measuring how the shopkeeper's response to this question changed as a result. Shopkeepers answered the question in different ways depending on how the question was phrased, saying, e.g., *"at* five o'clock" rather than "five o'clock" when the question included the additional preposition, e.g., "At what time do you close?", rather than "What time do you close?". This study provided ecological validity for the finding that the form of a question response reflects the form of the question itself, and inspired subsequent research on the phenomenon of structural priming in language production (Bock, 1986; Pickering & Garrod, 2004). By pairing studies of unscripted conversation with targeted investigations that afford a greater degree of experimental control, one can create a feedback loop between the two types of approaches in which studies of conversation validate findings from scripted settings and generate novel observations. Concurrently, studies in well-controlled settings can be used to replicate those ecologically valid findings while controlling for extraneous variables (e.g., see Brennan & Schober, 2001; Brennan & Clark, 1996; Brown-Schmidt, Gunlogson, & Tanenhaus, 2008; Brown-Schmidt & Tanenhaus, 2008; Garrod & Anderson, 1987).

The Referential Communication Task

A key method enabling naturalistic studies of language processing is the use of task-based conversation (Grosz & Sidner, 1986; Krauss & Weinheimer, 1964). For example, in the *referential communication task*, experimental participants work together to complete a task that requires reference to items in a co-present display. This method holds the topic of conversation constant across participants while allowing the dialogue to unfold naturally. A common variant is the *object sorting task* in which pairs of participants work together to re-arrange or match a set of abstract images (Krauss & Weinheimer, 1964). Typically, the participants see the same set of images, but in different orders. Participants are seated such that they can see each other's faces, but not each other's images. One participant is given the role of Director, and gives instructions to the other participant (the Matcher) to re-arrange the images into the same order as the Director's images. The same set of images is then sorted into different orders over a series of rounds (Figure 5.1).

The dependent measures of interest in this task have included the number of words used to describe each figure, the amount of time to describe each figure, as well as the Matcher's accuracy. In the first round of gameplay, Directors typically use many words to describe each image, but across rounds, the number of words needed to describe each figure reduces

Figure 5.1 Example tangram figures

quickly (Wilkes-Gibbs & Clark, 1992; Clark & Wilkes-Gibbs, 1986; Krauss & Weinheimer, 1964, 1966). For example, the tangram on the left side of Figure 5.1 would typically be described in great detail on the first round of game play (1), but by the ninth round, the speaker would be brief (2):

(1) *"ok it's a person flying off to the right but it's not they don't have two legs . . . there are . . . it's a diamond for a head and the wings are like flying off behind the body like it's only connected by like a point and then it looks like there's a triangle for the body . . . that's bigger than the head and pointing down and there's one leg that's big and there's no foot"*

(2) *"the flying guy"*

In other versions of this task, a speaker gives a listener instructions to pick up or select one of several objects (Metzing & Brennan, 2003). Stimuli in these tasks have included abstract drawings (Krauss & Weinheimer, 1964, 1966; Krauss, Garlock, Bricker, & McMahon, 1977), drawings of monsters (Gorman et al., 2013), familiar landmarks (Isaacs & Clark, 1987), and hard-to-name physical objects (Metzing & Brennan, 2003), though tangrams (Wilkes-Gibbs & Clark, 1992; Clark & Wilkes-Gibbs, 1986) are perhaps the most canonical.

Other common task-based conversational paradigms include the *map task* (Anderson et al., 1991), in which one participant describes a route on a map to another participant, and *construction and building tasks*, in which participants collaborate to build a structure (Clark & Krych, 2004; Grosz & Sidner, 1986). Other paradigms examine more *open-ended conversation*. For example, Richardson, Dale, and Kirkham (2007) monitored participants' eye-gaze as they discussed a popular television show and looked at a related image, providing insight into attention coordination in conversation. In other work, participants engaged in an open-ended conversation, after which their memory for the conversation was tested (e.g., Ross & Sicoly, 1979; Stafford & Daly, 1984).

Experimental Manipulations

Studies that manipulate the mode of communication (e.g., with or without visual feedback; Krauss & Weinheimer, 1966; Neider et al., 2010; Krauss et al., 1977; Clark & Krych, 2004) have been used to explore the relative contributions of audio and visual sources of information in referential communication. Manipulations of the intended audience, including friends vs. strangers (Krauss, 1987; Schober & Carstensen, 2010; Fussell & Krauss, 1989), have been used to understand how speakers tailor messages for specific partners. This work shows that speakers are sensitive to the knowledge of their partner, describing tangrams with brief labels for Matchers who know the labels, and longer descriptions for Matchers who are not familiar with the labels (Wilkes-Gibbs & Clark, 1992; Gann & Barr, 2012; Schober & Clark, 1989), a process termed *audience design* (Clark & Murphy, 1982). The longer descriptions for naïve partners are important for effective communication, since brief labels like *"the kick your butt guy"* would be difficult for a new, naïve partner to understand (Schober & Clark, 1989). Studies of the way speakers attempt to conceal meaning from overhearers (Clark & Schaefer, 1987) similarly address how language is designed for specific audiences.

Extensions of the Referential Communication Task into Multiparty Dialogue

Yoon and Brown-Schmidt (2014) examined audience design in situations where speakers must simultaneously address multiple addressees, each of whom may have different background knowledge. Pairs of participants first completed the sorting task with a set of 16 tangram images six times, establishing shared labels. In the second phase of the task, participants viewed four tangrams at a time, and the Director gave instructions to either the same Matcher (M1) or to both M1 and a new Matcher (M2) who did not participate during sorting and therefore had no knowledge of the established labels. When Directors simultaneously addressed M1 and M2, labels were longer and more disfluent, compared to when the Director addressed M1 alone, reflecting an attempt to accommodate M2's naïveté. Other work shows that as audience size increases, speakers use more words (Rogers, Fay, & Maybery, 2013; Anderson, 2006). Pairings of individuals within a larger group are also likely to be relevant to the way language is used in larger group conversations (see Fay, Garrod, & Carletta, 2000; Branigan, 2006), raising questions about the way in which the knowledge of mixed groups is represented and how these representations are used in dialogue.

Eye-Gaze Measures of Real-Time Language Comprehension in Conversation

Questions regarding the process of audience design in language production are complemented by similar questions regarding the way language comprehension is tailored to the perspective of the speaker. One way this question has been addressed in the literature is through the use of variants of the visual world paradigm (Tanenhaus, Spivey-Knowlton, Eberhard, & Sedivy, 1995) in which listeners' eye-gaze to referenced objects is monitored using eye-tracking technology. The study of perspective-taking in language processing has used this technique to examine if and when addressees use information about the speaker's perspective during language comprehension (e.g., Keysar, Lin, & Barr, 2003; Hanna et al., 2003; Barr, 2008; Brown-Schmidt & Fraundorf, 2015). Methodological approaches include listeners responding to a speaker's instructions to manipulate objects in situations where some objects are hidden from the speaker (Keysar et al., 2003; Hanna et al., 2003). In other approaches, participants listen to stories or watch videos in which the beliefs of actors are manipulated (Ferguson, Scheepers, & Sanford, 2010; Ferguson & Breheny, 2012).

For example, in addition to examining audience design, Yoon and Brown-Schmidt (2014) used eye-tracking to examine the knowledgeable Matcher's (M1) understanding of the Director's expressions. Recall that at test, Directors produced longer and more disfluent instructions when addressing both M1 and M2, compared to when the Directors just addressed M1. Analysis of M1's eye-gaze showed that M1s were slower to identify the target when M2 was present, in part because the Director's use of disfluency cued M1s to incorrectly gaze at a new tangram that did not have an established label (see Arnold et al., 2004). There was no evidence, however, that M2's presence per se affected M1's understanding when instruction form was held constant, though the lack of a balanced design may have been in play (as the instructions were spontaneously produced). In a second experiment, the Director was a lab assistant and the form of referring expressions (fluent or disfluent) was controlled. These findings *did* show that M1's processing of these instructions was sensitive to the presence of M2: M1s tended to discount disfluencies as due to the Director's need to accommodate M2. This pair of findings shows that both the production and comprehension of conversational language is guided by representations of the perspectives of the other conversational participants.

Challenges and Promise for the Future

A constant challenge in the study of language processing in conversation is the balance between ecological validity and experimental control. For example, testing whether a specific utterance form is hard to process may be difficult in unscripted conversation, as speakers are disinclined to produce difficult-to-understand utterances. A related concern is that if utterances are produced naturally, they may differ in subtle ways across conditions (see Metzing & Brennan, 2003; Barr, 2008). While much of the research in this domain uses pairs of naïve participants (Krauss & Weinheimer, 1964), others employ lab assistants (Yoon & Brown-Schmidt, 2014; Hanna & Tanenhaus, 2004), or confederates (Roßnagel, 2004), or have participants listen to recordings (Barr, 2008); see Kuhlen and Brennan (2013) for a discussion of these choices.

Multiple areas of active research hold promise for the future, including the study of the memory representations that support conversation (Horton & Gerrig, 2005; Knutsen & Le Bigot, 2014). Studies of multiparty conversation (Yoon & Brown-Schmidt, 2014), including computer-mediated discussions (Rogers et al., 2013), will add to our understanding of the cognitive limits on the representation of perspective, and how group dynamics influence conversational processes. Studies that monitor the eye-gaze of both participants in a dialogue (Richardson et al., 2007; Ryskin et al., 2015) show promise in the ability to examine different types of conversation, including those in larger groups. Examinations of how we achieve successful communication with individuals from other groups or cultures (e.g., Isaacs & Clark, 1987), and development of evidence-based models of how culture guides communicative processes (e.g., Nouri, Georgila, & Traum, 2014), are needed. Extensions to different populations show promise in revealing how conversational processes change across the lifespan, and in pinpointing the neural mechanisms that support conversation. These include studies of children (Graham, Sedivy, & Khu, 2014; Matthews, Lieven, & Tomasello, 2010; Nilsen & Graham, 2009; Cosgrove & Patterson, 1977), special populations including children with autism (Nadig, Vivanti, & Ozonoff, 2009), adults with Alzheimer's disease (Feyereisen, Berrewaerts, & Hupet, 2007), older adults (Filer & Scukanec, 1995; Hupet, Chantraine, & Nef, 1993; Horton & Spieler, 2007), and individuals with brain damage (Gupta, Duff, & Tranel, 2011; Duff et al., 2006).

References

Anderson, A. H. (2006). Achieving understanding in face-to-face and video-mediated multiparty interactions. *Discourse Processes, 41*, 251–287.

Anderson, A. H., Bader, M., Boyle, E., Bard, E. G., Doherty, G., Garrod, S., Isard, S. D., Kowtko, J., McAllister, J., Miller, J., Sotillo, C., Thompson, H. S., & Weinert, R. (1991). The H.C.R.C. Map Task Corpus. *Language and Speech, 34*, 351–366.

Arnold, J. E., Tanenhaus, M. K., Altmann, R., & Fagnano, M. (2004). The old and thee, uh, new. *Psychological Science, 15*, 578–582. doi:10.1111/ j.0956-7976.2004.00723.x.

Barr, D. J. (2008). Pragmatic expectations and linguistic evidence: Listeners anticipate but do not integrate common ground. *Cognition, 109*, 18–40.

Bock, J. K. (1986). Syntactic persistence in language production. *Cognitive Psychology, 18*, 355–387.

Branigan, H. (2006). Perspectives on multi-party dialogue. *Research on Language and Computation, 4*, 153–177.

Brennan, S. E., & Clark, H. H. (1996). Conceptual pacts and lexical choice in conversation. *Journal of Experimental Psychology: Learning, Memory, and Cognition, 22*, 1482–1493.

Brennan, S. E., & Schober, M. F. (2001). How listeners compensate for disfluencies in spontaneous speech. *Journal of Memory and Language, 44*, 274–296.

Brown-Schmidt, S., & Fraundorf, S. (2015). Interpretation of informational questions modulated by joint knowledge and intonational contours. *Journal of Memory and Language, 84*, 49–74.

Brown-Schmidt, S., Gunlogson, C., & Tanenhaus, M. K. (2008). Addressees distinguish shared from private information when interpreting questions during interactive conversation. *Cognition, 107*, 1122–1134.

Brown-Schmidt, S., & Tanenhaus, M. K. (2008). Real-time investigation of referential domains in unscripted conversation: A targeted language game approach. *Cognitive Science, 32*, 643–684.

Clark, H. H., & Krych, M. A. (2004). Speaking while monitoring addressees for understanding. *Journal of Memory and Language, 50*, 62–81.

Clark, H. H., & Murphy, G. L. (1982) Audience design in meaning and reference. In J. F. Le Ny & W. Kintsch (Eds), *Language and comprehension.* Amsterdam: North-Holland.

Clark, H. H., & Schaefer, E. F. (1987). Concealing one's meaning from overhearers. *Journal of Memory and Language, 26*, 209–225.

Clark, H. H., & Wilkes-Gibbs, D. (1986). Referring as a collaborative process. *Cognition, 22*, 1–39. doi:10.1016/0010-0277(86)90010-7.

Cosgrove, J. M., & Patterson, C. J. (1977). Plans and the development of listener skills. *Developmental Psychology, 13*, 557–564.

de Ruiter, J. P., Bangerter, A., & Dings, P. (2012). The interplay between gesture and speech in the production of referring expressions: Investigating the tradeoff hypothesis. *Topics in Cognitive Science, 4*, 232–248.

Duff, M. C., Hengst, J., Tranel, D., & Cohen, N. J. (2006). Development of shared information in communication despite hippocampal amnesia. *Nature Neuroscience, 9*, 140–146.

Fay, N., Garrod, S., & Carletta, J. (2000). Group discussion as interactive dialogue or as serial monologue: The influence of group size. *Psychological Science, 11*, 481–486.

Ferguson, H. J., & Breheny, R. (2012). Listeners' eyes reveal spontaneous sensitivity to others' perspectives. *Journal of Experimental Social Psychology, 48*, 257–263.

Ferguson, H. J., Scheepers, C., & Sanford, A. J. (2010). Expectations in counterfactual and theory of mind reasoning. *Language and Cognitive Processes, 25*, 297–346.

Feyereisen, P., Berrewaerts, J., & Hupet, M. (2007). Pragmatic skills in the early stages of Alzheimer's disease: An analysis by means of a referential communication task. *International Journal of Language & Communication Disorders, 42*, 1–17.

Filer, L., & Scukanec, G. P. (1995). Collaborative referencing in elderly women. *Perceptual and Motor Skills, 81*, 995–1000.

Fox Tree, J. E. (2001). Listeners' use of *um* and *uh* in speech comprehension. *Memory & Cognition, 29*, 320–326.

Fraundorf, S. H., & Watson, D. G. (2014). Alice's adventures in um-derland: Psycholinguistic dimensions of variation in disfluency production. *Language, Cognition and Neuroscience, 29*, 1083–1096.

Fussell, S. R., & Krauss, R. M. (1989). Understanding friends and strangers: The effects of audience design on message comprehension. *Journal of Experimental Social Psychology, 19*, 509–526.

Gann, T. M., & Barr, D. (2012). Speaking from experience: audience design as expert performance. *Language and Cognitive Processes, 29*, 744–760. http://dx.doi.org/10.1080/ 01690965.2011.641388.

Garrod, S., & Anderson, A. (1987). Saying what you mean in dialogue: A study in conceptual and semantic co-ordination. *Cognition, 27*, 181–218.

Gorman, K. S., Gegg-Harrison, W., Marsh, C. R., & Tanenhaus, M. K. (2013). What's learned together stays together: Speakers' choice of referring expression reflects shared experience. *Journal of Experimental Psychology: Learning, Memory, and Cognition, 39*, 843–853.

Graham, S. A., Sedivy, J., & Khu, M. (2014). That's not what you said earlier: Preschoolers expect partners to be referentially consistent. *Journal of Child Language, 41*, 34–50.

Grosz, B. J., & Sidner, C. L. (1986). Attention, intentions, and the structure of discourse. *Computational Linguistics, 12*, 175–204.

Gupta, R., Duff, M. C., & Tranel, D. (2011). Bilateral amygdala damage impairs the acquisition and use of common ground in social interaction. *Neuropsychology, 25*, 137–146.

Hanna, J. E., & Tanenhaus, M. K. (2004). Pragmatic effects on reference resolution in a collaborative task: Evidence from eye movements. *Cognitive Science, 28*, 105–115.

Hanna, J. E., Tanenhaus, M. K., & Trueswell, J. C. (2003). The effects of common ground and perspective on domains of referential interpretation. *Journal of Memory and Language, 49*, 43–61.

Horton, W. S., & Gerrig, R. J. (2005). The impact of memory demands on audience design during language production. *Cognition, 96*, 127–142. doi:10.1016/j.cognition.2004.07.001.

Horton, W. S., & Spieler, D. H. (2007). Age-related differences in communication and audience design. *Psychology and Aging, 22*, 281–290.

Hupet, M., Chantraine, Y., & Nef, F. (1993). References in conversation between young and old normal adults. *Psychology and Aging, 8*, 339–346.

Isaacs, E., & Clark, H. H. (1987). References in conversation between experts and novices. *Journal of Experimental Psychology: General, 116*, 26–37.

Keysar, B., Lin, S. H., & Barr, D. J. (2003). Limits on theory of mind use in adults. *Cognition, 89*, 25–41.

Knoeferle, P., & Crocker, M. W. (2006). The coordinated interplay of scene, utterance, and world knowledge: Evidence from eye-tracking. *Cognitive Science, 30*, 481–529.

Knutsen, D., & Le Bigot, L. (2014). Capturing egocentric biases in reference reuse during collaborative dialogue. *Psychonomic Bulletin & Review, 67*, 326–341.

Konopka, A. E. (2012). Planning ahead: How recent experience with structures and words changes the scope of linguistic planning. *Journal of Memory and Language, 66*, 143–162.

Krauss, R. M. (1987). The role of the listener: Addressee influences on message formulation. *Journal of Language and Social Psychology, 6*, 81–98.

Krauss, R. M., & Weinheimer, S. (1964). Changes in reference phrases as a function of frequency of usage in social interaction: A preliminary study. *Psychonomic Science, 1*, 113–114.

Krauss, R. M., & Weinheimer, S. (1966). Concurrent feedback, confirmation, and the encoding of referents in verbal communication. *Journal of Personality and Social Psychology, 4*, 343–346.

Krauss, R. M., Garlock, C. M., Bricker, P. D., & McMahon, L. E. (1977). The role of audible and visible back-channel responses in interpersonal communication. *Journal of Personality and Social Psychology, 35*, 523–529.

Kuhlen, A. K., & Brennan, S. E. (2013). Language in dialogue: When confederates might be hazardous to your data. *Psychonomic Bulletin & Review, 20*, 54–72.

Levelt, W. J. M., & Kelter, S. (1982). Surface form and memory in question answering. *Cognitive Psychology, 14*, 78–106.

Matthews, D., Lieven, E., & Tomasello, M. (2010). What's in a manner of speaking? Children's sensitivity to partner-specific referential precedents. *Developmental Psychology, 46*, 749–760.

Metzing, C., & Brennan, S. E. (2003). When conceptual pacts are broken: Partner specific effects on the comprehension of referring expressions. *Journal of Memory and Language, 49*, 201–213. doi:10.1016/S0749-596X(03)00028-7.

Meyer, A. S. (1996). Lexical access in phrase and sentence production: Results from picture-word interference experiments. *Journal of Memory and Language, 35*, 477–496.

Nadig, A., Vivanti, G., & Ozonoff, S. (2009). Adaptation of object descriptions to a partner under increasing communicative demands: A comparison of children with and without Autism. *Autism Research, 2*, 334–347.

Neider, M. B., Chen, X., Dickinson, C. A., Brennan, S. E., & Zelinsky, G. J. (2010). Coordinating spatial referencing using shared gaze. *Psychonomic Bulletin & Review, 17*, 718–724.

Nilsen, E. S., & Graham, S. A. (2009). The relations between children's communicative perspective-taking and executive functioning. *Cognitive Psychology, 58*, 220–249.

Nouri, E., Georgila, K., & Traum, D. (2014). Culture-specific models of negotiation for virtual characters: multi-attribute decision-making based on culture-specific values. *AI & Society, Online first*, 1–13.

Pickering, M. J., & Garrod, S. (2004). Toward a mechanistic psychology of dialogue. *Behavioral and Brain Sciences, 27*, 169–226.

Richardson, D. C., Dale, R., & Kirkham, N. Z. (2007). The art of conversation is coordination. *Psychological Science, 18*, 407–413.

Rogers, S. L., Fay, N., & Maybery, M. (2013). Audience design through social interaction during group discussion. *PLOS ONE, 8*, 1–7.

Roßnagel, C. S. (2004). Lost in thought: Cognitive load and the processing of addressees' feedback in verbal communication. *Experimental Psychology, 51*, 191–200.

Ross, M., & Sicoly, F. (1979). Egocentric biases in availability and attribution. *Journal of Personality and Social Psychology, 37*, 322–336.

Ryskin, R. A., & Brown-Schmidt, S. (2014). Do adults show a curse of knowledge in false-belief reasoning? A robust estimate of the true effect size. *PLOS ONE, 9*, 1–8.

Ryskin, R. A., Brown-Schmidt, S., Tullis, J., & Benjamin, A. S. (2015). Cognitive origins of perspective-taking. *Journal of Experimental Psychology: General, 144*, 898–915.

Sacks, H., Schegloff, E. A., & Jefferson, G. (1974). A simplest systematics for the organization of turn-taking for conversation. *Language, 50*, 696–735.

Saffran, J. R., Newport, E. L., & Aslin, R. N. (1996). Word segmentation: The role of distributional cues. *Journal of Memory and Language, 35*, 606–621.

Schober, M. F., & Carstensen, L. L. (2010). Does being together for years help comprehension? In E. Morsella (Ed.), *Expressing oneself/expressing one's self: Communication, cognition, language, and identity* (pp. 107–124). London: Taylor & Francis.

Schober, M. F., & Clark, H. H. (1989). Understanding by addressees and overhearers. *Cognitive Psychology, 21*, 211–232.

Stafford, L., & Daly, J. A. (1984). Conversational memory. *Human Communication Research, 10*, 379–402.

Tanenhaus, M. K., Spivey-Knowlton, M. J., Eberhard, K. M., & Sedivy, J. C. (1995). Integration of visual and linguistic information in spoken language comprehension. *Science, 268*, 632–634.

Wilkes-Gibbs, D., & Clark, H. H. (1992). Coordinating beliefs in conversation. *Journal of Memory and Language, 31*, 183–194. doi:10.1016/ 0749-596X(92)90010-U.

Yoon, S. O., & Brown-Schmidt, S. (2014). Adjusting conceptual pacts in three-party conversation. *Journal of Experimental Psychology: Learning, Memory, and Cognition, 40*, 919–937.

6

Research Methods

Big Data Approaches to Studying Discourse Processes

Michael N. Jones and Melody W. Dye

INDIANA UNIVERSITY

Discourse science has a deep tradition of analyzing naturally occurring linguistic sources to explore higher-order cognitive phenomena. However, the study of discourse presents unique challenges for quantitative analyses due to its relatively large unit of interest. Stable estimates of letter or phoneme frequency can be obtained from even small text corpora, and stable estimates of word frequency from corpora the size of the classic Brown Word Corpus (at least in the higher range of the frequency spectrum). But as the unit of analysis increases in size, the corresponding increase in text required to obtain stable estimates of a target unit or phenomenon goes *way* up. The multi-sentence unit of analysis that interests discourse scientists has traditionally made quantitative analyses elusive, imprecise, or even impossible due to a poverty of data sources. However, the recent growth of big data resources has opened a whole new methodological toolbox for discourse researchers.

Over the past decade, a number of significant advances have been made both in available technologies and resources, which have important implications for discourse analysis. The first is the advent of massive digital archives of human speech and text. As human interaction has increasingly shifted online, enormous streams of data have been generated in the wake of this shift, on the order of 2.5 quintillion bytes daily (McAfee et al., 2012). The web has thus established itself as a vast repository of social engagement and communication (Gernsbacher, 2014), which can be selectively crawled and mined to create curated text corpora. To date, researchers have mined texts from a wide array of online interactive environments, including social networks, blogs, comment boards, community forums, and review sites, among others. In principle, these digital traces can be harvested from any site within the public domain for subsequent processing and analysis.

At the same time, offline resources are now, increasingly, being digitized. This has led to the creation of multimillion-word subtitle corpora, which cover film, television, and radio; the digital archives of major national newspapers and periodicals; and the scanning of millions of books and articles. Today, one of the most promising ventures is the HathiTrust Digital Library, which represents a collaborative effort on the part of Google, the Internet Archive, and partner universities across the nation, to digitize and provide searchable access to the millions of volumes in America's research libraries. Liberman (2010) has likened the advent of such tools in this century to the invention of the telescope in the 17th. As he noted, these advances have begun to allow scholars to study discourse in a way that was never before thought possible: uncovering the intricacies of underlying patterns, revealing the idiosyncratic practices of individuals, collectives, and cultures, and informing scientific questions about mental processes.

New methodologies for quantifying discourse are very much intertwined with emerging big data resources. In some cases, the magnitude of text data has led to new insight techniques that did not previously exist, and in other cases old techniques have again become very relevant with the power that the massive scales of data provide. Hence we do not intend to separate data sources or methods in this chapter; they both go together to provide new tools for new insights in discourse processes. In this section, we will highlight two broad clusters of approaches that capitalize on these advances in especially fruitful and productive ways.

Surface-Level Natural Language Processing (NLP) Tools and Databases

The practice of counting and analyzing verbal sequences may seem a distinctly modern pursuit. In fact, its origins are ancient. Yule (1944) cites the practice of the Masoretes, Jewish scholars and scribes of classical antiquity, who were tasked with preserving scripture after the fall of the Jewish state in 70 AD. As guardians of the Hebrew Bible, they painstakingly recorded and tabulated the frequency of its words, phrases, and verses by hand, then clustered them by form and meaning, producing output not dissimilar to rudimentary count algorithms. The difference, of course, is that in modern times, scholars can apply such analytic techniques to any text (or collection of texts) of their choosing, while reaping the considerable benefits from automation and from significant advances in text modeling.

Progress in this domain should be of particular interest to discourse researchers, as rapid increases in the scale of corpora available over the past decade have finally yielded the data necessary to quantitatively evaluate theories that depend on multi-sentence units. But that increase in corpus scale has also produced a need for tools to mine these largely unstructured text sources. In addition, many of the early projects were funded by the private sector's need for machine translation and text-to-speech systems, which produced excellent data to study lexical and grammatical effects, but at too low a resolution for discourse analysis. For example, Google's announcement in 2006 that they were releasing a one-trillion-word corpus of web text was a huge excitement to discourse researchers. But when released, the database consisted of only decontextualized n-gram counts from the corpus, with the largest unit being a 5-gram.

Nonetheless, with the growth of raw text corpora, simple surface-level frequency counts of structural elements have proven to be quite useful in empirically testing intuitions about patterns of register variation, narrative structure, and to make genre comparisons. The largest collection of corpora currently available for these analyses is the ambitious HathiTrust Digital Library (www.hathitrust.org). The HathiTrust collection currently consists of 13.8 million volumes (618 terabytes) of digitized text sources from a wide range of registers, genres, and languages, and that number is currently growing by more than a thousand books a day. To put this massive scale in context, if all the books from HathiTrust were lined up on a shelf, the shelf would need to be 163 miles long, and the collection would weigh over 11,000 tons. HathiTrust has a variety of search tools and APIs that can be used by researchers interested in data-driven discourse analyses. In addition to HathiTrust's collection, which is largely composed of published book sources, Brian MacWhinney's group has compiled large sources of conversation, including child-directed speech, second-language tutoring, dementia transcripts, and conversation data linked with video (see http:// talkbank.org for data and tools).

The Brigham Young Corpus Repository (http://corpus.byu.edu), curated by Mark Davies, contains some of the most widely used large-scale corpora, including contemporary, historical, political speech, and book corpora, as well as other unconventional sources such as American soap operas. Each corpus is completely searchable with customizable tools. While the most common use of the site is determining simple frequencies of words, phrases, and collocates, the tools are well suited for discourse researchers to explore variation in register, dialect, or genre, to study historical change, and to create experimental stimuli balanced on a variety of contextual factors. The BYU corpus site sees over 130,000 unique visitors each month.

In addition to these unstructured text sources, considerable effort over the past decade has been put into the construction and validation of annotated text corpora. The largest repository of such databases is the Linguistic Data Consortium (www.ldc.upenn.edu). Annotated corpora allow for supervised training of language comprehension models and algorithms, compared to the unsupervised learning and surface text mining methods that must be applied to untagged corpora. While the vast majority of annotations have focused on units that are too small for many discourse researcher's questions—such as part-of-speech tagging, co-reference disambiguation, or semantic role labeling—there is great promise for such databases as the annotations grow to a higher level. For example, Banarescu et al.'s (2013) AMRs (Abstract Meaning Representations) afford discourse researchers a statistical representation of sentence meaning that is both precise and robust, and can be aggregated across multiple sentences to compare the meaning of larger contexts or to import into construction-integration frameworks.

Data such as those in the HathiTrust or BYU collections are largely free text, with their own proprietary analytic tools. But there are also ad hoc tools that researchers can feed their own corpora to evaluate usage patterns. The simplest—and perhaps most widely used—of these tools are count algorithms, which scan texts for words in user-defined dictionaries, and return count lists, organized by dimensions of interest (such as "personal pronouns" or "emotion words"). In the case of the popular Linguistic Inquiry and Word Count (LIWC) program, verbal categories have been devised to be psychologically meaningful, and usage patterns have been reliably linked to a range of traits, such as extroversion and depression (Tausczik & Pennebaker, 2010). This has led to the development of automated text scoring systems to assess personality, sociality, and mental health. A similar approach can be taken to annotated corpora. Multi-dimensional factor analysis was one of the first methods for quantifying variation among written registers, using the surface characteristics of the text as input to statistical models (Biber, 1998).

Another widely used tool to apply to unstructured text is CohMetrix (McNamara, Graesser, McCarthy, & Cai, 2014). CohMetrix was specifically designed to evaluate semantic coherence within texts, but computes 108 indices including metrics on referential cohesion, syntactic complexity, and pattern densities, and measures based on situation models. Crossley, Kyle, and McNamara (2015) have recently expanded on CohMetrix with their TAACO software (Tool for the Automatic Analysis of Text Cohesion), which allows for offline large-scale batch processing of texts, and expands to 150 indices that include both local and global cohesion measures. Crossley, Allen, Kyle, and McNamara (2014) have also produced a Python tool to provide simple access to a suite of NLP tools customized for discourse researchers.

Often, the curated text corpora and search tools are inadequate for a researcher's purposes, which may require exploring how language is used in the real world across very specific times or following the occurrence of specific social events. In cases such as these, a growing number of open-source tools exist to mine social media and discussion sites, allowing targeting of online conversations surrounding desired topics. For example, Dehghani et al.'s (2016) TACIT software (Text Analysis, Crawling, and Interpretation Tool; http://tacit.usc.edu) is a browser-based plugin that allows the user to target a range of real-time text sources (e.g., US Senate and Supreme Court speech transcriptions, Twitter, Reddit), and to automatically apply corpus preprocessing and count routines.

"Deep" Semantic Tools

The corpus mining methods discussed so far tend to focus on surface-level statistics of linguistic units, such as frequency of occurrence, incidence scores, or type-token ratios. While these surface-level counts can be very useful to study the commonality of constructions and how they vary across contexts, registers, and genres, they do tend to be rather shallow and limiting for many research questions in discourse. In addition, such methodologies have been criticized for their reliance on hand coded lists, their insensitivity to surrounding verbal context, and their unsophisticated handling of lexical statistics. More recent "deep" semantic tools have grown from techniques in data science and cognitive modeling. These methods allow the researcher to go beyond surface-level statistics and to explore topic, situational, and thematic shifts in larger units of text. It is beyond the scope of this chapter to describe all available deep semantic tools in detail; we instead focus on two that have been very prominent in the discourse literature (but see Jones, Willits, & Dennis, 2015, for a survey of these techniques).

The introduction of Latent Semantic Analysis (LSA; Landauer, Foltz, & Laham, 1998) was a significant advance for quantitative discourse analyses. LSA is an unsupervised learning algorithm, closely related to factor analysis, that infers a semantic vector representation for words based on co-occurrence patterns over a large corpus of text. Although two exact synonyms may be orthographically distinct, their resulting LSA vectors will be identical, projecting them into the same point in a high-dimensional space. The benefit of this transformation is that two text units that have roughly the same meaning, albeit with very different words, will be seen as extremely similar to LSA. This affords the discourse researcher a tool to evaluate higher-level semantic similarity independent of word overlap. LSA can be used as an exploratory tool when trained on a text corpus that a researcher wants to evaluate the higher-order discourse structure of. But more commonly, the "meaning-infused" vectors from an LSA model trained on a large corpus of text are used to evaluate discourse transitions, similarity, or cohesion in a new set of texts.

LSA has been widely applied in discourse analytic tools ranging from automated essay scoring to conversation analysis, to automated tutoring. It is a component of many of the offline tools described in the previous section as surface level (CohMetrix, TAACO, TACIT, etc.); indeed, this is why we selected these tools—they all have both surface-level and deep semantic indices. Despite its successes, a major issue that limits LSA's application to discourse analytics has to do with its fundamental geometric assumption that word meanings can be represented as points in a high-dimensional space. The meaning of a text is then simply the sum of the individual words occurring in that text. While the method has no doubt been fruitful, this simple vector summing produces saturation that makes it imprecise and insensitive when applied to discourse units either larger or smaller (because of the lack of syntax) than a few paragraphs.

More recently, there has been a great deal of interest surrounding probabilistic topic models for exploratory research in discourse. A topic model is an unsupervised machine-learning algorithm, similar to LSA, but it has several fundamental differences. When trained on a large text corpus, a topic model attempts to infer the main themes most likely to have generated the text. Each document in a text corpus is assumed to be generated by a mixture of these topics, and the algorithm then statistically infers the most likely set of topics given the text data at hand. The algorithm itself is a text generalization of Latent Dirichlet Allocation, which is used in a variety of data discovery fields including genetics, image analysis, and social networks (see Blei, 2012, for a review). Topic models have proven to be very useful insight tools that allow us to evaluate topic flow, thematic change over time, and situation models, or to zoom in and zoom out semantic resolution while analyzing a text to discover more specific or broader themes.

Topic models have been used to study linguistic change in online discussion communities, and to explore how group language and reference categories shift over time with discourse (e.g., McFarland et al., 2013). Recently, Murdock, Allen, and DeDeo (2015) have applied topic models to Darwin's reading notebooks, offering new insights into how his theory of natural selection emerged from the semantic path of his readings and writings. In addition, they provide an online tool for exploring the HathiTrust repository using topic models. Topic modeling is also an option in the aforementioned TACIT tool.

The growth of big data has also led to methodological developments in networks and complex systems, which are starting to see increased use in discourse analysis. Social networks of characters, events, and narrative schemas can be efficiently built and evaluated. While older generation architectures relied on extensive hand-crafted rules and external knowledge input, the field is moving towards automatic named-entity recognition and template extraction (Chambers & Jurafsky, 2008), vastly simplifying the problem for researchers seeking to investigate the structure of texts on a large-scale. At the same time, cross-recurrence analysis is now being used to explore alignment and synchrony in interpersonal communications in the real world, for example, by applying it to massive numbers of Twitter feeds during the US Presidential elections (Fusaroli et al., 2015).

In related work on online communities, complexity methods have been used to explore how social status influences linguistic alignment among members (Reitter, 2016; Vinson & Dale, 2016). Such investigations can also offer insight into the fine-grained temporal dynamics of these processes. For instance, when a local discourse adaptation spreads across the network, its cascading effects can be traced in time, revealing the reach and magnitude of change across both communities and time-steps (Danescu-Niculescu-Mizil et al., 2013). Similarly, systemic shifts in the language can be charted across historical corpora and related to changing social conditions. In a striking example of this line of research, Hills & Adelman (2015) report evidence that English-speakers have adopted increasingly concrete language over the past two hundred years, allowing them to communicate effectively in an ever more competitive information marketplace.

Discourse Relations

While for some analyses, treating discourse as a bag of words, sentences, or topics would suffice, in other analyses this approach fails to provide a suitable semantic representation. The interpretation of discourse not only depends on the pieces of information it contains but also on how they are organized. Discourse structure has been studied under the notions of cohesion and coherence for about five decades now (Asher & Lascarides, 2003; Grosz & Sidner, 1986; Halliday & Hasan, 1976; Webber & Joshi, 2012). Recent application-oriented research in machine translation, question answering, sentiment analysis, and text summarization has revealed that considering the local context of a sentence has a huge impact on a system's ability to comprehend and generate natural discourse.

A hot topic of research that benefits these applications as well as cognitive and computational theories of discourse processing is involved with identification of discourse relations, such as causal and temporal relations between neighboring sentences in a text. While surface cues such as discourse markers (*because, therefore, after*) are sometimes present, most semantic relations at this level are implicit in the way the deep meaning of two neighboring sentences are connected (*Mary was sick yesterday. She took a day off and visited a doctor*). Big data can help modeling word-knowledge that is required for understanding typical relations between familiar events (e.g., that being sick is a reason for taking a day off or visiting a doctor). Semi-supervised methods mine explicit discourse relations that occur in natural text with surface cues (*x therefore y*) and generalize the obtained relational knowledge to less familiar or unseen events (Hernault et al., 2011; Marcu & Echihabi, 2002; McKeown & Biran, 2013; Pitler et al., 2009; Sporleder, 2008; Zhou et al., 2010).

Challenges and Future Directions

In the tech industry, big data has already effected a sea change, as computer and data scientists have struck away from verbal conceptual theories founded on cherry-picked examples, to data-driven discovery. Yet while research in the private sector is driven by profit margins rather than basic science, the methods being developed there are increasingly relevant to the social and cognitive sciences. For scholars not versed in large-scale data extraction and analysis, the prospect of employing these methodologies in their own research can appear daunting. However, efforts are currently being mounted to make such tools more widely accessible. Powerful open-source scientific computing and data mining packages are being authored in various languages, significantly lowering the barrier to entry for novice coders, and more and more graphical applications are being developed that eliminate the need for code entirely. Large-scale text repositories have been made possible, in part, by optical character recognition technology, which converts the written and printed word into machine-readable text. As speech-to-text technology continues to advance, it will become possible to create parallel record keeping of spoken communication and oral histories.

How might the advent of big data begin to inform how discourse processes are studied? In the past, when such resources have been scarce or non-existent, discourse researchers have tended to rely on careful, sustained reading, on tightly controlled experimental studies, and on inferences from experience or "intuition". Big data in no way obviates the need for this foundational body of knowledge, or for the accumulated wisdom and insights of its experts, who are best positioned to ask productive questions of it. As Picasso was rumored to have opined of computers: "But they are useless. They can only give you answers."

Undoubtedly, the story here is rather more complex than Picasso had it. The prime advantages and opportunities are threefold: With scale, (1) old questions can be addressed with greater clarity or precision, reifying old knowledge, and with new technology, (2) old questions can be answered in new ways, and (3) new questions can be posed that would have previously been either unanswerable or inconceivable. In short, innovation is possible not only in our methods, but in our modes of thinking.

Suggested Reading

Baker, P. (2006). *Using corpora in discourse analysis*. London: A&C Black.
Biber, D., & Reppen, R. (2016). *The Cambridge handbook of English corpus linguistics*. Cambridge: Cambridge University Press.
Davies, M. (2014). Making Google Books n-grams useful for a wide range of research on language change. *International Journal of Corpus Linguistics, 19*(3), 401–416.
Dubey, A., Keller, F., & Sturt, P. (2013). Probabilistic modeling of discourse-aware sentence processing. *Topics in Cognitive Science, 5*(3), 425–451.
McNamara, D. S., Crossley, S. A., & McCarthy, P. M. (2009). Linguistic features of writing quality. *Written Communication, 27*(1), 57–86.

References

Asher, N., & Lascarides, A. (2003). *Logics of conversation*. Cambridge: Cambridge University Press.
Banarescu, L. et al. (2013). Abstract meaning representation for sembanking. In the *Proceedings of the 7th Linguistic Annotation Workshop and Interoperability with Discourse*.
Biber, D. (1998). *Variation across speech and writing*. Cambridge: Cambridge University Press.
Blei, D. M. (2012). Probabilistic topic models. *Communications of the ACM, 55*, 77–84.
Chambers, N., & Jurafsky, D. (2008). Unsupervised learning of narrative event chains. In *Proceedings of ACL/HLT 2008*.
Crossley, S. A., Allen, L. K., Kyle, K., & McNamara, D. S. (2014). Analyzing discourse processing using a simple natural language processing tool. *Discourse Processes, 51*, 511–534.
Crossley, S., Kyle, K., & McNamara, D. (2015). The tool for the automatic analysis of text cohesion (TAACO): Automatic assessment of local, global, and text cohesion. *Behavior Research Methods, 48*(4), 1227–1237.
Danescu-Niculescu-Mizil, C., West, R., Jurafsky, D., Leskovec, J., & Potts, C. (2013). No country for old members: User lifecycle and linguistic change in online communities. *Proceedings of WWW, 2013*.
Dehghani, M. et al. (2016). TACIT: An open-source text analysis, crawling, and interpretation tool. *Behavior Research Methods, 49*(2), 538–547.
Fusaroli, R., Perlman, M., Mislove, A., Paxton, A., Matlock, T., & Dale, R. (2015). Timescales of massive human entrainment. *PLOS ONE, 10*(4), e0122742.
Gernsbacher, M. A. (2014). Internet-based communication. *Discourse Processes, 51*, 359–373.
Grosz, B. J., & Sidner, C. L. (1986). Attention, intentions, and the structure of discourse. *Computational Linguistics, 12*(3), 175–204.
Halliday, M., & Hasan, R. (1976). *Cohesion in English*. London: Longman.
Hernault, H., Bollegala, D., & Ishizuka, M. (2011). Semi-supervised discourse relation classification with structural learning. *Computational Linguistics and Intelligent Text Processing*, 340–352.
Hills, T. T., & Adelman, J. (2015). Recent evolution in the learnability of American English from 1800 to 2000. *Cognition, 143*, 87–92.
Jones, M. N., Willits, J., & Dennis, S. (2015). Models of semantic memory. In J. R. Busemeyer, Z. Wang, J. T. Townsend, & A. Eidels (Eds), *Oxford handbook of mathematical and computational psychology* (pp. 232–254). Oxford: Oxford University Press.
Landauer, T. K., Foltz, P. W., & Laham, D. (1998). An introduction to latent semantic analysis. *Discourse Processes, 25*(2–3), 259–284.
Liberman, M. (2010). The future of computational linguistics: Or, what would Antonio Zampolli do? In *Antonio Zampolli Prize speech*, presented at LREC2010, Valletta, Malta.
Marcu, D., & Echihabi, A. (2002). An unsupervised approach to recognizing discourse relations. In *Proceedings of the 40th Annual Meeting of the Association for Computational Linguistics* (pp. 368–375).
McAfee, A., Brynjolfsson, E., Davenport, T. H., Patil, D. J., & Barton, D. (2012). Big data: The management revolution. *Harvard Business Review, 90*, 61–67.
McFarland, D. A., Ramage, D., Chuang, J., Heer, J., Manning, C. D., & Jurafsky, D. (2013). Differentiating language usage through topic models. *Poetics, 41*, 607–625.
McKeown, K., & Biran, O. (2013). Aggregated word pair features for implicit discourse relation disambiguation. In *Proceedings of the 51st Annual Meeting of the Association for Computational Linguistics* (pp. 69–73).

McNamara, D. S., Graesser, A. C., McCarthy, P. M., & Cai, Z. (2014). *Automated evaluation of text and discourse with Coh-Metrix.* Cambridge, MA: Cambridge University Press.

Murdock, J., Allen, C., & DeDeo, S. (2015). Exploration and exploitation of Victorian science in Darwin's reading notebooks. eprint arXiv:1509.07175

Pitler, E., Louis, A., & Nenkova, A. (2009). Automatic sense prediction for implicit discourse relations in text. In *Proceedings of the Joint Conference of the 47th Annual Meeting of the ACL* (pp. 683–691).

Reitter, D. (2016). Alignment in web-based dialogue: Who aligns, and how automatic is it? In M. N. Jones (Ed.), *Big data in cognitive science: From methods to insights.* London: Taylor & Francis.

Sporleder, C. (2008). Lexical models to identify unmarked discourse relations: Does WordNet help? *Lexical-Semantic Resources in Automated Discourse Analysis*, 20.

Tausczik, Y. R., & Pennebaker, J. W. (2010). The psychological meaning of words: LIWC and computerized text analysis methods. *Journal of Language and Social Psychology*, *29*, 24–54.

Vinson, D. W., & Dale, R. (2016). Social structure relates to linguistic information density. In M. N. Jones (Ed.), *Big data in cognitive science: From methods to insights.* London: Taylor & Francis.

Webber, B., & Joshi, A. (2012). Discourse structure and computation: Past, present and future. In *Proceedings of the ACL-2012 Special Workshop on Rediscovering 50 Years of Discoveries* (pp. 42–54).

Yule, G. U. (1944). *The statistical study of literary vocabulary.* Cambridge: Cambridge University Press.

Zhou, Z., Xu, Y., Niu, Z., Lan, M., Su, J., & Tan, C. (2010). Predicting discourse connectives for implicit discourse relation recognition. In *Proceedings of the 23rd International Conference on Computational Linguistics: Posters* (pp. 1507–1514).

7

Research Methods
Online Measures of Text Processing

Johanna K. Kaakinen

UNIVERSITY OF TURKU

Understanding how readers construct a coherent memory representation of text requires that in addition to measuring the outcome of the comprehension processes after reading, processes that occur during the course of reading need to also be examined. Methodological advancements in measuring online comprehension processes have been crucial for theoretical development (Lorch & van den Broek, 1997). For example, eye tracking has provided important information about how readers interact with text (Rayner, 1998, 2009), and as this technology has become more accessible and easy to use, it has proven its utility in exploring people's comprehension of connected discourse (Hyönä, Lorch, & Rinck, 2003).

This section will introduce some commonly used methods to study online processes occurring during reading: the self-paced reading time paradigm, eye movement recordings, and probe reaction time paradigms. After describing the advantages and restrictions of these methods, future directions in measuring comprehension processes during reading are discussed.

Self-Paced Reading Time Paradigm

The basic idea behind measuring reading times is that more complex or difficult processing takes more time than does simpler processing. In other words, reading time on a particular text segment is thought to reflect the complexity of processing required for the reader to comprehend it. In a typical study, text is presented on a computer screen line-by-line, sentence-by-sentence, or word-by-word, and the reader proceeds through the text by pressing a button. On each button press, the previous line, sentence, or word is erased from the screen, and the next text segment is presented on the screen. The time between the button presses is then used as the reading time measure for that particular text segment.

In a famous example (Albrecht & O'Brien, 1993), Mary, the protagonist of the story, is described as a strict vegetarian and a health nut. Later in the narrative, she is described as going to a restaurant with some friends, and readers encounter a target sentence "Mary ordered cheeseburger and fries." It is assumed that if readers maintain the information about Mary being a vegetarian in their minds despite intervening story information, there should be a slow-down in reading when they encounter the discrepant information that Mary, previously described as a vegetarian health freak, is ordering a cheeseburger. Indeed, using the self-paced reading paradigm, Albrecht and O'Brien showed that reading times for the target sentence were significantly slower when the beginning of the story described Mary as a vegetarian than when the beginning of the story described Mary as a junk food addict. Ever since this *inconsistency paradigm* (O'Brien & Albrecht, 1992) was introduced, it has been widely used to study the types of inferences that readers make during the course of reading.

However, one problem with the self-paced reading time paradigm is that deciding when to press the button in order to proceed through the text might introduce extra load to the readers. This overall slows down reading in comparison to a situation in which readers are allowed to inspect the text freely. Moreover, readers are not allowed to backtrack in text, which may cause them to utilize strategies that they might not otherwise use. These problems are overcome in the eye tracking paradigm, which typically allows readers to freely inspect the text.

Eye Tracking Paradigm

In a typical eye tracking study, participants read text presented on a computer screen while their eye movements are recorded. Readers may freely inspect the text, and they can also reread parts of text if they please. Modern eye tracking devices can compensate for head movements and do not necessarily require fixing the participant's head with a forehead-and-chin rest or a bite bar. The method thus allows researchers to examine reading under more ecologically valid conditions.

During reading, eyes do not smoothly slide across the text but make jerky movements, which are called *saccades* (see Rayner, 1998, for a review on eye movements during reading). Periods where the eyes stay relatively still are called *fixations*. Because the fovea, the area of accurate vision, extends only about 2 degrees of visual angle around the point of fixation, readers have to fixate almost every word in order to accurately recognize them. Short, frequent, and highly predictable words may be skipped, whereas long and less frequent words may require more than one fixation. Occasionally readers also regress to previous words.

Tracking the movements of the eyes during the course of reading provides extremely accurate information about the time-course of processing. According to the eye-mind hypothesis (Just & Carpenter, 1980), there is a tight link between where the eyes are gazing and what the reader is thinking of. Even though attention may be detached from the exact target of eye gaze during reading (e.g., attention may be directed to the upcoming word while fixating the previous word), the eye-mind hypothesis has proven to be sensible (see, e.g., Rayner, 1998). Eye movements can thus reveal how the reader interacts with text information as text unfolds during the course of reading.

The challenge is to decide what kind of measures should be computed from the eye fixation data (see Hyönä, Lorch, & Rinck, 2003). Word-level measures (see, e.g., Rayner, 1998) provide accurate information about how individual words are read within the text. Typical word-level measures distinguish between fixations that are made during the first-pass reading of a target word and fixations that are made during rereading. *First-fixation duration* refers to the duration of the initial fixation on a word, whereas *gaze duration* sums up all fixations that were made to a word during first-pass. *Regression path duration* is the summed duration of fixations that were made to previous words within the text, as well as to the target word itself, before the reader goes on to the next word. *Rereading time* is the duration of fixations that were made to the target word during second-pass (or even third-pass) reading.

An example of a study in which word-level measures were used is found in Camblin, Gordon, and Swaab (2007). They examined how an inconsistency at the global discourse

Research Methods: Text Processing

level (e.g., Mary ordering a cheeseburger even though she has been introduced as a vegetarian) influences eye fixation times (Experiments 2 and 3) during reading of connected discourse. In the study, participants read short stories in which a target word (e.g., cheeseburger) was embedded in a locally coherent sentence (e.g., Mary ordered a cheeseburger and fries). However, the target word was either consistent (Mary is a junk food addict) or inconsistent (Mary is a vegetarian) with the discourse context established in the first sentences of the story. Camblin et al. analyzed word skipping, first-fixation duration, gaze duration, regression path duration, and rereading time for the target word and the post-target word. The results showed that an inconsistency at the discourse level induced longer regression path durations from the target word and longer gaze durations as well as longer regression path durations from the post-target region. The results indicate that readers maintain the discourse context in mind during the course of reading and are sensitive to global inconsistencies in text.

Sometimes it might be more interesting to examine eye movements at the level of phrases, clauses, sentences, or even paragraphs (see Hyönä, Lorch, & Rinck, 2003). Eye fixation times can then be separated into first-pass reading of the segment and to later look backs to and from the segment. First-pass reading may be further divided into fixations that progress within the text segment and to rereadings done within the first-pass reading. The advantage is that if it is difficult to identify a single word in which the effect of interest should materialize, these sentence-level measures still provide detailed information about how readers inspect the text. Rinck, Gamez, Diaz, and De Vega (2003) examined whether readers maintain and update temporal order information during narrative reading using the inconsistency paradigm and eye tracking. They found that a temporal inconsistency did not influence the first-pass reading of the sentence, but resulted in more and longer looks back to a critical sentence that could have resolved the inconsistency. Moreover, this pattern was only found for readers who actually detected the inconsistency. Van der Schoot, Reijntjes, and van Lieshout (2012) used a similar approach for studying whether 10–12-year-old children update character-based information during narrative reading, and whether the inconsistency effect depends on reading skill. In addition to first-pass reading time, they also reported sentence wrap-up time (Rayner, Kambe, & Duffy, 2000), which is the total time spent on the last two words of the target sentence. This measure is thought to reflect the effort in integrating sentence-content before moving on in a text. The results showed that skilled readers do slow-down during first-pass reading, show longer wrap-up times, and are more likely to look-back to previous parts of text when they encounter an inconsistency, even if there is intervening text information between the character description and the target sentence.

Sometimes it might be fruitful to analyze both the word-level and phrase-level measures to fully understand how the effects unfold as the reader advances in text. A good example is found in a study by Wang, Chen, Yang, and Mo (2008), who examined how Chinese readers react to global discourse-level inconsistencies in text. In their study, the inconsistency could be localized to a single word consisting of a single Chinese character. Unfortunately, the target word was often skipped (53% of the time), resulting in great data loss in the word-level analyses. Thus, they also analyzed the data for regions consisting of more than one word. The target region was identified as the target word and the two adjacent characters around it. The pre-target region consisted of the words preceding the target region in the sentence, and the post-target region consisted of words following the target region until the end of the sentence. This way of defining the interest areas provided enough statistical power to detect inconsistency effects early during first-pass reading of the target region, in addition to increased rereading times in all regions.

An interesting approach to analyzing eye movement records during reading is to examine the scan path, i.e., the trace of eye gaze, in the text (see von der Malsburg, Kliegl, & Vasishth, 2014; von der Malsburg & Vasishth, 2011). For example, it might be interesting to examine the scan paths of readers after they have encountered an inconsistency in text (see Hyönä et al., 2003). The restriction of the typical eye fixation duration (and frequency) measures that are computed for certain interest areas is that transfers across the text segments – the scan path – might not readily be captured by these measures. Scan path measures capture the combined spatial and temporal similarity between readers. The similarities of the scan paths can then be used to identify clusters of readers who use similar strategies.

Even though eye movements provide temporally accurate information about how readers inspect text, it might be difficult to distinguish whether a slow-down in processing is caused by a processing difficulty, leading to comprehension failure, or "extra" processing required for successful comprehension. That is why eye movement records should always be accompanied by comprehension measures. Another challenge is that eye movements, just like any other reaction time measure, do not reveal the content of readers' thoughts. This can be overcome by collecting think-aloud protocols in combination with eye tracking either during the course of reading (Kaakinen & Hyönä, 2005) or retrospectively (Penttinen, Anto, & Mikkilä-Erdmann, 2013). In cued retrospective reporting (Van Gog, Paas, Van Merriëboer, & Witte, 2005), eye movements are visualized and played back to the reader, and the reader is then asked to comment on what s/he was thinking. Naturally, think-aloud reports only reveal information consciously available to the reader at the time of reporting (Ericsson & Simon, 1993). Nevertheless, they may help in defining the type of processing related to a specific pattern of eye movements.

Probe Reaction Time Paradigms

The problem with reaction time measurements such as self-paced reading time or eye movement recordings is that they reflect the time it takes to process a part of text, not what kind of information is active in the reader's mind. Probe reaction time paradigms are designed to tap into the type of information that is active in the reader's mind at a given point in text.

In the paradigm, a probe word, phrase, or question is presented at a certain point in text. The task, for example, is to indicate whether the probe is a real word or not (i.e. lexical decision task), name the word, answer a question, verify a statement, or indicate whether the word appeared earlier in the text. Response times are recorded either from the button press or using a voice trigger, and then used as a dependent variable in analyses. The basic logic is that response times are faster the more active the probed concept is in the reader's mind (see O'Brien & Myers, 1987).

Using modified versions of the texts used by Albrecht and O'Brien (1993), Cook and O'Brien (2014) asked participants to verify a probe ("Mary is a strict vegetarian") at different points in the text. They found that the strength of the relationship between reader's prior knowledge activated by information given in the beginning of a story (e.g., if Mary is said to be vegetarian then knowledge that vegetarians do not eat meat is likely activated) and the inconsistency presented in text ("Mary ordered a cheeseburger" or "Mary ordered a tuna salad") influenced probe verification speed and accuracy. Cook and O'Brien concluded that readers validate text information against their prior knowledge and that the stronger the link between the inconsistent information presented in text and prior knowledge, the faster prior knowledge becomes available.

Cook and O'Brien (2014) presented the texts using a self-paced reading paradigm, in which text was presented on the screen line-by-line. As noted above, this method does not allow natural reading in the sense that the reader cannot freely advance through the text (i.e., button presses are required to proceed to the next line) or return to previously read sentences. Kambe, Duffy, Clifton, and Rayner (2003) introduced an eye tracking variant of the probe reaction time paradigm, which overcomes these restrictions. In the eye-movement-contingent probe paradigm, readers are allowed to freely inspect the text until they reach a critical word. A probe is then presented in the location of the eye gaze, the participant responds to it, and the text returns on the screen allowing the reader to continue reading. This paradigm also allows researchers to vary the lag between readers reaching a certain point in text (e.g., the end of the target sentence) and the presentation of the probe. However, responding to probes in the middle of reading will necessarily disrupt "normal" reading, introducing extra load to the participant.

Future Directions: Combining Different Methods

In the future, it is likely that different research methods will be combined to gain better understanding of the comprehension processes occurring during reading. For example, some brain imaging techniques, such as electroencephalography (EEG) and event-related potentials (ERP), provide temporally extremely accurate information about the type of processing required to comprehend text. The restriction of the ERP method is that eye movements produce artefacts to the EEG data, and a simple solution to this problem has been to present text word-by-word. However, it is possible to combine EEG recordings with eye tracking (see e.g. Baccino & Manunta, 2005), which allows "normal reading" of text. Indeed, combining EEG recordings with eye tracking has already proven to be useful in understanding reading-related cognitive processes (see Dimigen, Sommer, Hohlfeld, Jacobs, & Kliegl, 2011).

Combining eye tracking with EEG is just one example of possible methodological triangulation to study online comprehension processes. Eye tracking can also be combined with other psychophysiological measures such as facial electromyography (EMG), galvanic skin response (GSR), and heart rate recordings, which will allow researchers to examine the role of affective responses in text comprehension. The development of automated facial recognition software that recognizes affective states from video images can also be combined with eye tracking. Moreover, combining eye tracking with motion capture systems will open up new avenues for researchers interested in theoretically important topics including embodied cognition.

There is no doubt that future theoretical work in text comprehension will benefit from these methodological developments. However, it might be good to remember that any online measure has only limited potential if not coupled with measures of comprehension. To fully understand how readers build a memory representation for what they read, and how the information presented in text is incorporated in a reader's knowledge base, online processing measures should be combined with measures of comprehension.

Suggested Reading

Liversedge, S., Gilchrist, I., & Everling, S. (2011). *The Oxford handbook of eye movements*. Oxford: Oxford University Press.

Rayner, K. (1998). Eye movements in reading and information processing: 20 years of research. *Psychological Bulletin, 124*(3), 372–422.

Rayner, K. (2009). Eye movements and attention in reading, scene perception, and visual search. *The Quarterly Journal of Experimental Psychology, 62*(8), 1457–1506.

Rayner, K., Schotter, E. R., Masson, M. E., Potter, M.C., & Treiman, R. (2016). So much to read, so little time: How do we read, and can speed reading help? *Psychological Science in the Public Interest, 17*(1), 4–34. doi: 10.1177/1529100615623267.

References

Albrecht, J. E., & O'Brien, E. J. (1993). Updating a mental model. *Journal of Experimental Psychology: Learning, Memory, and Cognition, 19*, 1061–1070.

Baccino, T., & Manunta, Y. (2005). Eye-fixation-related potentials: Insight into parafoveal processing. *Journal of Psychophysiology, 19*, 204–215.

Camblin, C. C., Gordon, P. C., & Swaab, T. Y. (2007). The interplay of discourse congruence and lexical association during sentence processing: Evidence from ERPs and eye tracking. *Journal of Memory & Language, 56*, 103–128.

Cook, A. E., & O'Brien, E. J. (2014). Knowledge activation, integration, and validation during narrative text comprehension. *Discourse Processes, 51*, 26–49.

Dimigen, O., Sommer, W., Hohlfeld, A., Jacobs, A., & Kliegl, R. (2011). Coregistration of eye movements and EEG in natural reading: Analyses and review. *Journal of Experimental Psychology: General, 140*, 552–572.

Ericsson, K. A., & Simon, H. (1993). *Protocol analysis: Verbal reports as data*. Cambridge, MA: MIT Press.

Hyönä, J., Lorch, R. F., Jr., & Rinck, M. (2003). Eye movement measures to study global text processing. In J. Hyönä, R. Radach, & H. Deubel (Eds), *The mind's eye: Cognitive and applied aspects of eye movement research* (pp. 313–334). Amsterdam: Elsevier Science.

Just, M. A., & Carpenter, P. A. (1980). A theory of reading: From eye fixations to comprehension. *Psychological Review, 87*(4), 329–354.

Kaakinen J. K., & Hyönä, J. (2005). Perspective effects on expository text comprehension: Evidence from think-aloud protocols, eyetracking, and recalls. *Discourse Processes, 40*, 239–257.

Kambe, G., Duffy, S. A., Clifton, C., & Rayner, K. (2003). An eye movement contingent probe paradigm. *Psychonomic Bulletin & Review, 10*, 661–666.

Lorch Jr., R. F., & Van den Broek, P. W. (1997). Understanding reading comprehension: Current and future contributions of cognitive science. *Contemporary Educational Psychology, 22*, 213–246.

O'Brien, E. J., & Albrecht, J. E. (1992). Comprehension strategies in the development of a mental model. *Journal of Experimental Psychology: Learning, Memory, and Cognition, 18*, 777–784.

O'Brien, E. J., & Myers, J. L. (1987). The role of causal connections in the retrieval of text. *Memory & Cognition, 15*, 419–427.

Penttinen, M., Anto, E., & Mikkilä-Erdmann, M. (2013). Conceptual change, text comprehension and eye movements during reading. *Research in Science Education, 43*(4), 1407–1434.

Rayner, K. (1998). Eye movements in reading and information processing: 20 years of research. *Psychological Bulletin, 124*(3), 372–422.

Rayner, K. (2009). Eye movements and attention in reading, scene perception, and visual search. *The Quarterly Journal of Experimental Psychology, 62*(8), 1457–1506.

Rayner, K., Kambe, G., & Duffy, S. A. (2000). The effect of clause wrap-up on eye movements during reading. *The Quarterly Journal of Experimental Psychology, 53A*(4), 1061–1080.

Rinck, M., Gamez, E., Diaz, J., & De Vega, M. (2003). Processing of temporal information: Evidence from eye movements. *Memory & Cognition, 31*, 77–86.

Van der Schoot, M., Reijntjes, A., & van Lieshout, E. C. D. M. (2012). How do children deal with inconsistencies in text? An eye fixation and self-paced reading study in good and poor reading comprehenders. *Reading and Writing, 25*(7), 1665–1690.

Van Gog, T., Paas, F., Van Merriëboer, J. J. G., & Witte, P. (2005). Uncovering the problem-solving process: Cued retrospective reporting versus concurrent and retrospective reporting. *Journal of Experimental Psychology: Applied, 11*, 237–244.

von der Malsburg, T., Kliegl, R., & Vasishth, S. (2014). Determinants of scanpath regularity in reading. *Cognitive Science*. doi: 10.1111/cogs.12208.

von der Malsburg, T., & Vasishth, S. (2011). What is the scanpath signature of syntactic reanalysis? *Journal of Memory and Language, 65*(2), 109–127.

Wang, S., Chen, H.-C., Yang, J., & Mo, L. (2008). Immediacy of integration in discourse comprehension: Evidence from Chinese readers' eye movements. *Language and Cognitive Processes, 23*, 241–257.

8

Research Methods

Neuroscientific Methods to Study Discourse Processes

Christopher A. Kurby

GRAND VALLEY STATE UNIVERSITY

Almost as long as discourse psychologists have been asking questions about what mechanics of the mind give rise to language understanding, they have been asking what parts of the brain implement those mechanics. Along the way, a number of quite useful techniques have been created to peek into the brain to see how the brain processes language. These methods range from imaging techniques to visualize which parts of the brain may be working harder than others during a task, to measuring its electrical signals, to manipulating the signals themselves. This section will offer a brief overview of some of the main methods, and some of the less used ones as well. This section is not meant to be a user's guide, but rather a primer to introduce new researchers to these methods. For more exhaustive descriptions of the procedures, good starting places would be Cabeza and Kingstone's book on neuroimaging (2006) and Luck's book on event-related potentials (ERPs) (2014).

Neuroimaging

Neuroimaging methods are meant to create visualizations of the brain and to map brain activity, usually in response to the presentation of a stimulus or event. In the case of discourse psychologists, researchers are interested in how the brain engages in processing language, broadly defined. The most widely used imaging techniques to measure functional brain activity are positron emission tomography (PET) and functional magnetic resonance imaging (fMRI). Both of these methods measure neuronal activity indirectly by assessing metabolic changes in the brain during a task (e.g., reading). The standard assumption is that brain regions that have more blood are likely working harder. In PET scans, the participant is injected with a radioactive isotope that distributes itself in the blood stream, including blood in the brain. These isotopes rapidly decay setting in motion a process that emits photons. The PET scanner detects these photons, which allows their point of origin to be measured. More photons indicate more blood. In fMRI experiments, brain activity is indirectly measured by assessing changes in blood flow across the brain; specifically, the ratio of oxygenated to deoxygenated hemoglobin. This is called the blood oxygen level dependent signal (BOLD).

A higher BOLD signal in a region is assumed to mean that region is working harder; it needs more oxygenated blood to keep up with demands. (As pointed out below, however, the assumption that a higher BOLD signal means more neuronal firing may be incorrect.) Both PET and fMRI provide good spatial resolution, with PET able to resolve activity down to 5 mm^3 and fMRI able to resolve activity down to 1–3 mm^3, and even smaller than that in some high-resolution applications (Harel, 2012). In modern applications of neuroimaging of language, fMRI is a preferred method, mostly because it allows for event-related measurement of activity, is less invasive than PET, and is more accessible because MR scanners are more common than computed tomography scanners (Cabeza & Kingstone, 2006).

What kinds of questions can be asked using neuroimaging methods in language experiments? Studies have assessed what brain regions are engaged when participants access the meanings of words in isolation (Bedny, Caramazza, Grossman, Pascual-Leone, & Saxe, 2008; Hauk, Johnsrude, & Pulvermüller, 2004; Kemmerer & Gonzalez-Castillo, 2010; Petersen, Fox, Posner, Mintun, & Raichle, 1989) and embedded in discourse (Yarkoni, Speer, Balota, McAvoy, & Zacks, 2008), perform syntactic parsing (Brennan et al., 2012), build coherence relations between sets of texts (Ferstl, Neumann, Bogler, & von Cramon, 2008), produce inferences (Mason & Just, 2004), build situation models (Speer, Reynolds, Swallow, & Zacks, 2009; Whitney et al., 2009), comprehend figurative language (Rapp, Mutschler, & Erb, 2012), generate perceptual representations during discourse processing (Chow et al., 2015; Kurby & Zacks, 2013), and construct multilevel representations of discourse (Friese, Rutschmann, Raabe, & Schmalhofer, 2008). (This is, of course, not an exhaustive list.) Clearly, neuroimaging techniques are well suited to investigating where in the brain different components of language processing are possibly conducted. However, a recent study also demonstrates the power of fMRI to assess the temporal dynamics of brain activity during the experience of language processing. Silbert and colleagues (Silbert, Honey, Simony, Poeppel, & Hasson, 2014) investigated the neural systems that become active during both language production, and language comprehension. They had participants tell a 15-minute story while their brain activity was recorded with fMRI. A separate group of participants then listened to that story while their activity was also recorded. Silbert et al. (2014) identified a common set of regions in temporal cortex that became active in both cases. More impressively, they found that those regions showed correlated dynamics across time between speaking and listening participants (i.e., moment-to-moment changes in BOLD signal were correlated across participants). This suggests that not only do certain regions participate in both modes of language processing, but that they may do so in a similar fashion across time. Studies such as these show that fMRI is valuable not only for spatial localization of processing, but also informative with respect to dynamic processing.

Although a notable strength of neuroimaging techniques is spatial localization, they have less than ideal temporal resolutions (Luck, 2014). The hemodynamic response is slow, with a peak around 6–10 seconds after onset (Cabeza & Kingstone, 2006). Thus, neuroimaging is not well suited to address questions regarding millisecond timing, or shorter timecourses of processes. Through proper experimental design and statistical techniques, however, one can separate the BOLD signal from events that occur in quicker succession, such as two different words appearing in the same sentence (Yarkoni et al., 2008), or two clauses in the same paragraph (Kurby & Zacks, 2013). But, inferences about the timing of successive neural events are typically not justified. Regarding PET, its use has become less common in part because the injection of radioactive isotopes into the participant make it more invasive than is typically desired. Lastly, one must be cautious about interpreting the meaning of the BOLD signal. It is tempting to assume that an increase indicates more neuronal firing; however, research suggests that changes in the hemodynamic response in the brain may better reflect changes in local field potentials driven by dendritic activity, and perhaps not changes in axonal firing (Cabeza & Kingstone, 2006). This is important because if a region is identified to increase in activity in response to an experimental event, it is unclear if that increase is driven by neural generators in that region, or because it is receiving signals from another region, or both.

Electrophysiological and Electromagnetic Methods

Other methods record or manipulate electrical potentials or magnetic fields, produced by the brain, on the scalp of the participant while they read text. The ERP technique is a common method to measure changes in electrical activity on the scalp (Luck, 2014), whereas magnetoencephalography (MEG) is used to measure changes in magnetic fields on the scalp. Transcranial magnetic stimulation (TMS), and repetitive magnetic transcranial stimulation (rTMS) apply magnetic fields to the scalp to stimulate or inhibit the underlying brain tissue. Transcranial direct-current stimulation (tDCS) applies an electrical current to the scalp to stimulate or inhibit neuronal activity. Each will briefly be discussed in turn.

In ERP experiments, participants wear a cap with 16–128 (or more) electrodes that simultaneously record electrical activity while they read units of text. An important advantage of using ERP is that it has high temporal resolution, sampling at rates from 250 Hz up to 1000 Hz. Additionally, measurements of cognitive processing can be done "covertly"; participants need not be asked to engage in an explicit judgment task during reading. Data are plotted and analyzed in relation to the onset of an event, such as the presentation of a word. Waveforms are produced which display average voltage differences recorded from an electrode across time. Typically, deflections of the waveform are observed at different delays from the onset of an event. These deflections or components of the ERP waveform are defined in a number of ways, including by their polarity, timing, and peak onset (Luck, 2014). There are a number of such components, with the N400 and the P600 two of the most studied (Luck, 2014). The N400 is a negative deflection with a peak between 300–500 ms after event onset. The magnitude of the N400 is typically interpreted as a sign of difficulty with semantic integration, with larger magnitudes associated with higher difficulty (Kutas & Hillyard, 1980; Luck, 2014; van Berkum, Hagoort, & Brown, 1999). The P600 is a positive deflection peaking between 500–900 ms after event onset, and has been associated with difficulty with syntactic processing (Hagoort, Brown, & Groothusen, 1993; Kaan, 2007), and may indicate additional processing of the text by the reader (Hagoort et al., 1993; Kuperberg, Paczynski, & Ditman, 2011).

The ERP methodology has been used to investigate many aspects of language processing (Kaan, 2007). A common method for ERP in language comprehension is to have participants read a unit of text (e.g., sentence) and then encounter a word that fits the previous sentential or discourse context to varying degrees of acceptability. The resulting ERP components to these violations are then measured. Using this general methodology, ERPs have revealed insights about syntactic parsing (e.g., Osterhout & Holcomb, 1992), word and sentence comprehension (e.g., Kutas & Hillyard, 1983, 1984), causal inferencing and situation model processing (e.g., Kuperberg et al., 2011), integration of information into discourse representations (e.g., van Berkum et al., 1999; Yang, Perfetti, & Schmalhofer, 2007), emotion processing during reading (e.g., Holt, Lynn, & Kuperberg, 2009), and word anticipation during discourse comprehension (e.g., Otten & Van Berkum, 2008).

Although ERP methods are quite powerful, they do have two major limitations. One is that they require a large amount of trials (usually in the hundreds) to obtain a reliable estimate of electrical changes (Luck, 2014), which may be impractical. The other is the well-known fact that they do not have good spatial resolution. In brief, a signal detected at any particular location on the scalp can be generated by any location from within the brain, rendering the location of the neural generator of the signal potentially unknowable. This so-called inverse problem has been argued to be mathematically unsolvable (Luck, 2014). Some efforts have been made on this front, such as sLORETA (Pascual-Marqui, 2002), which provides a low-resolution solution to find the center of regions that may contribute to an ERP signal. But, the use of these methods is not common (but see Louwerse & Hutchinson, 2012, for an interesting use of it).

Magnetoencephalography (MEG) is very similar to EEG, except instead of measuring electrical potentials, it measures magnetic fields. MEG may have even better temporal resolution than ERP with sampling rates near 3 kHz (Schmidt & Roberts, 2009). Additionally, because MEG measures magnetic fields, it has much better spatial resolution as well. (In contrast to ERP signals, magnetic fields are not distorted by the skull.) Thus, MEG provides a powerful method to investigate neural processing of discourse with both high temporal and spatial resolution. However, a main drawback is that the maintenance of an MEG system is quite expensive as it requires supercooling equipment and a magnetically shielded chamber (Luck, 2014), and as such the use of this technique in discourse comprehension is unfortunately uncommon. It is not surprising then that most of the use of MEG with language is conducted in medical facilities that investigate the relation between neurological disorders and language functioning (Breier et al., 2004; Moseley et al., 2014). (Though there are also uses outside of medical realms, such as joke comprehension, Marinkovic et al., 2011, and second language learning, Schmidt & Roberts, 2009.)

Transcranial magnetic stimulation (TMS), and repetitive magnetic transcranial stimulation (rTMS) are methods by which magnetic fields are applied to the scalp, and thus the underlying brain tissue, to affect neuronal activity of specific brain regions. Single-pulse TMS is used to excite specific brain regions during comprehension, with the assumption that if a brain region is important for a certain language function, then exciting that region should impact how that function is carried out. While there have not been that many published studies using single-pulse TMS in the context of discourse processing to date, the technique has been used in studies of sentence understanding. Researchers in embodied sentence comprehension, for example, have taken advantage of the fact that when a TMS pulse is applied to the motor cortex, a motor response is produced (a motor-evoked potential or *MEP*). Buccino et al. (2005), for example, found that MEPs induced by single-pulse TMS applied to either the hand or foot regions of the motor strip were modulated when reading sentences about hand or foot actions. Glenberg et al. (2008) found similar effects in regard to the reading of abstract transfer sentences. In rTMS, a train of pulses are applied on the scalp, and thus the underlying brain tissue, to interfere with neural activity causing a temporary lesion. This method allows for asking whether a brain region is causally important to some language function, similar to the logic used in standard lesion studies. rTMS has been used for studies of word processing, for example showing that the application of rTMS to left primary motor cortex interferes with verb processing of right handed individuals (Repetto, Colombo, Cipresso, & Riva, 2013). rTMS has also been used to investigate higher level language processes, such as idiom comprehension (Rizzo, Sandrini, & Papagno, 2007). Although these methods are important in the investigation of language processing, they have a few important limitations. First, they are not good methods for investigating the role of brain regions below the superficial layers of cortex. Second, the effects of TMS are relatively short lived, and as such they may be inappropriate to use when investigating the maintenance and revision of representations over time.

In contrast, tDCS has become more common, which provides a means of providing continuous electrical stimulation to a brain region (through the scalp) to affect processing during language tasks over time (Nozari, Arnold, & Thompson-Schill, 2014). Similar to TMS, stimulation of a brain region is assumed to enhance the functioning of that region, perhaps revealing its importance in a language task of interest. This technique has been used recently in investigations of language production (Marangolo et al., 2013). Nozari et al. (2014), for example, found that stimulation of the left prefrontal cortex, a region associated with executive functioning, caused participants to produce fewer error prone utterances compared to a sham stimulation condition. Because tDCS can stimulate tissue for longer durations than TMS, it could offer exciting applications for the investigation of situation model construction, which typically unfolds across time as the reader engages in working memory maintenance and updating processes (Zwaan & Radvansky, 1998). Additionally, tDCS is relatively cheap, in comparison to TMS or ERP setups, which makes the method potentially accessible to a large pool of researchers.

In summary, it is clear that discourse researchers have a large set of neuroscience methods available to investigate language processing. Some of these methods are well suited to asking what brain regions may contribute meaningfully to comprehension and others to investigating the neural timing of language processing. Researchers also have at their disposal methods to test causal relations between brain structures and comprehension, though at the moment the methods may be underused. Although discovery of the neural underpinnings of language comprehension is interesting in its own right, more broadly, it proves crucial for understanding how the brain implements language both practically and theoretically.

References

Bedny, M., Caramazza, A., Grossman, E., Pascual-Leone, A., & Saxe, R. (2008). Concepts are more than percepts: The case of action verbs. *The Journal of Neuroscience, 28*, 11347–11353.

Breier, J. I., Castillo, E. M., Boake, C., Billingsley, R., Maher, L., Francisco, G., & Papanicolaou, A. C. (2004). Spatiotemporal patterns of language-specific brain activity in patients with chronic aphasia after stroke using magnetoencephalography. *NeuroImage, 23*(4), 1308–1316. http://doi.org/http://dx.doi.org.ezproxy.gvsu.edu/10.1016/j.neuroimage.2004.07.069.

Brennan, J., Nir, Y., Hasson, U., Malach, R., Heeger, D. J., & Pylkkanen, L. (2012). Syntactic structure building in the anterior temporal lobe during natural story listening. *Brain and Language, 120*(2), 163–173. http://doi.org/10.1016/j.bandl.2010.04.002.

Buccino, G., Riggio, L., Melli, G., Binkofski, F., Gallese, V., & Rizzolatti, G. (2005). Listening to action-related sentences modulates the activity of the motor system: A combined TMS and behavioral study. *Cognitive Brain Research, 24*(3), 355–363. http://doi.org/http://dx.doi.org.ezproxy.gvsu.edu/10.1016/j.cogbrainres.2005.02.020.

Cabeza, R., & Kingstone, A. (Eds). (2006). *Handbook of functional neuroimaging of cognition (2nd ed.)*. Cambridge, MA: MIT Press. Retrieved from http://search.proquest.com.ezproxy.gvsu.edu/psycinfo/docview/621493890/F05BCBAF33B54B34PQ/1?.

Chow, H. M., Mar, R. A., Xu, Y., Liu, S., Wagage, S., & Braun, A. R. (2015). Personal experience with narrated events modulates functional connectivity within visual and motor systems during story comprehension. *Human Brain Mapping, 36*(4), 1494–1505. http://doi.org/10.1002/hbm.22718.

Ferstl, E. C., Neumann, J., Bogler, C., & von Cramon, D. Y. (2008). The extended language network: A meta-analysis of neuroimaging studies on text comprehension. *Human Brain Mapping, 29*(5). http://doi.org/10.1002/hbm.20422.

Friese, U., Rutschmann, R., Raabe, M., & Schmalhofer, F. (2008). Neural indicators of inference processes in text comprehension: An event-related functional magnetic resonance imaging study. *Journal of Cognitive Neuroscience, 20*(11), 2110–2124. http://doi.org/http://dx.doi.org.ezproxy.gvsu.edu/10.1162/jocn.2008.20141.

Glenberg, A. M., Sato, M., Cattaneo, L., Riggio, L., Palumbo, D., & Buccino, G. (2008). Processing abstract language modulates motor system activity. *The Quarterly Journal of Experimental Psychology, 61*, 905–919.

Hagoort, P., Brown, C., & Groothusen, J. (1993). The syntactic positive shift (SPS) as an ERP measure of syntactic processing. *Language and Cognitive Processes, 8*(4), 439–483. http://doi.org/http://dx.doi.org.ezproxy.gvsu.edu/10.1080/01690969308407585.

Harel, N. (2012). Ultra high resolution fMRI at ultra-high field. *NeuroImage, 62*(2), 1024–1028. http://doi.org/10.1016/j.neuroimage.2012.01.018.

Hauk, O., Johnsrude, I., & Pulvermüller, F. (2004). Somatotopic representation of action words in human motor and premotor cortex. *Neuron, 41*, 301–307.

Holt, D. J., Lynn, S. K., & Kuperberg, G. R. (2009). Neurophysiological correlates of comprehending emotional meaning in context. *Journal of Cognitive Neuroscience, 21*(11), 2245–2262. http://doi.org/http://dx.doi.org.ezproxy.gvsu.edu/10.1162/jocn.2008.21151.

Kaan, E. (2007). Event-related potentials and language processing: A brief overview. *Language and Linguistics Compass, 1*(6), 571–591. http://doi.org/http://dx.doi.org.ezproxy.gvsu.edu/10.1111/j.1749-818X.2007.00037.x.

Kemmerer, D., & Gonzalez-Castillo, J. (2010). The two-level theory of verb meaning: An approach to integrating the semantics of action with the mirror neuron system. *Brain and Language, 112*(1), 54–76. http://doi.org/http://dx.doi.org.ezproxy.gvsu.edu/10.1016/j.bandl.2008.09.010.

Kuperberg, G. R., Paczynski, M., & Ditman, T. (2011). Establishing causal coherence across sentences: An ERP study. *Journal of Cognitive Neuroscience, 23*(5), 1230–1246. http://doi.org/http://dx.doi.org.ezproxy.gvsu.edu/10.1162/jocn.2010.21452.

Kurby, C. A., & Zacks, J. M. (2013). The activation of modality-specific representations during discourse processing. *Brain and Language, 126*, 338–349.

Kutas, M., & Hillyard, S. A. (1980). Reading senseless sentences: Brain potentials reflect semantic incongruity. *Science, 207*(4427), 203–205. http://doi.org/http://dx.doi.org.ezproxy.gvsu.edu/10.1126/science.7350657.

Kutas, M., & Hillyard, S. A. (1983). Event-related brain potentials to grammatical errors and semantic anomalies. *Memory & Cognition, 11*(5), 539–550. http://doi.org/http://dx.doi.org.ezproxy.gvsu.edu/10.3758/BF03196991.

Kutas, M., & Hillyard, S. A. (1984). Event-related brain potentials (ERPs) elicited by novel stimuli during sentence processing. *Annals of the New York Academy of Sciences, 425*, 236–241. http://doi.org/http://dx.doi.org.ezproxy.gvsu.edu/10.1111/j.1749-6632.1984.tb23540.x.

Louwerse, M., & Hutchinson, S. (2012). Neurological evidence linguistic processes precede perceptual simulation in conceptual processing. *Frontiers in Psychology: Cognitive Science, 3*, 385. http://doi.org/10.3389/fpsyg.2012.00385.

Luck, S. J. (2014). *An introduction to the event-related potential technique (2nd ed.).* Cambridge, MA: MIT Press.

Mahon, B. Z., & Caramazza, A. (2008). A critical look at the embodied cognition hypothesis and a new proposal for grounding conceptual content. *Journal of Physiology - Paris, 102*, 59–70.

Marangolo, P., Fiori, V., Calpagnano, M. A., Campana, S., Razzano, C., Caltagirone, C., & Marini, A. (2013). tDCS over the left inferior frontal cortex improves speech production in aphasia. *Frontiers in Human Neuroscience, 7*. Retrieved from http://search.proquest.com.ezproxy.gvsu.edu/psycinfo/docview/1450175543/C74D73D76329440DPQ/1?.

Marinkovic, K., Baldwin, S., Courtney, M. G., Witzel, T., Dale, A. M., & Halgren, E. (2011). Right hemisphere has the last laugh: Neural dynamics of joke appreciation. *Cognitive, Affective and Behavioral Neuroscience, 11*(1), 113–130.

Mason, R. A., & Just, M. A. (2004). How the brain processes causal inferences in text. *Psychological Science, 15*(1), 1–7. http://doi.org/10.1111/j.0963-7214.2004.01501001.x.

Moseley, R. L., Pulvermüller, F., Mohr, B., Lombardo, M. V., Baron-cohen, S., & Shtyrov, Y. (2014). Brain routes for reading in adults with and without autism: EMEG evidence. *Journal of Autism and Developmental Disorders, 44*(1), 137–153. http://doi.org/http://dx.doi.org.ezproxy.gvsu.edu/10.1007/s10803-013-1858-z.

Nozari, N., Arnold, J. E., & Thompson-Schill, S. L. (2014). The effects of anodal stimulation of the left prefrontal cortex on sentence production. *Brain Stimulation, 7*(6), 784–792. http://doi.org/10.1016/j.brs.2014.07.035.

Osterhout, L., & Holcomb, P. J. (1992). Event-related brain potentials elicited by syntactic anomaly. *Journal of Memory and Language, 31*(6), 785–806. http://doi.org/http://dx.doi.org.ezproxy.gvsu.edu/10.1016/0749-596X(92)90039-Z.

Otten, M., & Van Berkum, J. J. A. (2008). Discourse-based word anticipation during language processing: Prediction or priming? *Discourse Processes, 45*(6), 464–496. http://doi.org/http://dx.doi.org.ezproxy.gvsu.edu/10.1080/01638530802356463.

Pascual-Marqui, R. D. (2002). Standardized low-resolution brain electromagnetic tomography (sLO-RETA): Technical details. *Methods and Findings in Experimental and Clinical Pharmacology, 24 Suppl D*, 5–12.

Petersen, S. E., Fox, P. T., Posner, M. I., Mintun, M., & Raichle, M. E. (1989). Positron emission tomographic studies of the processing of singe words. *Journal of Cognitive Neuroscience, 1*(2), 153–170. http://doi.org/10.1162/jocn.1989.1.2.153.

Pylyshyn, Z. W. (1981). The imagery debate: Analogue media versus tacit knowledge. *Psychological Review, 88*, 16–45.

Rapp, A. M., Mutschler, D. E., & Erb, M. (2012). Where in the brain is nonliteral language? A coordinate-based meta-analysis of functional magnetic resonance imaging studies. *NeuroImage, 63*(1), 600–610. http://doi.org/10.1016/j.neuroimage.2012.06.022.

Repetto, C., Colombo, B., Cipresso, P., & Riva, G. (2013). The effects of rTMS over the primary motor cortex: The link between action and language. *Neuropsychologia, 51*(1), 8–13. http://doi.org/http://dx.doi.org.ezproxy.gvsu.edu/10.1016/j.neuropsychologia.2012.11.001.

Rizzo, S., Sandrini, M., & Papagno, C. (2007). The dorsolateral prefrontal cortex in idiom interpretation: An rTMS study. *Brain Research Bulletin, 71*(5), 523–528. http://doi.org/http://dx.doi.org.ezproxy.gvsu.edu/10.1016/j.brainresbull.2006.11.006.

Schmidt, G. L., & Roberts, T. P. (2009). Second language research using magnetoencephalography: A review. *Second Language Research, 25*(1), 135–166. http://doi.org/http://dx.doi.org.ezproxy.gvsu.edu/10.1177/0267658308098999.

Silbert, L. J., Honey, C. J., Simony, E., Poeppel, D., & Hasson, U. (2014). Coupled neural systems underlie the production and comprehension of naturalistic narrative speech. *Proceedings of the National Academy of Sciences of the United States of America, 111*(43), E4687–96. http://doi.org/10.1073/pnas.1323812111.

Slotnick, S. (2013). *Controversies in cognitive neuroscience.* New York, NY: Palgrave Macmillan. Retrieved from http://search.proquest.com.ezproxy.gvsu.edu/psycinfo/docview/1312427287/39C4 21B2F2DB4CA8PQ/2?.

Speer, N. K., Reynolds, J. R., Swallow, K. M., & Zacks, J. M. (2009). Reading stories activates neural representations of visual and motor experiences. *Psychological Science, 20*, 989–999.

van Berkum, J. J. A., Hagoort, P., & Brown, C. M. (1999). Semantic integration in sentences and discourse: Evidence from the N400. *Journal of Cognitive Neuroscience, 11*, 657–671.

Whitney, C., Huber, W., Klann, J., Weis, S., Krach, S., & Kircher, T. (2009). Neural correlates of narrative shifts during auditory story comprehension. *NeuroImage, 47*(1). http://doi.org/10.1016/j.neuroimage.2009.04.037.

Yang, C. L., Perfetti, C. A., & Schmalhofer, F. (2007). Event-related potential indicators of text integration across sentence boundaries. *Journal of Experimental Psychology: Learning, Memory, and Cognition, 33*(1), 55–89. http://doi.org/http://dx.doi.org.ezproxy.gvsu.edu/10.1037/0278-7393.33.1.55.

Yarkoni, T., Speer, N. K., Balota, D. A., McAvoy, M. P., & Zacks, J. M. (2008). Pictures of a thousand words: Investigating the neural mechanisms of reading with extremely rapid event-related fMRI. *NeuroImage, 42*(2), 973–987. http://doi.org/10.1016/j.neuroimage.2008.04.258.

Zwaan, R. A., & Radvansky, G. A. (1998). Situation models in language comprehension and memory. *Psychological Bulletin, 123*, 162–185.

Part III
Topical Reviews

9

The Role of Sourcing in Discourse Comprehension

Ivar Bråten

UNIVERSITY OF OSLO

Marc Stadtler

UNIVERSITY OF MUENSTER

Ladislao Salmerón

UNIVERSITY OF VALENCIA

Introduction

The purpose of this chapter is to review theory and research on the role of sourcing in discourse comprehension and discuss implications for future research in this area. Focusing on textual discourse, we define sourcing as attending to, evaluating, and using available or accessible information about the sources of documents, such as who authored them and what kind of documents they are (Bråten, Strømsø, & Britt, 2009; Strømsø, Bråten, Britt, & Ferguson, 2013). Sourcing skills are generally considered essential among academics, displayed by experts in disciplines such as chemistry, physics, mathematics, history, law, and social science (Bazerman, 1985; Lundeberg, 1987; Shanahan, Shanahan, & Misischia, 2011; Weber & Mejia-Ramos, 2013; Wineburg, 1991; Wyatt et al., 1993). However, during the last decades, it has become increasingly clear that not only disciplinary experts but also students at different educational levels and laypersons out of school need considerable sourcing skills.

Presumably, the role of sourcing in discourse comprehension has become more important for everyone due to the abundance of information on almost every issue that characterizes the information age, as well as the fact that people increasingly learn from multiple documents that more often than not present conflicting perspectives on an issue (Alexander & the Disciplined Reading and Learning Research Laboratory, 2012; Goldman et al., 2011; Tabak, 2016). Moreover, professional gatekeeping is essentially lacking on the Internet, with posted documents often lacking explicit review policies and quality control, and with the kind of standard information about author and document that printed documents typically include often unavailable, masked, entirely missing, or, at best, hard to interpret on many websites (Britt & Gabrys, 2000; Flanagin & Metzger, 2008). In this situation, continuous vigilance and decision making are required by individual learners and information consumers regarding which sources to trust and which to mistrust.

The remainder of this chapter is divided into six main sections. In the first, we provide a theoretical background by discussing different frameworks relevant for understanding the role of sourcing in discourse comprehension. In the second, we review empirical work on students' sourcing skills and the role of individual and contextual factors in sourcing. In the third, we discuss the nature and particular challenges of sourcing in digital contexts and review research on sourcing in such contexts. In the fourth, we review intervention work aiming to improve students' consideration and evaluation of source features when dealing with multiple documents. In the fifth, we critically review measures used to assess sourcing skills in the research literature. Finally, in the sixth main section, we provide directions for future research on sourcing in relation to discourse comprehension.

Theoretical Frameworks

Systematic research on sourcing was initiated by social psychologists interested in persuasion, resulting in a large body of findings demonstrating effects of source credibility on persuasion (Pornpitakpan, 2004) and the building of theoretical frameworks such as the Heuristic-Systematic Model (HSM; Chaiken, 1987) and the Elaboration Likelihood Model (ELM; Petty & Cacioppo, 1986). The HSM focuses on how judgments are based on heuristic processing of source information; that is, low-effort activation and application of rules stored in memory (e.g., "never trust a journalist"). Such rules may be cued by salient and easily processed source characteristics, and their use may lead to judgments congruent or incongruent with judgments formed on the basis of more analytic and comprehensive processing of the actual content of the message (Chen & Chaiken, 1999). According to the ELM, however, information about the source (e.g., the author) of a message may affect people's evaluative judgments of an issue both when source information is effortfully processed and elaborated upon and when it is only superficially considered. Moreover, this model posits that the likelihood that people will think deeply about the source of a message in a persuasion context depends on individual (motivation and ability) as well as contextual (e.g., time and presence of distraction) factors, with considerable thinking about and elaboration upon source information often increasing its impact on judgments of an issue. Thus, whether people carefully scrutinize or just perform a cursory analysis of the same source information may sometimes have very different consequences for their judgments, with a source that seemed reliable at first glance, for example, judged to be strongly biased and unreliable when subjected to more scrutiny (Petty & Wegener, 1999).

It is important to note that the ELM emphasizes that source information can affect judgments of issues whether elaboration is high or low. Petty and colleagues (e.g., Petty & Briñol, 2012; Petty & Wegener, 1999) have repeatedly argued against the misunderstanding that the ELM identifies elaborative (i.e., central) processing with the message and low-effort, heuristic (i.e., peripheral) processing with source information, explaining that the message–source distinction is independent of the central–peripheral distinction.

Although discrepancies between sources may arise because they attempt to persuade people toward their positions, explanations, arguments, and conclusions presented by various sources may also conflict due to the tentative status of what is known. This highlights the need to complement social psychology models on persuasion with frameworks developed within discourse and literacy research when thinking about relationships between sourcing and discourse comprehension. One framework that emphasizes the importance of critical thinking and analysis directed toward the trustworthiness of sources is the new literacies perspective of Leu et al. (Leu, Kinzer, Coiro, Castek, & Henry, 2013). Still, it seems fair to say that sourcing plays a more distinct and prominent role in the documents model framework (DMF) of Britt, Rouet, and colleagues (Britt, Perfetti, Sandak, & Rouet, 1999; Britt & Rouet, 2012; Britt, Rouet, & Braasch, 2013; Perfetti, Rouet, & Britt, 1999; Rouet, 2006). The DMF is a theoretical account of multiple document comprehension, where readers need to move beyond the comprehension of single documents and, additionally, integrate information across different documents to create a global understanding of a situation or issue discussed across documents. When these documents present conflicting information about the same issue, the DMF posits that integrating information across documents may be facilitated by attention to the sources of the different documents (e.g., authors or publications), relationships between the sources and document contents (i.e., who says what), and relationships between the sources (e.g., that author A contradicts author B). In essence, the DMF explains how good readers deal with multiple documents presenting different or conflicting views on the same issue by constructing integrated mental representations of the issue and, at the same time, keeping track of the sources associated with the different pieces of information. According to the DMF, it is crucial to attend to, evaluate, and apply information about the sources of information because this allows readers to consider the trustworthiness of the information in light of the features of the sources. The perceived trustworthiness of information may, in turn, influence the weight and position that the information is assigned in readers' overall representations of the issue. Also, when readers note relationships between sources and contents as well as between different sources, such information will help them understand the conflict and reconcile the different perspectives (Bråten, Britt, Strømsø, & Rouet, 2011; Britt et al., 2013; Strømsø, Bråten, & Britt, 2010).

One recent extension of the DMF emphasizes the need to pay attention to sources cited or embedded within documents (i.e., embedded sources) in addition to the sources of separate documents (i.e., the main sources) (Britt et al., 2013; Strømsø et al., 2013). Presumably, there are several ways in which embedded sources may be mentally represented, with one possibility being that readers do not experience them as document entities and remember them as sources but simply see them as part of the content of the main documents. Another possibility is that readers attend to and remember embedded sources and the messages they convey detached from the main sources in which they are embedded, or even without taking note of or remembering the main sources at all. Finally, a more expert way would be to contextualize the embedded sources and their messages within the main sources; that is, by representing embedded sources as a second layer of source information (e.g., attributing a particular message to a particular author cited by a particular publication). The importance of contextualizing embedded sources and their messages within main sources may be illustrated by situations where people read to inform themselves about controversial issues, such as whether use of sunbeds may pose serious health risks, to make behavioral decisions. In such a situation, noting and remembering whether a message by a medical doctor stating that there is no reason to worry about sunbeds is included in a document published by an indoor tanning organization or in a document published by the National Cancer Association may help readers evaluate the trustworthiness of the embedded source and the message it conveys.

While the DMF mainly describes the additional representational structures needed to comprehend multiple documents in comparison to single documents, the Multiple-Document Task-based Relevance Assessment and Content Extraction (MD-TRACE) model of Rouet and Britt (2011) focuses on the processing steps involved in using multiple documents to complete a particular task (such as developing a class presentation or writing a letter to the editor). According to this model, multiple document use is an iterative cycle that includes five core processing steps: (1) task model construction, (2) assessment of information needs, (3) selection, processing, and integration of document information, (4) task product construction, and (5) assessment of product quality. In the complex third step, one criterion that readers use to determine the extent to which a document contributes to their goals, and ultimately is selected for use, is said to be document trustworthiness. This involves an evaluation of a document's source features, such as author expertise. Moreover, the integration process also included in step 3 involves attaching content information to its respective source as well as connecting sources through rhetorical predicates (e.g., noting whether sources support or oppose each other).

Recently, Stadtler and Bromme (2014) proposed the content-source integration (CSI) model to further explicate the cognitive processes and resources that readers draw on when encountering conflicting information about a particular issue. Like Britt, Rouet, and colleagues (Britt et al., 2013; Rouet, 2006; Rouet & Britt, 2011), these authors assumed that one way to restore a coherent representation of an issue after a conflict has been detected is to attribute the conflicting views to different sources. If readers, in addition, want to actually resolve the detected conflict, they may also need to evaluate the trustworthiness of the different sources, asking themselves "whom to believe". Such source evaluation becomes pertinent and even necessary when readers are not able to evaluate the validity of conflicting information directly by judging the truth-value of explanations and arguments, which is more often than not the case when laypersons read about complex socio-scientific issues of which they have only limited prior knowledge (Bromme & Goldman, 2014).

Finally, processes involved in encoding and reconstructing information about sources have been focused within the multiple-entry modular memory system framework (MEM) proposed by Johnson and colleagues (Higgins & Johnson, 2012; Johnson & Hirst, 1993). This framework reflects a memory-based view of how readers establish source-content connections and discusses whether such connections are well established during encoding or rely more on the reconstruction of source-content connections at a later point in time. According to the MEM framework, both automatic perceptual and more reflective processes may affect memory for sources, with these processes being influenced by factors such as readers' goals, the specificity of source information, and the time available to perceive and reflect on the presented information. The ability to remember the source of thoughts and memories, for instance, seems to depend on paying attention to and encoding source information upon one's first encounter with new information. Factors that disturb the encoding of source information have been demonstrated to affect people's ability to remember the source. One such factor is lack of specificity of source information (e.g., semantic similarity), leading, for example, to confusion between *The New York Post* and *The New York Times*. Another factor could be lack of attention to source due to emotional arousal concerning the content of the information, with readers paying more attention to their own emotions than to details of the source (Dunlosky & Metcalfe, 2009).

Taken together, frameworks developed within social psychology and memory research, as well as within literacy and discourse, highlight the need to expand conceptualizations of skilled comprehension to include attention to as well as evaluation and use of source information, especially in complex reading-task contexts where readers attempt to construct meaning from multiple conflicting information resources. Of note is that such expansion brings together perspectives that have largely been isolated in theory and research; that is, theory and research on how consumers of information evaluate the trustworthiness of the sources they encounter on the one hand, and theory and research on comprehending textual information on the other (Richter & Rapp, 2014). Thus, when social psychologists in the field of persuasion have investigated how recipients of persuasive messages evaluate the trustworthiness of information based on source features (e.g., author expertise), they have rarely taken into account how such evaluation is related to the comprehension of textual information, and when cognitive and discourse psychologists have investigated comprehension of text, they have rarely studied whether or how readers evaluate the trustworthiness of incoming information based on source features. Recent developments, especially within comprehension of multiple conflicting documents, however, suggest that sourcing and comprehension of text may be more closely interwoven than traditionally assumed (Britt, Richter, & Rouet, 2014; Kendeou, 2014).

In the best of all possible worlds, source-related representations and forms of processing described by theoretical frameworks such as the DMF and the MD-TRACE would also reflect what typical readers do in and out of school. Reality is more intractable than that, however, as our review of empirical work in the following section will show. At the same time, we will discuss empirical evidence suggesting that a range of individual differences and contextual factors may impact on readers' sourcing during discourse comprehension.

Research on Sourcing Skills

Developmental Roots

Developmental psychology research on social cognition has provided evidence on the antecedent foundations of sourcing. While young children are largely dependent on other people's testimony to gain information about the world, developmental psychologists have demonstrated that their trust in others' testimony is not blind (for reviews, see Clément, 2016; Harris, 2007). Rather, it depends on basic evaluations of trustworthiness referring to such features as the accuracy, competence, coherence, audience reception, and benevolence of sources (Clément, 2016; Harris, 2007). For example, when two sources make conflicting claims about the name of an unfamiliar object, 3- and 4-year-olds have been found to display selective trust based on the accuracy of those sources in naming a familiar object in the past (Corriveau & Harris, 2009; Koenig & Harris, 2005). Given that the building blocks for more mature sourcing seem to be formed at a very early age, it is somewhat surprising that sourcing is mostly conspicuous by its absence in older children and adolescents encountering multiple conflicting perspectives on controversial issues.

Students' Sourcing

Much empirical work demonstrates that students, from elementary through secondary and post-secondary levels, often fail to attend to source features (e.g., author and document type) to evaluate for trustworthiness when reading multiple documents to learn about controversial issues (Barzilai, Tzadok, & Eshet-Alkalai, 2015; Bråten, Strømsø, & Andreassen, 2016; Brem, Russell, & Weems, 2001; Britt & Aglinskas, 2002; Gerjets, Kammerer, & Werner, 2011; Kiili, Laurinen, & Marttunen, 2008; Kopp, 2013; Maggioni & Fox, 2009; Nokes, Dole, & Hacker, 2007; Sanchez, Wiley, & Goldman, 2006; Stadtler & Bromme, 2007; Stadtler, Thomm, Babiel, Hentschke, & Bromme, 2013; Stahl, Hynd, Britton, McNish, & Bosquet, 1996; Van Sledright & Kelly, 1998; Walraven, Brand-Gruwel, & Boshuizen,

2009; Wineburg, 1991). The landmark study in this area was conducted by Wineburg (1991), who compared expert historians and high-school students working through multiple documents about the battle of Lexington in the US War of Independence. In that study, historians were found to seek out and carefully consider the source of each document to determine its evidentiary value, paying attention to the author, document type, and place and date of document creation, and also using such source information in their interpretation of document content. In contrast, the high-school students often ignored source information and considered the textbook more trustworthy than documents written by persons directly involved in the event (primary sources) and documents written by persons commenting on the event (secondary sources).

The finding that students often fail to attend to relevant source information and make proper judgments about trustworthiness or potential bias when reading multiple documents has been corroborated by several studies in history (e.g., Britt & Aglinskas, 2002; Maggioni & Fox, 2009; Stahl et al., 1996; Van Sledright & Kelly, 1998) as well as in natural science (e.g., Barzilai et al., 2015; Bråten, Strømsø, & Andreassen, 2016; Sanchez et al., 2006). A particular challenge noted by Strømsø et al. (2013) is that students may link content information to sources embedded (i.e., cited) in a document while disregarding the source of the document itself. This involves a decontextualization of the content information that makes it harder to evaluate. Thus, Strømsø and colleagues (2013; Strømsø & Bråten, 2014) found that undergraduate students mostly referred to embedded sources in their essays without paying any attention to the sources in which they were embedded. Such findings suggest that students may have particular problems differentiating between and representing different layers of sources, with embedded sources sometimes suppressing or overshadowing main sources in readers' representations of documents (Bråten, Strømsø, & Andreassen, 2016).

Correlational Evidence

Although students at different educational levels more often than not seem to disregard source information and pay attention only to the content of documents, all students do not fare equally poorly in this regard. Thus, correlational studies have established that the extent to which students consider trustworthiness based on source features may predict their learning and comprehension when reading about controversial issues in multiple documents (Anmarkrud, Bråten, & Strømsø, 2014; Barzilai & Eseth-Alkalai, 2015; Barzilai et al., 2015; Bråten et al., 2009; Goldman, Braasch, Wiley, Graesser, & Brodowinska, 2012; Strømsø et al., 2010; Wiley et al., 2009). For example, Bråten et al. (2009) found that students' selective trust in information and attention to relevant source features (i.e., document type and publisher) predicted their single and cross-text comprehension independent of prior knowledge. More recently, Anmarkrud and colleagues (Anmarkrud et al., 2014) and Barzilai and colleagues (Barzilai & Eseth-Alkalai, 2015; Barzilai et al., 2015) demonstrated relationships between attention to and evaluation of information sources and argumentation sophistication and source use in post-reading essays. As a final example, Goldman et al. (2012) found that better learners, who were more likely than poorer learners to evaluate the trustworthiness of sources when reading multiple documents on a complex scientific issue, were also more likely to synthesize information within and across trustworthy documents and include relevant concepts in post-reading essays.

In brief, the findings from correlational research are consistent with theoretical frameworks such as the DMF and the MD-TRACE model, suggesting that sourcing plays an important role in the construction of integrated, accurate mental representations of controversial issues. In a later section, we will review intervention work that more directly speaks of a causal relationship between sourcing and discourse comprehension. In what immediately follows, however, we will discuss research on individual and contextual sources of variation in people's sourcing activity.

Individual and Contextual Factors

Individual Factors

A range of individual difference variables has been found to be positively related to sourcing activities when students read about controversial issues. These include working memory capacity (Braasch, Bråten, Strømsø, & Anmarkrud, 2014) and prior knowledge (Braasch, Bråten, Strømsø et al., 2014; Bråten, Strømsø, & Salmerón, 2011; Rouet, Britt, Mason, & Perfetti, 1996; Rouet, Favart, Britt, & Perfetti, 1997; Strømsø et al., 2010), as well as the view that intelligence is a malleable, increasable quality rather than a fixed, unchangeable quantity (Braasch, Bråten, Strømsø et al., 2014). Moreover, what people believe knowledge is like and how they believe people come to know in a particular domain have been linked to their sourcing activities in several recent studies (Barzilai et al., 2015; Barzilai & Eseth-Alkalai, 2015; Bråten, Ferguson, Strømsø, & Anmarkrud, 2014; Kammerer, Amann, & Gerjets, 2015; Kammerer, Bråten, Gerjets, & Strømsø, 2013; Strømsø, Bråten, & Britt, 2011). For example, Strømsø et al. (2011) presented evidence to suggest that students believing knowledge about an issue to be complex may be less likely to rely on information from sources that often simplify rather than elaborate upon complex issues, such as a newspaper. Finally, some studies suggest that people's prior attitudes, values, and motivations play a role in situations that require critical evaluation of source information (Andreassen & Bråten, 2013; Braasch, Bråten, Britt, Steffens, & Strømsø, 2014; Gottlieb & Wineburg, 2012; Strømsø et al., 2010; van Strien, Brand-Gruwel, & Boshuizen, 2014). For example, Gottlieb and Wineburg (2012) demonstrated how religious values and commitments may come into play when religious believers evaluate sources during the reading of sacred history, and Andreassen and Bråten (2013) showed that in-service teachers' source evaluation self-efficacy predicted their reliance on relevant source features when evaluating the trustworthiness of websites.

Contextual Factors

Among the contextual factors shown to play a role in people's sourcing is the presentation of primary documents. Thus, when Rouet et al. (1996) asked undergraduates to rank order the trustworthiness of different historical documents about a controversial event, they found that those who read primary documents in addition to other types of documents rated primary documents just as trustworthy as the textbook and more trustworthy than other document types. Students not exposed to primary documents rated the textbook as more trustworthy than all other document types, however. Rouet et al. (1996) also asked students to justify their trustworthiness rankings, finding that they evaluated the trustworthiness of documents mostly according to characteristics of the content. One notable exception was that the students who were exposed to primary documents evaluated those documents' trustworthiness mostly by document type.

McCrudden, Stenseth, Bråten, and Strømsø (2016) provided evidence that topic familiarity is another contextual factor influencing the extent to which people take source information into consideration. In their study, high-school students were presented with documents concerning two controversial topics varying in familiarity and selected the documents they deemed most useful for giving a presentation to their class about each of those topics. The extent to which participants took author expertise into consideration when selecting documents was context-dependent in the sense that it varied with the familiarity of the topic. Thus, participants distinguished much less between high and low author expertise when they selected documents for the more familiar topic than when they selected documents for the less familiar topic, consistent with the CSI model of Stadtler and Bromme (2014). Presumably, when participants were less familiar with the topic, they found it harder to evaluate the truthfulness of claims directly and therefore relied more on "second-hand evaluation", asking themselves "whom to believe" (Bromme & Goldman, 2014; Stadtler & Bromme, 2014). Of note is also that readers have been found to take source information more into consideration after working with multiple documents than during the selection phase (Kopp, 2013).

Other contextual factors investigated by Bråten, Strømsø, and Andreassen (2016) include source salience and emphasis on personal risk, based on the assumptions that highly salient sources and high emphasis on personal risk in document content might increase people's attention to and use of source information when reading documents to make behavioral decisions on controversial health-related issues. It was found, however, that the participating college students generally disregarded source information irrespective of such contextual factors, especially sources cited or embedded within documents.

Thus far, conflict is the contextual factor that has got the lion's share of attention in this area of research. Braasch, Rouet, Vibert, and Britt (2012) launched the idea that readers' attention to source information might increase when different sources provide conflicting accounts of the same situation. In support of this assumption, which they termed the Discrepancy-Induced Source Comprehension (D-ISC) assumption, these authors found that when undergraduates read brief news reports containing two claims that were either conflicting or consistent, conflicting claims promoted deeper processing of and better memory for the sources of the claims, as compared to consistent claims (see also Rouet, Le Bigot, de Pereyra, & Britt, 2016). De Pereyra, Belkadi, Marbach, and Rouet (2014) observed similar effects among lower-secondary students, but with stronger effects obtained for undergraduates than for 7th- and 9th-graders.

While the research cited above presented conflicting claims and their respective sources in a single text, the D-ISC assumption has also received support when conflicting claims about the same issue are presented in multiple documents with different sources (Kammerer & Gerjets, 2014a; Kammerer, Kalbfell, & Gerjets, 2016; Salmerón, Macedo-Rouet, & Rouet, 2016; Stadtler, Scharrer, Skodzik, & Bromme, 2014; Strømsø & Bråten, 2014; Strømsø et al., 2013). Kammerer et al. (2016), for example, found that when conflicting claims about a health-related issue were presented on two different web pages, university students paid more critical attention to source information during reading, referred more to source information in post-reading written reports, and discriminated better between more and less trustworthy sources than when the two web pages presented consistent claims about the issue. Additionally, Stadtler et al. (2014) found that when the existence of conflicting claims across multiple documents was explicitly signaled through rhetorical means, students included more source citations when generating essay responses than when conflicts were not explicitly signaled.

Interactions

Research on sourcing has also started to address how individual and contextual factors interactively may influence people's sourcing activities during reading (Barzilai & Eseth-Alkalai,

2015; Bråten, Salmerón, & Strømsø, 2016; Gottlieb & Wineburg, 2012; Maier & Richter, 2013). Thus, Gottlieb and Wineburg (2012) demonstrated that not only did the values of religiously committed historians influence the criteria they used for evaluating sources during the reading of historical documents, their values also came differentially into play depending on whether they were reading more or less religiously charged documents. Moreover, Maier and Richter (2013) suggested that a discrepancy between students' prior beliefs or attitudes regarding controversial issues and claims presented in documents may trigger attention to document source. In the same vein, Bråten, Salmerón, and Strømsø (2016) found that students' memory for source information may increase with the discrepancy between prior beliefs and textual claims. In that study, results also suggested that discrepancies between prior beliefs and textual claims might have different functional values in terms of promoting attention to source feature information depending on the exact nature of the discrepancy and how it is perceived by readers. Finally, Barzilai and Eseth-Alkalai (2015) showed that the influence of conflicts between sources on students' attention to and memory for "who said what" depended on their beliefs in uncertain knowledge and the need to justify knowledge claims through critical thinking and considering evidence.

Findings that individual as well as contextual factors contribute to readers' sourcing are consistent with theoretical frameworks relevant for the role of sourcing in discourse comprehension. For example, the individual difference factor of prior knowledge is highlighted in several of the theoretical frameworks discussed previously, as is the contextual factor of conflicting textual claims. At the same time, however, not all individual and contextual factors targeted in recent empirical work are equally well represented in the described frameworks, and interactions between individual and contextual factors, also highlighted in recent research, seem to be underspecified in those frameworks.

Sourcing in Digital Contexts

Particular Challenges for Sourcing in Digital Contexts

Sourcing is highly pertinent in a range of online interactions. These include simple search tasks, such as searching the Internet for the bus schedule, advanced inquiry tasks, such as performing a science inquiry task in high-school, and reading about a socio-scientific controversy on the Internet at home. In digital as well as in printed contexts, successful task completion may depend on people's attention to source information and processing of relevant source features (e.g., author expertise and document type). However, the Internet also offers new ways of interacting with documents that pose particular challenges compared to printed contexts. Three such challenges for sourcing will be discussed in the following.

A first challenge emerges from differences between documents typically used at school and those available on the Internet (Dede, 2008). At school, students are presented with coherent texts adapted to their reading level, written by expert authors with an informative purpose, and generally selected by their teachers. In contrast, on the Internet, students are confronted with documents that often present radically different views on an issue, and that vary greatly in completeness, rhetoric style, and legibility. In addition, those documents are typically written by authors differing with respect to competence and purpose and have different levels of editorial gatekeeping. Compared to working with pre-selected and already vetted documents at school, learners working in digital contexts thus face particular challenges in discarding web pages authored by non-experts and identifying web pages with non-informative purposes. Accordingly, digital contexts make it harder for students to find trustworthy sources of information (Purcell et al., 2012) and increase the likelihood that they acquire misconceptions about socio-scientific issues from untrustworthy sources (Kortum, Edwards, & Richards-Kortum, 2008).

A second challenge concerns how documents are delivered and displayed in digital contexts, usually by means of search engines presenting a list of documents. Given that most readers have been found to check only the first 2–3 results on a search engine results page (SERP) (Granka, Joachims, & Gay, 2004), the quality of those results plays a decisive role. It is therefore problematic that the documents listed at the top of SERPs may be one-sided or commercially biased (Lewandowski, 2011; Mansell & Read, 2009), and that readers generally have no knowledge about how results get ranked on SERPs (Gerhart, 2004). Further, the way search engines present documents (e.g., as a list, as categories) can influence the way readers process and comprehend the documents (Salmerón, Gil, Bråten, & Strømsø, 2010). Finally, digital documents come in a great variety of formats (e.g., personal blogs, "professional-looking" web pages), with online readers tending to perceive some formats as more trustworthy than others (Francke & Sundin, 2009).

A third challenge is that digital reading involves social activities traditionally reserved for face-to-face interactions. For example, readers use social networks to request advice on personal problems, comment on newspaper articles, or ask for advice on class assignments (Shah & Kitzie, 2012). However, digital contexts typically lack many credibility cues present in face-to-face communication, which enable even young children to consider the intentions and competence of speakers (Clément, 2016). Moreover, in many instances such cues can be easily faked in digital contexts.

The challenges discussed above have been researched within several disciplines, including information and communication sciences, education, and computer science. In the following sections, we review empirical work related to each of these challenges.

The Challenge of Dealing with Web Page Authors' Expertise and Intention

Students may have difficulties using information provided about author credentials when evaluating the trustworthiness of online sources and information (Coiro, Coscarelli, Maykel, & Forzani, 2015). For example, Eastin, Yang, and Nathanson (2006) found that elementary school students judged a web page that informed on the expertise of the author to be less trustworthy than a version of the same page without such author information, possibly because younger students may find a page more trustworthy if they perceive it as coming "from the Internet" than if they perceive it to be authored by an individual.

Another important source feature concerns the intention of the web page author. While high-school students may be able to identify the point of view of an author, they may have difficulties understanding how it influences the way information is presented (Coiro et al., 2015). Indeed, research suggests that even adults may struggle to understand web page authors' intentions and the implications of those intentions. For example, Iding, Crosby, Auernheimer, and Klemm (2009) provided a group of computer science students with web pages on a particular programming technique, finding that 40% of the participants considered a page from a consultant service "objective and accurate" although this page only briefly described the technique and included several paragraphs describing the service. Identifying and judging authors' intentions may be easier in commercially oriented online scenarios such as e-commerce forums, however (Willemsen, Neijens, & Bronner, 2012).

The Challenge of Dealing with Search Engine Delivery and Design of Web Pages

Search Engines

Eye-tracking studies have shown that readers tend to visually inspect, access, and use only the first 2–3 results on a SERP (Granka et al., 2004), with the effect of rank order overriding the effect of page content relevance (Pan et al., 2007). This effect is not limited to simple fact finding tasks (Pan et al., 2007; Westerwick, 2013) but can also be observed when students perform inquiry tasks concerning controversial socio-scientific issues. In such instances, students have been found to select more top than bottom search results on SERPs (Barzilai & Zohar, 2012; Gerjets et al., 2011) and include more information from top-ranked pages in post-reading essays, regardless of the trustworthiness of the web page (Kammerer & Gerjets, 2014b, Exp. 1).

The effect of rank order may be moderated by prior knowledge, however, with more knowledgeable undergraduate readers less likely to rely on rank order and more likely to rely on source trustworthiness when selecting web pages for a class assignment (Salmerón, Kammerer, & García-Carrión, 2013). The effect of rank order can also be reduced by alternative layouts, such as a tabular presentation labeling search results as objective, subjective, and commercial (Kammerer & Gerjets, 2012) or a grid presentation without any labeling (Kammerer & Gerjets, 2014b, Exp. 2).

Design of Web Pages

Johnson, Sbaffi, and Rowley (2016) found that although undergraduates judging the trustworthiness of online health information considered source information in addition to the accuracy of the content, they also took web page design factors such as ease-of-use and professional style into consideration. Similar results have been reported in studies of high-school students performing science inquiry tasks (Lorenzen, 2001; Walraven, Brand-Gruwel, & Boshuizen, 2008). The influence of design features may be moderated by prior knowledge, however, with readers lacking prior knowledge found to be particularly influenced by design features when judging the trustworthiness of Wikipedia entries (Lucassen, Muilwijk, Noordzij, & Schraagen, 2013).

Research has also analyzed the influence of design features on trustworthiness judgments by means of hoax pages; that is, professional-looking web pages that convey purposefully false information. Metzger, Flanagin, Markov, Grossman, and Bulger (2015), for example, presented 11–18-year-old students with two hoax pages about male pregnancy and hamster cheese farms, finding that almost half of the participants to some extent trusted the information on those pages. This effect was moderated by whether students applied elaborative or heuristic processing of source information (Petty & Wegener, 1999), with those applying thinking more deeply about the source less likely to trust information on the hoax pages than those applying heuristic processing, such as relying on web page design.

The Challenge of Dealing with Digital Reading as Social Activity

The Impact of Expertise and Personal Experience

When two authors provide conflicting information in digital contexts that allow for social interaction, such as web forums on daily life topics (Salmerón, Macedo-Rouet, & Rouet,

2016) and blogs on scientific controversies (Winter & Krämer, 2012), readers have been found to prefer messages from self-reported experts rather than from users writing under pseudonyms or lay users. Such preference may interact with the type of evidence provided by the author and reader educational level. Accordingly, Salmerón, Macedo-Rouet, and Rouet (2016) found that primary school students were more likely to recommend expert messages referring to personal experience whereas undergraduates were more likely to prefer expert messages referring to another information resource (e.g., a hospital web page) in support of author claims.

Moreover, the effect of reference to personal experience on reader preference may depend on the topic of the web forum and reader characteristics. Thus, when reading about risk-related topics, such as vaccination, even adults can put much emphasis on personal experience. For example, Betsch, Ulshöfer, Renkewitz, and Betsch (2011) found that after reading a forum reporting on negative personal experiences with vaccines, undergraduates' perceptions of risk increased and intentions to become vaccinated decreased as a function of the number of experiences reported. Additionally, empathic readers may be more influenced by references to personal experience. Thus, when Knobloch-Westerwick, Johnson, Silver, and Westerwick (2015) had undergraduates read web pages describing the pros and cons of different socio-scientific controversies, they found that participants with high trait empathy spent more time reading web pages describing personal experiences, whereas participants with high numerical ability spent less time reading such pages.

The Impact of Online Comments

Research has also explored to what extent online comments can influence readers' attitudes toward the content. Anderson, Brossard, Scheufele, Xenos, and Ladwig (2014) requested adults to read a newspaper article on the pros and cons of nanotechnology, which was followed by either civil (polite) or uncivil (insulting) comments. After reading uncivil comments, participants supporting nanotechnology before reading increased their support while participants opposing nanotechnology before reading increased their opposition. Such effects of uncivil comments add further complexity to the task of acquiring accurate information in digital contexts because comments on controversial issues may be highly inaccurate. When Regan et al. (2014) analyzed the content of approximately one thousand comments posted in response to two online media articles based on a US epidemiological study on the risks of red meat consumption, 75.6% of the comments criticized the risk message. Two major strategies were used: questioning the applicability of the risk message to the particularities of individual persons and questioning the trustworthiness of the source. Such comments may lead to more polarized attitudes (Miller, McHoskey, Bane, & Dowd, 1993), limiting the influence of the originally trustworthy source on readers' understanding of the issue.

Summary

Challenges for sourcing that seem peculiar to digital contexts, as well as the burgeoning research focusing on those challenges, have only partly been considered within the theoretical frameworks that we discussed in a previous section. For example, the individual and contextual factors that matter in coping with challenges posed by the nature of web-based documents, search engine delivery of information, and digital social interaction have not been adequately modeled within literacy and discourse, and the specific sourcing activities that mediate successfully between individuals and particular digital contexts on the one hand

Sourcing in Discourse Comprehension

and comprehension performance on the other are not well understood. Presumably, current frameworks developed within literacy and discourse will have to be supplemented with perspectives developed within areas such as information and communication science to more fully capture relationships between sourcing and discourse comprehension in digital contexts.

Sourcing Interventions

Recently, there has been increased interest in developing and evaluating interventions to promote consideration and evaluation of source features during reading. With respect to scope, some interventions have trained only sourcing skills (e.g., Kammerer et al., 2015; Stadtler, Paul, Globoschütz, & Bromme, 2015; Stadtler, Scharrer, Macedo-Rouet, Rouet, & Bromme, 2016; Walraven, Brand-Gruwel, & Boshuizen, 2013; Wiley et al., 2009) while others have targeted sourcing skills as part of more comprehensive skills, such as web literacy (e.g., Brand-Gruwel & Wopereis, 2006; Gerjets & Hellenthal-Schorr, 2008; Kuiper, Volman, & Terwel, 2009), historical reasoning (De La Paz & Felton, 2010; Nokes, 2014; Nokes et al., 2007; Reisman, 2012; Van Sledright & Kelly, 1998), and new literacies of online research and comprehension (Leu, Zawilinski, Forzani, & Timbrell, 2014). With respect to the underlying instructional principle, interventions have ranged from self-regulated learning with tutorial systems (e.g., Kammerer et al., 2015; Stadtler & Bromme, 2008; Wiley et al., 2009) to socio-constructionist classroom activities including group-discussions and reciprocal teaching (e.g., Colwell, Hunt-Barron, & Reinking, 2013; Kuiper et al., 2009). Finally, sourcing interventions have been conducted at elementary (Kuiper et al., 2009; Kuiper, Volman, & Terwel, 2008; Macedo-Rouet, Braasch, Britt, & Rouet, 2013; Zhang & Duke, 2011), secondary (Braasch, Bråten, Strømsø, Anmarkrud, & Ferguson, 2013; Britt & Aglinskas, 2002; De La Paz & Felton, 2010; Gerjets & Hellenthal-Schorr, 2008; Mason, Junyent, & Tornatora, 2014; Reisman, 2012; Stadtler et al., 2015; Walraven et al., 2013; Wooden, 2014), and post-secondary levels (Brand-Gruwel & Wopereis, 2006; Britt & Aglinskas, 2002; Calkins & Kelley, 2010; Graesser et al., 2007; Kammerer et al., 2015; Sanchez et al., 2006; Stadtler & Bromme, 2008; Wiley et al., 2009; Wopereis, Brand-Gruwel, & Vermetten, 2008). In the following, we present a brief overview of intervention programs, organized according to educational level, and discuss the current status of knowledge regarding "what works for whom".

Elementary School

Interventions aiming at fostering sourcing skills among elementary school students have suggested that it is possible to raise their level of vigilance regarding sources to some extent. For example, Zhang and Duke (2011) implemented an intervention that drew on the WWWDOT-framework, encouraging 4th- and 5th-graders to evaluate web-page credibility by determining who wrote the information, why it was written, and when it was written, among other things. Results of a randomized field trial indicated that four 30-minute lessons raised students' awareness of the need to evaluate Internet sources. Moreover, intervention students improved their ability to evaluate web pages on several dimensions after being prompted to do so. In the same vein, Kuiper et al. (2008, 2009), who conducted multiple case studies, found that 5th-graders could be taught to take a critical stance toward information from the Internet and learn about relevant criteria for evaluating sources. However, a major problem was that students might fail to translate a critical stance into concrete behavior. Kuiper et al.'s (2008, 2009) studies thus revealed that when searching the web after the intervention, students still relied on surface cues such as the appearance of a web page instead of source features in determining the appropriateness of the web page for their research project.

Later School Years

After transition to middle school, sourcing interventions are typically embedded within disciplinary education, especially within history (Britt & Aglinskas, 2002; De La Paz & Felton, 2010; Nokes, 2014; Nokes et al., 2007; Reisman, 2012; Wooden, 2014) and science education (Braasch et al., 2013; Mason et al., 2014; Stadtler et al., 2015). As such, source interventions introduce students to the disciplinary practices of interpreting primary and secondary sources of evidence and prepare them to interpret documentary evidence from the perspective of an informed citizen (De La Paz & Felton, 2010). Another characteristic of these interventions is that learners are interacting more with the learning materials in an independent, self-regulated way rather than just participating in whole-class instruction.

For example, Britt and Aglinskas (2002) developed a computer-based tutorial that prompted learners to identify source features while reading a set of documents on a historical controversy, with evaluation studies including 11th-graders showing positive effects on students' ability to identify and evaluate source information. Also addressing the sourcing skills of 11th-graders, Nokes et al. (2007) conducted a 3-week intervention in regular history classrooms. Results showed beneficial effects of working with multiple, authentic historical documents on students' sourcing skills whereas instruction in strategies typically used by expert historians (i.e., sourcing, corroboration, and contextualization) did not yield any notable effects.

Within science, Braasch et al. (2013) designed an intervention presenting students with contrasting cases that exemplified better versus poorer sourcing skills. In a study with 12th-graders, this intervention positively affected students' ability to assess the usefulness of documents for a particular inquiry task based on source feature evaluations of trustworthiness. Moreover, the positive effects of the intervention were reflected in the inclusion of more accurate, scientific concepts from reliable documents in post-reading essays. In another intervention in science, including 9th-graders, Stadtler et al. (2015) used a brief pre-reading instruction to introduce students to the concept of the division of cognitive labor (Keil, Stein, Webb, Billings, & Rozenblit, 2008). Thus, it was pointed out that people often have to rely on the knowledge of others when wanting to learn about scientific issues, and that this makes them dependent on the benevolence and competence of informants. Students were then prompted to check for the potential motive and competence of the source every time they retrieved a document. This intervention showed positive effects on students' attention to source information while reading and their use of source information in post-reading essays.

Post-Secondary Education

In one influential study with undergraduates, Wiley et al. (2009) tested the effects of an intervention where students first received declarative information about what they should look for when evaluating documents, including the source of the information in each document. They then practiced using this declarative information with a set of documents on a scientific controversy that varied in trustworthiness, and also rank-ordered these documents according to trustworthiness. Finally, students compared their rankings with those provided by topic experts. Compared to controls, participants discriminated better between more and less reliable documents on another controversy, more selectively studied reliable documents, included more accurate and less inaccurate causes in their essays, and acquired more conceptual knowledge from working with the documents. Of note is that Mason et al.

(2014) have successfully adapted this intervention for use with 9th-graders. Further sourcing interventions have been implemented with preservice teachers (Brand-Gruwel & Wopereis, 2006) and psychology students (Stadtler & Bromme, 2008; Wopereis et al., 2008), as well as with adults without any university education (Kammerer et al., 2015).

What Works for Whom?

Although no clear-cut answer can be given to the above question at this point, our review suggests three tentative conclusions. First, while notable improvements in sourcing skills can be obtained by means of brief interventions at secondary and post-secondary levels, promoting sourcing skills in elementary school children seems a lot more difficult, possibly because these children typically behave less reflectively and systematically than their older peers (Kuiper et al., 2009). Second, interventions seem to fare better when the protocol of learning activities is predefined, highly focused, and under the control of the experimenter (e.g., Braasch et al., 2013; Britt & Aglinskas, 2002; Mason et al., 2014; Stadtler & Bromme, 2008; Wiley et al., 2009; Zhang & Duke, 2011) than when carried out by the regular teacher within the dynamics of intact classes (e.g., Colwell et al., 2013; Kuiper et al., 2008, 2009; Walraven et al., 2013). Finally, our review informed us that very little is known about the sustainability of improvements in sourcing as a result of intervention. Rather, current intervention work can be said to mainly provide "proof of concept", demonstrating that it is possible to teach sourcing skills at particular age levels but providing no information on what may happen to these skills when the researchers "have left the building". Thus, pressing questions concern whether students will continue to evaluate sources when it is no longer obvious to them that today's lesson is about sourcing, and whether they will transfer newly acquired sourcing skills to other domains or to the use of information resources out of school.

Assessment of Sourcing Skills

The growing interest in sourcing skills among researchers requires that they try to develop valid, reliable, and efficient ways of assessing them. In keeping with our definition of sourcing, approaches to the assessment of sourcing may focus on attention to sources, evaluation of sources, and use of sources, respectively. In the following, we organize our discussion according to these three aspects of sourcing.

Attention to Source Information

Researchers have used various approaches to try to determine the extent to which individuals allocate their attention to source information during written discourse comprehension. These include analyses of navigation patterns (e.g., Kammerer et al., 2015; Salmerón et al., 2013; Stadtler et al., 2015), eye-tracking data (e.g., Braasch et al., 2012; Gerjets et al., 2011), think-aloud protocols (e.g., Barzilai et al., 2015; Leu et al., 2007; Strømsø & Bråten, 2014; Strømsø et al., 2013), or a combination of such approaches (e.g., Gerjets et al., 2011; Kammerer et al., 2016).

Although navigation logs may be relatively easy to analyze, the granularity of such analyses is rather coarse, making it impossible to determine which parts of a web page an individual is actually focusing on. This problem can be circumvented with the use of eye-tracking methodology because this approach enables researchers to define areas of interest within a given document. However, while eye-tracking data can be informative regarding the parts of a document processed by a reader, one limitation of this methodology is that the exact form of sourcing (e.g., mere attention to sources, evaluation of sources, or both) typically remains unclear. To address this issue, think-aloud methodology can be combined with eye-tracking or used alone. Because individuals may not consistently verbalize their evaluative thoughts, suggesting that some source mentions coded as attention to sources might actually involve more complex source evaluations, however, even think-alouds leave room for some speculation on the exact nature of sourcing during reading.

Of note is also that several studies have used performance on post-reading source memory tasks to indicate attention to source information, for example by asking participants to recall specific source features (Britt & Aglinskas, 2002; Steffens, Britt, Braasch, Strømsø, & Bråten, 2014) or match source information with document content after reading (Strømsø et al., 2010).

Source Evaluation

Approaches designed to assess evaluation of source information include asking participants to rank-order or rate sources in terms of trustworthiness, expertise, pertinence, usefulness, or benevolence (e.g., Barzilai & Eseth-Alkalai, 2015; Braasch et al., 2013; Bråten, Braasch, Strømsø, & Ferguson, 2015; Bromme, Stadtler, Scharrer, & Thomm, 2015; Eastin et al., 2006; Flanagin & Metzger, 2003; Rouet et al., 1996; Wineburg, 1991), to identify the most reliable and the most unreliable sources within a set of documents (e.g., Mason et al., 2014; Wiley et al., 2009), or to determine the most knowledgeable source in a controversy (e.g., Macedo-Rouet et al., 2013). A characteristic of such source evaluation assessments is that individuals are explicitly prompted to provide their evaluations. While this makes these approaches easy to administer and score and the data they provide unambiguous, it remains unclear whether individuals would have applied comparable source evaluation skills spontaneously; that is, without any explicit prompting. In fact, studies trying to assess students' spontaneous source evaluation during reading by means of think-alouds suggest that this form of processing is quite rare (Barzilai et al., 2015; Strømsø et al., 2013). Also, these approaches are not informative regarding individuals' use of source information, for example when making or justifying claims or interpreting content during discourse comprehension.

Use of Source Information

As an online measure of source use, researchers have studied navigation decisions, for example in terms of time spent on more or less reliable documents (e.g., Kammerer et al., 2015, 2016; Mason et al., 2014; Salmerón et al., 2013; Stadtler et al., 2015; Wiley et al., 2009). The idea is that individuals use their knowledge of sources to inform metacognitive decisions during discourse processing, for example to selectively process particular documents. Support for the validity of this approach comes from intervention studies showing that individuals can be trained to process documents more analytically and comprehensively when they are created by trustworthy sources (e.g., Mason et al., 2014). Using think-alouds, however, Barzilai et al. (2015) and Strømsø et al. (2013) found that students rarely used source information to predict and interpret document content during reading, which is typical of expert readers (Wineburg, 1991).

Offline, researchers have analyzed post-reading essays in terms of the origin of essay content (Braasch et al., 2013; Mason et al., 2014), with such work indicating that individuals may draw on source information in determining whether to incorporate document content into their own argumentation. The validity of this approach has also been supported by intervention studies (Braasch et al., 2013; Mason et al., 2014). Moreover, studies have validated the approach of analyzing students' post-reading essays in terms of source citations (Bråten et al., 2014; Britt & Aglinskas, 2002; Strømsø & Bråten, 2014; Strømsø et al., 2013), also distinguishing among mere mentioning of sources, source-content links, and evaluative statements regarding the sources (Strømsø et al., 2013).

Yet another assessment of source use asks people to make decisions on the validity of competing knowledge claims. For example, Kammerer et al. (2015) and Stadtler et al. (2016) presented participants with conflicting scientific claims set forth by sources varying in competence and intentions, finding that participants in sourcing interventions were more likely than controls to agree with knowledge claims made by competent and benevolent sources.

Finally, assessment of source use may ask people to justify their rank-ordering of documents or their personal stance on an issue. For example, Braasch et al. (2013) asked participants to justify their rankings of documents according to usefulness and coded their justifications in terms of considerations of trustworthiness based on source features (see also Rouet et al., 1996). Stadtler et al. (2015) asked participants to take a stance on a controversial scientific issue and provide written justifications for their stances, examining to what extent they mentioned source information in justifying their stance (see also Stadtler et al., 2016).

Future Directions

It should be clear by now that sourcing is an essential discourse process and that no model of discourse comprehension would be comprehensive without considering the role of sourcing. Judging the trustworthiness of sources is no longer a task primarily for professionals, such as researchers or editors of books, journals, and newspapers; it is increasingly the responsibility of students and lay readers who need sourcing skills to make sense of the almost unlimited range of information, opinions, and claims made easily accessible by the technologies of the 21st century. Yet, while there are several viable theoretical frameworks speaking to the importance of sourcing for discourse comprehension (see the section on Theoretical Frameworks), mainstream models of discourse comprehension that were mostly generated in the pre-Internet era are essentially devoid of any references to the role of sourcing (cf., McNamara & Magliano, 2009). Hopefully, the current chapter will provide an impetus for theorists and researchers in discourse comprehension to expand their conceptualizations and research agendas to encompass the process of sourcing and, thereby, increase our understanding of what it takes to be a competent comprehender as we move deeper into this century. In the following, we provide some directions for such future endeavors.

Despite the progress that has been made in this area of research, there is a great need to further investigate individual and contextual factors contributing to sourcing, especially when people read to comprehend controversial socio-scientific issues (Bromme & Goldman, 2014). Among additional, potentially contributing individual factors are general cognitive competencies such as cognitive reflection (Frederick, 2005) and critical-analytic thinking (Bonney & Sternberg, 2011), as well as general and domain-specific knowledge of relevant source features (Rouet, Ros, de Pereyra, Macedo-Rouet, & Salmerón, 2013). Likewise, non-cognitive individual factors such as values and emotions have hardly been studied in relation to sourcing during discourse comprehension (see, however, Gottlieb & Wineburg, 2012; Knobloch-Westerwick et al., 2015).

In addition, there are several additional contextual factors that need to be further researched, for example how distinct and elaborated the descriptions of main as well as embedded sources are, where they are located, and how clearly they are linked to content information (Britt et al., 2013; Strømsø et al., 2013). Other contextual factors wide open for further research concern the particular issue under investigation (Betsch et al., 2011) and the familiarity of that issue to readers (McCrudden et al., 2016).

More important than investigating individual and contextual factors separately, however, is further examination of how individual differences and contextual factors may interact to facilitate or constrain people's sourcing activities. For example, while the contributions of individual differences in prior knowledge and cross-referencing to sourcing have been investigated separately (e.g., Bråten, Strømsø, & Salmerón, 2011; Stadtler et al., 2014), an interesting issue concerns whether the effects of prior knowledge on sourcing might be moderated by explicit cross-referencing when people read to comprehend multiple conflicting documents. Within digital contexts, in particular, further research is needed on interaction effects of individual difference variables with credibility cues on online sourcing. For example, a reliable web sponsor referred to in the logo on top of a web page, such as Encyclopaedia Britannica, has been found to be rated as more trustworthy than a less reliable sponsor, such as Wikipedia, only when the encyclopedia entry contains high-quality information (Flanagin & Metzger, 2011). Moreover, Westerwick (2013) found that a reliable web sponsor might overshadow effects of other credibility cues, such as web design, on perceived trustworthiness. How the effects of different types of credibility cues on online sourcing might interact with individual differences variables, such as prior knowledge, beliefs, or emotions, is currently not known, however.

Of note is also that most previous research on sourcing in digital contexts has been conducted with children and youth. While other populations, such as atypical learners or elderly people, may also benefit from accessing online information and participating in online social networks, most evidence on such populations is merely anecdotic. One exception is Salmerón, Gómez, and Fajardo's (2016) investigation of students with intellectual disabilities identifying and evaluating source features in web forums. In that study, it was found that participants did not display selective trust in recommendations as a function of author expertise, indicating higher levels of credulity in this population than in typically developing students (Greenspan, Loughlin, & Black, 2001). Regarding elderly people, Chakraborty, Rao, and Uphadhyahy (2009) speculated that they, in general, might be particularly uncritical in digital contexts because they grew up in a more honest world and because they usually spend less time on the Internet. Also, at this point, nothing but speculation exists about how reading digital documents in a second language might affect people's sourcing activity. Cognitive psychology research has shown that when reading in a second language, people tend to be less influenced by decision-making heuristics (Keysar, Hayakawa, & An, 2012) and have less intense emotional reactions (Caldwell-Harris, 2015). Based on such findings, one hypothesis for future research might be that people also behave differently when assessing the trustworthiness of online sources in a second compared to a first language, such that they rely less on heuristics and more on rational thinking.

Despite the empirical work indicating that sourcing skills can be improved through instruction, longer-term classroom-based interventions targeting sourcing are essentially lacking. Within such interventions, it seems important to research how efforts to promote sourcing skills can be incorporated into regular content-area instruction conducted by classroom teachers being offered professional support. With respect to intervention effects, a desirable goal is to demonstrate positive effects on application tasks requiring that participants transfer newly learned sourcing skills to novel situations where they work on other issues. Preferably, assessment of sourcing skills in such situations should seek to combine different data sources, for example by relating data on source processing collected during reading to product data indicating use of source information after reading. Moreover, many existing procedures for assessing sourcing skills are quite labor-intensive in terms of completion or scoring, which makes them less suitable for large-scale studies requiring more efficient procedures with higher levels of standardization. Design and validation of more efficient assessment procedures that can be included in large-scale intervention work are therefore highly needed.

Importantly, outcomes of sourcing interventions should be measured in terms of not only sourcing skills but also participants' ability to build integrated understanding of an issue based on the most trustworthy information. Thus, researchers conducting sourcing interventions should consistently evaluate not only potential gains in sourcing but also in comprehension performance, allowing them to draw firmer conclusions regarding the causal relationship between participants' sourcing activity and discourse comprehension. Lack of follow-up data assessing long-term effects of sourcing interventions is also a serious limitation of prior work that needs to be addressed in future research. Finally, much more research is needed to design, implement, and evaluate interventions that prepare younger students for taking source information into consideration during discourse comprehension. Given the importance of functional sourcing skills in the 21st-century discourse context, efforts to help people become critical readers and learners by means of such skills should not be limited to a particular age group but include younger as well as older citizens.

Further Reading

Barzilai, S., Tzadok, E., & Eshet-Alkalai, Y. (2015). Sourcing while reading divergent expert accounts: Pathways from views of knowing to written argumentation. *Instructional Science, 43*, 737–766.
Britt, M.A., Rouet, J.F., & Braasch, J.L.G. (2013). Documents experienced as entities: Extending the situation model theory of comprehension. In M.A. Britt, S.R. Goldman, & J.F. Rouet (Eds), *Reading from words to multiple texts* (pp. 160–179). New York, NY: Routledge.
Gottlieb, E., & Wineburg, S. (2012). Between *veritas* and *communitas*: Epistemic switching in the reading of academic and sacred history. *The Journal of the Learning Sciences, 21*, 84–129.
Wiley, J., Goldman, S.R., Graesser, A.C., Sanchez, C.A., Ash, I.K., & Hemmerich, J.A. (2009). Source evaluation, comprehension, and learning in Internet science inquiry tasks. *American Educational Research Journal, 46*, 1060–1106.

References

Alexander, P.A., & the Disciplined Reading and Learning Research Laboratory (2012). Reading into the future: Competence for the 21st century. *Educational Psychologist, 47*, 259–280.
Anderson, A.A., Brossard, D., Scheufele, D.A., Xenos, M.A., & Ladwig, P. (2014). The "nasty effect": Online incivility and risk perceptions of emerging technologies. *Journal of Computer-Mediated Communication, 19*, 373–387.
Andreassen, R., & Bråten, I. (2013). Teachers' source evaluation self-efficacy predicts their use of relevant source features when evaluating the trustworthiness of web sources on special education. *British Journal of Educational Technology, 44*, 821–836.
Anmarkrud, Ø., Bråten, I., & Strømsø, H.I. (2014). Multiple-documents literacy: Strategic processing, source awareness, and argumentation when reading multiple conflicting documents. *Learning and Individual Differences, 30*, 64–76.
Barzilai, S., & Eseth-Alkalai, Y. (2015). The role of epistemic perspectives in comprehension of multiple author viewpoints. *Learning and Instruction, 36*, 86–103.
Barzilai, S., Tzadok, E., & Eshet-Alkalai, Y. (2015). Sourcing while reading divergent expert accounts: Pathways from views of knowing to written argumentation. *Instructional Science, 43*, 737–766.

Barzilai, S., & Zohar, A. (2012). Epistemic thinking in action: Evaluating and integrating online sources. *Cognition and Instruction, 30*, 39–85.

Bazerman, C. (1985). Physicists reading physics: Schema-laden purposes and purpose-laden schema. *Written Communication, 2*, 3–23.

Betsch, C., Ulshöfer, C., Renkewitz, F., & Betsch, T. (2011). The influence of narrative vs. statistical information on perceiving vaccination risks. *Medical Decision Making, 31*, 742–753.

Bonney, C., & Sternberg, R.J. (2011). Learning to think critically. In R.E. Mayer & P.A. Alexander (Eds), *Handbook of research on learning and instruction* (pp. 166–195). New York, NY: Routledge.

Braasch, J.L.G., Bråten, I., Britt, M.A., Steffens, B., & Strømsø, H.I. (2014). Sensitivity to inaccurate argumentation in health news articles: Potential contributions of readers' topic and epistemic beliefs. In D.N. Rapp & J.L.G. Braasch (Eds), *Processing inaccurate information: Theoretical and applied perspectives from cognitive science and the educational sciences* (pp. 117–137). Cambridge, MA: The MIT Press.

Braasch, J.L.G., Bråten, I., Strømsø, H.I., & Anmarkrud, Ø. (2014). Incremental theories of intelligence predict multiple document comprehension. *Learning and Individual Differences, 31*, 11–20.

Braasch, J.L.G., Bråten, I., Strømsø, H.I., Anmarkrud, Ø., & Ferguson, L.E. (2013). Promoting secondary school students' evaluation of source features of multiple documents. *Contemporary Educational Psychology, 38*, 180–195.

Braasch, J.L.G., Rouet, J.F., Vibert, N., & Britt, M.A. (2012). Readers' use of source information in text comprehension. *Memory & Cognition, 40*, 450–465.

Brand-Gruwel, S., & Wopereis, I. (2006). Integration of the information problem-solving skill in an educational programme: The effects of learning with authentic tasks. *Technology, Instruction, Cognition, and Learning, 4*, 243–263.

Bråten, I., Braasch, J.L.G., Strømsø, H.I., & Ferguson, L.E. (2015). Establishing trustworthiness when students read multiple documents containing conflicting scientific evidence. *Reading Psychology, 36*, 315–349.

Bråten, I., Britt, M.A., Strømsø, H.I., & Rouet, J.F. (2011). The role of epistemic beliefs in the comprehension of multiple expository texts: Toward an integrated model. *Educational Psychologist, 46*, 48–70.

Bråten, I., Ferguson, L.E., Strømsø, H.I., & Anmarkrud, Ø. (2014). Students working with multiple conflicting documents on a scientific issue: Relations between epistemic cognition while reading and sourcing and argumentation in essays. *British Journal of Educational Psychology, 84*, 58–85.

Bråten, I., Salmerón, L., & Strømsø, H.I. (2016). Who said that? Investigating the plausibility-induced source focusing assumption with Norwegian undergraduates. *Contemporary Educational Psychology, 46*, 253–262.

Bråten, I., Strømsø, H.I., & Andreassen, R. (2016). Sourcing in professional education: Do text factors make any difference? *Reading and Writing, 29*, 1599–1628.

Bråten, I., Strømsø, H.I., & Britt, M.A. (2009). Trust matters: Examining the role of source evaluation in students' construction of meaning within and across multiple texts. *Reading Research Quarterly, 44*, 6–28.

Bråten, I., Strømsø, H.I., & Salmerón, L. (2011). Trust and mistrust when students read multiple information sources about climate change. *Learning and Instruction, 21*, 180–192.

Brem, S.K., Russell, J., & Weems, L. (2001). Science on the Web: Student evaluations of scientific arguments. *Discourse Processes, 32*, 191–213.

Britt, M.A., & Aglinskas, C. (2002). Improving students' ability to identify and use source information. *Cognition and Instruction, 20*, 485–522.

Britt, M.A., & Gabrys, G.L. (2000). Teaching advanced literacy skills for the World Wide Web. In C.R. Wolfe (Ed.), *Learning and teaching on the World Wide Web* (pp. 73–90). San Diego, CA: Academic Press.

Britt, M.A., Perfetti, C.A., Sandak, R., & Rouet, J.F. (1999). Content integration and source separation in learning from multiple texts. In S.R. Goldman, A.C. Graesser, & P. van den Broek (Eds), *Narrative, comprehension, causality, and coherence: Essays in honor of Tom Trabasso* (pp. 209–233). Mahwah, NJ: Erlbaum.

Britt, M.A., Richter, T., & Rouet, J.F. (2014). Scientific literacy: The role of goal-directed reading and evaluation in understanding scientific information. *Educational Psychologist, 49*, 104–122.

Britt, M.A., & Rouet, J.F. (2012). Learning with multiple documents: Component skills and their acquisition. In J.R. Kirby & M.J. Lawson (Eds), *Enhancing the quality of learning: Dispositions, instruction, and learning processes* (pp. 276–314). New York, NY: Cambridge University Press.

Britt, M.A., Rouet, J.F., & Braasch, J.L.G. (2013). Documents experienced as entities: Extending the situation model theory of comprehension. In M.A. Britt, S.R. Goldman, & J.F. Rouet (Eds), *Reading from words to multiple texts* (pp. 160–179). New York, NY: Routledge.

Bromme, R., & Goldman, S. (2014). The public's bounded understanding of science. *Educational Psychologist, 49*, 59–69.

Bromme, R., Stadtler, M., Scharrer, L., & Thomm, E. (2015). *A scientist through and through? How the source's commitment to science affects readers' evaluation of source and content in the domain of medicine.* Paper presented at the Annual Meeting of the Society for Text and Discourse, Minneapolis, MN, USA.

Caldwell-Harris, C.L. (2015). Emotionality differences between a native and foreign language: Implications for everyday life. *Current Directions in Psychological Science, 24*, 214–219.

Calkins, S., & Kelley, M.R. (2010). Evaluating internet and scholarly sources across the disciplines: Two case studies. *College Teaching, 55*, 151–156.

Chaiken, S. (1987). The heuristic model of persuasion. In M.P. Zanna, J.M. Olson, & C.P. Herman (Eds), *Social influence: The Ontario Symposium* (Vol. 5, pp. 3–39). Hillsdale, NJ: Erlbaum.

Chakraborty, R., Rao, H.R., & Uphadhyahy, S.J. (2009). *BANDES: An adaptive decision support system for protecting online privacy for senior citizen centers.* Paper presented at the fourth Pre-ICIS Workshop on Information Security & Privacy.

Chen, S., & Chaiken, S. (1999). The Heuristic-Systematic Model in its broader context. In S. Chaiken & Y. Trope (Eds), *Dual-process theories in social psychology* (pp. 73–96). New York, NY: Guilford.

Clément, F. (2016). Social cognition. In J.A. Greene, W.A. Sandoval, & I. Bråten (Eds), *Handbook of epistemic cognition* (pp. 86–99). New York, NY: Routledge.

Coiro, J., Coscarelli, C., Maykel, C., & Forzani, E. (2015). Investigating criteria that seventh graders use to evaluate the quality of online information. *Journal of Adolescent & Adult Literacy, 59*, 287–297.

Colwell, J., Hunt-Barron, S., & Reinking, D. (2013). Obstacles to developing digital literacy on the Internet in middle school science instruction. *Journal of Literacy Research, 45*, 295–324.

Corriveau, K.H., & Harris, P.L. (2009). Choosing your informant: Weighing familiarity and recent accuracy. *Developmental Science, 12*, 426–437.

Dede, C. (2008). A seismic shift in epistemology. *Educause, 43*, 80–81.

De La Paz, S., & Felton, M.F. (2010). Reading and writing from multiple source documents in history: Effects of strategy instruction with low to average high school writers. *Contemporary Educational Psychology, 35*, 174–192.

De Pereyra, G., Belkadi, S., Marbach, L., & Rouet, J.F. (2014, August). *Do teenage readers' use source information when faced with discrepant information?* Paper presented at the Annual Meeting of the Society for Text and Discourse, Chicago, IL, USA.

Dunlosky, J., & Metcalfe, J. (2009). *Metacognition.* Los Angeles, CA: Sage.

Eastin, M.S., Yang, M.-S., & Nathanson, A.I. (2006). Children of the Net: An empirical exploration into the evaluation of internet content. *Journal of Broadcasting & Electronic Media, 50*, 211–230.

Flanagin, A.J., & Metzger, M.J. (2003). The perceived credibility of personal Web page information as influenced by the sex of the source. *Computers in Human Behavior, 19*, 683–701.

Flanagin, A.J., & Metzger, M.J. (2008). Digital media and youth: Unparalleled opportunity and unprecedented responsibility. In M.J. Metzger & A.J. Flanagin (Eds), *Digital media, youth, and credibility* (pp. 5–27). Cambridge, MA: The MIT Press.

Flanagin, A.J., & Metzger, M.J. (2011). From Encyclopaedia Britannica to Wikipedia. *Information, Communication, & Society, 14*, 355–374.

Francke, H., & Sundin, O. (2009). Format agnostics or format believers? How students in high school use genre to assess credibility. *Proceedings of the American Society for Information Science and Technology, 46*, 1–7.

Frederick, S. (2005). Cognitive reflection and decision making. *Journal of Economic Perspectives, 19*(4), 25–42.

Gerhart, S. (2004). Do Web search engines suppress controversy? *First Monday, 9*(1). Retrieved from http://firstmonday.org/article/view/1111/1031.

Gerjets, P., & Hellenthal-Schorr, T. (2008). Competent information search in the World Wide Web: Development and evaluation of a web training for pupils. *Computers in Human Behavior, 24*, 693–715.

Gerjets, P., Kammerer, Y., & Werner, B. (2011). Measuring spontaneous and instructed evaluation processes during web search: Integrating concurrent thinking-aloud protocols and eye-tracking data. *Learning and Instruction, 21*, 220–231.

Goldman, S.R., Braasch, J.L.G., Wiley, J., Graesser, A.C., & Brodowinska, K. (2012). Comprehending and learning from Internet sources: Processing patterns of better and poorer learners. *Reading Research Quarterly, 47*, 356–381.

Goldman, S.R., Ozuru, Y., Braasch, J.L.G., Manning, F.H., Lawless, K.A., Gomez, K.W., & Slanovits, M.J. (2011). Literacies for learning: A multiple source comprehension illustration. In N.L. Stein & S.W. Raudenbush (Eds), *Developmental cognitive science goes to school* (pp. 30–44). New York, NY: Routledge.

Gottlieb, E., & Wineburg, S. (2012). Between *veritas* and *communitas*: Epistemic switching in the reading of academic and sacred history. *The Journal of the Learning Sciences, 21*, 84–129.

Graesser, A.C., Wiley, J., Goldman, S.R., O'Reilly, T., Jeon, M., & McDaniels, B. (2007). SEEK Web Tutor: Fostering a critical stance while exploring the causes of volcanic eruption. *Metacognition and Learning, 2*, 89–105.

Granka, L.A., Joachims, T., & Gay, G. (2004). Eye-tracking analysis of user behavior in WWW search. In M. Sanderson, K. Järvelin, J. Allan, & P. Bruza (Eds), *Proceedings of the 27th Annual International ACM SIGIR Conference on Research and Development in Information Retrieval* (pp. 478–479). New York, NY: Association for Computing Machinery.

Greenspan, S., Loughlin, G., & Black, R.S. (2001). Credulity and gullibility in people with developmental disorders: A framework for future research. *International Review of Research in Mental Retardation, 24*, 101–135.

Harris, P.L. (2007). Trust. *Developmental Science, 10*, 135–138.

Higgins, J.A., & Johnson, M.K. (2012). Some thoughts on the interaction between perception and reflection. In J.M. Wolfe & L. Robertson (Eds), *From perception to consciousness: Searching with Anne Treisman* (pp. 390–397). New York, NY: Oxford University Press.

Iding, M.K., Crosby, M.E., Auernheimer, B., & Klemm, E.B. (2009). Web site credibility: Why do people believe what they believe? *Instructional Science, 37*, 43–63.

Johnson, F., Sbaffi, L., & Rowley, J. (2016). Students' approaches to the evaluation of digital information: Insights from their trust judgments. *British Journal of Educational Technology, 47*, 1243–1258.

Johnson, M.K., & Hirst, W. (1993). MEM: Memory subsystems as processes. In A.F. Collins, S.E. Gathercole, M.A. Conway, & P.E. Morris (Eds), *Theories of memory* (pp. 241–286). Sussex, UK: Erlbaum.

Kammerer, Y., Amann, D.G., & Gerjets, P. (2015). When adults without university education search the Internet for health information: The roles of Internet-specific epistemic beliefs and a source evaluation intervention. *Computers in Human Behavior, 48*, 297–309.

Kammerer, Y., Bråten, I., Gerjets, P., & Strømsø, H.I. (2013). The role of Internet-specific epistemic beliefs in laypersons' source evaluations and decisions during Web search on a medical issue. *Computers in Human Behavior, 29*, 1193–1203.

Kammerer, Y., & Gerjets, P. (2012). Effects of search interface and Internet-specific epistemic beliefs on source evaluations during Web search for medical information: An eye-tracking study. *Behaviour & Information Technology, 31*, 83–97.

Kammerer, Y., & Gerjets, P. (2014a). Quellenbewertungen und Quellenverweise beim Lesen und Zusammenfassen wissenschaftsbezogener Informationen aus multiplen Webseiten. *Unterrichtswissenschaft, 42*, 7–23.

Kammerer, Y., & Gerjets, P. (2014b). The role of search result position and source trustworthiness in the selection of web search results when using a list or a grid interface. *International Journal of Human-Computer Interaction, 30*, 177–191.

Kammerer, Y., Kalbfell, E., & Gerjets, P. (2016). Is this information source commercially biased? How contradictions between web pages stimulate the consideration of source information. *Discourse Processes, 53*, 430–456.

Keil, F.C., Stein, C., Webb, L., Billings V.D., & Rozenblit, L. (2008). Discerning the division of cognitive labor: An emerging understanding of how knowledge is clustered in other minds. *Cognitive Science, 32*, 259–300.

Kendeou, P. (2014). Validation and comprehension: An integrated overview. *Discourse Processes, 51*, 189–200.

Keysar, B., Hayakawa, S.L., & An, S.G. (2012). The foreign-language effect: Thinking in a foreign tongue reduces decision biases. *Psychological Science, 23*, 661–668.

Kiili, C., Laurinen, L., & Marttunen, M. (2008). Students evaluating Internet sources: From versatile evaluators to uncritical readers. *Journal of Educational Computing Research, 39*, 75–95.

Knobloch-Westerwick, S., Johnson, B.K., Silver, N.A., & Westerwick, A. (2015). Science exemplars in the eye of the beholder: How exposure to online science information affects attitudes. *Science Communication, 37*, 575–601.

Koenig, M., & Harris, P.L. (2005). Preschoolers mistrust ignorant and inaccurate speakers. *Child Development, 76*, 1261–1277.

Kopp, K.J. (2013). *Selecting and using information from multiple documents during argumentation.* Doctoral dissertation, Northern Illinois University.

Kortum, P., Edwards, C., & Richards-Kortum, R. (2008). The impact of inaccurate internet health information in a secondary school learning environment. *Journal of Medical Internet Research, 10, e17.* Retrieved from www.jmir.org/2008/2/e17.

Kuiper, E., Volman, M., & Terwel, J. (2008). Integrating critical Web skills and content knowledge: Development and evaluation of a 5th-grade educational program. *Computers in Human Behavior, 24*, 666–692.

Kuiper, E., Volman, M., & Terwel, J. (2009). Developing Web literacy in collaborative inquiry activities. *Computers & Education, 52*, 668–680.

Leu, D.J., Kinzer, C.K., Coiro, J., Castek, J., & Henry, L.A. (2013). New literacies: A dual-level theory of the changing nature of literacy, instruction, and assessment. In D.E. Alvermann, N.J. Unrau, & R.B. Ruddell (Eds), *Theoretical models and processes of reading* (6th ed., pp. 1150–1181). Newark, DE: International Reading Association.

Leu, D., Reinking, D., Carter, A., Castek, J., Coiro, J., Henry, L.A., . . . Zawilinski, L. (2007). *Defining online reading comprehension: Using think aloud verbal protocols to refine a preliminary model of Internet reading comprehension processes.* Paper presented at the Annual Meeting of the American Educational Research Association, Chicago, IL.

Leu, D.J., Zawilinski, L., Forzani, E., & Timbrell, N. (2014). Best practices in teaching the new literacies of online research and comprehension. In L.B. Gambrell & L.M. Morrow (Eds), *Best practices in literacy instruction* (pp. 343–364). New York, NY: Guilford.

Lewandowski, D. (2011). The influence of commercial intent of search results on their perceived relevance. In H. Bruce & J. Grudin (Eds), *iConference 2011 Proceedings* (pp. 452–458). New York, NY: Association for Computing Machinery.

Lorenzen, M. (2001). The land of confusion? High school students and their use of the World Wide Web for research. *Research Strategies, 18*, 151–163.

Lucassen, T., Muilwijk, R., Noordzij, M.L., & Schraagen, J.M. (2013). Topic familiarity and information skills in online credibility evaluation. *Journal of the American Society for Information Science and Technology, 64*, 254–264.

Lundeberg, M.A. (1987). Metacognitive aspects of reading comprehension: Studying understanding in legal case analysis. *Reading Research Quarterly, 22*, 407–432.

Macedo-Rouet, M., Braasch, J.L.G., Britt, M.A., & Rouet, J.F. (2013). Teaching fourth and fifth graders to evaluate information sources during text comprehension. *Cognition and Instruction, 31*, 204–226.

Maggioni, L., & Fox, E. (2009). *Adolescents' reading of multiple history texts: An interdisciplinary investigation of historical thinking, intertextual reading, and domain-specific epistemic beliefs.* Paper presented at the Annual Meeting of the American Educational Research Association, San Diego, CA.

Maier, J., & Richter, T. (2013). Text-belief consistency effects in the comprehension of multiple texts with conflicting information. *Cognition and Instruction, 31*, 151–175.

Mansell, P., & Read, J. (2009). Posttraumatic stress disorder, drug companies, and the Internet. *Journal of Trauma & Dissociation, 10*, 9–23.

Mason, L., Junyent, A.A., & Tornatora, M.C. (2014). Epistemic evaluation and comprehension of web-source information on controversial science-related topics: Effects of a short-term instructional intervention. *Computers & Education, 76*, 143–157.

McCrudden, M.T., Stenseth, T., Bråten, I., & Strømsø, H.I. (2016). The effects of author expertise and content relevance on document selection: A mixed methods study. *Journal of Educational Psychology, 108*, 147–162.

McNamara, D.S., & Magliano, J. (2009). Toward a comprehensive model of comprehension. *Psychology of Learning and Motivation, 51*, 297–384.

Metzger, M.J., Flanagin, A.J., Markov, A., Grossman, R., & Bulger, M. (2015). Believing the unbelievable: Understanding young people's information literacy beliefs and practices in the United States. *Journal of Children and Media, 9*, 325–348.

Miller, A.G., McHoskey, J.W., Bane, C.M., & Dowd, T.G. (1993). The attitude polarization phenomenon: Role of response measure, attitude extremity, and behavioral consequences of reported attitude change. *Journal of Personality and Social Psychology, 64*, 561–574.

Nokes, J. (2014). Elementary school students' roles and epistemic stances during document-based history lessons. *Theory & Research in Social Education, 42*, 375–413.

Nokes, J., Dole, J., & Hacker, D.J. (2007). Teaching high school students to be critical and strategic readers of historical texts. *Journal of Educational Psychology, 99*, 492–504.

Pan, B., Hembrooke, H., Joachims, T., Lorigo, L., Gay, G., & Granka, L. (2007). In Google we trust: Users' decisions on rank, position, and relevance. *Journal of Computer-Mediated Communication, 12*, 801–823.

Perfetti, C.A., Rouet, J.F., & Britt, M.A. (1999). Toward a theory of documents representation. In H. Van Oostendorp & S.R. Goldman (Eds), *The construction of mental representation during reading* (pp. 99–122). Mahwah, NJ: Erlbaum.

Petty, R.E., & Briñol, P. (2012). The Elaboration Likelihood Model. In P.A.M. Van Lange, A. Kruglanski, & E.T. Higgins (Eds), *Handbook of theories of social psychology* (Vol. 1, pp. 224–245). London: Sage.

Petty, R.E., & Cacioppo, J.T. (1986). *Communication and persuasion: Central and peripheral routes to attitude change.* New York, NY: Springer.

Petty, R.E., & Wegener, D.T. (1999). The Elaboration Likelihood Model: Current status and controversies. In S. Chaiken & Y. Trope (Eds), *Dual-process theories in social psychology* (pp. 41–72). New York, NY: Guilford.

Pornpitakpan, C. (2004). The persuasiveness of source credibility: A critical review of five decades' evidence. *Journal of Applied Social Psychology, 34*, 243–281.

Purcell, K., Rainie, L., Heaps, A., Buchanan, J., Friedrich, L., Jacklin, A., . . . Zickuhr, K. (2012). *How teens do research in the digital world.* Washington, DC: Pew Internet & American Life Project.

Reisman, A. (2012). A document-based history curriculum intervention in urban high schools. *Cognition and Instruction, 30*, 86–112.

Regan, A., Shan, L., Mcconnon, Á., Marcu, A., Raats, M., Wall, P., & Barnett, J. (2014). Strategies for dismissing dietary risks: Insights from user-generated comments online. *Health, Risk & Society, 16*, 308–322.

Richter, T., & Rapp, D.N. (2014). Comprehension and validation of text information. *Discourse Processes, 51*, 1–6.

Rouet, J.F. (2006). *The skills of document use: From text comprehension to Web-based learning.* Mahwah, NJ: Erlbaum.

Rouet, J.F., & Britt, M.A. (2011) Relevance processes in multiple documents comprehension. In M.T. McCrudden, J.P. Magliano, & G. Schraw (Eds), *Text relevance and learning from text* (pp. 19–52). Charlotte, NC: Information Age.

Rouet, J.F., Britt, M.A., Mason, R.A., & Perfetti, C.A. (1996). Using multiple sources of evidence to reason about history. *Journal of Educational Psychology, 88*, 478–493.

Rouet, J.F., Favart, M., Britt, M.A., & Perfetti, C.A. (1997). Studying and using multiple documents in history: Effects of discipline expertise. *Cognition and Instruction, 15*, 85–106.

Rouet, J.F., Le Bigot, L., de Pereyra, G., & Britt, M.A. (2016). Whose story is this? Discrepancy triggers readers' attention to source information in short narratives. *Reading and Writing, 29*, 1549–1570.

Rouet, J.F., Ros, C., De Pereyra, G., Macedo-Rouet, M., & Salmerón, L. (2013). *Teeenagers' developing awareness of source quality.* Paper presented at the Annual Meeting of the Society for Text and Discourse, Valencia, Spain.

Salmerón, L., Gil, L., Bråten, I., & Strømsø, H.I. (2010). Comprehension effects of signalling relationships between documents in search engines. *Computers in Human Behavior, 26*, 419–426.

Salmerón, L., Gómez, M., & Fajardo, I. (2016). How students with intellectual disabilities evaluate recommendations from Internet forums. *Reading and Writing, 29*, 1653–1675.

Salmerón, L., Kammerer, Y., & García-Carrión, P. (2013). Searching the Web for conflicting topics: Page and user factors. *Computers in Human Behavior, 29*, 2161–2171.

Salmerón, L., Macedo-Rouet, M., & Rouet, J.F. (2016). Multiple viewpoints increase students' attention to source features in social question and answer forum messages. *Journal of the Association for Information Science and Technology*, *67*, 2404–2419.

Sanchez, C.A., Wiley, J., & Goldman, S.R. (2006). Teaching students to evaluate source reliability during Internet research tasks. In S.A. Barab, K.E. Hay, & D.T. Hickey (Eds), *Proceedings of the Seventh International Conference on the Learning Sciences* (pp. 662–666). Bloomington, IN: International Society of the Learning Sciences.

Shah, C., & Kitzie, V. (2012). Social Q&A and virtual reference: Comparing apples and oranges with the help of experts and users. *Journal of the American Society for Information Science and Technology*, *63*, 2020–2036.

Shanahan, C., Shanahan, T., & Misischia, C. (2011). Analysis of expert readers in three disciplines: History, mathematics, and chemistry. *Journal of Literacy Research*, *43*, 393–429.

Stadtler, M., & Bromme, R. (2007). Dealing with multiple documents on the WWW: The role of metacognition in the formation of documents models. *International Journal of Computer Supported Collaborative Learning*, *2*, 191–210.

Stadtler, M., & Bromme, R. (2008). Effects of the metacognitive computer-tool met.a.ware on the web search of laypersons. *Computers in Human Behavior*, *24*, 716–737.

Stadtler, M., & Bromme, R. (2014). The content-source integration model: A taxonomic description of how readers comprehend conflicting scientific information. In D.N. Rapp & J.L.G. Braasch (Eds), *Processing inaccurate information: Theoretical and applied perspectives from cognitive science and the educational sciences* (pp. 379–402). Cambridge, MA: The MIT Press.

Stadtler, M., Paul, J., Globoschütz, S., & Bromme, R. (2015). Watch out! An instruction raising students' epistemic vigilance augments their sourcing activities. In D.C. Noelle, R. Dale, A.S. Warlaumont, J. Yoshimi, T. Matlock, C.D. Jennings, & P.P. Maglio (Eds), *Proceedings of the Annual Conference of the Cognitive Science Society* (pp. 2278–2283). Austin, TX: Cognitive Science Society.

Stadtler, M., Scharrer, L., Macedo-Rouet, M., Rouet, J.F., & Bromme, R. (2016). Improving vocational students' consideration of source information when deciding about science controversies. *Reading and Writing*, *29*, 705–729.

Stadtler, M., Scharrer, L., Skodzik, T., & Bromme, R. (2014). Comprehending multiple documents on scientific controversies: Effects of reading goals and signaling rhetorical relationships. *Discourse Processes*, *51*, 93–116.

Stadtler, M., Thomm, E., Babiel, S., Hentschke, J., & Bromme, R. (2013). *Ignorant albeit competent: Examining students' sourcing competencies and spontaneous use of source information while reading conflicting scientific texts*. Paper presented at the Workshop on Multiple Document Literacy, Muenster, Germany.

Stahl, S.A., Hynd, C.R., Britton, B.K., McNish, M.M., & Bosquet, D. (1996). What happens when students read multiple source documents in history? *Reading Research Quarterly*, *31*, 430–456.

Steffens, B., Britt, M.A., Braasch, J.L.G., Strømsø, H.I., & Bråten, I. (2014). Memory for scientific arguments and their sources: Claim-evidence consistency matters. *Discourse Processes*, *51*, 117–142.

Strømsø, H.I., & Bråten, I. (2014) Students' sourcing while reading and writing from multiple web documents. *Nordic Journal of Digital Literacy*, *9*, 92–111.

Strømsø, H.I., Bråten, I., & Britt, M.A. (2010). Reading multiple texts about climate change: The relationship between memory for sources and text comprehension. *Learning and Instruction*, *20*, 192–204.

Strømsø, H.I., & Bråten, I., & Britt, M.A. (2011). Do students' beliefs about knowledge and knowing predict their judgment of texts' trustworthiness? *Educational Psychology*, *31*, 177–206.

Strømsø, H.I., Bråten, I., Britt, M.A., & Ferguson, L.E. (2013). Spontaneous sourcing among students reading multiple documents. *Cognition and Instruction*, *31*, 176–203.

Tabak, I. (2016). Functional scientific literacy: Seeing science within the words and across the web. In L. Corno & E.M. Anderman (Eds), *Handbook of educational psychology* (3rd ed.). New York, NY: Routledge.

Van Sledright, B., & Kelly, C. (1998). Reading American history: The influence of multiple sources on six fifth graders. *The Elementary School Journal*, *98*, 239–265.

Van Strien, J.L.H., Brand-Gruwel, S., & Boshuizen, H.P.A. (2014). Dealing with conflicting information from multiple nonlinear texts: Effects of prior attitudes. *Computers in Human Behavior*, *32*, 101–111.

Walraven, A., Brand-Gruwel, S., & Boshuizen, H.P.A. (2008). Information-problem solving: A review of problems students encounter and instructional solutions. *Computers in Human Behavior, 24,* 623–648.

Walraven, A., Brand-Gruwel, S., & Boshuizen, H.P.A. (2009). How students evaluate information and sources when searching the World Wide Web for information. *Computers & Education, 52,* 234–246.

Walraven, A., Brand-Gruwel, S., & Boshuizen, H.P.A. (2013). Fostering students' evaluation behavior while searching the Internet. *Instructional Science, 41,* 125–146.

Weber, K., & Mejia-Ramos, J.P. (2013). The influence of sources in the reading of mathematical text: A reply to Shanahan, Shanahan, and Misischia. *Journal of Literacy Research, 45,* 87–96.

Westerwick, A. (2013). Effects of sponsorship, Web site design, and Google ranking on the credibility of online Information. *Journal of Computer-Mediated Communication, 18,* 80–97.

Wiley, J., Goldman, S.R., Graesser, A.C., Sanchez, C.A., Ash, I.K., & Hemmerich, J.A. (2009). Source evaluation, comprehension, and learning in Internet science inquiry tasks. *American Educational Research Journal, 46,* 1060–1106.

Willemsen, L.M., Neijens, P.C., & Bronner, F. (2012). The ironic effect of source identification on the perceived credibility of online product reviewers. *Journal of Computer-Mediated Communication, 18,* 16–31.

Wineburg, S.S. (1991). Historical problem solving: A study of the cognitive processes used in the evaluation of documentary and pictorial evidence. *Journal of Educational Psychology, 83,* 73–87.

Winter, S., & Krämer, N.C. (2012). Selecting science information in Web 2.0: How source cues, message sidedness, and need for cognition influence users' exposure to blog posts. *Journal of Computer-Mediated Communication, 18,* 80–96.

Wooden, J.A. (2014). *You have to consider the source: An investigation of 8th-grade students using history's sourcing heuristic to learn about America's past.* Doctoral dissertation, University of Maryland. Retrieved from: http://drum.lib.umd.edu/handle/1903/14053.

Wopereis, I., Brand-Gruwel, S., & Vermetten, Y. (2008). The effect of embedded instruction on solving information problems. *Computers in Human Behavior, 24,* 738–752.

Wyatt, D., Pressley, M., El-Dinary, P.B., Stein, S., Evans, P., & Brown, R. (1993). Comprehension strategies, worth and credibility monitoring, and evaluations: Cold and hot cognition when experts read professional articles that are important to them. *Learning and Individual Differences, 5,* 49–72.

Zhang, S., & Duke, N.K. (2011). The impact of instruction in the WWWDOT framework on students' disposition and ability to evaluate web sites as sources of information. *The Elementary School Journal, 112,* 132–154.

10

Discourse Updating
Acquiring and Revising Knowledge through Discourse

Tobias Richter

UNIVERSITY OF WÜRZBURG

Murray Singer

UNIVERSITY OF MANITOBA

Introduction

When readers comprehend a text, they continuously build a representation of the situations and events, termed a situation model. This cognitive activity involves the encoding of new information from the text and its integration with the existing representation and prior knowledge. However, in many cases, new information does not simply add another aspect or element to the existing representation but rather necessitates this representation to be altered in some way or another. This cognitive operation has been called *updating* (e.g., Albrecht & O'Brien, 1993). Consider, for example, a story describing a protagonist's activity followed by a sentence starting with the phrase *Three days later*. This phrase signals a temporal break to readers, prompting them to shift to a new representational structure, in this case a new event in the situation model of the story (Zwaan & Radvansky, 1998). Updating can also be necessitated by conflicting information, such as a character in a story performing an action (*Mary orders a cheeseburger*) that is at odds with a trait ascribed previously to that character (*Mary is a vegetarian*, Albrecht & O'Brien, 1993). Evolving news reports that include some piece of information that is corrected or discredited by later information also require readers to update their situation model of the reported events (Johnson & Seifert, 1994). Finally, text information can conflict with previously held knowledge and beliefs of the reader, potentially causing a more drastic *revision* of this knowledge. The attempt to change students' misconceptions in science education through appropriately designed texts is a case in point (Sinatra & Broughton, 2011).

For comprehension to be successful, readers need to update their mental representations in the appropriate way. Likewise, they need to revise their prior knowledge when new information renders it inaccurate or unreliable. At the same time, there is evidence that readers often do not engage in updating and revision even when they should do so. This chapter examines different instances of updating and knowledge-revision from the integrative perspective of an extended construction-integration model (Kintsch, 1988), which involves the component processes of activation, integration, and validation of information. Starting from an overview of relevant theoretical assumptions, we will discuss the available empirical evidence for when and how readers update or revise existing representations, and when they fail to do so. This discussion will prepare the ground for an outline of basic principles and cognitive processes that contribute to discourse updating and the revision of existing knowledge structures.

Theoretical Frameworks of Comprehension, Updating, and Revision

A thorough treatment of discourse updating must address the scientific methods for evaluating it and must rely on general theories of comprehension. Methods of studying discourse receive thorough treatment by Albert (this volume). Of particular relevance is the section about on-line methods. Other methodological issues will be considered when necessary. Here, we provide an overview of the frameworks that advance theories of updating.

Multiple Levels of Representation

Discourse representation is considered to comprise a verbatim or surface representation of the message, a "proposition" network of the idea units directly expressed in the message, and a representation of the situation to which the message refers (Johnson-Laird, 1983; van Dijk & Kintsch, 1983). This latter situation model integrates discourse information and world knowledge. Furthermore, it bears numerous dimensions, including but not restricted to temporal and spatial information, causation, and characters and their motivations (Zwaan, Magliano, & Graesser, 1995).

Evidence supporting multiple levels of representations converges from many sources. To cite just one example, consider a story with the sentences, *The bear was older than the hawk* and *The hawk was older than the wolf*. After reading, people are faster and more accurate to verify *The bear was older than the wolf* than the explicitly stated sentences. Because only the explicit sentences exactly match the story's surface form (Kintsch & Bates, 1977) and propositional content (Ratcliff & McKoon, 1978), this result must be explained in terms of a situation model representation of the story. Specifically, the more different the animals' ages in that model, the easier it is to distinguish them (Potts, 1972). It is considered that text comprehension results in verbatim, propositional, and situational encoding (van Dijk & Kintsch, 1983).

In addition, the representation levels have different qualities. For example, surface representations decay rapidly whereas situation models are enduring (Kintsch, Welsch, Schmalhofer, & Zimny, 1990; Sachs, 1967). Our treatment of discourse updating will address the different levels, with particular emphasis on the situation model.

The Construction-Integration Model (CI)

This influential model (Kintsch, 1988, 1998) posits two stages of processing of each successive discourse segment. Processing initially involves the *construction* of a network of the propositions stated in the message. Upon reading *The turtle ate lettuce*, its underlying ideas are extracted. However, the construction network is an enriched one: It includes generalizations, such as THE TURTLE WAS FEEDING, as well as ideas linking the current segment to the preceding discourse. The network also includes associated ideas both relevant (e.g., turtles are herbivores) and even irrelevant (turtles walk slowly) to the message.

Then, during *integration*, activation accumulates in the most highly interconnected message elements, effectively eliminating ideas less relevant to the message. A subset of highly activated ideas are retained in working memory as the comprehender proceeds to the next message constituent (Fletcher, 1981; Kintsch & van Dijk, 1978). These processes optimize the coherence of the representation.

The integration phase of CI is increasingly considered to itself comprise multiple phases, including validation and updating. *Validation* refers to the reader's continuous assessment of the accuracy, consistency, and congruence of the evolving message (Nieuwland & Kuperberg, 2008; Schroeder, Richter, & Hoever, 2008; Singer, Halldorson, Lear, & Andrusiak, 1992). Successful validation of novel discourse ideas with reference to the existing message representation and world knowledge enables the updating of the representation (Ferretti, Singer, & Harwood, 2013).

Structure Building

During comprehension, the reader continually initiates and completes structures at all levels of representation (Gernsbacher, 1990; Zwaan & Radvansky, 1998). At the syntactic level, for example, the word *the* routinely initiates a noun phrase. At the other end of the continuum, messages situate their circumstances in terms of specific places and times, and the traits and goals of their participants. Transitions on these dimensions may be signaled by explicit or subtle verbal expressions. Detecting that a narrative character has jumped ahead in time or has achieved an important goal is central to comprehension (Zwaan et al., 1995). Completing one structure and initiating a new one comprise a central aspect of discourse updating.

Relationship to Basic Memory Processes

Comprehension is widely considered to be based on general cognitive mechanisms rather than uniquely linguistic processes (e.g., Kintsch et al., 1990). Regarding updating, it is especially important to distinguish between mechanisms of working memory and long-term memory (LTM). Working memory comprises the active contents of cognition. It coordinates both storage and processing demands and is limited in its total capacity (Baddeley, 1986; Just & Carpenter, 1992; Miller, 1956). In comprehension processing, working memory is updated after every processing cycle to retain a few recent and highly relevant propositions (Fletcher, 1981; Kintsch & van Dijk, 1978).

These working memory updates reflect transitions both of surface and gist representations. Regarding surface structures, for example, people take less time to recognize a test word from the current clause than preceding clauses (Caplan, 1972; Jarvella, 1971). This indicates that when the reader proceeds to a new clause, the words of the preceding clause are purged from working memory (Kintsch & van Dijk, 1978). Accessibility is likewise affected by subtle situational cues. It takes less time to recognize a text word if it is associated with versus dissociated from a character (e.g., *the sweatshirt was pulled on/taken off*, respectively; Glenberg, Meyer, & Lindem, 1987). Likewise, it takes less time to verify that a phrase (*FIX FLAT*) accurately describes a text episode if the *aspect* of the relevant verb suggests that the activity was ongoing versus completed (*she was changing/changed the flat tire*; Magliano & Schleich, 2000). Discourse events such as a character walking through a doorway diminish the accessibility of objects associated with the abandoned location (Radvansky, 2012). These phenomena reflect the continual updating of working memory contents.

The long-term memory system, in contrast, is characterized by features such as a great if not unlimited capacity, effortful and slow retrieval, and the spread of activation among related concepts (e.g., J. R. Anderson, 2005). Memories may reside in long-term memory effectively for a lifetime (Bahrick, 1984). These qualities apply as much to long-term discourse representations as other memories (Ratcliff & McKoon, 1978).

Three fundamental qualities of memory clarify the relation between working memory and long-term memory, and bear special significance for discourse comprehension and updating. First, encoding information to long-term memory is promoted by *elaborative processing*; that is, detecting meaning relationships among ideas. For example, people exhibit better memory for *The fat man read the sign that warned of thin ice* than for *The fat man read the sign that was two feet tall* (Stein & Bransford, 1979). In discourse comprehension, enduring memory is superior when the reader's task emphasizes the consideration of meaning rather than a focus on surface qualities (e.g., proofreading; Mayer & Cook, 1981).

Second, the retrieval of relevant memories is promoted by mental models known as *long-term working memories* (*LT-WM*; Ericsson & Kintsch, 1995). LT-WMs bridge the gap between the very limited capacity of working memory and the need for efficient access to prior discourse ideas. In the language domain, LT-WMs comprise the situation model of the discourse up to the current segment. Effective LT-WMs are promoted by strong reading skills, which foster the construction of integrated situation models (Gernsbacher, Varner, & Faust, 1990; Radvansky & Copeland, 2001; Singer & Ritchot, 1996).

Third, all stimuli function as memory cues for the passive, nonstrategic retrieval of related ideas. The retrieved information is said to resonate to the cues, and it becomes available for integration with the current stimuli. In the comprehension domain, this analysis is called *memory-based text processing*. The elements of each text segment provide retrieval cues for antecedent discourse ideas and relevant world knowledge (McKoon & Ratcliff, 1998; O'Brien, Lorch, & Myers, 1998). As such, both the antecedent discourse representation and *all other memories* are, in principle, eligible to be incorporated in the evolving representation (Hintzman, 1988; Murdock, 1982). Thus, the full contents of working memory guide the continuous *updating* of all levels of text representation. In conclusion, the theoretical analysis of discourse updating draws heavily upon thoroughly evaluated formulations. The present treatment will refer extensively to those formulations.

Situation Model Updating During Comprehension

Surface, propositional, and situation representations must be continuously updated during reading. Two influential research approaches to discourse updating have focused on (a) the construction and refinement of these representational structures during comprehension and (b) the impact on encoding of detecting discourse inconsistencies. Both approaches bear on all representational levels but we will emphasize the situation model.

Constructing and Shifting Among Discourse Structures

Advances in this realm are captured by several complementary accounts: namely, the structure building framework (Gernsbacher, 1990); the event-indexing model (Zwaan, Langston, & Graesser, 1995; Zwaan & Radvansky, 1998); the event segmentation theory (Zacks, Speer,

Swallow, Braver, & Reynolds, 2007); and the event horizon model (Radvansky, 2012). These accounts hold, first, that understanders strive to map new information onto existing mental structures (Gernsbacher, 1990). Mapping is facilitated by syntactic cohesion, in the form of lexical repetition and transparent referential devices. Mapping is also promoted by coherence on situational dimensions such as cause, location, and time.

Conversely, disruptions and deficiencies in referential, causal, temporal, and spatial coherence initiate *shifts* to new structures (Gernsbacher, 1990; Radvansky, 2012). Shifting is cognitively demanding: It requires wrapping up the prior structure (Haberlandt & Graesser, 1985), a form of updating that resolves ambiguities in that structure and consolidates it in the discourse representation. Shifting also entails the initiation of a new structure.

One index of the cognitive demands of structure shifting is text reading time. Shifts can be signaled explicitly. For example, with reference to a lifeguard noticing a struggling child, reading time for *he jumped into the water* is inflated if it is preceded by the adverb, *Next* (Gernsbacher, 1990). This suggests that the adverb initiates a new structure. However, shifts are also routinely signaled semantically or implicitly. If a text describes the start of a marathon, for example, it takes less time to next read *Half an hour later, it began to rain*, which falls within the time frame of a marathon, than *Three days later, it began to rain*, which does not (Gernsbacher, 1990; Zwaan, Magliano et al., 1995). In this example, *Three days later* requires a shift to a new time frame.

Structure Building and Memory Updating

Constructing and shifting among structures continuously updates the contents both of working memory and long-term memory. As discussed earlier, superior word memory for the most recent clause indicates that the wording of prior clauses has been deleted from *working memory* (Jarvella, 1971). It is important that, in these studies, test words in the recent- versus prior-clause conditions were separated from their antecedent by exactly the same string of words. Gernsbacher (1985) observed that these findings therefore favored a structure-shift explanation over a memory-limitation hypothesis. Further evidence extended these phenomena to the comprehension of picture-stories and to transitions not only among syntactic structures but also between story episodes and between entire stories.

Other studies document pervasive and qualitatively varied effects of *situational shifts* on the contents of working memory. In one study, people made faster recognition judgments about objects (e.g., a lamp) in a protagonist's present story location, the reception room, than objects in a previous location, the library (Morrow, Greenspan, & Bower, 1987). Likewise, memory is worse for objects left behind in a different room (a spatial transition) than for those in the current room when people move among real and virtual spaces, holding the distance from the object constant (Radvansky & Copeland, 2006; Radvansky, Krawietz, & Tamplin, 2011).

A perhaps surprising claim is that working memory structures exhibit resistance to updating. Kurby and Zacks (2012) explained that such resistance protects the evolving structure from the impact of transient interruptions and distractions. Consistent with this proposal, when people read a narrative that interweaves two episodes, they spontaneously recall the episodes separately (Gernsbacher, 1990; Mandler, 1978). It would be counterproductive to update an episode in a manner that contaminated its features with those of a different episode.

After a shift, the former structure, although abandoned, becomes part of the evolving *long-term memory* (LTM) representation of the full discourse. In this regard, people can, of course, retrieve many details of messages even at great delays (Kintsch & van Dijk, 1978). The integration of the current segment with discourse information that has largely been backgrounded in LTM is at least partly accommodated by two of the basic memory processes discussed earlier. First, the contents of the current segment cue the full contents of memory (global matching). As a result, LTM antecedents that match this segment resonate to those cues (O'Brien, Rizzella et al., 1998). They are restored to working memory and become integrated with the current segment. Second, complex but well-organized LTM structures such as situation models may reside in the long-term working memory discussed earlier (LT-WM; Ericsson & Kintsch, 1995). Although the individual elements of LT-WMs cannot all be simultaneously active, they are efficiently accessed by suitable cues from working memory (Zwaan & Radvansky, 1998). Kurby and Zacks's (2012) view that *event representations* have a larger capacity than that measured for verbal materials suggests that those representations reside in LT-WM.

It is noteworthy that high-skill readers can construct and capitalize on the complex structures of long-term working memory more effectively than low-skill readers (Gernsbacher et al., 1990; Hannon & Daneman, 2001; Singer & Ritchot, 1996). In this regard, recall that people tend to read more quickly and make judgments more accurately about objects still associated with story characters (*sweatshirt – pulled on*) than dissociated from them (*sweatshirt – took off*) (Glenberg et al., 1987). However, this effect is largely restricted to readers diagnosed in a pretest to be highest in the ability to identify sentences compatible with a prior discourse situation model (Radvansky & Copeland, 2001). These individuals apparently make suitable updates to discourse structures in a manner that optimizes their comprehension of and memory for discourse.

To summarize, several event-oriented theories converge on the view that comprehension involves the continual construction of representational structures and that transitions among these structures require that they be suitably updated. Despite their similarities, these theories exhibit several subtle differences. For example, Radvansky (2012) noted that the event horizon model is inconsistent with some tenets of memory-based text processing. According to the latter view, access to antecedent text ideas is regulated by factors such as the degree of elaboration and distinctiveness of those ideas, and their text distance from the current segment. Beyond the current scope of memory-based processing, however, accessibility is also affected by text signals of a shift in events, even when all text-based variables are held constant. For example, readers exhibit worse memory for an object when they have left its room than when they are the same distance from that object but in a larger room that contains the object (Radvansky & Copeland, 2006). The possible incompatibility between the event horizon model and text-based processing merits further scrutiny.

Another example of differences among the structural theories is that Kurby and Zacks (2012) observed that Zwaan and Radvansky's (1998) event-indexing model demands continual, "incremental" updating on all situational dimensions, whereas the event segmentation theory (Zacks et al., 2007) emphasizes only global updating at major structural transitions. Kurby and Zacks used a variation of the think-aloud method (Albert, this volume) to distinguish these alternatives: They instructed the readers of an extended narrative to record instances of changes on situational dimensions and to segment the narrative into episodes. Their data indicated that readers are sensitive to dimensional changes, beyond those signaled by major episodic changes. They judged that Gernsbacher's (1990) structure building framework accommodates both incremental and global updating.

Detecting Discourse Inconsistency and Situational Updating

Informational inconsistency pervades language communication. In answering a press conference question about Russian involvement in conflicts in Syria, President Barack Obama stated that steps were being taken *so that we're not seeing U.S. AND AMERICAN firefights in the air* (an attentive listener might wonder why U.S. and American pilots might fight one another). As another case, a speaker might erroneously characterize a teenager as exhibiting *"autopsy"* rather than *"autism."* Or a story character might perform incongruent or impossible actions, such as making sandwiches in the absence of bread (Cohen, 1979). When understanders detect these kinds of inconsistencies, what impact does it have on the evolving discourse representation?

The role of inconsistency detection in representational updating has received extensive attention. At a general level, evidence is highly consistent across situational dimensions. In a seminal study documenting the consistency effect (O'Brien & Albrecht, 1992), readers encountered, toward the outset of a text, *Jane waited outside the door of her health club, waiting for the instructor*. Later, they read the target, *The instructor came in*, a statement inconsistent with Jane's location. Target reading times were greater in this condition than when Jane had been described as being inside the club. Likewise, in the temporal domain, it takes longer to read that Claudia was waiting for Markus on the railway platform when Claudia's train was set to arrive after Markus' rather than earlier (Rinck, Hahnel, & Becker, 2001). Regarding character traits, it takes longer to read about Mary ordering a cheeseburger when the text has previously described her as a vegetarian than a junk food fanatic (Albrecht & O'Brien, 1993).

These results confirm that readers monitor discourse congruence, but the findings also bear on knowledge updating in at least two distinct ways. First, detecting text inconsistencies and refutations enables the possible updating both of the message representation and world knowledge. Second, inconsistency detection diagnoses whether prior discourse ideas have been previously updated. We focus on the latter issue here, and the former issue later.

Diagnosing Prior Updating

Researchers have asked whether novel text information completely displaces prior inconsistent information or whether the outdated information continues to influence comprehension. In one familiar paradigm, critical sentences are either consistent or inconsistent with prior ideas: For example, ordering a cheeseburger is consistent with loving junk food but not healthier food. In an additional, crucial condition, ordering a cheeseburger invokes previously *qualified* information. Such qualifications include describing a character as a vegetarian who eats meat in restaurants or even as a *former* vegetarian (Albrecht & O'Brien, 1993). In the extreme, the qualification could be that the crucial information ("vegetarian") was a joke or a lie (O'Brien, Rizzella, Albrecht, & Halleran, 1998).

In these studies, reading times for the target sentence about ordering a cheeseburger have regularly been longer in the inconsistent than the qualified condition. However, the critical comparison is between the qualified and consistent conditions. According to the full-updating view posited by a *here-and-now* analysis, those reading times should be approximately equal (Morrow et al., 1987; Zwaan & Radvansky, 1998). That is, were it unequivocally encoded that Mary is no longer a vegetarian, then ordering a cheeseburger would be no more inconsistent with the reader's knowledge than if she had never been one. In contrast, a *memory-based text processing* view predicts that reading times in the qualified condition will exceed consistent ones, on the rationale that even outdated information continues to reside in long-term memory to influence comprehension.

Typically, evidence has supported the memory-based prediction: That is, reading is slowed when a former vegetarian orders a cheeseburger, relative to when the character never was one (Albrecht & O'Brien, 1993; O'Brien, Cook, & Guéraud, 2010; O'Brien, Rizzella et al., 1998). In contrast, evidence from Zwaan and Madden (2004) favored the here-and-now view. However, O'Brien et al. (2010) observed that some of Zwaan and Madden's critical concepts appeared at the end of their sentences, a position at which wrap-up processing might obscure differences between the consistent and qualified reading times. Using materials that avoided this problem, O'Brien et al. (2010) again documented greater qualified than consistent reading times.

Situational Dimensions of Consistency and Updating

Ostensibly, updating ought to proceed similarly for different dimensions of the situation model. However, the dimensions might differ in their relative importance to a message. Causal and motivational structures are particularly essential to message meaning (e.g., Schank & Abelson, 1977; Trabasso, Secco, & van den Broek, 1984), whereas spatial details, for example, may be more tangential (e.g., Zwaan & van Oostendorp, 1994). Dimensional differences might thus influence the degree to which revisions and inconsistencies impact updating.

In this regard, researchers have documented informative relations between character-trait information and *causes* pertaining to these traits. Consider a character named Albert whose shoes are buried under magazines and laundry, suggesting that he is messy. Participants in Rapp and Kendeou (2009) read about such situations. In one condition, called a "causal refutation," the text explained this circumstance by stating that Albert had just moved into his apartment. Immediately after the refutation, participants had to make a lexical decision about the relevant trait word, *messy*. Response time was greater in the presence than in the absence of a prior causal refutation. This suggested that causal refutations relatively deactivate the trait, inflating lexical decision time. This represents an instance of updating. Equally important, reading times for a subsequent sentence which portrayed Albert as behaving messily were *greater* with the prior refutation of Albert's messiness than without it. That is, an early refutation of Albert's messiness made subsequent sloppy behavior seem incongruent with the message meaning. The early updating of his character had a continued impact later in the text. It is noteworthy that a simple, noncausal refutation did not have this effect, such as the assertion that Albert was usually neat and that this circumstance was an exception (Rapp & Kendeou, 2009, Experiment 2; also see Mensink & Rapp, 2011).

Likewise, reading the causal explanation that Mary abandoned vegetarianism *because of her doctor's advice* resulted in participants needing no more time to subsequently read that she ordered a cheeseburger than in a *consistent* condition in which she is a junk food fanatic (Kendeou, Smith, & O'Brien, 2013; cf. O'Brien et al., 2010).

Conclusion

Updating is an essential, ongoing process of text comprehension. As a reader proceeds through a text, representational structures at the syntactic, propositional, and situational levels are continually initiated and completed. These transitions regulate the updating of the contents of both working memory and long-term memory in a manner that optimizes comprehension.

Detection of text inconsistencies constitute an important, special aspect of updating. Inconsistencies may appear at the syntactic level, such as when the reader must reanalyze a "garden-path" sentence such as *Sally ate up the street*. Alternatively, they may comprise situational inconsistencies or blatant contradictions of meaning. In either event, processes are initiated either to correct the inconsistency or to reconcile the contradictory facts.

Revision of Established Memories through Learning from Text

Encountering new information in a text can lead both to an updating of the current situation model and to a revision of knowledge stored in long-term memory. Such representations need to meet two seemingly antithetic criteria to be functional: They need to be stable over time, but also to be updated flexibly when new information challenges their validity (Ecker, Swire, & Lewandowsky, 2014; Schroeder et al., 2008). Research on the continued influence of misinformation (Johnson & Seifert, 1994) and on conceptual change (Vosniadou, 1994) describes situations in which stability wins over flexible updating: Readers often stick to acquired information even if this information has been discredited or corrected explicitly. In contrast, research on the impact of narrative texts on world knowledge and beliefs suggests that stories are particularly effective in changing mental representations, including the creation of misconceptions (Marsh, Meade, & Roediger, 2003).

Continued Influence of Misinformation

In a series of insightful experiments, Wilkes and Leatherbarrow (1988) had participants read a series of news messages about a warehouse fire that mentioned cans of paint and gas cylinders in the room where the fire started and other details inviting an inference that the paint and the gas had caused the fire. However, for one group of participants, the original information was explicitly corrected by a later message stating that the closet where the paint and the gas was usually kept was empty on that day. Interestingly, when asked open questions about the event described in the messages, participants who had received the correction were as likely to mention the paint and the gas as possible causes of the fire as were participants who had not received it, despite the fact that they accurately recalled the corrective message as well. This is reminiscent of the finding that readers of the garden-path (i.e., temporarily ambiguous) sentence, *While* Anna dressed the baby *spit up on the bed*, may misinterpret the sentence as meaning that Anna dressed the baby rather than herself (Ferreira, Christianson, & Hollingworth, 2001).

The participants in Wilkes and Leatherbarrow (1988) also based inferences about other aspects of the event on the misinformation. Several experiments based on variants of this paradigm have yielded highly similar results (e.g., Ecker, Lewandowsky, & Tang, 2010; Johnson & Seifert, 1994). In addition, experiments in social psychology on the perseverance of beliefs despite the presence of invalidating information support the continued influence of misinformation (e.g., C. A. Anderson, Lepper, & Ross, 1980; Ross, Lepper, Strack, & Steinmetz, 1977). For example, Ross et al. found that participants continue to embrace information from clinical case studies even if they learned later that this information was unsubstantiated.

Why and when do readers fail to revise mental representations in the light of correcting information? Interpreting their own results, Wilkes and Leatherbarrow (1988) suggested that despite the fact that readers recognized and remembered the correction, they were unable to alter the inferences they had made based on the original misinformation. However, Johnson and Seifert (1994) found that the misinformation showed a continued influence even if the correction was given immediately after the misinformation, which makes an influence on later inferences unlikely. Instead, they proposed that the central role of the misinformation in an explanation of the described events is crucial for the misinformation effect to occur. As long as no plausible alternative to the potential cause of the warehouse fire is available, the cans and gas cylinders keep their position on top of the causal chain organizing the situation model, even though their existence is denied by the corrective message. In fact, when Johnson and Seifert provided their participants with the potential alternative explanation that arson might have led to the warehouse fire, the correction was more effective in reducing inferences based on the misinformation.

Experiments on belief perseverance provide additional evidence that misinformation continues to be influential if it is integrated in a causal situation model of the described events. For example, C. A. Anderson et al. (1980) gave their participants case studies on the relationship between risk-taking and professional performance of firefighters. One group of participants provided written explanations of why such a relationship might occur. Later on, participants were debriefed that the case studies were purely fictitious. The instruction to generate explanations increased the degree to which participants still endorsed the belief that risk-taking and the performance of firefighters were related in the way described in the case studies (for similar results, see C. A. Anderson, 1983; Ross et al., 1977). Self-generated explanations for discredited information, which promote situation model construction through elaborative processing, seem to be even more effective in creating continued influence of misinformation than explanations provided by others (Davies, 1997). In contrast, generating explanations for alternative states of affairs can reduce misinformation effects (C. A. Anderson & Sechler, 1986).

In summary, integration of misinformation as a cause or an outcome in a causal situation model makes it more resistant to correction, whereas helping readers to construct an alternative causal situation model seems to be an effective way to counter the continued influence of misinformation. The latter conclusion converges with the findings by Rapp and Kendeou (2009) that causal refutations are particularly effective for updating during comprehension (see the section on Detecting Discourse Inconsistency and Situational Updating). However, a problem arises when no simple alternative explanation is available, as it is often the case when scientific accounts of complex phenomena compete with simple but incorrect pseudo-explanations. In such cases, the misinformation is likely to prevail even when readers know in principle that it is wrong.

What are the cognitive processes that mediate the continued influence of misinformation? Ecker et al. (2014) sketched a dual process model positing that misinformation effects occur when readers rely on passive memory processes to assess the plausibility of information but fail to apply strategic processes to monitor the accuracy of this assessment. The model is based on observations that individuals use metacognitive experiences such as the familiarity of information or the ease of retrieval as a heuristic to assess its plausibility (e.g., Schwarz, 2004). For example, when some piece of misinformation is tightly integrated in a causal situation model or in a network of a reader's beliefs, it is likely to be easily accessible and will be activated automatically by associated concepts, which will increase its subjective plausibility. Likewise, statements that have been encountered repeatedly are perceived as more plausible (truth effect, Dechêne, Stahl, Hansen, & Wänke, 2010). The positive effects of repetition on plausibility can occur even if the repetition is coupled with an explicit retraction of the information (e.g., Skurnik, Yoon, Park, & Schwarz, 2005). One way to explain these backfire effects for retractions is that the retracted information might be tagged as "false" in memory but activated later on without the "false" tag. In this case, comprehenders tend to accept false information as being true, especially when they lack the cognitive resources to process the information strategically. Supporting this assumption, Gilbert, Krull, and Malone (1990) demonstrated a confirmation bias when readers verified fantasy facts (e.g., *A Twyrin is a doctor*) that they had learned earlier together with a "true" or "false" label and under cognitive load. However, it should be noted that the confirmation bias occurs only for information that readers cannot validate based on their prior knowledge (Richter, Schroeder, & Wöhrmann, 2009) and when they are unable to establish a plausible alternative situation model of the negated state of affairs (Hasson, Simmons, & Todorov, 2005).

Conceptual Change

In educational and developmental psychology, problems similar to the continued influence of misinformation have been studied under the label of conceptual change. Conceptual change is a kind of learning that involves the revision or restructuring of existing preconceptions or misconceptions rather than enriching it or creating completely new knowledge. Most of the research in the area focuses on conceptual change in science learning. The preconceptions studied in conceptual change research are typically not experimentally induced but more or less deeply rooted in an individual's learning history (such as naïve physical concepts acquired in infancy; Vosniadou, 1994). Despite this difference in study topic from work on the continued-influence-of-misinformation effect, there are interesting parallels between the two lines of research. First, preconceptions can often be resistant to change. Second, this resistance to change depends in part on whether these preconceptions form more complex knowledge structures or are embedded in such structures. Third, a plausible and intelligible alternative needs to be presented to correct misconceptions (Posner, Strike, Hewson, & Gertzog, 1982).

Regarding the complexity of the underlying knowledge structures, Chi (2008) distinguished three different types of misconceptions. (1) When a misconception is based on single false beliefs, it can often be changed quite easily by direct refutation (e.g., Chi & Roscoe, 2002). (2) However, when the misconception is based on schema-like knowledge structures or a flawed mental model, a greater number of beliefs need to be changed to replace the mental model with an adequate one. For example, many children hold inadequate mental models about the shape of the earth, including conceptions that the earth is flat or a hollow sphere (Vosniadou & Brewer, 1992). To correct such models, it is insufficient to refute one single belief. Rather, a large number of beliefs that involve related concepts such as gravity, seasonal changes, and the day/night cycle need to be addressed as well. (3) Finally, the misconceptions most difficult to change are those that are based on category mistakes. Such mistakes occur when readers mistakenly think that a central concept belongs to a different branch in a conceptual hierarchy (lateral category) and, therefore, shares few features with the correct category. For example, in learning physics, misconceptions based on the category mistake that heat is an entity rather than a process cannot be corrected by simply refuting it (Chi, 2008).

Both typical expository texts and also persuasive texts that promote the correct alternative often fail to induce conceptual change, in particular if misconceptions are based on flawed mental models or category mistakes. In contrast, refutation texts are more effective in this regard (Guzetti, Snyder, Glass, & Gamas, 1993; Tippett, 2010). Refutation texts explicitly state a misconception, refute it, and provide an elaborate presentation of the correct alternative. For example, a refutation text aimed at correcting the misconception that global warming is caused only by natural causes could first introduce this view, then state that it is based on a misconception and explain why this is the case, and continue with presenting the alternative view about man-made causes of global warming along with scientific evidence. In terms of the comprehension processes outlined earlier in this chapter (Section 2), refutation texts support conceptual change in several ways (Sinatra & Broughton, 2011). First, they activate the misconception through a resonance-like mechanism, without requiring the reader to engage in any kind of strategic and effortful memory retrieval. The co-activation of the misconception and the correct information in working memory makes it likely that readers will notice that the two pieces of information are inconsistent, creating a cognitive conflict. Refutation texts facilitate resolving this conflict by making a plausible and intelligible alternative to the misconception available to the reader. In this regard, a refutation text on Newtonian mechanics promoted longer reading times and more knowledge-based infer-ences for critical sentences in readers who held misconceptions compared to readers without misconceptions, whereas a comparable non-refutation expository text did not produce these effects (Kendeou & van den Broek, 2007).

Acquiring Misinformation and Belief Change through Narrative Texts

Texts not only can be used to convey knowledge and help correct inadequate knowledge and beliefs. Sometimes, people also acquire false information and inadequate beliefs from texts. Social psychologists have a long-standing interest in the impact of persuasive texts that present arguments in favor or against certain claims on recipients' beliefs and attitudes. One tenet of this research is that strong and durable persuasive effects of such texts are quite limited and largely restricted to favorable conditions that include high-quality argu-ments and knowledgeable and motivated recipients (e.g., Petty & Wegener, 1999). Perhaps surprisingly, fictional stories seem to be more effective for conveying false information and changing recipients' beliefs, despite the fact that the authors of these texts do not claim to communicate true information. In one of the first experiments on this issue, Gerrig and Prentice (1991) presented participants with a story about a mock kidnapping that included false statements embedded in conversations between the story characters (e.g., *Most forms of mental illness are contagious*). In a subsequent verification task, participants were slower to reject the false statements. These results indicate that some information was learned from the story that interfered with real-world knowledge in the verification judgments.

Later research extended these results by showing that stories can even influence readers' responses to knowledge questions and belief ratings (Wheeler, Green, & Brock, 1999). In experiments by Marsh et al. (2003), participants read a number of short fictional stories that contained statements that either appeared in a true or false version (e.g., *A sextant/compass is the main tool used at sea to navigate via the stars*). After reading all stories, participants answered general knowledge questions in a cued recall format and indicated whether they knew the answer based on their general world knowledge. For correct story statements, more participants indicated that they had known the correct answer before the experiment, as compared to participants who did not read the story. This illusion of knowing was most pronounced after reading the story twice. More strikingly, however, participants who had read the story with false statements accepted a greater proportion of such statements as being true as compared to participants who had not read the same false statements. Furthermore, a con-siderable portion of these participants indicated that they had "known" the false answer before. At the same time, participants remembered quite well that they had read the false statement in the story. Thus, it seems that readers acquire correct information from fictional stories but that they also acquire false information to some degree. Moreover, the results for participants' source attributions militate against the view that information acquired from stories is stored in a completely compartmentalized way in memory, i.e. separate from general world knowledge. Rather, they suggest a hybrid view according to which both true and false information acquired from stories is integrated in readers' general world knowledge even though the source of the information seems to be retained as well (see also Potts & Peterson, 1985).

One limitation of Marsh et al.'s (2003) experiments is that they did not allow diagnosing misinformation effects on an individual basis. Subsequent work overcame this limitation by measuring prior knowledge in a pretest together with confidence ratings (Fazio, Barber, Rajaram, Ornstein, & Marsh, 2013). Two weeks later, participants read two stories that contained false information such as *Newton invented the theory of relativity* and responded to a knowledge test again. Participants used misinformation acquired from the stories on one fifth of the knowledge questions they had answered correctly in the pretest. Even for knowledge questions that were answered correctly and with high confidence in the pretest, misinformation effects occurred in one tenth of the answers given after reading the stories. In line with Marsh et al.'s (2003) aforementioned hybrid view, Fazio et al. interpreted these effects as intrusions of the misinformation from the stories into the knowledge tests rather than complete revisions of the original knowledge.

Again, for misinformation effects to occur, it may be crucial for the misinformation to have been processed recently and appear familiar to the reader. This interpretation is backed up by findings that misinformation effects decline when the knowledge test is applied after a delay of several weeks, which should reduce the recency of misinformation (Marsh et al., 2003, Experiment 3; but see Appel & Richter, 2007, for contrary results). Regarding the moderating role of familiarity, research by Rapp, Hinze, Slaten, and Horton (2014) is informative. These authors varied the familiarity of misinformation by presenting inaccurate statements either in a realistic or unrealistic (fantasy) story context. The unrealistic context greatly reduced the use of misinformation on a later knowledge test. Similarly, the plausibility of misinformation matters with respect to readers' uptake of false information (Hinze, Slaten, Horton, Jenkins, & Rapp, 2014).

While the misinformation effect through stories is well established, research on the cognitive processes during reading that might explain these effects is still scarce. Experiments by Rapp (2008, Experiments 1 and 2) shed light on the question of whether readers' acquisition of misinformation from stories might be a result of a failure to detect them while reading the story. In these experiments, participants read short stories that described historical events either in a way that conformed to readers' expectations, or in a way that suggested that the historical events might also have taken another turn, creating a suspenseful context. For example, one suspenseful story indicated that George Washington had doubts as to whether he should accept the offer to become president of the United States and seriously thought about retiring. A target sentence then described the historically correct outcome (*George Washington was elected First President of the United States*) or a counterfactual, historically incorrect outcome (*George Washington was not elected First President of the United States*). Reading times were longer for the historically incorrect than correct outcomes, indicating that readers detected the inconsistency given their prior knowledge. However, the suspenseful context reduced the penalty for inconsistent sentences, suggesting that stories may modulate the way readers use their world knowledge in validating the information communicated by the story. Importantly, reading tasks that promote the retrieval of accurate world knowledge when people read a story (such as the task to correct false information, Rapp, Hinze, Kohlhepp, & Ryskin, 2014) can greatly reduce the use of incorrect information in a later knowledge test. Thus, in principle, readers are able to protect themselves against the impact of misinformation by strategically recruiting their world knowledge for scrutinizing the veracity of story information.

Overall, these findings suggest that stories induce a kind of "suspension of disbelief" (Coleridge, 1817/1907) that might explain their power to shape readers' view of the world. To describe the psychological state that brings about this suspension of disbelief while reading stories, Gerrig (1993) proposed the metaphorical concept of transportation, which means that readers undertake a mental journey into the world of a narrative, with the result that "all mental systems and capacities become focused on the events occurring in the narrative" (Green & Brock, 2000, p. 701). The state of transportation is conceived of as a rather broad experiential state of being lost in a story (Nell, 1988), incorporating attentional and cognitive processes, imagery, and emotional reactions (e.g., Green, 2004; Green & Brock, 2000). Transportation is typically measured with a self-report scale developed by Green and Brock (2000). This scale captures cognitive-attentional processes ("I was mentally involved in the narrative while reading it"), emotional reactions ("The narrative affected me emotionally"), and visual imagery ("I had a vivid image of [character name]"). Psychometrically, items capturing these different types of processes form separable facets of the construct but nevertheless load on a common transportation factor, which supports the notion of transportation as a holistic experience (Appel, Gnambs, Richter, & Green, 2015). A number of experiments have used this scale to show that transportation is related to or even mediates the impact of stories on readers' beliefs (e.g., Appel & Richter, 2010; Green, 2004; Green & Brock, 2000; Vaughn, Hesse, Petkova, & Trudeau, 2009). However, relatively few studies have employed objective measures of the cognitive and emotional processes that supposedly constitute transportation. Regarding cognitive processes, evidence based on retrospective measures such as thought-listing procedures suggests that readers rely less on their world knowledge to counter information in a narrative when they are transported in the story world (Green & Brock, 2000). In an fMRI-experiment by Bezdek et al. (2015), participants watched an excerpt of a narrative movie while flashing checkerboards were presented in peripheral visual regions. During suspenseful parts of the movie, neural activity increased in the posterior calcarine sulcus of the primary visual cortex (associated with central vision) and decreased in the anterior calcarine sulcus (associated with peripheral vision), suggesting that higher transportation during the suspenseful sequences narrowed the focus of visual attention. Regarding emotional processes, one experiment measured physiological indicators of emotional arousal (electro-dermal and cardiac activity) while participants watched a video of a father telling a sad story of his son's illness (Barraza, Alexander, Beavin, Terris, & Zak, 2015). The more that participants were aroused during story reception, the more they were willing to donate money to a charity after the experiment. These findings complement other studies showing that the intensity of subjective feelings during story processing is correlated with story-consistent beliefs after reading (e.g., Busselle & Bilandzic, 2009).

Conclusion

The revision of existing knowledge and beliefs in long-term memory through text information is overall more difficult to achieve than the updating of episodic text representations. This resistance to change contributes to the stability of knowledge and beliefs but it can also cause readers to hold fast to misinformation and misconceptions. This section also reviewed research on the remarkable potential of narratives to change readers' beliefs and communicate false information, and discussed this research in terms of the cognitive/attentional and emotional processes that constitute an immersive reception of the narrative (transportation, Gerrig, 1993). In the next section, we will adopt an integrative perspective on the cognitive processes underlying discourse updating and knowledge-revision and discuss these phenomena in terms of memory access, integration, and validation.

Contexts of Updating: Validation and Revision

It was discussed at the outset that discourse updating and knowledge-revision, like all facets of comprehension, depend on general cognitive processes. Theoretical advances have increasingly converged on mechanisms that support updating. One important trend can be explicated using Kintsch's (1988, 1998) construction-integration framework. In particular, theorists have proposed that construction and integration can be further analyzed to comprise memory access (the basis of construction); and integration, validation, and updating (Cook & O'Brien, 2014; Ferretti et al., 2013).

Memory Access

Memory access in reading appreciably reflects the operation of the resonance processes of memory-based comprehension. As discussed earlier, the effectiveness of a discourse memory cue depends on its similarity to and text distance from its antecedent; and by the typicality, distinctiveness, and degree of elaboration of those antecedents (Albrecht & Myers, 1995, 1998; O'Brien & Albrecht, 1991; O'Brien, Albrecht, Hakala, & Rizzella, 1995; McKoon & Ratcliff, 1992). In this regard, consider that the target sentence, *Susan was tired and decided to go to bed*, is inconsistent with the fact that she needed to complete booking a flight before midnight. Albrecht and Myers (1995) reported that target reading times were greater when Susan had not previously booked the flight than when she had. However, the effect was detected only when Susan was in the same location, such as on a sofa, that she had occupied when previously thinking about the flight. As stipulated by memory-based processing, mentioning the sofa provided memory access to her prior intention to book a flight: This increase in cue similarity enhanced the salience of Susan's inconsistent action.

Another study that highlights the influence of access on possible updating scrutinized the joint impact of cue-antecedent distances and causal explanations (Blanc, Kendeou, van den Broek, & Brouillet, 2008). News report texts (similar to those used in the experiments on the continued influence of misinformation described in the section on Revision of Established Memories) presented one explanation of an event, followed by a different, conflicting explanation. For example, a factory explosion was attributed to (1) the volatility of materials and then (2) human negligence. Later, a target sentence favored either explanation 1 or 2. In subsequent testing, participants strongly preferred explanation 2 over explanation 1 when the target had supported explanation 2. The two explanations were about equally preferred when the target had supported explanation 1. This suggests that text distance influenced the relative preference for two explanations. That is, across the two versions of the target, explanation 2 was closer to the target sentence than was explanation 1. According to memory-based processing, explanation 2 would therefore be more eligible to be integrated with the target sentence than explanation 1. This accounts for why the closer explanation (viz. #2) was, on average, more preferred by the readers. Studies of this sort can expose the basic mechanisms contributing to the updating phenomena.

Memory access also plays a role in the persisting effects of misinformation. When misinformation stored in long-term memory can be retrieved easily, it appears to be familiar, increasing the likelihood that the information will be used in later inferences and judgments (Ecker et al., 2014). Difficulties in correcting misconceptions often arise when the correct information is less accessible than the misinformation, for example because the misinformation is embedded in a causal situation model whereas the correcting information is stored separately or only loosely linked to other information. Causal links are effective retrieval structures that will lead to the passive activation of information when other elements of the causal chain are presented (O'Brien & Myers, 1987). As a result, the misinformation but not the correcting information may be passively activated when relevant cues are available in later judgments and inferences. And even if both the misinformation and the correcting information are retrieved from long-term memory, the misinformation might still persist because its familiarity and relative ease of retrieval make it appear as more plausible than the correcting information (Schwarz, 2004). In contrast, adding a sufficient amount of causal information that supports updating can effectively prevent activation of the outdated information (Kendeou et al., 2013).

Integration, Validation, and Updating

The processes of discourse integration and validation were introduced earlier, in the framework of the construction-integration model. Cook and O'Brien (2014; O'Brien, 2015) characterized integration, validation, and updating as parallel and asynchronous components of discourse comprehension. The chronological relations among them were clarified in an event-related potential (ERP) study of Ferretti et al. (2013). ERPs are fast electrophysiological responses to "events," such as a word in a sentence (Jones et al., this volume). Early in stories, people read one of three versions of sentences like *Ken ate oranges/apples/<null> as he cycled to practice*. Later, all participants encountered the target sentence, *The coach knew that it was oranges that Ken had eaten*. This sentence was true, false, or of indeterminate truth, respectively, depending on which earlier version the subject had read. Comparing the false and the indeterminate conditions was especially revealing. Around 750 ms after the onset of *oranges*, ERPs were more negative in the false than in the indeterminate condition. This was interpreted as an extension of a familiar ERP response, the N400 (a negative response 400 ms after an event), reflecting a detection of the *apples-oranges* contradiction by validation processes. Importantly, this pattern was accompanied by *positive* deflections that were *greater* for the indeterminate than the false condition in the 800–1000 ms window. This late positivity is proposed to reflect representation updating (Burkhardt, 2006), an interpretation consistent with Ferretti et al.'s data. Their findings suggest that the indeterminate target is first successfully validated with respect to its antecedent because there is no incongruence between Ken having previously eaten something and the coach knowing that it was oranges. Then, assuming confidence in the author by the reader, the story representation should be updated to include the concept *oranges*.

Eye-tracking studies contrasting the processing of plausible and implausible sentences provide additional evidence for early effects of validation. For example, Staub, Rayner, Pollatsek, Hyönä, and Majewski (2007) manipulated plausibility in sentences with compound nouns such as *The new principal (talked to/visited) the CAFETERIA MANAGER at the end of the school day*. In the implausible version of the sentence, the head noun *cafeteria* creates an implausible scenario (because one cannot talk to a cafeteria) but plausibility is restored when readers encounter the second noun. Staub et al. found longer first eye fixations on the head noun in implausible compared to plausible sentences, suggesting that implausibilities of this type exert rapid and local effects even on nonstrategic comprehension processes. Moreover, the size of the effect was correlated with off-line plausibility ratings. Early effects of plausibility have also been found in eye-tracking experiments with typical versus atypical verb-instrument-patient combinations (e.g., *Donna used the shampoo/hose to wash her filthy hair/car*; Matsuki et al., 2011, Experiment 3; see Patson & Warren, 2011, Experiment 2, for similar results). However, when readers process less strong implausibilities and no strong cues are available that could activate validity-relevant prior knowledge, the detection of implausible information may be delayed and plausibility effects appear only in eye-tracking measures that are indicative of integration processes. For example, Patson and Warren (2011, Experiment 1) used sentences such as *After illustrating the research results in a poster/mosaic, David asked for help*. They found no effects on first fixations to the target region where the implausibility became apparent but longer fixations on the sentence region following this region (*mosaic*) and more and longer regressive fixations to the implausibility. This suggested that readers detected the implausibility only when they tried to integrate the information in the sentence into a coherent sentence meaning.

A self-paced experiment by Cook and O'Brien (2014) using the inconsistency paradigm further specifies the conditions when effects of implausible or inconsistent information may be delayed. Their participants read that Mary was either a junk food fanatic (consistent) or vegetarian (high inconsistent) and ordered a cheeseburger; or else that she was a vegetarian and ordered a tuna salad sandwich (low inconsistent). At the target sentence (*she ordered a cheeseburger/tuna salad sandwich*), reading time in the low-inconsistent condition was intermediate to the other two. This suggested that validation against world knowledge revealed greater incongruence for high- than low-inconsistent information. However, one sentence after the target, the high-low reading time pattern reversed. The authors suggested that low-inconsistent information engages relevant knowledge later than does high-inconsistent information, leading the reader to grapple with the incongruence subsequent to the target sentence.

Reading times, eye-tracking, and ERP data provide broad support for the assumption of routine validation during comprehension but they leave open the question of how readers react to implausible or inconsistent information. Experiments with the epistemic Stroop paradigm inform this issue by showing that information that is inconsistent with prior knowledge does indeed evoke a negative response tendency, indicating that readers routinely monitor plausibility and passively reject implausible information (Richter et al., 2009). In a typical epistemic Stroop experiment, participants see words appearing on the computer screen in rapid succession (e.g., for 300 milliseconds [ms]). These words progressively form sentences. At specific words, the presentation stops and participants are prompted to give a response that is unrelated to the content of the sentence. For example, they are prompted to respond to the word TRUE and the word FALSE with different keys (e.g., Isberner & Richter, 2013). When the prompt appears after words forming a false sentence (*Computers have emotions*), a negative response tendency occurs and interferes with responses to the word TRUE, leading to slower responses. Importantly, similar effects occur for information that is inconsistent with the discourse context. Isberner and Richter (2013) manipulated plausibility through a context sentence (e.g., *Frank has a broken pipe/leg. He called the plumber*). These mini-stories were combined with the task to respond with *yes* when the color of the critical word (*plumber*) changed from black to blue and *no* when it remained black. The *yes* responses were longer in the implausible version of the mini-story compared to the plausible version. Considering that the semantic content and the plausibility of the mini-story is completely irrelevant for the task of reacting to a change in font color, the slower yes responses indicate an involuntary, passive monitoring of discourse consistency.

Validation may be regarded as a precondition for updating because diagnosing an inconsistency may be seen as a precondition for a shift to a new structure (Gernsbacher, 1990). Examples include opening a new event node in reaction to situational inconsistencies in a story (Zwaan & Radvansky, 1998) or constructing a new situation model when novel information cannot be integrated into the existing one (Johnson-Laird, Girotto, & Legrenzi, 2004). Likewise, validation may be regarded as a precondition for revising existing knowledge structures in long-term memory. Conditions that enable validation, most notably the co-activation of inconsistent information (van den Broek & Kendeou, 2008), coincide with those that seem to be crucial for the correction of misconceptions. Moreover, there is a strong link between plausibility and comprehension, with information that is deemed as plausible being more likely to be integrated into the situation model of the text content (Schroeder et al., 2008).

Such findings suggest that validation can protect readers' mental representations from acquiring false information to some degree (e.g., Hinze et al., 2014). Sperber et al. (2010) proposed that language users possess a basic capacity called *epistemic vigilance* that capitalizes on a protective function of validation when acquiring knowledge from texts. However, it is important to note that this protection seems to be limited in two respects. First, if readers hold misconceptions or strong subjective beliefs, epistemic vigilance might backfire and hamper the construction of an adequate mental representation during text comprehension (e.g., Maier & Richter, 2013). One could speculate that in such cases, validation even contributes to the persistence of misinformation and misconceptions (Richter, 2011). Second, specific discourse contexts, most notably stories that create a fictional story world, seem to modulate validation to some degree. An eye-tracking experiment by Filik (2008) is instructive with regard to the underlying mechanism. She presented participants with pragmatically anomalous sentences (e.g., *He picked up the lorry and carried on down the road*) that were presented either in a realistic baseline context or in an established fictional context (e.g., the Incredible Hulk). In the realistic context, first fixation durations and first-pass reading times were prolonged for the region of the sentence immediately following the target word (*lorry*) in the implausible version as compared to a plausible version of the sentence (*He glared at the lorry . . .*). However, these effects did not occur when the same sentences were presented in an established fictional context. Apparently, knowledge about the fictional context (e.g. about the superior strength of the Incredible Hulk) was activated during reading and used for validating the critical sentence, rendering it plausible in the fictional world of the story (for ERP evidence suggesting a similar conclusion, see Nieuwland & van Berkum, 2006). It seems possible that this modulation of validation processes through story contexts contributes to the persuasive power of stories, although this hypothesis still needs to be tested.

Conclusion

To understand when and how readers update their mental representation of a text or revise their prior knowledge, it is important to consider the contributing cognitive processes. We propose that an elaborated construction-integration framework (Kintsch, 1988) clarifies both the temporal relations among the constituent comprehension phases and the qualities of their contributing processes, i.e. memory access, validation, integration, and updating. Memory access, in particular the relative strength of new and outdated information, seems to be crucial for updating and knowledge-revision. Misinformation continues to exert an influence on cognitive processes when it is easily activated through a resonance process. The ease of activation of the misinformation, in turn, depends on its degree of integration in a causal situation model (Kendeou et al., 2013). Likewise, the new information will outweigh the misinformation when it is presented together with a strong causal explanation that resolves the inconsistency. Moreover, for knowledge-revision to occur, both the misinformation and the new information must be co-activated in working memory. Refutation texts are likely to be effective in correcting misconceptions because they are structured according to interdependencies between updating and memory access. A second type of process that seems to be particularly relevant for updating and knowledge-revision is the validation of text information, as indicated by early consistency and plausibility effects. Of course, such effects do not inherently clarify discourse updating. However, it is a viable hypothesis that validation sets the stage for updating, although the relations between the two will necessarily be complex.

Acknowledgments

Tobias Richter's work on this chapter was supported by a grant from the German Research Association (Deutsche Forschungsgemeinschaft, DFG, grant RI 1100/8-1). The work was also supported by Discovery Grant OGP9800 from the Natural Sciences and Engineering Research Council (NSERC) of Canada to Murray Singer.

Suggested Reading

Kendeou, P., Smith, E. R., & O'Brien, E. J. (2013). Updating during reading comprehension: Why causality matters. *Journal of Experimental Psychology: Learning, Memory, and Cognition, 39*, 854–865.

Marsh, E. J., Meade, M. L., & Roediger, H. L. (2003). Learning facts from fiction. *Journal of Memory and Language, 49*, 519–536.

O'Brien, E. J., Cook, A. E., & Guéraud, S. (2010). Accessibility of outdated information. *Journal of Experimental Psychology: Learning, Memory, and Cognition, 36*, 979–991.

Radvansky, G. A. (2012). Across the event horizon. *Current Directions in Psychological Science, 21*, 269–272.

Rapp, D. N., Hinze, S. R., Kohlhepp, K., & Ryskin, R. A. (2014). Reducing reliance on inaccurate information. *Memory & Cognition, 42*, 11–26.

References

Albrecht, J. E., & Myers, J. L. (1995). Role of context in accessing distant information during reading. *Journal of Experimental Psychology: Learning, Memory, and Cognition, 21*, 1459–1468.

Albrecht, J. E., & O'Brien, E. J. (1993). Updating a mental model: Maintaining both local and global coherence. *Journal of Experimental Psychology: Learning, Memory, and Cognition, 19*, 1061–1070.

Anderson, C. A. (1983). Abstract and concrete data in the perseverance of social theories: When weak data lead to unshakable beliefs. *Journal of Experimental Social Psychology, 19*, 93–108.

Anderson, C. A., Lepper, M. R., & Ross, L. (1980). Perseverance of social theories: The role of explanation in the persistence of discredited information. *Journal of Personality and Social Psychology, 39*, 1037–1049.

Anderson, C. A., & Sechler, E. S. (1986). Effects of explanation and counterexplanation on the development and use of social theories. *Journal of Personality and Social Psychology, 50*, 24–34.

Anderson, J. R. (2005). *Cognitive psychology and its implications (6th ed.).* New York, NY: Worth Publishers.

Appel, M., Gnambs, T., Richter, T., & Green, M. (2015). The Transportation Scale: Short Form (TS-SF). *Media Psychology, 18*, 243–266.

Appel, M., & Richter, T. (2007). Persuasive effects of fictional narratives increase over time. *Media Psychology, 10*, 113–134.

Appel, M., & Richter, T. (2010). Transportation and need for affect in narrative persuasion: A mediated moderation model. *Media Psychology, 13*, 101–135.

Baddeley, A. D. (1986). *Working memory.* Oxford Psychology Series, Vol. 11. Oxford: Oxford University Press.

Bahrick, H. P. (1984). Semantic memory content in permastore: Fifty years of memory for Spanish learned in school. *Journal of Experimental Psychology: General, 113*, 1–29.

Barraza, J. A., Alexander, V., Beavin, L. E., Terris, E. T., & Zak, P. J. (2015). The heart of the story: Peripheral physiology during narrative exposure predicts charitable giving. *Biological Psychology, 105*, 138–143.

Bezdek, M. A., Gerrig, R. J., Wenzel, W. G., Shin, J., Pirog Revill, K., & Schumacher, E. H. (2015). Neural evidence that suspense narrows attentional focus. *Neuroscience, 303*, 338–345.

Blanc, N., Kendeou, P., van den Broek, P., & Brouillet, D. (2008). Updating situation models during reading of news reports: Evidence from empirical data and simulations. *Discourse Processes, 45*, 103–121.

Burkhardt, P. (2006). Inferential bridging relations reveal distinct neural mechanisms: Evidence from event-related brain potentials. *Brain and Language*, *98*, 159–168.

Busselle, R., & Bilandzic, H. (2009). Measuring narrative engagement. *Media Psychology*, *12*, 321–347.

Caplan, D. (1972). Clause boundaries and recognition latencies for words in sentences. *Perception and Psychophysics*, *12*, 73–76.

Chi, M. T. H. (2008). Three types of conceptual change: Belief revision, mental model transformation, and categorical shifts. In S. Vosniadou (Ed.), *Handbook of research on conceptual change* (pp. 61–82). Hillsdale, NJ: Erlbaum.

Chi, M. T. H., & Roscoe, R. (2002). The processes and challenges of conceptual change. In M. Limon & L. Mason (Eds.), *Reframing the process of conceptual change: Integrating theory and practice* (pp. 3–27). Dordrecht, The Netherlands: Kluwer.

Cohen, G. (1979). Language comprehension in old age. *Cognitive Psychology*, *11*, 412–429.

Coleridge, S. T. (1817/1907). *Biographia literaria*. London, UK: Oxford University Press.

Cook, A. E., & O'Brien, E. J. (2014). Knowledge activation, integration, and validation during narrative text comprehension. *Discourse Processes*, *51*, 26–49.

Davies, M. F. (1997). Belief persistence after evidential discrediting: The impact of generated versus provided explanations on the likelihood of discredited outcomes. *Journal of Experimental Social Psychology*, *33*, 561–578.

Dechêne, A., Stahl, C., Hansen, J., & Wänke, M. (2010). The truth about the truth: A meta-analytic review of the truth effect. *Personality and Social Psychology Review*, *14*, 238–257.

Ecker, U. K. H., Lewandowsky, S., & Tang, D. T. W. (2010). Explicit warnings reduce but do not eliminate the continued influence of misinformation. *Memory & Cognition*, *38*, 1087–1100.

Ecker, U. K. H., Swire, B., & Lewandowsky, S. (2014). Correcting misinformation: A challenge for education and cognitive science. In D. N. Rapp & J. L. G. Braasch (Eds.), *Processing inaccurate information: Theoretical and applied perspectives from cognitive science and the educational sciences* (pp. 13–18). Cambridge, MA: MIT Press.

Ericsson, K. A., & Kintsch, W. (1995). Long-term working memory. *Psychological Review*, *102*, 211–245.

Fazio, L. K., Barber, S. J., Rajaram, S., Ornstein, P. A., & Marsh, E. J. (2013). Creating illusions of knowledge: Learning errors that contradict prior knowledge. *Journal of Experimental Psychology: General*, *142*, 1–5.

Ferreira, F., Christianson, K., & Hollingworth, A. (2001). Misinterpretations of garden-path sentences: Implications for models of sentence processing and reanalysis. *Journal of Psycholinguistic Research*, *30*, 3–20.

Ferretti, T. R., Singer, M., & Harwood, J. (2013). Processes of discourse integration: Evidence from event-related brain potentials. *Discourse Processes*, *50*, 165–186.

Filik, R. (2008). Contextual override of pragmatic anomalies: Evidence from eye movements. *Cognition*, *106*, 1038–1046.

Fletcher, C. R. (1981). Short-term memory processes in text comprehension. *Journal of Verbal Learning and Verbal Behavior*, *20*, 564–574.

Gernsbacher, M. A. (1985). Surface information loss in comprehension. *Cognitive Psychology*, *17*, 324–363.

Gernsbacher, M. A. (1990). *Language comprehension as structure building*. Hillsdale, NJ: Erlbaum.

Gernsbacher, M. A., Varner, K. R., & Faust, M. E. (1990). Investigating differences in general comprehension skill. *Journal of Experimental Psychology: Learning, Memory, and Cognition*, *16*, 430–445.

Gerrig, R. J. (1993). *Experiencing narrative worlds*. New Haven, CT: Yale University Press.

Gerrig, R. J., & Prentice, D. A. (1991). The representation of fictional information. *Psychological Science*, *2*, 336–340.

Gilbert, D. T., Krull, D., & Malone, P. (1990). Unbelieving the unbelievable: Some problems in the rejection of false information. *Journal of Personality and Social Psychology*, *59*, 601–613.

Glenberg, A. M., Meyer, M., & Lindem, K. (1987). Mental models contribute to foregrounding during text comprehension. *Journal of Memory and Language*, *26*, 69–83.

Green, M. C. (2004). Transportation into narrative worlds: The role of prior knowledge and perceived realism. *Discourse Processes*, *38*, 247–266.

Green, M. C., & Brock, T. C. (2000). The role of transportation in the persuasiveness of public narratives. *Journal of Personality and Social Psychology*, *79*, 701–721.

Guzetti, B. J., Snyder, T. W., Glass, G. V., & Gamas, W. S. (1993). Promoting conceptual change in science: A comparative meta-analysis of instructional interventions from reading education and science education. *Reading Research Quarterly, 28*, 116–159.

Haberlandt, K. F., & Graesser, A. C. (1985). Component processes in text comprehension and some of their interactions. *Journal of Experimental Psychology: General, 114*, 357–374.

Hannon, B., & Daneman, M. (2001). A new tool for measuring and understanding individual differences in the component process of reading comprehension. *Journal of Educational Psychology, 93*, 103–128.

Hasson, U., Simmons, J. P., & Todorov, A. (2005). Believe it or not: On the possibility of suspending belief. *Psychological Science, 16*, 566–571.

Hintzman, D. L. (1988). Judgments of frequency and recognition memory in a multiple-trace memory model. *Psychological Review, 95*, 528–551.

Hinze, S. R., Slaten, D. G., Horton, W. S., Jenkins, R., & Rapp, D. N. (2014). Pilgrims sailing the Titanic: Plausibility effects on memory for facts and errors. *Memory & Cognition, 42*, 305–324.

Isberner, M.-B., & Richter, T. (2013). Can readers ignore implausibility? Evidence for nonstrategic monitoring of event-based plausibility in language comprehension. *Acta Psychologica, 142*, 15–22.

Jarvella, R. J. (1971). Immediate memory and discourse processing. In G. H. Bower (Ed.), *The psychology of learning and motivation* (Vol. 13, pp. 379–421). New York, NY: Academic Press.

Johnson, H. M., & Seifert, C. M. (1994). Sources of the continued influence effect: When discredited information in memory affects later inferences. *Journal of Experimental Psychology: Learning, Memory, and Cognition, 20*, 1420–1436.

Johnson-Laird, P. N. (1983). *Mental models*. Cambridge, MA: Harvard University Press.

Johnson-Laird, P. N., Girotto, V., & Legrenzi, P. (2004). Reasoning from inconsistency to consistency. *Psychological Review, 111*, 640–661.

Just, M. A., & Carpenter, P. A. (1992). A capacity theory of comprehension: Individual differences in working memory. *Psychological Review, 99*, 122–149.

Kendeou, P., Smith, E. R., & O'Brien, E. J. (2013). Updating during reading comprehension: Why causality matters. *Journal of Experimental Psychology: Learning, Memory, and Cognition, 39*, 854–865.

Kendeou, P., & van den Broek, P. (2007). The effects of prior knowledge and text structure on comprehension processes during reading of scientific texts. *Memory & Cognition, 35*, 1567–1577.

Kintsch, W. (1988). The role of knowledge in discourse comprehension: A construction-integration model. *Psychological Review, 95*, 163–182.

Kintsch, W. (1998). *Comprehension*. New York, NY: Cambridge University Press.

Kintsch, W., & Bates, E. (1977). Recognition memory for statements from a classroom lecture. *Journal of Experimental Psychology: Human Learning and Memory, 3*, 150–159.

Kintsch, W., & van Dijk, T.A. (1978). Toward a model of text comprehension and production. *Psychological Review, 85*, 363–394.

Kintsch, W., Welsch, D., Schmalhofer, F., & Zimny, S. (1990). Sentence memory: A theoretical analysis. *Journal of Memory and Language, 29*, 133–159.

Kurby, C. A., & Zacks, J. M. (2012). Starting from scratch and building brick by brick in comprehension. *Memory & Cognition, 40*, 812–826.

Magliano, J. P., & Schleich, M. C. (2000). Verb aspect and situation models. *Discourse Processes, 29*, 83–112.

Maier, J., & Richter, T. (2013). How nonexperts understand conflicting information on social science issues: The role of perceived plausibility and reading goals. *Journal of Media Psychology, 25*, 14–26.

Mandler, J. M. (1978). A code in the node: The use of a story schema in retrieval. *Discourse Processes, 1*, 14–35.

Marsh, E. J., Meade, M. L., & Roediger, H. L. (2003). Learning facts from fiction. *Journal of Memory and Language, 49*, 519–536.

Matsuki, K., Chow, T., Hare, M., Elman, J. L., Scheepers, C., & McRae, K. (2011). Event-based plausibility immediately influences on-line sentence language comprehension. *Journal of Experimental Psychology: Learning, Memory, and Cognition, 37*, 913–934.

Mayer, R. E., & Cook, L. K. (1981). Effects of shadowing on prose comprehension. *Memory & Cognition, 9*, 101–109.

McKoon, G., & Ratcliff, R. (1992). Inference during reading. *Psychological Review, 99*, 440–466.

McKoon, G., & Ratcliff, R. (1998). Memory-based language processing: Psycholinguistic research in the 1990s. *Annual Review of Psychology*, *49*, 25–42.

Mensink, M. C., & Rapp, D. N. (2011). Evil geniuses: Inferences derived from evidence and preferences. *Memory & Cognition*, *36*, 1103–1116.

Miller, G. A. (1956). The magical number seven, plus or minus two: Some limits on our capacity for processing information. *Psychological Review*, *63*, 81–97.

Morrow, D. G., Greenspan, S. L., & Bower, G. H. (1987). Accessibility and situation models in narrative comprehension. *Journal of Memory and Language*, *2*, 165–187.

Murdock, B. B. (1982). A theory for storage and retrieval of item and associative information. *Psychological Review*, *89*, 609–626.

Nell, V. (1988). *Lost in a book: The psychology of reading for pleasure*. New Haven, CT: Yale University Press.

Nieuwland, M. S., & Kuperberg, G. R. (2008). When the truth is not too hard to handle. *Psychological Science*, *19*, 1213–1218.

Nieuwland, M. S., & van Berkum, J. J. A. (2006). When peanuts fall in love: N400 effects for the power of discourse. *Journal of Cognitive Neuroscience*, *18*, 1098–1111.

O'Brien, E. J. (2015, July). *Mapping validation processes onto memory-based processing*. Paper presented at the 25th Annual Meeting of the Society for Text and Discourse, Minneapolis, MN.

O'Brien, E. J., & Albrecht, J. E. (1991). The role of context in accessing antecedents in text. *Journal of Experimental Psychology: Learning, Memory, and Cognition*, *17*, 94–102.

O'Brien, E. J., & Albrecht, J. E. (1992). Comprehension strategies in the development of a mental model. *Journal of Experimental Psychology: Learning, Memory, and Cognition*, *18*, 777–784.

O'Brien, E. J., Albrecht, J. E., Hakala, C. M., & Rizzella, M. L. (1995). Activation and suppression of antecedents during reinstatement. *Journal of Experimental Psychology: Learning, Memory, and Cognition*, *21*, 626–634.

O'Brien, E. J., Cook, A. E., & Guéraud, S. (2010). Accessibility of outdated information. *Journal of Experimental Psychology: Learning, Memory, and Cognition*, *36*, 979–991.

O'Brien, E. J., Lorch, R. F., & Myers, J. L. (1998). Memory-based text processing [Special issue]. *Discourse Processes*, *26*(2–3).

O'Brien, E., & Myers, J. (1987). The role of causal connections in the retrieval of text. *Memory & Cognition*, *15*, 419–427.

O'Brien, E. J., Rizzella, M. L., Albrecht, J. E., & Halleran, J. G. (1998). Updating a situational model: A memory based text processing view. *Journal of Experimental Psychology: Learning, Memory, and Cognition*, *24*, 1200–1210.

Patson, N. D., & Warren, T. (2011). Eye movements when reading implausible sentences: Investigating potential structural influences on semantic integration. *Quarterly Journal of Experimental Psychology*, *63*, 1516–1532.

Petty, R. E., & Wegener, D. T. (1999). The Elaboration Likelihood Model: Current status and controversies. In S. Chaiken & Y. Trope (Eds.), *Dual process theories in social psychology* (pp. 41–72). New York, NY: Guilford.

Posner, G. J., Strike, K. A., Hewson, P. W., & Gertzog, W. A. (1982). Accommodation of a scientific conception: Toward a theory of conceptual change. *Science Education*, *66*, 211–227.

Potts, G. R. (1972). Information processing strategies used in the encoding of linear orderings. *Journal of Verbal Learning and Verbal Behavior*, *11*, 727–740.

Potts, G. R., & Peterson, S. B. (1985). Incorporation versus compartmentalization in memory for discourse. *Journal of Memory and Language*, *24*, 107–118.

Radvansky, G. A. (2012). Across the event horizon. *Current Directions in Psychological Science*, *21*, 269–272.

Radvansky, G. A., & Copeland, D. E. (2001). Working memory and situation model updating. *Memory & Cognition*, *29*, 1073–1080.

Radvansky, G. A., & Copeland, D. E. (2006). Walking through doorways causes forgetting. *Memory & Cognition*, *34*, 1150–1156.

Radvansky, G. A., Krawietz, S. A., & Tamplin, A. K. (2011). Walking through doorways causes forgetting: Further explorations. *Quarterly Journal of Experimental Psychology*, *64*, 1632–1645.

Rapp, D. N. (2008). How do readers handle incorrect information during reading? *Memory & Cognition*, *36*, 688–701.

Rapp, D. N., Hinze, S. R., Kohlhepp, K., & Ryskin, R. A. (2014). Reducing reliance on inaccurate information. *Memory & Cognition, 42,* 11–26.

Rapp, D. N., Hinze, S. R., Slaten, D. G., & Horton, W. S. (2014). Amazing stories: Acquiring and avoiding inaccurate information from fiction. *Discourse Processes, 52,* 50–74.

Rapp, D. N., & Kendeou, P. (2009). Noticing and revising discrepancies as texts unfold. *Discourse Processes, 46,* 1–24.

Ratcliff, R., & McKoon, G. (1978). Priming in item recognition. *Journal of Verbal Learning and Verbal Behavior, 17,* 403–417.

Richter, T. (2011). Cognitive flexibility and epistemic validation in learning from multiple texts. In J. Elen, E. Stahl, R. Bromme, & G. Clarebout (Eds.), *Links between beliefs and cognitive flexibility* (pp. 125–140). Berlin, Germany: Springer.

Richter, T., Schroeder, S., & Wöhrmann, B. (2009). You don't have to believe everything you read: Background knowledge permits fast and efficient validation of information. *Journal of Personality and Social Psychology, 96,* 538–558.

Rinck, M., Hahnel, A., & Becker, G. (2001). Using temporal information to construct, update, and retrieval situation models of narratives. *Journal of Experimental Psychology: Learning, Memory, and Cognition, 27,* 67–80.

Ross, L. D., Lepper, M. R., Strack, F., & Steinmetz, J. (1977). Social explanation and social expectation: Effects of real and hypothetical explanations on subjective likelihood. *Journal of Personality and Social Psychology, 35,* 817–829.

Sachs, J. D. (1967). Recognition memory for syntactic and semantic aspects of connected discourse. *Perception and Psychophysics, 2,* 437–442.

Schank, R. C., & Abelson, R. P. (1977). *Scripts, plans, goals, and understanding.* Hillsdale, NJ: Erlbaum.

Schroeder, S., Richter, T., & Hoever, I. (2008). Getting a picture that is both accurate and stable: Situation models and epistemic validation. *Journal of Memory and Language, 59,* 237–259.

Schwarz, N. (2004). Metacognitive experiences in consumer judgment and decision making. *Journal of Consumer Psychology, 14,* 332–348.

Sinatra, G. M., & Broughton, S. H. (2011). Bridging reading comprehension and conceptual change in science education: The promise of refutation texts. *Reading Research Quarterly, 46,* 374–393.

Singer, M., Halldorson, M., Lear, J. C., & Andrusiak, P. (1992). Validation of causal bridging inferences. *Journal of Memory and Language, 31,* 507–524.

Singer, M., & Ritchot, K. (1996). Individual differences in inference validation. *Memory & Cognition, 24,* 733–743.

Skurnik, I., Yoon, C., Park, D. C., & Schwarz, N. (2005). How warnings about false claims become recommendations. *Journal of Consumer Research, 31,* 713–724.

Sperber, D., Clément, F., Heintz, C., Mascaro, O., Mercier, H., Origgi, G., & Wilson, D. (2010). Epistemic vigilance. *Mind & Language, 25,* 359–393.

Staub, A., Rayner, K., Pollatsek, A., Hyönä, J., & Majewski, H. (2007). The time course of plausibility effects on eye movements in reading: Evidence from noun-noun compounds. *Journal of Experimental Psychology: Learning, Memory, and Cognition, 33,* 454–475.

Stein, B. S., & Bransford, J. D. (1979). Constraints on effective elaboration: Effects of precision and subject generation. *Journal of Verbal Learning and Verbal Behavior, 18,* 769–777.

Tippett, C. D. (2010). Refutation text in science education: A review of two decades of research. *International Journal of Science and Mathematics Education, 8,* 951–970.

Trabasso, T., Secco, T., & van den Broek, P. (1984). Causal cohesion and story coherence. In H. Mandl, N. Stein, & T. Trabasso (Eds.), *Learning and comprehension of text* (pp. 83–111). Hillsdale, NJ: Erlbaum.

van den Broek, P., & Kendeou, P. (2008). Cognitive processes in comprehension of science text: The role of co-activation in confronting misconceptions. *Applied Cognitive Psychology, 22,* 335–351.

van Dijk, T. A., & Kintsch, W. (1983). *Strategies of discourse comprehension.* New York, NY: Academic Press.

Vaughn, L. A., Hesse, S. J., Petkova, Z., & Trudeau, L. (2009). "This story is right on": The impact of regulatory fit on narrative engagement and persuasion. *European Journal of Social Psychology, 39,* 447–456.

Vosniadou, S. (1994). Capturing and modeling the process of conceptual change. *Learning and Instruction, 4,* 45–69.

Vosniadou, S., & Brewer, W. F. (1992). Mental models of the earth: A study of conceptual change in childhood. *Cognitive Psychology, 24*, 535–585.

Wheeler, S. C., Green, M. A., & Brock, T. C. (1999). Fictional narratives change beliefs: Replications of Prentice, Gerrig, and Bailis (1997) with mixed corroboration. *Psychonomic Bulletin & Review, 6*, 136–141.

Wilkes, A. L., & Leatherbarrow, M. (1988). Editing episodic memory following the identification of error. *Quarterly Journal of Experimental Psychology, 40A*, 361–387.

Zacks, J. M., Speer, N. K., Swallow, K. M., Braver, T. S., & Reynolds, J. R. (2007). Event perception: A mind-brain perspective. *Psychological Bulletin, 133*, 273–293.

Zwaan, R. A., Langston, M. C., & Graesser, A. C. (1995). The construction of situation models in narrative comprehension: An event-indexing model. *Psychological Science, 6*, 292–297.

Zwaan, R. A., & Madden, C. J. (2004). Updating situation models. *Journal of Experimental Psychology: Learning, Memory, and Cognition, 30*, 283–288.

Zwaan, R. A., Magliano, J. P., & Graesser, A. C. (1995). Dimensions of situation-model construction in narrative comprehension. *Journal of Experimental Psychology: Learning, Memory, and Cognition, 21*, 386–397.

Zwaan, R. A., & Radvansky, G. A. (1998). Situation models in language comprehension and memory. *Psychological Bulletin, 123*, 162–185.

Zwaan, R. A., & van Oostendorp, H. (1994). Spatial information and naturalistic story comprehension. *Advances in Discourse Processes, 53*, 97–114.

11

Discourse Processing in Technology-Mediated Environments

Darren Gergle

NORTHWESTERN UNIVERSITY

Introduction

Communication technologies are rapidly evolving and shaping the ways we communicate and interact. It used to be that relatively clean distinctions existed between different communication forms: we read the travel section of the morning newspaper, wrote love letters to friends in faraway lands, listened to lectures in large auditoriums, or discussed politics in a local café. Nowadays, hundreds of millions of people communicate over vast distances using a variety of social network sites (e.g., Facebook), microblogs (e.g., Twitter), discussion forums (e.g., Reddit), wikis (e.g., Wikipedia), video-mediated communication systems, and live-streaming platforms (e.g., Skype, Periscope, or Facebook Livestream), they chat with robotic systems and conversational agents (e.g., Siri or Alexa), and they make use of mobile technologies for anytime, anywhere access.

These technological developments provide new ways and means to communicate, and they ease the fluidity with which we can switch among conversational platforms. We can post a "tweet" from our smartphone that contains a hyperlink to a longer news article where we can then engage others in the comments section to discuss the article. We can send ephemeral "snaps"[1] to our friends, and then follow up with a group text message to joke about the images; and we can converse directly with an individual while simultaneously broadcasting the conversation to a larger audience (e.g., by using the ".@" form of a direct message on Twitter).

While popular accounts of these technological advances often herald the "death of distance" and advocate widespread and equitable access to people and information (Biello, 2009; Cairncross & Cairncross, 2001), current scholarship paints a more complex picture. Video-mediated systems can support conversation and coordination, but a simple failure to provide the appropriate viewing angle can impair a pair's ability to establish common ground and lead to ineffective work (Clark & Krych, 2004; Kraut, Gergle, & Fussell, 2002). Online dating and social networking sites deliver new and effective ways to keep in touch and maintain relationships (Ellison, Hancock, & Toma, 2012; Tong & Walther, 2011; Vitak, 2012); however, relationships can also become strained, falter, or simply fail to develop in many online contexts (Clayton, Nagurney, & Smith, 2013; Dibble & Drouin, 2014; Northrup & Smith, 2016). And peer-production systems (Benkler, 2003; Duguid, 2006) such as Wikipedia provide global access to accurate and important information (Giles, 2005), but at the same time can introduce biased information (Hecht & Gergle, 2009) or suppress important minority viewpoints (Wagner, Garcia, Jadidi, & Strohmaier, 2015; Wagner, Graells-Garrido, Garcia, & Menczer, 2016).

In this rapidly evolving technological context for communication, how do we make use of the wide variety of options available? How do we decide on the best technology or device for a given task or conversational goal? What are the contexts and conditions under which certain technologies and technology use flourish?

The goal of this chapter is to help begin to address these questions by considering the changes taking place across the technological landscape—with a particular focus on communication technologies—and discussing the ways in which they challenge our current understanding of discourse processes. The chapter centers on ideas of grounding and mutual knowledge, and on understanding how these play out in the multimodal, multi-device, and multi-audience environments that are part of our everyday communication.

Fundamentals of Successful Communication

Successful communication—whether face-to-face or technologically mediated—relies upon jointly constructed meaning and a common ground of mutually acknowledged beliefs, goals, and perspectives. During a conversation, speakers and addressees jointly construct meaning through an interactive *grounding process* whereby they exchange evidence about what they do and do not understand (Brennan, 1990; Clark & Marshall, 1981; Clark & Wilkes-Gibbs, 1986). An important part of this process involves making new contributions, and this is achieved across two coordinated communication phases: the *presentation phase* and the *acceptance phase* (Clark & Schaefer, 1989).

In the presentation phase, speakers aim to produce effective utterances and they rely upon three factors that allow them to anticipate what an addressee may know: *community co-membership, linguistic co-presence*, and *physical co-presence* (Clark & Marshall, 1981). Community co-membership, for example, permits a member of a Python programming group to confidently use technical jargon such as "API," "namespace," or "dictionary" with her colleagues, while she would be unlikely to do so with outside members (see Isaacs & Clark, 1987 for related work). Linguistic co-presence permits a speaker to use a simple pronoun such as "he" to refer to a previously mentioned person—assuming the addressee was actively listening to the prior conversation. Physical co-presence allows a speaker to use exophoric references such as deictic pronouns (e.g., "that one") so long as she believes that her conversational partner shares a similar view of an object or environment.

During the acceptance phase, listeners demonstrate their understanding in a variety of ways, such as through explicit verbal acknowledgments (e.g., "okay" or "got it") or gestures (e.g., a head nod) that indicate they have understood the contribution well enough for current purposes (Clark & Wilkes-Gibbs, 1986). In some cases, the simple implicit demonstration of continued attention can be enough to serve as an acceptance and allow the conversation to move forward. In other cases, a failure to respond can signal confusion or misunderstanding, leading to further questions and clarifications to reach mutual understanding (Clark & Schaefer, 1989; Jefferson, 1972; Sacks, Schegloff, & Jefferson, 1974).

As the pairs engage in this active exchange of evidence, and as new contributions are presented and accepted, common ground is updated with new shared knowledge, beliefs, goals, etc. Furthermore, the ease and effectiveness of grounding are influenced by a variety of contextual, environmental, and social factors: differences in spatial orientation (Schober, 1993, 1995), levels of domain expertise (Isaacs & Clark, 1987), and socio-cultural background (Fussell & Krauss, 1992) have all been shown to influence various phases and aspects of the grounding process.

Grounding in Technologically Mediated Settings

While early research on conversational grounding focused on face-to-face language use, researchers soon began to investigate the role of technology. Clark and Brennan (1991) developed a framework to help predict and explain how communication technologies influence the grounding process. The central premise is that the cost of grounding is dependent upon the coordination constraints imposed by the technology. In other words, different technologies incur different costs as a result of the particular affordances or resources[2] they provide for establishing common ground, and these costs vary according to the communicative function being performed (e.g., timing an utterance to an action, establishing joint attention, or judging an addressee's level of comprehension).

It is important to note that this was a distinct departure from the literature of the time that tended to array communication technology along a single dimension of richness (e.g., Daft & Lengel, 1984). Such "bandwidth"-oriented theories treat technology-mediated communication as an impoverished form of interaction in comparison to the "gold standard" of face-to-face communication (see Hollan & Stornetta, 1992; Walther & Parks, 2002; Whittaker, 2003 for critiques and reviews of these theories), whereas an affordances-based view such as that proposed by Clark and Brennan is less deterministic and frames the analysis according to the goals of the interlocutors and multidimensional characteristics of the technologies.

Clark and Brennan (1991) propose eight primary resources for grounding that are often affected by technology: *Physical co-presence* is the degree to which the participants are mutually aware that they are collocated or occupy the same physical space; *Visibility* is the degree to which the participants are able to see one another, identify where one another are looking, or see objects that reside in the shared space; *Audibility* is the degree to which participants are able to hear one another as well as noises in the shared environment; *Cotemporality* is the degree to which participants share their experience in real-time and without delay (for example, when speaking in a face-to-face environment the addressee hears what is said almost without delay, whereas when sending an email there can be a substantial delay between what is being written and when it is read); *Simultaneity* is the degree to which participants can both produce and receive utterances or information at the same time; *Sequentiality* is the degree to which participants produce their utterances in ordered turns or sequences where temporal adjacency and temporal coherence are preserved; *Reviewability* is the degree to which participants can revisit their own utterances, messages, etc. as well as those of their conversational partners (in other words, it concerns the ephemerality of the messages and utterances); and *Revisability* is the degree to which the participants can alter or revise their message before it is sent.

Kraut and colleagues (Kraut, Fussell, Brennan, & Siegel, 2002) offer two more affordances that are important for many modern technological settings: *Tangibility* is the degree to which conversational partners are able to touch one another and other objects in the environment; and *Mobility* is the degree to which the conversational partners can move around within a shared space. While mobility was originally conceptualized as movement in a co-present physical space, it can also have an influence when interlocutors are physically remote. For example, mobile smartphones shift phone-based communication from a known spatial context (e.g., calling someone on their home landline) to an unknown spatial context (but one where you are more assured of the identity of the person you are contacting).

To better understand how the grounding framework can be applied, consider the video-calling component for a video-mediated communication (VMC) technology such as Skype[3] or Facetime. The video (and audio) allows you to see and hear the other person in real-time, both conversational partners can speak at the same time (in comparison to say a "push to talk" system like a walkie-talkie device), and dialogue and exchanges proceed in a relatively ordered fashion (in contrast with, for instance, an unthreaded exchange in a text-based IRC (Internet Relay Chat) channel). Furthermore—as is discussed in the following sections—the particular affordances can depend on the technological platform chosen and the details of its configuration. For example, visual angles can vary and provide more or less access to a partner's face and gestures, the positioning of the camera relative to the speaker can provide false cues regarding a partner's height and influence negotiation outcomes (Huang, Olson, & Olson, 2002), and the inclusion of "self-views" can affect self-disclosures that take place around sensitive information (Feuer & Schober, 2013).

In terms of Clark and Brennan's affordances, a relatively standard video-calling setup includes visibility, audibility, cotemporality, simultaneity, and sequentiality—and each of these can change costs for various techniques of grounding such as formulating an utterance, initiating a conversation, turn-taking, making reference to shared physical objects, acknowledging contributions, or correcting misunderstandings. In the video example, visibility and cotemporality can support temporally precise gaze functions that facilitate turn-taking (Argyle & Cook, 1976; Bavelas, Coates, & Johnson, 2002; Kendon, 1967). However, if there is lag or jitter in the system, or the video angles are set in such way that mutual gaze cannot be achieved, the capacity for effective turn-taking is diminished (Boyle, Anderson, & Newlands, 1994). As a result, speakers may take longer turns, there may be longer pauses during speaker transitions, higher rates of interruption can occur (Anderson et al., 1997; O'Malley, Langton, Anderson, Doherty-Sneddon, & Bruce, 1996), and if the amount of temporal lag or video degradation is substantial, then explicit turn-taking markers may be required (see Hancock & Dunham, 2001 for similar results on marked turn-taking in text-based computer-mediated communication environments).

Practical Extensions

While application of Clark and Brennan's conceptual framework is still quite useful today, there are a few ways it can be enriched when considering modern communication technologies. This includes a detailed consideration of the task features, the particular features of the technology, and the interaction of the two.

Features of the Task

The particular attributes of the task are important to consider for grounding: loose vs. tight coupling (e.g., planning a poster layout vs. performing in a string quartet), physical or sequential interdependence (e.g., interlocking vs. simple stackable elements), and attributes of the group and social organization (e.g., solo, instructional, or joint construction) all impose different requirements on the degree to which grounding processes need to be supported.

Consider again the case of understanding communication in the context of video-mediated communication systems. For a long time, researchers puzzled over a lack of evidence supporting benefits of video-mediated systems. Although, consistent with common intuitions, it was suggested that seeing one another's face was crucial for successful coordination and interaction (Short, Williams, & Christie, 1976), many experimental studies of the time failed to find evidence for such claims (see Williams, 1977 for a review). It turns out that for many tasks—especially those involving coordinated actions—it is more fruitful to show visual information about the activities and physical actions, the task objects, and the state of the joint task. It wasn't until researchers began to look closely at task features and the role they played that the particular benefits of technologies providing shared visual information became apparent (Nardi et al., 1993; Whittaker, Geelhoed, & Robinson, 1993).

The ability to visually share task-related context facilitates comprehension monitoring and reference to objects in a shared editor (Daly-Jones, Monk, & Watts, 1998), it improves performance and makes communication more efficient in collaborative physical tasks (Fussell, Setlock, & Kraut, 2003), and it can facilitate recovery from ambiguous help requests by supporting information gathering (Karsenty, 1999). The value of the visual feedback also varies depending on the contribution phase or the stage of the task. For example, visual feedback has the greatest impact during the acceptance phase (Brennan, 2005), and tighter coupling of the visual feedback to a partner's actions is more beneficial during stages of the task when the pairs are performing referential grounding (Ranjan, Birnholtz, & Balakrishnan, 2006). Furthermore, task experience plays a role whereby less experienced participants produce greater multimodal redundancy when referring to task objects (Anderson, Sanford, Thomson, & Ion, 2007). Together, these studies highlight the role that a precise understanding of the task features and goals can play in understanding the value of a particular technological context for grounding.

Features of the Technology

The second important consideration is a detailed understanding of the precise form of the technology and its specific design features. Much of the empirical work examining technology's role in communication follows a research tradition established by the Communications Study Group at British Telecom (Short et al., 1976) and Chapanis' research group in the US.[4] (Chapanis, Ochsman, Parrish, & Weeks, 1972)—a paradigm that tends to compare communication and interaction *across* major technology modes (e.g., face-to-face vs. video vs. audio-only vs. text). However, this can be too coarse of a distinction that obfuscates the role technology plays in discourse processes. In a similar way that task decomposition can be helpful for understanding discourse in various technological contexts, it is equally important to understand the differential effects particular features of the technology can have on communication, and to understand how the particular design features implemented *within* a mode affect communication (Gergle, 2006; Kraut et al., 2002).

Continuing with the example of video-mediated communication systems, most research tends toward a binary notion of visual information; it is either available or it is not. But, as is detailed in Gergle, Kraut, and Fussell (2013), consider the myriad forms that visual support can take in such a system: the viewing angle can be aligned or spatially offset (e.g., rotated 180°); the field of view can be narrow or wide-angle; voice may or may not be synchronized to actions; there can be delays, distortions, or low-fidelity visual renderings; colors and saturation levels may vary across displays; and choices need to be made regarding the setup as to whether each conversational participant can see the work area, each other's faces, gestures, both, neither, and so on. In other words, the technological choices made influence the amount, quality, and potential utility of the visual information being exchanged, and this formerly binary notion of shared visual context is now replaced by a graded and multidimensional construct.

The question then arises, how are these particular features and design decisions related to the coordination processes that serve successful communication and interaction? Numerous studies have demonstrated the extent to which small design changes can have a large impact on discourse processes and group outcomes. For example, the number of lines devoted to a dialogue history in a text-chat interface (see Figure 11.1) affects linguistic co-presence and reviewability, which then leads to changes in the rhythm of contributions and installment size (Gergle, Millen, Kraut, & Fussell, 2004). Similarly, varying a video-mediated system's field of view affects task awareness while shift in the viewing angle affects referential grounding (Gergle et al., 2013; also see Schober, 1993, 1995).

Task by Technology Interactions

Finally, it's important to acknowledge that the degree to which technological mediation will influence communication in any particular situation depends *both* on the technological choices made as well as the task the group is performing (Kraut, Fussell, & Siegel, 2003). For example, when examining the value of shared visual space, we might ask a number of questions that consider both the technological features and task components: How does a

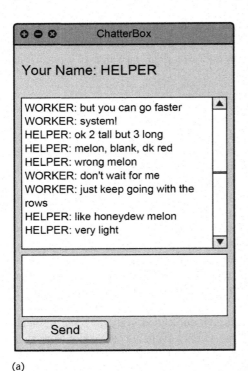 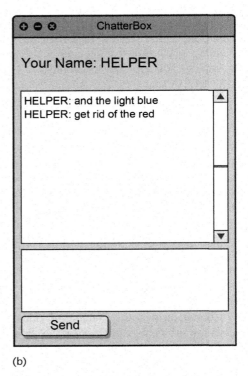

(a) (b)

Figure 11.1 Example chat interfaces from Gergle et al. (2004) that manipulate the degree of text persistence. The left image shows the high-persistence condition (a) with ten lines of history in comparison to the low-persistence condition (b) with only two lines of chat history visible. Reprinted with permission of ACM Press

Technology-Mediated Environments

small field of view affect the ability of pairs to plan subsequent actions? How do delays in the shared view affect grounding processes that rely on temporal precision? How is the generation and comprehension of referring expressions influenced by the availability of shared visual context?

Studies have shown, for instance, that different forms of shared visual space have differential effects on grounding and collaborative task performance (Gergle et al., 2013). This work makes use of a helper and worker paradigm where remote participants jointly assemble complex visual block puzzles (Kraut et al., 2002). Offsetting the spatial alignment through which the helper and worker see the shared visual space disrupts referential grounding and leads to lower production of spatial deixis (i.e., spatial phrases such as "in front of" or "to the left of"), but the pair's ability to track the overall task state remains intact as evidenced by little change in their use of verbal alignments (i.e., utterances that explicitly describe the state of the task such as "are you ready to continue?" or "got it . . . next one?") (Anderson et al., 1991). However, when spatial alignment is shared but we reduce the size of the common viewing area, referential grounding remains intact but the pair's ability to effectively track the overall task state is disrupted and they produce verbal alignments at a greater rate. This research, and related work (Anderson et al., 2007; Fussell et al., 2003), suggests that technological benefits depend on both the technology features and the task characteristics.

Current Trends and Issues

Prior research has identified the need to understand task components and technology features, but this can be challenging in a rapidly evolving technological world. The boundaries that previously existed between reading and writing are now blurred, and new ways of interacting are continually being developed. While discourse processing fundamentals remain, the practices around conversation and interaction have evolved in such a way as to necessitate a deeper investigation of the ways in which new technological features and group task properties influence discourse processes. The following focuses on identifying important trends in the technological sphere that affect discourse processes, centering on four important developments: (1) the rise in multimodality and mobility, (2) mode choice and mode switching, (3) social and network-based affordances, and (4) new audience forms.

Multimodality and Mobility

Popular accounts of technological innovation promise to lead us from the bygone era of the mouse and keyboard to a new world of "natural" user interfaces (e.g., Wigdor & Wixon, 2011). The vision is for interactive systems with the capacity to perform like good personal assistants who anticipate and understand a user's desires and everyday actions. It is argued that these interfaces will result in a more natural interaction paradigm for the user; however, before we can achieve this lofty goal, we need to better understand how humans interact naturally in a wide variety of multimodal configurations and environments.

We can communicate by just staring and not saying a word, raising an eyebrow, gesturing, or nodding. A friend can put pressure on our back and without words "ask" us to step forward in line. The value of a multimodal perspective can even be seen in something as simple as reference—in other words, how people specify the person, object, or entity that they are talking about (Carlson, 2004). As an example, consider the visual block study paradigm described earlier where a helper instructs a worker to select a puzzle piece by stating, "take a reddish brown colored block." This spoken segment establishes a licensed referent[5]—the object described as the "reddish brown colored block"—that can be specified later using a wide range of referential forms[6] such as pronominal expressions (e.g., "it," "that," or "this one"), definite or indefinite noun phrases (e.g., "the red-brown block"), etc. However, as the following example adapted from Gergle et al. (2007) demonstrates, a speaker's actions, gestures, or movements also serve as essential resources that can be used to evoke referential entities (see also Bangerter, 2004; Bavelas, Gerwing, Allison, & Sutton, 2011; Clark & Gergle, 2012):

1) **Helper:**   Okay, go and get <u>the bright red piece</u>.
   Worker: Yup.
   Worker: *[grabs the wrong piece – a pinkish-red piece]*
   Helper: Wait, no, <u>that</u>'s not <u>it</u>.

In the above excerpt, the helper requests that the worker grab "the bright red piece," and later uses the pronominal form "that" to specify the incorrect pinkish-red piece evoked by the worker's physical action and "it" to refer to the actual object evoked by the statement "the bright red piece." This simple example demonstrates how a model of spoken language alone does not suffice. Instead, a multimodal account is needed to accurately resolve the pronoun "that." In fact, it would be challenging for any conversational partner or computational system to correctly determine the referent of "that" without some form of shared visual access to the space (for further examples see Byron, Mampilly, Sharma, & Xu, 2005; Kehler, 2000).

This simple case highlights the need for a multimodal grounding framework, and the past couple of decades have seen remarkable growth in research exploring the role that various modalities such as gaze, gesture, haptics, and dynamic spatial cues play in support of grounding. The following covers a tiny portion of this work, with a particular focus on the modalities most often affected by technological innovation and mediation.

Gaze

Eye gaze patterns are an important resource for grounding that can provide evidence about a person's focus of attention (e.g., Vertegaal, Slagter, van der Veer, & Nijholt, 2001). They offer hints as to a partner's intentions, degree of understanding, or level of engagement, and they facilitate important conversational functions such as turn-taking and floor management. The ability to attend to a partner's gaze can support reference by minimizing the set of possible target objects (Brown-Schmidt, Campana, & Tanenhaus, 2002), reducing ambiguity before linguistic disambiguation occurs (Brennan, 2005; Hanna & Brennan, 2007), and providing evidence of the extent to which conversational pairs have successfully grounded their utterances (Ou, Oh, Yang, & Fussell, 2005).

Two noteworthy advances in eye-tracking technologies have been particularly helpful in furthering our understanding of the role that gaze plays in pair coordination and communication. Studies using *mobile eye-tracking* systems, which capture gaze patterns in unconstrained physical environments, have revealed that eye movements are often top-down processes that serve as precursors of task actions and are not simply reactions to external visual events (Land & Hayhoe, 2001; Land, Mennie, & Rusted, 1999; Pelz, Canosa, & Babcock, 2000). These studies lay the groundwork for understanding how conversational partners make use of gaze patterns to better coordinate their communication and interaction. *Dual user eye-tracking* is another developing technique that simultaneously tracks the gaze patterns of two individuals as they interact. This approach revealed that tighter coupling

Technology-Mediated Environments

between the speaker and listener's eye movements is associated with greater listener comprehension and increased mutual understanding (Richardson & Dale, 2005; Richardson, Dale, & Tomlinson, 2009). Recently, the method has been supplemented with gaze projection techniques (Velichkovsky, 1995) that provide visual representations of each speaker's gaze patterns to their partner, and this technique has been shown to support coordination and performance on time-sensitive spatial search tasks (Brennan, Chen, Dickinson, Neider, & Zelinsky, 2008). Studies of more complex tasks suggest it may also yield referential patterns that more closely approximate those of collocated pairs (D'Angelo & Gergle, 2016) and produce gains for remote students learning from complex diagrams (Schneider & Pea, 2013). However, gaze projection techniques are not always beneficial. "Always on" displays can actually disrupt referential processes and joint action (for examples see D'Angelo & Gergle, 2016), and the specific discourse processes supported remain elusive: Bard and colleagues found little evidence to support the notion that shared gaze systems increase the cognitive accessibility of referents (Bard, Hill, Foster, & Arai, 2014).

Gesture

Gesture is another important modality used to coordinate attention and ground conversation. It is highly sensitive to the spatial arrangement and configuration of interlocutors, with people adjusting their gestures depending upon where others are physically situated (Özyürek, 2002). Work by Bangerter (2004) provides a nice illustration of the coordinated nature of gesture and dialogue, revealing how pointing can be used to guide attention to spatial regions; but its utility hinges on the distance of the objects being referenced. When referential objects are nearby, conversational pairs rely more exclusively on pointing to identify them; however, when the objects are far away, pointing becomes more ambiguous and the pairs need to produce utterances with additional location and feature descriptions to successfully communicate. Other research has demonstrated this multimodal link between gesture and speech, suggesting that people use syntactically simpler language (Oviatt, 1997) and generate different surface forms (Cassell, Stone, & Yan, 2000) when their speech is accompanied by gestures or physical actions.

Tactile and Haptic Feedback

Tactile and haptic feedback can also be important resources for grounding and joint action. Consider the case of two people working together to move a piece of heavy furniture across a room. They can use language to describe where they will grab the object to lift it, discuss a plan for moving the piece around corners, describe where its final placement will be, etc. But the pair can also adjust to one another while actively moving the piece without saying a word—each person can feel the shifting weight of the piece and counter those forces in tandem with their partner. In other words, they maintain an awareness of where their partner is, how they may be holding the object and bearing the weight, and they can jointly produce "on-the-fly" adjustments while managing their goals (e.g., not dropping the furniture or banging it against the wall). However, while tactile and haptic feedback have been acknowledged as important coordination mechanisms for some forms of joint action (Brennan, 1991), they have been relatively underexplored in discourse research.

Nonetheless, researchers in the closely affiliated human-computer interaction field have developed new technologies that provide haptic and tactile feedback—often with supporting remote communication and coordination as the goal. Early work such as the InTouch

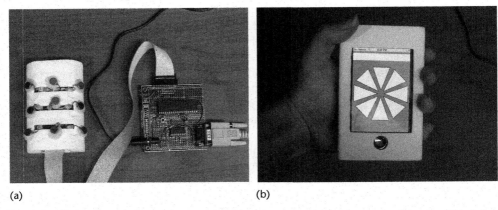

Figure 11.2 The hardware prototype developed and used by Yatani and colleagues. The left photo shows the hardware controller that drives the nine vibration motors used to provide spatial tactile feedback to a remote user. The right photo shows the device in the user's hand and the screen used during the spatial coordination task. From Yatani et al. (2012). Reprinted with permission of ACM Press

system allowed a user to transmit simple motion to a remote partner via Internet-connected mechanical cylinders (Brave, Ishii, & Dahley, 1998). Work by Oakley and colleagues developed a system for producing "haptic gestures" using the PHANTOM device that could be used to guide a remote partner to a specific region in a shared virtual workspace (Oakley, Brewster, & Gray, 2001). And Young and colleagues built a chair with a vibration-based tactor array that lets you "tap" on the back of a remote partner (Young, Tan, & Gray, 2003), and they showed that this technique could be used to successfully guide a remote partner to a targeted spatial region on a display.

More recently, researchers have focused on the development of systems with vibro-tactile feedback to directly support grounding and joint activity. One example uses an array of vibration motors on the back of a mobile smartphone device to provide "spatial tactile feedback" (see Figure 11.2) (Sahami, Holleis, Schmidt, & Häkkilä, 2008; Yatani & Truong, 2009). Yatani and colleagues used this approach to support spatial coordination between remote partners performing a joint task on their mobile devices that required them to jointly touch and "scrub clean" a triangular tile before it filled (for further details see Yatani et al., 2012). They showed that the combination of visual and tactile feedback was more beneficial than either visual or tactile feedback alone (see Figure 11.3 for an illustration of the experimental task and condition). The benefit stemmed, in part, from the fact that visual occlusions diminished the value of the visual feedback and thereby increased the benefit of the tactile feedback as a redundant cue to support spatial coordination. These are just a few examples of exciting new developments in tactile and haptic feedback design to support joint activity.

Mobility and Spatial Cues

The physical and spatial contexts in which grounding takes place are also important factors to consider, regardless of the particular modalities involved. For example, speakers have been shown to vary their descriptions and perspectives based on cues they draw from the surrounding spatial context (Schober, 1993), and spatial perspective marking is important for reducing cognitive costs and supporting effective communication (Steels & Loetzsch, 2009).

Technology-Mediated Environments

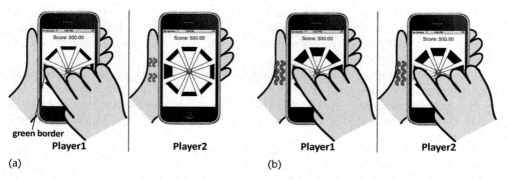

Figure 11.3 The panel on the left illustrates that when Player 1 touches a piece the relevant tactile feedback is provided to Player 2. When Player 2 touches the screen, Player 1 receives tactile feedback on the same area of the device. From Yatani et al. (2012). Reprinted with permission of ACM Press

Speakers vary their use of proximity markers (e.g., "this" or "here" vs. "that" or "there") in technologically mediated environments according to whether they perceive themselves to be physically co-present with their addressees (Bao & Gergle, 2009; Byron & Stoia, 2005; Fussell et al., 2004). Speakers also shift their spatial descriptions in ways that account for both their own spatial abilities as well as the perceived abilities of their partners (Schober, 2009). These interactions become even more complex when speakers are mobile and the objects move about in space around the speakers. For example, mobile pairs have been shown to use more proximal deixis (e.g., "this"), provide less location-based information and more feature-based information in their referential descriptions, and exhibit a lower incidence of joint gaze overlap in comparison to seated, stationary pairs performing a similar conversational task (Gergle & Clark, 2011). These findings highlight the importance of the pairs' access to physical movement as a coordination mechanism—something previous studies of collaborative reference have tended to overlook.

Emerging Research Challenges and Directions

Studies of gaze, gesture, haptics, and mobility all highlight the need to understand multimodality as it relates to grounding and discourse processes. While substantial progress has been made over the past two decades, the majority of experiments still take place in laboratories with static referential domains where participants are immobile and conversational roles are stable. There is room for methodological innovation that brings more natural context to discourse studies. For example, work in our laboratory fuses a mobile eye-tracking system with dual user eye-tracking techniques and automated object recognition techniques from computer vision to explore more complex, real-time collaboration in natural settings (for further details on the system and approach, see Gergle & Clark, 2011). This approach may be especially fruitful for revealing the complex relationship that exists between gaze, proxemics, and referential forms, but also for revealing how gaze patterns relate to higher-level cognitive and communicative processes in complex interaction settings. Gaze patterns are likely to vary according to stages of cognitive development, they may vary depending on levels of expertise and conversational roles, or even depend on the dialogue acts (e.g., questions, acknowledgments, hedges, requests for clarification, etc.) being performed in specific modalities and contexts. The merger of mobile and dual user eye-tracking approaches can be used to answer research questions about the multimodal communication and coordination processes in more complex, natural, and dynamic physical contexts, as well as inform the development of new gaze awareness tools, and in doing so continue to advance our understanding of world-situated language use (Trueswell & Tanenhaus, 2005).

A second area for multimodal advancement stems from closer integration with computer science research. Technological advances provide new platforms and integrate multimodality in novel and interesting ways, and this work serves dual purpose. On the one hand, it makes use of our knowledge of discourse processes to develop innovative forms of technological support. On the other hand, these new technologies can, in turn, help to reveal gaps in our theoretical understanding. In other words, a mutually beneficial synergy exists whereby computational modeling and technological development can both benefit from, and lead to deeper understanding of, discourse processes.

Consider interactive spoken dialogue systems as an example. Engineering practice has long adopted a model of communication and coordination that consists of simple message passing: a sender encodes information in a message, the message is transmitted through a technological mode, and the receiver then decodes the information. For many engineers this serves to quantize communication into convenient packages and simplifies the process of communication. However, this message-passing approach has numerous inadequacies compared to what we know about the coordination processes that characterize everyday interaction (Clark & Schaefer, 1989; Schober, 1995). Instead of this simplistic model of packaging and transferring messages, people engage in grounding processes and joint coordination. However, while the grounding framework provides an excellent conceptualization of communication as a joint activity, it was initially modest in the details it provided—from an engineering perspective—for building systems that can properly ground and engage with users. It has taken some time for researchers to adopt and develop models with these coordinative capacities (for notable early achievements see DeVault, Kariaeva, Kothari, Oved, & Stone, 2005; Nakano, Reinstein, Stocky, & Cassell, 2003; Traum, 1999), but recent systems (e.g., Nuance or Google Assistant) have begun to implement grounding aspects (e.g., backchannels and acknowledgments such as "got it," or requests for clarification such as "You said, [X]—is that correct?") into their dialogue management systems.

One particularly promising avenue for bringing discourse processes research to engineering centers on multimodal dialogue and communication in the development of the next generation of social robotics systems (see, e.g., Kim, Leyzberg, Tsui, & Scassellati, 2009; Mutlu, Kanda, Forlizzi, Hodgins, & Ishiguro, 2012). The design of robotic systems with cognitive and socio-emotional capacity is important for providing social support for human users in the areas of healthcare and education, among others. However, the current capacity of many social robotic platforms is still quite limited and lacks a computational underpinning based on embodied human behaviors such as gestures, body positioning and posture, gaze patterns, interpersonal distancing, and spatial configurations—as well as the ways in which these behaviors lead to important phenomena such as effectively guiding attention, establishing social roles, etc.

Mutlu and colleagues demonstrate the potential of this approach in their investigations exploring how the ATR Robovie social robotic platform can use head position and gaze to guide engagement with others involved in multiparty interactions (Mutlu, Shiwa, Kanda, Ishiguro, & Hagita, 2009), and better support the development of rapport and allocation of task attention (Mutlu et al., 2012). Figure 11.4 provides an illustration of their study design examining a model of conversational gaze mechanisms as they relate to turn-taking in three-party, human–robot conversations.

Technology-Mediated Environments

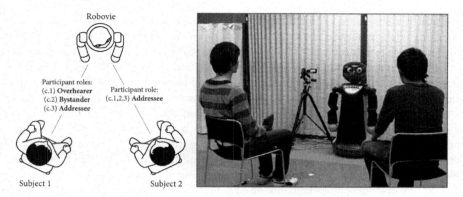

Figure 11.4 Work by Mutlu and colleagues uses a robotic agent, Robovie, to explore computational and generative models of role-signaling, turn-taking, and topic-signaling in multiparty environments. From Mutlu et al. (2012). Reprinted with permission of ACM Press

Work by Bohus and Horvitz (2010) expanded on this research to develop a real-time computational model for turn-taking in multiparty environments. Their multimodal behavioral control model leverages dialogue acts, deictic markers, time, and other factors to orchestrate a conversational agent's use of gaze, gesture, and speech to effectively control multiparty turn-taking. Researchers have also begun to integrate the numerous roles that gaze serves for grounding (e.g., establishing joint visual attention, disambiguating speech, and supporting turn-taking), and integrating these roles with dialogue and task management modules (Mehlmann et al., 2014).

Mode Choice and Mode Switching

One of the biggest changes to communication over the past decade is the integration of technological mediation into everyday life. The traditional distinction between "online" and "offline" interactions has blurred and people regularly make use of a wide variety of communication modes to interact with others and achieve work goals, develop personal relationships or simply have fun (Baym, Zhang, & Lin, 2004). They also routinely make use of different communication modes (e.g., phone calls, texting, emailing, video-chat) during a single communication episode—for example, you might send a text message to notify your significant other that you are coming home late from work and then follow up immediately with a phone call to clarify what groceries you need to pick up for dinner.

How do people decide on which communication mode to use? How do they determine when to switch between modes and what factors influence these decisions? How do discourse factors relate to the effectiveness of these decisions? And how do these choices affect grounding and broader communication outcomes? These are all questions that can be explored through research on mode choice (e.g., Conrad et al., 2017) and the related behavior of mode switching (e.g., Scissors & Gergle, 2013; Walther, 2004).[7] Mode choice generally refers to the decisions being made, and the factors influencing those decisions, about which communication mode to use, whether broadcasting via social media, directly emailing another person, group texting, or making a person-to-person phone call, and how these choices vary according to one's conversational needs.

The ability to choose a communication mode is not a new phenomenon—after all, people could always decide between writing a letter, sending a telegram, or making a phone call. What is new is that we now make these choices on a daily, hourly, or even minute-to-minute basis and we have a much greater variety of immediately available modes. As detailed in Conrad et al. (2017), this stems, in part, from the rapid increase in smart mobile device ownership with 68% of all U.S. adults owning smartphones in 2015 (a number that increases to 98% for 18–29-year-olds) (Anderson, 2015), and a consequence of this is that smartphones now serve as the primary communication device for a large portion of the world's population. Couple this with the fact that smartphones aggregate a number of communication modes onto a single device, and now hundreds of millions of people have the ability to instantly choose their preferred mode of communication at any point in time.

The growth in media choice behavior also results from the wide variety of communication modalities and broadcast levels available within a single software application (Oeldorf-Hirsch & Sundar, 2015). For example, social media platforms like Facebook allow a person to connect with others in numerous ways: you can post on another's timeline, send a message to a customized group of people, or use Facebook's Messenger application to send messages directly to a partner's mobile device or even initiate a live video-chat.

Furthermore, the ubiquity of the smartphone device also influences when and where communication is possible. We routinely communicate and interact while performing other activities and as a result we need to make choices about the best mode given the current situation or context. For example, mobility means the physical location we are in when we receive a call is often unknown (in comparison to older landlines that tied the receiver to a particular location such as their home), and as a result callers have to deal with a wide range of potential contextual factors when deciding whether to call (e.g., Avrahami, Gergle, Hudson, & Kiesler, 2007). We can be on a noisy commute, pushing a stroller, standing in line at a coffee-shop, or sitting in a public space where we don't want to speak loudly about a private matter. We can also be doing other things on our device: checking status updates or skimming a news announcement, playing video games, or watching videos. These situations and contexts can influence how and when we choose to communicate and what mode we choose to use when doing so.

When thinking about mode choice, earlier work in the organizational communication literature on the related construct of "media choice" bears mention. This literature focused on understanding managerial decision-making regarding the purchase and use of communication technology infrastructure in an organizational setting. Broadly speaking, it tends to disregard the nuanced distinctions that can exist within a given communication mode (as detailed in the first half of this chapter), and instead focuses on coarser comparisons between face-to-face and telephone-based communication and, to a lesser extent, video-chat systems. Much of the work applies an extension of media richness theories, which focused on communication performance, to technology choice with the assumption that group performance is equated with media choice decisions (Daft, Lengel, & Trevino, 1987; George, Carlson, & Valacich, 2013). The majority of these studies do not examine dialogue or natural interaction but instead focus on self-reported managerial perceptions. Nevertheless, the literature identifies a number of important factors that may be influential in mode choice research: the urgency or time pressure associated with an information need (Straub & Karahanna, 1998), the likelihood of recipient availability (Muller, Raven, Kogan, Millen, & Carey, 2003), and the physical distance of a partner (Webster & Trevino, 1995) may all play a role in how individuals make mode choices.

Early work on mode choice behavior tended to focus on its relationship to initiating contact with another person (e.g., Nardi, Whittaker, & Bradner, 2000). This research explored how mode choice related to interruption and availability, and came in response to concerns regarding workplace interruptions and information overload that coincided with the introduction of new communication technologies (e.g., Fogarty, Lai, & Christensen, 2004). More recently, mode choice research has focused directly on discourse processes. For example, in the context of survey research, people respond differently depending on the mode they choose: text-based SMS responses have been shown to be more precise, report more socially undesirable behaviors, and permit multitasking at higher rates, but they are slower and unfold over fewer conversational turns (Schober et al., 2015). This work is just the tip of the iceberg in understanding natural contexts for interaction, and understanding how mode choices can influence what we say, what we report, and how we interpret others.

Another important direction for mode choice research focuses on how people shift and change the modes they use over the course of a conversation or interaction. Mode switching[8] studies focus on the strategic shifts that take place between modes during a single communication episode. Early work highlighted this behavior in the context of Instant Messaging (IM) in the workplace and revealed that individuals engaged in mode switching from IM to another communication mode to overcome the times when a discussion needed better "interaction," when the participant felt there was a "misunderstanding," or when the group felt it would be better to have access to a shared physical workspace (Nardi et al., 2000).

Isaacs and colleagues (Isaacs, Walendowski, Whittaker, Schiano, & Kamm, 2002) performed a content analysis and found that mode switching occurs in almost 18% of the IM conversations they examined. People switched from IM to face-to-face meetings more than half the time, and the remainder of the time they switched from IM to the phone or email. It's important to note that at the time of the study switching often required the participants to switch devices (e.g., from a desktop computer to a landline phone) or even a switch locations such as from an office phone call to a collocated face-to-face meeting. With today's smartphone devices, the changing cost is even lower. As Nardi and colleagues show, mode switching has also been shown to occur at times judged to be appropriate points in a dialogue:

> Note that John asked [to switch to a] phone call after Bonnie provided an opening for a longer conversation with the question, "How are things going?" John judged the moment to be a reasonable time to request a longer conversation, using a different medium.
>
> *(Nardi et al., 2000, pp. 85–86)*

While most of the switching described in studies of IM use centered on coordinating other meetings or switching to environments that better suited group task requirements, there is also empirical evidence to suggest that mode selection can be a conversational strategy that depends on in-the-moment relational needs. For example, Scissors and colleagues performed structured interviews and surveys and found that participants were likely to perform mode switching (what they call "channel switching") during times of heightened relational conflict (2013; Scissors, Roloff, & Gergle, 2014). These results suggest that people strategically switch, sometimes in the middle of a conversation, and they exhibit a variety of switching patterns (e.g., from face-to-face to text chat and back; from text-messaging to a phone call to face-to-face; or from email to face-to-face to text-messaging). A number of interpersonal and relational motivations for initiating switches included: avoiding escalation in conflict, managing emotions (either one's own or one's partner's), adjusting to a partner's preferences, or resolving conflict.

However, a cautionary note is in order as mode choice and mode switching may not always be associated with positive outcomes. One instance of this is that individuals with low self-esteem are often drawn to communication technology that mediates interactions, likely because the technologies are perceived to lower face-threat and support distancing behaviors (Joinson, 2004; Scissors et al., 2014). But these choices can actually be poorly suited to an individual's interpersonal and relational needs (Forest & Wood, 2012). While low self-esteem individuals might have a preference for IM based interactions, when they make use of it to interact with their partner to discuss a prior conflict they report lower satisfaction with the interaction and their perceptions of changes in relational quality are more negative than when discussing face-to-face (Scissors & Gergle, 2016). In short, low self-esteem individuals' preferred mode choice can actually disadvantage their attempts at relational development and maintenance.

Emerging Research Challenges and Directions

Mode choice research is a nascent field, especially as it relates to discourse processes research. Much of the research to date focuses on identifying the presence of the behavior and is primarily descriptive in nature. There remains a need for greater theoretical integration and a broader range of studies exploring the phenomenon. How, why, and when do people make decisions regarding the choice of a communication mode? Do they strategically choose different modes for different purposes or in different social or environmental contexts? How do people vary their choices based on conversational goals (e.g., negotiating vs. apologizing)? To what extent do these choices vary depending on one's speaking partner (e.g., communicating with a stranger vs. a loved one) and their comfort or capacity with a given mode?

The holy grail for discourse processes research would be to develop a theoretical understanding that allows us to predict when and why certain mode choices are made, as well as determine when we might switch from one mode to another, and to understand what role mode choice plays in broader discourse and communication outcomes. Clark and Brennan's (1991) grounding framework may help to get us some of the way there. Certain choices, especially as they relate to issues around the establishment of mutual understanding, would likely benefit from applying the grounding framework. For example, ideas around least collaborative effort and grounding criteria may suggest the adoption of certain modes. Yet, while motivations for mode choice and channel switching are likely driven by a desire to ground and establish mutual understanding, there are a number of other important factors: personal preferences, environmental, situational, and temporal factors all play a significant role. Further, it remains to be explained how mode choices and mode switching affects core discourse topics such as conversational coherence, comprehension, learning, or a host of other communication outcomes.

There are also numerous social aspects around mode choice that are likely to be important to developing a comprehensive understanding of the behavior. In this regard, earlier research on "media" choice may be instructive. While this work tends to focus on general technology adoption and is less focused on the particular modes or features and attributes of the communication technology itself or how it may relate to messages, utterances, or discourse processes, it does provide a number of lessons regarding important social factors that may be integrated with choices made around the suitability of particular technological features for particular tasks (Webster & Trevino, 1995). For example, people with close relational ties are more likely to use a greater variety of modes with each other (Haythornthwaite, 2005), and an individual's choices may be influenced by prior experiences or exposure to other people's choices (Walther, 2011), as well as self-presentation and identity goals (Lampinen, Lehtinen, & Cheshire, 2014; Marwick & boyd, 2011; Papacharissi, 2011). Social influence, compliance with group norms (Fulk, Schmitz, & Steinfield, 1990), and reciprocal interdependence (Markus, 1987) are additional forces that have been shown to influence more general media choice and may be applicable when considering mode choice behaviors.

Finally, from a research perspective this topic poses significant methodological challenges. Naturalistic data collection often isolates the data collection to a single mode, whether a behavioral trace of interactions happening on a social network platform or a complete record of text-messaging (Smith, Hancock, Reynolds, & Birnholtz, 2014), but we often lose track of an individual as they move across major communication or interaction modalities. While survey methods, diary methods, or ecological momentary assessment approaches can be useful techniques, the development and application of new methods of data collection such as sensor-based and context-sensing approaches (e.g., Choudhury et al., 2008), especially those based on smartphone platforms, may be especially fruitful for future mode choice studies.

Social and Network-Based Affordances

Another important advance in communication technologies is the rapid introduction of network-based platforms. Social network sites[9] (SNSs) and social media platforms constitute many of today's most frequently visited online sites and they are part of everyday communication practices for a large portion of the world's population (ComScore, 2017). A defining feature of these technologies is their network-based structure—or the explicit and observable ties that exist between and among individuals and content—that both enrich and complicate the ways we think about addressees, overhearers, and audience, and they can have a profound effect on grounding processes and common ground.

As previously discussed, an affordances-based view can be particularly powerful as it abstracts away from the surface details of a technology and focuses instead on the particular components that are used to support the users' tasks and conversational goals. Researchers have begun to enumerate a set of network-based affordances that are important to consider when studying communication on SNS platforms (Ellison & Vitak, 2015; Treem & Leonardi, 2012). This work builds upon Clark and Brennan's framework by theorizing the particular ways in which SNSs, and the network-based properties they entail, influence available conversational resources. Treem and Leonardi (2012) describe four essential affordances of SNSs: association, visibility, persistence, and editability.[10]

Association refers to the connections that exist between and among users and their content (e.g., connected friends on Facebook), and it is one of the most unique affordances of network-based communication platforms. From a grounding perspective, associative structures provide the technical underpinning for users to become privy to the exchanges of others that would typically be outside of their view. It works in tandem with the visibility affordance (described next) to provide a greater sense of shared experience, community co-membership, and an understanding of "who knows who" and "who knows what." Furthermore, these structures provide SNS users with a way to actively signal to others their associations to various groups and content.

Visibility relates to the access users have to the connections among individuals and to the content with which they interact. This information provides users with insight into relationships, knowledge, behaviors, and personalities of others in their social network, as well as highlighting community activity patterns (e.g., noticing when a large group of peers engage in discussion around a recent news event). While Clark and Brennan's definition of visibility focuses more exclusively on the visual modality, Treem and Leonardi's concept of visibility centers more on the general accessibility of associative information (i.e., social ties are made "visible"), regardless of whether it's available in visual form or not. Visibility is enhanced by the fact that users can quickly publish what they know, what they experience, who they work with, etc., and this information is often searchable and widely available to others. One example of the value of visibility can be seen in an organizational context where workers draw upon visible information about their colleagues' backgrounds, interests, and activities to form a deeper understanding of one another (DiMicco, Geyer, Millen, Dugan, & Brownholtz, 2009); and newcomers to an organization use SNS content to help develop their understanding of an organization's culture, values, beliefs, and norms (Thom-Santelli, Millen, & Gergle, 2011).

Persistence, which has many similarities to Clark and Brennan's concept of reviewability, has to do with the fact that a message or post remains available for people to see at a future time. As noted earlier in the chapter, a clear record of prior conversation can be useful for grounding and coordination; however, in the context of network-based platforms, persistence also provides a communally shared record that endures over long periods of time. Furthermore, Treem and Leonardi argue that social media persistence creates more robust forms of communication because important information can be appropriated, reused, or remixed in various ways, ultimately proving to be beneficial for a wider variety of individuals. However, a potential downside to persistence is that the content can also be difficult to rescind, remove, or destroy—sometimes leading to substantial user regrets (e.g., Wang et al., 2011).

Editability is similar to Clark and Brennan's notion of revisability; however, there is a greater focus on the user's ability to edit a message after it has been posted. Also, because editing occurs in the context of a larger social setting, it is often done with a greater eye toward how others will perceive and react to the person or post. In other words, because SNS profiles are often used to create public-facing personas (Nie & Sundar, 2013), identity management becomes a more central concern when editing and revising messages for the SNS environments.

Treem and Leonardi also point out that it is the *set of affordances* as a whole that make SNSs unique relative to more traditional communication technologies. Furthermore, these are not the only affordances of SNSs. For example, the visible connections to others can reveal community co-membership as well as provide an important set of social credentials for future interactions (Lin, 1999)—being able to see that another individual interacts with a high-status individual may affect the likelihood or manner in which others communicate with them. Broadcast affordances, lowered transaction costs (Vitak & Ellison, 2013), replicability, and searchability (boyd, 2010) have all been posited as unique affordances of SNSs and social media platforms that support communication and provide more effortless access to resources.

Emerging Research Challenges and Directions

Similar to the earlier discussion on task and technology features and their interaction, further investigation of the specific platform features and conversational goals is needed to

Technology-Mediated Environments

secure our understanding of the degree to which social media platforms will influence communication in any given situation. On Facebook, for example, ties are reciprocal and primarily to known individuals with profiles based on everyday identities; and posting can be targeted to an individual, to groups, or to the general public. Twitter, on the other hand, does not require you to use a real identity, relations may or may not be reciprocal, and posting can be done to an individual in private or in public as well as to curated groups (i.e., "lists"). When considering social media platforms, close inspection of these features is just as important as it is in other forms of mediated communication. Many early studies of Facebook treated it as a single, monolithic entity even though usage and activities vary widely and take on highly differentiated forms (Baym et al., 2004; Smock, Ellison, Lampe, & Wohn, 2011). A simple activity like posting a "status message" update can take many different forms and be routed in different ways to different people (e.g., as a status update to one's full network or to a custom subset of one's network, as a post on a friend's wall, or as a direct message to an individual). Furthermore, these choices can be more or less effective depending on the sender's conversational goals or information needs (e.g., looking for restaurant recommendation vs. seeking health information for a set of symptoms) as well as one's audience in a given network (Oeldorf-Hirsch & Gergle, 2014; Oeldorf-Hirsch, Hecht, Morris, Teevan, & Gergle, 2014).

While this section has focused primarily on social network sites, there are numerous social computing technologies that have unique features and affordances that merit further investigation including wikis, microblogging platforms such as Twitter, discussion forums like Reddit, blogs, social tagging systems, and network-based video and multimodal systems such as Instagram, Snapchat, etc. Each of these technologies has a particular constellation of features, and as a result provides a set of affordances that are important to consider when investigating interaction and communication.

New Audience Forms

Another critical development over the past decade is the increasingly complex notion of audience, especially in the context of modern social media platforms. Network-based platforms can obscure the view of an audience in a way that affects message formulation and comprehension, as well as disrupt the conventional distinctions that exist between one-to-one and one-to-many communication environments.

Why Does Audience Matter?

An accurate understanding of audience plays a critical role in the process of audience design (Clark & Carlson, 1982), or the intentional tailoring of utterances and messages for specific listeners, which in turn serves as a basis for understanding (Clark & Murphy, 1982). Speakers make use of shared culture, joint experiences, prior conversation, and so on to better craft their contributions for addressees. Addressees, in turn, make use of this information to establish understanding as well as guide their pursuit of missing details (e.g., through requests for clarification). People that simply overhear a conversation, but do not have direct control over the conversation or the ability to interject, do not fare as well (Schober & Clark, 1989). Together these two components—the audience characteristics that influence message formulation and the conversational roles played by audience members—are crucial to conversational success. Yet, it is precisely these two audience features that are difficult to determine on modern social media platforms.

Who Comprises the Audience?

One prerequisite for effective audience design follows from the common adage, "know your audience," but this can be hard to accomplish on today's social media platforms. Bernstein and colleagues describe the challenges associated with determining audience on Facebook: "posting to a social network site is like speaking to an audience from behind a curtain. The audience remains invisible to the user: while the invitation list is known, the final attendance is not" (Bernstein, Bakshy, Burke, & Karrer, 2013, p. 21). Contrast this with a traditional face-to-face environment where speakers interact with a known audience that occupies the space around them.

On many social media platforms, the audience is ill-defined and its size, composition, degree of common ground, and the attentiveness of its members are less apparent and highly variable. As a result, speakers engage with an "imagined audience" (Litt, 2012) that is either too broad and abstract (e.g., "everyone in the world!") or too homogenous and overly focused on friends and family in comparison to the actual members of the audience (Litt & Hargittai, 2016). Even estimating the size of the audience is hard to do well: Facebook users were found to underestimate their actual audience size by a factor of four (Bernstein et al., 2013). It goes without saying that misalignments between an imagined and actual audience can pose significant challenges for grounding, as well as lead to a host of rather sobering social blunders.

A second audience challenge stems from the fact that social media platforms bring together previously distinct audiences. This is known as "context collapse" (Marwick & boyd, 2011), whereby formerly compartmentalized social groups come together in the melting pot that is a platform's audience. Friend groups, work colleagues, family members, fellow hobbyists, political allies, etc. are amalgamated into a single audience. What is clear and meaningful for one audience member or group may not be for another, and a statement that relies on common ground for one person or group may carry different meaning or simply be incomprehensible for another.

A third audience challenge stems from the fact that it is often unclear who actually receives a message. In face-to-face conversations, it's relatively easy to assess whether spoken utterances are heard by an addressee. However, the inability to accurately assess audience membership clouds one's ability to know whether a message was received or understood, and the flood of messages and news streams makes it easy for any given post to get lost in the morass. The problem of knowing "who saw what" is further complicated by the influence of invisible curation algorithms that determine which messages are displayed to whom and when—often in unpredictable ways that go unnoticed by senders and addressees (Eslami et al., 2015).

Emerging Research Challenges and Directions

Future research could take a number of directions to pursue an understanding of audience issues on social media platforms. But studying audience issues with large-scale, real-world communities has several important challenges that first need to be overcome.

One of the more enduring challenges to studying audience results from a need for a large and active user population to study.[11] One solution is for researchers to build their own community as a research platform (e.g., Harper & Konstan, 2015), and while this approach has the advantage that you know more about your audience demographics and have greater awareness of the algorithms and system affordances at play, it is also labor intensive and can be prone to failure, particularly when trying to populate the system with new users. Another approach is to work directly with commercial platforms and corporations (e.g., Kramer, Guillory, & Hancock, 2014). This has the advantage of providing access to a large, active, and diverse audience, but it suffers from a lack of algorithmic transparency and the fact that platform owners can change how the site operates on a whim, leaving the researcher to scramble to redesign their study (or worse, invalidate the study). While some of these challenges can be mitigated by working with successful open-source projects (e.g., Wikipedia or the Zooniverse platform), these communities can be limited in scope and scale.

A promising approach was recently described by Grevet and Gilbert (2015). They devised a hybrid technique known as "piggyback prototyping" that leverages existing commercial platforms (e.g., Twitter or Facebook) to answer research questions through the use of semi-autonomous bots. Their approach exploits existing platforms and services in a way that gets past the hurdle of having to attract a large number of people to your system, and instead lets you focus on research questions or design solutions in the context of a large-community operating at scale. This technique could provide discourse processes researchers with the ability to quickly prototype studies, expose flaws in their approach, and then iterate on their study design without having to spend all of their efforts building out a study that may or may not work out. In other words, the approach provides the ability to quickly iterate on study design—as one would with more traditional laboratory experiments—but in the context of a functioning, large-scale, online community. Another example of such a hybrid approach can be seen in Gilbert's (2012) study that explores how revealing audience exposure to common information can affect retweeting practices. They developed a tool named Link Different that helps a user to make a more informed decision about retweeting by showing them how many of their Twitter followers have already seen a tweet that links to a separate article or news story. The tool was used over 1.3 million times by nearly 150,000 users, with the result that users tended to retweet information that 20% or less of their audience had seen (perhaps not so surprising), but they also retweeted information that 95%+ of their followers had already seen (perhaps wanting to be seen as "in the know").

Another challenge for discourse researchers pursuing audience-related studies stems from the fact that discourse, exposure, and interaction all take unique forms in online settings, and specialized theories and methods are needed to work with large-scale, networked-based data. For example, to study macro-level phenomena such as social influence or sentiment contagion, researchers need to deal with both the aforementioned challenges around audience and exposure, as well as the unique properties associated with network-based communication structures and message forms that exist in many online domains. New techniques and theories are needed to "scale up" discourse process approaches. One potentially promising avenue may be to develop multilevel theories of discourse with corresponding statistical approaches that simultaneously capture individual, group, and network properties (e.g., Monge & Contractor, 2003). Purpose-built techniques are also needed for automated processing of language data available on social media platforms; for example, tools to deal with the unique properties of social media data such as parsing and sentiment analysis on tweets (e.g., Hutto & Gilbert, 2014; Owoputi et al., 2013).

Summary and Future Directions

Communication technologies are continuously evolving and in doing so they shape, and are shaped by, the ways we interact and communicate. These changes bring with them a host of research opportunities ranging from innovative ways to explore multimodal interaction to the need for computational models that integrate conversational grounding processes to whole new domains of research that focus on behaviors such as mode choice and mode switching. Researchers need to consider the special issues surrounding scale and network-based communication structures, and they can make use of new techniques and tools from computer vision as well as introduce statistical and machine learning approaches to enhance the study of discourse processes, whether from dyadic conversations or large-scale, massive online conversations. Furthermore, there are a number of topics and domains that are just beginning to blossom: new multilingual methods are being developed to study the semantic makeup of user-generated content repositories (Hecht & Gergle, 2010); cross-lingual interactions and their effect on grounding are being explored (Gao, Yamashita, Hautasaari, & Fussell, 2015); and we are on the cusp of many new innovations in two-way conversational interfaces as they are rapidly integrated into commodity devices (e.g., Alexa, Siri, Cortana, or Google Assistant). The study of technology-mediated discourse, and related problems at the intersection of technology and communication, continues to push the limits of our theoretical and practical understanding and will provide discourse processes researchers with new challenges for years to come.

Acknowledgments

I would like to thank a number of colleagues who have helped to form and inspire many of the ideas covered throughout this chapter, including Justine Cassell, Alan Clark, Sarah D'Angelo, Susan Fussell, Sid Horton, Robert Kraut, Eden Litt, Anne Marie Piper, Michael Schober, Lauren Scissors, Khai Truong, and Koji Yatani, as well as my many colleagues in the area of Technology and Social Behavior at Northwestern University.

Notes

1 "Snaps" refer to Snapchat messages. These are pictures or short video messages that can be recorded and sent to other Snapchat friends. They are then made available for the receiver to view but once they are opened the message is only available for up to ten seconds.
2 While Clark and Brennan originally refer to these as constraints, they can also be effectively thought of as affordances or resources for grounding and communication (Kraut, Fussell, & Siegel, 2003).
3 The Skype platform provides a number of features such as screen-sharing, a text-based chat interface, etc. While we focus on the video-calling component here for ease of exposition, these additional features provide a wider set of affordances that may or may not be used during a given interaction.
4 The earliest of these studies centered on comparing typewriting with handwriting, which more closely resembles the more fine-grained approach espoused here.
5 Licensed referents are the objects (or entities in a more general sense) that are syntactically available to be referenced.
6 Each of these expressions offer clues about the cognitive status of the referent in the pair's shared model of the activity (Ariel, 1988; Gundel, Hedberg, & Zacharski, 1993).
7 Media-multiplexity theory is a related theory that explores how groups add to their repertoire of communication media as group ties become stronger (Haythornthwaite, 2002).
8 Mode switching goes by a number of other terms in the literature including "media switching" (Nardi, Whittaker, & Bradner, 2000) and "channel switching" (e.g., Scissors & Gergle, 2013; Walther, 2004).
9 Ellison and boyd (2013, p. 158) define SNSs as networked communication platforms where users have identifiable profiles, publicly articulated connections to others, a traversable network structure, and user-generated content provides much of the information on the site.

10 While this research was originally constrained to workplace and organizational settings, it generally highlights the unique aspects a network-based perspective brings in comparison to more traditional non-network forms of technology-mediated communication.
11 This is more generally known as the "cold start" problem in social computing research.

References

Anderson, A. H., Bader, M., Bard, E. G., Boyle, E., Doherty, G., Garrod, S., . . . Weinert, R. (1991). The Hcrc map task corpus. *Language and Speech, 34*(4), 351–366. https://doi.org/10.1177/002383099103400404.

Anderson, A. H., O'Malley, C., Doherty-Sneddon, G., Langton, S., Newlands, A., Mullin, J., . . . Van der Velden, J. (1997). The impact of VMC on collaborative problem solving: An analysis of task performance, communicative process, and user satisfaction. In K. E. Finn, A. J. Sellen, & S. B. Wilbur (Eds), *Video-mediated communication* (pp. 133–155). Mahwah, NJ: Lawrence Erlbaum Publishers.

Anderson, M. (2015). Technology device ownership: 2015. *Pew Research Center*. Retrieved from www.pewinternet.org/2015/10/29/technology-device-ownership-2015.

Anderson, T., Sanford, A., Thomson, A., & Ion, W. (2007). Computer-supported and face-to-face collaboration on design tasks. *Discourse Processes, 43*(3), 201–228. https://doi.org/10.1080/01638530701226188.

Argyle, M., & Cook, M. (1976). *Gaze and mutual gaze*. Cambridge, UK; New York, NY: Cambridge University Press.

Ariel, M. (1988). Referring and accessibility. *Journal of Linguistics, 24*(1), 65–87.

Avrahami, D., Gergle, D., Hudson, S. E., & Kiesler, S. (2007). Improving the match between callers and receivers: A study on the effect of contextual information on cell phone interruptions. *Behaviour & Information Technology, 26*(3), 247–259. https://doi.org/10.1080/01449290500402338.

Bangerter, A. (2004). Using pointing and describing to achieve joint focus of attention in dialogue. *Psychological Science, 15*(6), 415–419. https://doi.org/10.1111/j.0956-7976.2004.00694.x.

Bao, P., & Gergle, D. (2009). What's "this" you say? The use of local references on distant displays. In *Proceedings of the 27th International Conference on Human Factors in Computing Systems* (pp. 1029–1032). New York, NY: ACM. https://doi.org/10.1145/1518701.1518858.

Bard, E. G., Hill, R. L., Foster, M. E., & Arai, M. (2014). Tuning accessibility of referring expressions in situated dialogue. *Language, Cognition and Neuroscience, 29*(8), 928–949. https://doi.org/10.1080/23273798.2014.895845.

Bavelas, J. B., Coates, L., & Johnson, T. (2002). Listener responses as a collaborative process: The role of gaze. *Journal of Communication, 52*(3), 566–580. https://doi.org/10.1111/j.1460-2466.2002.tb02562.x.

Bavelas, J., Gerwing, J., Allison, M., & Sutton, C. (2011). Dyadic evidence for grounding with abstract deictic gestures. In G. Stam & M. Ishino (Eds), *Integrating gestures: The interdisciplinary nature of gesture*. Amsterdam: John Benjamins Publishing Co.

Baym, N. K., Zhang, Y. B., & Lin, M.-C. (2004). Social interactions across media interpersonal communication on the internet, telephone and face-to-face. *New Media & Society, 6*(3), 299–318. https://doi.org/10.1177/1461444804041438.

Benkler, Y. (2003). Freedom in the commons: Towards a political economy of information. *Duke Law Journal, 52*(6), 1245–1276.

Bernstein, M. S., Bakshy, E., Burke, M., & Karrer, B. (2013). Quantifying the invisible audience in social networks. In *Proceedings of the SIGCHI Conference on Human Factors in Computing Systems* (pp. 21–30). New York, NY: ACM. https://doi.org/10.1145/2470654.2470658.

Biello, D. (2009, March 18). Can videoconferencing replace travel? *Scientific American*.

Bohus, D., & Horvitz, E. (2010). Facilitating multiparty dialog with gaze, gesture, and speech. In *International Conference on Multimodal Interfaces and the Workshop on Machine Learning for Multimodal Interaction* (pp. 5:1–5:8). New York, NY: ACM. https://doi.org/10.1145/1891903.1891910.

boyd, danah. (2010). Social network sites as networked publics: Affordances, dynamics, and implications. In Z. Papacharissi (Ed.), *Networked self: Identity, community, and culture on social network sites* (pp. 39–58).

Boyle, E. A., Anderson, A. H., & Newlands, A. (1994). The effects of visibility on dialogue and performance in a cooperative problem solving task. *Language and Speech, 37*(1), 1–20. https://doi.org/10.1177/002383099403700101.

Brave, S., Ishii, H., & Dahley, A. (1998). Tangible interfaces for remote collaboration and communication. In *Proceedings of the 1998 ACM Conference on Computer Supported Cooperative Work* (pp. 169–178). New York, NY: ACM. https://doi.org/10.1145/289444.289491.

Brennan, S. E. (1990). *Seeking and providing evidence for mutual understanding.* Stanford, CA: Stanford University.

Brennan, S. E. (1991). Conversation with and through computers. *User Modeling and User-Adapted Interaction, 1*(1), 67–86.

Brennan, S. E. (2005). How conversation is shaped by visual and spoken evidence. In J. C. Trueswell & M. K. Tanenhaus (Eds), *Approaches to studying world-situated language use: Bridging the language-as-product and language-as-action traditions* (pp. 95–129).

Brennan, S. E., Chen, X., Dickinson, C. A., Neider, M. B., & Zelinsky, G. J. (2008). Coordinating cognition: The costs and benefits of shared gaze during collaborative search. *Cognition, 106*(3), 1465–1477. https://doi.org/10.1016/j.cognition.2007.05.012.

Brown-Schmidt, S., Campana, E., & Tanenhaus, M. K. (2002). Reference resolution in the wild: Online circumscription of referential domains in a natural interactive problem-solving task. In *Proceedings of the 24th Annual Meeting of the Cognitive Science Society* (pp. 148–153).

Byron, D., Mampilly, T., Sharma, V., & Xu, T. (2005). Utilizing visual attention for cross-modal coreference interpretation. In *Proceedings of the 5th International Conference on Modeling and Using Context* (pp. 83–96). Berlin; Heidelberg: Springer-Verlag. https://doi.org/10.1007/11508373_7.

Byron, D. K., & Stoia, L. (2005). An analysis of proximity markers in collaborative dialog. In *In Proceedings of 41st Annual Meeting of the Chicago Linguistic Society.* Chicago, IL: Chicago Linguistic Society.

Cairncross, F., & Cairncross, F. C. (2001). *The death of distance: How the communications revolution is changing our lives* (Revised Edition). Boston, MA: Harvard Business Review Press.

Carlson, G. (2004). Reference. In L. R. Horn & G. Ward (Eds), *The handbook of pragmatics* (pp. 74–96). New York: Wiley.

Cassell, J., Stone, M., & Yan, H. (2000). Coordination and context-dependence in the generation of embodied conversation. In *Proceedings of the First International Conference on Natural Language Generation: Volume 14* (pp. 171–178). Stroudsburg, PA: Association for Computational Linguistics. https://doi.org/10.3115/1118253.1118277.

Chapanis, A., Ochsman, R. B., Parrish, R. N., & Weeks, G. D. (1972). Studies in interactive communication: I—The effects of four communication modes on the behavior of teams during cooperative problem-solving. *Human Factors, 14*, 487–509.

Choudhury, T., Borriello, G., Consolvo, S., Haehnel, D., Harrison, B., Hemingway, B., . . . Wyatt, D. (2008). The mobile sensing platform: An embedded activity recognition system. *IEEE Pervasive Computing, 7*(2), 32–41. https://doi.org/10.1109/MPRV.2008.39

Clark, A. T., & Gergle, D. (2012). Know what I'm talking about? Dual eye-tracking in multimodal reference resolution. *Workshop Paper Appearing in DUET 2012: Dual Eye Tracking Workshop at CSCW 2012.*

Clark, H. H., & Brennan, S. E. (1991). Grounding in communication. In *Perspectives on socially shared cognition* (pp. 127–149). New York: American Psychological Association.

Clark, H. H., & Carlson, T. B. (1982). Hearers and speech acts. *Language*, 332–373.

Clark, H. H., & Krych, M. A. (2004). Speaking while monitoring addressees for understanding. *Journal of Memory and Language, 50*(1), 62–81. https://doi.org/10.1016/j.jml.2003.08.004.

Clark, H. H., & Marshall, C. R. (1981). Definite reference and mutual knowledge. In A. K. Joshi & I. A. Sag (Eds), *Elements of discourse understanding* (pp. 10–63). Cambridge, UK: Cambridge University Press.

Clark, H. H., & Murphy, G. L. (1982). Audience design in meaning and reference. *Advances in Psychology, 9*, 287–299. https://doi.org/10.1016/S0166-4115(09)60059-5.

Clark, H. H., & Schaefer, E. F. (1989). Contributing to discourse. *Cognitive Science, 13*(2), 259–294. https://doi.org/10.1207/s15516709cog1302_7.

Clark, H. H., & Wilkes-Gibbs, D. (1986). Referring as a collaborative process. *Cognition, 22*(1), 1–39.

Clayton, R. B., Nagurney, A., & Smith, J. R. (2013). Cheating, breakup, and divorce: Is Facebook use to blame? *Cyberpsychology, Behavior, and Social Networking, 16*(10), 717–720. https://doi.org/10.1089/cyber.2012.0424.

ComScore. (2017, January 23). Revised top 50 digital media properties for October and November 2016. Retrieved from www.comscore.com/Insights/Rankings/Revised-Top-50-Digital-Media-Properties-for-October-and-November-2016.

Conrad, F.G., Schober, M.F., Antoun, C., Yan, H.Y., Hupp, A.L., Johnston, M., ... Zhang, C. (2017). Respondent mode choice in a smartphone survey. *Public Opinion Quarterly, 81*(S1), 307–337.

Daft, R. L., & Lengel, R. (1984). Information richness: A new approach to managerial behavior and organizational design. *Research in Organizational Behavior, 6*, 191–233.

Daft, R. L., Lengel, R. H., & Trevino, L. K. (1987). Message equivocality, media selection, and manager performance: Implications for information systems. *MIS Quarterly, 11*(3), 355–366. https://doi.org/10.2307/248682

Daly-Jones, O., Monk, A., & Watts, L. (1998). Some advantages of video conferencing over high-quality audio conferencing: Fluency and awareness of attentional focus. *International Journal of Human-Computer Studies, 49*(1), 21–58. https://doi.org/10.1006/ijhc.1998.0195.

D'Angelo, S., & Gergle, D. (2016). Gazed and confused: Understanding and designing shared gaze for remote collaboration. In *Proceedings of the 2016 CHI Conference on Human Factors in Computing Systems* (pp. 2492–2496). New York, NY: ACM. https://doi.org/10.1145/2858036.2858499.

DeVault, D., Kariaeva, N., Kothari, A., Oved, I., & Stone, M. (2005). An information-state approach to collaborative reference. In *Proceedings of the ACL 2005 on Interactive Poster and Demonstration Sessions* (pp. 1–4). Stroudsburg, PA: Association for Computational Linguistics. https://doi.org/10.3115/1225753.1225754.

Dibble, J. L., & Drouin, M. (2014). Using modern technology to keep in touch with back burners: An investment model analysis. *Computers in Human Behavior, 34*, 96–100. https://doi.org/10.1016/j.chb.2014.01.042.

DiMicco, J. M., Geyer, W., Millen, D. R., Dugan, C., & Brownholtz, B. (2009). People sensemaking and relationship building on an enterprise social network site. In *2009 42nd Hawaii International Conference on System Sciences* (pp. 1–10). https://doi.org/10.1109/HICSS.2009.343.

Duguid, P. (2006). Limits of self-organization: Peer production and "laws of quality." *First Monday, 11*(10).

Ellison, N. B., & boyd, danah. (2013). Sociality through social network sites. In W. H. Dutton (Ed.), *The Oxford handbook of internet studies* (pp. 151–172). Oxford: Oxford University Press.

Ellison, N. B., Hancock, J. T., & Toma, C. L. (2012). Profile as promise: A framework for conceptualizing veracity in online dating self-presentations. *New Media & Society, 14*(1), 45–62. https://doi.org/10.1177/1461444811410395.

Ellison, N. B., & Vitak, J. (2015). Social network site affordances and their relationship to social capital processes. In S. S. Sundar (Ed.), *The handbook of the psychology of communication technology* (pp. 203–227). New York, NY: John Wiley & Sons, Ltd. https://doi.org/10.1002/9781118426456.ch9.

Eslami, M., Rickman, A., Vaccaro, K., Aleyasen, A., Vuong, A., Karahalios, K., . . . Sandvig, C. (2015). "I always assumed that I wasn't really that close to [her]": Reasoning about invisible algorithms in news feeds. In *Proceedings of the 33rd Annual ACM Conference on Human Factors in Computing Systems* (pp. 153–162). New York, NY: ACM. https://doi.org/10.1145/2702123.2702556.

Feuer, S., & Schober, M. F. (2013). Self-view can increase disclosure in videomediated survey interviews. *23rd Annual Meeting of the Society for Text and Discourse.*

Fogarty, J., Lai, J., & Christensen, J. (2004). Presence versus availability: The design and evaluation of a context-aware communication client. *International Journal of Human-Computer Studies, 61*(3), 299–317. https://doi.org/10.1016/j.ijhcs.2003.12.016.

Forest, A. L., & Wood, J. V. (2012). When social networking is not working: Individuals with low self-esteem recognize but do not reap the benefits of self-disclosure on Facebook. *Psychological Science, 23*(3), 295–302. https://doi.org/10.1177/0956797611429709.

Fulk, J., Schmitz, J., & Steinfield, C. (1990). A social influence model of technology use. In J. Fulk & C. Steinfield (Eds), *Organizations and communication technology* (pp. 117–140). Thousand Oaks, CA: SAGE Publications.

Fussell, S. R., & Krauss, R. M. (1992). Coordination of knowledge in communication: Effects of speakers' assumptions about what others know. *Journal of Personality and Social Psychology, 62*(3), 378–391.

Fussell, S. R., Setlock, L. D., & Kraut, R. E. (2003). Effects of head-mounted and scene-oriented video systems on remote collaboration on physical tasks. In *Proceedings of the SIGCHI Conference on Human Factors in Computing Systems* (pp. 513–520). New York, NY: ACM. https://doi.org/10.1145/642611.642701.

Fussell, S. R., Setlock, L. D., Yang, J., Ou, J., Mauer, E., & Kramer, A. D. I. (2004). Gestures over video streams to support remote collaboration on physical tasks. *Human–Computer Interaction*, *19*(3), 273–309. https://doi.org/10.1207/s15327051hci1903_3.

Gao, G., Yamashita, N., Hautasaari, A. M. J., & Fussell, S. R. (2015). Improving multilingual collaboration by displaying how non-native speakers use automated transcripts and bilingual dictionaries. In *Proceedings of the 33rd Annual ACM Conference on Human Factors in Computing Systems* (pp. 3463–3472). New York, NY: ACM. https://doi.org/10.1145/2702123.2702498.

George, J. F., Carlson, J. R., & Valacich, J. S. (2013). Media selection as a strategic component of communication. *MIS Quarterly*, *37*(4), 1233–A4.

Gergle, D. (2006). *The value of shared visual information for task-oriented collaboration*. Pittsburgh, PA: Carnegie Mellon University Press.

Gergle, D., & Clark, A. T. (2011). See what I'm saying? Using dyadic mobile eye tracking to study collaborative reference. In *Proceedings of the ACM 2011 Conference on Computer Supported Cooperative Work* (pp. 435–444). New York, NY: ACM. https://doi.org/10.1145/1958824.1958892.

Gergle, D., Kraut, R. E., & Fussell, S. R. (2013). Using visual information for grounding and awareness in collaborative tasks. *Human–Computer Interaction*, *28*(1), 1–39. https://doi.org/10.1080/07370024.2012.678246.

Gergle, D., Millen, D. R., Kraut, R. E., & Fussell, S. R. (2004). Persistence matters: Making the most of chat in tightly-coupled work. In *Proceedings of the SIGCHI Conference on Human Factors in Computing Systems* (pp. 431–438). New York, NY: ACM. https://doi.org/10.1145/985692.985747.

Gergle, D., Rosé, C. P., & Kraut, R. E. (2007). Modeling the impact of shared visual information on collaborative reference. In *Proceedings of the SIGCHI Conference on Human Factors in Computing Systems* (pp. 1543–1552). New York, NY: ACM. http://doi.acm.org/10.1145/1240624.1240858

Gilbert, E. (2012). Designing social translucence over social networks. In *Proceedings of the SIGCHI Conference on Human Factors in Computing Systems* (pp. 2731–2740). New York, NY: ACM. https://doi.org/10.1145/2207676.2208670.

Giles, J. (2005). Internet encyclopaedias go head to head. *Nature*, *438*(7070), 900–901. https://doi.org/10.1038/438900a.

Grevet, C., & Gilbert, E. (2015). Piggyback prototyping: Using existing, large-scale social computing systems to prototype new ones. In *Proceedings of the 33rd Annual ACM Conference on Human Factors in Computing Systems* (pp. 4047–4056). New York, NY: ACM. https://doi.org/10.1145/2702123.2702395.

Gundel, J. K., Hedberg, N., & Zacharski, R. (1993). Cognitive status and the form of referring expressions in discourse. *Language*, *69*(2), 274–307. https://doi.org/10.2307/416535.

Hancock, J. T., & Dunham, P. J. (2001). Language use in computer-mediated communication: The role of coordination devices. *Discourse Processes*, *31*(1), 91–110. https://doi.org/10.1207/S15326950dp3101_4.

Hanna, J. E., & Brennan, S. E. (2007). Speakers' eye gaze disambiguates referring expressions early during face-to-face conversation. *Journal of Memory and Language*, *57*(4), 596–615. https://doi.org/10.1016/j.jml.2007.01.008.

Harper, F. M., & Konstan, J. A. (2015). The MovieLens datasets: History and context. *ACM Trans. Interact. Intell. Syst.*, *5*(4), 19:1–19:19. https://doi.org/10.1145/2827872.

Haythornthwaite, C. (2002). Strong, weak, and latent ties and the impact of new media. *The Information Society*, *18*(5), 385–401.

Haythornthwaite, C. (2005). Social networks and Internet connectivity effects. *Information, Communication & Society*, *8*(2), 125–147. https://doi.org/10.1080/13691180500146185.

Hecht, B., & Gergle, D. (2009). Measuring self-focus bias in community-maintained knowledge repositories. In *Proceedings of the Fourth International Conference on Communities and Technologies* (pp. 11–20). New York, NY: ACM.

Hecht, B., & Gergle, D. (2010). The tower of Babel meets web 2.0: User-generated content and its applications in a multilingual context. In *Proceedings of the 28th International Conference on Human Factors in Computing Systems* (pp. 291–300). New York, NY: ACM.

Hollan, J., & Stornetta, S. (1992). Beyond being there. In *Proceedings of the SIGCHI Conference on Human Factors in Computing Systems* (pp. 119–125). New York, NY: ACM. https://doi.org/10.1145/142750.142769.

Huang, W., Olson, J. S., & Olson, G. M. (2002). Camera angle affects dominance in video-mediated communication. In *CHI '02 Extended abstracts on human factors in computing systems* (pp. 716–717). New York, NY: ACM. https://doi.org/10.1145/506443.506562.

Hutto, C. J., & Gilbert, E. (2014). Vader: A parsimonious rule-based model for sentiment analysis of social media text. In *Eighth International AAAI Conference on Weblogs and Social Media*.

Isaacs, E. A., & Clark, H. H. (1987). References in conversation between experts and novices. *Journal of Experimental Psychology: General, 116*(1), 26.

Isaacs, E. A., Walendowski, A., Whittaker, S., Schiano, D. J., & Kamm, C. (2002). The character, functions, and styles of instant messaging in the workplace. In *Proceedings of the 2002 ACM Conference on Computer Supported Cooperative Work* (pp. 11–20). New York, NY: ACM. https://doi.org/10.1145/587078.587081.

Jefferson, G. (1972). Side sequences. In D. Sudnow (Ed.), *Studies in social interaction* (pp. 294–338). New York, NY: The Free Press.

Joinson, A. N. (2004). Self-esteem, interpersonal risk, and preference for e-mail to face-to-face communication. *Cyberpsychology & Behavior: The Impact of the Internet, Multimedia and Virtual Reality on Behavior and Society, 7*(4), 472–478. https://doi.org/10.1089/cpb.2004.7.472.

Karsenty, L. (1999). Cooperative work and shared visual context: An empirical study of comprehension problems in side-by-side and remote help dialogues. *Human–Computer Interaction, 14*(3), 283–315. https://doi.org/10.1207/S15327051HCI1403_2.

Kehler, A. (2000). Cognitive status and form of reference in multimodal human-computer interaction. In *AAAI/IAAI* (pp. 685–690).

Kendon A. (1967). Some functions of gaze-direction in social interaction. *Acta Psychologica, 26*(1), 22–63.

Kim, E. S., Leyzberg, D., Tsui, K. M., & Scassellati, B. (2009). How people talk when teaching a robot. In *Proceedings of the 4th ACM/IEEE International Conference on Human Robot Interaction* (pp. 23–30). New York, NY: ACM. https://doi.org/10.1145/1514095.1514102.

Kramer, A. D. I., Guillory, J. E., & Hancock, J. T. (2014). Experimental evidence of massive-scale emotional contagion through social networks. *Proceedings of the National Academy of Sciences, 111*(24), 8788–8790. https://doi.org/10.1073/pnas.1320040111.

Kraut, R. E., Fussell, S. R., Brennan, S. E., & Siegel, J. (2002). Understanding effects of proximity on collaboration: Implications for technologies to support remote collaborative work. In P. Hinds & S. Kiesler (Eds), *Distributed work* (pp. 137–162). Cambridge, MA: MIT Press.

Kraut, R. E., Fussell, S. R., & Siegel, J. (2003). Visual information as a conversational resource in collaborative physical tasks. *Human-Computer Interaction, 18*(1), 13–49.

Kraut, R. E., Gergle, D., & Fussell, S. R. (2002). The use of visual information in shared visual spaces: informing the development of virtual co-presence. In *Proceedings of the 2002 ACM Conference on Computer Supported Cooperative Work* (pp. 31–40). New York, NY: ACM. https://doi.org/10.1145/587078.587084.

Lampinen, A., Lehtinen, V., & Cheshire, C. (2014). Media choice and identity work: A case study of information communication technology use in a peer community. In *Communication and information technologies annual* (Vol. 8, pp. 103–130). Emerald Group Publishing Limited.

Land, M. F., & Hayhoe, M. (2001). In what ways do eye movements contribute to everyday activities? *Vision Research, 41*(25–26), 3559–3565. https://doi.org/10.1016/S0042-6989(01)00102-X.

Land, M., Mennie, N., & Rusted, J. (1999). The roles of vision and eye movements in the control of activities of daily living. *Perception, 28*(11), 1311–1328. https://doi.org/10.1068/p2935.

Lin, N. (1999). Building a network theory of social capital. *Connections, 22*(1), 28–51.

Litt, E. (2012). Knock, knock: Who's there? The imagined audience. *Journal of Broadcasting & Electronic Media, 56*(3), 330–345. https://doi.org/10.1080/08838151.2012.705195.

Litt, E., & Hargittai, E. (2016). The imagined audience on social network sites. *Social Media + Society, 2*(1), 2056305116633482. https://doi.org/10.1177/2056305116633482.

Markus, M. L. (1987). Toward a "critical mass" theory of interactive media universal access, interdependence and diffusion. *Communication Research, 14*(5), 491–511. https://doi.org/10.1177/009365087014005003.

Marwick, A. E., & boyd, danah. (2011). I tweet honestly, I tweet passionately: Twitter users, context collapse, and the imagined audience. *New Media & Society*, *13*(1), 114–133. https://doi.org/10.1177/1461444810365313.

Mehlmann, G., Häring, M., Janowski, K., Baur, T., Gebhard, P., & André, E. (2014). Exploring a model of gaze for grounding in multimodal HRI. In *Proceedings of the 16th International Conference on Multimodal Interaction* (pp. 247–254). New York, NY: ACM. https://doi.org/10.1145/2663204.2663275.

Monge, P. R., & Contractor, N. S. (2003). *Theories of communication networks*. Oxford; New York: Oxford University Press.

Muller, M. J., Raven, M. E., Kogan, S., Millen, D. R., & Carey, K. (2003). Introducing chat into business organizations: Toward an instant messaging maturity model. *SIGGROUP Bull.*, *24*(1), 5–5. https://doi.org/10.1145/1027232.1027241.

Mutlu, B., Kanda, T., Forlizzi, J., Hodgins, J., & Ishiguro, H. (2012). Conversational gaze mechanisms for humanlike robots. *ACM Trans. Interact. Intell. Syst.*, *1*(2), 12:1–12:33. https://doi.org/10.1145/2070719.2070725.

Mutlu, B., Shiwa, T., Kanda, T., Ishiguro, H., & Hagita, N. (2009). Footing in human-robot conversations: How robots might shape participant roles using gaze cues. In *Proceedings of the 4th ACM/IEEE International Conference on Human Robot Interaction* (pp. 61–68). New York, NY: ACM. https://doi.org/10.1145/1514095.1514109.

Nakano, Y. I., Reinstein, G., Stocky, T., & Cassell, J. (2003). Towards a model of face-to-face grounding. In *Proceedings of the 41st Annual Meeting on Association for Computational Linguistics: Volume 1* (pp. 553–561). Association for Computational Linguistics.

Nardi, B. A., Schwarz, H., Kuchinsky, A., Leichner, R., Whittaker, S., & Sclabassi, R. (1993). Turning away from talking heads: The use of video-as-data in neurosurgery. In *Proceedings of the INTERACT '93 and CHI '93 Conference on Human Factors in Computing Systems* (pp. 327–334). New York, NY: ACM. https://doi.org/10.1145/169059.169261.

Nardi, B. A., Whittaker, S., & Bradner, E. (2000). Interaction and outeraction: Instant messaging in action. In *Proceedings of the 2000 ACM Conference on Computer Supported Cooperative Work* (pp. 79–88). New York, NY: ACM. https://doi.org/10.1145/358916.358975.

Nie, J., & Sundar, S. S. (2013). Who would pay for Facebook? Self-esteem as a predictor of user behavior, identity construction and valuation of virtual possessions. In *Human-computer interaction –INTERACT 2013* (pp. 726–743). Berlin; Heidelberg; Springer. https://doi.org/10.1007/978-3-642-40477-1_50.

Northrup, J., & Smith, J. (2016). Effects of Facebook maintenance behaviors on partners' experience of love. *Contemporary Family Therapy*, *38*(2), 245–253. https://doi.org/10.1007/s10591-016-9379-5.

Oakley, I., Brewster, S., & Gray, P. (2001). Can you feel the force? An investigation of haptic collaboration in shared editors. In *Proceedings of Eurohaptics* (pp. 54–59).

Oeldorf-Hirsch, A., & Gergle, D. (2014). Audience targeting strategies for seeking information on Facebook. Presented at the International Communication Association (ICA 2014).

Oeldorf-Hirsch, A., Hecht, B., Morris, M. R., Teevan, J., & Gergle, D. (2014). To search or to ask: The routing of information needs between traditional search engines and social networks. In *Proceedings of the 17th ACM Conference on Computer Supported Cooperative Work and Social Computing* (pp. 16–27). New York, NY: ACM. https://doi.org/10.1145/2531602.2531706.

Oeldorf-Hirsch, A., & Sundar, S. S. (2015). Posting, commenting, and tagging: Effects of sharing news stories on Facebook. *Computers in Human Behavior*, *44*, 240–249. https://doi.org/10.1016/j.chb.2014.11.024.

O'Malley, C., Langton, S., Anderson, A., Doherty-Sneddon, G., & Bruce, V. (1996). Comparison of face-to-face and video-mediated interaction. *Interacting with Computers*, *8*(2), 177–192. https://doi.org/10.1016/0953-5438(96)01027-2.

Ou, J., Oh, L. M., Yang, J., & Fussell, S. R. (2005). Effects of task properties, partner actions, and message content on eye gaze patterns in a collaborative task. In *Proceedings of the SIGCHI Conference on Human Factors in Computing Systems* (pp. 231–240). New York, NY: ACM. https://doi.org/10.1145/1054972.1055005.

Oviatt, S. (1997). Multimodal interactive maps: Designing for human performance. *Human-Computer Interaction 12*(1), 93–129. https://doi.org/10.1207/s15327051hci1201&2_4.

Owoputi, O., O'Connor, B., Dyer, C., Gimpel, K., Schneider, N., & Smith, N. A. (2013). Improved part-of-speech tagging for online conversational text with word clusters. Association for Computational Linguistics.

Özyürek, A. (2002). Do speakers design their cospeech gestures for their addressees? The effects of addressee location on representational gestures. *Journal of Memory and Language, 46*(4), 688–704. https://doi.org/10.1006/jmla.2001.2826.

Papacharissi, Z. (2011). *A networked self: Identity, community and culture on social network sites.* New York, NY: Routledge.

Pelz, J. B., Canosa, R., & Babcock, J. (2000). Extended tasks elicit complex eye movement patterns. In *Proceedings of the 2000 Symposium on Eye Tracking Research and Applications* (pp. 37–43). New York, NY: ACM. https://doi.org/10.1145/355017.355023.

Ranjan, A., Birnholtz, J. P., & Balakrishnan, R. (2006). An exploratory analysis of partner action and camera control in a video-mediated collaborative task. In *Proceedings of the 2006 20th Anniversary Conference on Computer Supported Cooperative Work* (pp. 403–412). New York, NY: ACM. https://doi.org/10.1145/1180875.1180936.

Richardson, D. C., & Dale, R. (2005). Looking to understand: The coupling between speakers' and listeners' eye movements and its relationship to discourse comprehension. *Cognitive Science, 29*(6), 1045–1060.

Richardson, D. C., Dale, R., & Tomlinson, J. M. (2009). Conversation, gaze coordination, and beliefs about visual context. *Cognitive Science, 33*(8), 1468–1482. https://doi.org/10.1111/j.1551-6709.2009.01057.x.

Sacks, H., Schegloff, E. A., & Jefferson, G. (1974). A simplest systematics for the organization of turn-taking for conversation. *Language, 50*(4), 696–735. https://doi.org/10.2307/412243.

Sahami, A., Holleis, P., Schmidt, A., & Häkkilä, J. (2008). Rich tactile output on mobile devices. In E. Aarts, J. L. Crowley, B. de Ruyter, H. Gerhäuser, A. Pflaum, J. Schmidt, & R. Wichert (Eds), *Ambient intelligence* (pp. 210–221). Berlin; Heidelberg: Springer. https://doi.org/10.1007/978-3-540-89617-3_14.

Schneider, B., & Pea, R. (2013). Real-time mutual gaze perception enhances collaborative learning and collaboration quality. *International Journal of Computer-Supported Collaborative Learning, 8*(4), 375–397. https://doi.org/10.1007/s11412-013-9181-4.

Schober, M. F. (1993). Spatial perspective-taking in conversation. *Cognition, 47*(1), 1–24. https://doi.org/10.1016/0010-0277(93)90060-9.

Schober, M. F. (1995). Speakers, addressees, and frames of reference: Whose effort is minimized in conversations about locations? *Discourse Processes, 20*(2), 219–247. https://doi.org/10.1080/01638539509544939.

Schober, M. F. (2009). Spatial dialogue between partners with mismatched abilities. In K. R. Coventry, T. Tenbrink, & J. A. Bateman (Eds), *Spatial language and dialogue* (pp. 23–39). Amsterdam: John Benjamins.

Schober, M. F., & Clark, H. H. (1989). Understanding by addressees and overhearers. *Cognitive Psychology, 21*, 211–232.

Schober, M. F., Conrad, F. G., Antoun, C., Ehlen, P., Fail, S., Hupp, A. L., . . . Zhang, C. (2015). Precision and disclosure in text and voice interviews on smartphones. *PLOS ONE, 10*(6), e0128337. https://doi.org/10.1371/journal.pone.0128337.

Scissors, L. E., & Gergle, D. (2013). "Back and forth, back and forth": Channel switching in romantic couple conflict. In *Proceedings of the 2013 Conference on Computer Supported Cooperative Work* (pp. 237–248). New York, NY: ACM. https://doi.org/10.1145/2441776.2441804.

Scissors, L. E., & Gergle, D. (2016). On the bias: Self-esteem biases across communication channels during romantic couple conflict. In *Proceedings of the 19th ACM Conference on Computer-Supported Cooperative Work and Social Computing* (pp. 383–393). New York, NY: ACM. https://doi.org/10.1145/2818048.2820080.

Scissors, L. E., Roloff, M. E., & Gergle, D. (2014). Room for interpretation: The role of self-esteem and CMC in romantic couple conflict. In *Proceedings of the 32nd Annual ACM Conference on Human Factors in Computing Systems* (pp. 3953–3962). New York, NY: ACM. https://doi.org/10.1145/2556288.2557177.

Short, J., Williams, E., & Christie, B. (1976). *The social psychology of telecommunications.* London; New York: Wiley.

Smith, M. E., Hancock, J. T., Reynolds, L., & Birnholtz, J. (2014). Everyday deception or a few prolific liars? The prevalence of lies in text messaging. *Computers in Human Behavior, 41*, 220–227. https://doi.org/10.1016/j.chb.2014.05.032.

Smock, A. D., Ellison, N. B., Lampe, C., & Wohn, D. Y. (2011). Facebook as a toolkit: A uses and gratification approach to unbundling feature use. *Computers in Human Behavior, 27*(6), 2322–2329. https://doi.org/10.1016/j.chb.2011.07.011.

Steels, L., & Loetzsch, M. (2009). Perspective alignment in spatial language. In K. R. Coventry, T. Tenbrink, & J. A. Bateman (Eds.), *Spatial language and dialogue* (pp. 70–88). Amsterdam: John Benjamins.

Straub, D., & Karahanna, E. (1998). Knowledge worker communications and recipient availability: Toward a task closure explanation of media choice. *Organization Science*, *9*(2), 160–175. https://doi.org/10.1287/orsc.9.2.160.

Thom-Santelli, J., Millen, D. R., & Gergle, D. (2011). Organizational acculturation and social networking. In *Proceedings of the ACM 2011 Conference on Computer Supported Cooperative Work* (pp. 313–316). New York, NY: ACM. https://doi.org/10.1145/1958824.1958871.

Tong, S., & Walther, J. B. (2011). Relational maintenance and CMC. In K. B. Wright & L. M. Webb (Eds), *Computer-mediated communication in personal relationships* (pp. 98–118). New York, NY: Peter Lang Publishing.

Traum, D. R. (1999). Computational models of grounding in collaborative systems. In *Psychological models of communication in collaborative systems: Papers from the AAAI Fall Symposium* (pp. 124–131).

Treem, J. W., & Leonardi, P. M. (2012). *Social media use in organizations: Exploring the affordances of visibility, editability, persistence, and association* (SSRN Scholarly Paper No. ID 2129853). Rochester, NY: Social Science Research Network.

Trueswell, J. C., & Tanenhaus, M. K. (2005). *Approaches to studying world-situated language use: Bridging the language-as-product and language-as-action traditions*. Cambridge, MA: MIT Press.

Velichkovsky, B. M. (1995). Communicating attention: Gaze position transfer in cooperative problem solving. *Pragmatics & Cognition*, *3*(2), 199–223. https://doi.org/10.1075/pc.3.2.02vel.

Vertegaal, R., Slagter, R., van der Veer, G., & Nijholt, A. (2001). Eye gaze patterns in conversations: There is more to conversational agents than meets the eyes. In *Proceedings of the SIGCHI Conference on Human Factors in Computing Systems* (pp. 301–308). New York, NY: ACM. https://doi.org/10.1145/365024.365119.

Vitak, J. (2012). *Keeping connected in the Facebook age: The relationship between Facebook use, relationship maintenance strategies, and relational outcomes*. East Lansing, MI: Michigan State University Press.

Vitak, J., & Ellison, N. B. (2013). "There's a network out there you might as well tap": Exploring the benefits of and barriers to exchanging informational and support-based resources on Facebook. *New Media & Society*, *15*(2), 243–259. https://doi.org/10.1177/1461444812451566.

Wagner, C., Garcia, D., Jadidi, M., & Strohmaier, M. (2015). It's a man's wikipedia? Assessing gender inequality in an online encyclopedia. *International AAAI Conference on Web and Social Media*.

Wagner, C., Graells-Garrido, E., Garcia, D., & Menczer, F. (2016). Women through the glass ceiling: Gender asymmetries in Wikipedia. *EPJ Data Science*, *5*(1). https://doi.org/10.1140/epjds/s13688-016-0066-4.

Walther, J. B. (2004). Language and communication technology introduction to the special issue. *Journal of Language and Social Psychology*, *23*(4), 384–396. https://doi.org/10.1177/0261927X04269584.

Walther, J. B. (2011). Theories of computer-mediated communication and interpersonal relations. In M. L. Knapp & J. A. Daly (Eds), *The handbook of interpersonal communication* (4th ed., pp. 443–479). Thousand Oaks, CA: Sage.

Walther, J. B., & Parks, M. R. (2002). Cues filtered out, cues filtered in. In M. L. Knapp & J. A. Daly (Eds), *Handbook of interpersonal communication* (pp. 529–563). Thousand Oaks, CA: Sage.

Wang, Y., Norcie, G., Komanduri, S., Acquisti, A., Leon, P. G., & Cranor, L. F. (2011). I regretted the minute I pressed share: A qualitative study of regrets on Facebook. In *Proceedings of the Seventh Symposium on Usable Privacy and Security* (p. 10). ACM.

Webster, J., & Trevino, L. K. (1995). Rational and social theories as complementary explanations of communication media choices: Two policy-capturing studies. *The Academy of Management Journal*, *38*(6), 1544–1572. https://doi.org/10.2307/256843.

Whittaker, S. (2003). Theories and methods in mediated communication. In A. C. Graessser, M. A. Gernsbacher, & S. R. Goldman (Eds), *Handbook of discourse processes* (pp. 243–286). Mahwah, NJ: Erlbaum.

Whittaker, S., Geelhoed, E., & Robinson, E. (1993). Shared workspaces: How do they work and when are they useful? *International Journal of Man-Machine Studies*, *39*(5), 813–842. https://doi.org/10.1006/imms.1993.1085.

Wigdor, D., & Wixon, D. (2011). *Brave NUI world: Designing natural user interfaces for touch and gesture* (1st ed.). San Francisco, CA: Morgan Kaufmann Publishers Inc.

Williams, E. (1977). Experimental comparisons of face-to-face and mediated communication: A review. *Psychological Bulletin, 84*(5), 963–976. https://doi.org/10.1037/0033-2909.84.5.963.

Yatani, K., Gergle, D., & Truong, K. (2012). Investigating effects of visual and tactile feedback on spatial coordination in collaborative handheld systems. In *Proceedings of the ACM 2012 Conference on Computer Supported Cooperative Work* (pp. 661–670). New York, NY: ACM. https://doi.org/10.1145/2145204.2145305.

Yatani, K., & Truong, K. N. (2009). SemFeel: A user interface with semantic tactile feedback for mobile touch-screen devices. In *Proceedings of the 22nd Annual ACM Symposium on User Interface Software and Technology* (pp. 111–120). New York, NY: ACM.

Young, J. J., Tan, H. Z., & Gray, R. (2003). Validity of haptic cues and its effect on priming visual spatial attention. In *11th Symposium on Haptic Interfaces for Virtual Environment and Teleoperator Systems, 2003* (pp. 166–170). https://doi.org/10.1109/HAPTIC.2003.1191265.

12

Discourse and Expertise

The Challenge of Mutual Understanding between Experts and Laypeople[1]

Rainer Bromme and Regina Jucks

UNIVERSITY OF MUENSTER

For some time now, Mr. A. has been finding it painful to breathe. After searching the Internet with the phrase "painful to breathe," he is afraid of having a pulmonary embolism or bronchitis. So he makes an appointment with his general practitioner (Dr. B.) and describes his troubles to her. The doctor examines him and asks him to describe the type and duration of his pains. She proposes a further examination with an ultrasound scan and says she would like to refer him for an MRT examination. At one point, she mentions *spiral CT angiography*. Later she talks about "imaging" his legs. Based on what he has heard from a relative who has long been suffering from vein problems, Mr. A. starts to think that this will call for the administration of a contrast agent and be painful. He asks Dr. B. about this and tells her he does not like the thought of undergoing an MRT examination. She gives him an answer designed to reassure him. It is only after the consultation that he realizes that the key question that he wanted to ask is what does painful breathing have to do with his legs.

Dr. B. is pleased that she has succeeded in initiating the process of diagnosing the pain, which is the most important thing. She hopes she has strengthened Mr. A.'s commitment, but is not quite sure about that. At the same time, she has gained the impression that her patient is unnecessarily upset by his Internet search. Nevertheless, she is pleased that his relative's experiences made him ask about the contrast agent, so that she could allay his fears (in her mind) about that. It is only afterwards that she realizes that he might not have understood the relation between venous thrombosis and pulmonary embolism. Because she knows that Mr. A. is an educated and sensitive patient, she is not sure whether to address this topic during the next appointment. The connection might seem too obvious, and she does not want to be impolite and embarrass him if it turns out that he has been informing himself about various diagnoses on the Internet but has not understood the basic principle of pulmonary embolism.

This interaction between Dr. B. and Mr. A. illustrates several aspects of expert–laypeople communication. Expert–laypeople communication is an interaction between interlocutors who have different background knowledge about the topic (Isaacs & Clark, 1987; Jucks & Bromme, 2011). The interaction is motivated by the needs of laypeople who expect support from the expert. It entails the *exchange* of knowledge. Often the support is given via the provision of knowledge, for example if Dr. B. advised Mr. A. about what he could do to cope with the breathing pains. Knowledge may also be used in support of practical actions, for example when Dr. B explains the reasons for doing an MRT. Expert–laypeople communication works in both directions. Before experts provide specialist knowledge, they must learn about laypeople's experiences and understanding. Actually, expert–laypeople communication typically starts by the conveyance of information from laypeople to experts (Bromme, Jucks, & Runde, 2005). In our example, Mr. A. opened the conversation by describing his breathing problems. Both interlocutors produce and interpret their contributions against the background of their knowledge and understanding of the topic at stake (Schober, 2006). Therefore, mutual understanding is only possible if this background has some degree of overlap, the so-called "common ground" (Clark, 1996). Problems of understanding arise when this common ground is too small, due to qualitative and quantitative differences of the knowledge base held by the interlocutors. For example, Dr. B.'s understanding of breathing problems is based on medical knowledge and Mr. A.'s understanding of breathing problems is based on his personal theories about body functions. Additional problems might arise when the interlocutors adhere to conversational rules which are deleterious for the expansion of common ground (Clark & Brennan, 1991). This could happen because several conversational rules which are well suited for everyday conversation do not work well in expert–laypeople communication (Jucks, Bromme, & Runde, 2007; Brummernhenrich & Jucks, 2013). For example, Dr. B. has avoided providing further explanations because she wanted to be polite and henceforth did not want to poke into her patient's shortcomings of medical understanding. For successful expansion of common ground it is necessary to *anticipate* what the interlocutors already know and which conversational rules they will adhere to and then to *adapt* their own conversational input accordingly (Bromme, Rambow, & Nückles, 2001). It would have been helpful if Dr. B. had anticipated what Mr. A. actually understands about his condition. Because of the different roles of experts and laypeople, the expert has special responsibility for establishing and maintaining common ground (Bromme, Jucks, & Runde, 2005). Nevertheless, even in the best of cases, expert knowledge cannot be fully transferred to laypeople. Therefore, the understanding being achieved in expert–laypeople communication must be embedded in the establishment of mutual *trust* (Hendriks, Kienhues, & Bromme, 2016b). When Dr. B. explains how an MRT works she aims not only for an understanding, but also for her patient's trust in her competence.

Expert–laypeople communication is not confined to the medical domain; it is ubiquitous (Bromme & Goldman, 2014). It is challenging in all contexts where expertise matters. The constraints for establishing mutual understanding, which follows from the huge and qualitative knowledge differences between the interlocutors, are similar across domains. Salespeople in computer shops are another example of experts who have to anticipate their customers' background understanding. At one moment, they might have to deal with a computer nerd and in the next with a complete newbie who has trouble understanding that computers have windows, but no curtains (Nückles, Ertelt, Wittwer, & Renkl, 2007). Likewise, citizens engaged in online discussions of climate change with scientists or ways to overcome the debt crisis with economists are other examples of laypeople coping with experts' explanations (McBride & Burgman, 2012). Unfortunately, expert–laypeople communication is much less researched in these domains than in the realm of medicine. Therefore, we shall illustrate our arguments mainly with examples taken from communication between medical doctors and patients (Lehtinen, 2013), but we will point out how these illustrate general processes and obstacles of expert–laypeople communication. This rather general perspective is enabled by the theoretical account of conversation as cooperation (sensu Clark, 1996), which will be detailed in this chapter. Starting from this theory, we will develop the following theoretical assumption: The mechanisms for establishing mutual understanding work best when the interlocutors bring with them a similar knowledge base. When, in contrast, this knowledge base is fundamentally different, these same mechanisms can give rise to problems. Indeed, they must be scrutinized by experts as well as by laypeople in order to adapt their contributions to the interlocutor. This assumption is the core of the present chapter.

In the following, we explain what *experts* are and what distinguishes them from a special kind of non-expert: Laypeople (first section). Then we discuss structural features of experts' (second section) and laypeople's (third section) knowledge. In the fourth section the *common ground model of communication*, as it has been suggested by Clark (1996), will be introduced. It allows for modeling the impact of knowledge on mutual understanding. By means of this model we can then describe how problems in expert–laypeople communication might be characterized as *collateral damage of developing expertise*. We illustrate this in detail for three challenges confronting experts: Building common ground on technical concepts, being polite as well as clear, and establishing and maintaining trust. Finally, lines for further research will be sketched.

Fundamental Concepts: Experts, Expertise, Novices, and Laypeople

Modern industrial societies are characterized by specializations in tasks and functions. Houses are designed by architects and they are built by craftsmen. Patients are treated by physicians using drugs which are provided by pharmacists and which have been developed by chemists. These specializations have led to an enormous growth and differentiation of knowledge. Many tasks within a society require special (not commonly shared) knowledge, a state which is called the *division of cognitive labor* (Kitcher, 1990). A person who addresses a task by means of special knowledge and skills is called an *expert*. *Experts* and *expertise* (we shall use the latter term for expert-specific knowledge and abilities) are always relational concepts. Collins and Evans (2007, p. 3) illustrate this aptly with language abilities: A person speaking fluent French in England might be an expert there, whereas the same competence in France will not be seen as expertise.

What Is an Expert? Three Approaches

Expertise is not just a description of one's knowledge, but also an attribution accorded by social groups. Providing expertise depends not only on the individual's possession of specialized knowledge and abilities but also on the general recognition of that individual's expert status by a relevant social group (Evetts, Mieg, & Felt, 2006). A person is considered to be an engineer when having the knowledge and the skills for engineering and furthermore if he has the approval (for example, a diploma) certifying that he has the capabilities to do his job. The relevant social groups are the board who defines the procedure for certification and the public (his customers) who know about the meaning of such certificates. Hence, an initial definition of experts contains both *cognitive* and *social* aspects. Experts are persons possessing a combination of knowledge and abilities that are not commonly shared in their environment and who are socially recognized as *experts*. In the following, our analysis will start from this initial definition. Psychological as well as sociological approaches to expertise vary regarding the definition of "expert". In the following section, three of these approaches will be briefly introduced. Each approach brings with it a definition of *expert* that emphasizes different aspects of expert–laypeople communication.

Within psychological research on experts there are different research traditions. In the first that we consider, experts are defined as outstanding performers in a domain (Feltovich, Prietula, & Ericsson, 2006; Ericsson, 2015). Achieving such high performance is viewed as the product of years of education or, more specifically, years of deliberate practice (Ericsson, 2006). This approach focuses on the structure of experts' knowledge representations (de Groot, 1965; Koedinger & Anderson, 1990). The large body of psychological research within the expert–novice paradigm has delivered many insights into the structure of experts' knowledge in various disciplines (Chase & Simon, 1973; Ericsson, 2015; Ferrari, Didierjean, & Marmèche, 2006). Later, we will argue that those specific features of experts' knowledge structures that enable high performance are also the reasons for communication problems between experts and laypeople.

A second research tradition emphasizes the function of the expert: that is, solving problems in a domain that is typically conceived as a profession (Mieg, 2001). This means that experts are persons who have successfully mastered the complex challenges of their work after many years of—in most cases—*academic* education followed by professional training. The accumulation of practical experience then refines and extends the expertise of these persons. In this research tradition, experts are typically identified by their functional role, e.g., teachers have expertise in classroom teaching (Bromme, 2001) and physicians have expertise in diagnosing illnesses (Lehtinen, 2007), along with some kind of performance indicator but without an emphasis on outperforming their peers. This approach directly addresses the setting of expert–laypeople communication as a certain task or request from a layperson as the starting point for experts' work. Typically such experts perform their work in an institutional context (a school or a hospital) and conform to clearly defined roles. Their behavior is constrained by the goals and expectations which are related to these roles.

A third research tradition has arisen around a definition proposed by the sociologists Stehr and Grundmann (2011). They confine the concept of *experts* to those specialists who are mediating between the realm of knowledge production and the realm of knowledge use. *Experts* in this sense focus on transferring knowledge generated by *scientists* to the users of this knowledge. For example: Chemists, physicists, and meteorologists have produced the scientific evidence about climate change, but practical problems, such as finding ways carbon emissions could be reduced, are still open questions. Any application of the basic scientific evidence about climate change requires the communication of this evidence to non-experts. Politicians as well as citizens who have to judge and act with regard to climate change cannot directly understand this evidence—they require the assistance of specialists who synthesize and communicate this evidence in practical terms. Although we shall not follow the terminological confinement suggested by Stehr and Grundmann (2011) their argument is of interest here. They point out that expert–laypeople communication is not just about the *transmission* of "ready-made" knowledge. Experts have not only to *translate* the specialized knowledge but also to *transform* it by tailoring it to fit a concrete problem and, above all, by selecting and weighting information from the range of competing offers available. Experts have to solve practical problems and prepare decisions for laypeople.

The second and third definitions that we have presented both address the challenge of expert communication with laypeople. We briefly consider the question of what laypeople are and why it's important for experts to communicate with them.

Laypeople Versus Novices

The concept of expert always implies the concept of a *non-expert* as an opposite. There are two kinds of non-experts: *novices* and *laypeople*. Psychological research on expertise mostly compares experts with *novices* or *intermediates*. These are persons on their educational way to becoming an expert (Ericsson, 2015). It is important to grasp the difference between such *novices* and *laypeople*. A novice is a student of some skill or discipline who is at an early stage of training. Laypeople, in contrast, may hold some knowledge about a certain domain, but lack specialized expertise and do not want to acquire it in the sense of becoming an expert themselves. Instead, they seek support from an expert about an issue they already have a certain idea about—otherwise they would not have approached the expert. Hence, laypeople and novices differ systematically in their aims. As a consequence, to take research on novices' knowledge structures as evidence about a laypeople's perspective might lead to wrong conclusions. We will discuss laypeople's knowledge structures further below.

Why Communication with Laypeople Is Essential for Experts

In many situations, an expert is required as a representative or substitute for laypeople. People ask physicians to diagnose and treat their medical condition. They ask an engineer to design a technical device or a lawyer to represent them in court. The expert is needed to *do* something *for* a customer, client, or patient. At first glance, it appears that the expert's main focus is on the problem at stake, not the laypeople. People ask an expert for help with some kind of concrete problem but not primarily to acquire that expert's specialized knowledge—they want the problem fixed, not explained. Therefore the question has to be answered why expert–laypeople communication is not peripheral to expert problem solving in most domains?

One answer is that even when an expert represents or substitutes for a client or customer, his or her work requires communication with laypeople (as patients, clients, or customers). When laypeople assign their problem to an expert, information (a problem description, including the problem history, goals, beliefs, and sometimes even emotions) has to be transferred successfully to the expert. Conversely, much expert problem solving inherently requires some kind of knowledge transmission from the expert to the patient, client, or customer. A doctor who wants her patient to comply with her treatment recommendation has to consider the patient's subjective beliefs about illness and correct these if necessary, while simultaneously explaining the diagnostic and therapeutic procedures she wishes to apply. Furthermore, all kinds of *counseling* require expert knowledge to be passed on to laypeople. In order to adapt this knowledge to the needs of a specific client, the interaction between expert and laypeople must be mutual. Elements of counseling are even present in domains in which the expert's role does not focus mainly on communication but on dealing with artifacts, as in engineering or informatics. For example, fixing a complex technical device often involves some explanations about the causes of the problem. Such explanations are the basis for further advice on how the customer should handle the device.

Since the knowledge base of the interlocutors is so crucial in the theoretical approach underlying this chapter, we have to consider in detail the features of experts' as well as laypeople's knowledge.

Experts' Cognitive Frameworks: Foundations for High Performance, but Obstacles for Communication

In our earlier example, Mr. A. lacks relevant medical knowledge that would help him to relate Dr. B.'s questions to his well-being. Dr. B., in contrast, holds specialized knowledge and competence that are needed for her to answer Mr. A.'s questions. However, the training she has undergone while becoming an expert have altered her whole way of thinking, perceiving, and communicating. The abilities acquired while developing expertise are not fully conscious, but create a perception of the world that is simply taken for granted (*tacit knowledge*, Collins & Evans, 2007).

Psychological research on experts has shown that experts and laypeople do not just differ in the extent and content of their knowledge (Schmidt & Rikers, 2007). At some stage on the way to becoming an expert, the knowledge acquired in education undergoes a complex restructuring (Feltovich, Prietula, & Ericsson, 2006; Murphy & Wright, 1984). One's education on the way to expertise starts with the acquisition of separate units of knowledge, consisting typically of abstract concepts and inference rules (Woods, 2007): Medical students, for example, start with learning chemistry, biology, anatomy, and concepts about basic pathophysiological mechanisms. Later, this knowledge becomes more integrated and focused on illnesses, their conditions and their treatment. Then, based on further practical experiences with real cases medical students learn more about the contextual conditions under which a certain piece of knowledge applies and when it does not. It would not be possible simply to incrementally add layers of knowledge and still find out rapidly which piece of knowledge applies and when. Instead the knowledge has to be reconstructed (compare the notion of conceptual change, Vosniadou, 2013).

Chase and Simon (1973) described the aggregation of many single pieces of information into parts of a more complex structure as a general feature of expert knowledge. Such a reconstruction of previously acquired knowledge helps to explain, for example, the extraordinary performance of successful chess players. Since these early studies on chess expertise (Chase & Simon, 1973), the appropriate organization of knowledge units within long-term memory has been shown to be critical for the high performance of experts in all semantically rich domains (Ericsson, 2014). The problem- and context-related organization of knowledge enables rapid problem solving, but it also makes the knowledge less accessible for talking about it. This has been observed in several studies in the domain of medicine. Rikers, Schmidt, and Boshuizen (2000) found that so-called intermediates (advanced medical students) remember more detailed information than do experts after reading a unit of information describing a clinical case. Sullivan, Yates, Inaba, Lam, and Clark (2014) provide further evidence for this effect. Experts form a more abstract mental representation of the clinical case as an entity and therefore need to make more mental effort to remember the underlying concrete elements. Schmidt and Rijkers (2007) describe this restructuring of knowledge (scientific basics, clinical observations, and causal assumptions about particular illnesses) as *knowledge encapsulation* (van de Wiel, 1997; van de Wiel, Boshuizen, & Schmidt, 2000; Rikers, Schmidt, & Moulaert, 2005). Expert knowledge is highly *contextualized*. It is organized according to the context. If, for example, a medical doctor works in a hospital context where a certain type of virus disease is highly prevalent, his/her general knowledge of viruses is reorganized in a way that it fits to this kind of disease and to the available procedures and tools. In the medical domain it has been shown that experts do not process all information from a blood test the same but concentrate on those parameters that fit the patients' profile. Novices, on the other hand, take information into account piece by piece even if for a certain diagnosis one piece of information might be out of relevance. *Routinization* is also a specific of experts' knowledge. Experts engage in routine actions; they neither question nor decide on each single step of an action. Instead, they develop a certain fluency within their actions. Categorical perception forms the basis for quick and adequate action (Nakashima et al., 2015). For example, experienced doctors see structures in X-ray photographs that novices (and, we can conclude, also laypeople) are less able to detect (Ericsson, 2015). Doctors seem to experience the visual perception of these structures intuitively. They do not experience that they are drawing on the cognitive availability of the appropriate professional concept. The categorical perception simultaneously activates concepts regarding possible treatments, relevant constraints, and typical circumstances of the specific medical condition (Ericsson, 2015). In other words, an experienced medical doctor's *seeing* of an X-ray picture is a good example of how experts' performances are based on *knowledge encapsulation, contextualization*, and *routinization of knowledge*.

The abstract concepts of experts are the building blocks of their expert theories and these theories sum up to form an overarching perspective. In the case of the doctor–patient relationship, this is the medical perspective. A medical doctor does not just know more about medical conditions; she also has a professional perspective on illnesses and on the ways to cope with these. Besides the expert knowledge and skills, which we have discussed so far, such a perspective includes goals, values, foci of attention, a self-perception as expert and the perception of the differences between the own group (the experts) and others (laypeople, experts from other fields etc.). Perspectives are shared by the members of an expert community and they serve as the source of assumptions brought into communication with laypeople. The expert perspective typically differs qualitatively from the laypeople's conceptions (described in the following section).

The structural characteristics of expert knowledge (knowledge encapsulation, contextualization, and routinization of knowledge) could impede conveyance of information to laypeople. Knowledge has to be unpacked and extra mental effort must be made in speech-planning. In the next section, some detrimental effects of these structural characteristics for mutual understanding will be detailed. We will also elaborate on how some obstacles in the communication between experts and laypeople could be conceived as a kind of *collateral damage* of the knowledge transformation on the long way to becoming an expert.

Laypeople's Cognitive Frameworks

Laypeople have, by definition (see above), less knowledge about the issues on which they are consulting an expert than does the expert. Nevertheless, they often have at least some ideas about the issue at stake (Becker, Bromme, & Jucks, 2008). Laypeople asking experts for support (for practical actions like fixing a computer or for advice on how to fix the computer themselves) necessarily have some mental representation about the critical issue (computers and why they fail) as well as about the relevant domain of expertise which could be pertinent for the problem at hand (an electrical engineer or a software specialist). Laypeople do not enter the conversation as tabula rasa, but bring along their own ideas, expectations, beliefs, and pieces of knowledge about the topic (Becker, Bromme, & Jucks, 2008). When interacting with experts, these cognitive structures encounter and sometimes clash with the knowledge and belief structures of experts. Understanding the problems of expert–laypeople communication therefore requires an understanding of experts' (section above) as well as laypeople's knowledge structures (this subsection).

Concepts and Features of Laypeople's Beliefs

Research on so-called naïve theories (Anderson & Lindsay, 1998), laypeople's theories (Furnham, 1988), or folk theories (Keil, 2003, 2010) allows for some conclusions about the cognitive representations brought into the conversation with experts. These accounts, though slightly different, agree with regard to the features of laypeople's knowledge structures.

Laypeople's knowledge is rich and complex. Laypeople's *theories* are *complex belief systems.* We have termed these beliefs as *knowledge* because beliefs are assumptions which are conceived to be true. Sometimes these beliefs are actually true. They could also be characterized as *knowledge* from a scientific point of view. In this case, they are justified because they are based on evidence which is generally accepted, like the belief that the earth is a globe. Sometimes they are only subjectively true, like the belief that the earth is flat.

Laypeople's knowledge consists of related pieces, e.g. of cross-linked information. Although this knowledge may be fragmented and sometimes also false, it generally does not consist of isolated single facts, but tends to be organized. Therefore several researchers refer to such knowledge structures as "theories". Sometimes, such theories might contain logically incoherent elements. Kalish, Lewandowsky, and Kruschke (2004) describe such incoherence between mutually contradictory information as *knowledge partitioning.* They have shown that people use different and incoherent parts of their knowledge adaptively for different tasks. Laypeople also have not only separate beliefs referring to separate issues but a system of beliefs which makes up their *perspective.* Again, just as is the case for experts, such perspective includes goals, values, foci of attention, a self-perception as laypeople, and the perception of the differences between the own group (for example the patients) and the others (for example medical doctors, nurses, lawyers etc.).

Laypeople's theories can be remarkably resistant to change. New, discrepant information is often integrated into the deficient structure rather than changing it (Sinatra & Chinn, 2012). This can lead to the maintenance of misconceptions. These are inherently coherent assumptions that are flexible enough to integrate contradicting experiences and contain even scientifically correct claims. For example, both students and adults tend to have a rather Aristotelian personal theory about force, movement, and gravity, even when they have been taught Newtonian theory.

Laypeople's theories are seldom totally wrong. They often entail and integrate correct assumptions leading to true conclusions even when based on false assumptions (Jee, Uttal, Spiegel, & Diamond, 2015). This makes it difficult to recognize underlying false assumptions when laypeople provide conclusions which are true, but were based on wrong reasons.

We illustrate the impact of these features of laypeople's theories on expert–laypeople communication with a fictitious example. Imagine a citizen reading on the Internet a report on water pollution due to pipe corrosion in Michigan, USA. He might then want to ask experts if this problem might also occur within his community. When encountering an expert (for example, an engineer from the local water company) he has of course some knowledge about the problems of old pipe systems. But this knowledge is embedded in a whole belief system about technical infrastructure, water, and the impact of water on health. Some of these assumptions might be true, others might be wrong. It might not even be clear for him what exactly he should ask about. He might, for example, assume that it is possible to "clean" old lead pipes, based on a misconception of lead as "dirt" which could be washed out from the pipes. The expert might also mention "cleaning" the pipes, but she might be referring to the insertion of a layer of fabric separating the metal from the water. Thus, they could both talk about "cleaning" the pipes and not be aware that their understanding refers to completely different things. Alternatively, the interaction may be based on the tacit assumption on the citizen's side that "more is better". Laypeople might take it for granted that pressing more water through the system would dilute the lead. The expert, in contrast, might implicitly take for granted that within such a system the turbulence of water should be kept low as long as it is not possible to separate the corrosion from the water. Both assumptions are as strong as they are tacit and hence they impact on the mutual understanding of all contributions. Processing all contributions is furthermore embedded in further assumptions about the goals of both sides. The engineer might assume that the citizen has a basic mistrust in the local water company. The citizen instead mistrusts the state's supervision boards and considers his counterpart to be a servant of this authority. Such mutual assumptions make up the overarching perspective contributing to the understanding of each utterance.

So far, we have emphasized the obstacles which follow from the differences between experts' and laypeople's knowledge. With regard to the latter we have mainly emphasized the incompleteness of and also the distortions within laypeople's knowledge. This emphasis is justified because it is precisely these differences which motivate laypeople to ask experts for help. Nevertheless, it is also important to acknowledge that in most contexts experts must listen to laypeople and recognize that they can provide important information and insights. For example, in the domain of health, subjective experiences are "true" for the persons involved and therefore relevant for their interaction with experts. This could blur the distinction between expert and laypeople in the cognitive sense (see above). Patients naturally have much more knowledge about their body and pain perceptions than the doctor and often more precise information on their individual patient history. Insofar as laypeople are also experts regarding some aspects of the issue that is in the focus of their interaction with the "real" experts, the possible positive result of communication can be an increase in mutual understanding—and not just on the laypeople's side. Experts, as well, can profit from actively taking the laypeople's perspective into account. The arguments put forward by laypeople, which do not consider the premises that are taken for granted within the experts' community, can function as a productive opposition that may broaden the expert's thinking and open up new paths (Mercier, 2011). To come back to our example of the water pipes: Citizens' observations of the water quality in their house could be taken (and in the real case mentioned above should have been) as empirical evidence on the issue at stake and henceforth the non-expert's contribution could entail knowledge which should be conceived as expert knowledge. The fact that laypeople could also have some kinds of expertise is important here because it is a further reason why the knowledge of both interlocutors matter for successful conversation. In other words, it matters when the beliefs are false, because then they are an obstacle for mutual understanding, but it matters even more when they are correct because then they could contribute to the joint goal of solving the shared problem.

The Psychology of Reciprocal Understanding: The "Common Ground" Communication Model

To understand where the special challenges in expert–laypeople communication come from, it is first necessary to ask how understanding in communication can be achieved in general. According to the psycholinguistic communication theory formulated by Herbert H. Clark and his colleagues, reciprocal understanding can be defined as an exchange of messages produced and received against the background of what are, in each case, *individual frames of reference* (Clark, 1996; see Schober, 2006, for an overview; see Shintel & Keysar, 2009 as well as Raczaszek-Leonardi, Debska, & Sochanowicz, 2014, for critiques). It is called "frames of reference" because the communication ground model is about the reduction of ambiguity with regard to the *referential* meaning of the contributions. Imagine a couple, sitting at a breakfast table. "Please pass the coffee" is understood as referring to the pot standing in front of them because both are aware that they are within a breakfast setting and they also share the visual impression of the pot in front. Twenty minutes earlier when they prepared the breakfast "Please pass the coffee" would have referred to the can with the ground coffee powder on the kitchen shelf. The ambiguity of the referent "coffee" was eliminated because both interlocutors used frames of references which allowed for the context-dependent identification of the references meant by the word "coffee". Based on such examples and on studies with such scenarios of *referential* ambiguity, Herbert H. Clark and his colleagues have developed the "common ground" communication model. In our view the common ground model could be applied in conversational settings where the content processed is more complex. Within these settings, ambiguity results not only from different objects of reference, for example of different instances of the word "coffee", but also from the conceptual complexity of the matters that expert–laypeople communication is about.

A frame of reference includes individuals' knowledge, beliefs, attitudes, and feelings. As such, every message is understood according to what an individual knows, feels, and is able and willing to accept. The frame of reference is composed of stable elements such as prior knowledge, attitudes, beliefs, and stereotypes as well as dynamic elements such as current contents of perception, situation-specific information, and the development of the conversation so far. For the most part it is the same as what has been called "perspective" above, which we occasionally use because it is the notion used in other research traditions. A message, like "I would recommend using imaging to diagnose this", from our introductory example, is produced against the background of an expert's frame of reference and is received against the background of laypeople's frame of reference. Hence it might be that the expert suggests one method of diagnosis as the most straightforward in contrast to another. Laypeople might interpret the use of imaging techniques as an indicator of a severe illness, because the usage of high-end technology is in their view indicative for the severity of an illness.

Establishing Common Ground

For successful mutual understanding, both communication partners have to build a *shared* frame of reference—the so-called *common ground* (Clark, 1996). This shared frame of reference is not a simple overlap between the individual frames of references, e.g. the overlap of knowledge from both parties. It contains knowledge about what the other is thinking and feeling as well as knowledge about how far this knowledge is shared (Heller, Gorman, & Tanenhaus, 2012; Brown-Schmidt, Yoon, & Ryskin, 2015). Hence, two people might share a lot of knowledge and beliefs, but if they are not aware of this, their common ground is low.

As has been shown by numerous experiments using the Referential Communication Task (Krauss & Fussell, 1991) building common ground happens stepwise: Communication partners learn from the others' knowledge and gain insights into the others' perspectives and beliefs. Clark and colleagues (e.g., Clark & Schaefer, 1989) reconstructed the process of building common ground as follows: At the beginning, information that only one conversation partner has, is introduced into the communication. If the other has shown that this information has been processed, then it becomes part of the common ground. Through the interaction, common ground not only accumulates but is also, when necessary, revised. In the seminal study on the impact of expertise on the process of establishing common ground by Susan Isaacs and Herbert H. Clark (1987), participants were asked to sort a number of postcards from New York. The degree of expertise (knowing New York well versus having never been there) was an experimental condition. One participant (the director) explained how the postcards of New York famous buildings were placed on his/her table. The other participant (the matcher) should sort his/her cards in the same way. It was not possible to see the other's cards; hence communication was the only vehicle to solve the task. The process went as follows: They explicitly (by naming) and implicitly (by analyzing the communication behavior of each other) learn about one another's individual frame of reference (e.g., that the matcher was not knowledgeable about the famous New York buildings). In doing so, they *build up* common ground. If the director was an expert and the matcher was a non-expert he/she suggested names for the building which were quickly accepted and then continuously used in further trials. If the matcher was the expert and the director the non-expert, the latter came up with suggestions. If both sides were non-experts, they gradually developed their own special concepts for objects on the postcards. In all conditions, further trials were sorted faster due to a stepwise extended common ground.

Various grounding methods make sure that a certain piece of information is part of the common ground. In direct verbal communication, the three most important grounding methods (Clark, 1996) are (1) verbal affirmation or disaffirmation, (2) the initiation of a speaker change (e.g., a continuative question) signalizing that the offered information has been processed, and (3) the use of nonverbal signals (e.g., eye contact or frowning) showing that the conversation partner follows (or does not follow) the speaker's statements (Brennan & Clark, 1996). Once a statement has been accepted, it can be regarded as part of the common ground. Moreover, Clark emphasizes that both conversation partners try to achieve understanding with a minimum of effort. The degree of effort that is considered adequate to reach understanding depends on contextual factors (e.g., how important understanding is) and situational factors (e.g., how much time is available). In the end, the conviction that both have understood each other sufficiently for the current purpose (Clark & Murphy, 1982) determines how grounding takes place (Garrod & Anderson, 1987; Hilliard & Cook, 2016).

Certainly, it is neither possible nor necessary to build up the shared frame of reference (common ground) from scratch (Clark, 1996). Moreover, conversation partners bring their own assumptions about the knowledge and the perspective of the other (Isaacs & Clark, 1987). These can be *general*, e.g. based on the others' group membership. For example, some doctors may hold expectations about the knowledge and perspectives of adult patients who are using the Internet to acquire medical information. Furthermore, these assumptions can be based on the prior experiences and interactions with the *specific* interaction partner. For example, Dr. B. has expectations about the knowledge and perspectives of Mr. A. after having explained the procedure of MRT examination. Communication partners expand the *common ground* gradually (Clark & Brennan, 1991). They present and accept each other's contributions or ask for clarification (Clark & Schaefer, 1989). Each contribution provides two kinds of information relevant for common ground: the direct information gained from what has been said and assumptions that occur due to the interpretation of what and how something has (not) been said. Hence, common ground is more precise the better one is able to *anticipate* what the partner already knows and feels. Based on these anticipations the interlocutors could then *adapt* their utterances accordingly.

Expert Knowledge Could Hamper the Building of Common Ground

The common ground approach is fruitful for modeling expert–laypeople communication because it emphasizes the role of personal perspectives (including knowledge and belief systems as well as personal goals and values) for mutual understanding. As we have suggested in the preceding sections, it is the difference of perspectives which comprises the distinction between experts and laypeople. Therefore, a psycholinguistic approach that starts from such differences in interlocutors' knowledge is especially appropriate here. Research on the development of expertise has shown that expert knowledge is encapsulated, related to professional routines, and immersed in the perspectives of a profession. These processes of encapsulation and immersion have to be reverted to elaborate the expert knowledge in a way that is adapted to laypeople's understanding. This does not of course mean that an expert should think about his/her domain of expertise again like he/she has done when being a novice. But it could be helpful to become aware of these former ways of thinking about and perceiving the issues which are within the realm of his/her expertise. For example, abstract concepts, which structure the thinking of experts and foreshadow the solution, have to be transformed to a less abstract level and then conveyed. The seemingly self-evident complex perception of the situation has to be explicated so that laypeople will be able to comprehend it. In other words, those characteristics of an expert's knowledge, thinking, and perceptions that have proved to be of value and even necessary for solving professional tasks become a problem when it comes to communication about this knowledge. This applies to both processes which are essential for establishing and expanding common ground: *anticipation* and *adaptation* (Jucks & Bromme, 2011).

There is some evidence that experts' extensive and highly integrated knowledge of their field makes it difficult for them to anticipate laypeople's rather different perspective. These difficulties have been called the *curse-of-expertise* effect (Hinds, 1999) or the *knowledge effect* (Hayes & Bajzek, 2008). An estimation of the other person's knowledge is based on one's own knowledge which is referred to as standard (Nickerson, 1999; Royzman, Cassidy, & Baron, 2003). This explains the systematic overestimation of the knowledge of laypeople (the expert cannot imagine how much less laypeople see in an X-ray image). However, experts do not always tend to *over*estimate the knowledge of laypeople; they also reveal systematic *under*estimations. The quality of estimation is influenced by the expert's experience with laypeople and the type of professional vocabulary. When computer experts have to estimate laypeople's knowledge of concepts in their field, their estimates differ depending on their own professional background. If they have professional experience in giving advice to laypeople (e.g., through working at the hotline of a computer center), their estimations are less biased (Bromme, Rambow, & Nückles, 2001). The quality of these estimations then impacts their adaptation in discourse with laypeople (Nückles & Bromme, 2002; Rambow, 2000; Wittwer, Nückles, & Renkl, 2008). Keysar, Barr, and Horton (1998) demonstrated that, even in everyday interactions, people erroneously use *privileged information*; that is, information that is available only to them and not to their interlocutor. For example, people are asked to judge whether a sentence like "This is a wonderful restaurant" would be understood as being ironic. Without the privileged information about the actual quality of the restaurant a listener cannot recognize the ironic quality of the statement. Nevertheless, subjects make use of their own knowledge (privileged information) about the restaurant (which was actually bad). They do not take into account what the listener knows. When experts instruct laypeople, their expert knowledge can also be regarded as privileged information.

When for example Dr. B. from our introductory example refers to "imaging" the patients' legs, she makes use of her *privileged information* about the concept of "imaging" without taking into account that her patient might not have this information.

The combination of theories on expertise and experts' perspective and Clark's theory on common ground brings up fruitful insights and empirical paradigms that we are going to outline in the following. In doing so, we will discuss three challenges for experts when communicating with laypeople. These challenges derive from different aspects of expert–laypeople communication, but they all show that establishing and expanding "common ground" is crucial for mutual understanding.

- Experts are in charge of anticipating laypeople's perspective on terminology, e.g. what meaning laypeople create out of an expert's explanation (see next section) and adapt their language accordingly.
- Experts are in charge of anticipating the emotional needs that laypeople encounter during expert–laypeople communication, e.g. how they feel about being advised and instructed and adapt their language accordingly.
- Experts are in charge of establishing mutual trust. Laypeople are dependent on experts and therefore they should not only be helped to understand but also engendered with trust.

The following paragraphs focus on experts' special responsibility for engaging in communication with laypeople. This was a deliberate decision. According to H. Clark's (1996) theory, mutual understanding is a cooperative activity and hence asks for both communication partners to contribute to mutual understanding. With regard to everyday conversations, the common ground model emphasizes the cooperative nature of communication, with both sides contributing equally toward establishing and expanding common ground. However, in expert–laypeople communication the balance is different. Experts have a greater responsibility for successful communication. They possess exclusive knowledge and have more possibilities for shaping the conversation. As we have described above, laypeople must have some beliefs about the issue at stake, otherwise they would not have approached the expert. Nevertheless, it is not easy for them to choose the right expert and then to ask the right questions, when not knowing about the underlying structure of their problem. Therefore, we refer to the following aspects of expert–laypeople communication primarily as challenges for experts, but we would like to argue that this is still reconcilable with the basic tenet of the common ground model that communication is a *cooperative* activity.

The Challenge of Building Common Ground on Technical Concepts

Whenever we engage in communication we build common ground; we interpret the words from our communication partner; anticipate his/her knowledge background; and adapt our contributions to those of our communication partners (Jucks, Linnemann, Thon, & Zimmermann, 2016).

Specialized Terminology

Exchanging meaning and anticipating others' individual frames of reference includes analyzing word usage. In expert–laypeople communication technical language plays a key role. Technical languages have their own syntax tied to domain-related genres. Medical reports, legal texts, and this *Handbook of Discourse Processes* are examples of different genres;

they each have their own lexicon of specialist concepts. Some of these specialist concepts are encoded in special words from other languages (e.g., from Latin in medicine); some are based on conventions and make use of the history of the field of knowledge (when referring to important contributors to the field, e.g., Ohm, Volt, and Kelvin in physics); others are fully artificial conventions (*chi square*). There are also many specialist concepts that are encoded in words taken from everyday language but have a much more specific meaning within the field (such as *anxiety* in the field of psychology). Specialist terms refer to concepts possessing complex meanings that can be understood only with reference to their position within expert theories and also with reference to their practical use within the social practices of communities of experts (Engberg, 2010, 2012). It is important to note that these are not only conventions used for conversational purposes but also cognitive units of knowledge. Experts acquire their knowledge through the use of technical language. Hence, they come to automatically think in these technical terms and with an individual frame of reference that is technical. Nevertheless, these frames of reference are also individual; the representation of technical concepts is not the same for all experts within a field (Murphy & Wright, 1984; Medin, Lynch, Coley, & Atran, 1997). For example, Bromme, Rambow, and Wiedmann (1998) have shown that chemists, while being aware of the technical definition of the well-defined concepts *acid* and *base*, still have a flexible representation of these concepts. Depending on the specific contexts in which their expertise is required, they will emphasize different features as elements of the specialist concept. Whereas such a flexibility of concept representation is common for everyday concepts that often have no exact definition at all, it is remarkable to see that it can also be found in well-defined concepts. These individualizations of concept meaning go beyond technical definitions and are acquired during the social practice of expertise in specific professional contexts. Thus, individualizations are especially critical for transforming the rich conceptual content of technical concepts into *privileged information* (see prior section).

Establishing Common Ground on Technical Concepts

During communication, specialized language serves as an indicator for an individual's frame of reference. Experts build their anticipation of laypeople's understanding from the way laypeople use specialized language. Bromme, Rambow, and Nückles (2001) found that experts' estimations of laypeople's understanding of the same concepts vary depending on the status of the concepts. If a layperson introduced a concept as a technical concept, experts judged the layperson as more knowledgeable than if the same concept was introduced as a general concept.

Laypeople also assess their own knowledge background by reflecting on the words that encode a technical concept: Jucks and Paus (2012) asked college students to judge the difficulty, familiarity, competence, accessibility, and their knowledge of 17 everyday language terms such as *Kleinhirn* (*little brain*, a common German everyday language word for the anatomical structure called *cerebellum* in English) and their specialist language synonyms such as "cerebellum". The influence of word frequency was controlled. As expected, students judged everyday language terms to be less difficult than specialist language terms. Consequently, comprehension of these terms was rated as higher. However, their comprehension ratings were less accurate for everyday language than for specialist language terms.

Hence, when it comes to developing common ground, many technical concepts (e.g., words of Latin or Greek origin or abbreviations) clearly and explicitly signal that expert knowledge is needed to understand their meaning. They are clearly recognizable as specialist concepts, and both sides are aware that they are based on a large body of expert knowledge. This makes it easier for experts to anticipate laypeople's lack of background knowledge on the specific concept. Those technical concepts that are encoded in everyday language are more problematic for expert–laypeople communication. An *illusion of common ground* might occur on both sides, experts and laypeople, that conceals differences in the individual frames of references (Runde, Bromme, & Jucks, 2007).

Fallacies of Adaptation

In an everyday conversation context, the use of lexical encodings that are "on the table" is economical and mostly reasonable. For example, a person having a dialogue about a missing computer might ask "Where is your *notebook*?" and the interlocutor may respond "Yesterday my *notebook* was on the shelf". She will not respond "Yesterday my *computer* was on the shelf". This constraint is called *lexical alignment* (Garrod & Pickering, 2004) and its effect on expert–laypeople communication can sometimes be problematic. Not only experts, but also laypeople use technical concepts (Fage-Butler & Jensen, 2015), though not necessarily correctly. If, for example, laypeople refer to migraine, a medical doctor should not take it for granted that they are actually referring to a correct diagnosis—they may well have overgeneralized this concept to all kinds of headaches. Nevertheless, this is a frequent occurrence, as an analysis of "Ask the Doctor" websites revealed (Jucks & Bromme, 2007). Bromme, Jucks, and Wagner (2005) have shown experimentally that laypeople's use of expert terminology impacts the way experts communicate with laypeople. Advanced medical students (the experts in this study in contrast to laypeople) responded to fictitious requests from persons who made explicitly clear that they had the status of medical laypeople. These requests made use of either medical technical language (diabetes mellitus) or everyday medical language (*Zuckerkrankheit* [sugar illness], which is a common German term for diabetes mellitus). Experts adapted their answers with regard to the exact language terms used by the laypeople in their requests. Furthermore, their answers varied in complexity and technicality accordingly to the word usage. This unreflecting reuse of technical language was also shown when the technical concept was introduced by another source (e.g., a textbook) and not by the addressees (Jucks, Becker, & Bromme, 2008). The mere alignment of word usage is not a fully conscious decision (see Linnemann & Jucks, 2016, for the convergence in word use in human–computer interaction). Results clearly indicate a gap between correct anticipations of laypeople's frame of reference and the communication behavior triggered through the presence of specialized language (Jucks, Paus, & Bromme, 2012).

To sum up, technical concepts in expert–laypeople communication need special attention: They are, especially when worded very technically in Greek or Latin, obvious clues to a lack of common ground between experts and laypeople and so might be used as explicit signals to build common ground. It is also necessary for experts to be aware of the underlying meaning of those technical concepts that don't "look that hard to be understood" and avoid their reflexive, unconsidered use.

The Challenge of Being Polite and Clear: Individuals' Frames of Reference and the Application of Politeness Rules in Communication

As has been outlined so far, establishing common ground happens through exchanging and anticipating others' frames of reference. Communication partners need to interpret each other's communication behavior and anticipate underlying knowledge, attitudes, and beliefs. Furthermore, they need to anticipate their partners' emotional states. Insights into the process of gauging communication partners' emotional states can be gained from *politeness theory*: Brown and Levinson (1987) have argued that every person has a public self-perception, their so-called *face*, and that a face needs to be shaped positively. *Face* consists of the need for independence and autonomy (called *negative face*) plus the need for affiliation and benevolence (*positive face*). Indeed, there are many situations in which *face* is threatened, be it through direct orders, which restrict autonomy and independence, or through corrections, which can be seen indirectly as a rejection of the person. Thus, politeness serves the need to maintain a positive relationship to the conversation partner: to save one's own and the other's face. Hence, mitigating face threats whenever autonomy or affiliation is threatened is a natural communication behavior. Communicators take these two needs into account in communication (Schneider, Nebel, Pradel, & Rey, 2015).

However, in expert–laypeople communication, polite formulations might have negative effects on clarity and understandability. When doctors deliver bad news by saying that the test results indicate "possibly" negative consequences, patients may be unsure whether the consequences really are unpredictable or whether negative consequences definitely are going to occur and the doctor is simply softening the bad news out of politeness (Pighin & Bonnefon, 2011). Hence, politeness issues impact both, the way information is presented by experts (as they anticipate and mitigate face threats) and the way information is interpreted by laypeople (as they assume avoiding face threats is part of experts' communication behavior).

The needs related to the social balance between communication partners might counteract the cognitive need of laypeople to gain, for example, a clear, direct explanation. Empirical research supports this assumption (Brummernhenrich & Jucks, 2015): In an online tutor-tutee discourse, tutors' politeness was varied in a 1×3 between-subject design. Face threats were either mitigated politely, addressing the positive or negative face, or expressed without redress. Participants rated their perception of the tutor and the tutor's contribution, and provided alternative formulations of the presented face threats. Results showed that avoiding negative face threats, e.g. those that restrict autonomy, are valued positively by participants. Hence, it is worthwhile for tutors to mitigate instructional face threats. Data from studies with experts also show that politeness issues are taken into account in expert–laypeople communication. Experts try to avoid face threats, e.g. they do not communicate directly and address misconceptions on laypeople's side straightforwardly (Bromme, Brummernhenrich, Becker, & Jucks, 2012; Brummernhenrich & Jucks, 2013; Jucks, Päuler, & Brummernhenrich, 2016).

Hence, not only *conceptual* elements, but also feelings and values are part of the common ground and impact both experts' and laypeople's communication behavior. Politeness theory provides a helpful reference in identifying biases in gauging perspective and hence "mistakes" in building a precise mental model of an individual's frame of reference.

The Challenge of Establishing and Maintaining Trust in Expert–Laypeople Communication

The common ground model assumes that all contributions within a conversation are made and understood in the context of the interlocutors' aims. Imagine again the sentence "Pass me the coffee please". It is produced and understood in a context where both interlocutors have the aim of having breakfast together. The common ground entails the assumptions that both sides have the *intention* as well as the *capabilities* to act according to mutually assumed goals as well as according to the context (here: breakfast). These assumptions are not processed as conscious inferences. Interlocutors will only become aware of them when there are reasons for doubt. When, for example, one of the interlocutors is a child, the mother might deliberately reflect the child's ability to handle a large and hot pot of coffee.

Mutual assumptions about the interlocutors' intentions as well as capabilities are even more critical when the interlocutors cannot control whether they will actually be fulfilled. This is frequently the case in expert–laypeople communication, especially when the domain of expertise is based on complex scientific and technological knowledge. Because the general public can have only a *bounded understanding of science* (Bromme & Goldman, 2014), laypeople have only limited means of independently testing an expert's knowledge claims, judgments, and problem solutions. A person asking for medical advice cannot—as laypeople can't—judge whether the underlying knowledge base of these interventions was valid and relevant. He might—in the long run—be able to judge the quality of the advice. But at first, within the conversation with the expert he has to assume that the expert is actually willing as well as capable of acting coherently with the assumed intentions. In this example, this means that the patient assumes that the medical doctor actually wants to help and knows how to help.

These assumptions about intentions as well as about capabilities are part of the individual's frame of reference, in other words, they are part of the common ground. At the same time, they can be conceptualized as *trust*. This concept is important for the analysis of expert–laypeople communication because it allows for an inspection of an imbalance between the interlocutors. In the preceding sections, we have pointed to the imbalance of knowledge between experts and laypeople. In the first section, we had already emphasized that specialization, the differentiation of knowledge, and the division of cognitive labor lead to the general public being dependent on experts. Laypeople may consult with experts and request, for example, a second opinion about a suggested medical treatment, but, ultimately, laypeople always have to *trust* experts. *Trust* is an attribution under the condition of an imbalance of power. Mayer, Davis, and Schoorman (1995, p. 712) define it as follows:

> Trust is the willingness of a party [here laypeople] to be vulnerable to the actions of another party [here experts] based on the expectation that the other will perform a particular action important to the trustor, irrespective of the ability to monitor or control that other party.

This imbalance of control and—at least in some contexts—of power is an important contextual constraint of expert–laypeople communication. *Trust* is a set of assumptions about the other (in our examples so far: about the expert) which help to cope with this imbalance of control. These assumptions must be part of the *common* ground because the expert must know if laypeople actually trust her. (Of course, there is also a need for the expert to trust laypeople.)

Trust as Requirement as well as Outcome of Expert–Laypeople Communication

The common ground model explains why common ground is a prerequisite as well as a result of communication. This applies also for trust. What is said within the interaction that rests on the trust assumption will modify (amplify or weaken) this trust assumption. Trust is therefore not only a precondition, but also a result of expert–laypeople communication. What is said by the expert, how it is understood by laypeople, and vice versa will affect the above-mentioned hidden assumption and sometimes make it more overt. When an expert comes up with a treatment that runs counter to a patient's expectation, this patient might

Discourse and Expertise

start having doubts about the doctor's underlying knowledge base—an issue that had not been critical until then. When the medical expert manages to explain her treatment very well, she might amplify the trust attribution of her patient. In summary, expert–laypeople communication will succeed when there is a reciprocal communication that serves the intended problem solving and when mutual trust either exists or can be developed. The emphasis on the reciprocity of communication and trust does not imply a symmetric responsibility. Just as laypeople must not necessarily know what they do not know (see above), their dependency is a reason to be vigilant against violations of expectations about appropriate and helpful actions provided by the expert being trusted (Hendriks, Kienhues, & Bromme, 2016b).

How to Tell Who Is Trustworthy? Context-, Content-, and Communication-Related Criteria

This raises the question regarding what makes a person (the *trustee*) trustworthy to an interlocutor (the *trustor*). If, for example, laypeople (patients) have reasons to assume that the expert's main aim is financial gain even if this means not giving the best treatment to her patients, this would endanger trust (Sperber et al., 2010). By means of factor analysis Mayer, Davis, and Schoorman (1995) have identified three aspects that account for a trustor to attributed trust by the trustee (ABI-Model): (1) *ability*, which refers to expertise (does the expert have the most relevant and the most valid knowledge base?), (2) *benevolence* (does the expert actually try to do the very best for her patient, client, or customer?), and (3) *integrity* (does the expert adhere to the rules and codes of her profession?). On the basis of this research Hendriks, Kienhues, and Bromme (2015) provided an inventory that addresses the context of expert–laypeople communication.

Judgments about the trustworthiness of an interlocutor are not confined to criteria which are tight to the communication setting. An overview of these criteria would go beyond the scope of this chapter (Lewandowsky, Ecker, Seifert, Schwarz, & Cook, 2012, provide such an overview). But we will provide a few examples. Representative surveys have shown that trust in scientists depends on their institutional affiliation. This is an example of a *context*-related criterion. Scientists working in publicly funded research contexts (e.g., state universities) are trusted much more than their colleagues in private, industry-related research institutions (Ipsos Mori Social Research Institute, 2011). This is in line with the above-mentioned criteria of benevolence and integrity. Along with awareness of the aforementioned features of the source, people also consider compatibility with their existing beliefs and knowledge as well as the coherence of the message. These are examples of *content*-related criteria.

In the context of this chapter, *communication*-related criteria for judging the trustworthiness of experts and of the credibility of their assertions are of special interest. An important criterion for trustworthiness here is the size and the homogeneity of the communication arena. Are there other experts supporting or contradicting each other? It has been mentioned already that one way for laypeople to cope with their dependence on experts is to seek the advice of other experts. It is almost as if individual experts have just one voice in a choir. This strategy reflects the fact that there are many domains in which expert knowledge on important topics is not unequivocal (Carpenter et al., 2015). The Internet strengthens laypeople's impression that different experts in many fields of expertise give very different recommendations regarding how to act (Britt, Richter, & Rouet, 2014). This makes the development and maintenance of trust in communication with laypeople more difficult—but also more relevant. Not only do people look for a consensus opinion among experts but they ask themselves whether others would believe this information.

239

A further example of communication-related criteria are the ways that the information is presented (Jucks, Linnemann, Thon, & Zimmermann, 2016; Jucks & Thon, 2017). For example, the simplicity of the information processing itself contributes to whether the transmitted information seems credible or not. For example, Lev-Ari and Keysar (2010) have shown that statements made with a foreign accent are perceived to be less credible than accent-free statements in the recipient's native language. They also showed that this effect is not due to stereotypes about the speaker's nationality, but to the impediment of language processing. Scharrer, Bromme, Britt, and Stadtler (2012) have shown that people judge assertions from mainly understandable (for them) scientific texts to be more credible than conclusions from texts that are difficult to read due to scientific terminology. This is remarkable, because in this study the topic at stake (what the expert–laypeople communication was about) was evidently based on scientific findings concerning very complex issues.

Conclusions and Open Questions

Expert–laypeople communication is relevant to many domains. In this chapter, we have outlined the cognitive prerequisites for successful communication between these parties and the practical challenges in communicating successfully. We have introduced the challenges of establishing and maintaining common ground. The theoretical perspective suggested here makes use of the common ground communication theory but it is not confined to it. Originally this psycholinguistic account was developed to model how people reduce referential ambiguity (how do interlocutors establish a common understanding of what is meant by an utterance?). In contrast, the challenges in communication between experts and laypeople are not confined to only *referential* ambiguity, as they have been, for example, in the seminal Isaacs and Clark (1987) study on the impact of expertise on grounding in conversation. Therefore, we have introduced further critical aspects, like politeness and trust. Nevertheless, the common ground model is inspiring because of its focus on the interplay between knowledge and mutual understanding. In this chapter, we have applied the common ground model to expert–laypeople communication, but it might prove fruitful to reverse the perspective, using the specific conversational setting of experts and laypeople as a testbed for further developing the psycholinguistic theory of "common ground". Beyond that, we identify three further areas of research being helpful for improving (the understanding of) expert–laypeople communication.

Research on Domain-Specific Conceptual Perspectives of Experts and Laypeople

For communication to be successful, it is necessary for an expert to have a veridical anticipation of the laypeople's knowledge. Because of the quantitative and qualitative differences in knowledge, common ground does not develop by accident. Studies on the domain-specific conceptual perspectives of experts and laypeople are needed. Such content-specific studies serve two functions: (1) to inform experts about the average laypeople's perspective on the content, e.g. what can be taken for granted and what needs explanations; and (2) to help laypeople assess their own (lack of) knowledge and gain insights into typical illusions of understanding.

Research on Communication Trainings for Experts and Laypeople

Both experts and laypeople need training in communication with members from the other group. Insights into how common ground is built up help to define the specific tasks. Experts need to

Discourse and Expertise

analyze what laypeople say to further anticipate laypeople's individual frame of reference. Here specific language takes a key role as it is necessary to question its usage. Experts are to be trained in communication strategies such as straightforward asking about prior knowledge and current understanding. Laypeople are to be encouraged to ask questions and to question an experts' explanation. Empirical research needs to analyze how communication training can be effective.

Extending the Content and Context of Expert–Laypeople Communication

For the sake of clarity this chapter was focused on a context where a single expert interacts with laypeople. We have already emphasized the role of context as well as content for mutual understanding. Further accounts on expert–laypeople communication should expand (and compare) contexts as well as content. An extension of contexts could include conversations within groups where the status of the interlocutors as experts or laypeople is more fragile than in our examples. Internet forums of citizens who focus on research projects (citizen science) as well as science blogs where researchers communicate about their research to inform their colleagues as well as the general public (Hendriks, Kienhues, & Bromme, 2016a) would be interesting cases here.

Throughout this chapter we have confined our examples to areas of expertise which are science and technology related. There are other domains of expertise (for example, art, politics, and economy) where—for example—the criteria for the truth of knowledge as well as for whom it is trustworthy might differ from the cases discussed in this chapter. It would be interesting to scrutinize such criteria because it could help us to understand how common ground is established and expanded in such further contexts.

Further Reading

Clark, H. H. (1996). *Using language*. Cambridge, MA: Cambridge University Press.
Ericsson, K. A. (2015). Acquisition and maintenance of medical expertise: A perspective from the expert-performance approach with deliberate practice. *Academic Medicine, 90,* 1471–1486. doi:10.1097/ACM.0000000000000939.
Garrod, S., & Pickering, M. J. (2004). Why is conversation so easy? *Trends in Cognitive Science, 8,* 8–11. doi:10.1016/j.tics.2003.10.016.
Keil, F. C. (2010). The feasibility of folk science. *Cognitive Science, 34*(5), 826–862. doi:10.1111/j.1551-6709.2010.01108.x.
Nickerson, R. S. (1999). How we know—and sometimes misjudge—what others know: Imputing one's own knowledge to others. *Psychological Bulletin, 125*(6), 737–759.
Rikers, R., Schmidt, H., & Boshuizen, H. (2000). Knowledge encapsulation and the intermediate effect. *Contemporary Educational Psychology, 25,* 150–166. doi:10.1006/ceps.1998.1000.
Stehr, N., & Grundmann, R. (2011). *EXPERTS: The knowledge and power of expertise*. Milton Park, UK: Routledge.

Note

1 This is an extensively modified and extended version of a chapter published in German. We wish to thank the publisher, W. Kohlhammer, for allowing its use here. Reference: Bromme, R., & Jucks, R. (2014). Fragen Sie Ihren Arzt oder Apotheker: Die Psychologie der Experten-Laien-Kommunikation. [Ask your doctor or pharmacist: The psychology of expert–laypeople communication]. In M. Blanz, A. Florack, & U. Piontkowski (Eds), *Kommunikation: Eine interdisziplinäre Einführung* [Communication: An interdisciplinary introduction] (pp. 237–249). Stuttgart: Kohlhammer. Thanks to Alessa Hillbrink and Jonathan Harrow for translating the German chapter, to Maria Zimmermann for help in finalizing the chapter, and to the *Handbook* editors (esp. A.B.) for advice and comments.

References

Anderson, C. A., & Lindsay, J. J. (1998). The development, perseverance, and change of naive theories. *Social Cognition, 16*, 8–30. doi:10.1521/soco.1998.16.1.8.

Becker, B. M., Bromme, R., & Jucks, R. (2008). College students' knowledge of concepts related to the metabolic syndrome. *Psychology, Health & Medicine, 13*, 367–379. doi:10.1080/13548500701405525.

Brennan, S. E., & Clark, H. H. (1996). Conceptual pacts and lexical choice in conversation. *Journal of Experimental Psychology: Learning, Memory, and Cognition, 22*(6), 1482–1493.

Britt, M. A., Richter, T., & Rouet, J.-F. (2014). Scientific literacy: The role of goal-directed reading and evaluation in understanding scientific information. *Educational Psychologist, 49*, 104–122. doi:10.1080/00461520.2014.916217.

Bromme, R. (2001). Teacher expertise. In N. J. Smelser, P. B. Baltes, & F. E. Weinert (Eds), *International encyclopedia of the behavioral sciences: Education* (pp. 15459–15465). London, UK: Pergamon.

Bromme, R., Brummernhenrich, B., Becker, B. M., & Jucks, R. (2012). The effects of politeness-related instruction on medical tutoring. *Communication Education, 61*, 358–379. doi:10.1080/036 34523.2012.691979.

Bromme, R., & Goldman, S. (2014). The public's bounded understanding of science. *Educational Psychologist, 49*(2), 59–69. doi:10.1080/00461520.2014.921572.

Bromme, R., Jucks, R., & Runde, A. (2005). Barriers and biases in computer-mediated expert-layperson-communication: An overview and insights into the field of medical advice. In R. Bromme, F. W. Hesse, & H. Spada (Eds), *Barriers and biases in computer-mediated knowledge communication – and how they may be overcome* (pp. 89–118). New York, NY: Springer.

Bromme, R., Jucks, R., & Wagner, T. (2005). How to refer to "diabetes"? Language in online health advice. *Applied Cognitive Psychology, 19*, 569–586. doi:10.1002/acp.1099.

Bromme, R., Rambow, R., & Nückles, M. (2001). Expertise and estimating what other people know: The influence of professional experience and type of knowledge. *Journal of Experimental Psychology: Applied, 7*, 317–330. doi:10.1037/1076-898X.7.4.317.

Bromme, R., Rambow, R., & Wiedmann, J. (1998). Typizitätsvariationen bei abstrakten Begriffen: Das Beispiel chemischer Fachbegriffe [Typicality of abstract concepts: The example of chemistry specialist concepts]. *Sprache & Kognition, 17*, 3–20.

Brown, P., & Levinson, S. C. (1987). *Politeness: Some universals in language usage.* Cambridge, UK: Cambridge University Press.

Brown-Schmidt, S., Yoon, S. O., & Ryskin, R. A. (2015). People as contexts in conversation. *Vol. 62. Psychology of Learning and Motivation – Advances in Research and Theory* (pp. 59–99).

Brummernhenrich, B., & Jucks, R. (2013). Managing face threats and instructions in online tutoring. *Journal of Educational Psychology, 105*, 341–350. doi:10.1037/a0031928.

Brummernhenrich, B., & Jucks, R. (2015). "He shouldn't have put it that way!" How face threats and mitigation strategies affect person perception in online tutoring. *Communication Education*, 1–17. doi:10.1080/03634523.2015.1070957.

Carpenter, D. M., Geryk, L. L., Chen, A. T., Nagler, R. H., Dieckmann, N. F., & Han, P. (2015). Conflicting health information: A critical research need. *Health Expectations*, 1–10. doi:10.1111/hex.12438.

Chase, W. G., & Simon, H. A. (1973). Perception in chess. *Cognitive Psychology, 4*, 55–81. doi:10.1016/0010-0285(73)90004-2.

Clark, H. H. (1996). *Using language.* Cambridge, MA: Cambridge University Press.

Clark, H. H., & Brennan, S. E. (1991). Grounding in communication. In L. B. Resnick, J. M. Levine, & S. D. Teasley (Eds). *Perspectives on socially shared cognition* (pp. 127–149). Washington, DC: APA Books.

Clark, H. H., & Murphy, G. L. (1982). Audience design in meaning and reference. In J. F. LeNy & W. Kintsch (Eds), *Language and comprehension* (pp. 287–299). Amsterdam: North Holland.

Clark, H. H., & Schaefer, E. F. (1989). Contributing to discourse. *Cognitive Science, 13*, 259–294. doi:10.1207/s15516709cog1302_7.

Collins, H., & Evans, R. (2007). *Rethinking expertise.* Chicago, IL: University of Chicago Press.

de Groot, A. D. (1965). *Thought and choice in chess.* The Hague: Mouton Publishers.

Engberg, J. (2010). Knowledge construction and legal discourse: The interdependence of perspective and visibility of characteristics. *Journal of Pragmatics, 42*(1), 48–63. doi:10.1016/j.pragma.2009.05.011.

Engberg, J. (2012). Specialized communication and culture, practice, competence and knowledge: Implications and derived insights. In L. Pon, V. Karabalic, & S. Cimer (Eds), *Applied linguistics today: Research and perspectives: Proceedings from the CALS Conference 2011* (pp. 109–130). Frankfurt/Main, Germany: Pabst.

Ericsson, K. A. (2006). The influence of experience and deliberate practice on the development of superior expert performance. In K. A. Ericsson, N. Charness, P. J. Feltovich, & R. R. Hoffmann (Eds), *The Cambridge handbook of expertise and expert performance* (pp. 683–703). Cambridge, MA: Cambridge University Press.

Ericsson, K. A. (2014). Why expert performance is special and cannot be extrapolated from studies of performance in the general population: A response to criticisms. *Intelligence, 45*, 81–103. doi:10.1016/j.intell.2013.12.001.

Ericsson, K. A. (2015). Acquisition and maintenance of medical expertise: A perspective from the expert-performance approach with deliberate practice. *Academic Medicine, 90*, 1471–1486. doi:10.1097/ACM.0000000000000939.

Evetts, J., Mieg, H. A., & Felt, U. (2006). Professionalization, scientific expertise, and elitism: A sociological perspective. In K. A. Ericsson, N. Charness, P. J. Feltovich, & R. R. Hoffmann (Eds), *The Cambridge handbook of expertise and expert performance* (pp. 105–123). New York, NY: Cambridge University Press.

Fage-Butler, A. M., & Jensen, N. M. (2015). Medical terminology in online patient-patient communication: Evidence of high health literacy? *Health Expectations, 19*(3), 643–653. doi: 10.1111/hex.12395.

Feltovich, P. J., Prietula, M. J., & Ericsson, K. A. (2006). Studies of expertise from psychological perspectives. In K. A. Ericsson, N. Charness, P. J. Feltovich, & R. R. Hoffmann (Eds), *The Cambridge handbook of expertise and expert performance* (pp. 41–68). Cambridge, UK: Cambridge University Press.

Ferrari, V., Didierjean, A., & Marmèche, E. (2006). Dynamic perception in chess. *The Quarterly Journal of Experimental Psychology, 59*(2), 397–410. doi: 10.1080/17470210500151428.

Furnham, A. (1988). *Lay theories: Everyday understanding of problems in the social sciences.* Oxford, UK: Pergamon Press.

Garrod, S., & Anderson, A. (1987). Saying what you mean in dialogue: A study in conceptual and semantic co-ordination. *Cognition, 27*, 181–218. doi:10.1016/0010-0277(87)90018-7.

Garrod, S., & Pickering, M. J. (2004). Why is conversation so easy? *Trends in Cognitive Science, 8*, 8–11. doi:10.1016/j.tics.2003.10.016.

Hayes, J. R., & Bajzek, D. (2008). Understanding and reducing the knowledge effect: Implications for writers. *Written Communication, 25*(1), 104–118. doi: 10.1177/0741088307311209.

Heller, D., Gorman, K. S., & Tanenhaus, M. K. (2012). To name or to describe: Shared knowledge affects referential form. *Topics in Cognitive Science, 4*(2), 290–305. doi: 10.1111/j.1756-8765.2012.01182.x.

Hendriks, F., Kienhues, D., & Bromme, R. (2015). Measuring laypeople's trust in experts in a digital age: The Muenster Epistemic Trustworthiness Inventory (METI). *PLOS ONE 10*(10): e0139309. doi:10.1371/journal.pone.0139309.

Hendriks, F., Kienhues, D., & Bromme, R. (2016a). Evoking vigilance: Would you (dis)trust a scientist who discusses ethical implications of research in a science blog? *Public Understanding of Science, 25*(8), 992–1008. doi:10.1177/0963662516646048.

Hendriks, F., Kienhues, D., & Bromme, R. (2016b). Trust in science and the science of trust. In B. Blöbaum (Ed.), *Trust and communication in a digitized world: Models and concepts of trust research* (pp. 143–159). Berlin, Germany: Springer.

Hilliard, C., & Cook, S. W. (2016). Bridging gaps in common ground: Speakers design their gestures for their listeners. *Journal of Experimental Psychology: Learning Memory and Cognition, 42*(1), 91–103. doi:10.1037/xlm0000154.

Hinds, P. J. (1999). The curse of expertise: The effects of expertise and debiasing methods on predictions of novice-performance. *Journal of Experimental Psychology: Applied, 5*, 205–221. doi:10.1037/1076-898X.5.2.205.

Ipsos Mori Social Research Institute (2011). *Public attitudes to science 2011: Main report.* Retrieved from www.ipsos-mori.com/researchpublications/researcharchive/2764/Public-attitudes-to-science-2011.aspx.

Isaacs, E. A., & Clark, H. H. (1987). References in conversation between experts and novices. *Journal of Experimental Psychology: General, 116*(1), 26–37. doi:10.1037/0096-3445.116.1.26.

Jee, B. D., Uttal, D. H., Spiegel, A., & Diamond, J. (2015). Expert–novice differences in mental models of viruses, vaccines, and the causes of infectious disease. *Public Understanding of Science, 24*(2), 241–256. doi:10.1177/0963662513496954.

Jucks, R., Becker, B.-M., & Bromme, R (2008). Lexical entrainment in Written Discourse: Is experts' word use adapted to the addressee? *Discourse Processes, 45*, 497–518. doi:10.1080/01638530802356547.

Jucks, R., & Bromme, R. (2007). Choice of words in doctor-patient-communication: An analysis of health-related Internet Sites. *Health Communication, 21*, 267–277. doi:10.1080/10410230701307865.

Jucks, R., & Bromme, R. (2011). Perspective taking in computer-mediated instructional communication. *Journal of Media Psychology, 23*, 192–199. doi:10.1027/1864-1105/a000056.

Jucks, R., Bromme, R., & Runde, A. (2007). Explaining with non-shared illustrations: How they constrain explanations. *Learning and Instruction, 17*, 204–218. doi:10.1016/j.learninstruc.2007.01.006.

Jucks, R., Linnemann, G. A., Thon, F. M., & Zimmermann, M. (2016). Trust the words. Insights into the role of language in trust building in a digitalized world. In B. Blöbaum (Ed.), *Trust and communication in a digitized world* (pp. 225–237). New York, NY: Springer International Publishing.

Jucks, R., Päuler, L., & Brummernhenrich, B. (2016). "I need to be explicit: You're wrong": Impact of face threats on social evaluations in online instructional communication. *Interacting with Computers, 28*, 73–84. doi:10.1093/iwc/iwu032.

Jucks, R., & Paus, E. (2012). What makes a word difficult? Insights into the mental representation of technical terms. *Metacognition & Learning, 7*, 91–111. doi:10.1007/s11409-011-9084-6.

Jucks, R., Paus, E., & Bromme, R. (2012). Patients' medical knowledge and health counseling: What kind of information helps to make communication patient-centered? *Patient Education and Counseling, 88*, 177–183. doi:10.1016/j.pec.2012.01.011.

Jucks, R., & Thon, F. M. (2017). Better to have many opinions than one from an expert? Social validation by one trustworthy source versus the masses in online health forums. *Computers in Human Behavior, 70C*, 375–381. doi:10.1016/j.chb.2017.01.019.

Kalish, M. L., Lewandowsky, S., & Kruschke, J. K. (2004). Population of linear experts: Knowledge partitioning and function learning. *Psychological Review, 111*, 1072–1099. doi:10.1037/0033-295X.111.4.1072.

Keil, F. C. (2003). Folkscience: Coarse interpretations of a complex reality. *Trends in Cognitive Sciences, 7*(8), 368–373. doi:10.1016/S1364-6613(03)00158-X.

Keil, F. C. (2010). The feasibility of folk science. *Cognitive Science, 34*(5), 826–862. doi:10.1111/j.1551-6709.2010.01108.x.

Keysar, B., Barr, D. J., & Horton, W. S. (1998). The egocentric bias of language use: Insights from a processing approach. *Current Directions in Psychological Science, 7*, 46–50. doi:10.1111/1467-8721.ep13175613.

Kitcher, P. (1990). The division of cognitive labor. *Journal of Philosophy, 87*, 5–22.

Koedinger, K. R., & Anderson, J. R. (1990). Abstract planning and perceptual chunks: Elements of expertise in geometry. *Cognitive Science, 14*, 511–550. doi:10.1207/s15516709cog1404_2.

Krauss, R. M., & Fussell, S. R. (1991). Perspective-taking in communication: Representations of others' knowledge in reference. *Social Cognition, 9*, 2–24.

Lehtinen, E. (2007). Merging doctor and client knowledge: On doctors' ways of dealing with clients' potentially discrepant information in genetic counseling. *Journal of Pragmatics, 39*, 389–427. doi:10.1016/j.pragma.2006.05.006.

Lehtinen, E. (2013). Hedging, knowledge and interaction: Doctors' and clients' talk about medical information and client experiences in genetic counseling. *Patient Education and Counseling, 92*(1), 31–37. doi:10.1016/j.pec.2013.02.005.

Lev-Ari, S., & Keysar, B. (2010). Why don't we believe non-native speakers? The influence of accent on credibility. *Journal of Experimental Social Psychology, 46*, 1093–1096. doi:10.1016/j.jesp.2010.05.025.

Lewandowsky, S., Ecker, U. K. H., Seifert, C. M., Schwarz, N., & Cook, J. (2012). Misinformation and its correction: Continued influence and successful debiasing. *Psychological Science in the Public Interest, 13*, 106–131. doi:10.1177/1529100612451018.

Linnemann, G. A., & Jucks, R. (2016). "As in the question, so in the answer?": Language style of human and machine users affects interlocutors' convergence on wording. *Journal of Language and Social Psychology.* doi:10.1177/0261927X15625444.

Mayer, R. C., Davis, J. H., & Schoorman, D. F. (1995). An integrative model of organisational trust. *The Academy of Management Review*, *20*, 709–734. doi:10.5465/AMR.1995.9508080335.

McBride, M. F., & Burgman, M. A. (2012). What is expert knowledge, how is such knowledge gathered, and how do we use it to address questions in landscape ecology? In A. H. Perera & C. A. Drew (Eds), *Expert knowledge and its application in landscape ecology* (pp. 11–38). New York, NY: Springer.

Medin, D. L., Lynch, E. B., Coley, J. D., & Atran, S. (1997). Categorization and reasoning among tree experts: Do all roads lead to Rome? *Cognitive Psychology*, *32*(1), 49–96.

Mercier, H. (2011). When experts argue: Explaining the best and the worst of reasoning. *Argumentation*, *25*(3), 313–327. doi:10.1007/s10503-011-9222-y.

Mieg, H. A. (2001). *The social psychology of expertise: Case studies in research, professional domains, and expert roles*. Mahwah, NJ: Lawrence Erlbaum Associates.

Murphy, G. L., & Wright, J. C. (1984). Changes in conceptual structure with expertise: Differences between real-world experts and novices. *Journal of Experimental Psychology: Learning, Memory, and Cognition*, *10*, 144–155.

Nakashima, R., Watanabe, C., Maeda, E., Yoshikawa, T., Matsuda, I., Miki, S., & Yokosawa, K. (2015). The effect of expert knowledge on medical search: Medical experts have specialized abilities for detecting serious lesions. *Psychological Research*, *79*(5), 729–738. doi:10.1007/s00426-014-0616-y.

Nickerson, R. S. (1999). How we know—and sometimes misjudge—what others know: Imputing one's own knowledge to others. *Psychological Bulletin*, *125*(6), 737–759.

Nückles, M., & Bromme, R. (2002). Internet experts' planning of explanations for laypersons: A web experimental approach in the Internet domain. *Experimental Psychology*, *9*(4), 1–13. doi:10.1026//1618-3169.49.4.292.

Nückels, M., Ertelt, A., Wittwer, J., & Renkl, A. (2007). Scripting laypersons' problem descriptions in internet-based communication with experts. In F. Fischer, I. Kollar, H. Mandl, & J. M. Haake (Eds), *Scripting computer-supported collaborative learning* (pp. 73–89). New York, NY: Springer. doi:10.1007/978-0-387-36949-5_5.

Pighin, S., & Bonnefon, J. F. (2011). Facework and uncertain reasoning in health communication. *Patient Education and Counseling*, *85*, 169–172. doi:10.1016/j.pec.2010.09.005.

Raczaszek-Leonardi, J., Debska, A., & Sochanowicz, A. (2014). Pooling the ground: Understanding and coordination in collective sense making. *Frontiers in Psychology*, *5*(Oct). doi:10.3389/fpsyg.2014.01233.

Rambow, R. (2000). *Experten- Laien-Kommunikation in der Architektur [Expert-layperson communication in the architecture domain]*. Münster, Germany: Waxmann.

Rikers, R., Schmidt, H., & Boshuizen, H. (2000). Knowledge encapsulation and the intermediate effect. *Contemporary Educational Psychology*, *25*, 150–166. doi:10.1006/ceps.1998.1000.

Rikers, R. M. J. P., Schmidt, H. G., & Moulaert, V. (2005). Biomedical knowledge: Encapsulated or two worlds apart? *Applied Cognitive Psychology*, *19*(2), 223–231. doi:10.1002/acp.1107.

Royzman, E., Cassidy, K., & Baron, J. (2003). "I know, you know": Epistemic egocentrism in children and adults. *Review of General Psychology*, *7*, 38–65. doi:10.1037/1089-2680.7.1.38.

Runde, A., Bromme, R., & Jucks, R. (2007). Scripting in net-based medical consultation: The impact of external representations on giving advice and explanations. In F. Fischer, I. Kollar, H. Mandl, & J. M. Haake (Eds), *Scripting computer-supported collaborative learning: Cognitive, computational, and educational perspectives* (pp. 57–72). New York, NY: Springer. doi:10.1007/978-0-387-36949-5_4.

Scharrer, L., Bromme, R., Britt, M. A., & Stadtler, M. (2012). The seduction of easiness: How science depictions influence laypeople's reliance on their own evaluation of scientific information. *Learning and Instruction*, *22*, 231–243. doi:10.1016/j.learninstruc.2011.11.004.

Schmidt, H. G., & Rijkers, R. M. J. P. (2007). How expertise develops in medicine: Knowledge encapsulation and illness script formation. *Medical Education*, *41*, 1133–1139. doi:10.1111/j.1365-2923.2007.02915.x.

Schneider, S., Nebel, S., Pradel, S., & Rey, G. D. (2015). Mind your Ps and Qs! How polite instructions affect learning with multimedia. *Computers in Human Behavior*, *51*, 546–555. doi:10.1016/j.chb.2015.05.025.

Schober, M. F. (2006). Dialogue and interaction. In K. Brown (Ed.), *Encyclopedia of language and linguistics* (2nd ed., Vol. 3, pp. 564–571). Oxford, UK: Elsevier.

Shintel, H., & Keysar, B. (2009). Less is more: A minimalist account of joint action in communication. *Topics in Cognitive Science*, *1*, 260–273. doi:10.1111/j.1756-8765.2009.01018.

Sinatra, G. M., & Chinn, C. A. (2012). Thinking and reasoning in science: Promoting epistemic conceptual change. In K. R. Harris, S. Graham, T. Urdan, A. Bus, S. Major, & H. L. Swanson (Eds), *APA educational psychology handbook* (Vol. 3, pp. 257–282). Washington, DC: American Psychological Association.

Sperber, D., Clément, F., Heintz, C., Mascaro, O., Mercier, H., Origgi, G., & Wilson, D. (2010). Epistemic vigilance. *Mind & Language*, *25*(4), 359–393. doi:10.1111/j.1468-0017.2010.01394.x.

Stehr, N., & Grundmann, R. (2011). *EXPERTS: The knowledge and power of expertise.* Milton Park, UK: Routledge.

Sullivan, M. E., Yates, K. A., Inaba, K., Lam, L., & Clark, R. E. (2014). The use of cognitive task analysis to reveal the instructional limitations of experts in the teaching of procedural skills. *Academic Medicine*, *89*(5), 811–816. doi:10.1097/ACM.0000000000000224.

van de Wiel, M. (1997). *Knowledge encapsulation: Studies on the development of medical expertise.* PhD thesis, University of Maastricht. Maastricht, Netherlands.

van de Wiel, M. W. J., Boshuizen, H. P. A., & Schmidt, H. G. (2000). Knowledge restructuring in expertise development: Evidence from pathophysiological representations of clinical cases by students and physicians. *European Journal of Cognitive Psychology*, *12*(3), 323–355.

Vosniadou, S. (2013). Conceptual change in learning and instruction: The framework theory approach. In S. Vosniadou (Ed.), *International handbook of research on conceptual change* (pp. 11-30). New York, NY: Routledge.

Wittwer, J., Nückles, M., & Renkl, A. (2008). Is underestimation less detrimental than overestimation? The impact of experts' beliefs about a layperson's knowledge on learning and question asking. *Instructional Science*, *36*, 27–52. doi:10.1007/s11251-007-9021-x.

Woods, N. N. (2007). Science is fundamental: The role of biomedical knowledge in clinical reasoning. *Medical Education*, *41*(12), 1173–1177. doi:10.1111/j.1365-2923.2007.02911.x.

13

Discourse Processing and Development through the Adult Lifespan

Elizabeth A. L. Stine-Morrow
UNIVERSITY OF ILLINOIS AT URBANA-CHAMPAIGN

Gabriel A. Radvansky
UNIVERSITY OF NOTRE DAME

Participation in the discourse world in its varied forms (e.g., reading a novel or newspaper, watching a movie, or engaging in conversation) is essential to effective functioning throughout the adult lifespan. Adult development is characterized by multidimensional change in cognition, encompassing both gain and loss (Baltes, 1987; Linderberger, 2014), which can impact the way in which language and discourse are processed (Radvansky & Dijkstra, 2007; Stine-Morrow, Miller, & Hertzog, 2006). The possibility that discourse understanding might be compromised with aging, or otherwise change in quality, is a practically important issue given the fact of population aging. It has been recognized for some time in the scholarly literature and popular press that increased life expectancy is contributing to a dramatic increase in the relative proportion of older adults (United Nations Department of Economic and Social Affairs Population Division, 2013). While the percentage of the world's population aged 60 and over was 12% in 2013 (up from 8% in 1950), the projection is that this will increase to 21% by 2050.

Thus, understanding how discourse processing functions in late life is not only a matter of scientific accuracy, but also of interest in translational applications for promoting effective communication (e.g., media, workplace training, and health care). Moreover, individual trajectories of cognitive development are themselves shaped by experiences and activities (Hertzog, Kramer, Wilson, & Lindenberger, 2008), among which are literacy practices and habitual engagement with discourse. This dynamic is intriguing, and yet, understudied, and population aging heightens the urgency of understanding this reversal in causal effects – how engagement in discourse processing impacts the experience of aging. Our goals in the next few pages, then, are to explore the myriad ways in which age-related change in cognition can impact discourse comprehension and production, and to consider how engagement

Change and Stability in Discourse Processing with Age

Age differences in memory for information from text are well documented, whereas evidence for age differences in comprehension is more mixed (Johnson, 2003; Meyer & Pollard, 2006; Wingfield & Stine-Morrow, 2000). Most of this research has depended on extreme-group designs in which the performance of younger adults (typically, college students) is compared with that of adults over the age of 60. The relatively few studies that have examined the effects of age as a continuous variable are not consistent, at times suggesting that such declines may occur relatively late, with middle-aged to young-old adults performing quite well but others suggesting more continuous change through the lifespan (Ferstl, 2006; Payne et al., 2014; Stine-Morrow, Miller, Gagne, & Hertzog, 2008). An approach to understanding this complexity depends on an appreciation of both the multifaceted nature of aging as well as of discourse processing, and how these map onto one another.

The Nature of Cognitive Aging

Age declines in processing speed, working memory capacity, reasoning, executive control, and other fluid abilities are normative, with effect sizes for cross-sectional differences between the ages of 20 and 80 estimated to be as high as two standard deviations (Salthouse, 2010); estimates for within-person change are more modest, up to about one standard deviation (Schaie, 2005). Knowledge-based processes, such as acquired skill, semantic memory, and crystallized verbal ability (e.g., vocabulary) are quite well preserved at least into the eighth decade (Baltes, 1997; Li et al., 2004).

Domain-specific knowledge also shows stability into late life, as well as the capacity to grow, dependent on the habitual engagement with the domain (Ackerman & Rolfhus, 1999). Some evidence suggests that older adults engage in more gist-based processing (Chapman et al., 2002; Koustaal & Schacter, 1997; Tun, Wingfield, Rosen, & Blanchard, 1998). Insofar as gist-based processing, in part, reflects efforts at semantic elaboration that support memory, it may have some adaptive value (Schacter, Guerin, & St. Jacques, 2011). While cognition shows multidimensional change through the adult lifespan, its role in relation to other psychological systems may also change. Some researchers have suggested that cognition becomes more tightly integrated with socioemotional concerns (Carstensen, Mikels, & Mather, 2006). Also, because cognitive processes can become more resource-consuming with age, effort may be engaged more selectively (Hess, 2014). This dynamic in gain and loss in cognitive processes, as well as the changing role of cognition in relation to other psychological systems, can impact language and discourse processing.

The Nature of Discourse Processing

Like any meaningful task, discourse processing requires the coordination and cooperation of multiple systems (e.g., van Dijk & Kintsch, 1983). Much adult developmental work has been concerned with differential effects of age-graded influences on three levels of processing, namely, the surface form, textbase, and situation model levels. Briefly, the surface form encompasses the exact words and syntactic phrasing of the discourse. Successful discourse processing requires that individuals be fairly accurate for most of this information for either production or comprehension. This level of representation is the most transitory of the three, with information being lost from memory soon after it is used (Kintsch, Welsch, Schmalhofer, & Zimny, 1990).

While small errors in processing can be tolerated, the majority of the critical elements of the surface form need to be successfully processed so that the comprehender can access the relevant background knowledge and develop a reasonably accurate understanding. At the same time, as we will discuss later, individuals can use the larger context of discourse to circumvent some of the lower-level processing demands. While there is some evidence that successful discourse processing can be attenuated by age-related declines in hearing and vision (Wingfield & Lash, in press), for our purposes we will assume that younger and older adults are able to encode surface form information to a reasonable degree.

At the intermediate level is the textbase, the integrated collection of propositions that represent the semantic content actually conveyed in the discourse (e.g., Kintsch, 1998; van Dijk & Kintsch, 1983). A proposition is essentially an idea, defined as a relationship among concepts. For example, the text *Liz raved about the stout, but G.A. preferred the merlot*, conveys three ideas, two defining a relationship between characters and a beverage, and a contrastive relationship between the first two ideas. So, like the surface form, this information is tied to the actual discourse itself. The textbase is important for a discourse comprehender to get the gist of what is being communicated without being tied to the actual words and linguistic structure involved. This information is retained in memory for a longer time than the surface form (e.g., one might later recall that *G.A. likes merlot*, which is consistent with the ideas conveyed even if expressed differently). Nevertheless, it is still forgotten within a short period of time, relative to the more enduring representation given by the situation model.

Of most primary relevance in models of discourse understanding is the situation model level of processing (Zwaan & Radvansky, 1998), also known as the mental model level (Johnson-Laird, 1983; Morrow, Bower, & Greenspan, 1989) or the event model level (Radvansky & Zacks, 2014). Situation models differ from the surface form and textbase levels in that they are not representations of the text itself, but are referential representations of the circumstances described by the text. That is, situation models capture not what the text is, but what the text is about. This includes information that may be in a text, as well as any inferences a person may draw using general world knowledge (e.g., based on the ideas conveyed above about Liz and G.A., one might infer that they were at a restaurant). In narratives, situation models are typically built around the protagonist(s) and their interactions that are tracked in space and time, so as to constitute a mental simulation of events; in expository texts, situation models can comprise lines of argumentation and mental simulations of systems. Also, unlike the surface form and textbase levels, situation models are more enduring in memory. That is, they may remain highly available and relatively unaltered even a week later (Radvansky et al., 2001). This may be because the representations capture our interactions with and understandings of the world, whereas the surface form and textbase levels comprise the actual expression and ideas that are a means for transferring the situation model understanding in one person's mind to another person's.

The importance of the situation model level is evident if one takes a broader view of comprehension and memory. Specifically, think of all of the stories/narratives a person is tracking at any time. This includes events transpiring in their own lives (autobiographical memory) and the lives of others in their family, work, friends, etc., the stories they are tracking in terms of the books they are reading, the television and film series they are watching, and so on.

The situation model is the representational level on which the comprehension and memory of these diverse kinds of events depend for encoding and retrieval.

Age Effects on the Memory and Comprehension of Discourse Content

Undoubtedly, age-related changes in the speed of processing, working memory capacity, and executive control can impact the ability to construct a robust and distinctive textbase representation, so that learning from text can be compromised (Borella, Ghisletta, & de Ribaupierre, 2011; Payne et al., 2014; Thomas & Hasher, 2012). Interestingly, while sentence processing is reliably affected by these mechanisms, the more language becomes forms of discourse (i.e., interconnected sentences that cohere into larger information structures, such as argument exposition or stories), the less the involvement of working memory, and the less consistent age declines become (Shake, Noh, & Stine-Morrow, 2009; Stine & Wingfield, 1990b; Stine-Morrow et al., 2008).

There is some evidence that the ability to extract the gist or interpretive meaning of a text may be preserved (Adams, 1991; Adams, Labouvie-Vief, Hobart, & Dorosz, 1990; Adams, Smith, Nyquist, & Perlmutter, 1997), but the story here is likely to be complex. Chapman et al. (2006) has distinguished between the *transformed gist*, which is the interpretative meaning of a text that is based in world knowledge (e.g., the ability to extract a moral) and the *main-idea gist*, which is the differential recall of main ideas. Chapman et al. showed that while transformed gist is relatively preserved with age, main-idea gist is more likely to show declines.

These paradoxical findings perhaps speak to the difference between the representation of discourse as a set of ideas as compared to a mental simulation of events that is integrated into larger knowledge structures and personal meanings. The ability of older adults to selectively retain the main ideas of a text can vary with text demands. For example, while older adults often show good discrimination in memory among ideas that vary in importance (i.e., showing better recollection for major over minor ideas, just as younger adults do), when the density of ideas within sentences is increased or discourse structures don't afford cues to organization, the ability to select out the more important ideas (i.e., main-idea gist) can be compromised (Stine & Wingfield, 1988, 1990a). As discussed below, the ability to create mental simulations of events, which would presumably support memory for transformed gist, appears to be quite well maintained into old age (Dijkstra et al., 2004; Radvansky & Dijkstra, 2007). The relative preservation of the situation model even when the retention of particular ideas is compromised has been explained in terms of a scaffolding metaphor in which older adults construct a more fragile textbase representation to support the construction of a situation model that endures with decay of the textbase (Radvansky, Zwaan, Curiel, & Copeland, 2001).

Age Effects on Understanding Situations from Discourse

While there is a great deal of evidence to suggest that age-related declines in fluid abilities may bring difficulty with sentence processing (i.e., parsing complex syntax, proposition assembly; Wingfield & Grossman, 2006; Payne & Stine-Morrow, 2016), to a large extent, situation model processing appears to be intact in later adulthood, leading to the suggestion that older adults are often more reliant on, or attend more to this level of representation (Morrow, Leirer, Altieri, & Fitzsimmons, 1994; Morrow et al., 1997; Radvansky, Copeland, Berish, & Dijkstra, 2003; Radvansky, Copeland, & Zwaan, 2003;

Radvansky & Curiel, 1998; Radvansky & Dijkstra, 2007; Radvansky, Gerard, Zacks, & Hasher, 1990; Radvansky et al., 2001; Stine-Morrow, Gagne, Morrow, & DeWall, 2004; Stine-Morrow, Miller, & Leno, 2001; Stine-Morrow, Morrow, & Leno, 2002). We address this suggestion by considering how aging influences situation model use during the process of event segmentation and comprehension.

The first issue we consider is the ability to segment a stream of action into separate situation models. For example, when a person is comprehending a story there is often a series of events, rather than a static description of a scene. For comprehension to be successful, people need to track those changes. This ability is important because it allows the comprehender to strategically organize material as it is being comprehended. If event segments are missed, then a person is left trying to handle too much information as part of a single unit. If segmentation occurs at inappropriate places, then this leaves a person's understanding unnecessarily fragmented or inappropriately disjointed. In considering how aging affects event segmentation, we first consider work involving the explicit segmentation of information followed by work in which evidence of segmentation is more ongoing and implicit.

The explicit marking of event boundaries is often done using a version of the Newtson task (e.g., Newtson, 1973; Newtson & Engquist, 1976; Magliano & Zacks, 2011; Zacks & Swallow, 2007). In this task, people are given a narrative to comprehend. This can be either a written narrative or a narrative film. The task is to indicate, in some way, when a person thinks that a new event has started. Despite this seemingly vague instruction, people are actually quite consistent at doing this, both within and across individuals. For simplicity, we assume that at each point a person marks as an event boundary, this is the point at which a new situation model is created.

While this is a simple and straight-forward task, the results regarding the influence of aging on event segmentation are somewhat mixed. On the one hand, there is some evidence that aging does not have much of an influence on event segmentation. In a study by Magliano, Kopp, McNerney, Radvansky, and Zacks (2012), younger and older adults were asked to segment text and picture versions of stories. Younger and older adults were similar in their event segmentations, although the older adults showed some proclivity for identifying smaller segments than did the younger adults. That said, there is some evidence from Kurby and Zacks (2011) of age-related differences in the event segmentation of videos of everyday activities. Specifically, the older adults' segmentation was more variable and different from normative segmentations produced by younger adults. Why is there a difference between studies investigating age differences in event segmentation? While a systematic assessment of this difference has not yet been produced, it likely has something to do with the fact that in the Magliano et al. study the events were more drawn out, with larger changes from one event to another (such as changes in spatial location or characters). In comparison, in the Kurby and Zacks study, the videos were of single, continuous activities, with much more subtle markers of different events. As such, there are fundamental differences in the types of events that are being assessed in these studies, and it may be that while older adults have trouble with the more fine-grained segmentation of individual activities, they do not appear to have much trouble with the segmentation of larger events.

Aside from methods that explicitly ask people to segment a stream of information, there are also less disruptive, more natural ways to assess the segmentation of a stream of information into events. Perhaps one of the most well known of these is an analysis of reading times. In particular, reading times tend to show an increase when readers encounter event boundaries (e.g., Zwaan et al., 1995, 1998). For example, when a comprehender reads that the story protagonist went from the gym out to the parking lot, there is a change in spatial location.

As such, this is an event boundary that separates the event of being in the gym from the event of being in the parking lot. The increase in reading time at this point is thought to reflect the increased effort needed to update one's situation models, such as by shifting to a new model. In terms of aging, younger and older adults appear to perform similarly (Radvansky, Zwaan, Curiel, & Copeland, 2001), showing similar increases in reading time at event boundaries. Together with the explicit segmentation data, this supports the idea that there are small to no age-related changes in the basic process of detecting changes from one event to another. As such, one would expect younger and older adults to create similar situation models, at least in terms of the extent to which people interpret one event to end and another to begin.

For processing at the situation model level to be successful, a person needs not only to detect when one event ends and another begins, but also to update the representation of the information relative to the developing events. That is, information that is tied to prior events should become less available in working memory so that it does not intrude on one's under-standing of the current event. This is particularly relevant in terms of issues of aging, as it is well known that older adults have greater difficulty removing newly irrelevant information from the current stream of processing (Hasher & Zacks, 1988).

Despite this, there are a variety of sources of evidence suggesting that older adults man-age the contents of their situation models as effectively as do younger adults. For example, Radvansky, Copeland, Berish, and Dijkstra (2003) found that when there were changes in the spatial or temporal framework of described events, such as when a story character moved from one location to another, or there was a big jump in time in the story (e.g., a day later), younger and older adults were similarly able to remove event-specific information from their situation models. For example, if a story protagonist moved from the gym to the park-ing lot, then information about the lighting in the gym would no longer be relevant, and if information about the lighting were probed at that point, it would be similarly unavailable for younger and older adults. This comprehension process is not isolated to linguistic materi-als. Radvansky, Pettijohn, and Kim (2015) have found that when younger and older adults move from one room to another in a virtual environment, there is a similar decline in the availability of information about objects with which the person interacted in a prior room. Thus, there is substantial evidence that older adults do not show any broad-based decline in the ability to update their understanding of unfolding events.

Keeping that in mind, there is some evidence that older adults can have difficulty with some aspects of situation model processing. First, there is a study by Noh and Stine-Morrow (2009) in which younger and older adults were asked to read texts that involved multiple characters. Under these circumstances, where the demand on the processing of the situation model is increased, older adults have difficulty tracking the larger number of event entities. Another source of evidence is a study by Copeland and Radvansky (2007), which assessed younger and older adults' ability to integrate information in brief, unfold-ing descriptions. When discontinuous orders were presented, in which people needed to wait to learn how all of the elements could be integrated together, older adults showed difficulty integrating the information, particularly when the information was presented in the form of sentences and word diagrams (although not when presented in the form of picture diagrams). Again, as in the Noh and Stine-Morrow study, when the older adults needed to coordinate multiple sources of information within and across situation models, they were less effective than the younger adults. This difficulty may be a result of decline in working memory capacity as there is a need to manage multiple sources of information in these tasks.

Aging and the Use of Discourse Context in Language Understanding

Age-related declines in speed of processing in working memory impact language under-standing, in particular, by decreasing the rate of propositional coding (Hartley et al., 1994; Stine & Hindman, 1994). However, older readers take disproportionate use of discourse context to support the comprehension and encoding of lower-level information (Miller & Stine-Morrow, 1998), such that while such deficits are readily detected in sentence process-ing, they are much reduced, and often undetectable, in discourse processing. For example, measuring "reading efficiency" as the time allocated to reading relative to the number of propositional idea unit recalled (ms/idea), Miller, Cohen, and Wingfield (2006) showed that older readers took longer than younger adults to encode information from ambiguous texts, but differentially improved in efficiency when the text was preceded by a title that made the discourse coherent. Such effects were exaggerated among those with relatively low working memory capacity, as well as by a dual-task condition that was designed to reduce working memory demands. These findings support the view that creating a textbase representation of the ideas from a text is resource-consuming, especially so with aging, but that these processes can be supported by the larger discourse context (Stine & Wingfield, 1990b; Stine-Morrow et al., 2008).

Discourse context can facilitate processing for older adults through a number of routes. Shake and Stine-Morrow (2011) measured eye movements while younger and older adults read texts containing a pronoun that referenced a noun that was either matched or mismatched in stereotypical gender roles to the pronoun (e.g., The firefighter pulled himself/herself up the ladder). When such sentences were read in isolation, younger adults took a little extra time on the pronoun when it did not match their expectations (in this case, *herself*). Older adults, on the other hand, did not slow down on the pronoun, but were more likely to regress back from a subsequent word when there was a mismatch. In other words, younger readers immediately recognized the mismatch (e.g., features of *firefighter*, including gender, were activated and within two words integrated with the features of the pronoun to create an error signal), but older readers were not able to do this until they were past the pronoun. When these sentences were embedded in a short narrative that provided some context for the sentence, older readers responded immediately to the mismatch just as the younger adults did – regardless of whether the context revealed the gender of the referent. Discourse context, then, appeared to enable the older adults to instantiate the character in the narrative and be prepared to process the dis-tinctive feature of gender within a single sentence. Also instructive were the age differences in processing in the discourse condition as a function of whether it revealed the gender of the character or not. In the gender-disambiguating condition, both groups of readers still took a little extra time on the mismatch, but younger and older readers showed virtually identical effects. In the gender-neutral condition that allowed the reader to instantiate the character in the narrative without revealing the gender, the older adults took much longer to process the target sentence. Thus, older adults can exploit the richer semantic representation afforded by discourse, both for instantiating discourse entities into the narrative (which then enables faster elaboration), and to constrain possible specific meanings.

Aging and the Effects of Knowledge on Discourse Processing

One of the great advantages of growing older is the opportunity for knowledge growth, both in terms of shared cultural and world knowledge, but also in particularized knowledge that can be derived from the investment in work and leisure activities that are more person-specific (Ackerman & Rolfhus, 1999). Older adults are often shown to differentially rely on domain-specific and schematic knowledge, which can be a double-edged sword (Umanath & Marsh, 2014).

On one hand, there is considerable evidence that knowledge can have beneficial effects on discourse processing with age. Crystallized knowledge, typically measured as vocabulary level, develops in part through habitual engagement with print (Stanovich, West, & Harrison, 1995). As we discuss below, such knowledge may have broad effects on cognition, but more proximally, verbal skill can have a number of positive effects on language and discourse processes. It has been recognized for some time that underdeveloped word recognition skills can compromise comprehension processes among both children (Perfetti & Hogaboam, 1975) and college-aged adults (Bell & Perfetti, 1994), but variation in word knowledge can have continuing effects into later adulthood. Older adults with higher levels of vocabulary and/or print exposure are more efficient in word processing during reading and allocate more effort to semantic integration processes (Payne et al., 2012; Stine-Morrow et al., 2008), and are more tuned to the statistical properties of attachment in language (Payne et al., 2014). Age deficits in discourse memory are very often found to be reduced or eliminated among those with high levels of verbal ability (Johnson, 2003; Meyer & Pollard, 2006), which may be attributable in part to deeper semantic and situational processing that is afforded by verbal efficiency.

Experience more generally may afford advantages with discourse processing among older adults. Interestingly, it has been shown that college professors, who presumably spend much of their lives engaged with processes of knowledge acquisition and organization, show no age deficits at all in discourse memory with texts outside of their domain of expertise (Shimamura et al., 1995). Younger adults reading narratives that include erroneous factual details (e.g., a story about someone going to St. Petersburg, the capital of Russia) are likely to inadvertently "learn" this information and later endorse it as factual in the context of a general knowledge questionnaire. As we discuss in more detail below, Umanath and Marsh (2012) have found that older adults are less vulnerable to false information, arguing that this is a consequence of the protective effects of a more developed knowledge base.

Domain-specific knowledge very typically is shown to produce enhanced discourse memory for texts among both younger and older adults in various domains of expertise, including aviation (Morrow, Leirer, & Altieri, 1992), baseball (Hambrick & Engle, 2002), and cooking (Miller, 2003). There is surprisingly little evidence that domain-related knowledge reduces age differences in recall in this literature (i.e., knowledge does not appear to differentially enhance memory performance among older adults). However, domain-related expertise has been shown to mitigate aging effects in other aspects of performance. For example, knowledge about cooking has been shown to differentially enhance the efficiency with which information is encoded from expository texts about cooking techniques and recipes (Miller, 2009). Also, Morrow et al. (2009) showed that relative to novices, expert pilots reading scenarios of aviation-related problems allocated particular attention to problem-relevant information, and then generated more effective solutions; interestingly, the solutions generated by the older experts were just as effective as those developed by the younger pilots, in contrast to the age difference observed among the novices. Domain knowledge may also differentially enhance inferencing processes among older readers (Miller, Stine-Morrow, Kirkorian, & Conroy, 2004).

In general, crystallized verbal knowledge is correlated with domain knowledge (because high-verbal people are likely to use these skills to learn new things), but verbal and domain-related knowledge can have distinctive effects on text processing. For example, Chin et al. (2015) showed in a sample of older adults that verbal ability enhanced conceptual integration for both health-related and domain-general texts, but controlling for verbal ability, health knowledge produced specific advantages for conceptual integration for health texts. Conceptual integration, in turn, enhanced later recall performance.

On the other hand, when discourse understanding depends on overriding well-learned schemas, older adults can be put at a disadvantage. For example, older adults have differential difficulty learning narratives that are variations on well-learned fairy tales (Attali & Dalla Barba, 2013; Dalla Barba, Attali, & La Corte, 2010).

Aging, Resource Allocation, and Engagement in Discourse Processing

Reading time is remarkably sensitive to demands that the text places on decoding the surface form, constructing the propositional textbase, and the need to repair discontinuities in the situation model. Statistical decomposition of reading time has been used to show that older adults are especially attentive to situation model features, and often less so to binding concepts into propositional idea units (Radvansky et al., 2001; Stine-Morrow et al., 2004; Stine-Morrow et al., 2008).

A consequence of reduced allocation to propositional analysis is that it may appear that older adults engage in more shallow and superficial processing of materials during comprehension. That is, there is not as much processing effort devoted to the comprehension of the meaning of exactly what is read. As a result, older adults are more likely to miss inconsistencies or irregularities in the language that is being comprehended. For example, in a series of studies, Umanath and Marsh (2012, 2014) assessed the performance of younger and older adults on semantic illusions, such as the Moses illusion. The Moses illusion is the finding that when asked the question, "How many animals of each kind did Moses take on the ark?," people will often respond with the answer, "2," even though nearly all of them know that it was Noah, not Moses, who took the animals on the ark. What they found was that older adults were more likely to fall prey to this illusion and give the inappropriate answer.

In another demonstration, older adults read texts that contained factually inaccurate information, such as a sentence that contained the phrase ". . . paddling across the largest ocean, the Atlantic, . . ." Here, younger and older adults were similarly disrupted during their comprehension. However, for both of these studies, when world knowledge was subsequently tested, older adults were less likely than younger adults to fall prey to the misinformation from the earlier part of the study. Instead, older adults were more likely to rely on their correct, long-term semantic knowledge. Thus, while there is some evidence that older adults may be compromised in terms of the depth with which they process information during comprehension, the long-lasting negative consequences for their long-term semantic memories is more limited than that for younger adults.

Older adults may generally adopt a heuristic of relying more on knowledge-based understanding of the situation with concomitant shallow processing of the surface form. For example, at syntactic levels of processing, work by Christianson, Williams, Zacks, and Ferreira (2006) had younger and older adults read garden paths sentences, such as "While Anna dressed the baby played in the crib." Younger and older adults were similarly disrupted in online comprehension, as measured by reading times, and both age groups were often likely to misinterpret the sentence, endorsing that "Anna dressed the baby." However, older adults endorsed the inappropriate interpretations at a higher rate, relative to control sentences, than did the younger adults. Christianson et al. argued that readers maintain the original interpretation while also encoding that the baby was playing in the crib (in fact, participants are also likely to endorse this meaning as well) even though the co-existence of these two meanings is not allowed by the sentence structure. They suggest that rather than deriving meaning strictly based on the rules of language, that we use heuristics to create situational representations that are consistent with world knowledge. Because older adults tend to rely on knowledge-based heuristics, they are more likely to engage in such shallow processing.

Another example of this, at a more complex level of representation, was demonstrated by Hamm and Hasher (1992). In this study, people read passages in which the readers were led to interpret the situation in a particular way, and then were given further information that rendered that original interpretation incorrect. For example, people might be reading a story about a big game hunter out on the savanna who sees the animal he has been looking for, and how he is getting ready to take a shot. Then the person reads about the shutter clicking. At that point the reader needs to shift from the schematic/implied interpretation that the hunter is on a hunting safari to the interpretation that the hunter is on a photographic safari. While younger and older adults drew inferences about the revised interpretation at the same rate, older adults were also more likely to continue to maintain the original, incorrect interpretation. Thus, in both of these studies, younger and older adults seem similarly able to detect when some modification of their understanding is needed. However, older adults appear to hang on to inappropriate representations and understanding after it has become very clear that they are wrong.

Note that these findings may appear to differ from those of Umanath and Marsh described earlier in showing that older adults retain the "misinformation," but there is a subtle, but important, difference in these bodies of research. In the Umanath and Marsh work, the surface form and textbase introduce information that is inconsistent with well-established knowledge. The tendency for older adults to be more knowledge-driven and less likely to attend to propositional analysis results in less attention to the "revised" information and to rely on their stored knowledge. In the studies by Christianson, and by Hamm and Hasher, the pieces of conflicting information are both encoded from the text so that their relative value cannot be adjudicated based on existing knowledge.

Another issue that arises for older adults when comprehending is the degree to which they can stay engaged in the materials. Given that, according to many studies, they have reduced cognitive resources, it would intuitively be expected that they would be less likely to maintain focus on the comprehension task itself, and be more likely to have thoughts drift to off-topic ideas. The disengagement of normal comprehension, and the movement to off-topic, internally generated thoughts, is called *mind-wandering* (Barron, Riby, Greer, & Smallwood, 2011; Giambra, 1995; Smallwood & Schooler, 2006, 2015). The classical illustration of this is when one is reading a page and realizes when the bottom is reached that there is no memory for what was just read. Mind-wandering has been linked to a shift in cortical activity toward the default mode network (DMN) (e.g., Buckner, Andrews-Hanna, & Schacter, 2008; Weissman, Roberts, Visscher, & Woldorff, 2006).

Again, the expectation based on work on cognitive control is that older adults should mind wander more than younger adults when they are comprehending because they are less able to control their attention. However, what is interesting is that there are several studies showing that older adults actually mind wander either at the same rate as younger adults (Giambra & Arenberg, 1993), or *less* so (Jackson & Balota, 2012; Krawietz, Tamplin, & Radvansky, 2012). For example, in a study by Krawietz et al., younger adults were asked to read the first

Discourse Processing in the Adult Lifespan

five chapters of *War and Peace* (Tolstoy, 1869). During reading, people were occasionally interrupted with probes asking if they were mind-wandering. Using this method, they found that older adults were less likely to report mind-wandering. Supporting these claims, they also found that older adults were as able as younger adults to answer questions about the text when they reported not mind-wandering, suggesting that some active comprehension was occurring. More generally, this is further evidence that during comprehension, older adults can perform as well as or better than younger adults, particularly when comprehension is being assessed in terms of more global, situation model levels of understanding.

That said, there is also evidence of preservation with age in the use of surface form cues to selectively focus on discourse elements. One way this is accomplished is through syntactic form. For example, notice the difference in emphasis when a story begins, "*It was Paul who lost his daughter*," as opposed to, "*What Paul lost was his daughter*." This is a syntactic device, called *clefting*, which puts the focus on Paul in the first case and on his daughter in the second case, and leads to certain expectations about how the story will proceed. Price and Sanford (2012) conducted a series of experiments in which older and younger adults were presented with passages in which cleft constructions were used to manipulate the focus of entities in the discourse. As the story continued with the sentence, "*He/She had wandered off in the shop*," reading time was facilitated when the continuation matched the focus implied by the syntactic form. Older adults were just as able as young adults to use these syntactic cues to guide their attention to the focused elements and maintain them in working memory, thus facilitating comprehension and enhancing episodic memory for the focused elements.

Similarly, older adults have been shown to be able to use stress patterns in spoken discourse as a cue to selectivity. Fraundorf, Watson, and Benjamin (2012) presented younger and older adults with short spoken narratives with target sentences (e.g., "*The family decided to visit the Rockies in the fall*"), in which they systematically manipulated the prosodic pattern so as to differentially emphasize the importance of certain discourse elements. So the sentence was spoken with the stress accent on one element (e.g., "*The family decided to visit the **Rockies** in the fall*"), or the other (e.g., "*The family decided to visit the Rockies in the **fall***"), both (e.g., ***Rockies . . . fall***), or neither (e.g., *Rockies . . . fall*). In a delayed memory task, both younger and older adults were more likely to remember the concepts that had been spoken with a stress accent (cf. also Cohen & Faulkner, 1986). However, Fraudorf et al. showed that age-related declines in working memory may set limits on how much information can be focused on at once. While younger participants showed a benefit for each focused item regardless of the number of accented items in the text, the benefit for older adults was decreased when both items were accented, a phenomenon they called the "other accent penalty." Because low-span younger adults also showed the other accent penalty, they argued that working memory resources are required to manage the elements held in focus and that age-related declines in working memory reduced older adults' ability to maintain multiple elements in focus. Thus, older adults appear to be quite good at using cues to process the discourse more selectively, but there may be boundary conditions on this ability. Selectivity in discourse focus is only useful inasmuch as it allows individuals to manage information given their existing working memory capacity.

Collectively, these studies indicate that older adults are able, and perhaps in some cases, more able than younger adults to selectively attend to the larger discourse situation rather than the individual idea units. They are also able to use focus cues in discourse to guide their more limited working memory capacities toward important information.

Aging and Conversation

Conversation with other people serves myriad functions throughout the lifespan. We use conversation both to exchange information, and to establish and maintain social relationships that nurture our emotional lives. We can consider how aging impacts this critical function from different angles.

One consideration is the impact of sensory hearing loss on understanding conversation. Age-related declines in auditory function can impact comprehension directly through decreased sensitivity and through a compromised ability to discriminate among speech sounds, but there is growing evidence that the secondary effects are also significant. Aging listeners are often quite good at using top-down control to compensate for an impoverished speech signal, but this can require cognitive resources so that attention needed to create the textbase and situational representations are diminished (Wingfield & Lash, in press). In fact, comprehension among older adults is especially compromised in noisy environments (Schneider, Daneman, Murphy, & Kwong See, 2000). Older adults also have particular difficulty in following multi-talker conversations, and the ability to engage top-down control mechanisms can depend on complex interactions between the quality of the acoustic environment (e.g., separation between speakers and/or extraneous noise) as well as the cognitive resources of the individual (Avivi-Reich, Daneman, & Schneider, 2014). A substantial body of work has investigated age-related changes in language production, which would be expected to impact participation in conversation. It has long been known that language production shows a shift toward simpler syntactic forms with age, and to a lesser degree, reduced informational density, measured as idea units per utterance (Kemper et al., 2001; Kemper, Thompson, & Marquis, 2001). That said, older adults are sometimes found to be quite comparable to the young in producing informationally rich stories (Wright, Capilouto, Srinivasan, & Fergadiotis, 2011). Furthermore, there is considerable variability among individuals, with greatest effects related to late-life cognitive pathologies. Simplification in surface form (and perhaps, in propositional content) may, in part, represent a shift in attention toward higher order discourse forms, given evidence that older adults produce narratives that are structurally more complex (Kemper, Rash, Kynette, & Norman, 1990).

Another aspect of production that can impact conversation is the ability to maintain a coherent flow of topics. Findings on this using structured interviews or personal recollections are somewhat mixed, with some studies showing less coherent production among older adults relative to young (Glosser & Deser, 1992), and others suggesting a great deal of variability as a function of the structure of the task and the cognitive abilities of the participants (Wright, Koutsoftas, Capilouto, & Fergadiotis, 2014). Some have argued that age-related changes in executive control make older adults more vulnerable to engaging in off-topic speech (Arbuckle & Gold, 1993), conforming to the unfortunate stereotype of the verbose older adults. However, other work has demonstrated that older adults are more likely to produce elaborations off the main story line ("asides") when recounting personal narratives, but not when describing a picture (James, Burke, Austin, & Hulme, 1998) or when recounting a narrative that was learned in the laboratory session (Bluck, Alea, Baron-Lee, & Davis, 2016). Such findings strongly imply that any cohort differences in "verbosity" may serve a social function, rather than reflecting age-related changes in cognition.

Finally, participating in conversation requires sensitivity to the listener, tailoring production to the partner's understanding. One way in which this has been investigated is with the referential communication task, in which conversational partners work together to arrange ambiguous items without access to the other's viewpoint. Participants take turns serving as the director, who can see the arrangement of items, and the partner, who has the items but has to create the arrangement based on conversation with the director. A key challenge to this task is developing a common terminology with which to refer to the ambiguous items that must be arranged. Older partners often take longer to achieve the common arrangement because it takes them longer to achieve terms of reference, which has been attributed to memory deficits (Hupet, Chantraine, & Nef, 1993; Lysander & Horton, 2012).

For example, Horton and Spieler (2007) manipulated the familiarity of the partner in a second session after common ground had been established in a referential communication task and found that while younger adults took advantage of the earlier experience to selectively abbreviate communication with familiar partners with whom common ground had already been established, older adults did not. They argue that older adults were less likely to engage in such "audience design," because of difficulties in encoding listener-specific perspectives and then retrieving them on the fly in the new situation. Other research, however, suggests that older adults can be quite sensitive in tailoring conversation to the listener. Adams et al. (2002) found that when retelling a narrative to a child, as opposed to an adult experimenter, older adults were better than the young in simplifying the story for the child. Incidentally, the typical text memory deficits for older adults that were observed with the experimenter listener were also eliminated when the listener was a child, suggesting that socioemotional dimensions of motivation may offset declines in cognitive resources in recalling discourse, which is certainly likely to play a role in conversation.

Aging and Discourse Processing in New Ecologies

The little work that has been conducted in multimedia environments with younger and older adults suggests similar age-related patterns to those found with conventional text studies. For example, Cavanaugh (1983) compared younger and older adults' memory for television programs and found that older adults showed the same advantage in memory for points central to the plot as did the young; and interestingly, as we have discussed earlier in connection with text, age effects depended on verbal ability such that it was only the older adults with lower verbal ability who showed deficits in memory.

The contexts in which discourse processing and development is studied are expanding. For example, there are increases in the study of conversations. Also, nonlinguistic aspects of communication, such as gesture, are being more deeply considered, and the time is ripe for these new discoveries and theories to be applied to older adult populations. What is particularly notable are the recent expansions into new media in which discourse can occur. Specifically, this can include work on the comprehension that occurs when watching videos and other multimedia, as well as interacting with virtual environments. In terms of film, there has been a dramatic increase in work assessing how people process and comprehend narrative film. Some of this work is being done by researchers whose background is in discourse processing, and they bring the perspective and tools of discourse analysis to the study of narrative film (e.g., Magliano, Miller, & Zwaan, 2001; Zacks, Speer, & Reynolds, 2009). The results of this work reveal that many of the same principles that guide comprehension for narrative texts can be extended to the comprehension of narrative film. In terms of aging, it may be that older adults are more adept at processing narrative film than narrative texts. For example, a study by Kurby, Asiala, and Mills (2014) found no age differences in older and younger adults' event segmentation of a narrative film.

More recent cognitive science advances in computer technology have led to an explosion of research using virtual environments in which a participant can actively navigate and interact with objects and entities in multi-space settings. This technology allows for the assessment of various aspects of human cognition. Aside from the obvious studies of spatial navigation and memory (e.g., Richardson, Montello, & Hegarty, 1999; Riecke, Cunningham, & Bülthoff, 2007), there are also studies that assess how the structure of the environment influences memory processing in that environment.

One example of this is the finding that walking through doorways causes forgetting (Radvansky & Copeland, 2006; Radvansky, Krawietz, & Tamplin, 2011; Radvansky, Tamplin, & Krawietz, 2010). Essentially, in this paradigm, people are asked to navigate through a virtual environment picking up and setting down objects as they move through the space. The critical finding is that people are less accurate at remembering what objects they are currently carrying if they move from one room to another as compared to if they simply move across a large room of the same distance. This work was inspired by and parallels work in discourse comprehension that has found that the availability of objects mentioned previously in a text grows worse as a story protagonist moves away from the object in the story world (e.g., Glenberg, Meyer, & Lindem, 1987; Morrow, Bower, & Greenspan, 1987). Similarly, like the finding that younger and older adults similarly update their event models during written discourse processing by removing no longer relevant objects from their event models, work using these virtual environments has found that older adults are similar to younger adults in terms of how they update their understanding of the unfolding interactive environment. Given these parallels, one can think of written or spoken discourse as a means for comprehenders to create vicarious autobiographical experiences, as the same cognitive mechanisms seem to be involved in both.

With the rise of electronic media (e.g., Internet, electronic books), another feature of new discourse ecologies is that readers play more of a role in selecting texts and managing multiple sources (Pirolli, 2005). In such a context, discourse understanding depends not only on textbase and situation model processes, but also skills in search, and strategies for selective investment of attentional resources into particular sources. To the extent that such processes are age-sensitive, one might expect age differences in how older adults process discourse in such environments. On the one hand, age declines in executive control might be expected to compromise performance with age when navigational demands are high, but at the same time, self-regulation afforded in these new ecologies may yield special advantages for older adults. For example, older adults' search strategies for obtaining health information in web environments has been characterized as more top-down relative to those of younger adults in relying on existing knowledge (Chin, Fu, & Kannampallil, 2009).

Other research indicates that older adults may be especially adaptive in responding to the constraints of a search environment. In a recent study by Liu et al. (submitted) younger and older adults were asked to learn about a topic by selecting a series of short texts to read on an electronic tablet. Programmed into the tablet was a short random delay between when the participant selected the text and when it appeared, during which a spinning wheel appeared (indicating the tablet was loading the text). There were two conditions in which the total amount of study time was controlled but the presentation delay (a "switch cost" in moving from one passage to another) was varied (0–2 sec vs. 6–8 sec). It can be shown that optimal information gain from the whole environment requires that the learner increase persistence within a text as the switch cost increases. In fact, both younger and older adults adopted this strategy, and showed benefits in recall as a result. Older adults were somewhat

Discourse Processing in the Adult Lifespan

more adaptive to the change in switch cost, so that age differences in delayed recall were eliminated when switch cost was high.

How Discourse Processing Can Shape Aging

While the myriad ways in which aging impacts discourse processing have been of interest in the scientific literature for some time, questions about how engagement with language and discourse impacts aging are only recently coming into focus (Stine-Morrow, Hussey, & Ng, 2015). Even with the normative age-related declines in some aspects of cognition that we have already discussed, there is also evidence of great plasticity and considerable interest in the pathways to promote cognitive resilience with aging (Hertzog et al., 2008; Stine-Morrow & Chui, 2012), in particular through engagement with everyday activities (Carlson et al., 2011; Stine-Morrow et al., 2014). Habitual engagement with discourse through sustained literacy practices is quite plausibly an activity with the potential to promote cognitive health. Because self-reports of reading habits can be inflated by demand characteristics, habits of engagement with print are typically measured with tasks requiring recognition of the names of authors or magazines (Mol & Bus, 2011). Such measures tend to correlate with self-reports and other measures that plausibly reflect a predilection toward engagement with written discourse (e.g., number of books in the home, the ability to name a favorite author).

Print exposure has been found to account for age-related growth in vocabulary and crystallized ability (Stanovich et al., 1995). Early in the lifespan, the magnitude of cross-sectional correlations between print exposure and language abilities tend to increase with age, and cross-lagged correlations between measures of these constructs in longitudinal data have prompted some to argue for a causal spiral between print exposure that contributes to more fluent reading, on the one hand, and abilities that afford access to an ever wider range of texts, on the other (e.g., Mol & Bus, 2011). Older readers with higher levels of print exposure process words more efficiently and allocate more attention to semantic processing, even when controlling for differences in vocabulary (Payne et al., 2012). In addition, readers with higher levels of print exposure are more attuned to the statistical properties of syntactic structure (Payne et al., 2014). Finally, print exposure has been shown to modulate the well-replicated relationship between working memory (a fluid ability) and text memory, such that at the highest levels of print exposure, text recall is not at all constrained by poor working memory (Payne et al., 2012). Older adults with poorer literacy skills show steeper declines in cognition measured longitudinally (Manly et al., 2004), and there is some evidence that avid readers are more resistant to the effects of late-life cognitive pathology (Wilson et al., 2000).

Perhaps the most striking evidence for the long-term effects of language use and literacy practices on mind and brain comes from natural experiments examining individuals who are deprived of literacy instruction for reasons unrelated to the ability to acquire literacy (Dehaene et al., 2010; Huettig & Mishra, 2014; Petersson, Ingvar, & Reis, 2009). This work suggests that literacy engagement has a number of effects on cognition, including enhanced verbal working memory, semantic fluency, and episodic memory, as well as effects on neural structure and function. Reading engagement may have effects beyond cognition. Consistent with the idea that narrative comprehension affords immersion into worlds with new places with new people, evoking the simulation of social experiences in particular (Gerrig & Jacovina, 2009; Mar & Oatley, 2008; Nell, 1988), adults higher in narrative print exposure score higher on objective measures of empathy (Mar, Oatley, & Peterson, 2009).

Knowledge Gaps and New Frontiers

There has been a great deal of research assessing the influence of the aging process on comprehension, particularly language comprehension, and more particularly, written language comprehension. Moreover, the materials that people are being asked to comprehend are quite limited in scope and importance, as is typical of many laboratory studies. While research using these sorts of materials can illuminate individual mechanisms, comprehension is much broader than this. There have been major advances in extending the range of contexts and paradigms in which aging and comprehension are being explored. The work on conversation is one example of this. That noted, there are still a number of areas that are severely understudied.

A moment's reflection will reveal that the majority of what younger and older adults are comprehending is not covered by traditional laboratory studies. As is the case earlier in the lifespan, many older adults spend a great deal of time reading books, as well as watching television programs and movies. A common element that is found in many of these cases is that there is a need for the comprehender to keep large amounts of complex information available in memory to understand the unfolding events. In the case of books, a reader often puts the book down to do other things. The book is then picked up some time later. This may be hours, days, weeks, or even months later. Often, the reader can continue reading, picking up where they left off without much difficulty, although we do acknowledge that the longer it has been since the person was reading, the harder this will be to do.

Similarly, when people watch television shows, they track various events that occur over an episode, with the need to refer to elements that may have been encountered several minutes earlier, often with interfering and distracting information in commercials. Even more importantly, in many televisions shows, viewers may need to refer back to events from episodes that may have been seen weeks, months, or even years earlier. Along the same lines, when viewers watch narrative feature films, they may need to remember back to events that occurred quite a while earlier in the movie. There may also be cases in which there is reference to earlier films if they are part of a series, which may have been seen years prior. Even more interesting is the ability of readers and viewers to make and appreciate references to other narratives that may not even be part of the current series, again, even if the narrative events had not been read about or viewed in many years or decades.

Despite these obstacles, most comprehenders seem to have no difficulty doing this. Nor do they seem to have difficulty remembering and tracking large numbers of life "narratives" about themselves, family members, friends, co-workers, and so on. More importantly, many of the age-related comprehension and memory complaints that are mentioned by older adults tend to fall along the lines of the kinds of unrelated, less systematic information that is typically studied in the laboratory. Older adults are not known for regularly complaining about not being able to comprehend and remember things that are described in the books that they read, or the television shows and movies that they watch. Thus, there are great swaths of comprehension and memory abilities that are largely preserved during the natural aging process that have not been intensively studied to date. If anything, older adults may be in a better position to comprehend and remember such "real life" narratives because they have a larger base of narrative memories on which to draw.

Technology is radically changing the ecology in which discourse processing occurs, not just in the delivery of conventional texts in electronic formats (e.g., e-books, Internet) but also in creating a culture in which we are deeply embedded in diverse forms of discourse through social media. For the current cohort of older adults, this creates avenues of cognitive and social enrichment that are unprecedented, but also within a context that is historically novel in terms of discourse forms and the roles of participants. These new forms of discourse are shaping our collective understanding of narrative forms and information exchange, so that future cohorts of older adults are aging into new modes of discourse with knowledge schemas for communication and information transmission that are very different from those of current cohorts. Of interest is how age-graded change in cognition impacts, and is impacted by, participation in these new ecologies.

References

Ackerman, P. L., & Rolfhus, E. L. (1999). The locus of adult intelligence: Knowledge, abilities, and nonability traits. *Psychology and Aging, 14*, 314–330.

Adams, C. (1991). Qualitative age differences in memory for text: A life-span developmental perspective. *Psychology and Aging, 6*, 323–336.

Adams, C., Labouvie-Vief, G., Hobart, C. J., & Dorosz, M. (1990). Adult age group differences in story recall style. *Journal of Gerontology: Psychological Sciences, 45*, P17–27.

Adams, C., Smith, M. C., Nyquist, L., & Perlmutter, M. (1997). Adult age-group differences in recall for the literal and interpretive meanings of narrative text. *Journal of Gerontology: Psychological Sciences, 52B*, P187–P195.

Adams, C., Smith, M. C., Pasupathi, M., & Vitolo, L. (2002). Social context effects on story recall in older and younger women: Does the listener make a difference? *Journal of Gerontology: Psychological Sciences, 57B*, P28–P40.

Arbuckle, T. Y., & Gold, D. P. (1993). Aging, inhibition, and verbosity. *Journal of Gerontology: Psychological Sciences, 48*, P225–P232.

Attali, E., & Dalla Barba, G. (2013). Confabulation in healthy aging is related to poor encoding and retrieval of over-learned information. *Aging, Neuropsychology, and Cognition, 20*, 339–355.

Avivi-Reich, M., Daneman, M., & Schneider, B. A. (2014). How age and linguistic competence alter the interplay of perceptual and cognitive factors when listening to conversations in a noisy environment. *Front Syst Neurosci, 8*, Article 21.

Baltes, P. B. (1987). Theoretical propositions of life-span developmental psychology: On the dynamics between growth and decline. *Developmental Psychology, 23*, 611–626.

Baltes, P. B. (1997). On the incomplete architecture of human ontogeny: Selection, optimization, and compensation as foundation of developmental theory. *American Psychologist, 52*, 366–380.

Barron, E., Riby, L. M., Greer, J., & Smallwood, J. (2011). Absorbed in thought: The effect of mind wandering on the processing of relevant and irrelevant events. *Psychological Science, 22*, 596–601.

Bell, L. C., & Perfetti, C. A. (1994). Reading skill: Some adult comparisons. *Journal of Educational Psychology, 86*, 244–255.

Bluck, S., Alea, N., Baron-Lee, J. M., & Davis, D. K. (2016). Story asides as a useful construct in examining adult story recall. *Psychology and Aging*. doi: http://dx.doi.org/10.1037/a0039990.

Borella, E., Ghisletta, P., & de Ribaupierre, A. (2011). Age differences in text processing: The role of working memory, inhibition, and processing speed. *Journal of Gerontology: Psychological Sciences, 66B*, 311–320.

Buckner, R. L., Andrews-Hanna, J. R., & Schacter, D. L. (2008). The brain's default network. *Annals of the New York Academy of Sciences, 1124*, 1–38.

Carlson, M. C., Parisi, J. M., Xia, J., Xue, Q.-L., Rebok, G. W., Bandeen-Roche, K., & Fried, L. P. (2011). Lifestyle activities and memory: Variety may be the spice of life: The Women's Health and Aging Study II. *Journal of the International Neuropsychological Society, 18*, 1–9.

Carstensen, L. L., Mikels, J. A., & Mather, M. (2006). Aging and the intersection of cognition, motivation, and emotion. In J. E. Birren & K. W. Schaie (Eds), *Handbook of the psychology of aging* (6th ed., pp. 343–362). New York, NY: Academic Press.

Cavanaugh, J. C. (1983). Comprehension and retention of television programs by 20- and 60-year olds. *Journal of Gerontology, 38*, 190–196.

Chapman, S. B., Anand, R., Sparks, G., & Cullum, C. M. (2006). Gist distinctions in healthy cognitive aging versus mild Alzheimer's Disease. *Brain Impairment, 7*, 223–233.

Chapman, S. B., Zeintz, J., Weiner, M., Rosenberg, R., Frawley, W., & Burns, M. H. (2002). Discourse changes in early Alzheimer Disease, mild cognitive impairment, and normal aging. *Alzheimer Dis Assoc Disord, 16*, 177–186.

Chin, J., Fu, W.-T., & Kannampallil, T. (2009). Adaptive information search: Age-dependent interactions between cognitive profiles and strategies. *Proceedings of the 27th ACM Conference on Human Factors in Computing Systems CHI'09*, 1683–1692. doi: 10.1145/1518701.1518961.

Chin, J., Madison, A., Gao, X., Graumlich, J. F., Conner-Garcia, T., Murray, M. D., . . . Morrow, D. G. (2015). Cognition and health literacy in older adults' recall of self-care information. *The Gerontologist*. doi: 10.1093/geront/gnv091.

Christianson, K., Williams, C. C., Zacks, R. T., & Ferreira, F. (2006). Younger and older adults' "good-enough" interpretations of garden-path sentences. *Discourse Processes, 42*, 205–238.

Cohen, G., & Faulkner, D. (1986). Does "elderspeak" work? The effect of intonation and stress on comprehension and recall of spoken discourse in old age. *Language and Communication, 6*, 91–98.

Copeland, D. E., & Radvansky, G. A. (2007). Aging and integrating spatial situation models. *Psychology and Aging, 22*, 569–579.

Dalla Barba, G., Attali, E., & La Corte, V. (2010). Confabulation in healthy aging is related to interference of overlearned, semantically similar information on episodic memory recall. *Journal of Experimental and Experimental Neuropsychology, 32*, 655–660.

Dehaene, S., Pegado, F., Braga, L. W., Ventura, P., Filho, G. N., Jobert, A., . . . Cohen, L. (2010). How learning to read changes the cortical networks for vision and language. *Science, 330*, 1359–1364.

Dijkstra, K., Yaxley, R. H., Madden, C. J., & Zwaan, R. A. (2004). The role of age and perceptual symbols in language comprehension. *Psychology and Aging, 19*, 352–356.

Ferstl, E. C. (2006). Text comprehension in middle aged adults: Is there anything wrong? *Aging, Neuropsychology, and Cognition, 13*, 62–85.

Fraundorf, S. H., Watson, D. G., & Benjamin, A. S. (2012). The effects of age on the strategic use of pitch accent in discourse: A processing-resource account. *Psychology and Aging, 27*, 88–98.

Gerrig, R. J., & Jacovina, M. E. (2009). Reader participation in the experience of narrative. In B. H. Ross (Ed.), *Psychology of learning and motivation* (Vol. 51, pp. 223–254). New York, NY: Elsevier.

Giambra, L. M. (1995). A laboratory method for investigating influences on switching attention to task-unrelated imagery and thought. *Consciousness and Cognition, 4*, 1–21.

Giambra, L. M., & Arenberg, D. (1993). Adult age differences in forgetting sentences. *Psychology and Aging, 8*, 451–462.

Glenberg, A. M., Meyer, M., & Lindem, K. (1987). Mental models contribute to foregrounding during text comprehension. *Journal of Memory and Language, 26*, 69–83.

Glosser, G., & Deser, T. (1992). A comparison of changes in macrolinguistic and microlinguistic aspects of discourse production in normal aging. *Journal of Gerontology: Psychological Sciences, 47*, P266–P272.

Hambrick, D. Z., & Engle, R. W. (2002). Effects of domain knowledge, working memory capacity, and age on cognitive performance: An investigation of the knowledge-is-power hypothesis. *Cognitive Psychology, 44*, 339–387.

Hamm, V. P., & Hasher, L. (1992). Age and the availability of inferences. *Psychology and Aging, 7*, 56–64.

Hartley, J. T., Stojack, C. C., Mushaney, T. J., Annon, T. A. K., & Lee, D. W. (1994). Reading speed and prose memory in older and younger adults. *Psychology and Aging, 9*, 216–223.

Hasher, L., & Zacks, R. T. (1988). Working memory, comprehension, and aging: A review and a new view. In G. H. Bower (Ed.), *The psychology of learning and motivation*, Vol. 22 (pp. 193–225). New York, NY: Academic Press.

Hertzog, C., Kramer, A. F., Wilson, R. S., & Lindenberger, U. (2008). Enrichment effects on adult cognitive development: Can the functional capacity of older adults be preserved and enhanced? *Psychological Science in the Public Interest, 9*, 1–65.

Hess, T. M. (2014). Selective engagement of cognitive resources: Motivational influences on older adults' cognitive functioning. *Perspectives on Psychological Science, 9*, 388–407.

Horton, W. S., & Spieler, D. H. (2007). Age-related differences in communication and audience design. *Psychology and Aging, 22*, 281–290.

Huettig, F., & Mishra, R. K. (2014). How literacy acquisition affects the illiterate mind: A critical examination of theories and evidence. *Language and Linguistics Compass, 8*, 401–427.

Hupet, M., Chantraine, Y., & Nef, F. (1993). References in conversation between young and old normal adults. *Psychology and Aging, 8,* 339–346.

Jackson, J. D., & Balota, D. A. (2012). Mind-wandering in younger and older adults: Converging evidence from the sustained attention to response task and reading for comprehension. *Psychology and Aging, 27,* 106–119.

James, L. E., Burke, D. M., Austin, A., & Hulme, E. (1998). Production and perception of "verbosity" in younger and older adults. *Psychology and Aging, 13,* 355–367.

Johnson, R. E. (2003). Aging and the remembering of text. *Developmental Review, 23,* 261–346.

Johnson-Laird, P. N. (1983). *Mental models.* Cambridge, MA: Harvard University Press.

Kemper, S., Greiner, L. H., Marquis, J. G., Prenovost, K., & Mitzner, T. L. (2001). Language decline across the life span: Findings from the Nun Study. *Psychology and Aging, 16,* 227–239.

Kemper, S., Rash, S., Kynette, D., & Norman, S. (1990). Telling stories: The structure of adults' narratives. *European Journal of Cognitive Psychology, 2,* 205–228.

Kemper, S., Thompson, M., & Marquis, J. (2001). Longitudinal change in language production: Effects of aging and dementia on grammatical complexity and propositional content. *Psychology and Aging, 16,* 600–614.

Kintsch, W. (1998). *Comprehension: A paradigm for cognition.* New York, NY: Cambridge University Press.

Kintsch, W., Welsch, D., Schmalhofer, F., & Zimny, S. (1990). Sentence memory: A theoretical analysis. *Journal of Memory and Language, 29,* 133–159.

Koustaal, W., & Schacter, D. L. (1997). Gist-based false recognition of pictures in older and younger adults. *Journal of Memory and Language, 30,* 555–583.

Krawietz, S. A., Tamplin, A. K., & Radvansky, G. A. (2012). Aging and mind wandering during text comprehension. *Psychology and Aging, 27,* 951–958.

Kurby, C. A., Asiala, L. K. E., & Mills, S. R. (2014). Aging and the segmentation of narrative film. *Aging, Neuropsychology, and Cognition, 21,* 444–463.

Kurby, C. A., & Zacks, J. M. (2011). Age differences in the perception of hierarchical structure in events. *Memory & Cognition, 39,* 75–91.

Li, S.-C., Lindenberger, U., Hommel, B., Aschersleben, G., Prinz, W., & Baltes, P. B. (2004). Transformations in the couplings among intellectual abilities and constituent cognitive processes across the life span. *Psychological Science, 15,* 155–163.

Linderberger, U. (2014). Human cognitive aging: Corriger la fortune? *Science, 346,* 572–578.

Liu, X., Chin, J., Fu, W.-T., Morrow, D. G., & Stine-Morrow, E. A. L. (submitted). Adult age differences in information foraging in an interactive reading environment.

Lysander, K., & Horton, W. S. (2012). Conversational grounding in younger and older adults: The effect of partner visibility and referent abstractness in task-oriented dialogue. *Discourse Processes, 49,* 29–60.

Magliano, J., Kopp, K., McNerney, M. W., Radvansky, G. A., & Zacks, J. M. (2012). Aging and perceived event structure as a function of modality. *Aging, Neuropsychology, and Cognition, 19,* 264–282.

Magliano, J. P., Miller, & Zwaan, R. A. (2001). Indexing space and time in film understanding. *Applied Cognitive Psychology, 15,* 533–545.

Magliano, J. P., & Zacks, J. M. (2011). The impact of continuity editing in narrative film on event segmentation. *Cognitive Science, 35,* 1489–1517.

Manly, J. J., Byrd, D., Touradji, P., Sanchez, D., & Stern, Y. (2004). Literacy and cognitive change among ethnically diverse elders. *International Journal of Psychology, 39,* 47–60.

Mar, R. A., & Oatley, K. (2008). The function of fiction in the abstraction and simulation of social experience. *Perspectives on Psychological Science, 3,* 173–192.

Mar, R. A., Oatley, K., & Peterson, J. B. (2009). Exploring the link between reading fiction and empathy: Ruling out individual differences and examining outcomes. *Communications, 34,* 407–428.

Meyer, B. J. F., & Pollard, C. K. (2006). Applied learning and aging: A closer look at reading. In J. E. Birren & K. W. Schaie (Eds), *Handbook of the psychology of aging* (6th ed., pp. 233–260). New York, NY: Elsevier.

Miller, L. M. S. (2003). The effects of age and domain knowledge on text processing. *Journal of Gerontology: Psychological Sciences, 58B,* P217–P223.

Miller, L. M. S. (2009). Age differences in the effects of domain knowledge on reading efficiency. *Psychology and Aging, 24,* 63–74.

Miller, L. M. S., Cohen, J. A., & Wingfield, A. (2006). Contextual knowledge reduces demands on working memory during reading. *Memory & Cognition, 34,* 1355–1367.

Miller, L. M. S., & Stine-Morrow, E. A. L. (1998). Aging and the effects of knowledge on on-line reading strategies. *Journal of Gerontology: Psychological Sciences, 53B,* P223–P233.

Miller, L. M. S., Stine-Morrow, E. A. L., Kirkorian, H., & Conroy, M. (2004). Age differences in knowledge-driven reading. *Journal of Educational Psychology, 96,* 811–821.

Mol, S. E., & Bus, A. G. (2011). To read or not to read: A meta-analysis of print exposure from infancy to early childhood. *Psychological Bulletin, 137,* 267–296.

Morrow, D. G., Bower, G. H., & Greenspan, S. L. (1989). Updating situation models during comprehension. *Journal of Memory and Language, 28,* 292–312.

Morrow, D. G., Leirer, V. O., & Altieri, P. A. (1992). Aging, expertise, and narrative processing. *Psychology and Aging, 7,* 376–388.

Morrow, D. G., Leirer, V., Altieri, P., & Fitzsimmons, P. (1994). Age differences in updating situation models from narratives. *Language and Cognitive Processes, 9,* 203–220.

Morrow, D. G., Miller, L. M. S., Ridolfo, H. E., Magnor, C., Fischer, U. M., Kokayeff, N. K., & Stine-Morrow, E. A. L. (2009). Expertise and age differences in pilot decision making. *Aging, Neuropsychology, and Cognition, 16,* 33–55.

Morrow, D. G., Stine-Morrow, E. A. L., Leirer, V. O., Andrassy, J. M., & Kahn, J. (1997). The role of reader age and focus of attention in creating situation models from narratives. *Journal of Gerontology: Psychological Sciences, 52B,* P73–P80.

Nell, V. (1988). *Lost in a book: The psychology of reading for pleasure.* New Haven, CT: Yale University Press.

Newtson, D. (1973). Attribution and the unit of perception of ongoing behavior. *Journal of Personality and Social Psychology, 28,* 28–38.

Newtson, D., & Engquist, G. (1976). The perceptual organization of ongoing behavior. *Journal of Experimental Social Psychology, 12,* 436–450.

Noh, S. R., & Stine-Morrow, E. A. L. (2009). Age differences in tracking characters during narrative comprehension. *Memory & Cognition, 37,* 769–778.

Payne, B. R., Gao, X., Noh, S. R., Anderson, C. J., & Stine-Morrow, E. A. L. (2012). The effects of print exposure on sentence processing and memory in older adults: Evidence for efficiency and reserve. *Aging, Neuropsychology, and Cognition, 19,* 122–149.

Payne, B. R., Grison, S., Gao, X., Christianson, K., Morrow, D., & Stine-Morrow, E. A. L. (2014). Aging and individual differences in binding during sentence understanding: Evidence from temporary and global syntactic attachment ambiguities. *Cognition, 130,* 157–173.

Payne, B. R., Gross, A. L., Parisi, J. M., Sisco, S. M., Stine-Morrow, E. A. L., Marsiske, M., & Rebok, G. W. (2014). Modeling longitudinal changes in older adults' memory for spoken discourse: Findings from the ACTIVE cohort. *Memory, 22,* 990–1001.

Payne, B. R., & Stine-Morrow, E. A. L. (2016). Risk for mild cognitive impairment is associated with semantic integration deficits in sentence comprehension. *Journal of Gerontology: Psychological Sciences, 71,* 243–253.

Perfetti, C. A., & Hogaboam, T. (1975). Relationship between single word decoding and comprehension skill. *Journal of Educational Psychology, 67,* 461–469.

Petersson, K. M., Ingvar, M., & Reis, A. (2009). Language and literacy from a cognitive neuroscience perspective. In D. R. Olson & N. Torrance (Eds), *Cambridge handbook of literacy* (pp. 152–181). Cambridge: Cambridge University Press.

Pirolli, P. (2005). Rational analysis of information foraging on the web. *Cognitive Science, 29,* 343–373.

Price, J. M., & Sanford, A. J. (2012). Reading in healthy aging: The influence of information structuring in sentences. *Psychology and Aging, 27,* 529–540.

Radvansky, G. A., & Copeland, D. E. (2006). Walking through doorways causes forgetting. *Memory & Cognition, 34,* 1150–1156.

Radvansky, G. A., Copeland, D. E., Berish, D. E., & Dijkstra, K. (2003). Aging and situation model updating. *Aging, Neuropsychology, and Cognition, 10,* 158–166.

Radvansky, G. A., Copeland, D. E., & Zwaan, R. A. (2003). Aging and functional spatial relations in comprehension and memory. *Psychology and Aging, 18,* 161–165.

Radvansky, G. A., & Curiel, J. M. (1998). Narrative comprehension and aging: The fate of completed goal information. *Psychology and Aging, 13,* 69–79.

Radvansky, G. A., & Dijkstra, K. (2007). Aging and situation model processing. *Psychonomic Bulletin and Review*, *14*, 1027–1042.

Radvansky, G. A., Gerard, L., Zacks, R. T., & Hasher, L. (1990). Younger and older adults' use of mental models as representations for text materials. *Psychology and Aging*, *5*, 209–214.

Radvansky, G. A., Krawietz, S. A., & Tamplin, A. K. (2011). Walking through doorways causes forgetting: Further explanations. *The Quarterly Journal of Experimental Psychology*, *64*, 1632–1645.

Radvansky, G. A., Pettijohn, K. A., & Kim, J. (2015). Walking through doorways causes forgetting: Younger and older adults. *Psychology and Aging*, *30*, 259–265.

Radvansky, G. A., Tamplin, A. K., & Krawietz, S. A. (2010). Walking through doorways causes forgetting: Environmental integration. *Psychonomic Bulletin & Review*, *17*, 900–904.

Radvansky, G. A., & Zacks, J. M. (2014). *Event cognition.* Oxford: Oxford University Press.

Radvansky, G. A., Zwaan, R. A., Curiel, J. M., & Copeland, D. E. (2001). Situation models and aging. *Psychology and Aging*, *16*, 145–160.

Richardson, A. E., Montello, D. R., & Hegarty, M. (1999). Spatial knowledge acquisition from maps and from navigation in real and virtual environments. *Memory & Cognition*, *27*(4), 741–750.

Riecke, B. E., Cunningham, D. W., & Bülthoff, H. H. (2007). Spatial updating in virtual reality: The sufficiency of visual information. *Psychological Research*, *71*(3), 298–313.

Salthouse, T. A. (2010). *Major issues in cognitive aging.* New York, NY: Oxford University Press.

Schacter, D. L., Guerin, S. A., & St. Jacques, P. L. (2011). Memory distortion: An adaptive perspective. *Topics in Cognitive Science*, *15*, 467–474.

Schaie, K. W. (2005). *Developmental influences on adult intelligence: The Seattle Longitudinal Study.* New York, NY: Oxford University Press.

Schneider, B. A., Daneman, M., Murphy, D. R., & Kwong See, S. (2000). Listening to discourse in distracting settings: The effects of aging. *Psychology and Aging*, *15*, 110–125.

Shake, M. C., Noh, S. R., & Stine-Morrow, E. A. L. (2009). Age differences in learning from text: Evidence for functionally distinct text processing systems. *Applied Cognitive Psychology*, *23*, 561–578.

Shake, M. C., & Stine-Morrow, E. A. L. (2011). Age differences in resolving anaphoric expressions during reading. *Aging, Neuropsychology, and Cognition*, *18*, 678–707.

Shimamura, A. P., Berry, J. M., Mangels, J. A., Rusting, C. L., & Jurica, P. J. (1995). Memory and cognitive abilities in university professors: Evidence for successful aging. *Psychological Science*, *6*, 271–277.

Smallwood, J., & Schooler, J. W. (2006). The restless mind. *Psychological Bulletin*, *132*, 946–958.

Smallwood, J., & Schooler, J. W. (2015). The science of mind wandering: Empirically navigating the stream of consciousness. *Annual Review of Psychology*, *66*, 487–518.

Stanovich, K. E., West, R. L., & Harrison, M. R. (1995). Knowledge growth and maintenance across the life span: The role of print exposure. *Developmental Psychology*, *31*, 811–826.

Stine, E. A. L., & Hindman, J. (1994). Age differences in reading time allocation for propositionally dense sentences. *Aging and Cognition*, *1*, 2–16.

Stine, E. A. L., & Wingfield, A. (1988). Memorability functions as an indicator of qualitative age differences in text recall. *Psychology and Aging*, *3*, 179–183.

Stine, E. A. L., & Wingfield, A. (1990a). The assessment of qualitative age differences in discourse processing. In T. M. Hess (Ed.), *Aging and cognition: Knowledge organization and utilization* (pp. 33–92). New York, NY: Elsevier.

Stine, E. A. L., & Wingfield, A. (1990b). How much do working memory deficits contribute to age differences in discourse memory? *European Journal of Cognitive Psychology*, *2*, 289–304.

Stine-Morrow, E. A. L., & Chui, H. (2012). Cognitive resilience in adulthood. In B. Hayslip, Jr. & G. C. Smith (Eds), *Annual Review of Gerontology and Geriatrics* (Vol. 32, pp. 93–114). New York, NY: Springer.

Stine-Morrow, E. A. L., Gagne, D. D., Morrow, D. G., & DeWall, B. H. (2004). Age differences in rereading. *Memory & Cognition*, *32*, 696–710.

Stine-Morrow, E. A. L., Hussey, E. K., & Ng, S. (2015). The potential for literacy to shape lifelong cognitive health. *Policy Insights from the Behavioral and Brain Sciences*, *2*. doi: 10.1177/2372732215600889.

Stine-Morrow, E. A. L., Miller, L. M. S., Gagne, D. D., & Hertzog, C. (2008). Self-regulated reading in adulthood. *Psychology and Aging*, *23*, 131–153.

Stine-Morrow, E. A. L., Miller, L. M. S., & Hertzog, C. (2006). Aging and self-regulated language processing. *Psychological Bulletin, 132*, 582–606.

Stine-Morrow, E. A. L., Miller, L. M. S., & Leno, R. (2001). Patterns of on-line resource allocation to narrative text by younger and older readers. *Aging, Neuropsychology, and Cognition, 8*, 36–53.

Stine-Morrow, E. A. L., Morrow, D. G., & Leno, R. (2002). Aging and the representation of spatial situations in narrative understanding. *Journal of Gerontology: Psychological Sciences, 57B*, P291–P297.

Stine-Morrow, E. A. L., Payne, B. R., Gao, X., Roberts, B., Kramer, A. F., Morrow, D. G., . . . Parisi, J. M. (2014). Training versus engagement as paths to cognitive optimization with aging. *Psychology and Aging, 29*, 891–906.

Thomas, R., & Hasher, L. (2012). Reflections of distraction in memory: Transfer of previous distraction improves recall. *Journal of Experimental Psychology: Learning, Memory, and Cognition, 38*, 30–39.

Tolstoy, L. (1869). *War and Peace*. London: Penguin.

Tun, P. A., Wingfield, A., Rosen, M. J., & Blanchard, L. (1998). Response latencies for false memories: Gist-based processes in normal aging. *Psychology and Aging, 13*, 230–241.

Umanath, S., & Marsh, E. B. (2012). Aging and memorial consequences of catching contradictions with prior knowledge. *Psychology and Aging, 27*, 1033–1038.

Umanath, S., & Marsh, E. J. (2014). Understanding how prior knowledge influences memory in older adults. *Perspectives on Psychological Science, 9*, 408–426.

United Nations Department of Economic and Social Affairs Population Division. (2013). *World population ageing 2013*. Retrieved from www.un.org/en/development/desa/population/publications/pdf/ageing/WorldPopulationAgeing2013.pdf.

van Dijk, T. A., & Kintsch, W. (1983). *Strategies of discourse comprehension*. New York, NY: Academic Press.

Weissman, D. H., Roberts, K. C., Visscher, K. M., & Woldorff, M. G. (2006). The neural bases of momentary lapses in attention. *Nature Neuroscience, 9*, 971–978.

Wilson, R. S., Bennett, D. A., Gilley, D. W., Beckett, L. A., Barnes, L. L., & Evans, D. A. (2000). Premorbid reading activity and patterns of cognitive decline in Alzheimer Disease. *Archives of Neurology, 57*, 1718–1723.

Wingfield, A., & Grossman, M. (2006). Language and the aging brain: Patterns of neural compensation revealed by functional brain imaging. *Journal of Neurophysiology, 96*, 2830–2839.

Wingfield, A., & Lash, A. (in press). Audition and language comprehension in adult aging: Stability in the face of change. In K. W. Schaie & S. L. Willis (Eds), *Handbook of the psychology of aging* (8th ed.). New York, NY: Elsevier.

Wingfield, A., & Stine-Morrow, E. A. L. (2000). Language and speech. In F. I. M. Craik & T. A. Salthouse (Eds), *The handbook of aging and cognition* (2nd ed., pp. 359–416). Mahwah, NJ: Erlbaum.

Wright, H. H., Capilouto, G. J., Srinivasan, C., & Fergadiotis, G. (2011). Story processing ability in cognitively healthy younger and older adults. *Journal of Speech, Language, and Hearing Research, 54*, 900–917.

Wright, H. H., Koutsoftas, A. D., Capilouto, G. J., & Fergadiotis, G. (2014). Global coherence in younger and older adults: Influence of cognitive processes and discourse type. *Aging, Neuropsychology, and Cognition, 21*, 174–196.

Zacks, J. M., Speer, N. K., & Reynolds, J. R. (2009). Segmentation in reading and film comprehension. *Journal of Experimental Psychology: General, 138*, 307–327.

Zacks, J. M., & Swallow, K. M. (2007). Event segmentation. *Current Directions in Psychological Science, 16*, 80–84.

Zwaan, R. A., Langston, M. C., & Graesser, A. C. (1995). The construction of situation models in narrative comprehension: An event-indexing model. *Psychological Science, 6*, 292–297.

Zwaan, R. A., Magliano, J. P., & Graesser, A. C. (1995). Dimensions of situation model construction in narrative comprehension. *Journal of Experimental Psychology: Learning, Memory, and Cognition, 21*, 386–397.

Zwaan, R. A., & Radvansky, G. A. (1998). Situation models in language comprehension and memory. *Psychological Bulletin, 123*, 162–185.

14

The Cognitive Neuroscience of Discourse
Covered Ground and New Directions

Jeffrey M. Zacks

WASHINGTON UNIVERSITY IN SAINT LOUIS

Raymond A. Mar

YORK UNIVERSITY

Navona Calarco

CENTRE FOR ADDICTION AND MENTAL HEALTH

Cognitive neuroscience and discourse processing are both young fields, yet their intersection has already produced a surprisingly rich body of results. In this chapter, we outline the major findings of past work and then describe some exciting new directions in discourse processing research. We begin with a discussion of the evolutionary origins of discourse processing, follow this with a discussion of the mechanisms of interest to neuroscientists who study discourse, and conclude with an overview of the new directions in which this work has recently begun to move. Our hope is to provide a useful overview of what neuroscience has to offer researchers interested in discourse, as well as to push the field forward by highlighting new methodological advances and what they have revealed.

Evolution and the Neurobiology of Language and Discourse

The neurobiology of language is a wide scientific field, encompassing systems from insects to humans and levels of analysis ranging from neurotransmitter systems to multiple communicating organisms. Within humans, it encompasses both oral-gestural language and written language. Oral and gestural language resulted from the influence of natural selection over millions of years and comprises a species-general capacity that emerges in most humans without tutelage. Written language, in contrast, is a relatively recent cultural invention that only arises in the presence of deliberate instruction and practice. These differences have important implications for the neurobiology of language. Most fundamentally, the neural mechanisms for oral and gestural communication are explained in terms of how they evolved from non-language abilities into language-specific functions, whereas writing systems must be explained by the co-option of mechanisms that evolved for other purposes.

Recognizing these evolutionary differences can be useful when theorizing about language and the brain. For example, the dual-stream account of auditory speech recognition proposes an account of how speech recognition evolved (Hickok & Poeppel, 2007). According to this theory, one route to recognizing spoken language builds on mechanisms involved in motor control. Regions in the lateral prefrontal cortex (lPFC) and the anterior-superior parietal lobe are important for goal-directed action in many species. These regions evolved to take input from the auditory cortex and map gestures (both heard and seen) onto motor plans. In other words, the perception of communicative gestures (both visual and auditory) depends on referencing the motor plans required to produce these gestures. This system now forms what is commonly referred to as the dorsal language comprehension stream. In most people, this system is located more in the left cerebral hemisphere than the right. This lateralization reflects the dorsal system's evolutionary roots in the motor control system, as the left hemisphere controls the right side of the body, which is dominant for action in most individuals. Over the same evolutionary time-course, a ventral language comprehension stream developed to map auditory features onto the semantic features of words. This stream involves projections from the auditory cortex posterior to the superior temporal gyrus (STG) and anterior to the inferior temporal sulcus (ITS) and middle temporal gyrus (MTG). These projection zones (STG, ITS, MTG) also receive converging input from the visual object recognition system, providing a locus for representing semantic features. This dual-stream model has received wide support, providing a parsimonious account for a large body of patient and neuroimaging data.

Whereas the dual-stream account of spoken language comprehension is based on evolutionary processes, accounts of visual word recognition rely on exaptation. One example is the recent debate over the visual word form area (VWFA), a region in the left inferior temporal lobe that is selectively activated during the viewing of words but not other visual stimuli (Dehaene, Le Clec'H, Poline, Le Bihan, & Cohen, 2002). Activity in the VWFA is modulated by many lexical features, including word frequency, length, and orthographic regularity (Yarkoni, Speer, Balota, McAvoy, & Zacks, 2008). Some have argued that this region evolved to process configural cues for complex visual stimuli such as faces and objects (McCandliss, Cohen, & Dehaene, 2003), but its processing is co-opted and reapplied during the long developmental process of learning to read. Counter to this, others have argued that there is no functional unit that is remolded by learning to read (Price & Devlin, 2003). From this view, the VWFA is part of a processing stream that is sensitive to several features associated with words, but processes these features across stimuli with no special selectivity for words. Whereas the first account proposes that reading re-wires readers' brains, the second account denies this. But most importantly, both accounts agree that the brain regions undergirding language were fixed before written language was phylogenetically acquired.

Within the broad field of the neurobiology of language, the cognitive neuroscience of discourse is a much more focal subfield (Willems, 2015). The term "cognitive" tells us that we are dealing with the mechanisms of thought, rather than those of sensation, perception, or action. The word "discourse" indicates that we are concerned with the construction and use of language structures that span sentences, rather than being composed of single sentences or parts thereof. Work in this area has demonstrated that the neural mechanisms of language processing at the discourse level differ from those at the level of smaller language units.

The Cognitive Neuroscience of Discourse

In part, whereas discourse processing relies on low-level language processing, it also employs numerous other mechanisms that evolved to represent the structure of events in the world (and our reactions to them) rather than language processing *per se*.

Mechanisms and Phenomena

Predictive Processing

As other chapters in this volume note, there is not a coherent unified theory of discourse processing in terms of computation and behavior. Thus, it is not surprising that we also lack a unified neurobiological theory of discourse processing. What we have at this point is a growing set of replicable phenomena that are suggestive of mechanisms, and descriptions of some of those mechanisms. One particularly robust finding is that language processing is predictive. Comprehenders of discourse continually make predictions about what is coming next in the language stream, monitoring the quality of those inferences by computing the error between what is predicted and what actually occurs. The occurrence of a prediction error produces changes in reading time and in the electrical activity of the brain, as measured by electroencephalography (EEG).

Two kinds of predictive processing errors have been well characterized, at both the discourse level and lower levels of language processing. The first prediction error is based in semantic processing. The classic paradigm involves presenting words that are semantically incongruous within a sentence context (Kutas & Hillyard, 1980). For example, if one reads the sentence "I like my coffee with cream and dog," reading times for the final word, "dog," will be high compared to that for a semantically congruous word such as "sugar" (Marton & Szirtes, 1988). EEG recordings show that the incongruous word elicits an increase in a negative-going evoked response potential (ERP) approximately 400 ms after onset; because of the timing and polarity, this potential is known as the N400.

The second kind of prediction error involves predictions about syntax. For example, if one was to read "The child throw the ball," reading the word "child" induces a prediction that the verb will be singular. As a result, "throws" is predicted and encountering "throw" leads to a prediction error. This error once again results in a characteristic ERP, but one different from the N400 (Osterhout & Holcomb, 1992). In this case, the ERP peaks at around 600 ms and is positive-going; hence, it is known as a P600. In addition, behaviorally, syntactic violations lead to slowing on the word that produces the violation, but *speeding* on the sentence-final word. This is possibly because the language processing system has "given up" resolving the error (Ditman, Holcomb, & Kuperberg, 2007).

Although most studies of prediction errors examine violations at the level of the sentence, both semantic prediction (N400) and syntactic prediction (P600) effects have been observed in studies of discourse. For example, van Berkum and colleagues asked participants to read stories that set up a semantic expectation about a character or situation, which was then violated (van Berkum, Hagoort, & Brown, 1999). One story described an older sister that went to wake her younger brother but found him already dressed and ready to go. The target word was always congruous at the level of the individual sentence, but could either be congruous or incongruous at the discourse level. For example, after learning that the sister discovered her brother already dressed, participants read "Jane told her brother that he was exceptionally quick/slow." Reading the unexpected word "slow" led to a larger N400 response. Similar results were also observed when the materials were presented aurally (van Berkum, Zwitserlood, Hagoort, & Brown, 2003).

271

An example of discourse-level syntactic prediction comes from a study by Knoeferle and colleagues (2008). In this experiment, participants viewed pictures with three characters and then listened to sentences describing the pictures. The pictures were deliberately silly, so that both the characters and the actions were easy to observe and name. For example, one of the pictures showed a pirate washing a princess, while the princess painted a fencer. After viewing the picture, a sentence was presented that contained either a predictable verb (e.g., "The princess paints the fencer") or an unpredicted verb (e.g., "The princess washes the pirate"). Both sentences were syntactically appropriate at the level of the sentence, but one conflicted with the syntax of the action. These anomalies produced a P600 ERP, similar to what is observed for sentence-level syntactic violations.

Segmentation

A second robust mechanism of discourse processing is segmentation. When people listen or read, they segment language into phonemes, syllables, words, clauses or phrases, and sentences. At the discourse level, sentences (or sometimes clauses or phrases) are assembled into larger units. For both written and spoken discourse, a critical kind of segmentation is the segmentation of the ongoing language stream into events.

One account of discourse-level segmentation is given by *event segmentation theory* (EST; Zacks, Speer, Swallow, Braver, & Reynolds, 2007). EST is a model of how comprehenders segment ongoing activity into events, not just for discourse but also during live perception of actions. Briefly, EST is rooted in the predictive mechanisms discussed in the previous section. It proposes that listeners and readers constantly make predictions about features of a discourse that are relevant for maintaining comprehension; features often include characters, objects, locations, time, goals, and causes. To make these predictions, EST proposes that comprehenders construct and update situation models (or "event models") that maintain a representation of "what is happening now" (Kintsch & van Dijk, 1978; Zwaan & Radvansky, 1998). Event boundaries correspond to a cascade of processing in which the presence of increasing prediction errors leads to an updating of one's situation model. Updating based on rapid increases in prediction error allows a comprehender to negotiate a balance between maintaining a situation model that is stable enough to be useful for prediction, but not so rigid as to produce perseverative errors. For example, reading that a new character has arrived reduces the predictability of a situation, and errors should occur. At this time it would be adaptive to update one's situation model to incorporate information about the new character (cf. Rapp, Gerrig, & Prentice, 2001).

EST is closely related to two other cognitive theories of discourse processing. One is Gernsbacher's (1990) *structure building theory*. In that theory, the mechanism of *shifting* to construct a new discourse representation is similar to the event segmentation mechanism proposed by EST. The other related theory is Zwaan's (1999) *event indexing model*. From that model, EST borrows the idea that dimensions of experience in a situation described by discourse are monitored and represented in a situation model. EST's proposal that updating results from prediction failure is one unique feature of the model. A second unique feature is that it proposes mechanisms with both neurophysiological and information-processing aspects. A key mechanism in the model is the signaling of prediction error spikes, which may be implemented by midbrain neuromodulatory systems including the phasic dopamine system (Zacks, Kurby, Eisenberg, & Haroutunian, 2011). The consequences of prediction error signals are proposed to include broad phasic responses in the neocortex corresponding to situation model updating. This has been observed for narrative

The Cognitive Neuroscience of Discourse

reading (Speer, Reynolds, & Zacks, 2007; Whitney et al., 2009) as well as for the viewing of visual narratives in movies (Zacks et al., 2001; Zacks, Speer, Swallow, & Maley, 2010; Zacks, Swallow, Vettel, & McAvoy, 2006). For example, Speer and colleagues (2007) asked participants to read a set of stories about a young boy while brain activity was measured with functional magnetic resonance imaging (fMRI). After the initial reading, the participants read the stories again and marked off boundaries between meaningful units. When readers' brain activity was time-locked to those boundaries, phasic increases were observed in the posterior parietal, temporal, and anterior occipital lobes bilaterally, and in right dorsal frontal cortex. In a set of behavioral experiments, it was found that the points in the narrative that readers identified as event boundaries were those points at which more features of the narrated situation were changing. This is consistent with EST's prediction that situation changes lead to prediction errors, which in turn lead to event model updating.

Situation Model Construction: dmPFC

The construction of a situation model is itself an important mechanism of discourse comprehension. Going back to classic studies of sentence and story memory conducted by Bransford and colleagues, behavioral research finds that coherent discourse affords the construction of a mental representation, in turn supporting better comprehension and memory (Bransford, Barclay, & Franks, 1972; Bransford & Johnson, 1972). In terms of the neurophysiology of situation model construction, Zacks and colleagues (2007) proposed that situation models are a specialized form of working memory that are maintained primarily by subregions of the prefrontal cortex. Support for this idea comes from a study by Yarkoni, Speer, and Zacks (2008). In this experiment, participants read two sorts of paragraphs while brain activity was recorded with fMRI. The coherent paragraphs described coherent situations, excerpted from a larger narrative. Scrambled paragraphs included the same sentences, but with each sentence randomly assigned to a different paragraph. This manipulation controls language structure up to the level of the sentence, allowing for the isolation of situation model construction mechanisms. In the dorsomedial prefrontal cortex (dmPFC), reading coherent paragraphs produced an activity profile consistent with situation model building: activity increased at the onset of the paragraph and remained high. In contrast, the dmPFC showed no change in activity in the scrambled condition. Sustained activity in the story condition was also observed for regions in the lateral PFC and the cerebellum; these regions also showed smaller increases during the scrambled condition. In all of these regions, the level of activation in each block was correlated with subsequent memory for that block, which suggests that these regions contribute to the formation of stable long-term memories.

Early in the neuroscientific study of discourse processing, it was proposed that the right hemisphere is specialized for processing language at the discourse level—that is, for building situation models (Beeman, 1993; Robertson et al., 2000; St. George, Kutas, Martinez, & Sereno, 1999). This is an attractive proposal: Whereas the left hemisphere is specialized for language processing up to the sentence level in most right-handed adults (Hickok & Poeppel, 2007), perhaps the right hemisphere is specialized for language processing at the discourse level. This idea received early support from some neuropsychological studies (Beeman, 1993) and neuroimaging studies (Robertson et al., 2000; St. George et al., 1999). However, the right hemisphere hypothesis has not been supported by the bulk of subsequent work. Instead, meta-analyses identify a bilateral set of brain regions as being important for comprehension at the discourse level—particularly the dmPFC (Ferstl, Neumann, Bogler, & von Cramon, 2008; Mar, 2011). Focused studies have indicated that this

273

region is activated in circumstances that require integrating information across sentences (Ferstl & von Cramon, 2001, 2002; Kuperberg, Lakshmanan, Caplan, & Holcomb, 2006). For example, Yarkoni and colleagues found that when story paragraphs that allowed for discourse-level processing were directly contrasted to scrambled paragraphs that did not, the resulting activity was distinctly bilateral (Yarkoni, Speer, & Zacks, 2008).

Embodied Language Effects

A phenomenon that has attracted considerable interest and debate in discourse comprehension is embodiment. In discourse, embodiment means using experience in one's body to understand a text. Pinning down exactly what that means has elicited some contentious debate (Meteyard, Cuadrado, Bahrami, & Vigliocco, 2012; Wilson, 2002; Zwaan, 2014). The strongest and most interesting construal claims that we use modality-specific neural representations to comprehend language. Modality-specific brain regions obligatorily encode information about perceptual and motor dimensions such as spatial location (visual areas V1, V2, and others), color (visual area V4), and body part (primary somatosensory and motor cortex, and others). Much of the ongoing debate has concerned whether this claim is true and what sorts of evidence bear decisively on it.

Striking embodied language processing effects were first reported in behavioral studies of language processing. When people make judgments about sentences, they are generally faster when any accompanying nonlinguistic features are congruent with the language compared to when those features are incongruent. This is so even when the nonlinguistic features are irrelevant to the task being performed. (For reviews, see Barsalou, 2008; Fischer & Zwaan, 2008.) For example, Zwaan and colleagues (2002) presented readers with sentences such as "The ranger saw the eagle in the sky" or "The ranger saw the eagle in its nest," followed by a picture, and asked them to judge whether the picture depicted an object in the sentence. Judgments were faster when the picture showed the eagle in a pose that matched the sentence description, even though the shape of the eagle was not relevant to the task.

Neuroimaging studies of language comprehension have also provided evidence for embodied language processing, mostly in the motor domain. For example, Hauk and colleagues (2004) showed that making judgments about action words such as "pick," "lick," and "kick" led to localized activity within somatosensory and motor cortices that corresponded to areas involved with actual body movements (Hauk, Johnsrude, & Pulvermuller, 2004). An important question about such findings is whether they generalize to naturalistic discourse processing. Speer and colleagues (2009) tested this by measuring brain activity when specific dimensions of a narrative changed during a long story (Speer, Reynolds, Swallow, & Zacks, 2009). For example, in a classroom situation, reading "he crumpled the paper" is a change in the object acted on (i.e., paper), and reading "returned to her desk" signals a change in location. Changes in causes, characters, goals, objects, space, and time were all indexed. The authors found large cortical regions that responded to multiple changes, but also found many regions that responded selectively to a single type of change. For example, object changes selectively evoked activity in motor and somatosensory cortex that was lateralized to the hemisphere responsible for control of participants' dominant hands, which is suggestive of a modality-specific representation. To follow this up, Kurby and Zacks (2013) asked a new group of participants to rate each clause in these stories for the strength of the sensory or motor experience they evoked. They also had the new participants rate the paragraphs studied by Yarkoni and colleagues (2008). What they found was that high-imagery clauses—coded as visual, auditory, or motor—evoked localized responses in regions known to be specialized for these respective modalities.

The Cognitive Neuroscience of Discourse

One critique of embodied language theories proposes that embodiment is epiphenomenal. Like the heat given off by a light bulb, it occurs along with the mechanisms that are responsible for comprehension, but is not itself causally involved in comprehension (Chatterjee, 2010; Mahon & Caramazza, 2008, 2009). Another critique argues that embodied effects reflect task demands or other artificial constraints during discourse processing tasks in the laboratory (Speer et al., 2009). At this point, the weight of the evidence seems to support the strong embodied language processing claim for the necessity of modality-specific regions for some kinds of language comprehension (Pulvermüller & Fadiga, 2010). However, it is clear that the degree to which reading and listening comprehension is embodied depends on the text, the task, and a reader's abilities and goals. When a skilled and motivated reader is immersed in a text and reading for deep comprehension, it is likely that perceptual-motor representations play a causal role in processing the discourse. However, when a reader is struggling or skimming a text, there may be little sign of embodiment.

Theory-of-Mind

The last phenomenon we will discuss is theory-of-mind (ToM) or mentalizing, which involves the ability to infer another person's mental state(s). Cognitive neuroscience studies of ToM are inextricably tied with studies of discourse in part because the initial, influential, neuroimaging study of ToM involved reading stories about characters' mental states (Fletcher et al., 1995; for a recent study involving implicit mental inferences, see Kandylaki et al., 2015). This experiment found increased activity in the mPFC, posterior STS, temporal poles, and posterior cingulate (PCC) when participants attributed mental states to others, and this pattern has been consistently observed in subsequent studies (e.g., Gallagher & Frith, 2003). Two features of this neuroanatomy are important. First, it overlaps heavily with a network of regions that is highly active when participants lie quietly in the scanner, awake but with no fixed task, which has come to be known as the default network (Buckner, Andrews-Hanna, & Schacter, 2008; McGuire et al., 1996). Second, the most robust activation, in the mPFC, corresponds to the region we previously noted as associated with situation model construction.

A number of different studies have examined this overlap in the brain regions associated with discourse processing and those associated with theory-of-mind (e.g., Ferstl & von Cramon, 2002; Ferstl et al., 2008; Mason & Just, 2009, 2011). In a recent investigation, a series of meta-analyses were used to quantify the degree of overlap between discourse processing regions and mentalizing regions across a number of past studies (Mar, 2011). First, two separate meta-analyses were conducted on ToM: one for story-based studies and one for studies that employed other types of stimuli to isolate the mentalizing network. A comparison of brain regions implicated in both meta-analyses revealed a conservative estimate of the mentalizing network. These regions were then compared to the results of a meta-analysis of narrative-processing regions (see Figure 14.1). A number of the ToM areas were also implicated in the set of narrative-processing studies, including the mPFC, bilateral posterior STS and temporoparietal junction, bilateral anterior middle temporal gyri (just posterior to the temporal poles), and a small region in the inferior frontal gyrus. What these regions of overlap represent is open to interpretation. It could be that they support mentalizing about fictional characters while processing narratives, or it might be that some more basic process underlying both mentalizing and discourse comprehension is being represented by this network. In favor of the former possibility, one study found that a sub-network of the default network appears to be closely linked to mentalizing during reading, with follow-up analyses

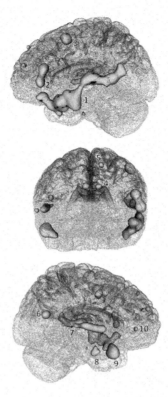

Figure 14.1 Meta-analytic results from Mar (2011) visualizing brain regions associated with narrative comprehension. Clusters include: (1) pSTS/TPJ, STS, STG, MTG, aTL, IFG; (2) IFG; (3) dorsal precentral gyrus; (4) bilateral mPFC; (5) mPFC/aSFG; (6) pSTS; (7) STG; (8) MTG; (9) aTL; (10) IFG. Additional clusters not visible; for full details see Table 7 of Mar (2011). For a color version of this figure, see https://osf.io/jxdnw/

supporting the idea that frequent reading could hone or improve mentalizing abilities (Mar & Oatley, 2008; Tamir, Bricker, Dodell-Feder, & Mitchell, 2016).

In sum, the cognitive neuroscience of discourse at this point has discovered a set of robust empirical phenomena and provided sketches of mechanisms to explain these phenomena, but has not yet offered up a comprehensive theory of discourse-level language processing in the brain. As we move toward such a theory, building on past work, the field is also growing in exciting new directions. It is to these new directions that we now turn.

New Directions

Cognitive neuroscience continues apace to build on the studies of the past with the goal of developing a comprehensive theory of discourse processing informed by brain science. The field has expanded in exciting new directions, employing new research populations, broadening the aspects of reader behavior that are considered, and using innovative stimuli, methods, and analyses. As is to be expected, branching out in all these different ways often means that there are only one or two studies of a kind, rendering it difficult to knit these branches into a cohesive whole or draw firm conclusions regarding these topics. In light of

Texts

Cognitive neuroscience investigations of language processing focused initially on single words, moving only recently to sentences and connected discourse. For that reason, most early studies of discourse paid little attention to what type of text was being presented as the presentation of connected sentences was itself rather novel. However, neuroscientists have now begun to explore how different genres of texts are processed and received. Because this direction is rather new, it is especially difficult to draw conclusions regarding different types of texts. A majority of past studies of discourse have employed simple narrative texts. Although some researchers presented expository texts (e.g., Kansaku, Yamaura, & Kitazawa, 2000), this was often without providing any rationale for choosing this genre or acknowledging any possible genre effects. This has changed, with neuroscientists now increasingly sensitized to the importance of genre differences, reflecting past work by behavioral scientists (e.g., Zabrucky & Ratner, 1992). Swett and colleagues, for example, frame their own study of discourse as one that specifically investigates the neural correlates of comprehending expository text (Swett et al., 2013). To arrive at a clearer picture of how stories and exposition are differentially processed, however, it is necessary to present both types of text within the same study. An EEG study on inferencing did just this, presenting participants with narrative and expository passages of about four sentences in length (Baretta, Tomitch, MacNair, Lim, & Waldie, 2009). Few differences in brain activity were observed between genres, although the authors did find neural evidence that readers detected unpredicted and incongruent information more readily for the expository texts (as evidenced by a greater N400) compared to narrative texts. This is consistent with the behavioral data, which found that participants were superior at drawing inferences when reading the expository texts. In light of these demonstrated differences, future work on prediction might benefit from including different genres of text as stimuli.

Texts in the real world exist in far greater variety than simply being either narrative or expository in nature and bold researchers have begun to delve into these other genres. Zeman and colleagues, for example, conducted an *f*MRI study of responses to both poetry and prose (Zeman, Beschin, Dewar, & Sala, 2013b). The texts included practical as well as evocative prose passages, rather accessible as well as somewhat difficult sonnets, along with some poems that the participants selected themselves. The researchers found that a number of brain regions were similarly activated in response to both poetry and prose, perhaps not surprising since both involve discourse-level language processing. There were, however, some regions differentially activated by the two forms of text. Poetry led to greater activation in key memory regions (i.e., bilateral hippocampi) as well as the right temporal pole. Prose, in contrast, led to greater activation in a central information-processing hub (the PCC) as well as visual areas in the occipital lobe. When self-selected poetry was contrasted with the experimenter-chosen texts, greater activation was observed in the parietal lobes (bilaterally), likely reflecting the fact that participants knew these passages well and recognized them, reading them "by heart" rather than for the first time. The variety in the stimuli employed here is highly admirable and something that future studies will hopefully emulate. In particular, allowing the participants to choose some texts presents an intriguing design element, allowing for a clearer understanding of how personally meaningful texts are processed. This study also included a unique element with respect to its target population, in that experts in the form of faculty and graduate students from an English department participated. Unfortunately, the data from these experts was not contrasted with naïve controls. This would have allowed for an exploration of how expertise interacts with discourse comprehension, an interesting question that remains to be answered.

In addition to different genres of text, there are also unique aspects within a text that deserve special interest. A single story can have moments that are evocative in different ways, with descriptions that make the reader laugh out loud at one point and experience crushing dread at another. One study by Lehne and colleagues examined an emotion that is rather unique to discourse: suspense (Lehne, Engel, Rohrmeier, Menninghaus, Jacobs, & Koelsch, 2015). Although single words and sentences can generate many of the basic emotions like happiness and sadness, building suspense relies upon a longer time-scale to create anticipation and is not easily achieved at lower levels of language. The creation of suspense is likely rooted in the construction of situation models for the story's plot and prediction in the form of anticipating the potential for a negative outcome (de Graaf & Hustinx, 2011). In the study by Lehne and colleagues (2015), the short story *Der Sandmann* (The Sandman) by E.T.A. Hoffmann was further shortened by experimenters and then portioned into 65 separate segments, to be read by participants who judged how suspenseful each segment was while being scanned using *f*MRI. Explicit ratings of suspense predicted activation in a number of different brain regions, many of which had previously been observed in past studies of narrative comprehension and social cognition (e.g., posterior STS, TPJ, mPFC; see Figure 14.1). This approach—breaking a longer text into many smaller segments and gathering rating data after each segment—provides a nice way of collecting behavioral data as participants read a lengthier text. Emulating this technique would help researchers to employ longer and more ecologically valid story stimuli in their designs. There are risks associated with this approach, however: Readers may find the constant need to provide ratings to be disruptive and the type of rating requested likely sensitizes readers to particular aspects of the text. That said, moving toward longer, more ecologically valid texts is key for the neuroscience of discourse and collecting explicit judgments to accompany neural data will always be valuable. Both would allow this neuroscientific work to be more easily integrated with behavioral research on discourse processes, allowing for more rapid development of cross-disciplinary models of discourse comprehension.

In addition to emotions, different texts can also engage the reader to varying degrees. Richard Gerrig (1993) described narrative engagement as transportation, employing a metaphor of the reader being transported into the narrative world. Some texts can be more or less successful in engaging readers. In a reanalysis of *f*MRI data from bilinguals reading emotional Harry Potter passages (Hsu, Jacobs, Citron, & Conrad, 2015a), an entirely separate group of readers rated how immersed they felt after reading each excerpt (Hsu et al., 2014). Immersiveness ratings were then related to the neural activity observed in the group of participants who read these same passages while being scanned with MRI. Activity in a region of the middle cingulate cortex was found to correlate more highly with immersion ratings for the fear-related passages compared to the neutral passages. This study illustrates how various qualities of a text can be associated with neural responses long after the *f*MRI data have been collected. Subjective responses to the text, like immersiveness or elicited emotion, can be assessed by separate groups of participants as may more objective text qualities like type-token ratio or average word frequency. These data can then be combined with neuroimaging data for analysis.

The Cognitive Neuroscience of Discourse

Fictional narratives contain a wealth of unique aspects, not limited to their potential to evoke emotions or engage readers. For example, there are no limits to what can be represented by a story, with characters, objects, and settings that are rarely or even never experienced in the real world commonly occurring. One research group conducted a fascinating study that highlights the potential to study these unique aspects of narrative, by examining the supernatural events within the Harry Potter series (Hsu, Jacobs, Altmann, & Conrad, 2015b). When brain activity elicited by supernatural excerpts was contrasted with activity observed during reality-consistent passages, a number of brain regions related to attention and emotion were found to be more strongly engaged (e.g., bilateral inferior frontal gyrus [IFG] and inferior parietal lobule [IPL], as well as the left amygdala). Future studies could take a similar approach with other types of narrative content, such as interactions with future technology or shifts in time in the form of flash-backs or flash-forwards.

The fact that fictional narratives can contain elements not found in reality is often a helpful way for us to distinguish fiction from fact. But things are not often so easy and another promising direction for research on discourse is how people make this distinction (Abraham, von Cramon, & Schubotz, 2008). One way in which we can identify a piece of text as representing fiction or reality is when it is explicitly labeled as one or the other. Altmann and colleagues examined this very question, by presenting different participants with identical short narratives that were labeled as either "real" or "invented" (Altmann, Bohrn, Lubrich, Menninghaus, & Jacobs, 2014). In this way, differences in brain activity for the two conditions can be inferred to result from the expectations surrounding a text based on its purported source, rather than the actual words being read (which were identical for both conditions). Some brain regions were more active when texts were labeled as fiction (e.g., frontal poles, mid-line areas throughout the cingulate and precuneus), whereas other regions were more active when texts were presented as factual (e.g., temporal pole, cerebellum, left MTG/STG). These researchers associated the fiction expectation regions with the fronto-parietal control network and the default network, conjecturing that an expectation of fiction results in a more flexible situation model that invites imagination about what may have been. This labeling of a text, as invented or real, is known as paratextual information, or information about a text. Other examples of paratextual information include whether a story is written by a man or woman, whether a text is critically acclaimed or universally panned, and whether a text has been translated from a foreign language. The potential influences of these other forms of paratextual information have been investigated with behavioral paradigms and it would be interesting to see more neuroscience work on these kinds of questions.

Populations

In addition to expanding the purview of what texts are studied with cognitive neuroscience, researchers have also begun to better appreciate that interesting differences may be occurring across different types of readers. This mirrors advances in behavioral research on discourse processing, many of which are outlined in Chapters 8 and 9. Within neuroscience, one approach to studying different types of readers has been to examine the discourse processing abilities of people with neurological and psychiatric disorders. For example, researchers have used narratives to delineate the language capacities of individuals with amnesia (Zeman et al., 2013a), schizophrenia (Marini et al., 2008), and autism (Barnes, 2012). A related approach involves studying special populations to better understand how specific brain regions support discourse processes. An obvious example involves

279

studying the performance of lesion patients to identify which brain regions are necessary and/or sufficient for narrative processes (Mar, 2004). Continuing along this line of research are investigations into how the neural correlates of discourse processing might differ for special populations compared to typically developing ones (e.g., individuals with autism; Mason, Williams, Kana, Minshew, & Just, 2008; Williams et al., 2013).

In addition to studying special populations, researchers are becoming increasingly curious about individual and group differences within typically developing language users. For example, it is a well-recorded fact that numerous gender differences exist with respect to reading. A 2009 survey of 65 countries found that girls outperform boys in reading ability for every single country examined (OECD, 2011). In addition, there have been a number of studies demonstrating neural differences between men and women with respect to lower-level language processing, such as at the word or sentence level (e.g., Burmann, Bitan, & Booth, 2008; Clements et al., 2006; Pugh et al., 1996; Shaywitz et al., 1995; cf. Wallentin, 2009). But what about gender differences in the processing of discourse?

An early fMRI investigation into gender differences for discourse comprehension presented auditory versions of short essays to men and women, with the same audio presented in a reversed form as a control (Kansaku, Yamaura, & Kitazawa, 2000). When listening to the essays, men exhibited more left-lateralized activations (around the superior and middle temporal gyrus, relative to the control condition), whereas women exhibited more bilateral activations (in approximately the same areas). In a follow-up study, the researchers compared chopped-up versions of these essays to their reversed counterparts and observed no such differences in lateralization between men and women. This led the researchers to conclude that the lateralization differences in posterior language areas observed for men and women are specifically tied to the processing of coherent narratives. Unfortunately, the use of reversed language as a control is less than ideal, as the resulting contrast does not isolate the unique contributions of discourse-level language; there are too many differences between the experimental and control stimuli to draw meaningful conclusions from the contrast (e.g., simple meaningfulness at the word level). Meaningful, but sentence-level, language is the most appropriate control condition to isolate processes specific to discourse.

Meaningful sentences were employed as a control in an imaging study on gender differences in discourse comprehension by Frank and colleagues (Frank, Baron-Cohen, & Ganzel, 2015). These researchers presented men and women with a series of very simple stories to read in the scanner, and contrasted these images with those resulting from the reading of very similar unlinked sentences. They found few differences in activation between men and women. The sole difference was that women deactivated a region within the right ventromedial PFC more so than men. Regrettably, both of these studies likely suffered from low statistical power (Button et al., 2013), as neither included more than 30 participants per group. (Assuming an average effect-size of $d = .5$ and 80% power, 64 participants per group is required for a simple two-tailed t-test.) This means that there is a high risk of false negatives and so a failure to detect differences is somewhat difficult to interpret. Although there are very real economic hurdles to collecting adequate sample sizes for neuroimaging research, higher statistical power should be a future goal of work in this area (Mar et al., 2013). A future study, with greater power, may well answer the question of whether differences exist between men and women in how situation models are constructed and updated.

Another interesting population for the study of discourse is bilingual (or multilingual) individuals. Although past work has determined that for those highly proficient in their second language there are few differences in brain activation when processing words or sentences in either language (Fabbro, 2001), what about responses to stories? Hsu and

The Cognitive Neuroscience of Discourse

colleagues asked Germans also proficient in English to read four-line passages from the Harry Potter books that were either emotional in tone (happy or fearful) or neutral (Hsu et al., 2015a). These excerpts were also presented in either German or in English. Using the neutral passages as a control, happy passages presented in the participants' native tongue (German) elicited more activation in key emotion areas of the brain (i.e., the amygdala, bilaterally) as well as a portion of the precentral gyrus, compared to the same contrast in their second language. In other words, first-language processing of happy passages selectively increased activation in these areas relative to second-language processing of happy passages. No such interactions were found for the fearful passages. Additional analyses confirmed that passages read in a second language resulted in an attenuated emotional response, though readers were highly proficient at reading in that language. By taking a long, naturalistic text and breaking it down into specific excerpts associated with particular aspects of interest (i.e., certain emotions), the researchers were able to achieve several notable aims: (1) employing a naturalistic stimulus in the form of a professionally written long-form narrative, (2) highlighting key components of this text by excerpting portions, thereby (3) creating a stimulus set appropriate for a neuroimaging study.

Across both special and normally developing populations, individuals can also differ with respect to experience or trait tendencies, and these differences may be associated with different neural responses to discourse. For example, behavioral studies have established that personal experience with the topics addressed in a piece of fiction can affect how that text is processed (Bartlett, 1932; Green, 2004). Having personal experience with a situation described in a text might lead the reader to resonate more with the content, perhaps allowing him or her to better imagine what it would be like to see or do something similar. In a neuroimaging study investigating this possibility, Chow and colleagues asked whether experience with a topic would result in more coherent brain activity when reading a story about that same topic (Chow, Mar, Xu, Liu, Wagage, & Braun, 2015; for a related study on familiarity with the topics of nonfiction essays, see Buchweitz, Mason, Meschyan, Keller, & Just, 2014). To test this, the authors first pilot-tested story topics to identify those with which participants would have varying levels of experience, such as performing a musical piece in front of an audience. They then wrote short three-paragraph stories around these topics, with certain paragraphs designed to focus on either perceptual content (i.e., visually vivid details) or action content (i.e., movements and physical behaviors). Coherence of brain activity was measured in the form of correlations within the brain networks responsible for visual and motor processing. Individuals who reported more personal experience with the topic of the story had more tightly correlated activity in the visual network while reading visually vivid details. Similarly, when reading about actions, those with more experience exhibited higher correlations within the motor processing network. These results suggest that the degree to which language processing is an embodied process depends in part on our level of past experience with what's being represented.

There are several noteworthy aspects to this study that could be applied to future investigations of discourse processing. For one, pilot-testing was employed to maximize the variability in responses, helping to compensate for the small sample size; small samples are a common and nontrivial problem for correlational analyses in neuroimaging (Mar, Spreng, & DeYoung, 2013). Second, the texts for this study were carefully prepared to capture both variability in experience as well as the processing of either visual details or motor actions. These details and actions were described over the course of several sentences to allow for a block of neural activity to be isolated for the analysis of correlations within brain networks. Methods such as these could easily be adapted to explore other characteristics of readers

281

(e.g., levels of reading ability; Prat, Mason, & Just, 2011, 2012) and different aspects of texts using neuroimaging (e.g., emotional segments, instances of free indirect discourse).

Individual readers not only differ from one another with respect to their personal experiences, but also in trait tendencies closely related to literary discourse. For example, people differ in their tendency to become highly absorbed or transported into fictional narratives. Although we have previously discussed how different texts can differ in their ability to engage readers, people also differ in their natural tendencies to become engaged regardless of the text. One oft-used measure of trait empathy includes a subscale closely related to transportation: the Fantasy subscale of the Interpersonal Reactivity Index (IRI; Davis, 1980). All but one of the seven items in this subscale describes a tendency to become absorbed in books, movies, and television. In a study examining how scores on the IRI relate to differences in brain structure, the Fantasy subscale was found to predict greater gray matter volume in a portion of the right dlPFC (Banissy, Kanai, Walsh, & Rees, 2012). One of the most impressive aspects of this study was its large sample size, with data from 118 individuals being included. Future research on this topic would benefit from a multi-dimensional approach to measuring trait tendencies toward transportation, distinguishing emotional engagement from attentional focus, for example (Busselle & Bilandzic, 2009).

A tendency to become highly engaged or transported into a narrative world is highly related to the construct of character identification (Tal-Or & Cohen, 2010). Character identification is unlikely to emerge in the context of single sentences and cannot occur for discourse that lacks characters. As a result, identifying with fictional characters is relatively unique to literature and a ripe topic for investigation for cognitive neuroscientists interested in discourse. In a study on this topic, Cheetham and colleagues employed a German version of the IRI that includes the four positively worded items of the Fantasy subscale, isolating those that relate to character identification (Cheetham, Hänggi, & Jancke, 2014). Employing a similar approach to the previous study on transportation, but with a smaller sample, they found that cortical thickness varied with self-ratings of character identification for areas in the left dmPFC (negatively) and IFG (positively). The volume of a region in the left dlPFC was also positively related to these scores.

These two studies of trait transportation and character identification illustrate the potential to examine how self-reports of tendencies related to discourse processing can be related to structural MRI data, such as brain volume and cortical thickness. The method could also be extended to other forms of neural data, such as resting-state connectivity analyses and white-matter organization (i.e., diffusion tensor imaging; DTI). One important factor to keep in mind with these approaches, however, is the importance of sample size and statistical power when examining correlations.

Reader Response

Although it is true that different types of individuals may react differently to a text, a single text can also evoke a variety of reactions among individuals belonging to a similar population of readers. Examining the variability in how readers respond to a text is yet another fertile area of inquiry for cognitive neuroscientists interested in discourse.

One subjective response that seems ripe for investigation is how the brain reflects varying levels of engagement or immersion in a narrative text. Studies examining narrative engagement have previously been discussed based on trait tendencies or as a quality of the text, but no study to date has examined evaluations of immersion by readers also providing neural

The Cognitive Neuroscience of Discourse

data, with transportation measured either in vivo or directly after reading. Hopefully this gap in the literature will be filled in the near future.

For a successful example of investigating variability in reader responses for a single population, one need only look to the previously discussed study on poetry and prose (Zeman et al., 2013b). In this study, readers reported their evaluations of the texts, including each text's emotionality and literariness. Both are subjective responses to a text, with emotionality being familiar to lay readers and literariness an elaborated construct for this population of literary scholars. Drawing on past neuroaesthetic work on music that elicits "shivers down the spine" (Blood & Zatorre, 2001), a similar network of brain regions was found to track with increasing ratings of emotionality: the thalamus, anterior cingulate, insula, cerebellum, and supplementary motor area (SMA). For literariness, higher ratings were associated with left-hemisphere regions and parts of the basal ganglia. These regions are components of the dorsal speech comprehension pathway described above, which is specialized for analyzing the sequential structure of language (Hickok & Poeppel, 2007). One possibility is that the processing of more literary texts taxes these components more heavily. To adopt this paradigm for future studies, almost any type of reader response or evaluation could be studied in this way and there exist a great number of possibilities still outstanding. Neuroaesthetics, for example, has explored beauty judgments for several kinds of stimuli (Skov & Vartanian, 2009), but not for literary discourse (e.g., Blood & Zatorre, 2001; Cupchik, Vartanian, Crawley, & Mikulis, 2009; Kawabata & Zeki, 2004; cf. Jacobs, 2015). Perhaps the closest example that exists involved participants reading single-line proverbs and rating them for beauty after leaving the scanner, with implicit aesthetic judgments associated with areas of the brain linked to reward (Bohrn, Altmann, Lubrich, Menninghaus, & Jacobs, 2013). But beauty can also be found in longer passages and it would be informative to learn if these responses were similar or different to finding beauty in visual art forms or music.

Measuring different responses to a text and associating these responses with neural data is one approach to studying variability in reader responses; another is to study the variability in the neural responses themselves. This latter approach was taken in an fMRI study by Nijhof and Willems (2015), who had participants listen to three short stories, with reversed versions of these stories serving as a control. For each story, sentences dealing with either actions or mental inference were identified. The authors observed great variability in the degree to which action-processing and mentalizing brain regions were activated during reading (identified using localizer tasks), with a negative correlation emerging across the group. In other words, the participants that tended to activate mentalizing regions more while reading the passages were less likely to activate action-processing areas, and vice versa. The researchers interpreted these data as demonstrating variability in reader responses at the neural level. It would be interesting to relate this variability in network activations to other reading outcomes or responses, such as immersion, identification, comprehension, recall, event segmentation, or perhaps the updating of situation models.

Responses to a text are not only subjective, but can also be evaluated objectively such as with comprehension and memory. Comprehension and recall for text material is linked to the ability to focus on the text material and not be distracted by unrelated thoughts. To explore how the two relate, Yarkoni and colleagues recorded brain activity while participants read narrative paragraphs, and then tested verbatim memory and comprehension for those paragraphs (Yarkoni, Speer, & Zacks, 2008). Better subsequent memory was associated with greater activation in the regions that were selectively engaged by a coherent discourse structure. This suggests that successfully constructing a situation model supports performance on later tests of comprehension and memory.

283

To construct, maintain, and update a coherent situation model, one must avoid distraction from unrelated thoughts. The effects of such distraction were also investigated in another study that asked participants to read excerpts of a nonfiction book, rate their own level of distraction, and then complete a series of comprehension questions (Smallwood et al., 2013). In an entirely separate session, a subset of these participants was scanned at rest with *f*MRI and inter-correlations between active brain regions were employed to form a resting-state functional connectivity analysis (rs-fcMRI; Biswal et al., 1995). Distraction or mind-wandering has been linked to the default mode network, which tends to readily emerge from rs-fcMRI data (Mason et al., 2007). Smallwood and colleagues (2013) found that connectivity between a key region of the default network, the PCC, and other brain regions was modulated by comprehension. Individuals exhibiting greater comprehension across the texts had stronger links between the PCC and right anterior insula while lying at rest. Worse comprehension was associated with stronger links between the PCC and the ventral striatum/amygdala. This study demonstrates that reader responses measured at one time can be meaningfully related to neural data collected on a separate occasion, even when that neural data is not tied to reading of any task at all.

Conversation

Most work in the cognitive neuroscience of discourse has studied solitary participants comprehending a fixed text. But a great deal of real-world language use involves conversation—a dynamic interchange among two or more partners (Hasson, Ghazanfar, Galantucci, Garrod, & Keysers, 2012) that takes place within a complex social interaction fundamentally different from classic laboratory paradigms (Schilbach et al., 2013). Researchers are increasingly taking on the dynamic complexity of conversation, producing more ecologically valid investigations of language production and comprehension.

In everyday conversation, much of significance is never spoken but is only implied. Jang and colleagues investigated the neural basis of comprehending conversational implicatures, specifically focusing on those that violate the Gricean maxim of relevance (Jang et al., 2013). Participants observed an exchange between two speakers, with the first asking a question (e.g., "Have gas prices gone up a lot?") and the second providing an answer that required either an explicit inference ("Prices have gone up a lot"), a moderately implicit inference ("I am saving gas nowadays"), or a highly implicit inference ("My dad takes the bus these days"). Participants then indicated if the answer meant "yes" or "no." Comprehension of moderately and highly implicit answers, as compared to explicit answers, showed greater activation in the anterior temporal lobe (ATL), angular gyrus (AG), and posterior middle temporal gyrus (MTG), all left lateralized. When highly implicit answers were compared to moderately implicit ones, there were increased activations in all of these regions, in addition to unique activation in the left inferior frontal gyrus (IFG), left medial prefrontal cortex (mPFC), left PCC, and right anterior temporal lobe (ATL). Interestingly enough, activation in many of these areas is also observed in studies of reading narrative texts, perhaps reflecting the predictive inferencing that occurs during both types of discourse processing.

Bašnáková, Weber, Petersson, van Berkum, and Hagoort (2014) investigated implicature in a slightly richer social context. Participants were introduced to a speaker and a listener, and then heard a four-turn dialogue. The first two utterances established the communicative context and the final two utterances were a question and an answer. Depending on the preceding context, the answer (e.g., "It is hard to give a good presentation") could be interpreted as either a direct reply to the question ("Is it hard to give a good presentation?"),

The Cognitive Neuroscience of Discourse

an indirect-informative reply requiring an inference ("Will you give a presentation?"), or an indirect-emotional reply requiring an inference ("Did you find my presentation convincing?"). Thus, unlike the study by Jang et al. (2013), the same answers served as direct or indirect replies based on prior context. Relative to direct replies, indirect replies activated a common set of frontal regions including dmPFC, bilateral superior medial frontal gyrus, the right SMA, and parts of the bilateral IFG, extending into the insula in the left hemisphere, as well as right TPJ and right middle temporal gyrus.

Recent neuroimaging studies have begun to map the neural mechanisms underlying the coordination of speakers and listeners in naturalistic conversation. Stephens, Silbert, and Hasson (2010) used ƒMRI to compare the time courses of neural activity for speakers and listeners. In most brain regions that shared activation for listeners and speakers, the listeners' brain activity also displayed temporal coupling with a few seconds of delay, suggesting that the speaker's discourse causally shapes the brain activity of the listener. Coupling occurred in brain areas associated with auditory and facial motor processing, as expected, but also throughout brain networks associated with language processing and beyond. Interestingly, in brain regions including the dlPFC and dmPFC, activity in the listener preceded that of the speaker. This finding supports the significance of predictive processing for language comprehension. In particular, the fact that these effects were prominent in the PFC and the fact that the degree of coupling predicted the degree of listeners' comprehension suggest that listeners may construct a situation model that enables prediction, in line with our earlier discussion. Also of note, the coupled areas were highly bilateral, supporting the view that discourse comprehension is a bilateral rather than right-lateralized function. In a subsequent study, the same research group coached speakers to tell a once-spontaneous story repeatedly (Silbert, Honey, Simony, Poeppel, & Hasson, 2014). The original storyteller repeated the story multiple times, and other tellers learned it as well. The regions previously found to correlate between speaker and listeners also correlated across multiple retellings of the story, both within and between speakers.

One study has used simultaneous ƒMRI recordings of two people engaged in a live conversation to track coordination in truly spontaneous conversation (Spiegelhalder et al., 2014). Activity in the speaker's motor cortex was found to predict activity in the listener's auditory cortex. In this study, the broader coupling reported by Stephens and colleagues was not found, but this could reflect the lower statistical power of the study by Spiegelhalder and colleagues (2014). The degree of coupling between speaker and listener has been found to vary as a function of the discourse environment, with, for example, more rhetorically powerful speeches resulting in more coherent brain synchrony (Schmälzle, Häcker, Honey, & Hasson, 2015).

Although these studies clarify the neural bases of conversation, they fall short of fully approximating naturalistic conversation in important ways. Perhaps most obviously, all have retained the classic distinction between a speaker and listener, in which the speaker essentially produces an uninterrupted monologue and the listener acts as passive receiver, with no conversational turn-taking. This is due to the practical difficulties of producing interactive scenarios in an MRI scanner, and the complexity of disentangling and analyzing components of multifaceted behavior. However, there have been interesting developments on this front. In the first study of its kind, Derix and colleagues performed *post hoc* analyses of electrocorticography (ECoG) data recorded from pre-surgical epilepsy patients (Derix, Iljina, Schulze-Bonhage, Aertsen, & Ball, 2012). Based on the patients' electrode placement and common behavior, the authors were able to compare activity in the temporal lobe as patients freely conversed with their life partners as compared to physicians. The authors found that alpha and theta bands in the bilateral TP and entire ATL showed increased power when participants talked to life partners relative to physicians, although some electrodes in the posterior left ATL also showed higher power when talking to physicians. This study shows that non-experimental studies and *post hoc* analyses may be a promising way of investigating the neural basis of unscripted real-world conversation.

How we might develop better methods to explore naturalistic conversation is an important question for future research. One exciting direction is to simultaneously measure, or "hyperscan," the brain activity of two or more people engaged in conversation. Over a decade ago, Montague et al. (2002) demonstrated hyperscanning in MRI, and others have since demonstrated the method using magnetoencephalography (MEG) and EEG (for a review, see Babiloni & Astolfi, 2014). To the best of our knowledge, with the exception of the study by Spiegelhalder et al. (2014) noted above, no study has yet employed hyperscanning to investigate real-time conversation. This is unfortunate, because it is presently unclear if the neural dynamics of conversation differ from what is suggested by studies that isolate production and comprehension. On the basis of recent neuroscience investigations of interpersonal, nonverbal communication, it seems possible—and we think likely—that interactive conversation will bear a neural signature distinct from that of simple comprehension and production. For example, in a study of gaze behavior, Saito et al. (2010) found that brain-to-brain coupling is greater when participants follow another's gaze toward a target, rather than obey an instruction to do so. Similarly, in a study of hand gestures, Dumas, Nadel, Soussignan, Martinerie, and Garnero (2010) found that brain-to-brain coupling is greater when participants spontaneously started and ended a movement simultaneously. Although the reasons for the lack of uptake of hyperscanning are several and too lengthy to be discussed here (see Hari & Kujala, 2009, for a review), we think it will play a crucial role in future neuroscience studies of conversation.

Advanced Neuroimaging Designs

As the preceding section indicates, one source of excitement in the cognitive neuroscience of discourse is the development of new neuroimaging methods. For example, some studies have paired neuroimaging with a longitudinal design, an impressive feat in light of the cost of the former and the threat of attrition associated with the latter. One group that managed to overcome these hurdles, led by Szaflarski (Szaflarski et al., 2012; see also Horowitz-Kraus et al., 2013) recruited 30 children between the ages of five and seven, and scanned them each year for up to 10 years. During scanning, the children listened to simple stories of around 30 seconds in length, with random pure tones presented as a control. As the children aged, the researchers witnessed an increased involvement of middle and superior temporal areas during story comprehension, even after controlling for anticipated confounds such as IQ and linguistic abilities. These increases demonstrate that the lateral temporal parts of the language processing network continue to mature bilaterally over this age span, perhaps reflecting a growth in semantic networks. Relative decreases during story comprehension associated with maturation were observed in the PCC and cuneus, as well as regions of the occipital cortex. The meaning of these decreases is less clear, but it could be tied to greater activity during the control condition over time as the resting-state control might be more likely to promote spontaneous thought. This impressive study brings us closer to understanding how the processing of narrative texts develops over childhood. Another longitudinal study of narrative processing involving adults (both participants with schizophrenia and controls) found that the neural activity elicited by a story-listening task is highly stable within individuals across a period of 21 months (Maïza et al., 2011). This stability in activation provides an important baseline reference when examining longitudinal effects. Knowing that story-listening activations in adults are reproducible over relatively long periods of time allows for changes observed across a longitudinal study to be attributed to changes within the individual (e.g., treatment, experience, learning) and not low test-retest reliability. Together these two studies demonstrate that longitudinal neuroimaging research on discourse processes is certainly possible, opening the door for fascinating future work.

A rather unique type of longitudinal neuroimaging study was undertaken by Berns and colleagues, who wanted to know how reading a novel would affect functional connectivity in the brain (Berns, Kristina, Prietula, & Pye, 2013). They acquired a resting-state scan of 21 individuals every day for 19 days in a row, with the initial five days of scanning serving to establish a baseline control (i.e., "wash in" period) and five days at the end serving to examine the timeline of any effects post-reading (i.e., "wash out" period). For the nine days in the middle, participants read 1/9th of a novel (*Pompeii: A Novel*, by Robert Harris) prior to being scanned while at rest. A network of regions within the cerebellum showed significantly more connectivity after reading the entire novel. On the days when participants read the novel, three separate networks became more tightly connected, including one that involved the left angular gyrus, precuneus, and mPFC. This highly innovative approach to studying discourse achieved what not too long ago seemed like an impossible feat: studying the reading of an entire novel with neuroimaging. This success was achieved by two main methodological decisions: (1) breaking the novel into nine parts, and (2) not scanning participants as they read, but rather while they lay at rest after reading. The latter certainly raises the question of whether one is studying the process of reading a novel or rather studying a person who is thinking about parts of a novel that have recently been read (which is distinct, but not uninteresting). As pragmatic decisions are made to adapt reading paradigms for neuroimaging methods, it is important to examine how the questions being asked are also altered. Limitations aside, one could imagine modifying this paradigm to examine all kinds of related questions, such as comparing the reading of fiction to nonfiction, and reading something new to re-reading a familiar book.

Another novel methodology that has been applied to the neuroscientific study of discourse involves building computational models based on neuroimaging data. Wehbe and colleagues, for example, scanned nine individuals as they read an entire chapter of a Harry Potter book, presented one word at a time (using rapid serial visual presentation), over the course of 45 minutes (Wehbe, Murphy, Talukdar, Fyshe, Ramdas, & Mitchell, 2014). They then took this *f*MRI data and trained a computational model to predict the observed brain activity based on 195 different features of the text. These features included syntactic, semantic, and narrative information about the current state of the text (e.g., characters, actions, emotions, dialogue), updated with every new word. After training, the computational model achieved above-chance accuracy for classifying which of two novel passages was being "read" based solely on observed neural activity (74% correct, with 50% representing chance). The researchers were then able to isolate story features and identify the brain areas associated with processing different aspects of a text. Dialogue between characters, for example, was processed in bilateral temporal and inferior frontal areas, along with the right TPJ. Strikingly, these regions show some overlap with those identified in the study on conversation by Bašnáková and colleagues (2014). Given the richness of both neuroimaging data and discourse, employing computational network models seems to be a promising way to take a bottom-up approach to identifying relations between the two, possibly resulting in new hypotheses that can be pursued with more theoretically informed study designs.

Conclusion

Surveying this terrain, we are encouraged by the rapid progress that has been made in the cognitive neuroscience of discourse. When the first edition of this handbook on discourse processes was being prepared 15 years ago, it was perfectly reasonable to omit consideration of neuroscience approaches. Now there is enough to say that we have had to be highly selective in our treatment and we can point to books that devote many or all of their pages to this topic (Hickok & Small, 2015; Schmalhofer & Perfetti, 2007; Willems, 2015). However, it is clear that this is early in the journey. We think the next 15 years will likely be characterized by two trends. First, we expect the field to look back at the path traveled thus far, sort through the phenomena we have described (and doubtless a few we have missed), separate the replicable wheat from the false positive chaff, and consolidate what remains into coherent mechanistic theories. In what we have described in the latter sections of this chapter, it is important to emphasize that these investigations are in their early stages and will likely be revised as more data are collected. Second, we expect that new neuroimaging and neurostimulation methods will allow the field to carve bold new paths. Three neuroimaging developments that we are particularly excited about are sophisticated time-series analysis (evident in the Conversation section above), machine learning methods that will help illuminate how patterns in brain activity map onto mental representation (Kriegeskorte, Goebel, & Bandettini, 2006; Norman, Polyn, Detre, & Haxby, 2006), and the use of computational models to predict moment-by-moment changes in neural activity. All in all, we have ample reason to hope for a very exciting future for the cognitive neuroscience of discourse processes.

References

Abraham, A., von Cramon, D. Y., & Schubotz, R. I. (2008). Meeting George Bush versus meeting Cinderella: The neural response when telling apart what is real from what is fictional in the context of our reality. *Journal of Cognitive Neuroscience*, *20*(6), 965–976.

Altmann, U., Bohrn, I. C., Lubrich, O., Menninghaus, W., & Jacobs, A. M. (2014). Fact vs. fiction: How paratextual information shapes our reading processes. *Social Cognitive and Affective Neuroscience*, *9*(1), 22–29.

Babiloni, F., & Astolfi, L. (2014). Social neuroscience and hyperscanning techniques: Past, present and future. *Neuroscience and Biobehavioral Reviews*, *44*, 76–93. doi:http://dx.doi.org/10.1016/j.neubiorev.2012.07.006.

Banissy, M. J., Kanai, R., Walsh, V., & Rees, G. (2012). Inter-individual differences in empathy are reflected in human brain structure. *NeuroImage*, *62*(3), 2034–2039.

Baretta, L., Tomitch, L., MacNair, N., Lim, V. K., & Waldie, K. E. (2009). Inference making while reading narrative and expository texts: An ERP study. *Psychology & Neuroscience*, *2*(2), 137–145.

Barnes, J. L. (2012). Fiction, imagination, and social cognition: Insights from autism. *Poetics*, *40*(4), 299–316.

Barsalou, L. (2008). Grounded cognition. *Annual Review of Psychology*, *59*, 617–645.

Bartlett, F. (1932). *Remembering: A study in experimental and social psychology*. Cambridge: Cambridge University Press.

Bašnáková, J., Weber, K., Petersson, K. M., van Berkum, J., & Hagoort, P. (2014). Beyond the language given: The neural correlates of inferring speaker meaning. *Cerebral Cortex*, *24*(10), 2572–2578.

Beeman, M. (1993). Semantic processing in the right hemisphere may contribute to drawing inferences from discourse. *Brain and Language*, *44*(1), 80–120.

Berns, G. S., Kristina, B., Prietula, M. J., & Pye, B. E. (2013). Short- and long-term effects of a novel on connectivity in the brain. *Brain Connectivity*, *3*(6), 590–600.

Biswal, B., Yetkin, F. Z., Haughton, V. M., & Hyde, J. S. (1995). Functional connectivity in the motor cortex of resting human brain using echo-planar MRI. *Magnetic Resonance in Medicine*, *34*(4), 537–541.

The Cognitive Neuroscience of Discourse

Blood, A. J., & Zatorre, R. J. (2001). Intensely pleasurable responses to music correlate with activity in brain regions implicated in reward and emotion. *Proceedings of the National Academy of Sciences, 98*(20), 11818–11823.

Bohrn, I. C., Altmann, U., Lubrich, O., Menninghaus, W., & Jacobs, A. M. (2013). When we like what we know: A parametric fMRI analysis of beauty and familiarity. *Brain and Language, 124*(1), 1–8.

Bransford, J. D., Barclay, J. R., & Franks, J. J. (1972). Sentence memory: A constructive versus interpretive approach. *Cognitive Psychology, 3*(2), 193–209.

Bransford, J. D., & Johnson, M. K. (1972). Contextual prerequisites for understanding: Some investigations of comprehension and recall. *Journal of Verbal Learning & Verbal Behavior, 11*(6), 717–726.

Buchweitz, A., Mason, R. A., Meschyan, G., Keller, T. A., & Just, M. A. (2014). Modulation of cortical activity during comprehension of familiar and unfamiliar text topics in speed reading and speed listening. *Brain & Language, 139*, 49–57.

Buckner, R., Andrews-Hanna, J., & Schacter, D. (2008). The brain's default network: Anatomy, function, and relevance to disease. *Year in Cognitive Neuroscience, 1124*, 1–38. http://doi.org/10.1196/annals.1440.011.

Burmann, D. D., Bitan, T., & Booth, J. R. (2008). Sex differences in neural processing of language among children. *Neuropsychologia, 46*(5), 1349–1362.

Busselle, R., & Bilandzic, H. (2009). Measuring narrative engagement. *Media Psychology, 12*, 321–347.

Button, K. S., Ioannidis, J. P. A., Mokrysz, C., Nosek, B. A., Flint, J., Robinson, E. S. J., & Munafò, M. R. (2013). Power failure: Why small sample size undermines the reliability of neuroscience: Erratum. *Nature Reviews Neuroscience, 14*(6), 442.

Chatterjee, A. (2010). Disembodying cognition. *Language & Cognition, 2*, 79–116.

Cheetham, M., Hänggi, J., & Jancke, L. (2014). Identifying with fictive characters: Structural brain correlates of the personality trait "fantasy." *Social Cognitive and Affective Neuroscience, 9*(11), 1836–1844.

Choi, S., Park, J., Kim, Y., Hwang, J., Seo, J., Jin, S., Lee, Y., Lee, H. J., Lee, J., Lee, M., & Chang, Y. (2015). Neural correlates of second language reading comprehension in the presence of congruous and incongruous illustrations. *Journal of Neurolinguistics, 35*, 25–38.

Chow, H. M., Mar, R. A., Xu, Y., Liu, S., Wagage, S., & Braun, A. R. (2015). Personal experience with narrated events modulates functional connectivity within visual and motor systems during story comprehension. *Human Brain Mapping, 36*, 1494–1505.

Clements, A. M., Rimrodt, S. L., Abel, J. R., Blankner, J. G., Mostofsky, S. H., Pekar, J. J., Denckla, M. B., & Cutting, L. E. (2006). Sex differences in cerebral laterality of language and visuospatial processing. *Brain and Language, 98*(2), 150–158.

Cupchik, G. C., Vartanian, O., Crawley, A., & Mikulis, D. J. (2009). Viewing artworks: Contributions of cognitive control and perceptual facilitation to aesthetic experience. *Brain and Cognition, 70*(1), 84–91.

Davis, M. H. (1980). A multidimensional approach to individual differences in empathy. *JSAS Catalogue of Selected Documents in Psychology, 10*, 85.

de Graaf, A., & Hustinx, L. (2011). The effect of story structure on emotion, transportation, and persuasion. *Information Design Journal, 19*, 142–154.

Dehaene, S., Le Clec'H, G., Poline, J.-B., Le Bihan, D., & Cohen, L. (2002). The visual word form area: A prelexical representation of visual words in the fusiform gyrus. *NeuroReport: For Rapid Communication of Neuroscience Research, 13*(3), 321–325. http://doi.org/10.1097/00001756-200203040-00015.

Derix, J., Iljina, O., Schulze-Bonhage, A., Aertsen, A., & Ball, T. (2012). "Doctor" or "darling"? Decoding the communication partner from ECoG of the anterior temporal lobe during non-experimental, real-life social interaction. *Frontiers in Human Neuroscience, 6*(25), 1–14.

Ditman, T., Holcomb, P. J., & Kuperberg, G. R. (2007). An investigation of concurrent ERP and self-paced reading methodologies. *Psychophysiology, 44*(6), 927–935. http://doi.org/10.1111/j.1469-8986.2007.00593.x.

Dumas, G., Nadel J., Soussignan, R., Martinerie, J., & Garnero, L. (2010). Inter-brain synchronization during social interaction. *PLOS ONE, 5*(8), e12166. doi:10.1371/journal.pone.0012166.

Fabbro, F. (2001). The bilingual brain: Cerebral representation of languages. *Brain and Language, 79*(2), 211–222.

Ferstl, E. C., Neumann, J., Bogler, C., & von Cramon, D. Y. (2008). The extended language network: A meta-analysis of neuroimaging studies on text comprehension. *Human Brain Mapping*, *29*(5), 581–593.

Ferstl, E. C., & von Cramon, D. Y. (2001). The role of coherence and cohesion in text comprehension: An event-related fMRI study. *Cognitive Brain Research*, *11*(3), 325–340.

Ferstl, E. C., & von Cramon, D. Y. (2002). What does the frontomedian cortex contribute to language processing: Coherence or theory of mind? *Neuroimage*, *17*(3), 1599–1612.

Fischer, M. H., & Zwaan, R. A. (2008). Embodied language: A review of the role of the motor system in language comprehension. *The Quarterly Journal of Experimental Psychology*, *61*(6), 825–850.

Fletcher, P. C., Happé, F., Frith, U., Baker, S. C., Dolan, R. J., Frackowiak, R. S. J., & Frith, C. D. (1995). Other minds in the brain: A functional imaging study of "theory of mind" in story comprehension. *Cognition*, *57*(2), 109–128. http://doi.org/10.1016/0010-0277(95)00692-R.

Frank, C. K., Baron-Cohen, S., & Ganzel, B. L. (2015). Sex differences in the neural basis of false-belief and pragmatic language comprehension. *NeuroImage*, *105*, 300–311.

Gallagher, H. L., & Frith, C. D. (2003). Functional imaging of "theory of mind." *Trends in Cognitive Sciences*, *7*(2), 77–83.

Gernsbacher, M. A. (1990). *Language comprehension as structure building*. Hillsdale, NJ: Lawrence Erlbaum Associates.

Gerrig, R. J. (1993). *Experiencing narrative worlds: On the psychological activities of reading*. New Haven, CT: Yale University Press.

Green, M. C. (2004). Transportation into narrative worlds: The role of prior knowledge and perceived realism. *Discourse Processes*, *38*(2), 247–266.

Hari, R., & Kujala, M.V. (2009). Brain basis of human social interaction: From concepts to brain imaging. *Physiological Reviews*, *89*(2), 453–479. http://doi.org/10.1152/physrev.00041.2007.

Hasson, U., Ghazanfar, A. A., Galantucci, B., Garrod, S., & Keysers, C. (2012). Brain-to-brain coupling: A mechanism for creating and sharing a social world. *Trends in Cognitive Sciences*, *16*(2), 114–121.

Hauk, O., Johnsrude, I., & Pulvermuller, F. (2004). Somatotopic representation of action words in human motor and premotor cortex. *Neuron*, *41*(2), 301–307.

Hickok, G., & Poeppel, D. (2007). The cortical organization of speech processing. *Nature Reviews Neuroscience*, *8*(5), 393–402.

Hickok, G., & Small, S. (Eds) (2015). *Neurobiology of language*. London, UK: Elsevier Science.

Horowitz-Kraus, T., Vannest, J. J., & Holland, S. K. (2013). Overlapping neural circuitry for narrative comprehension and proficient reading in children and adolescents. *Neuropsychologia*, *51*(13), 2651–2662.

Hsu, C., Conrad, M., & Jacobs, A. M. (2014). Fiction feelings in Harry Potter: Haemodynamic response in the mid-cingulate cortex correlates with immersive reading experience. *NeuroReport: For Rapid Communication of Neuroscience Research*, *25*(17), 1356–1361.

Hsu, C., Jacobs, A. M., Citron, F. M. M., & Conrad, M. (2015a). The emotion potential of words and passages in reading Harry Potter: An fMRI study. *Brain and Language*, *142*, 96–114.

Hsu, C., Jacobs, A. M., Altmann, U., & Conrad, M. (2015b). The magical activation of left amygdala when reading Harry Potter: An fMRI study of how descriptions of supra-natural events entertain and enchant. *PLOS ONE*, 10(2), e0118179.

Hsu, C. T., Jacobs, A. M., Citron, F. M., & Conrad, M. (2015c). The emotion potential of words and passages in reading Harry Potter: An fMRI study. *Brain and Language*, *142*, 96–114.

Jacobs, A. M. (2015). Neurocognitive poetics: Methods and models for investigating the neuronal and cognitive-affective bases of literature reception. *Frontiers in Human Neuroscience*, *9*, 186.

Jang, G., Yoon, S., Lee, S., Park, H., Kim, J., Ko, J. H., & Park, H. (2013). Everyday conversation requires cognitive inference: Neural bases of comprehending implicated meanings in conversations. *NeuroImage*, *81*, 61–72.

Kandylaki, K. D., Nagels, A., Tune, S., Wiese, R., Bornkessel-Schlesewsky, I., & Kircher, T. (2015). Processing of false belief passages during natural story comprehension: An fMRI study. *Human Brain Mapping*, *36*, 4231–4246.

Kansaku, K., Yamaura, A., & Kitazawa, S. (2000). Sex differences in lateralization revealed in the posterior language areas. *Cerebral Cortex*, *10*(9), 866–872.

Kawabata, H., & Zeki, S. (2004). Neural correlates of beauty. *Journal of Neurophysiology*, *91*, 1699–1705.

The Cognitive Neuroscience of Discourse

Kintsch, W., & Van Dijk, T. A. (1978). Toward a model of text comprehension and production. *Psychological Review, 85*(5), 363–394.

Knoeferle, P., Habets, B., Crocker, M., & Munte, T. (2008). Visual scenes trigger immediate syntactic reanalysis: Evidence from ERPs during situated spoken comprehension. *Cerebral Cortex, 18*(4), 789–795. http://doi.org/10.1093/cercor/bhm121.

Kriegeskorte, N., Goebel, R., & Bandettini, P. (2006). Information-based functional brain mapping. *Proceedings of the National Academy of Sciences of the United States of America, 103*(10), 3863–3868.

Kuperberg, G. R., Lakshmanan, B. M., Caplan, D. N., & Holcomb, P. J. (2006). Making sense of discourse: An fMRI study of causal inferencing across sentences. *Neuroimage, 33*(1), 343–361.

Kurby, C. A., & Zacks, J. M. (2013). The activation of modality-specific representations during discourse processing. *Brain and Language, 126*(3), 338–349. http://doi.org/10.1016/j.bandl.2013.07.003.

Kutas, M., & Hillyard, S. A. (1980). Reading senseless sentences: Brain potentials reflect semantic incongruity. *Science, 207*(4427), 203–225.

Lehne, M., Engel, P., Rohrmeier, M., Menninghaus, W., Jacobs, A. M., & Koelsch, S. (2015). Reading a suspenseful literary text activates brain areas related to social cognition and predictive inference. *PLOS ONE, 10*(5), e0124550.

Mahon, B. Z., & Caramazza, A. (2008). A critical look at the embodied cognition hypothesis and a new proposal for grounding conceptual content. *Journal of Physiology-Paris, 102*(1–3), 59–70. http://doi.org/10.1016/j.jphysparis.2008.03.004.

Mahon, B. Z., & Caramazza, A. (2009). Concepts and categories: A cognitive neuropsychological perspective. *Annual Review of Psychology, 60*, 27–51. http://doi.org/10.1146/annurev.psych.60.110707.163532.

Maïza, O., Mazoyer, B., Hervé, P., Razafimandimby, A., Dollfus, S., & Tzourio-Mazoyer, N. (2011). Reproducibility of fMRI activations during a story listening task in patients with schizophrenia. *Schizophrenia Research, 128*(1–3), 98–101.

Mar, R. A. (2004). The neuropsychology of narrative: Story comprehension, story production and their interrelation. *Neuropsychologia, 42*(10), 1414–1434.

Mar, R. A. (2011). The neural bases of social cognition and story comprehension. *Annual Review of Psychology, 62*, 103–134.

Mar, R. A., & Oatley, K. (2008). The function of fiction is the abstraction and simulation of social experience. *Perspectives on Psychological Science, 3*, 173–192.

Mar, R. A., Spreng, R. N., & DeYoung, C. G. (2013). How to produce personality neuroscience research with high statistical power and low additional cost. *Cognitive, Affective & Behavioral Neuroscience, 13*(3), 674–685.

Marini, A., Spoletini, I., Rubino, I. A., Ciuffa, M., Bria, P., Martinotti, G., Banfi, G., Boccascino, R., Strom, P., Siracusano, A., Caltagirone, C., & Spalletta, G. (2008). The language of schizophrenia: An analysis of micro and macrolinguistic abilities and their neuropsychological correlates. *Schizophrenia Research, 105*(1–3), 144–155.

Marton, M., & Szirtes, J. (1988). Context effects on saccade-related brain potentials to words during reading. *Neuropsychologia, 26*(3), 453–463. http://doi.org/10.1016/0028-3932(88)90098-X.

Mason, M. F., Norton, M. I., Van Horn, J. D., Wegner, D. M., Grafton, S. T., & Macrae, C. N. (2007). Wandering minds: The default network and stimulus-independent thought. *Science, 315*(5810), 393–395.

Mason, R. A., & Just, M. A. (2009). The role of the theory-of-mind cortical network in the comprehension of narratives. *Language & Linguistic Compass, 3*, 157–174.

Mason, R. A., & Just, M. A. (2011). Differential cortical networks for inferences concerning people's intentions versus physical causality. *Human Brain Mapping, 32*, 313–329.

Mason, R. A., Williams, D. L., Kana, R. K., Minshew, N., & Just, M. A. (2008). Theory of mind disruption and recruitment of the right hemisphere during narrative comprehension in autism. *Neuropsychologia, 46*, 269–280.

McCandliss, B. D., Cohen, L., & Dehaene, S. (2003). The visual word form area: Expertise for reading in the fusiform gyrus. *Trends in Cognitive Sciences, 7*(7), 293–299. http://doi.org/10.1016/S1364-6613(03)00134-7.

McGuire, P. K., Silbersweig, D. A., Wright, I., & Murray, R. M. (1996). The neural correlates of inner speech and auditory verbal imagery in schizophrenia: Relationship to auditory verbal hallucinations. *The British Journal of Psychiatry, 169*(2), 148–159.

Meteyard, L., Cuadrado, S. R., Bahrami, B., & Vigliocco, G. (2012). Coming of age: A review of embodiment and the neuroscience of semantics. *Cortex, 48*(7), 788–804. http://doi.org/10.1016/j.cortex.2010.11.002.

Montague, P. R., Berns, G. S., Cohen, J. D., McClure, S. M., Pagnoni, G., Dhamala, M., Wiest, M. C., Karpov, I., King, R. D., Apple, N., & Fisher, R. E. (2002). Hyperscanning: Simultaneous fMRI during linked social interactions. *Neuroimage, 16*(4), 1159–1164.

Nijhof, A. D., & Willems, R. M. (2015). Simulating fiction: Individual differences in literature comprehension revealed with fMRI. *PLOS ONE,* 10(2), e0116492.

Norman, K., Polyn, S., Detre, G., & Haxby, J. (2006). Beyond mind-reading: Multi-voxel pattern analysis of fMRI data. *Trends in Cognitive Sciences, 10*(9), 424–430.

OECD (2011). How do girls compare to boys in reading skills?, in PISA 2009 at a Glance, OECD Publishing. http://dx.doi.org/10.1787/9789264095250-5-en.

Osterhout, L., & Holcomb, P. J. (1992). Event-related brain potentials elicited by syntactic anomaly. *Journal of Memory and Language, 31*(6), 785–806.

Prat, C. S., Mason, R. A., & Just, M. A. (2011). Individual differences in the neural basis of causal inferencing. *Brain & Language, 116,* 1–13.

Prat, C. S., Mason, R. A., & Just, M. A. (2012). An fMRI investigation of analogical mapping in metaphor comprehension: The influence of context and individual cognitive capacities on processing demands. *Journal of Experimental Psychology: Learning, Memory, and Cognition, 38,* 282–294.

Price, C. J., & Devlin, J. T. (2003). The myth of the visual word form area. *Neuroimage, 19*(3), 473–481.

Pugh, K. R., Shaywitz, B. A., Shaywitz, S. E., Constable, R. T., Skudlarski, P., Fulbright, R. K., Bronen, R. A., Shankweiler, D. P., Katz, L., Fletcher, J. M., & Gore, J. C. (1996). Cerebral organization of component processes in reading. *Brain, 119*(4), 1221–1238.

Pulvermüller, F., & Fadiga, L. (2010). Active perception: Sensorimotor circuits as a cortical basis for language. *Nature Reviews Neuroscience, 11*(5), 351–360.

Rapp, D. N., Gerrig, R. J., & Prentice, D. A. (2001). Readers' trait-based models of characters in narrative comprehension. *Journal of Memory and Language, 45,* 737–750.

Robertson, D. A., Gernsbacher, M. A., Guidotti, S. J., Robertson, R. R., Irwin, W., Mock, B. J., & Campana, M. E. (2000). Functional neuroanatomy of the cognitive process of mapping during discourse comprehension. *Psychological Science, 11*(3), 255–260.

Saito, D. N., Tanabe, H. C., Izuma, K., Hayashi, M. J., Morito, Y., Komeda, H., Uchiyama. H., Kosaka, H., Okazawa, H., Fujibayashi. Y., & Sadato, N. (2010). "Stay tuned": Inter-individual neural synchronization during mutual gaze and joint attention. *Frontiers in Integrative Neuroscience.* doi:http://dx.doi.org/10.3389/fnint.2010.00127.

Schilbach, L., Timmermans, B., Reddy, V., Costall, A., Bente, G., Schlicht, T., & Vogeley, K. (2013). Toward a second-person neuroscience. *Behavioral and Brain Sciences, 36*(4), 393–414.

Schmalhofer, F., & Perfetti, C. A. (Eds). (2007). *Higher level language processes in the brain: Inference and comprehension processes.* Mahwah, NJ: Lawrence Erlbaum Associates. Retrieved from http://libproxy.wustl.edu/login?url=http://search.ebscohost.com/login.aspx?direct=true&db=psyh&AN=2007-05815-000&site=ehost-live&scope=site.

Schmälzle, R., Häcker, F. E. K., Honey, C. J., & Hasson, U. (2015). Engaged listeners: Shared neural processing of powerful political speeches. *Social Cognitive and Affective Neuroscience, 10*(8), 1137–1143.

Shaywitz, B. A., Shaywitz, S. E., Pugh, K. R., Constable, R. T., Skudlarski, P., Fulbright, R. K., Bronen, R. A., Fletcher, J. M., Shankweller, D. P., Katz, L., & Gore, J. C. (1995). Sex differences in the functional organization of the brain for language. *Nature, 373*(6515), 607–609.

Silbert, L. J., Honey, C. J., Simony, E., Poeppel, D., & Hasson, U. (2014). Coupled neural systems underlie the production and comprehension of naturalistic narrative speech. *Proceedings of the National Academy of Sciences, 111*(43), E4687–E4696.

Skov, M., & Vartanian, O. (Eds.) (2009). *Neuroaesthetics.* Amityville, NY: Baywood Publishing.

Smallwood, J., Gorgolewski, K. J., Golchert, J., Ruby, F. J., Engen, H., Baird, B., Vinski, M. T., Schooler, J. W., & Margulies, D. S. (2013). The default modes of reading: modulation of posterior cingulate and medial prefrontal cortex connectivity associated with comprehension and task focus while reading. *Frontiers in Human Neuroscience, 7.*

Speer, N. K., Reynolds, J. R., Swallow, K. M., & Zacks, J. M. (2009). Reading stories activates neural representations of perceptual and motor experiences. *Psychological Science, 20,* 989–999.

Speer, N. K., Reynolds, J. R., & Zacks, J. M. (2007). Human brain activity time-locked to narrative event boundaries. *Psychological Science, 18*(5), 449–455.

Spiegelhalder, K., Ohlendorf, S., Regen, W., Feige, B., van Elst, L. T., Weiller, C., Hennig, J., Berger, M., & Tüscher, O. (2014). Interindividual synchronization of brain activity during live verbal communication. *Behavioural Brain Research, 258*, 75–79.

St. George, M., Kutas, M., Martinez, A., & Sereno, M. I. (1999). Semantic integration in reading: Engagement of the right hemisphere during discourse processing. *Brain, 122*(Pt 7), 1317–1325.

Stephens, G. J., Silbert, L. J., & Hasson, U. (2010). Speaker–listener neural coupling underlies successful communication. *PNAS Proceedings of the National Academy of Sciences of the United States of America, 107*(32), 14425–14430.

Swett, K., Miller, A. C., Burns, S., Hoeft, F., Davis, N., Petrill, S. A., & Cutting, L. E. (2013). Comprehending expository texts: The dynamic neurobiological correlates of building a coherent text representation. *Frontiers in Human Neuroscience, 7*, 853.

Szaflarski, J. P., Altaye, M., Rajagopal, A., Eaton, K., Meng, X., Plante, E., & Holland, S. K. (2012). A 10-year longitudinal fMRI study of narrative comprehension in children and adolescents. *NeuroImage, 63*(3), 1188–1195.

Tal-Or, N., & Cohen, J. (2010). Understanding audience involvement: Conceptualizing and manipulating identification and transportation. *Poetics, 38*, 402–418.

Tamir, D. I., Bricker, A. B., Dodell-Feder, D., & Mitchell, J. P. (2016). Reading fiction and reading minds: The role of the default network. *Social Cognitive Affective Neuroscience, 11*(2), 215–224.

van Berkum, J. J. A., Hagoort, P., & Brown, C. M. (1999). Semantic integration in sentences and discourse: Evidence from the N400. *Journal of Cognitive Neuroscience, 11*(6), 657–671.

van Berkum, J. J. A., Zwitserlood, P., Hagoort, P., & Brown, C. M. (2003). When and how do listeners relate a sentence to the wider discourse? Evidence from the N400 effect. *Cognitive Brain Research, 17*(3), 701–718.

Wallentin, M. (2009). Putative sex differences in verbal abilities and language cortex: A critical review. *Brain and Language, 108*(3), 175–183.

Wehbe, L., Murphy, B., Talukdar, P., Fyshe, A., Ramdas, A., & Mitchell, T. (2014). Simultaneously uncovering the patterns of brain regions involved in different story reading subprocesses. *PLOS ONE, 9*(11), e112575.

Whitney, C., Huber, W., Klann, J., Weis, S., Krach, S., & Kircher, T. (2009). Neural correlates of narrative shifts during auditory story comprehension. *NeuroImage, 47*(1), 360–366. http://doi.org/10.1016/j.neuroimage.2009.04.037.

Willems, R. M. (2015). *Cognitive neuroscience of natural language use*. Cambridge, UK: Cambridge University Press.

Williams, D. L., Cherkassky, V. L., Mason, R. A., Keller, T. A., Minshew, N. J., & Just, M. A. (2013). Brain function differences in language processing in children and adults with autism. *Autism Research, 6*, 288–302.

Wilson, M. (2002). Six views of embodied cognition. *Psychonomic Bulletin & Review, 9*(4), 625–636. http://doi.org/10.3758/BF03196322.

Yarkoni, T., Speer, N., Balota, D., McAvoy, M., & Zacks, J. (2008). Pictures of a thousand words: Investigating the neural mechanisms of reading with extremely rapid event-related fMRI. *Neuroimage, 42*, 973–987.

Yarkoni, T., Speer, N., & Zacks, J. (2008). Neural substrates of narrative comprehension and memory. *Neuroimage, 41*, 1408–1425.

Zabrucky, K., & Ratner, H. H. (1992). Effects of passage type on comprehension monitoring and recall in good and poor readers. *Journal of Reading Behavior, 24*(3), 373–391.

Zacks, J. M., Braver, T. S., Sheridan, M. A., Donaldson, D. I., Snyder, A. Z., Ollinger, J. M., Buckner, R. L., & Raichle, M. E. (2001). Human brain activity time-locked to perceptual event boundaries. *Nature Neuroscience, 4*(6), 651–655.

Zacks, J. M., Kurby, C. A., Eisenberg, M. L., & Haroutunian, N. (2011). Prediction error associated with the perceptual segmentation of naturalistic events. *Journal of Cognitive Neuroscience, 23*, 4057–4066. http://doi.org/10.1162/jocn_a_00078.

Zacks, J. M., Speer, N. K., Swallow, K. M., Braver, T. S., & Reynolds, J. R. (2007). Event perception: A mind/brain perspective. *Psychological Bulletin, 133*(2), 273–293.

Zacks, J. M., Speer, N. K., Swallow, K. M., & Maley, C. J. (2010). The brain's cutting room floor: Segmentation of narrative cinema. *Frontiers in Human Neuroscience, 4*(168), 1–15. http://doi.org/10.3389/fnhum.2010.00168.

Zacks, J. M., Swallow, K. M., Vettel, J. M., & McAvoy, M. P. (2006). Visual movement and the neural correlates of event perception. *Brain Research, 1076*(1), 150–162.

Zeman, A., Milton, F., Smith, A., & Rylance, R. (2013a). By heart: An fMRI study of brain activation by poetry and prose. *Journal of Consciousness Studies, 20*(9–10), 132–158.

Zeman, A. Z. J., Beschin, N., Dewar, M., & Sala, S. D. (2013b). Imagining the present: Amnesia may impair descriptions of the present as well as of the future and the past. *Cortex, 49*(3), 637–645.

Zwaan, R. A. (1999). Five dimensions of narrative comprehension: The event-indexing model. In S. R. Goldman, A. C. Graesser, & P. van den Broek (Eds), *Narrative comprehension, causality, and coherence: Essays in honor of Tom Trabasso* (pp. 93–110). Mahwah, NJ: Lawrence Erlbaum Associates.

Zwaan, R. A. (2014). Embodiment and language comprehension: Reframing the discussion. *Trends in Cognitive Sciences, 18*(5), 229–234.

Zwaan, R. A., & Radvansky, G. A. (1998). Situation models in language comprehension and memory. *Psychological Bulletin, 123*(2), 162–185.

Zwaan, R. A., Stanfield, R. A., & Yaxley, R. H. (2002). Language comprehenders mentally represent the shape of objects. *Psychological Science, 13*(2), 168–171.

15
Beliefs and Discourse Processing

Michael B. Wolfe

GRAND VALLEY STATE UNIVERSITY

Thomas D. Griffin

UNIVERSITY OF ILLINOIS AT CHICAGO

Imagine two students studying the genetic influences on homosexuality. One student believes that homosexuality is genetically determined and the other believes it is not. A Google search returns articles with some headlines stating that homosexuality is and some that it is not genetically determined. Next, imagine that the students read the following section from an Introductory Psychology textbook (Lilienfeld, Lynn, Namy, & Woolf, 2014):

> In another study, they found concordance rates for lesbians of 48 percent in identical twins and 16 percent in fraternal twins (Bailey, et. al., 1993). The finding that a substantial percentage of identical twins aren't concordant tells us that environmental influences play a key role in homosexuality, although it doesn't tell us what these influences are.

This text passage is inconsistent with the beliefs of both students to some extent because it suggests that both genetic and environmental influences are at play in determining sexual orientation.

In this chapter, we address several questions that arise in situations such as this. How do the prior beliefs of students influence the way in which they process this information? Will students comprehend information with more or less success if it matches or does not match their prior beliefs? Under what circumstances might students change their beliefs? Do students change beliefs to make them consistent with data reported in scientific studies, or are other factors at play? We also argue that the traditional methods and theories from text comprehension are well suited to examine the influences of beliefs on the processing students do and the mental representations they form when reading belief-related texts.

Defining Beliefs

The literature on beliefs contains a number of review papers that define beliefs or discuss variations in definitions across fields (Abelson, 1979; Alexander & Dochy, 1994; Murphy & Mason, 2006; Southerland, Sinatra, & Matthews, 2001). Many definitions involve beliefs as things that a person wishes to be true based on some affective component. This approach borrows from Plato's distinction between a *belief* in which some claim is accepted without rational justification, versus *knowledge* in which the believer has justification and the claim is objectively true (Fine, 2003). This philosophical distinction is problematic for empirical investigations of belief formation/revision processes, because it confounds the variables of what a person believes with why they believe it, and involves a third non-psychological variable of X actually being objectively true, which is not scientifically measureable independent of rational justification for believing it. In contrast, cognitive and educational science refers to knowledge in terms of mentally represented perceptions and ideas without regard to whether this knowledge is believed or accurate. For example, learners can acquire knowledge of fictional creatures and make hypothetical predictions about their survival without actually believing in the existence of these fictional creatures (Jee & Wiley, 2014).

We confine our definition of these constructs to distinct psychological states and distinguish them from epistemic and psychological processes that give rise to them. We define knowledge as mental representation of concepts or propositions about relations among them. In contrast, we define belief as a position about the truth value of a proposition (Griffin & Ohlsson, 2001; Quine & Ullian, 1978; Wolfe, Tanner, & Taylor, 2013). This makes beliefs independent of the actual truth or preponderance of evidence related to the proposition. Two important distinctions are relevant to our definition. First, beliefs are different from knowledge. A person can understand the principles of evolution that are taught in school (knowledge), but have a personal opinion that the information is false (belief). Second, beliefs are different from attitudes. More so than beliefs, attitudes are a focus in social psychology. They reflect valenced affective preferences toward something, but that preference might or might not form the basis of one's beliefs about that thing (Greenberg, Schmader, Arndt, & Landau, 2015). For example, many people who believe that the theory of evolution is true still have a negative attitude toward the theory and prefer that it was not true (Brem, Ranney, & Schindel, 2003). A similar distinction between beliefs and attitudes may exist for students' judgments about the genetic influences on homosexuality mentioned earlier. The belief-attitude distinction is important because the inherent affective nature of attitudes could make their role in text processing different from beliefs. However the literature on attitudes is more extensive than that on beliefs, so we do discuss research on attitudes where the tasks and findings are related to our questions.

Beliefs are a position on a question of fact, but they can arise from affective reactions. They can also follow from logical reasoning about knowledge and factual premises in the absence of emotional considerations. Beliefs can be logically contradicted or supported by factual premises, and a person following those logical implications may be compelled to hold a particular belief. Even with factual scientific subjects, beliefs can be based in either affective preferences or consideration of supporting information. Griffin (2008) developed a belief-basis scale to determine the affective or evidence-based nature of beliefs for a subject within a topic. Example items include "I trust my heart and not my head on this topic" and "I considered the evidence that I'm personally aware of." These differences appear to be influenced by features of the specific topic (Griffin & Ohlsson, 2001) as well as dispositional individual differences across domains (Griffin, 2008). The basis of a belief represents what and how information was processed when a person arrives at a belief. Thus, belief-basis might impact what new information is processed, how it is processed, and what the outcomes (both learning and belief revision) of the discourse processing will be.

Discourse Comprehension

Our discussion of beliefs is placed within a context of research on discourse comprehension. Typically, the process of reading results in a mental representation of the information (McNamara & Magliano, 2009). According to Kintsch's prominent Construction Integration (CI) theory (Kintsch, 1998), comprehension begins with a construction phase in which components of a sentence are connected into a preliminary mental representation of what the sentence says. Some related knowledge is automatically activated and added to the preliminary representation. Next, an integration phase takes place in which mental activation spreads through this representation until it reaches a stable state. Relevant knowledge and important concepts remain part of the representation and are transferred to long-term memory (LTM). Irrelevant knowledge and weakly related concepts are deactivated. The result is a mental representation in LTM of the text information, relevant knowledge, and inferences that have been generated.

But comprehension is not always typical. As Kintsch (1998) states, "Text comprehension depends as much on the reader and the pragmatic situation as on the text itself" (p. 188). Readers can exert control over their comprehension processes by generating more elaborate inferences, forming opinions, thinking about how they might use the content, or other processes "beyond" simple memory of what they read. These processes vary based on the reader's knowledge and goals at the time they read (Rapp & van den Broek, 2005). The CI theory proposes that the mental representation of the text can be conceptualized as existing at three levels. The *surface structure* represents the literal wording of the sentences. The *textbase* represents the content of the text in the way the text describes it. This is the representation a reader would have if they only attempted to remember what they read. Finally, the *situation model* contains the textbase, but also the activated knowledge, inferences, and reactions to the text. The situation model describes not just what was said, but the broader situation being described by the text.

Several aspects of this process are potentially subject to belief influences. Beliefs and basic reasons supporting them are part of our LTM representation, and therefore individual differences in beliefs or belief-basis will result in differences in what knowledge gets automatically activated (Voss, Fincher-Kiefer, Wiley, & Silfies, 1993). Also, the affective basis of some beliefs could motivate controlled processing strategies that result in different situation models. For example, readers may attempt to argue against a position while they read (Kunda, 1990).

Comprehension research supports an important distinction between mental processes during reading and the resulting mental representation. We propose that methods of evaluating belief influences should be understood as addressing one of three aspects of comprehension. First, *processing* of information refers to the on-line mental processes readers engage in while they consume discourse (Graesser, Singer, & Trabasso, 1994). Measures of processing include reading times, think aloud protocols, or response times to probes presented during reading. Second, processing results in a *mental representation* in LTM (Kintsch, 1998). Mental representation tasks require a memory of the content (e.g., word recognition, free or cued recall), or potentially elaboration and integration of what was read (e.g., inference-verification-tasks, concept maps, explanatory essays). Performance on these task should rely on accurate memory or understanding of the text rather than the reader's personal opinions. Finally, *evaluation* refers to performance on tasks in which the subject provides a critical evaluation of the text content against either some external standard (objective) or their own beliefs and attitudes (subjective). Evaluative responses should not be taken as direct assessments of a mental representation. Optimal performance on objective evaluation tasks require accurate mental representations, but also require knowledge of and skill in applying the standards (e.g., evaluating the claim-evidence structure of a text). Subjective evaluation tasks often lack any requirement of accurate understanding, mostly reflecting the readers' subjective reactions (e.g., pre/post beliefs or attitudes on the topic, thought listing) to whatever their mental representation is along with any demand characteristics.

Why Study Beliefs?

One motivation for studying beliefs is that people regularly encounter information that is consistent or inconsistent with beliefs. In educational settings, students read scientific information that is inconsistent with beliefs they may have developed outside of school. Adults consume belief-relevant information through both print and audio-visual media about topics such as history, science, or politics. These situations involve aspects of comprehension. People vary in their beliefs, knowledge, desire to maintain beliefs, motivations for engaging in belief-related information, and affective responses to information. These influences will likely lead people to alter their processing and influence the mental representations they construct when encountering belief-related information.

Next, we are interested in beliefs because society benefits from a scientifically literate populace, and yet many people hold misconceptions about scientific topics. Students have inaccurate beliefs, such as that humans use only 10% of our brains (Taylor & Kowalski, 2004). People hold beliefs contradicted by scientific evidence (Sinatra, Southerland, McConaughy, & Demastes, 2003) as indicated by a number of recent Gallup polls. For example, among Americans, 42% do not believe in biological evolution, 9% believe that vaccines are more dangerous than the diseases they prevent, and 6% believe vaccines cause autism and another 52% are unsure, despite overwhelming evidence refuting these beliefs. Even in 2015, 35% of Americans do not believe that global warming is happening or will happen in their lifetimes, which is up from 25% in 2008. Discourse processing researchers can potentially help address these misconceptions by understanding why they are so often resistant to change.

Finally, beliefs can trigger affective reactions that change readers' goals to differ dramatically from assigned tasks or presumed goals. People often are resistant to changing their beliefs, either because they think beliefs should not be changed (Alexander & Dochy, 1994), or out of a desire to maintain a consistent sense of self (Aronson, 1968; Gawronski & Strack, 2012). Readers can process belief-related information with a goal of reaching a certain pre-determined conclusion (Kunda, 1990). When beliefs contradict text content, readers can also experience a sense of psychological threat (Hayes et al., 2015). Much of this research has not traditionally been undertaken by discourse processing researchers. In fact, the first edition of this *Handbook* (Graesser, Gernsbacher, & Goldman, 2003a) did not have a chapter on beliefs or related issues. In short, it is important to understand belief influences because they introduce a number of potential factors that can influence processing and mental representation of information.

Processing and Mental Representation of Information as a Function of Beliefs

How do beliefs influence what we do with discourse? Do we put more effort into understanding information that is consistent or inconsistent with beliefs? Do we remember information better if we believe or don't believe it? What factors mediate or moderate the relationship between beliefs and comprehension? The distinctions between processing, representation, and evaluation are important in addressing these questions. For example, research suggests that inferences that connect clauses in a text are sometimes generated during processing, and other times generated after processing when readers are responding to questions about the text (Kintsch & Keenan, 1973; Noordman & Vonk, 1992). Reader knowledge, the demands of the task, and linguistic cues like sentence connectives can all influence these processes. If readers only tend to think further about what they read *because* they are responding to others' questions, it is important to understand that.

Processing Belief-Consistent and Belief-Inconsistent Information

In any research study, on-line processing measures can provide information about the effort subjects put into reading. However, processing changes may not have a direct or obvious relationship to the reader's mental representation or evaluation of the content. A reader can take longer, pause on a word, or reread more prior sentences either because they are struggling to form even a superficial representation, or because they are slowing down to generate inferences and create an elaborate situation model.

There are few studies that actually measure on-line processing as a function of belief in the text content. In one study, Kardash and Howell (2000) had subjects think out loud as they read a text about HIV as the cause of AIDS. They found that when subjects read belief-consistent content, they made more metacognitive comments about their understanding or lack of understanding of the content. Belief-inconsistent content triggered more disagreements with the content. The distinction between metacognitive comments and disagreements illustrates the point that processing effort needs to be further differentiated in terms of the type of effort readers are engaged in (i.e., to understand versus discount the text content). However, all subjects in the study believed that HIV caused AIDS, so the belief-inconsistent content was always arguing that HIV did not cause AIDS. Any seeming effect of belief inconsistency could be simply due to the different nature of the content itself, regardless of its relation to prior beliefs. Wolfe et al. (2013) measured sentence reading times for extended texts about evolution and TV violence. Reading times were analyzed as a function of the extent to which individual sentences were consistent or inconsistent with subjects' beliefs. Critically, belief consistency was orthogonal to the person's or the text's position on the topic, because there were both believers and disbelievers on each topic who were randomly assigned to read either a pro or anti text. Results showed that subjects slowed down reading for belief-inconsistent sentences for the evolution topic but not for the TV violence topic. Off-line assessments of the mental representations showed that these reading times were not associated with readers' memory for the text information, suggesting elaboration (e.g., counter-arguing) was responsible rather than readers struggling to form a basic representation of belief-inconsistent information.

In terms of potential variables that moderate processing, some evidence suggests that the reason why readers claim to hold their beliefs influences how they process texts. Griffin (2008; Griffin & Ohlsson, 2001) showed that some people are more *evidence-based* and others are more *affect-based* in terms of the reasons they claim to hold particular beliefs. These belief-basis differences are proposed to reflect qualitative differences in how people arrive at their beliefs (based on evidence vs. emotional reasons), and in how they process and evaluate new evidence relating to them. Belief-basis is measured with a self-report questionnaire, and is specific to a particular topic for each person. Wolfe et al. (2013) found that for texts about evolution, subjects' belief-basis moderated whether they focused on arguments while reading. Evidence-based subjects showed stronger evidence of argument-focused processing than affect-based subjects, particularly for sentences that were inconsistent with the overall position of the text. In an eye-tracking study, Griffin and Salas (under review) found that readers with more evidence-based beliefs about evolution spent longer reading both belief-consistent and inconsistent texts, which was partially due to them looking back more often and rereading previously read sentences. These reading-time differences were found while controlling for prior evolution knowledge and their reading times and look-backs while reading on a different topic. Also, path model analyses suggested that while poor comprehenders more often reread prior sentences, these evidence-based readers actually had superior comprehension, suggesting they reread as a way to engage in elaboration and improve their understanding. More research on belief-basis is needed, but preliminary data suggest that subjects who claim to hold their beliefs because of evidence may put greater effort toward integrating new information with existing knowledge.

In a number of other studies, terms are used that might imply conclusions about text processing, but processing is either not measured, or is combined with other tasks. Terms such as *biased assimilation* (Corner, Whitmarsh, & Xenias, 2012; Munro & Ditto, 1997), *motivated reasoning* (Hart & Nisbet, 2012; Kunda, 1990), *message scrutiny* (Petty & Cacioppo, 1984), and *processing* (Clark, Wegener, & Fabrigar, 2008) might imply that readers alter text processing based on the match between beliefs or attitudes and text content. Despite these terms, these experiments do not measure processing as a function of beliefs.

Some lessons can be gleaned from studies examining processing of attitude-inconsistent (rather than belief-inconsistent) texts. In an oft-cited study, Edwards and Smith (1996) found that subjects spent longer processing attitude-inconsistent arguments about a range of topics compared to attitude-consistent arguments. This paper is cited as evidence that readers put more effort into processing attitude-inconsistent than consistent information. The task in Edwards and Smith's (1996) study was to read and rate the strength of a series of arguments. Reading times for argument premises were collected and reported as a function of text position, but never analyzed as a function of attitude-consistency. Reading times for argument conclusions were combined with the time it took to make the argument-strength judgment, which means the processing and evaluation components of the task cannot be distinguished. Similarly, Taber and Lodge (2006) and Taber, Cann, and Kucsova (2009) found that people with more general political knowledge or stronger prior attitudes spent longer reading and rating attitude-inconsistent arguments about political policies. They also did not separate reading times from evaluation response times.

It is common for these "effortful processing" results to be interpreted as readers being motivated to protect their attitudes, or to mentally generate arguments against the attitude-inconsistent points as they read them. This conclusion is also reached, for example, in reasoning studies in which subjects list more thoughts about attitude-inconsistent arguments after reading (Munro & Ditto, 1997). Thought listing is an evaluation task, however, so it is possible that the influence of attitudes on thoughts takes place during post-reading thought generation rather than text processing. Thought listing also involves potential demand characteristics in which readers might consider it more relevant to note points of disagreement than agreement, especially since they just reported their own attitude. In addition, these attitude studies are often discussed, including by their authors, in terms of "belief" consistency effects. But the texts and the participants' prior positions dealt with attitudes regarding preference for various political policies, such as the acceptability of using the death penalty, corporal punishment of children, and taxation of junk foods. Unlike beliefs, such attitudes cannot be objectively refuted by arguments any more than a preference for chocolate can be shown incorrect. Beliefs may trigger different reactions.

Much more research is needed to understand the influence of beliefs on processing. There seems to be a common assumption that belief-inconsistent information is processed in greater depth, or more critically, compared to belief-consistent information. We find relatively little evidence supporting this conclusion. We emphasize a few points that researchers should pay attention to. First, a clear distinction between processing, mental representation, and evaluation should be adhered to when researchers make conclusions. Second, the relationship between different types of processing effort and their influences on representation and evaluation should be examined. For example, if readers slow down reading for particular types of information, or some readers slow down more than others, what is this increased effort being devoted to? A combination of processing and representation measures may be needed to interpret processing effects. Finally, researchers should be mindful that different topics could affect processing differently. Some researchers have suggested that beliefs or attitudes function like schemas, which are organized bodies of knowledge about specific topics (Maier & Richter, 2013; Pratkanis, 1989; Wiley, 2005). If so, we may expect beliefs to be automatically activated during comprehension. Voss et al. (1993) presented evidence that informal arguments activate associated attitudes and reasons. But for many topics, such as the genetic bases of homosexuality, it is not clear whether most readers have beliefs that are well developed enough to function in a similar fashion.

Mental Representation of Belief-Consistent and Inconsistent Information

Do readers' mental representations of text information differ based on the match between their beliefs and text content? A more focused question has been addressed extensively in the attitude literature; do people remember attitude-consistent information better than attitude-inconsistent information? Meta-analyses have evaluated studies in which subjects read lists of arguments on each side of an issue, then recall the arguments (Eagly, Chen, Chaiken, & Shaw-Barnes, 1999; Eagly, Kulsea, Chen, & Chaiken, 2001; Roberts, 1985). The lists of arguments are likely to produce a textbase type of representation, not an integrated situation model. Topics include abortion, gay soldiers in the military, or communism. Two main findings emerge. First, there does appear to be a small but significant attitude-consistency advantage, in which attitude-consistent information is recalled better than inconsistent information. Second, there is large variability in this finding, and there appear to be several moderators of this relationship. Two significant moderators of the consistency advantage were that studies with topics that were highly relevant to the subjects showed larger benefits for attitude-consistent information, while more highly controversial topics showed smaller benefits of attitude-consistent information (Eagly et al., 1999). More controversial topics may produce greater processing for both sides of the issue, thus decreasing the attitude-consistency advantage (Eagly et al., 2001). In one experiment on abortion attitudes, Eagly et al. (2001) found no difference in recall of attitude-consistent vs. inconsistent arguments. After reading, subjects listed more counterattitudinal thoughts than proattitudinal thoughts, which the authors interpreted as students putting more processing effort into counterattitudinal than proattitudinal arguments, although argument processing was not measured. The assumption that biased processing in favor of attitude-inconsistent information leads to a lack of overall memory differences cannot be evaluated without experiments that evaluate processing in more detail.

In comparison to the attitude and memory literature, studies that examine beliefs and memory have used more extended texts, and assessed textbase as well as situation model representations. Wolfe et al. (2013) found no difference in recall of information about evolution or TV violence as a function of belief consistency. Griffin and Salas (under review) found no belief-consistency effects for textbase or situation model representations (using both closed and open-ended assessments) of texts on the topics of evolution and racial differences in intelligence. Britt, Kurby, Dandotkar, and Wolfe (2008) found no relationship between agreement with simple arguments and memory for the arguments. Maier and Richter (2013) found stronger memory for text content that was belief-inconsistent, but a stronger situation model understanding for belief-consistent information. Their results were moderated by text order and blocked or alternating presentation format. However, this was another study in which the belief consistency of the texts was confounded with the text content itself; the belief-inconsistent texts always argued for the non-scientific viewpoints that global warming is not impacted by humans and that vaccines are useless and more harmful than helpful.

In an examination of belief-basis, Griffin and Salas (under review) found that the more a reader's prior beliefs about evolution or racial differences in intelligences were evidence-based rather than affect-based, the better they performed on situation model measures for texts on those topics, regardless of belief consistency. They replicated these effects and showed that they emerge even after controlling for on-line reading behaviors, topic knowledge, general thinking dispositions, and ability to comprehend texts on other topics. Wolfe et al. (2013) had subjects read a one-sided text, then a neutral text, then write a summary of the neutral text. Affect-based subjects wrote summaries that contained more biased content from the one-sided text compared to evidence-based subjects, who wrote summaries with more balanced content. The results suggest that evidence-based subjects created situation models that reflected an effort to understand both sides of the topic even when reading a one-sided text. Overall, there is little evidence for the common assumption that belief consistency directly impacts the quality of the mental representation or comprehension of discourse, but some evidence that belief-basis does have such effects.

Various accounts for the belief-basis effect exist. Kunda (1990) discussed how information processing can be guided by either accuracy goals or directional goals. Accuracy goals exist when the person seeks to understand the information and make their own views as accurate as possible. Directional goals exist when information is processed in a biased manner to reach preferred conclusions. Affect-based beliefs can be seen as the result of directional goals, whereas evidence-based beliefs result from accuracy goals that direct the person to first understand the information and its implications before evaluating it. Alternatively, Griffin and Ohlsson (2001) postulated that evidence-based beliefs mean the person has already gone through a reasoning process to some extent. This should create greater coherence among their relevant concepts and knowledge representations that better enable them to represent any new information they encounter. More research is needed to test between these alternative (though not mutually exclusive) accounts of the belief-basis effects.

Belief Change

One of the most important challenges in belief-related research is to understand the circumstances under which people will change or revise their beliefs. In the first edition of the *Handbook of Discourse Processes*, Graesser, Gernsbacher, and Goldman (2003b) argued that research on discourse processes should become more interdisciplinary, meaning that researchers collaborate across disciplines to create an integrated understanding or theory to explain the issue. Current research on belief change comes from researchers in social psychology, educational psychology, cognitive psychology, science education, communications, health, political science, and other fields. However, each discipline approaches it in their own way, making it multidisciplinary, but lacking the integration of interdisciplinary research. Several summaries of the multidisciplinary nature of research on belief change have been published (Dole & Sinatra, 1998; Murphy & Mason, 2006; Southerland, Sinatra, & Matthews, 2001; Vosniadou & Mason, 2012). In this section, we summarize research suggesting that people sometimes (but not always) change beliefs after exposure to new information. We describe factors that influence, mediate, or moderate the belief change process, and offer suggestions for how discourse researchers might contribute to this field.

It is well established that in laboratory experiments, subjects change beliefs after reading evidence or arguments suggesting they are incorrect. In many experiments, subjects first report beliefs (or attitudes) about a controversial topic, often in a separate session from the main experiment. Next, subjects read evidence or arguments on one side of the topic or the other (or both). Finally, subjects report beliefs or attitudes again, and often complete mental representation or evaluation tasks. Many of these studies show that on average, when subjects read evidence or arguments supporting a position, their beliefs change in the direction of the text position (Buehl et al., 2001; Clark, Wegener, & Fabrigar, 2008; Cobb & Kuklinski, 1997; Hart & Nisbet, 2012; Hayes et al., 2015; Kendeou, Walsh, Smith, & O'Brien, 2014; Murphy, Long, Holleran, & Esterly, 2003; Petty & Cacioppo, 1984; Sinatra, Kardash, Taasoobshirazi, & Lombardi, 2012; Slusher & Anderson, 1996). The picture of when beliefs change in response to evidence is complicated by a subset of studies that do not show reliable belief changes in response to belief-inconsistent evidence (Cobb & Kuklinski, 1997; Nyhan, Reifler, Richey, & Freed, 2014; Prasad et al., 2009). It is important to note that belief change is typically small and along a continuum, not a binary change from one belief to its opposite. Also, belief change is rarely measured in a separate session after a delay (Kendeou et al., 2014, and Slusher & Anderson, 1996, are exceptions). In some experiments, subjects read evidence or arguments on both sides of the topic, which makes it unclear what belief change to expect.

Text Factors in Belief Change

What aspects of a text affect belief change? Probably the most consistent set of findings deals with refutation texts (Hynd, 2001). In a refutation text, misconceptions about topics are made explicit, then refuted. This text format has been shown to result in greater change in readers' beliefs than texts that merely present the more accurate alternative conception without mentioning the misconceptions. An important caveat about the research on refutation texts, however, is that the majority of studies examining them use topics that are unlikely to challenge students' worldviews or deeply held beliefs. Students reduce misconceptions about topics such as the visual system, or correct basic conceptual errors such as believing that humans only use 10% of their brain or that ostriches hide their head in the ground (Kowalski & Taylor, 2009). Not only are such beliefs less likely to have a strong affective component, but they may lack coherence with relevant knowledge and stand largely isolated as trivia facts repeated often in pop-culture. Other prior beliefs refuted in these studies are "implicit", where a person might find a misconception intuitively appealing without having formed an explicit belief about it (e.g. "heavier objects fall faster"). It is an important topic for future research to examine whether refutation texts would be effective at changing beliefs about topics that are more central to students' worldviews such as evolution, vaccines, or climate change.

Argument structure is another text factor that impacts belief change. Slusher and Anderson (1996) had subjects read one of two texts that both explained that AIDS does not spread through casual contact. Only one text included a causal explanation about why that is the case, and this text led to more change in beliefs about AIDS transmission. Mediation analyses suggested that this greater change was due to greater memory for the causal text. Cobb and Kuklinski (1997) found that opinions changed more when subjects read easy to understand arguments than when the arguments were more complex. This pattern only held for the topic of free-trade, and not for health care.

Moderating Factors in Belief Change

A moderating factor in belief change is one in which people differ on some characteristic that predicts greater or lesser amounts of belief change. Prior knowledge influences on comprehension success are well known; high-knowledge readers generally comprehend information better than low-knowledge readers (e.g. Spilich, Vesonder, Chiesi, & Voss, 1979). However, readers with low knowledge on the topic may be more likely to change beliefs in the direction of the text position. Nyhan, Reifler, and Ubel (2013) found that reading a text refuting the existence of "death panels" related to the U.S. Affordable Care Act led to reduced belief in such panels among readers with low knowledge of the topic but increased belief among readers with high knowledge. However, Buehl et al. (2001) found no difference in belief change about educational reform as a function of prior knowledge. Higher knowledge people may better understand the text and how it contradicts their belief, yet this knowledge can also make the texts' arguments insufficient to trigger belief change. The moderating effect of knowledge may itself be moderated by additional factors.

Mediating Factors in Belief Change

A factor that serves as a mediator in belief change is one in which readers encountering belief-consistent or inconsistent information may have some sort of psychological reaction to the information, and that reaction, in turn, would influence potential changes in beliefs. One potential mediating factor in belief change is psychological threat. According to cognitive dissonance theory (Aronson, 1968; Festinger, 1957) and terror management theory (Schimel, Hayes, Williams, & Jahrig, 2007), when people encounter information that is inconsistent with beliefs that relate to important values the person holds, they may feel some level of threat or dissonance. Changing beliefs to better align with new information is one response that would reduce threat. For example, Hayes et al. (2015) had subjects read a belief-inconsistent text about evolution. Psychological threat was manipulated by subjects writing a short essay about their own mortality. Belief change was greater when threat was active at the time of the post belief reporting compared to when subjects had an opportunity to reduce threat before reporting post beliefs. Williams, Schimel, Hayes, and Faucher (2012) manipulated threat by having subjects write an essay about their own mortality (or a control essay). They found that readers under this mortality threat answered more conceptual questions about a belief-inconsistent evolution text compared to the low-threat readers. The authors suggest that psychological threat triggers subjects to put extra processing effort into the text to defend their worldviews. Psychological threat is relatively unexamined by the discourse processing community, however. One important topic for future research is to examine the generalizability of this phenomenon beyond issues such as evolution, which is a topic that is likely to be centrally related to readers' worldview. For example, researchers who study refutation texts in science learning do not tend to discuss threat as a potential mechanism or explanation for their results.

Other experiments examine strategies that readers employ when faced with belief-inconsistent information but do not directly examine belief change. Most of these studies suggest reasoning strategies readers may employ in an effort to maintain current beliefs. For example, one response subjects may have to reading belief-inconsistent information about scientific topics is to lessen the extent to which the topic is considered something that is open to scientific study. Munro (2010) found that when subjects read evidence relating to stereotypes about homosexuality, those who read belief-inconsistent texts rated the topic as a whole to be less amenable to scientific investigation than subjects who read belief-consistent texts. Similarly, Friesen, Campbell, and Kay (2015) found that when highly religious subjects read an article on the discovery of the Higgs-Boson particle that suggested religion is invalid, they altered their reasons for being religious to be more unfalsifiable. In another experiment, both opponents and proponents of same-sex parenting rated the issue as more unfalsifiable after reading an article that was inconsistent with their belief about the psychological outcomes of children of same-sex parents.

Awareness of Belief Change

When people change their beliefs after reading, do they have metacognitive awareness that their beliefs have changed? One way to determine this is to have people read a belief-inconsistent text that changes their belief, then have them recall their prior belief. Research on this question with scientific beliefs is sparse. But research on attitudes and behaviors suggest that recollections of previous attitudes and behaviors are highly biased by current estimates (Goethals & Reckman, 1973; Ross, 1989; Safer, Levine, & Drapalski, 2002). In the standard procedure, subjects rate an attitude about something in an initial session. Then subjects either learn some new information that may change their attitude, or time passes and attitudes change naturally. In a different session, subjects report their current attitudes again and recollect their previous attitudes. With topics ranging from bussing to achieve racial integration to anxiety about exam performance, results indicate that recollection of previous attitudes is biased toward current attitudes. These results suggest that when attitudes change, people may lack awareness that they have done so. In recent work, Wolfe, Williams, Geers, Hessler, and Simon (2014) found strong evidence of this memory bias with scientific beliefs about TV violence influences. Subjects changed beliefs toward the text position after reading a belief-inconsistent text. Recollections of previous beliefs were much closer to current beliefs than to actual previous beliefs. This preliminary evidence suggests that with beliefs about science topics, subjects may also lack metacognitive awareness of having changed beliefs.

Backfire/Polarization Effects in Belief Change?

In a classic social psychology study, Lord, Ross, and Lepper (1979) found attitude polarization about capital punishment, where attitudes became more extreme and shifted away from the position supported by the texts. Munro and Ditto (1997) replicated that result with attitudes about homosexuality. These results are cited as "belief polarization" or "backfire" effects, and assumed to apply to beliefs. However, these seminal studies actually showed that only general attitudes (e.g., support for capital punishment) became polarized whereas prior beliefs about the specific claims that were targeted by the texts (e.g., capital punishment reduces crime rates) changed in the direction argued by the belief-inconsistent texts. When readers were later given additional texts that supported their beliefs and critiqued the belief-inconsistent research they had just read about, then they became more extreme in their beliefs. But this is not a "backfire" effect so much as selective use of mixed evidence. Subsequent research has either measured only attitude and not belief change (Hart & Nisbet, 2012; Taber et al., 2009), or belief change only in response to mixed evidence (Corner, Whitmarsh, & Xenias, 2012).

The studies supporting "backfire effects" have a particular methodology in common. In all cases, the effect only emerged when participants themselves subjectively rated the degree their attitudes or beliefs changed over the course of the experiment. In fact, some studies show backfire effects for this *perceived change* measure, but found no evidence of it based upon the empirical difference between separate pre and post-reading attitude ratings (Corner et al., 2012; Munro & Ditto, 1997; Munro et al., 2002). Given the evidence that subjects have poor metacognitive awareness of belief or attitude change, it is plausible that the backfire effect is a byproduct of incorrectly recalling prior beliefs or attitudes. On the other hand, demonstrating evidence of a more extreme pre-post change would be difficult if subjects are selected for experiments for their already polarized beliefs on the topics.

A final note about backfire effects is that they may not be consistent between beliefs about information and intentions to act on that information. Nyhan, Reifler, Richey, and Freed (2014) had one group of subjects read a text discrediting the link between vaccines and autism. After reading, these subjects overall did report lower levels of belief in the link between vaccines and autism. Within that group, however, subjects who were the most negative about vaccines to begin with reported *less* willingness to vaccinate their children than before reading. These results suggest that beliefs changed to be more consistent with text content, but intentions to act on those beliefs showed a backfire effect. The disconnect between beliefs and stated intentions to take an action is an important issue that should be studied more.

Theories of Belief Change

The Knowledge Revision Components (KReC) framework of Kendeou and O'Brien (2014) addresses the updating of incorrect knowledge or misconceptions when new information is incorporated into a mental representation. One of the key components of the framework is that, consistent with theories of memory, once knowledge is encoded into long-term memory, it does not get deleted or overwritten. As a result, new information and old information continually compete for mental activation. Another important assumption is that for new information to correct a misconception, the new and old information must be activated in working memory at the same time. This co-activation of new and old information in working memory is proposed as a key component in refutation texts' effectiveness at correcting misconceptions. The KReC framework, however, has been tested mostly with beliefs that either lack a strong affective component, or lack a rich network of knowledge related to the belief. With such beliefs it could be difficult (and perhaps irrelevant) to empirically distinguish between knowledge-revision (i.e., an updated mental representation) versus belief revision.

Some models of knowledge/conceptual change are often applied as models of belief change. For example, Dole and Sinatra (1998) reviewed and integrated some of these models from social, cognitive, and educational psychology (e.g., Petty & Cacioppo, 1986; Posner, Strike, Hewson, & Gertzog, 1982; Thagard, 1992) into the Cognitive Reconstruction of Knowledge Model (CRKM). Although Dole and Sinatra (1998) discuss "conceptions" as the objects of change, they also make frequent reference to "belief" and provide examples that entail a learner's personal beliefs on a topic being changed. According to the CRKM the likelihood of conceptual change after encountering inconsistent information is based on three factors. Prior conceptions are less likely to change when they have greater *strength* (well formed), are more *coherent* and the person has a high level of *commitment* to the conception.

There is an important caveat when describing or evaluating theories related to belief change. Beliefs and knowledge as defined here are distinct mental states that can change independently, and thus must have partially distinct process models of how and when they change. In principle (and likely in practice), conceptual change and knowledge reconstruction can occur in the absence of any belief revision. For example, a Biblical creationist who rejects evolution on an affective basis may have a prior misconception that evolution presumes that animals intentionally adapt their biological traits to suit their environment. Through instruction, they may realize their conception of evolution is incorrect and acquire a new conception of random variation and natural selection of traits. Such a change in the learner's conception of evolutionary processes would qualify as "strong conceptual change" under the CRKM. But the learner's disbelief in evolution may remain unchanged. In contrast, the same conceptual change could trigger a belief change and acceptance of evolution if the learner's prior disbelief was based in thinking that intentional adaptation is implausible, but they find their new conception for adaptive change more plausible.

Narrative Texts and Belief Change

This chapter has focused on the relation between prior beliefs and processing of non-fiction expository/argumentative texts that explicitly make claims and arguments about the real world, to alter the reader's knowledge and beliefs related to those claims. Narrative texts tell stories of specific events, typically lacking any effort to connect to and alter readers' real-world beliefs. Texts that do attempt to alter beliefs are expositional, using the narratives primarily as rhetorical devices to support a more explicit argument (Wolfe & Mienko, 2007). For these reasons, the literatures on how prior beliefs relate to expository and narrative texts cannot be assumed to apply to one another.

Fictional events are generally free to vary without direct conflict with real-world beliefs. Given that narratives lack general real-world implications, readers may limit how much they critically evaluate ideas and claims in narratives. This point is aligned with the notion that narratives trigger *a willing suspension of disbelief*, in which readers are *transported* into the narrative world, making aspects of their real world less accessible (Prentice, Gerrig, & Bailis, 1997). One implication is that this chapter's focus upon the impact of belief consistency on text processing and comprehension is less relevant to narrative texts. Although recent research shows that the *plausibility* of inaccurate claims impacts their acceptance, plausibility is orthogonal to whether the claim is directly consistent with beliefs, instead reflecting the degree of latent-semantic overlap between various inaccurate claims and the accurate claim that is commonly believed (Hinze, Slaten, Horton, Jenkins, & Rapp, 2014).

Another implication of the transportation theory is that narratives could have a strong passive impact on belief revision, due to their claims being processed less critically and accepted within the local story context. This hypothesis is supported by research showing that readers' beliefs about even well established and widely accepted facts (e.g., seatbelts save lives) can be weakened or altered by reading fictional narratives with events that run counter to these ideas (e.g., Prentice et al., 1997). Also, Jacovina, Hinze, and Rapp (2014) found no reliable reading-time slow down when readers read blatantly inaccurate versus accurate historical claims (e.g., the South won the US civil war), so long as the preceding narrative context supported and foreshadowed that inaccurate claim. Thus, local narrative context can override the influence of prior beliefs on how readers process inaccurate information.

There is also support for a presumed passive mechanism whereby narrative claims are not evaluatively processed in relation to prior beliefs. Appel and Richter (2007) found that the impact of fictional narratives on prior beliefs increased after a two-week delay, and that the effect was unrelated to dispositions toward more elaborative processing. Those findings support the idea that narratives impact beliefs via passive processes rather than direct persuasion. As readers forget the source of the information (fictional text), the isolated ideas that made their way into memory without critical examination now simply count as a piece of information that impact construction of a response to a belief prompt. In addition, Green and Brock (2000) showed that the degree of impact of narratives on beliefs was tied to readers' degree of "transportation" into the narrative, whether due to individual differences or contextual manipulations. Disrupting transportation by instructing readers to correct inaccuracies within narratives can reduce the impact of those inaccuracies on readers' beliefs (Rapp, Hinze, Kohlhepp, & Ryskin, 2014). In sum, narrative texts tend to be processed in a manner that reduces the impact of prior beliefs on that processing, and yet allows ideas within those texts to have a kind of back-door influence on beliefs.

Conclusions and Future Directions

Existing research on belief influences on comprehension and belief change has been characterized by multidisciplinarity, but not interdisciplinarity. Researchers from different fields study different topics, people, and types of tasks. Not surprisingly the results, conclusions, and even definitions of beliefs themselves are not consistent across the literature. We propose that one guideline for future researchers is to be mindful of the distinction between processing, mental representation, and evaluation as experimental tasks and levels of interpretation. In proposing these distinctions, we are guided by previous research on discourse processing, much of which is summarized in the chapters of this *Handbook*. In the remainder of this section, we suggest a few general issues and directions for future research.

In considering the research on processing of belief-related information and belief change, there is a seemingly inconsistent pattern in the results and conclusions of these studies. In the majority of studies that show belief change, that change is consistent with the position argued for in the text, suggesting that readers are partially persuaded to change beliefs by the text content. This change does not always take place, and when it does it is incremental rather than absolute. In terms of processing, however, the most common interpretation of the data (mostly from attitude studies) is that subjects put extra scrutiny or processing attention on information they do not agree with. It seems potentially contradictory to suggest that subjects put mental effort into discrediting information that is inconsistent with their beliefs, but are more likely to shift beliefs toward those arguments than away from them. We suggest that systematic research examining the relationship between processing, mental representation, and belief change be undertaken to better understand these findings. Also, researchers should be mindful of the distinction between beliefs and attitudes. The circumstances are not clear under which beliefs and attitudes may influence processing differently, and whether they change in similar ways in response to conflicting discourse.

Another topic that should receive more systematic study is the influence of worldview on belief-related phenomena. Worldview refers to the set of shared values, beliefs, and practices within a culture that serve to give people a kind of meaning beyond their existence as an individual person. Traditional text comprehension research is guided by an often unstated assumption that the reader's goal is to understand the text and update their mental model to be consistent with the text content. This assumption may be reasonable when addressing beliefs related to rather benign topics such as those sometimes addressed in the conceptual change literature (e.g. physics conceptions, the visual system, or basic factual misconceptions). But other topics are likely to be affect-laden, or address topics that are central to the self-concept of people, or are likely to trigger fears and anxieties (e.g., vaccines, race issues, or evolution). These topics may differ in the reactions and reading behaviors they elicit. This point has been addressed by a number of previous researchers (Cobern, 1996; Dole & Sinatra, 1998; Pintrich, Marx, & Boyle, 1993; Schimel et al., 2007). However the literature does not contain a systematic means for quantifying the extent to which topics may vary in terms of how central or peripheral they are to readers' worldviews, nor how readers' worldviews may vary within a single topic. We suggest that interdisciplinary collaboration between discourse researchers and social psychologists may be fruitful in addressing worldview influences.

A couple of methodological points are also worth considering. First, there is a possibility that some belief-related comprehension phenomena may suffer from the file drawer problem. This name refers to the situation in which a researcher conducts an experiment and the results fail to reject the null hypothesis. The standard interpretation of null results is that they are not interpretable, and thus they do not tend to be published. Consider, for example, students reading to study for an exam in a class. There is an external motivation to learn all of the assigned content equally regardless of belief consistency. Under these circumstances, processing effort may not differ between belief-consistent and belief-inconsistent information. Valid evidence supporting this conclusion would be interesting and relevant, but such null findings would be unlikely to be published. In fact, we (authors of this chapter) have multiple such studies in our file drawers, and you (readers) will not read about them. One possible remedy for the file drawer problem is the use of Bayesian statistics in which traditional null hypotheses can be tested (Lee & Wagenmakers, 2005). Another possible remedy is the use of experimental designs in which an interaction is predicted such that an independent variable is expected to influence a dependent variable at one level of a second independent variable but not at the other level of the second variable. Second, belief-consistency effects cannot be tested adequately unless such consistency is fully orthogonal to the two variables of reader beliefs and text position within a topic. Readers with different beliefs should be crossed with texts that take opposing positions. Without this design, there is no way to determine whether any effects are simply due to the content of the texts, or to other general individual differences that happen to covary with differing prior beliefs on a topic. Third, it is important to consider how our research contexts may underestimate the impact of beliefs in less formal contexts where people encounter belief-relevant discourse, such as when someone chooses to read a news article about climate change or listen to a podcast about gun control. Our research settings may impose external goals and expectations on readers that override the influence of their own intrinsic motivations tied to their beliefs. Beliefs and the variable knowledge, emotions, and goals they trigger could have their greatest impact in those situations where the reader chooses what and when to read, and chooses how they will elaborate and think about the text beyond what is minimally required for the most basic understanding.

Finally as a general point, it seems implausible that many valid conclusions could be drawn about the effects of prior beliefs on discourse processing at the most general level. Prior beliefs are themselves the result of discourse processing, with variable processing motivated by variable goals. Any given belief is likely to be tied to particular processing goals and to a mental representation shaped by past processing. Those goals and current representation features are likely to impact future processing of belief-relevant discourse. Belief-basis is one construct aimed at capturing some of this variability in goals and representations stemming from an interaction between the nature of the topic and the individual-level factors. However, the current context (e.g., reading for a grade versus personal interest or discussing to persuade versus to learn about a topic) can alter the goals that influence how prior beliefs are used in discourse processing. Thus, even when consistent findings appear to emerge across studies, it is critical to question whether that consistency arises because of shared focus on narrow and non-representative types of readers, topics, or contexts.

Acknowledgement

This work was partially supported by the National Science Foundation (NSF) under DUE grant 1535299, and by the Institute of Education Sciences, U.S. Department of Education, through Grants R305B07460 and R305A160008. Any opinions, findings, conclusions, or recommendations are those of the authors and do not necessarily reflect the views of either of these organizations.

References

Abelson, R. P. (1979). Differences between belief and knowledge systems. *Cognitive Science, 3*(4), 355–366. doi:http://dx.doi.org/10.1207/s15516709cog0304_4.

Alexander, P. A., & Dochy, F. J. R. C. (1994). Adults' views about knowing and believing. In R. Garner & P. A. Alexander (Eds), *Beliefs about text and instruction with text* (pp. 223–244). Hillsdale, NJ: Lawrence Erlbaum Associates, Inc.

Appel, M., & Richter, T. (2007). Persuasive effects of fictional narratives increase over time. *Media Psychology, 10*, 113–134.

Aronson, E. (1968). Dissonance theory: Progress and problems. In R. P. Abelson, E. Aronson, W. J. McGuire, T. M. Newcomb, M. J. Rosenberg, & P. H. Tannenbaum (Eds), *Theories of cognitive consistency: A sourcebook* (pp. 5–27). Skokie, IL: Rand-McNally.

Bailey, J. M., Pillard, R. C., Neale, M. C., & Agyei, Y. (1993). Heritable factors influence sexual orientation in women. *Archives of General Psychiatry, 50*(3), 217–223. doi:http://dx.doi.org/10.1001/archpsyc.1993.01820150067007.

Brem, S. K., Ranney, M., & Schindel, J. E. (2003). The perceived consequences of evolution: College students perceive negative personal and social impact in evolutionary theory. *Science Education, 87*, 181–206.

Britt, M. A., Kurby, C. A., Dandotkar, S., & Wolfe, C. R. (2008). I agreed with what? Memory for simple argument claims. *Discourse Processes, 45*(1), 52–84. doi:10.1080/01638530701739207.

Buehl, M. M., Alexander, P. A., Murphy, P. K., & Sperl, C. T. (2001). Profiling persuasion: The role of beliefs, knowledge, and interest in the processing of persuasive texts that vary by argument structure. *Annual Meeting of the National Reading Conference, Dec 1998, 33*(2), 269–301. doi:10.1080/10862960109548112.

Clark, J. K., Wegener, D. T., & Fabrigar, L. R. (2008). Attitude accessibility and message processing: The moderating role of message position. *Journal of Experimental Social Psychology, 44*(2), 354–361. doi:http://dx.doi.org/10.1016/j.jesp.2006.12.001.

Cobb, M. D., & Kuklinski, J. H. (1997). Changing minds: Political arguments and political persuasion. *American Journal of Political Science, 41*(1), 88–121.

Cobern, W. W. (1996). Worldview theory and conceptual change in science education. *Science Education, 80*(5), 579–610. doi:http://dx.doi.org/10.1002/(SICI)1098-237X(199609)80:5.

Corner, A., Whitmarsh, L., & Xenias, D. (2012). Uncertainty, skepticism and attitudes towards climate change: Biased assimilation and attitude polarisation. *Climatic Change, 114*(3–4), 463–478. doi:http://dx.doi.org/10.1007/s10584-012-0424-6.

Dole, J. A., & Sinatra, G. M. (1998). Reconceptualizing change in the cognitive construction of knowledge. *Educational Psychologist, 33*(2–3), 109–128. doi:10.1207/s15326985ep3302&3_5.

Eagly, A. H., Chen, S., Chaiken, S., & Shaw-Barnes, K. (1999). The impact of attitudes on memory: An affair to remember. *Psychological Bulletin, 125*, 64–89.

Eagly, A. H., Kulesa, P., Brannon, L. A., Shaw, K., & Hutson-Comeaux, S. (2000). Why counterattitudinal messages are as memorable as proattitudinal messages: The importance of active defense against attack. *Personality and Social Psychology Bulletin, 26*(11), 1392–1408. doi:10.1177/0146167200263007.

Eagly, A. H., Kulesa, P., Chen, S., & Chaiken, S. (2001). Do attitudes affect memory? Tests of the congeniality hypothesis. *Current Directions in Psychological Science, 10*(1), 5–9.

Edwards, K., & Smith, E. E. (1996). A disconfirmation bias in the evaluation of arguments. *Journal of Personality and Social Psychology, 71*(1), 5–24. doi:10.1037/0022-3514.71.1.5.

Festinger, L. (1957). *A theory of cognitive dissonance*. Stanford, CA: Stanford University Press.

Fine, G. (2003). *Plato on knowledge and forms: Selected essays*. Oxford: Clarendon Press.

Friesen, J. P., Campbell, T. H., & Kay, A. C. (2015). The psychological advantage of unfalsifiability: The appeal of untestable religious and political ideologies. *Journal of Personality and Social Psychology, 108*(3), 515–529. doi:http://dx.doi.org/10.1037/pspp0000018.

Gawronski, B., & Strack, F. (2012). Cognitive consistency as a basic principle of social information processing. In B. Gawronski & F. Strack (Eds), *Cognitive consistency: A fundamental principle in social cognition* (pp. 1–16). New York, NY: Guilford Press.

Goethals, G. R., & Reckman, R. F. (1973). The perception of consistency in attitudes. *Journal of Experimental Social Psychology, 9*(6), 491–501. doi:http://dx.doi.org/10.1016/0022-1031(73)90030-9.

Graesser, A. C., Gernsbacher, M. A., & Goldman, S. R. (Eds). (2003a). *Handbook of discourse processes*. Mahwah, NJ: Lawrence Erlbaum Associates.

Graesser, A. C., Gernsbacher, M. A., & Goldman, S. R. (2003b). *Introduction to the handbook of discourse processes* (pp. 1–23). Mahwah, NJ: Lawrence Erlbaum Associates.

Graesser, A. C., Singer, M., & Trabasso, T. (1994). Constructing inferences during narrative text comprehension. *Psychological Review, 101*, 371–395.

Green, M. C., & Brock, T. C. (2000). The role of transportation in the persuasiveness of public narratives. *Journal of Personality and Social Psychology, 79*, 701–721.

Greenberg, J., Schmader, T., Arndt, J., & Landau, M. (2015). *Social psychology: The science of everyday life*. New York, NY: Worth Publishers.

Griffin, T. D. (2008). Faith: Serving emotional epistemic goals rather than evidence coherence. In V. Sloutsky, B. Love, & K. McRae (Eds), *Proceedings of the 30th Annual Conference of the Cognitive Science Society*, pp. 2059–2064. Austin, TX: Cognitive Science Society, Inc.

Griffin, T. D., & Ohlsson, S. (2001). Beliefs versus knowledge: A necessary distinction for explaining, predicting, and assessing conceptual change. In J. D. Moore & K. Stenning (Eds), *Proceedings of the Twenty-Third Annual Conference of the Cognitive Science Society* (pp. 392–397). Mahwah, NJ: Lawrence Erlbaum Associates, Inc.

Griffin, T. D., & Salas, C. R. (2015). Affect-based prior beliefs impair comprehension of science texts. Manuscript submitted for publication.

Hart, P. S., & Nisbet, E. C. (2012). Boomerang effects in science communication: How motivated reasoning and identity cues amplify opinion polarization about climate mitigation policies. *Communication Research, 39*(6), 701–723. doi:http://dx.doi.org/10.1177/0093650211416646.

Hayes, J., Schimel, J., Williams, T. J., Howard, A. L., Webber, D., & Faucher, E. H. (2015). Worldview accommodation: Selectively modifying committed beliefs provides defense against worldview threat. *Self and Identity, 14*(5), 521–548. doi:http://dx.doi.org/10.1080/15298868.2015.1036919.

Hinze, S. R., Slaten, D. G., Horton, W. S., Jenkins, R., & Rapp, D. N. (2014). Pilgrims sailing the Titanic: Plausibility effects on memory for misinformation. *Memory & Cognition, 42*, 305–324.

Hume, D. (2000). *A treatise of human nature*, edited by David Fate Norton and Mary J. Norton. Oxford/New York, NY: Oxford University Press.

Hynd, C. R. (2001). Refutational texts and the change process. *International Journal of Educational Research, 35*(7), 669–714.

Jacovina, M. E., Hinze, S. R., & Rapp, D. N. (2014). Fool me twice: The consequences of reading (and rereading) inaccurate information. *Applied Cognitive Psychology, 28*, 558–568.

Jee, B. D., & Wiley, J. (2014). Learning about the internal structure of categories through classification and feature inference. *Quarterly Journal of Experimental Psychology, 67*(9), 1786–1807.

Kardash, C. M., & Howell, K. L. (2000). Effects of epistemological beliefs and topic-specific beliefs on undergraduates' cognitive and strategic processing of dual-positional text. *Journal of Educational Psychology, 92*, 524–535.

Kendeou, P., & O'Brien, E. J. (2014). The Knowledge Revision Components (KReC) framework: Processes and mechanisms. In D. N. Rapp & J. L. Braasch (Eds), *Processing inaccurate information: Theoretical and applied perspectives from cognitive science and the educational sciences.* (pp. 353–377). Cambridge, MA: MIT Press.

Kendeou, P., Walsh, E. K., Smith, E. R., & O'Brien, E. J. (2014). Knowledge revision processes in refutation texts. *Discourse Processes, 51*(5–6), 374–397. doi:http://dx.doi.org.ezproxy.gvsu.edu/1 0.1080/0163853X.2014.913961.

Kintsch, W. (1998). *Comprehension: A paradigm for cognition.* New York, NY: Cambridge University Press.

Kintsch, W., & Keenan, J. M. (1973). Reading rate and retention as a function of the number of propositions in the base structure of sentences. *Cognitive Psychology, 5*, 257–274.

Kowalski, P., & Taylor, A. K. (2009). The effect of refuting misconceptions in the introductory psychology class. *Teaching of Psychology, 36*(3), 153–159. doi:http://dx.doi.org.ezproxy.gvsu.edu/10.1080/00986280902959986.

Kunda, Z. (1990). The case for motivated reasoning. *Psychological Bulletin, 108*(3), 480–498. doi:http://dx.doi.org/10.1037/0033-2909.108.3.480.

Lee, M. D., & Wagenmakers, E. (2005). Bayesian statistical inference in psychology: Comment on Trafimow (2003). *Psychological Review, 112*(3), 662–668. doi:http://dx.doi.org/10.1037/0033-295X.112.3.662.

Lilienfeld, S. O., Lynn, S. J., Namy, L. L., & Woolf, N. J. (2014). *Psychology: From inquiry to understanding* (3rd ed.). Upper Saddle River, NJ: Pearson Education, Inc.

Lord, C. G., Ross, L., & Lepper, M. R. (1979). Biased assimilation and attitude polarization: The effects of prior theories on subsequently considered evidence. *Journal of Personality and Social Psychology, 37*(11), 2098–2109. doi:10.1037/0022-3514.37.11.2098.

Maier, J., & Richter, T. (2013). Text-belief consistency effects in the comprehension of multiple texts with conflicting information. *Cognition and Instruction, 31*(2), 151–175. doi:http://dx.doi.org/10.1080/07370008.2013.769997.

McNamara, D. S., & Magliano, J. (2009). Toward a comprehensive model of comprehension *The psychology of learning and motivation (Vol 51). T3 – The psychology of learning and motivation* (pp. 297–384). San Diego, CA: Elsevier Academic Press.

Munro, G. D. (2010). The scientific impotence excuse: Discounting belief-threatening scientific abstracts. *Journal of Applied Social Psychology, 40*(3), 579–600. doi:10.1111/j.1559-1816.2010.00588.x.

Munro, G. D., & Ditto, P. H. (1997). Biased assimilation, attitude polarization, and affect in reactions to stereotype-relevant scientific information. *Personality and Social Psychology Bulletin*, *23*(6), 636–653.

Munro, G. D., Ditto, P. H., Lockhart, L. K., Fagerlin, A., Gready, M., & Peterson, E. (2002). Biased assimilation of sociopolitical arguments: Evaluating the 1996 US presidential debate. *Basic and Applied Social Psychology*, *24*(1), 15–26.

Murphy, P. K., Long, J. F., Holleran, T. A., & Esterly, E. (2003). Persuasion online or on paper: A new take on an old issue. *Learning and Instruction*, *13*(5), 511–532. doi:http://dx.doi.org/10.1016/S0959-4752(02)00041-5.

Murphy, P. K., & Mason, L. (2006). Changing knowledge and beliefs. In P. A. Alexander & P. H. Winne (Eds), *Handbook of educational psychology* (pp. 305–324). Mahwah, NJ: Lawrence Erlbaum Associates.

Noordman, L. G., & Vonk, W. (1992). Readers' knowledge and the control of inferences in reading. *Language and Cognitive Processes*, *7*(3–4), 373–391. doi:http://dx.doi.org/10.1080/016909 69208409392.

Nyhan, B., Reifler, J., Richey, S., & Freed, G. L. (2014). Effective messages in vaccine promotion: A randomized trial. *Pediatrics*, *133*(4), e835–842. doi:10.1542/pEds2013-2365.

Nyhan, B., Reifler, J., & Ubel, P. A. (2013). The hazards of correcting myths about health care reform. *Medical Care*, *51*(2), 127–132. doi:http://dx.doi.org.ezproxy.gvsu.edu/10.1097/MLR.0b013e318279486b.

Petty, R. E., & Cacioppo, J. T. (1984). The effects of involvement on responses to argument quantity and quality: Central and peripheral routes to persuasion. *Journal of Personality and Social Psychology*, *46*(1), 69–81. doi:http://dx.doi.org.ezproxy.gvsu.edu/10.1037/0022-3514.46.1.69.

Petty, R. E., & Cacioppo, J. T. (1986). The elaboration likelihood model of persuasion. In L. Berkowitz (Ed.), *Advances in experimental social psychology* (Vol. 19, pp. 123–205). New York, NY: Academic.

Pintrich, P. R., Marx, R. W., & Boyle, R. A. (1993). Beyond cold conceptual change: The role of motivational beliefs and classroom contextual factors in the process of conceptual change. *Review of Educational Research*, *63*(2), 167–199. doi:http://dx.doi.org/10.2307/1170472.

Posner, G. J., Strike, K. A., Hewson, P. W., & Gertzog, W. A. (1982). Accommodation of a scientific concept: Towards a theory of conceptual change. *Science Education*, *67*, 489–508.

Prasad, M., Perrin, A. J., Bezila, K., Hoffman, S. G., Kindleberger, K., Manturuk, K., & Powers, A. S. (2009). "There must be a reason": Osama, Saddam, and inferred justification. *Sociological Inquiry*, *79*(2), 142–162. doi:http://dx.doi.org.ezproxy.gvsu.edu/10.1111/j.1475-682X.2009.00280.x.

Pratkanis, A. R. (1989). The cognitive representation of attitudes. In A. R. Pratkanis, S. J. Breckler, & A. G. Greenwald (Eds), *Attitude structure and function* (pp. 71–98). Hillsdale, NJ: Lawrence Erlbaum Associates.

Prentice, D. A., Gerrig, R. J., & Bailis, D. S. (1997). What readers bring to the processing of fictional texts. *Psychonomic Bulletin & Review*, *4*, 416–420.

Quine, W., & Ullian, J. (1978). *The web of belief* (2nd ed.). New York, NY: Random House.

Rapp, D. N., Hinze, S. R., Kohlhepp, K., & Ryskin, R. A. (2014). Reducing reliance on inaccurate information. *Memory & Cognition*, *42*, 11–26.

Rapp, D. N., & van den Broek, P. (2005). Dynamic text comprehension: An integrative view of reading. *Current Directions in Psychological Science*, *14*(5), 276–279. doi:10.1111/j.0963-7214.2005.00380.x.

Roberts, J. V. (1985). The attitude-memory relationship after 40 years: A meta-analysis of the literature. *Basic & Applied Social Psychology*, *6*(3), 221–241. doi:10.1207/s15324834basp0603_3.

Ross, M. (1989). Relation of implicit theories to the construction of personal histories. *Psychological Review*, *96*(2), 341–357. doi:10.1037/0033-295X.96.2.341.

Safer, M. A., Levine, L. J., & Drapalski, A. L. (2002). Distortion in memory for emotions: The contributions of personality and post-event knowledge. *Personality and Social Psychology Bulletin*, *28*(11), 1495–1507. doi:http://dx.doi.org/10.1177/014616702237577.

Schimel, J., Hayes, J., Williams, T., & Jahrig, J. (2007). Is death really the worm at the core? Converging evidence that worldview threat increases death-thought accessibility. *Journal of Personality and Social Psychology*, *92*(5), 789–803. doi:http://dx.doi.org.ezproxy.gvsu.edu/10.1037/0022-3514.92.5.789.

Sinatra, G. M., Kardash, C. M., Taasoobshirazi, G., & Lombardi, D. (2012). Promoting attitude change and expressed willingness to take action toward climate change in college students. *Instructional Science*, *40*(1), 1–17. doi:http://dx.doi.org/10.1007/s11251-011-9166-5.

Sinatra, G. M., Southerland, S. A., McConaughy, F., & Demastes, J. W. (2003). Intentions and beliefs in students' understanding and acceptance of biological evolution. *Journal of Research in Science Teaching*, *40*(5), 510–528. doi:10.1002/tea.10087.

Slusher, M. P., & Anderson, C. A. (1996). Using causal persuasive arguments to change beliefs and teach new information: The mediating role of explanation availability and evaluation bias in the acceptance of knowledge. *Journal of Educational Psychology*, *88*(1), 110–122. doi:http://dx.doi.org.ezproxy.gvsu.edu/10.1037/0022-0663.88.1.110.

Southerland, S. A., Sinatra, G. M., & Matthews, M. R. (2001). Belief, knowledge, and science education. *Educational Psychology Review*, *13*(4), 325–351.

Spilich, G. J., Vesonder, G. T., Chiesi, H. L., & Voss, J. F. (1979). Text processing of domain-related information for individuals with high and low domain knowledge. *Journal of Verbal Learning and Verbal Behavior*, *18*, 275–290.

Taber, C. S., Cann, D., & Kucsova, S. (2009). The motivated processing of political arguments. *Political Behavior*, *31*(2), 137–155. doi:http://dx.doi.org/10.1007/s11109-008-9075-8.

Taber, C. S., & Lodge, M. (2006). Motivated skepticism in the evaluation of political beliefs. *American Journal of Political Science*, *50*(3), 755–769.

Taylor, A. K., & Kowalski, P. (2004). Naïve psychological science: The prevalence, strength, and sources of misconceptions. *The Psychological Record*, *54*(1), 15–25.

Thagard, P. (1992). *Conceptual revolutions*. Princeton, NJ: Princeton University Press.

Vosniadou, S., & Mason, L. (2012). Conceptual change induced by instruction: A complex interplay of multiple factors. In K. R. Harris, S. Graham, T. Urdan, S. Graham, & J. M. Royer (Eds), *APA educational psychology handbook, Vol. 2: Individual differences and cultural and contextual factors. T3 – APA handbooks in psychology* (pp. 221–246). Washington, DC: American Psychological Association.

Voss, J. F., Fincher-Kiefer, R., Wiley, J., & Silfies, L. N. (1993). On the processing of arguments. *Argumentation*, *7*(2), 165–181. doi:10.1007/BF00710663.

Wiley, J. (2005). A fair and balanced look at the news: What affects memory for controversial arguments? *Journal of Memory and Language*, *53*, 95–109.

Williams, T. J., Schimel, J., Hayes, J., & Faucher, E. H. (2012). The effects of existential threat on reading comprehension of worldview affirming and disconfirming information. *European Journal of Social Psychology*, *42*(5), 602–616. doi:http://dx.doi.org.ezproxy.gvsu.edu/10.1002/ejsp.1849.

Wolfe, M. B. W., & Mienko, J. A. (2007). Learning and memory of factual content from narrative and expository text. *British Journal of Educational Psychology*, *77*, 541–564.

Wolfe, M. B., Tanner, S. M., & Taylor, A. R. (2013). Processing and representation of arguments in one-sided texts about disputed topics. *Discourse Processes*, *50*(7), 457–497. doi:http://dx.doi.org/10.1080/0163853X.2013.828480.

Wolfe, M. B., Williams, T. J., Geers, C. G., Hessler, J. K., & Simon, I. D. (August 2014). *Belief change and memory for previous beliefs after comprehension of contentious scientific information*. Paper presented at the conference of the Society for Text & Discourse, Chicago, IL.

16

Classroom Discourse
What Do We Need to Know for Research and for Practice?

Catherine O'Connor

BOSTON UNIVERSITY

Catherine Snow

HARVARD UNIVERSITY

Introduction: The Analytical and Operational Complexity of Classroom Discourse

Our goal in this chapter is to probe some recurrent puzzles in the study of oral classroom discourse. By *classroom discourse* we mean here the talk that is conducted as part of instruction, and that is intended to function as a vehicle of instruction. Our overarching purpose in this chapter is to explicate challenges that teachers must manage in putting into practice certain forms of classroom discourse. We focus on these challenges to (a) shed light on what it takes to successfully implement classroom discussion, and (b) inform researchers who need to understand these dimensions to design and interpret research on classroom instruction. We selectively review some strands of the literature on classroom discourse to describe a set of dimensions that we think are important for teacher practice and development, and for researchers who seek to better understand certain forms of classroom discourse.

We also attempt to lay out important distinctions in the discourse itself. As the other chapters in this Handbook demonstrate, the contents of human discourse are varied, complex, and difficult to summarize. By looking at classroom discourse we may seem to be taking a narrow slice of the giant array of routines, devices, positionings, and linguistic structures found in the larger world of discourse and its processes. However, even our narrow slice contains tremendous variety, and this variety must be better accounted for if we want research to reveal what works in studies of instruction that uses discussion.

Three Classroom Discourse Prototypes

First consider a simple typology of what we'll call *discourse formats* found in classrooms. Both research literature and pedagogical sources contain many terms that can be roughly grouped into two clusters. One is arrayed around the words *lecture* or *recitation*. This cluster contains the terms *monologic, closed, known-answer, quizzing,* and *teacher-centered*. In the prototypical version of this format the teacher provides information by "telling," and checks for student understanding by eliciting short answers to "closed" or "display" questions.

The other cluster is focused on the word *discussion*. Descriptors include *authentic, dialogic, open, conversational, academically productive,* and *student-centered*. This cluster can be further split into two prototypical discourse formats. One prototype is *teacher-orchestrated whole-class discussion*, in which the teacher poses open-ended questions that allow students to contribute their thinking to the whole class, and facilitates the ongoing conversation, aiming for "dialogic" talk. The goal is to allow students to respond to one another's contributions to deepen their individual and collective thinking about some consequential topic. The other prototype is *small-group student-led discussion*, in which students are given a question or task and are asked to talk about it together with little or no input from the teacher.

It's often the case that the first type, *lecture/recitation*, is held up as bad practice while the second and third are valorized. Some hold the third prototype, *small-group discussion*, as the pinnacle of classroom discourse, and assert that it is of greater value than either of the others in terms of student learning. But these valuations are asserted against a backdrop of the realities of practice. As many have pointed out, lecture/recitation is by far the most ubiquitous type of classroom discourse (e.g. Applebee et al., 2003; Parker & Hess, 2001). Even with professional development support, many teachers do not implement discussion-based classroom discourse consistently, if at all (Roberts, 2009). So one persistent question concerns the obstacles that stand in the way of putting these valued forms of discourse into practice.[1] Why should it be that most classrooms revert to lecture/recitation as their normal discourse format, when two more highly valued formats are increasingly called for by educators?

For researchers, a different question arises: one source of complexity is an increasing number of programs or approaches that feature some form of our "discussion" prototypes as part of their pedagogy. Examples include Junior Great Books (Bird, 1984), Collaborative Reasoning (Clark et al., 2003), Questioning the Author (Beck, McKeown, Sandora Kucan, & Worthy, 1996), Accountable Talk (Michaels, O'Connor, & Resnick, 2008), Reciprocal Teaching (Palincsar & Brown, 1984), Socratic or Paideia Seminars (Billings, & Fitzgerald, 2002), Book Clubs (Goatley, Brock, & Raphael, 1995), Academic Conversations (Zwiers & Crawford, 2011), Intentional Talk (Kazemi & Hintz, 2014), Word Generation (Lawrence, Crosson, Paré-Blagoev, & Snow, 2015), NGSX (Moon et al., 2014), Talk Science (Michaels & O'Connor, 2012), and Classroom Discussions in Math (Chapin, O'Connor, & Anderson, 2009), among others.

This set of programs spans all content areas and grades. What are the complex relations among discourse formats, content, and other aspects of talk (discussed further below) within each of these? While it is certainly possible to conduct studies of some of the better-structured, thus more unvarying of these approaches (cf. Wilkinson, Murphy, & Binici, 2015), the specific discourse characteristics of each approach remain a black box.

Finally, from a research standpoint, another principal goal is to deeply understand the impact of different forms of classroom discourse on student learning. But this understanding will depend on our understanding of relationships among discourse formats and a variety of possible *mechanisms* and *outcomes*. What aspects of a discourse format or practice have an impact on what aspects of learning, and why? For example, researchers might study the associations between a "discussion" format and *memory of content*, for example, measured by tests of vocabulary or problem solving. Another target might be *deeper understanding of content*, measured by transfer tasks. Some might pursue the relationship between participation in discussion pedagogy and social-emotional factors such as *long-term motivation*, or *growth mindset*, or *self-efficacy*. Still others might focus on *argumentation skills* or impact on *writing*. The mechanisms whereby a classroom discussion might influence one or more of these features are various. But to deeply understand any of these relationships, we need a relatively precise understanding of relevant aspects of the discourse formats themselves.

Our focus in this chapter arises from a long-term goal that we share with many people: to facilitate the introduction of productive discussion into default classroom practice and to better understand what results it brings and what mechanisms are at work in these results. We have worked separately and together on various approaches to achieve this goal: programs of professional development with teachers to support their use of discussion techniques in math (Chapin, O'Connor, & Anderson, 2009) and science (Michaels & O'Connor, 2012), promotion of "accountable talk" as a district-wide reform effort (Michaels, O'Connor, & Resnick, 2008), and the development of curriculum designed to facilitate and scaffold discussion (Duhaylongsod, Snow, Selman, & Donovan, 2015; Lawrence, Rolland, Branum-Martin, & Snow, 2014; Lawrence et al., 2015; Snow, Lawrence, & White, 2009). We have also conducted research on some of these, to various effects.

At the same time, we recognize that our various efforts have been inadequate, not because teachers are incapable or districts unwilling (and not for lack of trying on our parts), but because the many complexities of instruction can so easily derail attention to the discourse structures being implemented. Moreover, our own knowledge of how and what to convey to teachers is still a work in progress, as is our understanding of what is involved in teachers' development as they take on these practices. In this chapter, we focus on adumbrating a few of the complexities introduced so far, in the hope of moving toward better ways to support practitioners, while also alerting researchers to the multiple dimensions they need to take into account when studying instruction that involves classroom discourse.

We think it is an important time to turn our attention to the issue of obstacles faced by teachers in orchestrating classroom discourse. The Common Core State Standards (CCSS) indirectly call for more discussion-based learning. As the CCSS (or their analogs) start to influence classroom practice, we anticipate that teachers might well be evaluated on the frequency and quality of their classroom discussions. Before that happens, it makes sense to consider the many demands teachers encounter that may reduce their opportunities to promote classroom discussion. Articulating those demands may, in turn, help us see ways to reduce, circumvent, or manage the challenges that impede an appropriate use of discussion-based pedagogy. And as researchers become more interested in how discussion pedagogy impacts students' progress toward college and career, they will increasingly attempt to study the learning outcomes associated with particular pedagogies. Some will want to make progress in understanding the mechanisms by which discussion pedagogy brings about certain outcomes. The further we can move toward explicating the complex discursive substrate of these approaches, the better we will be able both to support teachers and to interpret the findings of researchers.

In the following section, we provide a brief overview of some basic instructional desiderata that teachers must keep in mind during any kind of teaching, and explore how they interact with the properties of our three classroom discourse prototypes. Following that, we review some of the literature on each of these three prototypes, calling attention to what is not yet well understood for purposes of practice or research. In the penultimate section entitled "Understanding the Infrastructure," we describe several additional dimensions that are central to our understanding of classroom discourse. In the Discussion section we discuss next steps.

Classroom Discourse and Instructional Concerns: Affordances and Constraints

Here we will provide a few simple examples that are intended to introduce a basic but important idea: *Teachers approach an instructional episode with a large set of immediate concerns and long-term goals. These immediate concerns and goals, however, interact in complex ways with the basic formats of classroom discourse.* We think that this idea may help us illuminate the question about why *discussion* is a rare discourse format.

Our point here is not to make judgments about yield or value yet, but rather to point to some constraints and affordances of each prototypical classroom discourse configuration so that we may begin to better understand their typical distribution and variable enactments in classrooms. We will do this by briefly imagining the same fragment of curriculum enacted in each of these three prototype discourse configurations. Further, we will consider how these three configurations enable (or disable) the teacher in succeeding in relation to a small but core set of requirements for any instruction. This simplified scenario is at the center of our attempt in this chapter to provide helpful ways of conceptualizing challenges to practitioners and to researchers.

Five Constant Concerns of Moment-to-Moment Instruction

Instruction in any content area—e.g. a lesson in math or history or literature—ideally requires thorough mastery of the content by the teacher. While this ideal is often not met, we will not include teacher content knowledge as a factor in our consideration of different discourse formats. Although such knowledge is crucial for instructional success, we will assume that readers can work out its importance on their own; we will assume in the examples below that the teacher has a sufficient mastery of content.

The view of instruction we develop involves five instructional *goals* or *constant concerns*. These concerns are persistently present no matter what choices the teacher makes about classroom discourse format. When one of these goals is not achieved, at least to some degree, there are consequences for student learning. On the other hand, resources devoted to reaching one goal may divert attention from others—the ecology of instruction is a delicate and difficult balancing act.

1   Clarity and intelligibility. If an instructional enactment is to convey information to students (no matter by what means), it must be intelligible and clear. All students have to be able to hear or see or read *and* understand what is said in or about the content.
2   Coherence and correctness. If the content of an instructional interaction is a single word or phrase, or a simple fact reiterated, coherence is not a concern, and correctness is usually trivial. But as soon as the content has any connection to past material, or needs to point to upcoming material, coherence becomes a concern. While the coherence dimension may be more obvious in complex college-level instruction, it is a concern even in 1st grade. *Will the students be able to connect the three things I have to tell them about, to understand where this is going? Will it all make sense?* And as soon as it has any complexity at all, *correctness* may be an issue. Particularly in math and science, teachers generally carry a concern: will students understand the content in the way that it is canonically understood in the relevant field? In addition, teachers have a concern that students will draw incorrect conclusions from the instruction, or will misunderstand it.

Classroom Discourse

3   Engagement. This requirement is more global and perhaps more unpredictable. Are students engaged in the instruction, no matter what its form? If they are not, its contents may not take up residence in their thinking. And notice that this concern is independent of the first two sets of concerns. Clarity/intelligibility and coherence/correctness may be in place, but students may be completely disengaged.

4   Equity. Most teachers are committed to the learning of all their students. But in many classrooms, different students need different things: in addition to the opportunity gap between affluent and poor students, there are differential access issues for English learners and for students with disabilities. The management of access, support, and differentiation where necessary is a constant concern, moment to moment. And while success in the first three goals or concerns can be helpful in securing equity, equity is an independent need which must be managed on its own.

5   Time. Anyone who has had experience in classroom teaching will note that we have left until last perhaps the most pervasive concern of all: *time*. Time pressure is omnipresent. Content coverage is a primary dimension of teacher responsibility, and teaching requires a constant calculation: for this piece of curriculum or content, how much time is required to ensure that most students can take it in? Part of this calculation is of course how much time a particular pedagogical approach to the content will take, and if one approach takes more time than another, what is the offsetting benefit? Obviously, time is most under the teacher's control in the lecture/recitation format. As soon as open discussion is introduced, a dimension of potential conflict emerges: students can be slow, verbose, hard to understand, or off-topic in a multitude of ways. As the clock ticks, the teacher must decide who to shut down or who to ignore, which presents another level of difficulty. And in the small-group setting, as the teacher circulates among multiple small groups, the time-talk calculation becomes even more complex.

These five are constant concerns; they don't fade or "get taken care of." They persist as long as instruction is going on.[2] And these five ongoing concerns have no necessary connection with any particular discourse format—they persist as concerns no matter what type of talk is going on. Yet each of them will *interact* with the teacher's choice of discourse format.

To illustrate interactions between these constant concerns and our three discourse formats, we need a sample instructional topic. So imagine a classroom in which the topic is a species classification question: is a killer whale—an Orca—a whale or not (Engle & Conant, 2002)? The teacher wants the students to begin to understand the difference between an informal use of a species term and the biological basis for a classification decision. In our imaginary classroom, students have been given a pamphlet from a local marine amusement park and a handout about species and Linnaean classification.

Orcas in Lecture/Recitation

Consider the teacher who introduces students to the problem of classification of Orcas in the lecture/recitation format. First, how is *clarity/intelligibility* managed? It is under the teacher's control. Her printed materials, what she writes on the board, her verbal speed and verbal repetition of material are completely up to her. If she asks a student a question and the student's response is unintelligible, she can ignore it or repeat it so that others can follow. In this format, the importance of a student's response to others' learning is low, so management of the *intelligibility* of the material resides in the teacher's own talk.

319

Similarly, the teacher is in charge of creating and maintaining *coherence* and *correctness*. She can decide how to tell the story so that students get the discrepancy between the common name of the animal and its classification, and the layers of embedded terms in the taxonomy within which we find whales, killer whales, dolphins, and so on. She can leave out or highlight certain facts or features to create a story that hangs together.

Many would argue that lecture/recitation is not an *engaging* form of classroom discourse (though eager students flocking to listen to renowned lecturers in massive on-line open-access courses might disagree). Whether lectures (with or without "recitation" questions) are compelling and engaging depends on what the materials look like, how they are presented, what students already know, and how the lecture is structured. Even a lecture laden with the famous "I-R-E" sequence (teacher Initiation move followed by student Response followed by teacher Evaluation; see our review of the literature below) can be engaging if it is well designed; in fact, this is one finding in the research literature: teachers who believe they are engaging their students in "discussion" are often in fact engaging in lectures with IRE turns (Alvermann et al., 1990). This is understandable: highly attentive students in a well-designed lecture/recitation may display the level of engagement often associated with "true" discussion.

How is *equity* handled in a lecture/recitation format? Materials can be presented in a way that makes them available to English learners, and background can be presented that "levels the playing field" so that all students can follow the thread. It may be that not all students will have access in the same way, but adjuncts and supports can be planned ahead of time.

Time is to a large extent also under the teacher's control in this discourse format. Lecture material can be presented in predictable time slots, and only if too many students ask too many clarification questions is the lesson plan disrupted.

Notice that there are trade-offs in this format (as in all others). For example, *engagement* of some students may suffer if they become restless because the teacher takes too much *time* in attempts to address *equity* by providing supports to make sure that all students find the thread of *coherence*. But by and large, all five requirements can be managed by the teacher in this format, with more or less success, because the teacher has maximal control over each.

Orcas in Whole-Class Discussion

How are *clarity* and *intelligibility* managed when the teacher is leading a whole-class discussion? If she asks a student a question and the student's response is unintelligible, she cannot ignore it—the student's response is supposed to count as a contribution toward the understanding of others. She can resort to repeating it or can ask for clarification. But as each student is assigned status as a contributor to the group's thinking, the teacher essentially becomes a manager of the clarity of students, whose minds and articulation she does not control. As more students participate, threats to intelligibility can become more omnipresent.

Similarly, as the teacher invites contributions, she invites threats to *coherence* and *correctness*. She is no longer in complete control of which facts or features will emerge, and so must be ready for a variety of interpretations and storylines that will start to compete for students' attention as other students bring them up. In our example lesson, these may or may not result in divergent accounts of the terminology and taxonomy of whales and dolphins. If the teacher cannot assume that coherence will emerge from student contributions, and if she cannot assert control over the narrative completely, it will give rise to a moment-to-moment challenge for order and coherence. (This can be solved in many ways, but our point is that the challenge is there, continually. It is a constant concern.)

Many have asserted that whole-class discussion leads to higher *engagement* for most students, and it is fairly obvious that students do listen to the contributions of peers in ways that are different from their attention to the teacher (Franke et al., 2015). It also changes the teacher's role in ways that may allow her to manage *engagement* with less effort.

But at the same time that the teacher is getting a break on the requirement of *engagement* overall, the *equity* dimension becomes more challenging. As student contributions to group reasoning become the focus, some students quickly come to the fore, hands raised, ready and eager to monopolize the floor. And some are very good at it. So this format can present a constant challenge: a good and knowledgeable student speaker can somewhat ameliorate the challenges to *clarity* and *coherence* while the teacher focuses on the complex task of managing the class contributions. Yet such speakers can send a message to those who are less ready or willing to contribute, a message that their contributions are not needed. This lowers engagement and can undermine the teacher's efforts at equity. And concomitantly, the teacher may subvert her own attempts at equity by systematically favoring those students who are better able to fit into the teacher's plan for coherence and clarity.

Finally, *time* planning is very difficult in whole-class discussions. Covering a unit of material almost always takes more time in a discussion format than in a lecture. High student engagement may make it harder to cut off discussion at some predetermined time limit. Furthermore, validating student contributions may require the teacher to allow excursions from the topic, which undermine coherence unless the time is available to reorient the discussion and achieve the goal for the day's lesson. Practitioners frequently mention time management as an obstacle to managing whole-class discussions.

Orcas in Small-Group Discussion

How are *clarity* and *intelligibility* managed when the teacher has assigned students to small-group discussion? Here, students are on their own. This can lead to more focused attempts by students to make sure they understand one another as they talk face to face, or it can lead to unclarity and/or avoidance. Students' capacity to ask a peer to clarify what they mean is not something the teacher can count on; in fact, most programs that attempt to introduce discussion include a period of developing "norms" to support students' capacity to do this. Thus the use of this discourse format reveals social dimensions to the intellectual work that are less evident in the other two formats. In fact, as we will discuss below, the literature on small-group discussion devotes a great deal of attention to this dimension because of its importance in blocking or facilitating productive learning.

As small groups converse, the teacher has no control over the *coherence* and *correctness* of the material. In this format what may result is five or six versions of the material, one or more per small group, depending upon what question is posed for the groups. (This is neither inherently bad nor good; its significance depends upon the larger instructional purpose.) Again, these different versions may or may not result in divergent accounts of the terminology and taxonomy of whales and dolphins, depending in part upon the materials students are given to prepare. They may or may not lead to productive dialogue about the question. Furthermore, different groups may well need different amounts of *time* to achieve similar levels of coherence and clarity, creating a management problem for the class as a whole.

Many have asserted that small-group student-led discussions lead to higher *engagement* for most students, but others have made the case that small-group work leads to many problems not evident in teacher-orchestrated large-group discussion, because of the social challenges. Finally, the *equity* dimension is perhaps most challenging in small-group work. As discussed further below, when students are left to their own devices, a number of socially mediated negative consequences can ensue, which we return to below.

Managing Instruction within Discourse Formats

Readers who are deeply familiar with the complex typology of classroom discourse may ask: aren't these three discourse "prototypes" described in an overly simple fashion? Isn't it possible to ameliorate the challenges to our five "constant concerns" with various tools, curricula, discursive moves, or "talk tools" (Michaels & O'Connor, 2015), as well as various kinds of explicit classroom discussion norms? The answer, of course, is yes; these three radically simplified examples were chosen to highlight the interdependent nature of the enterprise of classroom discourse, and to make plain the need for such materials, norms, and tools. There are many ways to ameliorate the challenges. Yet we think it unwise for either educators or researchers to assume that these challenges can be consistently headed off. They are a core part of the challenges that we think lead to the reported low incidence of productive discussion. Rarely, however, are they considered systematically, all together, in either research or instruction-focused efforts. We present them for consideration as a simplified glimpse into the problem before providing an overview of some of the literature that attempts to report research on one or more of these three prototypes.

Research on the Three Discourse Prototypes

In this section we selectively review research on each of the three instructional discourse prototypes exemplified above, to highlight both the history of the preference for discussion-based formats and the evidence supporting their effectiveness.

Research on Lecture/Recitation

Beginning in the 1960s (Bellack et al., 1966) a number of scholars—education researchers, anthropologists, and linguists—began to take note of the special characteristics of the classroom discourse most commonly found in elementary and secondary classrooms. Much of the early research on the "recitation" format focuses on the key discourse structure that defines it, specifically the three-part sequence of discourse moves that is its core: the IRF, described by Sinclair and Coulthard (1975) as the sequence of "Initiation"—a question or prompt by the teacher, "Response"—a response by a student, and "Follow-Up"—a designation for any "third turn" move by the teacher that responds to the student response. While this third turn can actually include many different kinds of responses, Mehan and Cazden focused on the ubiquitous version where the teacher asks a "known answer" question and then evaluates the response, in an "IRE" sequence (Mehan, 1979; Cazden, 2001; Mehan & Cazden, 2015).

This three-part structure is so deeply internalized by those who have been schooled in the US that it is a psychological backdrop to any classroom interaction: in the Evaluation slot, a teacher need not even utter an explicit negative evaluation to convey that the answer is wrong:

> *Teacher: Who remembers one of the kinds of eclipse we studied?*
> *Student: Annual?*
> *T: Hmm . . .*

Because the IRE sequence is so different from ordinary conversation between peers, some studies (e.g. Hellermann, 2003) examine the IRE sequence as a linguistic entity, exploring the fine-grained features of each of the discourse moves that constitute the IRE sequence, including its prosody and unique patterns that differentiate it from other three-part sequences in non-school "ordinary" talk. Conversation analysts studied its relation to talk in other special settings like courtrooms (Drew & Heritage, 1992) and its divergences from talk-in-interaction more generally (MacBeth, 2004).

Most discussions of the recitation format document its ubiquity and focus on the intellectual authority and control maintained by the teacher in this format. Many critiques center on the issues with authority in the IRF/IRE sequence, i.e. that the teacher maintains full intellectual and interpretive authority and students are positioned merely as "getters of the correct answer" and are evaluated only for this (Gutierrez et al., 1995; Gee, 1996). Others point to the fact that its structure does not afford any room for deeper investigation of more complex issues, or of questions that may not have a simple right or wrong answer (Lemke, 1990; Nystrand & Gamoran, 1990, 1991). In science and mathematics education this is particularly problematic, because many influential educators have been attempting to shift learning in STEM areas from memorization and regurgitation of facts to deeper consideration of contestable issues, and engagement in scientific and mathematical practices of the profession (Lemke, 1990; Lampert, 1990). Finally, it does not provide any opportunity for students to build understandings together, a critical dimension of democratic education (Mayer, 2012, 2015; Michaels et al., 2008).

On the other hand, several scholars have argued that there is more to the triadic sequence of IRF than the evaluative IRE, and that there are pedagogical purposes that are served by triadic sequences, even though these may be anchored in "known-answer" questions (Wells, 1993; Nassaji & Wells, 2000; Boyd & Rubin, 2006; Macbeth, 2003).

The strongest critiques are directed to its use with elementary and middle-grade students. The inevitability of lectures in secondary and tertiary education is not widely challenged, though attempts to interject opportunities for authentic interaction and student feedback are increasingly valued, as described below, particularly in post-secondary science, technology, engineering, and math (STEM) education.

Research on Whole-Class Discussion

The research strongly supports the basic position that whole-class discussion promotes some set of desirable student outcomes, but there are issues here: different researchers focus on different outcomes that are said to emerge from discussion (e.g. content learning, conceptual change, reading comprehension, participation, communicative ability), and so the research, while containing much of value, sheds little light on either the mechanism(s) by which discussion works or the complexity of launching and maintaining it.

A variety of approximations of whole-class discussions may be a feature of classrooms at every grade level, starting at prekindergarten. Demonstrably productive instructional procedures and interactions during "circle time" or the literacy block in preK–3rd-grade classrooms share many features with what is described as good discussion in the higher grades: focus on a shared experience or text, open-ended and genuine questions, engaging content, opportunities for all children to participate, and norms for how participation will occur. These features are present, for example, in "cognitively engaged talk" (Dickinson, 2001), which has been shown to predict child language outcomes in a correlational study, and are reflected in measures of classroom quality that relate to academic, language, and social skills (Mashburn et al., 2008). They are also implemented in programs shown in small-scale experimental studies to support young children's language and emergent literacy skills, e.g., Dialogic Reading (Whitehurst et al., 1994) and Text Talk (Beck et al., 1996). But scaling up programs like this and maintaining the large effect sizes observable in small-scale implementations is no easier in early childhood settings than it has been shown to be in middle or high school years (Yoshikawa et al., 2015).

Philosophy for Children (www.montclair.edu/cehs/academics/centers-and-institutes/iapc; see also http://p4c.com) is a program focused on improving young children's thinking and argumentation. It provides professional development and curricular materials to teachers of early childhood and elementary students, to help them ask "big questions" of their students and guide the subsequent discussion (Chamberlain, 1993; Lipman, 1975; Yeazell, 1982). These big questions derive from a shared experience, typically with young children, of a story read aloud. Children are encouraged to develop their own questions in response, and subsequent discussions center around those questions. While the evidence in support of the effectiveness of Philosophy for Children is limited (but see Resnick, Asterhan, & Clarke, 2015), it has developed a world-wide network of practitioners. The ultimate test of its effectiveness will derive from longitudinal studies of the children who have experienced it. One key question is whether the academic productivity of discussion is greater for students in later grades when those same students have had early experiences with an intensive discussion-focused curriculum.

Murphy, Wilkinson, Soter, Hennessey, and Alexander (2009) identified the whole-class approaches that were least likely to vary in their fidelity of implementation, and conducted a meta-analysis of those nine discussion-based pedagogies. They showed variable levels of impact on the two key outcomes tracked—reading comprehension and critical thinking. The largest effect sizes on critical thinking of whole-class approaches were obtained for Philosophy for Children, and Junior Great Books Shared Inquiry. Approaches used with primary grade students (TextTalk: Beck & McKeown, 2001; Beck et al., 1996; Instructional Conversations: Echevarria, 1995, 1996; Saunders & Goldenberg, 1998, 1999; Junior Great Books Shared Inquiry: Junior Great Books, 1992) showed the largest effects on comprehension.

It is striking that far more research on classroom discussion looks for effects on critical thinking, on comprehension skills, or on student participation measures than on content learning, though the studies by O'Connor et al. (2015) and by Ma et al. (2013) (see below) represent exceptions.

The Murphy et al. (2009) meta-analysis presented rather little data on the Paideia Seminar, in part because it was designed to improve writing rather than reading comprehension (Chesser, Gellalty, & Hale, 1997). The Paideia approach did show positive effects on factual reading comprehension, but the Paideia approach was only tried in a few classrooms and fully implemented in only some of those. In fact, partial or incorrect implementation of good programs is a recurrent finding (La Russo, Donovan, & Snow, 2016), but one that we would argue is often misinterpreted. The default interpretation is that teachers were incompetent, or perhaps insufficiently trained. We think it important to consider the possibility that teachers were juggling multiple instructional and interpersonal decisions on-line, with the result that full attention to the complexities of supporting discussion within the guidelines of any of the programs was just not feasible. Thus our attention in this chapter to the many dimensions that intersect in any analysis of classroom discourse.

Some insights about the complexities of managing discussion emerge more clearly in qualitative studies. In an intensive, teacher-focused study, Hsiao (2015) videotaped teachers implementing a discussion-based curriculum, then showed them clips of their own classrooms shortly afterwards, to elicit reactions and information about their on-line thinking and decision-making. One teacher, for example, reported experiencing considerable tension when trying to extend wait time, to allow a student with learning disabilities to participate fully in representing his group's thinking. The teacher was balancing the desire to honor one (halting and hesitant) student's right to speak with the need to keep the other students from becoming restive and losing focus. In this particular case, the teacher waited and the class cooperated, with the result that the learning-disabled student managed a helpful contribution to the discussion; dozens of other such cases may well have produced a different outcome under similar circumstances.

Hsiao's study offers considerable detail about how one teacher balanced the need for clarity and coherence with engagement and equity concerns, while also managing time allocated to discussion. Such detail is, of course, not feasibly integrated into every study of the impact of discussion on student outcomes, but ultimately any impact that is found must reflect adequate attention to all those dimensions.

The Teacher's Role: Central, Orchestrating, Neutral, Fading?

Some definitions of discussion emphasize that peer talk should be prioritized, with teachers serving only as time-keepers and referees, whereas others give the teacher a more central role as a participant, perhaps even a privileged participant, in the discussion. We think it crucial to take a micro-developmental perspective on this question. In classrooms being inducted into discussion, the teacher might be an active participant—managing turn-taking, redirecting contributions to ensure their relevance to the central topic, correcting errors of fact or interpretation, and reminding students of both social and epistemic norms. In many contexts, an active teacher role may persist for weeks or months. As students ultimately become more familiar with and more competent at discussion, though, teachers may move to the sidelines, setting up the purpose and format, but then intervening only when matters go awry. Of course, if the discussion becomes particularly difficult for any reason, many assume that the teacher should be available to step in and redirect it.

It is worthwhile noting that this process of the teacher "stepping back" or "fading" is irreducibly complex, because one must discern what it is that the teacher is stepping back from—what is already in place, what is the role the students are taking in the discussion, and as described above, what are the constraints on clarity, coherence, correctness, equity, and time? For example, in a discussion of opinions about whether a fictional character should or should not have followed a particular course of action, the teacher's stepping back may provide needed space for students to interact. In a discussion of a science experiment to determine whether weight or volume determine water displacement, that stepping back may need to be followed by a judicious reentry into the conversational fray to avoid a situation in which many students leave the class with incorrect conclusions.

Mayer (2012, 2015) makes the important point that there is complex structure to the teacher role in classroom discourse, because the intellectual activity is itself complex. Her analytic framework contrasts with those that assume that a teacher speaking is a teacher taking full authority for the intellectual content, not allowing students to share that authority. She notes that productive intellectual activity generally includes three phases: *framing* a question, *developing* responses or positions with respect to that question, and *evaluating* those responses. Her "FDE" framework explores who is responsible for each phase in a variety of discussions situated within a range of schools. While in some formats, such as lectures, teachers are responsible for all three phases, in other formats they may share with students responsibility for any one of these phases, or hand over responsibility for one or more completely.

A specific challenge in discussion is to what degree teachers should reveal their own positions on the topic under consideration. A key element contributing to the effectiveness of discussion, in our opinion, is the opportunity for students to articulate and defend their own views. That opportunity can be undermined if the teacher has an authoritative role within the discussion, as of course is the default case when the discussion centers around facts in history or science. Thus we see considerable value in focusing discussion on processes (how did you arrive at that answer? How do you know that?) or on true dilemmas, controversies for which it is acknowledged that arguments can be offered on both sides. Research offers no guidance, though, for the teacher trying to put on the "poker face" of impartiality and conceal his/her true views. One Maryland teacher implementing the Word Generation unit about restricting access to guns summarized the problem: "My students know I'm from West Virginia and I have a gun rack in my truck. Am I supposed to act like I'm not in favor of legalizing firearms?"

As students and teachers become more skilled with discussion routines and formats, though, the relevant procedures can be extended to discussion of a wider array of topics, including topics on which a majority of experts may have reached consensus, e.g., did the North win the Civil War? Is marriage a defensible institution? Can any fraction be represented as a decimal? The selection of topic for a discussion, though, ideally reflects decisions on many levels: what preparation have students had to engage in this particular discussion about this particular topic, what is the goal for which discussion is being used, and is discussion the most effective and most efficient procedure for reaching that goal?

Research on Small-Group Discussion

There is considerable research showing the value of small-group, student-managed discussions, but limited evidence about its value in comparison to whole-class formats. Richard Anderson and his laboratory, for example, have generated a robust research program exploring Collaborative Reasoning (CR), an approach to promoting discussion in which 6–8 students work together to answer a question, with limited guidance from a teacher. The questions are typically moral or social dilemmas derived from a brief narrative read by everyone in the group; control students read the same material but without the discussion component. CR activities have been shown to produce more student talk than equivalent whole-class discussions (Chinn, Anderson, & Waggoner, 2001). Experience with CR promotes an increase in relational thinking (Lin et al., 2012), an increase in quality of oral narration and argumentation, and an increase in aspects of writing quality (syntactic complexity, lexical diversity) among students in the US, including English language learners and minority students (Zhang, Anderson, & Nguyen-Jahiel, 2013; Ma et al., 2013). Studies abroad have demonstrated that CR produces better argumentation among Chinese 5th graders (Dong, Anderson, Kim, & Li, 2008) and Korean 4th graders (Kim, Anderson, Miller, Jeong, & Swim, 2011).

Given the increased opportunity for student talk in CR sessions, it is not surprising that the format supports foreign as well as second language learning. CR has also been found to enhance students' engagement and attention (Wu, Anderson, Nguyen-Jahiel, & Miller, 2013). Yet a challenge is to sort out the primary and secondary mechanisms of action; do students' thinking and literacy skills improve simply because they are more engaged, or because the back-and-forth of the discussion forces them to think more deeply?

A limitation of CR is that the discussions are typically launched by narratives that revolve around particular social issues, e.g., lying to protect a friend. In other words, the approach focuses on promoting critical thinking and reading rather than content learning, thus reducing the complexity of demands the discussion must meet. Ma et al. (2013) extended the underlying CR principles, though, to the design of collaborative group work on a science topic. Their outcome of interest was topic-related vocabulary knowledge, and they compared small-group work to direct, teacher-led instruction covering the same content. The group-work students used more vocabulary from the unit both during classroom discussions and in individually administered interviews about a related topic. Thus, it seems that the opportunity for student-student talk may be directly responsible for the positive impacts of CR, and that the approach can be combined with content learning goals.

CR typically focuses the student talk on a moral or social question drawn from a relatively simple text; the primary goal is critical thinking. Other small-group discussion approaches may focus more directly on promoting the comprehension of challenging texts. Reciprocal teaching (Palincsar & Brown, 1984), for example, is typically used with the goal of understanding a text. Student participants are given roles (predictor, questioner, clarifier, summarizer) whose actions are initially modeled by the teacher but ultimately performed independently by the students. Many other instructional techniques may use small-group discussions to varying degrees, for example project-based learning, jigsaw configurations, and partner reading or editing.

Project-based learning often involves a mix of participation structures. For example, a class decides on a joint project, but then specific tasks (e.g. writing up subparts) are undertaken by smaller task groups. Jigsawing (forming new groups with one member from each of the task groups so that each new group has an "expert" in one facet of the task) might then be introduced to ensure that everyone in the class can be exposed to all the content and can review all the entries. Such approaches can provide rich opportunity for student talk, high engagement, and accountability to get the content right, but may offer challenges in managing equity and time.

Cohen and Lotan (1995, 2014 i.a.) and Howe and Abedin in an extensive review (2013) have pointed out the fragile social net that holds together the four to six students working together on their own. Status differences, including race and ethnicity, contribute to inequitable treatment within small groups. Bossiness, bullying, ignoring, and other forms of difficult interaction can and do take place with no teacher present. And while engagement can take off in a positive direction, it can also deteriorate into off-task aimlessness. Finally, the equity dimension is perhaps most challenging in small-group work. As many have shown (Cohen, Lotan, Wortham Galton, & Williamson, 1992 i.a.), when students are left to their own devices, a number of socially mediated negative consequences can ensue, which we return to below.

Summary

In this section we have very selectively reviewed three broad categories of classroom discourse: lecture, whole-class discussion, and small-group or partner discussion. Our goal has been to sample the research on these topics to demonstrate both its contributions and its limitations. Researchers have focused on describing discourse formats and their consequences for ratios of student to teacher talk, as well as for student outcomes in literacy and critical thinking. Despite considerable agreement that it is difficult to implement discussion-based teaching consistently and effectively, there has been less attention directed to the question of why. We argue that pedagogical demands to build student engagement, promote equitable access to learning, ensure that content is presented correctly and coherently, and manage all these tasks within appropriate time limits have to be managed simultaneously, no matter what the class format. Managing them all in real time is a constant challenge, whether in lectures or in discussions.

It is crucial to note, though, that the relevant experiences of teachers and students implementing any particular program are highly variable. What is called Philosophy for Children, or Dialogic Reading, Text Talk, Reciprocal Teaching, Collaborative Reasoning, or Socratic Dialogues may vary enormously even within program exemplar. Some of that variation may derive from poor or partial implementation, but much more is likely accounted for by teacher adaptations to the needs of students, by students' prior knowledge and prior experience, by the use of the program for varying purposes and in varying contexts. Thus, we suggest that researchers interested in evaluating the consequences of such programs attend carefully to the several dimensions we have outlined in this chapter, to understand the instructional and interactive engine underneath the program label.

Wilkinson et al. (2015) address the issue of whether there is a coherent framework underlying all of the research on classroom discourse. In a survey based in part on their earlier meta-analysis, they find, not surprisingly, there is not. Researchers cite Piaget, Vygotsky, Bakhtin, Dewey, and other more nebulous formulations to provide a theoretical base for their work. In the same volume, Sfard (2015) trenchantly points out that others simply assert that "it is widely believed" that talk of some varieties is supportive of learning. She questions the generally vague connections asserted between the features of a "talking classroom" and the kinds of learning outcomes that are posited most frequently.

This weakness in the literature is not entirely, we think, the fault of the researchers. Rather, again, it points to the complexity of the central phenomenon: discourse in all its many levels of social and structural detail is linked with almost every aspect of human functioning. And each of the frameworks cited (Vygotsky, Dewey, Piaget, etc.) offers some account of most of those aspects, as does a non-theorized pragmatic view of human activity within the settings of teaching and learning. So we are unlikely to find a single framework that all will adopt to push this research forward.

Understanding the Infrastructure: Other Dimensions of Classroom Discourse

While the "orca" examples given above are simplified, we hope they serve to point to the challenges for both practitioners and researchers. But these discourse formats themselves exist within larger discourse contexts, and also are composed of smaller elements. What does the full infrastructure look like? While it will not be possible for us here to spell out a model that generates all dimensions of the multi-dimensional space of classroom discourse, we will in this section briefly introduce a few dimensions that often have an impact on the outcomes of classroom discourse and its feasibility in the first place.

Participant Structures: Configurations, Rights, and Responsibilities

In an early contribution to the study of classroom discourse, Philips (1983) examined basic configurations of classroom interaction, including whole-class talk, small-group talk, seat work, and one-on-one talk between teacher and student. Her study took place at the Warm Springs Indian Reservation, and examined how the rights and obligations associated with a variety of "participant structures" posed challenges for children in the Native American communities living there. The basic dimensions of how many people are involved, who they are, and what their rights and obligations are with respect to talk, give rise to a plethora of possible configurations, but the ones Philips discussed are basic to virtually all classrooms. Since that work, the notion of participant structure has been further elaborated to include the positioning of participants with respect to the contents of instruction in ways that make clearer the power relations involved (Herrenkohl & Guerra, 1998). Some researchers have closely studied specialized discourse formats as embodying types of social and cultural knowledge that students must acquire. A good example is Michaels' (1981) study of "sharing time" in a 1st grade. This is not a study of outcomes or effectiveness; rather it is a close analysis of conversation that shows the cultural particularity of this routine, which may seem transparent to White middle class teachers and students.

We can adapt the term *participant structure* to further specify a wide variety of specialized discourse routines that exist as special techniques within education. Approaches adopted in elementary classes but also in university classes teaching economics and microbiology include debates using "fishbowl" and "four corners" formats (e.g., Asha, 2011; Shaw, 2012); the "interview grid" (Zwiers & Crawford, 2011), and small-group discussion with role assignment (as in Reciprocal Teaching; Palinscar & Brown, 1984).

Beyond our three discourse format prototypes lie a number of these interactional routines—smaller amalgams of discourse activities and functions that have particular purposes. For example, "partner talk" appears to be a minimal version of small-group discussion, but it is often used at a very short time-scale (a minute or so) to prepare students to take part in whole-class discussion. It also occurs in more fixed routines like "Think-Pair-Share" (TPS; McTighe & Lyman, 1988), a technique that originated within the cooperative learning movement in the 1980s. The teacher asks a question or provides a prompt. Students are directed to think silently, to themselves, for some brief specified period of time, and then to confer with a partner about their response. After a specified time for pairs to talk, all pairs then orient toward the whole class and share their response.

In K-8 education, TPS is widely used, but has not, to our knowledge, been formally studied. This may be because it is transparently useful: to most educators, positive outcomes like increased individual participation, wider participation among students, and higher quality exchanges may seem commonsensical. Among other things, with TPS, students have time to think, they have the opportunity to practice what they might say, as well as possibly get reassurance from hearing what another student has to say. Teachers can allocate turns more equitably, knowing that all students have had a chance to think about and talk about the question.

Interestingly, there is research on it carried out at the college level. Fitzgerald (2013) discusses a study of TPS in an associate nursing degree program. The process is adapted for college-level learning, including long (10–15-minute) periods of thinking and writing about a series of questions, then partnering for 10–15 minutes and attempting to come to consensus on answers to each, and then sharing answers with the whole class in a teacher-orchestrated whole-class discussion format. The author cites outcomes that include increased engagement and a 20% increase in students reaching proficiency on the end-of-course assessment. Kothiyal et al. (2013) report on a study of the use of TPS in an introductory university computer science class, but their focus is solely on engagement, measured by an observation protocol and triangulated with surveys. They found that 83% of their CS-1 students ($n = 228$) were engaged most of the time during the TPS sequence. (See also Siburian (2013) and Ledlow (2001) for other college examples.)

TPS is structurally very similar to a technique called "Peer Instruction" or PI, developed by Mazur and colleagues (Crouch et al., 2007). It has been widely used in universities, particularly in physics instruction. The core principle is constant student engagement throughout the class. This is accomplished by short segments of lecture (e.g. 15 minutes) followed by a short test that is designed to highlight misunderstandings or incorrect conceptions. Each student then thinks about the test items, answers them individually, then discusses their answer choices with other students (they are encouraged to "find someone who disagrees with you"). After this the instructor holds a whole-class discussion of the results of each pair or small group and re-explains where necessary. They then move on to another topic. Crouch et al. report on surveys taken by over 400 instructors at many institutions, and find significant increases in student learning, teacher satisfaction, student satisfaction, and student retention.

Why should this simple 3-part discourse practice be of such interest to secondary and post-secondary educators in STEM fields? We think that as the information load gets greater in higher grades, the chance for dialogue and discussion becomes more difficult—the information is coming from the teacher, and the creation of opportunities for meaningful peer discussion is more challenging. In almost every case, the authors of these STEM discourse studies are acutely aware of the challenges that will make productive discussion difficult in teaching science at the post-secondary level.

We also find some qualitative studies looking closely at *how* productive discussion is or is not emerging in secondary science classes. Scott and Mortimer (2005) study the "movement between authoritative and dialogic discourse" in high school science classes in Brazil. Their approach is largely qualitative, and their conclusion, like those of other high school and college educators, acknowledges the unavoidability of recurrent "authoritative" and "non-dialogic" uses of discourse, in which the teacher is instructing students about the canonical knowledge of the field. However, they describe cases where "the authoritative introduction of new ideas is followed by the opportunity for dialogic application and exploration of those ideas. In these ways, one communicative approach follows from the other, authoritativeness acting as a seed for dialogicity and vice versa" (p. 605).

Alozie, Moje, and Krajcik (2010) study two teachers' high school project-based science classes to better understand how characteristics of typical science instruction provide obstacles to teacher attempts to orchestrate discussion; most of their sample of lessons consists of IRE sequences. They find that "curricular supports" can ameliorate these challenges to some extent, but not enough. They call for more research to better understand how teachers can be supported to use discussion in high school science.

Participation Frameworks: Incorporating the Utterance

The examples we have given so far are all focused at the level of the participants and their orientation to the task, and to one another. However, a great deal of work on everyday conversation outside of the classroom focuses on the utterance level. One important strand of this work focuses on the shifting roles and "footing" of participants in the talk (van Langenhove & Harré, 1999; Goffman, 1981): e.g. Speaker 1 explains why he's late to work, Speaker 2 (the "accuser") takes in the explanation, while a third person stands by, not yet a "ratified participant." If that third person produces an utterance defending Speaker 1, she then becomes a ratified participant and takes on the role of "defender." Thus a single utterance can change the configuration of roles or statuses in ongoing talk, as well as adding to the discourse topic.

Goodwin (1990) lays out a compelling instance of this in her study of an interactional routine among children, a routine that she dubbed "He said she said." Here, a single utterance creates and applies a set of participant roles to the interactants: *"Well, SHE said that YOU said that I wasn't wearing the right CLOTHES for that."* Such utterances configure a participation framework containing an accuser, a defendant, and an informer.

O'Connor and Michaels (2007) extended the notion of participant framework to certain forms of classroom talk by teachers, arguing that moves such as *revoicing* ("So are you saying that you agree that the divisor has to be less than four? Do I have that right?") create complex and productive participant frameworks within the classroom, positioning students as thinkers who are temporarily on equal footing with the teacher. Aligned with this work are studies that look closely at other "discourse moves." These include studies of moves that "press for reasoning" e.g. *Why do you think that?* (McElhone, 2013), as well as others that attempt to position students to think with ideas of other students (e.g. *Why do you think she said that?* and *Can you put what Jake said in your own words?* and *Who can add on to that?*). Each of these "talk moves" positions both teacher and students with respect to one another and with respect to the content of a particular utterance that has preceded it.

Although five or six basic categories recur in most accounts, the construct of "talk move" denotes an open class. Reznitskaya (in press) describes a move originating in Philosophy for Children which she calls "tracking the thread": the teacher intentionally brings together the divergent threads of a classroom discussion, drawing students' attention to the consequences for the larger discussion, and positioning them to take up the claims of previous speakers: *"So what have we got here? Joey said this, and then Jada said that, so where does that leave us?"* This is a move that is invaluable in keeping everybody on the same page and keeping things moving—it jointly "manages" the five concerns we describe above.

Considering this dimension takes us into the micro-analytic world of transcript analysis. It is not possible for us to review that extensive literature here, but there are many examples of papers that provide beautiful insights into the workings of classroom discourse and the complexities of its analysis (e.g. MacBeth, 2003). A recent collection of studies of classroom discourse residing at this micro-level is Heller and Morek (2015) and papers therein.

Amount of Talk by Students vs. Teacher

Consider two basic dimensions of classroom talk, *words uttered* (by teacher or students) and *turns taken*. Roughly, a turn consists of a speaker's production from when they begin an utterance until they stop to let another speaker talk, or are stopped by another speaker, who then begins their own turn. The unmarked norm for classroom discourse in the US is for the teacher to take long turns at talk, and then to ask a question of a student, who provides a short answer. The teacher responds briefly with an evaluation, and then moves on to another student. This results in a norm of roughly equal numbers of turns by the teacher and the students—we have seen that a one-to-one ratio is typical across a wide variety of classrooms. However, the ratio of teacher words to student words is widely variable, and depends on the length of student turns and teacher turns.

Many of the approaches to implementing discussion-based teaching have been shown to increase the ratio of student talk to teacher talk. Murphy et al. (2009), for example, document that the nine discussion formats they analyze all decrease teacher talk and increase the amount of student talk over control or comparison conditions, though they also note that variation across programs in amount of student talk is not associated with variation in outcomes. Some forms of instruction (e.g., formal debates, fishbowls) are designed, in their full-fledged forms at least, to exclude any teacher contributions to content, limiting teacher talk to management.

The Question of Question Type

A key element of successful discussion-oriented instruction is having a good question. In the research literature on discussion, "good questions" have generally been defined as open-ended, in contrast to the "known-answer" or "display" or "test" questions that initiate IRE sequences. (This widespread assumption is countered by Boyd and Rubin (2006), who argue that it is not the nature of the question itself: even "display" questions can promote substantive engagement if they are contingent on a previous student utterance.)

Open-ended questions, however, themselves vary on multiple dimensions: content focus (see above), source of the answer (e.g., personal experience vs. text; stored knowledge vs. thinking process), student capacity that the answer is meant to reveal (e.g., fact recall, text analysis, synthesis of information, provision of evidence, creativity), and degree of connection to the topic on the table. Though the value of having an overarching "big question" to guide a classroom discussion is widely attested (Goldman, Snow, & Vaughn, 2016), the effective teacher also deploys multiple questions at varying levels of openness and challenge to engage different students effectively. Thus, for example, Word Generation teachers preparing their 6th graders to debate the big question "were the Pharaohs wise investors or wasteful spenders?" posed many process-oriented requests designed to ensure that the students provided warrants (*"I want you, independently before we discuss it as a group, to tell me why you think that"*) and considered counterarguments (*"So how, if they present that to us as it's not wise, how can we flip that on its head and say that it is wise?"*) (Duhaylongsod, 2016).

In posing any such question or question sequence, teachers are recurrently confronted with the endemic challenges we have outlined above. Do the questions effectively promote clarity and coherence, in ways that are accessible to all the students? Are they engaging enough to promote active participation? Will extracting answers to them be worth the time invested? We envision the value of providing teachers with a deep repertoire of question types and some guidance about when and how to use them, but also of alerting researchers to the inadequacy of traditional question coding schemes in representing the complexity of decisions and challenges encountered in any classroom discussion. Bloom's taxonomy of types of thinking, graduated by their cognitive complexity (1956), has been used as a base for attempts to categorize types of questions, but this has not led to reliable tools for eliciting engaged discussion.

Summary

Even these few dimensions give rise to many permutations. Imagine a 6th-grade class in which students have been given a homework assignment to create a solution for a text-based problem (e.g. *read these three passages and decide what you think the main character should do and why*). Then each student is expected to give a brief presentation of their response, and then answer questions from their classmates. Is this "student-centered discourse"? How does it compare to the same assignment, given to small groups of four students, who must come to consensus during class in their own independent discussions, and then must present their solution to the whole class? What are the opportunities and costs for the teacher and for the students of these relatively small differences in discourse format?

Or imagine a 4th-grade class in which the teacher poses an "open" question, not a test question, to his students, asking them to project or predict the narrative: "Who is more likely to win the favor of the leader in Chapter 3?" He then asks ten students in succession, not commenting on their answers, but also not asking them to weigh in on one another's answers. How does that compare to a "fishbowl" in which four students hold a 5-minute discussion of the same question, while being observed by their classmates, who are then allowed to ask questions? These examples are simply intended to get readers to ponder the many dimensions of classroom discourse and content and instruction, and the permutations and interactions that we do not yet fully understand.

Discussion

The issues presented in this chapter offer more questions than answers. One goal has been to provide a broad framework, into which the available empirical work on classroom discourse can be slotted. A second goal, though, has been to raise awareness of the complexity faced by teachers in managing classroom discourse, so as to modify commitments to overly simple prescriptions for improvement, and to inform researchers studying these phenomena about the limitation of simple analytic approaches.

Beliefs vs. Empirical Evidence

People in many different relationships to education (teachers, administrators, researchers, coaches, professional development providers) hold strong and generalized beliefs about classroom discourse, beliefs based largely on personal experience. Here are some common examples: Teachers should hang back and say as little as possible. The best discussions are highly animated and the teacher should be highly involved. Group work is always better than IRE. IRE has its useful functions and is sometimes more efficacious than group work. Ideally, every student should talk during every discussion. Partner talk is an ideal precursor to large-group discussion but should be used sparingly. Partner talk should be used frequently during discussion. Talk stems (signs posted with conversational starters such as "I agree with you about ___ but . . .") can help students participate. Talk stems are a sign that the teacher is not active enough in the discussion. Talk stems are a disempowering crutch.

Individuals who hold these beliefs may have a firm basis in their experience, but what we don't know about their situations (and what they may be taking for granted) may be crucial elements in the successes or failures that shaped these beliefs. Someone who believes that, ideally, everyone should talk during every discussion may have students who are generally quite facile at using English to express their reasoning. Thus the time pressures may not be as severe. But is it necessary for everyone to talk during each discussion for equity to be achieved, or for students to benefit cognitively? Obviously, over the long haul, we want each student to have enough instances of participation in discussion centering on reasoning to get the benefits of identity, agency, practice. There is some evidence that students who do talk during a whole-class discussion do not derive any greater benefit in terms of content understanding than those who do not talk (Inagaki, Hatano, & Morita, 1998; O'Connor et al., 2017) as long as students do expect to be called on (Stahl & Clark, 1987).

Someone who believes that partner talk should be used sparingly may not have good control over the classroom norms needed to train students to come right back to large-group discussion after a moment or two of pair talk. Or it may be that their pre-adolescent students are harder to control when faced with the opportunity (or the threat) of having to talk to a partner. Or it may be that the teacher has not yet figured out what kinds of questions are most usefully meted out to partners for a brief discussion. And the other beliefs are similarly subject to a wide range of variable causes and conditions.

Issues That Deserve Further Study

Our major goal in this chapter was to articulate some of the complexity associated with defining, describing, and evaluating forms of classroom talk, either from the point of view of the educator choosing a discourse format for a lesson, or of the researcher trying to figure out whether and how that lesson benefited students. It is easy enough to condemn the lecture mode after observing a classroom of sleepy, disengaged students listening to a teacher, but it is would be a mistake to think that "simply" shifting to a whole-class discussion would be an automatic improvement. We have identified five persistent challenges that teachers need to contend with in making instructional choices, and suggested the various ways in which choice of a classroom talk format eases some while exacerbating others. And we have suggested that researchers observing instruction could usefully go beyond simple measures like percent student talk, or incidence of open-ended questions, to articulate the ways in which issues of clarity/intelligibility, coherence/correctness, equity, engagement, and time are being juggled.

We recognize, however, that it is impractical to address all the details of these issues in any single research study. There is a strong and informative history of classroom research focused on the analytic detail of student-teacher interactions. Such research is labor-intensive and time-consuming and rarely informs practice, in part because it is particular to the context in which it was carried out. We urge the field to generate methods for characterizing classroom talk formats that are relatively straightforward, easy to take to scale, and capable of providing immediate feedback, recognizing that such methods will miss much of the texture we have tried to sketch in this chapter. The task is to not lose sight of that texture, the many challenges being balanced, when interpreting the observations about classroom talk, rather than simply assuming more lecturing is bad or more discussion is good.

As we have mentioned, it is difficult to study discourse formats like small-group discussion or teacher-orchestrated whole-class discussion in the necessary detail to get a strong theory of the mechanisms by which they bring about their impacts. Not surprisingly, smaller and more tightly constrained routines like Think-Pair-Share are easier to study, as discussed above, and have been studied in more rigorous ways. Another striking example includes studies of "wait time"—the practice of a teacher (a) waiting for at least 3 seconds after asking a question before calling on a student, and (b) waiting for at least 3 seconds after a student responds before saying something else. Mary Budd Rowe, a university science educator, describes two decades of findings (Bianchini, 2008), including profound changes in how, when, and which students participate in classroom talk, the quality of talk, the quality of learning, and the ways teachers interact with students at micro- and macro-interactional levels, at all grade levels from preschool to university classes. These studies were enabled by the discrete, simple, and observable nature of the practice. This also helped researchers to pursue many different types of outcomes. In some sense, a complete theory of *why* wait time has the effects it has is less important—there are many plausible candidates for mechanisms. (Unfortunately, these outstanding results are not seen in most classrooms: wait time is very hard to perform consistently.)

Perhaps the closest approximation to the ideal studies we envision containing extensive analysis of discourse characteristics and associated outcomes is a series of papers by

Wilkinson, Soter, and Murphy in various combinations, in the development of a model they call "Quality Talk" (Wilkinson et al., 2015; Murphy et al., 2009). Grounded in a meta-analysis of the programs and approaches discussed above in the literature review, as well as in close observation of classroom discussions, their model spans four dimensions that integrate discourse and pedagogical considerations, including (a) an ideal instructional frame, (b) discourse signs and tools used to promote productive talk about text, (c) teacher conversational moves, and (d) a set of pedagogical principles (Wilkinson et al., 2015). While their focus has been on narrative fiction, they are working to expand it to expository texts. The model is specific (e.g. the ideal instructional frame is where teachers have "control over choice of text and topic, but students have interpretive authority and control of turns" (p. 149)), but allows for a range of types of discussion (e.g. efferent, expressive, critical-analytic stance).

But here there are more challenges: models like these are complex interventions, usually grounded in particular disciplines, with particular configurations of resources, such as texts, computer equipment, and so on, and particular curricular choices. It is possible to demonstrate success on a variety of outcomes. How do we organize and use those findings across content areas of learning? Across ages? Second, how do we begin to explore more deeply what aspects of the talk are having what impacts? But this still leaves our original question: if results continue to accrue that talk of some kinds is supportive of learning and supportive of the cognitive and emotional capacities that surround content learning, then why is it so rare? And how can we come to support teachers in their use of it?

We have noted many points on which future research could provide illumination. What are the optimal procedures for preparing students to participate in discussions, and for avoiding or defusing the micro-aggressions and unintended offenses that are likely to occur? How do discussion skills develop over the course of a school year? Should teachers gradually take a back seat, or continue to participate actively? Are the affordances and consequences of discussion the same for elementary, secondary, and higher education students, or should different techniques be used in different education settings? How do the ideas and arguments developed in discussion transfer to students' writing, or to their thinking? These and many other questions deserve ongoing research attention. But perhaps the most pressing question is what advice we should be giving teachers about when, how, and how much discussion to introduce into their classrooms.

Type, Intensity, Duration, Frequency

Consider the complexity of exercise science. Muscle strength, cardiac health, and mood adjustment are all affected by exercise, but they are differentially responsive to different types, intensities, durations, and frequencies of exercise. In a recent well-controlled study, one minute of high-intensity exercise within a ten-minute moderate exercise period improved cardiometabolic health as well as 50 minutes of moderate exercise three times per week (Gillen et al., 2016). Now consider some comparable basic questions about classroom discourse and its outcomes. How much discussion is necessary for a benefit to accrue? This will obviously depend upon the outcome we are interested in. Intuitively, three significant and productive discussions per year are unlikely to result in a significant change in students' "growth mindset" about their own abilities to reason. It may not contribute to their *communicative stamina*—their ability to persist in trying to understand others, and clarify their own contribution. But it may be that infrequent discussions of high-leverage topics make a difference in motivation and in content learning of the relevant topics, beyond what one would predict. We do not yet know.

Student Opportunity to Learn vs. Teacher Burnout

Why is it important to know these things? We started out making the point early in the chapter that each discourse format has its own constraints and affordances, its own way of supporting or complexifying the instructional goals and constant concerns that a teacher has. We need to understand better what the outcomes are for these three formats (and their many subvarieties) for the following reasons.

As many researchers and policy analysts are increasingly articulating, we have major issues with opportunity to learn for many students. For students in under-resourced settings, and students who have lacked access to language and literacy resources, rich and productive discussion that involves them may provide a high-quality experience—an opportunity to learn content, language, reasoning, and argumentation all at the same time. It may offer these benefits *if it is structured in a productive way and is delivered with adequate frequency and duration*. But what are those values? We don't fully know.

Our lack of knowledge has a cost. It may be that we are asking teachers to conduct discussions in formats that are more demanding than they need to be. Just as fitness programs lose many participants by featuring demanding routines that only those with the most leisure time (or other sources of support) can keep up with, it may be that we are asking teachers to do something that has so many dimensions of variation, so many degrees of freedom, so much to manage, that it is unlikely to go well in the majority of cases. Even if students benefit, teachers may lose resolve through exhaustion or lack of support from supervisors who do not realize the challenges some forms of discussion present.

A similar problem has motivated exercise scientists to explore whether there are more moderate ways to get essentially the same benefits without the risk of exhaustion and burnout, or injury. With more and better research, we might be able to establish whether a minimal increment of discussion is required for a particular level of benefit in a particular kind of classroom. To do this, we need to be able to track the key dimensions of importance inside the discussion space, as well as the key factors in the larger situation that impinge on decisions about discussion. We have attempted in this chapter to start to sketch those dimensions and factors, in the hope of stimulating more research targeted at these crucial questions.

Acknowledgments

We gratefully acknowledge the advice and encouragement of our editor, Anne Britt. During the writing of this chapter the authors were supported by the Institute of Education Sciences, U.S. Department of Education, through Grant R305F100026 to the Strategic Educational Research Partnership Institute and grant R305F100005 to Educational Testing Service as part of the Reading for Understanding Research Initiative. The opinions expressed are those of the authors and do not represent views of the Institute or the U.S. Department of Education.

Further Reading

Duhaylongsod, L., Snow, C. E., Selman, R., & Donovan, M. S. (2015). Toward disciplinary literacy: Dilemmas and challenges in designing history curriculum to support middle school students. *Harvard Educational Review, 85*, 587–608.

Howe, C., & Abedin, M. (2013). Classroom dialogue: A systematic review across four decades of research. *Cambridge Journal of Education, 43*(3), 325–356.

Mayer, S. J. (2012). *Classroom discourse and democracy: Making meanings together. Educational Psychology: Critical Pedagogical Perspectives. Volume 13*. New York, NY: Peter Lang.

Michaels, S., & O'Connor, C. (2017). From recitation to reasoning: Implementing scientific and engineering practices through talk. In C. Schwarz, C. Passmore, & B. J. Reiser (Eds), *Helping Students Make Sense of the World Using Next Generation Science and Engineering Practices* (pp. 311–336). Arlington, VA: NSTA Press.

Reznitskaya, A. G., Glina, M., Carolan, B., Michaud, O., Rogers, J., & Sequeira, L. (2012). Examining transfer effects from dialogic discussions to new tasks and contexts. *Contemporary Educational Psychology, 37*(4), 288–306.

Wilkinson, I. A. G., Murphy, P. K., & Binici, S. (2015). Dialogue-intensive pedagogies for promoting reading comprehension: What we know, what we need to know. In L. B. Resnick, C. Asterhan, and S. Clarke (Eds), *Socializing Intelligence through Academic Talk and Dialogue*, Ch. 3, pp. 37–50. DOI: 10.3102/978-0-935302-43-1_3. Washington, DC: American Educational Research Association.

Notes

1 Choice of discourse format is also related to the teacher's specific goal. In reviewing the research on classroom talk, we found some lack of specificity among those who advocate the use of discussion formats about the purpose of discussion or the mechanism by which it is presumed to operate. We make an effort in the following sections to identify the nature of any measured impacts (student participation, student engagement, critical thinking, argumentation skills, literacy skills, content learning), but whether teachers choosing a particular participation format for a lesson have those specific goals in mind is not always clear.

2 Similar or parallel constant concerns can be found in other high-demand occupations, such as surgery, e.g. adequate light and access to tools; support for connected physical subsystems; monitoring patient status; and attention to individual pre-existing conditions and needs. These don't usually garner individual attention from outsiders unless they are missing and disaster results.

References

Alozie, N. M., Moje, E. B., & Krajcik, J. S. (2010). An analysis of the supports and constraints for scientific discussion in high school project-based science. *Science Education, 94*(3), 395–427.

Alvermann, D. E., O'Brien, D. G., & Dillon, D. R. (1990). What teachers do when they say they're having discussions of content area reading assignments: A qualitative analysis. *Reading Research Quarterly, 4*, 296–322.

Applebee, A. N., Langer, J. A., Nystrand, M., & Gamoran, A. (2003). Discussion-based approaches to developing understanding: Classroom instruction and student performance in middle and high school English. *American Educational Research Journal, 40*(3), 685–730.

Arnold, J. E., Tanenhaus, M. K., Altmann, R. J., & Fagnano, M. (2004). The old and thee, uh, new disfluency and reference resolution. *Psychological Science, 15*(9), 578–582.

Asha, R. (2011). Benefits of in-class debates as an instructional strategy. *Economic Affairs, 56*, 139–145.

Beck, I. L., & McKeown, M. G. (2001). Capturing the benefits of read-aloud experiences for young children. *Reading Teacher, 55*, 10–20.

Beck, I. L., McKeown, M. G., Sandora, C., Kucan, L., & Worthy, J. (1996). Questioning the author: A year-long classroom implementation to engage students with text. *The Elementary School Journal, 96*, 385–414.

Bellack, A., Kliebard, H. K., Hyman, R.T., & Smith, F. L., Jr. (1966). *The language of the classroom*. New York, NY: Teachers College Press.

Bianchini, J. A. (2008). Mary Budd Rowe: A storyteller of science. *Cultural Studies of Science Education, 3*(4), 799–810.

Billings, L., & Fitzgerald, J. (2002). Dialogic discussion and the Paideia Seminar. *American Educational Research Journal, 39*, 907–941.

Bird, J. B. (1984). *Effects of fifth graders' attitudes and critical thinking/reading skills resulting from a Junior Great Books program*. Unpublished doctoral dissertation, Rutgers: The State University of New Jersey, New Brunswick.

Bloom, B. S. (1956). *Taxonomy of educational objectives: The classification of educational goals: Cognitive domain*. London: Longman.

Boyd, M. P., & Rubin, D. L. (2002). Elaborated student talk in an elementary ESoL classroom. *Research in the Teaching of English*, 495–530.

Boyd, M. P., & Rubin, D. L. (2006). How contingent questioning promotes extended student talk: A function of display questions, *Journal of Literacy Research, 38*(2), 141–169.

Cazden, C. (2001). *Classroom discourse: The language of learning and teaching.* Portsmouth, NH: Heinemann.

Chamberlain, M. A. (1993). *Philosophy for Children program and the development of critical thinking of gifted elementary students.* Unpublished doctoral dissertation, University of Kentucky, Lexington.

Chapin, S. H., & O'Connor, C. (2007). Academically productive talk: Supporting students' learning in mathematics. *The Learning of Mathematics,* 113–128.

Chapin, S., O'Connor, C., & Anderson, N. C. (2009). *Classroom discussions: Using math talk to help students learn, Grades K-6,* 2nd edition. New York, NY: Math Solutions.

Chesser, W. D., Gellalty, G. B., & Hale, M. S. (1997). Do Paideia Seminars explain higher writing scores? *Middle School Journal, 29,* 40–44.

Chinn, C. A., Anderson, R. C., & Waggoner, M. A. (2001). Patterns of discourse in two kinds of literature discussion. *Reading Research Quarterly, 36,* 378–411.

Clark, A. M., Anderson, R. C., Kuo, L. J., Kim, I. H., Archodidou, A., & Nguyen-Jahiel, K. (2003). Collaborative reasoning: Expanding ways for children to talk and think in school. *Educational Psychology Review, 15*(2), 181–198.

Cohen, E. G., & Lotan, R. A. (1995). Producing equal-status interaction in the heterogeneous classroom. *American Educational Research Journal, 32*(1), 99–120.

Cohen, E. G., & Lotan, R. A. (2014). *Designing groupwork: Strategies for the heterogeneous classroom,* 3rd edition. New York, NY: Teachers College Press.

Crouch, C. H., Watkins, J., Fagen, A. P., & Mazur, E. (2007). Peer instruction: Engaging students one-on-one, all at once. *Research-Based Reform of University Physics, 1*(1), 40–95.

Dickinson, D. K. (2001). Large-group and free-play times: Conversational settings supporting language and literacy development. In D. K. Dickinson & P. O. Tabors (Eds), *Beginning literacy with language* (pp. 223–255). Baltimore, MD: Brookes.

Dong, T., Anderson, R. C., Kim, I. H., & Li, Y. (2008). Collaborative reasoning in China and Korea. *Reading Research Quarterly, 43*(4), 400–424.

Donovan, M. S., & Bransford, J. D. (Eds). (2005). *How students learn: History, mathematics, and science in the classroom.* Washington, DC: National Academies Press.

Drew, P., & Heritage, J. (1992). *Analyzing talk: An introduction. Talk at work: Interaction in institutional settings.* Cambridge: Cambridge University Press.

Dudley-Marling, C., & Michaels, S. 2012. Shared inquiry: Making students smart. In C. Dudley-Marling & S. Michaels (Eds), *High expectation curricula: Helping all students succeed with powerful learning.* New York, NY: Teachers College Press.

Duhaylongsod, L. (2016). *Promoting the intellectual skills of argumentation: Case studies of teachers and students in urban middle schools using a debate-based social studies curriculum.* Unpublished doctoral dissertation, Harvard Graduate School of Education.

Duhaylongsod, L., Snow, C. E., Selman, R., & Donovan, S. (2015). Toward disciplinary literacy: Design principles for curriculum to support both teachers and students in urban middle schools. *Harvard Educational Review, 85,* 587–608.

Echevarria, J. (1995). Interactive reading instruction: A comparison of proximal and distal effects of instructional conversations. *Exceptional Children, 61,* 536–552.

Echevarria, J. (1996). The effects of instructional conversations on the language and concept development of Latino students with learning disabilities. *The Bilingual Research Journal, 20,* 339–363.

Engle, R., & Conant, F. (2002). Guiding principles for fostering productive disciplinary engagement: Explaining an emergent argument in a community of learners' classroom. *Curriculum and Instruction, 20,* 399–483.

Fitzgerald, D. (2013). Employing think–pair–share in associate degree nursing curriculum. *Teaching and Learning in Nursing, 8*(3), 88–90.

Franke, M. L., Turrou, A. C., Webb, N. M., Ing, M., Wong, J., Shin, N., & Fernandez, C. (2015). Student engagement with others' mathematical ideas: The role of teacher invitation and support moves. *The Elementary School Journal, 116,* 126–148.

Galton, M., & Williamson, J. (1992). *Group work in the primary classroom.* London: Routledge.

Gee, James (1996). *Social linguistics and literacies: Ideology and discourses,* 2nd edition. London: Taylor & Francis.

Gillen, J. B., Martin, B. J., MacInnis, M. J., Skelly, L. E., Tarnopolsky, M. A., & Gibala, M. J. (2016). Twelve weeks of sprint interval training improves indices of cardiometabolic health similar to traditional endurance training despite a five-fold lower exercise volume and time commitment. *PLOS One*, *11*(4), e0154075.

Goatley, V. J., Brock, C. H., & Raphael, T. E. (1995). Diverse learners participating in regular education "Book Clubs." *Reading Research Quarterly*, *30*, 352–380.

Goffman, E. (1978). Response cries. *Language*, 787–815.

Goffman, E. (1981). Footing. *Forms of Talk*, 124–159.

Goldman, S., Snow, C., & Vaughn, S. (in press). Common themes in teaching reading for understanding: Lessons from three projects. *Journal of Adolescent and Adult Literacy*.

Goodwin, M. H. (1990). *He-said-she-said: Talk as social organization among black children.* Bloomington, IN: Indiana University Press.

Gutierrez, K., Larson, J., & Kreuter, B. (1995). Cultural tensions in the scripted classroom: The value of the subjugated perspective. *Urban Education*, *29*, 410–442.

Heller, V., & Morek, M. (2015). Academic discourse as situated practice: An introduction. *Linguistics and Education*, *31*, 174–186.

Hellermann, J. (2003). The interactive work of prosody in the IRF exchange: Teacher repetition in feedback moves. *Language in Society*, *32*(1), 79–104. DOI:10.23074169241.

Herrenkohl, L. R., & Guerra, M. R. (1998). Participant structures, scientific discourse, and student engagement in fourth grade. *Cognition and Instruction*, *16*(4), 431–473.

Howe, C., & Abedin, M. (2013). Classroom dialogue: A systematic review across four decades of research. *Cambridge Journal of Education*, *43*(3), 325–356.

Howe, C., Tolmie, A., Duchak-Tanner, V., & Rattray, C. (2000) Hypothesis testing in science: Group consensus and the acquisition of conceptual and procedural knowledge. *Learning and Instruction*, *10*(4), 369–391.

Hsiao, L. (2015). *Moving the discussion through surprises and dilemmas: Teacher learning in academic discussion.* Unpublished doctoral dissertation, Harvard Graduate School of Education.

Hymes, D. (1974). *Foundations of sociolinguistics: An ethnographic approach.* Philadelphia, PA: University of Pennsylvania Press.

Inagaki, K., Hatano, G., & Morita, E. (1998). Construction of mathematical knowledge through whole-class discussion. *Learning and Instruction*, *8*(6), 503–526.

Junior Great Books. (1992). *The Junior Great Books curriculum of interpretive reading, writing and discussion.* Chicago, IL: Great Books Foundation.

Kazemi, E., & Hintz, A. (2014). *Intentional talk: How to structure and lead productive mathematical discussions.* Portland, ME: Stenhouse Publishers.

Kim, I. H., Anderson, R. C., Miller, B., Jeong, J., & Swim, T. (2011). Influence of cultural norms and collaborative discussions on children's reflective essays. *Discourse Processes*, *48*(7), 501–528.

Kothiyal, A., Majumdar, R., Murthy, S., & Iyer, S. (2013, August). Effect of think-pair-share in a large CS1 class: 83% sustained engagement. In *Proceedings of the Ninth Annual International ACM Conference on International Computing Education Research* (pp. 137–144). New York, NY: ACM.

Lampert, M. (1990). When the problem is not the question and the solution is not the answer: Mathematical knowing and teaching. *American Educational Research Journal*, *27*(1), 29–63.

La Russo, M., Donovan, S., & Snow, C. (2016), Implementation challenges for tier one and tier two school-based programs for early adolescents. In B. Foorman (Ed.), *Challenges and solutions to implementing effective reading intervention in schools, new directions in child and adolescent development* (p. 152). New York, NY: Wiley.

Lawrence, J., Crosson, A., Paré-Blagoev, J., & Snow, C. (2015). Word generation randomized trial: Discussion mediates the impact of program treatment on academic word learning. *American Educational Research Journal*. DOI: 10.3102/0002831215579485.

Lawrence, J., Rolland, R., Branum-Martin, L., & Snow, C. (2014). Generating vocabulary knowledge for at-risk middle school readers: Contrasting program effects and underlying growth trajectories. *Journal of Education for Students Placed at Risk (JESPAR)*, *19*, 76–97. DOI: 10.1080/10824669.2014.958836.

Ledlow, S. (2001). *Using think-pair-share in the college classroom.* Arizona State University Press: Center for Learning and Teaching Excellence.

Lemke, J. (1990). *Talking science: Language, learning and values.* Westport, CN: Ablex Publishing.

Lin, T.-J., Anderson, R. C., Hummel, J. E., Jadallah, M., Miller, B. W., Nguyen-Jahiel, K., & Dong, T. (2012). Children's use of analogy during collaborative reasoning. *Child Development, 83,* 1429–1443. DOI: 10.1111/j.1467-8624.2012.01784.x.

Lipman, M. (1975). *Philosophy for Children.* (ERIC Document Reproduction Service No. ED103296.)

Ma, S., Anderson, R. C., Lin, T.-J., Zhang, J., Morris, J. A., Nguyen-Jahiel, K., . . . Latawiec, B. (2013). Influence of collaborative group work on English language learners' oral narratives. Manuscript submitted for publication.

Martin, J. (1998). Literature circles. *Thresholds in Education, 24,* 15–19.

Mashburn, A. J., Pianta, R. C., Hamre, B. K., Downer, J. T., Barbarin, O. A., Bryant, D., . . . Howes, C. (2008). Measures of classroom quality in prekindergarten and children's development of academic, language, and social skills. *Child Development, 79,* 732–749.

Mayer, S. J. (2009). Conceptualizing interpretive authority in practical terms. *Language and Education, 23*(3), 199–216.

Mayer, S. J. (2012). *Classroom discourse and democracy: Making meanings together. Educational Psychology: Critical Pedagogical Perspectives. Volume 13.* New York, NY: Peter Lang.

Mayer, S. J. (2015). Representing Dewey's constructs of continuity and interaction within classrooms. *Education and Culture, 31*(2), Article 5. Available at: http://docs.lib.purdue.edu/eandc/vol31/iss2/art5.

Macbeth, D. (2003). Hugh Mehan's learning lessons reconsidered: On the differences between the naturalistic and critical analysis of classroom discourse. *American Educational Research Journal, 40*(1), 239–280.

Macbeth, D. (2004). The relevance of repair for classroom correction. *Language in Society, 33*(5), 703–736.

McElhone, D. (2013). Pressing for elaboration in student talk about texts. *Journal of Classroom Interaction, 48*(1), 4–15.

McTighe, J., & Lyman, F. T. (1988). Cueing thinking in the classroom: The promise of theory-embedded tools. *Educational Leadership, 45*(7), 18–24.

Mehan, H. (1979). *Learning lessons.* Cambridge, MA: Harvard University Press.

Mehan, H., & Cazden, C. (2015). The study of classroom discourse: Early history and current developments. In L. Resnick, C. Asterhan, & S. Clarke (Eds), *Socializing intelligence through academic talk and dialogue* (pp. 13–34). Washington, DC: American Educational Research Association.

Mercer, N., Dawes, L., Wegerif, R., & Sams, C. (2004). Reasoning as a scientist: Ways of helping children to use language to learn science. *British Educational Research Journal, 30*(3), 359–377.

Michaels, S. (1981). "Sharing time": Children's narrative styles and differential access to literacy. *Language in Society, 10*(3), 423–442.

Michaels, S., & O'Connor, C. (2012). *Talk science primer.* Cambridge, MA: TERC.

Michaels, S., & O'Connor, C. (2015). Conceptualizing talk moves as tools: Professional development approaches for academically productive discussions. In L. Resnick, C. Asterhan, & S. Clarke (Eds), *Socializing intelligence through academic talk and dialogue* (pp. 347–362). Washington, DC: American Educational Research Association.

Michaels, S., O'Connor, C., & Resnick, L. (2008). Deliberative discourse idealized and realized: Accountable talk in the classroom and in civic life. *Studies in Philosophy and Education, 27*(4), 283–297. DOI: 10.1007/s11217-007-9071-1.

Moon, J., Passmore, C., Reiser, B., & Michaels, S. (2014). Beyond comparisons of online versus face-to-face PD: Commentary in response to Fishman et al., "Comparing the Impact of Online Versus Face-to-Face Professional Development in the Context of Curriculum Implementation." *Journal of Teacher Education, 65*(2), 172–176.

Murphy, K., Wilkinson, I., Soter, A., Hennessey, M., & Alexander, J. (2009). Examining the effects of classroom discussion on student comprehension of text: A meta-analysis. *Journal of Educational Psychology, 101,* 740–764.

Nassaji, H., & Wells, G. (2000). What's the use of "triadic dialogue"?: An investigation of teacher-student interaction. *Applied Linguistics, 21*(3), 376–406.

Nystrand, M., & Gamoran, A. (1990). Student engagement: When recitation becomes conversation. Available at https://eric.ed.gov/?id=ED323581.

Nystrand, M., & Gamoran, A. (1991). Instructional discourse, student engagement, and literature achievement. *Research in the Teaching of English,* 261–290.

O'Connor, C., & Michaels, S. (2007). When is dialogue "dialogic"? *Human Development, 50*(5), 275–285.

O'Connor, C., Michaels, S., & Chapin, S. (2015). "Scaling down" to explore the role of talk in learning: From district intervention to controlled classroom study. *Socializing Intelligence through Talk and Dialogue*. Washington, DC: American Educational Research Association.

O'Connor, C., Michaels, S., Chapin, S., & Harbaugh, A. G. (2017). The silent and the vocal: Participation and learning in whole class discussion. *Learning and Instruction, 48*, 5–13.

Palincsar, A. M., & Brown, A. (1984). Reciprocal teaching of comprehension-fostering and comprehension-monitoring activities. *Cognition and Instruction, 1*, 117–185.

Parker, W. C., & Hess, D. (2001). Teaching with and for discussion. *Teaching and Teacher Education, 17*, 273–289.

Philips, S. U. (1983). *The invisible culture: Communication in classroom and community on the Warm Springs Indian Reservation*. Long Grove, IL: Waveland Press.

Resnick, L., Asterhan, C., & Clarke, S. (Eds) (2015). *Socializing intelligence through academic talk and dialogue*. Washington, DC: American Educational Research Association.

Reznitskaya, A., Kuo, L. J., Clark, A. M., Miller, B., Jadallah, M., Anderson, R. C., & Nguyen-Jahiel, K. (2009). Collaborative reasoning: A dialogic approach to group discussion. *Cambridge Journal of Education, 39*(1), 29–48.

Reznitskaya, A., & Wilkinson, I. A. G. (2017). *The most reasonable answer: Helping students build better arguments together*. Boston, MA: Harvard Education Press.

Roberts, A. M. (2009). *In search of discussion in the standards-based middle school social studies classroom*. Unpublished dissertation, Virginia Polytechnic Institute and State University.

Saunders, W., & Goldenberg, C. (1998). The effects of an instructional conversation in Latino students' concepts of friendship and story comprehension. In R. Horowitz (Ed.), *The evolution of talk about text: Knowing the world through classroom discourse*. Newark, DE: International Reading Association.

Saunders, W. M., & Goldenberg, C. (1999). Effects of instructional conversations and literature logs on limited- and fluent-English-proficient students' story comprehension and thematic understanding. *The Elementary School Journal, 99*, 277–301.

Scott, P., & Mortimer, E. (2005). Meaning making in high school science classrooms: A framework for analysing meaning making interactions. *Research and the Quality of Science Education*, 395–406.

Sfard, A. (2015). Why all this talk about talking classrooms? Theorizing the relation between talking and learning. Available at www.academia.edu/19958936/Why_All_This_Talk_About_Talking_Classrooms_Theorizing_the_Relation_Between_Talking_and_Learning.

Shaw, J. (2012). Using small group debates to actively engage students in an introductory microbiology course. *Journal of Microbiology Education, 13*, 155–160.

Siburian, T.A. (2013). Improving students' achievement on writing descriptive text through Think Pair Share. *The International Journal of Language Learning and Applied Linguistics World, 3*, 32–44.

Sinclair, J. M., & Coulthard, M. (1975). *Towards an analysis of discourse*. New York, NY: Oxford University Press.

Snow, C., Lawrence, J., & White, C. (2009). Generating knowledge of academic language among urban middle school students. *Journal of Research on Educational Effectiveness, 2*, 325–344. Available at www.informaworld.com/smpp/content~db=all~content=a915824847.

Stahl, S., & Clark, C. (1987). The effects of participatory expectations in classroom discussion on the learning of science vocabulary. *American Educational Research Journal, 24*, 541–555.

van der Veen, C., de Mey, L., van Kruistum, C., & van Oers, B. (2016). The effect of productive classroom talk and metacommunication on young children's oral communicative competence and subject matter knowledge: An intervention study in early childhood education. *Learning and Instruction*. DOI: 10.1016/j.learninstruc.2016.06.001.

Van Langenhove, L., & Harré, R. (1999). *Introducing positioning theory*. New York, NY: Blackwell.

Wells, Gordon (1993). Reevaluating the IRF sequence: A proposal for the articulation of theories of activity and discourse for the analysis of teaching and learning in the classroom. *Linguistics in Education, 5*, 1–37.

Whitehurst, G. J., Arnold, D. S., Epstein, J. N., Angell, A. L., Smith, M., & Fischel, J. E. (1994). A picture book reading intervention in day care and home for children from low-income families. *Developmental Psychology, 30*, 679–689. http://dx.doi.org/10.1037/0012-1649.30.5.679.

Wilkinson, I. A., Murphy, P. K., & Binici, S. (2015). Dialogue-intensive pedagogies for promoting reading comprehension: What we know, what we need to know. *Socializing Intelligence through Academic Talk and Dialogue*, 1–12.

Williams, B. G. (1999). Emergent readers and Literature Circle discussions. In J. R. Dugan, P. E. Linder, W. M. Linek, & E. G. Sturtevant (Eds), *Advancing the world of literacy: Moving into the 21st century* (pp. 44–53). Carrollton, GA: The College Reading Association.

Wu, X., Anderson, R. C., Nguyen-Jahiel, K., & Miller, B. (2013). Enhancing motivation and engagement through collaborative discussion. *Journal of Educational Psychology, 105*(3), 622–632.

Yeazell, M. I. (1982). Improving reading comprehension through philosophy for children. *Reading Psychology: An International Quarterly, 3*, 239–246.

Yoshikawa, H., Leyva, D., Snow, C., Treviño, E., Arbour, M., Barata, C., . . . & D'Sa, N. (2015). Experimental impacts of a teacher professional development program in Chile on preschool classroom quality and child outcomes. *Developmental Psychology, 51*, 309–322.

Zhang, J., Anderson, R. C., & Nguyen-Jahiel, K. (2013). Language-rich discussions for English language learners. *International Journal of Educational Research, 58*, 44–60.

Zhang, X., Anderson, R. C., Dong, T., Nguyen-Jahiel, K., Li, Y., Lin, T.-J., & Miller, B. (2013). Children's moral reasoning: Influence of culture and collaborative discussion. *Journal of Cognition and Culture*, 497–516.

Zwiers, J., & Crawford, M. (2011). *Academic conversations: Classroom talk that fosters critical thinking and content understanding*. Portland, ME: Stenhouse Publishers.

17

The Modern Reader

Should Changes to How We Read
Affect Research and Theory?

Joseph P. Magliano

NORTHERN ILLINOIS UNIVERSITY

Matthew T. McCrudden

VICTORIA UNIVERSITY OF WELLINGTON

Jean-Francois Rouet

CNRS AND UNIVERSITY OF POITIERS

John Sabatini

EDUCATIONAL TESTING SERVICES

In this chapter we introduce the construct of the Modern Reader, which implies that the reader, the reading context, or both have somehow changed from the past. This is not a new idea and has been discussed at great length in the context of the new literacies (e.g., Coiro, Knobel, Lankshear, & Leu, 2008; Goldman & Scardamalia, 2013; Leu, Kinzer, Coiro, Castek, & Henry, 2013; New London Group, 1996), which argue that new technologies and an increase in the number of ways that texts can be accessed and used have created new opportunities and challenges. If the Modern Reader is different from a reader who primarily accesses print-based texts, then *how* is the Modern Reader different?

We are by no means the first to explore this question from the perspective of discourse psychology (e.g., Goldman, 2011). However, in this chapter we anchor our exploration on 40 years of theory and research in discourse comprehension to explore if it can help guide research on reading in the modern era. To do so, we first identify key assumptions that arise from theories and models of comprehension that have shaped our field over the past 40 years (McNamara & Magliano, 2009b). Next, we discuss what has changed for the reader in the modern era. Finally, we discuss implications of being a Modern Reader on the key assumptions specified in the first section, and in doing so pose an initial set of questions that could guide future research.

What Is Comprehension?

To better learn about the Modern Reader, it is useful to define what is meant by *comprehension*, as it has been described and studied in discourse psychology (e.g., Graesser, Millis, & Zwaan, 1997; McNamara & Magliano, 2009b). While we draw from discourse psychology for this conception, we recognize that the study of comprehension is spread across disciplines, and there is no consensus on its definition (New London Group, 1996). A theoretically grounded perspective of comprehension does not afford a simple definition, but rather a set of key assumptions regarding the mental processes and products that support it. In this section, we specify key assumptions that are common across psychological theories/formal models of comprehension (see also McNamara & Magliano, 2009b). In the subsequent section, we explore how the circumstances that the Modern Reader faces may affect these assumptions. In doing so, we hope to inspire future research.

It is important to acknowledge the fact that most of the research on text comprehension over the past 40 years was conducted in an idealized environment from the perspective of psychological science (Magliano & Graesser, 1991; McNamara & Magliano, 2009b). That is, texts are carefully constructed such that a few features are varied, while others are controlled. Texts are typically presented in a controlled fashion, often via computer, and participants are given general instructions to read for understanding. This controlled environment clearly does not reflect the typical reading circumstances in any era, much less the modern digital age. Nonetheless, we argue that this research has provided important insights that can guide future research for understanding the Modern Reader.

Reading Is Inherently Goal-Directed

Reading is always done for a purpose or goal (Graesser et al., 1994; McNamara & Magliano, 2009b; Rouet, 2006; Snow, 2002; White, Chen, & Forsyth, 2010, for an empirical survey of everyday reading practices). Reading to answer a question (Graesser & Lehman, 2012), reading to solve self-generated problems (e.g., I want to find out what flat-screen TV I should buy), or assigned problems (e.g., a teacher assigns a task to write a paper on how human activities influence the environment; McCrudden & Schraw, 2007), or even reading to pass the time in a doctor's office are all instances of reading for a goal or purpose.

Importantly, reading goals can substantially affect processes that support mental model construction (Magliano, Trabasso, & Graesser, 1999; McCrudden & Schraw, 2007; Rouet, 2006; van den Broek, Bohn-Gettler, Kendeou, & Carlson, 2011). Specifically, goals can affect strategic processing, such as the allocation of attentional resources and the use of particular strategies to achieve one's goals (McCrudden, Magliano, & Schraw, 2010; van den Broek, Risden, & Husbye-Hartmann, 1995). In other words, reading strategically is something more than simply understanding text; it also involves the use of goals and their subsequent impact on processes and behaviors used to achieve those goals (McCrudden & Schraw, 2007; Rouet, 2006).

Additionally, reading strategically involves determining the relevance of text content to one's reading goals. Information within and across texts differs in the extent to which it is relevant to an individual's goals or purposes for reading. *Text relevance* is the perceived

The Modern Reader

instrumental value of text content with respect to a reading goal (McCrudden et al., 2010). Content with greater perceived value is deemed more relevant than content with lesser perceived value. When readers assess the content relevance of text, they apply *standards of relevance*, which are the criteria readers use to establish the comparative value or usefulness of ideas in a text (McCrudden et al., 2011). Thus, relevance processing involves the ability to selectively attend to and process content that is critical to answering questions or solving problems. Moreover, information that is deemed relevant to a goal, may be different from information that is important to the coherence of the text (McCrudden & Schraw, 2007; Schraw, Wade, & Kardash, 1993). Therefore, reading strategically may lead one to extract and process information from a text that may be very different than the purpose for which it was written.

Comprehension Is Grounded in Mental Models

The process of constructing a *mental model* for a specific document leads to comprehension. A *coherent* mental model of a text consists of a network of interrelated propositions that reflect the explicit information within that text, and the inferences that establish how the explicit content is interconnected and related to background knowledge (Kintsch, 1988, 1998; Zwaan & Radvansky, 1998). A mental model is coherent to the extent that the reader is able to establish how text constituents (e.g., propositions) are related to one another (Kintsch, 1988). These relations can occur at a relatively shallow semantic level (overlap between arguments, lexical relationships) or at a relatively deep semantic level (e.g., causal, spatial-temporal, explanatory, comparative; Wolfe, Magliano, & Larsen, 2005). However, the nature of the relations that support coherence for any given text is contingent upon the nature of that text. For instance, situational relations, such as causality, agency, goals, spatiality, and temporality (e.g., Zwaan & Radvansky, 1998) tend to establish coherence for narrative texts, whereas relations that establish coherence for informational text typically reflect rhetorical structures (e.g., cause-effect, comparison, description; Meyer, 1985; Meyer & Freedle, 1984) and argumentative structure (e.g., claim-reason; Toulmin, 1958).

Inferences Are Required to Build Mental Models

Mental models are constructed by generating inferences (Graesser et al., 1994). A variety of taxonomies of inferences have been proposed (Magliano & Graesser, 1991; Kintsch, 1998; Trabasso & Magliano, 1996), but we draw upon a simple distinction that McNamara and Magliano (2009b) argue is common across models/theories of comprehension, and which focuses on the function that inferences play in establishing coherence. Some inferences serve to establish how two elements of the text are related, which have been referred to as *bridging inferences*. These inferences can establish a variety of relations, ranging from anaphoric resolution to deeper semantic relationships (e.g., causal inferences). Bridging inferences are deemed necessary for establishing a coherent mental model (e.g., Graesser et al., 1994), and virtually all models of comprehension consider them to be important (McNamara & Magliano, 2009b). Other inferences involve the use of background knowledge to elaborate upon text content, which are referred to as *knowledge-based inferences* (McNamara & Magliano, 2009a, b). Knowledge-based inferences are not always necessary for establishing coherence (i.e., establishing how discourse constituents are connected) and therefore may not be generated unless the reader has extensive relevant background knowledge or has a specific goal to do so (Magliano et al., 1999).

345

Passive Knowledge Activation Is Necessary for Constructing Mental Models

Knowledge is activated during reading to support mental model construction (Kintsch, 1988). This knowledge can be activated directly during mental model formation for the document that is currently being read, indirectly from mental models formed from previously read documents, or from associated world knowledge. Regardless of its origin, knowledge activation is a passive, bottom-up process (Kintsch, 1988; Long & Lea, 2005; Myers & O'Brien, 1998). That is, content from the sentence being read sends out a retrieval signal that activates semantically similar knowledge via a process of spreading activation (Kintsch, 1988). Content that "resonates" with this signal becomes activated in working memory (Myers & O'Brien, 1998) and can potentially contribute to the construction of inferences that become incorporated into the mental model. However, it is important to emphasize that the reader's attentional focus likely affects the strength of retrieval signals (McCrudden, Magliano, & Schraw, 2011). The more closely a reader is attending to a particular text constituent, the stronger the retrieval signal.

Mental Models Are Validated against Relevant World Knowledge

The process of validation has received considerable attention in recent years (Richter & Rapp, 2014). Validation in the context of reading involves evaluating the plausibility of text content against relevant world knowledge (e.g., Richter, Schroeder, & Wöhrmann, 2009; Singer, 2013). There is a growing body of evidence (Lombardi, Sinatra, & Nussbaum, 2013; Richter et al., 2009; Singer & Halldorson, 1996; Voss, Fincher-Keifer, Wiley, & Silfies, 1993) and theoretical conjecture (Cook & O'Brien, 2014) that suggests that validation is an important part of discourse comprehension. For example, Singer and colleagues have shown that validation supports causal inferences that establish how an action is connected to an outcome (Singer & Halldorson, 1996). In addition to supporting mental model construction, validation has also been assumed to be important for learning complex concepts in science because the learner must evaluate how the to-be-learned content is aligned with existing knowledge (Stadtler, Scharrer, Skodzik, & Bromme, 2014; Steffens, Britt, Braasch, Strømsø, & Bråten, 2014; Wittwer & Ihme, 2014). Moreover, validation may be critical in evaluating the credibility of a text's source and affect the extent to which readers should believe its content.

Summary

In this section we identified several core assumptions about comprehension. In exploring the implications of being a Modern Reader on comprehension, we next review a set of prominent features of reading in the modern era and reflect upon how those features affect the constructs and processes delineated in these assumptions. In doing so, we hope to stimulate fruitful avenues of research regarding the Modern Reader.

The Modern Reader

What is the Modern Reader and how might this construct inform theories of comprehension in discourse psychology (e.g., Kintsch, 1988)? The Modern Reader engages in a variety of literacy practices while attempting to comprehend and potentially use a variety of *text-based information products*, a term we use to refer to discourse artifacts that are exchanged between senders and receivers. These products are conveyed through a variety of modalities (text, sequential art such as comic books, film, video games), accessible through different informational delivery systems (print, screen/TV, Internet, audio, game console), and can serve a variety of purposes (entertainment, self-chosen exploration, assigned or required task). Moreover, the literacy practices readers use to interact with these modalities and delivery systems are not generic, but rather vary across discipline (Shanahan & Shanahan, 2008), genre (Bazerman, 2004), and context (Gee, 2001, 2007) including educational, social, family, citizen, and professional networks.

Does the Modern Reader differ from the reader as conceptualized in contemporary theories of text comprehension? One could argue that the Modern Reader is no different than the reader from past eras because comprehension still requires the building of a mental model. However, many aspects of how the Modern Reader consumes text can potentially affect the processes that support mental model construction in non-trivial, and unexplored ways (Goldman, 2011; Goldman & Scardamalia, 2013). Below we discuss several of the factors associated with reading in the modern era that we believe researchers need to consider.

An Increase in the Accessibility of Texts

The advent of the Internet and other technological developments has increased the amount of information available to the Modern Reader. On one hand, more information means that more people can gain access to and use that information. On the other hand, increased accessibility can flood a search space with a sea of information (Goldman, 2011). For instance, a search for texts pertaining to the causes of the United States Civil War using Google's search engine yields over 48 million hits! It is not surprising that students require training to optimize how they search, select, and use information from a search that yields such a large number of hits (Graesser et al., 2007).

The digital systems that support access to texts feature a number of devices that facilitate searches for specific content. These extend from simple "find" functions in word processing applications, to sophisticated search engines accessible via web browsers. However, the competent use of these devices requires specific forms of literacy (Graesser et al., 2007). For instance, when adolescent readers are given a search task, they often rely on surface cues to signal relevance rather than the semantic content of search engine results when selecting links (Rouet, Ros, Goumi, Macedo-Rouet, & Dinet, 2011), and this is more so the case for less successful learners (Goldman, Braasch, Wiley, & Brodowinska, 2012). Moreover, reading online involves a specific "navigation" component due to the scattering of information across pages and nonlinear linking of pages (Naumann, 2015; OECD, 2011). Readers with a lesser visuo-spatial capacity are more prone to become lost in hypertext networks (Rouet, Vörös, & Pléh, 2012).

Increased accessibility is concomitant with an increase in reader effort. The Modern Reader needs to identify, evaluate, and integrate information within and across various texts that may contain overlapping, unique, and conflicting messages (Goldman et al., 2012). Thus, readers must not only devote resources toward identifying relevant information and credible sources, they must also build mental models of individual texts as well as links across texts (Rouet & Britt, 2011). Given that working memory resources used to support comprehension are limited (e.g., Just & Carpenter, 1992), it stands to reason that the more resources one uses to locate and evaluate information within and across texts, the fewer resources that would be available to build a mental model or that more effort would be needed to construct a coherent mental model. Ultimately, accessibility may affect whether and how that information is used to achieve some goal.

Changes in Who Produces Content

The broadest level we consider here concerns the publishers or media channels of information products. In the pre-digital era, publishing and media industries tightly controlled published sources. For better or worse, this placed constraints on the accessibility of books (fiction and non-fiction) and periodicals (academic articles, popular magazines, newspapers). Previously, personal communications (letters, journals, diaries) also had limited circulation to the general public.

Even today, large publishers and media corporations exercise wide control over the availability of information products. Critical and cultural researchers study how publishers control or shape content (Fabos, 2008). A benign example of these influences would be a magazine editor who assigns a staff writer to develop an article on a topic that meets specific content and format guidelines. The magazine targets a certain circulation audience and simultaneously seeks the sponsorship of companies who market products to that audience. One might expect an editorial process that favors certain points of view that are favorable to the audience and advertisers, and censures content that is not consistent with that viewpoint. In this case, interpreting the author's (or researcher's or reader's) point of view without considering the broader media context provides an incomplete view of the information product. The Modern Reader makes choices (intentionally or unintentionally) about how and where they access information, and how they process and form beliefs about the credibility of media channels (Scharrer, Bromme, Britt, & Stadtler, 2012; Stadtler, Scharrer, Brummernhenrich, & Bromme, 2013). These choices may, over time, condition their expectations and cognitive processing when confronting novel products from novel sources.

Whereas the traditional publishing industry vetted most content that was available to the reader in some manner, the Internet has also greatly democratized the process of producing and disseminating content. Nearly anyone from any background can publish on the web. This has created a situation in which the Modern Reader should demonstrate some form of "epistemic vigilance" (Sperber et al., 2010); that is, to question the source credibility of any document that one has accessed. Unfortunately, most people are not overly sensitive to author intentions without training (Britt & Aglinskas, 2002; Claassen, 2012) or even adept at identifying and keeping track of the authors when processing a set of documents without training (Bråten, Strømsø, & Britt, 2009; Britt & Rouet, 2012). There are potential dangers in accessing content from an unfiltered source. For example, in October 2015, hundreds of high school students in the French town of Péronne assembled into a street protest after a false rumor that the government was planning to cut summer vacation time had been peddled on social networks (francetvinfo.fr, October 16, 2015). Historically, theories of text comprehension typically do not make predictions regarding whether or how readers attend to the source of a text. That said, sourcing has become an issue that has been increasingly addressed in the literature (e.g., Britt & Aglinskas, 2002; Wineburg, 1991).

An Increase in the Variety of Devices That Can Deliver Content

Modern Readers can access information from a variety of devices including TV, smart phones/tablet computers, personal computers, etc. – even paper-based devices (e.g., a book)! Does the device matter? After all, content is content. However, to the extent that a device changes how we interact with content, then it will have an impact on how the Modern Reader engages with information and the resulting mental model. For example, suppose people are filling time and use a digital device to access news sites. This could easily lead people to use this device to primarily skim texts, rather than read them for deep understanding. There is, in fact, evidence that reading from computers results in more shallow processing of the information (Santana et al., 2013; Tewksbury & Althaus, 2000), higher cognitive load (Macedo-Rouet, Rouet, Epstein, & Fayard, 2003), and poorer text comprehension (Mangen, Walgermo, & Brønnick, 2013). On the other hand, we could adopt strategies when reading traditionally printed text that may involve deeper reading, such as reading a textbook for a class. If there are systematic ways in which readers use devices, then strategies will likely emerge that are linked to those content delivery systems.

Another issue to consider is the fact that having access to multiple devices at any one time can have both positive and negative implications. Suppose a modern reader is watching a movie at home and wants to know who directed it. This information can be easily accessed on a variety of digital devices. This could lead to an enriched representation of the movie, leading to a better understanding of it than if such access was not available in the moment. On the other hand, accessing such devices requires attentional resources that would not be allocated to processing the movie (that is, assuming the individual chose not to pause it while searching for the director), which may detract from the person's mental model of the movie. As another example, a modern reader can use devices that have no bearing on the primary task. For example, a viewer could watch a movie and browse social media at the same time. This dual tasking could possibly lead to a relatively shallower understanding of the movie than if the viewer's attention was not split between two tasks.

An Increase in the Number of Modalities to Consume Content

The Modern Reader has access to content in a variety of modalities, such as traditional linear texts, diagrams, films, graphic novels, video games, etc. Is comprehension specific to verbal language, or does it extend across various communication modalities, such as still or animated pictures? One answer to this question is that theories of text comprehension are generalizable beyond the medium of text and can be construed as general models of comprehension (Gernsbacher, Varner, & Faust, 1990; Kintsch, 1998). Relatively speaking, only a few studies have directly explored the similarities and differences in comprehension processes across modalities while controlling for content (Baggett, 1979; Gernsbacher et al., 1990; Kintsch, 1998; Magliano, Loschky, Clinton, & Larson, 2013). Two of these studies have shown that there is indeed a high degree of overlap in mental models for visual and text-based narrative content (Baggett, 1979; Magliano, Kopp, McNerney, Radvansky, & Zacks, 2011).

However, consider the classic Kennedy–Nixon debate in the 1960 US presidential race in which the delivery system had a profound influence on inferences drawn about the two candidates and the perceived outcome of the debate (Druckman, 2003). John F. Kennedy and Richard Nixon were opponents in the first televised presidential debate in American history, which was also broadcast via radio. People who listened on the radio thought Nixon had won a close debate, whereas those who watched on television thought that Kennedy was the clear winner. Thus, modality was related to different states of comprehension, which impacted the task at hand; deciding who to vote for in the upcoming election. This classic illustration of the power of visual media on the influence of public thinking challenges the claim that comprehension is the same independently of medium.

Magliano et al. (2013) provided a framework to explore how and why media might matter that draws a gross distinction between front- and back-end processes. Front-end processes are involved in the moment-to-moment encoding of information (e.g., lexical processing), and back-end processes are involved in building mental models of an experience (e.g., inferences). While there are obvious differences in front-end processes across modalities of experiences (e.g., viewing a film involves perceptual processes that support encoding not likely used during reading), Magliano et al. (2013) argued that back-end processes are similar independently of format, modality, or context (though still dependent on goal orientation). While this may be the case (e.g., Magliano et al., 2011), we contend that differences in front-end process and differences in the affordances of different modalities can affect comprehension. More specifically, differences in processing constraints across media and the affordances of the presentation formats will likely impact what kinds of knowledge gets encoded or activated, which would have implications for mental model construction. The paradigm of comparing and contrasting content across media could be a fruitful avenue of future research into understanding mental model construction (Sabatini, 2005).

For example, with film or video, the viewer does not have self-paced control (albeit one can choose to pause or rewind in most media except live broadcast), and additionally, visual media (e.g., film makers) producers use well-documented techniques to control the viewer's attentional processes (Bordwell, 1985; Smith, 2012). In contrast, readers of text or graphic narratives (i.e., comic books) have control over how they read the materials, such as where they direct or focus their attention, or whether they review or reread to enhance or confirm their understanding. These differences in level of control may have important implications for what kinds of knowledge are available moment-to-moment, but the impact of these differences has been largely unexplored.

Additionally, different media have different affordances, as the Kennedy–Nixon debate nicely illustrates. Visual media allow one to see facial expressions, which afford different inferences about internal states of agents (e.g., Ekman, 1992) that only voice inflection (available still via radio broadcast) does not. As such, viewers of the debate likely had a different set of knowledge activated regarding Kennedy and Nixon than the radio audience, who have different knowledge than those reading a transcript of the debate. Authors can choose to provide rich descriptions of not just characters' emotions, but complex belief and goal states. When viewing a film version of a narrative, the viewer must infer those states based on what they see. It is quite reasonable to predict a more enriched representation of the characters' internal states for a text version than a film version by virtue of difference in knowledge that is activated by what the two media afford. On the other hand, perhaps inferring internal states of characters depends more on what information the story teller chooses to present or not present than on whether the narrative is visual or text-based (Sabatini, 2005).

We posit that while it may be the case that the basic mechanisms that support comprehension are general and apply across modalities of experience (Gernsbacher et al., 1990; Kintsch, 1998), this does not mean that the products of comprehension are the same across media. Different media have different affordances that may affect comprehension in non-trivial ways.

Using Multiple Texts in the Moment

The Internet and mobile devices afford immediate access to multiple documents in the moment (Goldman, 2011). We can be watching a movie, and decide to get information about its production or how others have reviewed it. We can share our thoughts in the moment through the use of social media. We can access text to support complex activities, such as cooking a meal or building a fence in the backyard. This ability to access text surely affects how we think about the utility of different text to support our goals. Additionally, it likely requires skills that enable us to comprehend the content of a text(s) and use that knowledge in the activity that motivated reading the text in the first place. There are a host of factors that could both facilitate and hinder that coordination. For example, a text describing cooking instructions is well aligned with the activity of cooking. However, a text describing the filmography of an actor or director of a film will not be semantically aligned with the movie we may be currently watching. As such, while reading that text may enhance one's understanding of the film in some ways, it certainly could affect how well we comprehend the section of film that unfolds as we search for, access, and read the text.

Summary of Implications for the Modern Reader

One main conclusion that can be drawn from this discussion is that reading in the modern era changes the demands placed on a reader's cognitive resources. An increase in the accessibility of texts means readers have more information available. To succeed in such an environment, the Modern Reader must be goal-directed and discern the extent to which various texts and information within those texts is relevant to answering questions or solving problems and selectively allocate processing resources accordingly. Changes in who produces content means that the Modern Reader should not access text with blind trust of the quality of content and therefore should adopt a relatively high level of epistemic vigilance. An increase in the variety of devices that can deliver content, the number of modalities to consume content, and the possibility of using multiple texts in the moment means that modern readers must integrate information across multiple documents, devices, and media within a short time frame. Different contextual situations may afford such integration, whereas other situations could present challenges. We have come to the conclusion that reading in the modern era creates new challenges in terms of cognitive demands, such that we need to consider implications on the core processes delineated by theories of comprehension, which is the purpose of the next section.

Implications of Being a Modern Reader on Comprehension and Future Research

In the remainder of this chapter, we explore answers to the question posed in the title of this chapter. In this exploration, we discuss how the challenges of being a Modern Reader affect the processes specified in the common assumptions of comprehension specified in the first section.

Implications for Goal-Directed Reading

The nature of goal-directed reading has been discussed at great length in recent discussions of reading literacy, whether in general (McCrudden & Schraw, 2007; Rouet & Britt, 2011), or in the context of the new literacies of online reading (Goldman & Scardamalia, 2013; Leu et al., 2013). At least four general skills have been identified as essential to goal-directed reading in the modern era: locating, evaluating, and synthesizing online content, and communicating that content (e.g., OECD, 2008). While these skills have always been important (e.g., Guthrie, 1988; Guthrie & Kirsch, 1987), reading in the modern era has amplified both their need and the ability to execute them skillfully. As discussed above, relevance processing is a critical component of goal-directed reading (McCrudden & Schraw, 2007; McCrudden et al., 2011), in part because it supports these skills.

Modern readers need to be able to identify and select documents that are useful to their goals. In the context of an Internet search that can yield thousands or perhaps millions of hits, this can be extremely challenging. Thus, an increase in the accessibility of texts means that relevance processing plays a key role in locating goal-related information. Relevance processing was initially conceptualized as an intra-textual process; nonetheless, it is required to support inter-textual processes as well (Rouet & Britt, 2011). When relevant information is spread across multiple documents, the Modern Reader needs a variety of skills for selecting information and deciding whether it will be useful (Goldman et al., 2012). Readers need to distinguish between more and less relevant documents and content within those documents. Several variables, such as topic familiarity, surface cues (e.g. key words), or deep semantic cues can affect the extent to which content is deemed relevant, and sensitivity to these cues is particularly important in the modern era (Goldman et al., 2012; Keil & Kominsky, 2013; Leu et al., 2013; Rouet & Britt, 2011). Reading the titles of articles from an Internet search can provide potentially useful criteria for document selection, but the deep semantic cues may not be well represented in document titles (Keil & Kominsky, 2013). As such, relevance processing may require targeted reading of documents to determine the extent to which they are useful and contain relevant content.

Given the changes to publishing afforded by the modern era, simply selecting information that is semantically aligned with one's goal does not guarantee that the information is reputable. As such, selecting information also requires one to evaluate the quality of that information based on a variety of criteria, such as who produced the content, what were their goals when producing the content, did they rely on reputable practices when producing the content, was the content vetted by an appropriate community, etc. Thus, readers must exercise a certain level of epistemic vigilance when selecting and evaluating documents and content in the modern era.

An increase in the variety of devices that can deliver content and an increase in the number of modalities to consume content has further implications for goal-directed reading. Such changes can potentially decrease the amount of time taken to answer questions or solve problems. Information can be accessed more rapidly and in numerous settings or contexts. That is, the proliferation of modes of delivery (i.e., device) and consumption (i.e., modality) can increase processing efficiency. However, challenges can potentially arise. On one hand, readers may invest more energy in seeking to find corroboration across different documents and modalities. On the other hand, readers may be reluctant to invest energy if they are unable to answer a question or solve a problem in a short time frame. This may in fact change how content is delivered, such that content is packaged in smaller information units that provide less depth on a particular topic. Thus, device delivery and modality consumption may affect processing efficiency and strategic processing. Thus, tasks that require one to synthesize information across documents, devices, and types of information sources may affect goal-directed reading.

Implications for Constructing a Coherent Mental Model

As discussed above, discourse comprehension theories universally assume that building a coherent mental model involves building mental representations that establish how ideas are connected (e.g., McNamara & Magliano, 2009a, b). However, most of these theories of mental model construction did not take into consideration the variety of reasons why one accesses content (see Graesser et al., 1994; van den Broek et al., 1995, for exceptions), and in particular in the context of the Internet. Certainly, planning out a train travel schedule requires the formulation of a goal, accessing texts that provide information about train schedules, identifying the trains and times that fit one's schedule, and creating a mental model of the schedule (and probably external representation of that information as well). This is clearly a literacy activity (Guthrie, 1988; New London Group, 1996), but it is arguably a very different kind of literacy activity than theories of discourse comprehension were intended to explain (for an early discussion see Guthrie & Kirsch, 1987).

As another example, consider someone who is participating in a discussion thread on Facebook. While clearly a form of discourse that warrants scientific exploration (Gernsbacher, 2014), do people actually construct a coherent mental model for discussion threads, and if so under what conditions? What is the nature of these representations? What phenomena in the modern era should theories and models explain? Answering these questions is beyond the scope of this chapter, but we assume that one necessary criterion for models of discourse comprehension is that the experience requires the construction of a mental model, given the centrality of coherence-building to theories of comprehension (McNamara & Magliano, 2009b). However, as specified above, the nature of a coherent representation is based in part on the nature of the discourse. As such, understanding the nature and structure of new forms of discourse that have emerged in the modern era, such as discussion threads and Twitter feeds, is warranted.

What constitutes a coherent mental model in the modern era? This question has arguably been most thoroughly explored in the context of multiple documents (e.g., Goldman, 2011; Goldman et al., 2012; Graesser et al., 2007; Rouet & Britt, 2011; Sanchez et al., 2006), and as such the rest of our reflection on mental model construction in the modern era is framed in this context. Perfetti, Rouet, and Britt (1999) conceptualized mental models for multiple documents as a *documents model* (see also Rouet, 2006; Rouet & Britt, 2011). A key assumption is that documents models reflect the individual's goal or purpose for reading. For instance, if one's goal was to accurately represent each document in a set, then the documents model would consist of separate representations of each document, and their structure would represent important ideas. Conversely, if one's goal was to build an argument, then the documents model would contain a coherent representation of the content aligned with that purpose and not necessarily for each document.

Constructing mental models based on multiple documents on the Internet presents new challenges for relevance processing (Bråten, Ferguson, Anmarkrud, & Strømsø, 2013; Britt & Gabrys, 2000; Goldman, 2004; Rouet, 2006; Sabatini, 2005) that lead to important questions that warrant exploration. The variety of texts that can be accessed in any given search certainly makes relevance processing more challenging. This is in part due to the fact that the texts that are accessed from an Internet search typically written by different authors, for different audiences, and often for very different purposes. The balance between reading enough to understand what information is in a text and locating and extracting only that content that is most germane to a given purpose likely requires skill and practice. How does one build a coherent mental model that stems from relevance processing and in the context of multiple documents accessed through an Internet search? What are the features of these mental models? How are they different from those constructed from a single text, if at all? Do readers generate inter-textual bridging inferences during moment-to-moment processing, or are these generated when engaged in a post-reading task?

It has been a common practice in discourse psychology to classify inferences and empirically explore which types are typically generated to support the construction of a mental model (Graesser et al., 1994; Magliano & Graesser, 1991; McNamara & Magliano, 2009a, b;

McKoon & Ratcliff, 1998; Singer, 2006). For example, above we discussed the functional distinction between bridging and elaborative inferences. Do these classifications of inferences make sense in the context of building mental models for multiple documents? Certainly readers need to connect ideas across documents through bridging inferences and draw upon background knowledge to generate inferences consistent with the reading goal when learning from multiple documents. However, given that the mental model for a set of documents will be different than the intended purposes of the individual texts, it could be relatively more challenging to distinguish between bridging and elaborative processes. That is, making connections across documents (i.e., inter-textual bridging inferences) may be inherently elaborative in nature and require more background knowledge than making connections within a text that are consistent with the text structure (e.g., causal, claim-reason, comparison).

As noted above, there has been some speculation as to whether there are similarities and differences in the nature of mental models across media (e.g., Magliano et al., 2013). Differences in representational format may involve non-trivial differences in front-end processes (Magliano et al., 2013) and require literacy skills specific to some forms of media (OECD, 2008). Extracting relevant information from a visual display and then integrating it with text content can present challenges (e.g., Mayer, 2009, 2013; McCrudden & Rapp, in press), much less doing so across documents (Wineburg, 1991). Research that systematically explores the similarities and differences in front-end and back-end processes across media is arguably lacking (Magliano et al., 2013), and this must change if we are to have a better understanding of the challenges presented for mental model construction when documents in a documents set vary in forms of media.

Another issue for consideration stems from the fact that the Modern Reader can access documents on multiple devices in the moment. Presumably, this would allow them to make connections between documents on different devices (i.e., generate inter-textual bridging inferences). Given that there is strong evidence that memory is linked to context (e.g., Godden & Baddeley, 1975), it may be the case that using different devices could impede the inter-textual processes that are required to build a documents model. Of course that would be contingent upon the extent to which devices are associated with situational context, such that using different devices creates different contexts. Additionally, there is some speculation and evidence that reading on digital devices, such as computers or smart phones, tends to be shallower than print texts (Macedo-Rouet et al., 2003; Mangen et al., 2013). There are a variety of reasons why this might be the case, such as affordances of the devices (small window may affect standards of comprehension) or reasons why one might typically read from a device (people may use smart phones to access texts to pass the time, and thereby read more shallowly than when reading to learn).

How might the modern era affect memory retrieval, which is critical to establish connections across multiple documents (Kurby, Britt, & Magliano, 2005; McCrudden et al., 2011)? The strength of a retrieval cue is likely contingent on how attentional resources have been devoted to it, and as such, information that is deemed more relevant will likely provide a stronger signal than content deemed less relevant. However, this is an idea that to our knowledge has been little investigated in the context of text comprehension and memory (though see de Pereyra, Britt, Braasch, & Rouet, 2014). Moreover, it may be the case that certain kinds of semantic overlap have a greater impact on inter-text retrieval. For example, Kurby et al. (2005) showed that college readers were more likely to integrate across documents when the documents shared common events than when they simply shared common agents. Finally, if some devices do indeed lead to relatively shallow processing of texts as noted above, then it stands to reason that this will have implications of the memory-based processes that support inference generation and mental model construction.

A final issue that warrants consideration with respect to mental model construction in the context of multiple documents is source evaluation. Ideally, a documents model requires one to evaluate the credibility of the sources (i.e., credibility of the Internet sites) and credentials of the authors (e.g., expertise, trustworthiness; Fogg & Tseng, 1999; McCrudden, Stenseth, Bråten, & Strømsø, 2016; Sundar & Nass, 2001). This places high cognitive demands in the form of epistemic vigilance, and in a manner that may not come naturally to readers who do not have specialized training to evaluate texts in such a manner (e.g., Wineburg, 1991). To this end, a documents model should ideally represent some key features of the sources, such as the authors' names or occupations, and convey any discrepancies amongst the sources (Britt, Perfetti, Sandak, & Rouet, 1999; Rouet, 2006). Doing so is challenging with print text, even though authorship is typically clearly marked (Britt & Aglinskas, 2002). One can speculate that it may be even more challenging with Internet documents where authorship may not be clearly specified (Britt, Rouet, & Braasch, 2013).

Implications for Validation

Validation has been construed as a memory-based process, and in particular in the context of supporting narrative comprehension (e.g., Cook & O'Brien, 2014; Richter, Schroeder, & Wöhrmann, 2009; Singer, 2006). However, a more deliberate form of validation may be important for learning from text (Stadtler et al., 2014; Steffens et al., 2014; Wittwer & Ihme, 2014; see also Britt, Richter, & Rouet, 2014, for a discussion). As such, the notion of epistemic vigilance may be an important aspect of deliberate forms of validation. One can speculate that deliberate validation is essential in the modern era. Specifically, given changes in the ability to disseminate information in the modern era, evaluating the veracity of the information based on the assessment of the source of a given document (i.e., whether the source is competent and benevolent) takes on greater importance.

However, there is mounting evidence that readers find it challenging to evaluate the accuracy, reliability, and bias of online information (Bråten et al., 2009; Sanchez, Wiley, & Goldman, 2006; Wallace, Kupperman, Krajcik, & Soloway, 2000). Further, modern readers need to distinguish between more and less credible sources. Source credibility can be affected by author expertise and author trustworthiness (Rouet et al., 1997). Once content has been deemed relevant and source features (i.e., source credibility) have been vetted, readers need to remember who said what, and to identify corroborative, discrepant, and unique features within and across documents (Britt et al., 1999). Thus, the mental model for such an activity can consist of an *intra*-textual model and an *inter*-textual model (Perfetti et al., 1999). To date, however, the conditions that enable readers to form such sophisticated memory representations of text information remain to be specified.

Important Research Questions for Consideration

Research is obviously well underway to explore the challenge of reading in the modern era from within the disciplines that study discourse comprehension (e.g., Goldman et al., 2012; Graesser et al., 2007; Sanchez et al., 2006). However, we believe that the exploration of dimensions specified by theories of comprehension and implications of the central challenges of reading in the modern era point to questions that warrant further exploration to better understand the Modern Reader. These include:

- How do the reasons for reading in the modern era affect the process of locating, evaluating, and synthesizing content, and communication of that content?
- How do standards of relevance (i.e., criteria used to judge the extent to which documents and content within those documents are relevant) affect locating, evaluating, and synthesizing content, and communicating content in the modern era?

  o Further, to what extent are standards of relevance predictive of strategic processing and mental model construction?

- What are the implications for accessing multiple documents and through multiple devices on mental model construction?

  o How does the context (materials, goals, tasks, reader characteristics) influence intra- and inter-textual inferences?
  o How does the context influence the memory-based processes that support mental model construction?

- How does modality affect mental model construction and in particular in the context of learning from multiple documents that vary in modality?
- Under what conditions does integration across multiple documents occur in the moment or after reading?
- When is validation based on implicit memory processes and when is it based on more deliberate reasoning about the contents and/or sources?

  o Does the concept of epistemic vigilance play a role in validation?

Conclusion

In this chapter, we introduced the construct of the Modern Reader, which reflects the fact that the modern era has changed the game for reading literacy (Leu et al., 2013; New London Group, 1996). In the chapter we have tried to ground this discussion in the existing literature on discourse comprehension. We hope that the motivation for doing so is transparent. Scholars who study discourse comprehension have much to contribute to understanding the Modern Reader, but research questions should be grounded in what we have learned about comprehension thus far in discourse psychology and related fields. While there may be new skills required to read in the modern era, as speculated by scholars of the new literacies (Coiro et al., 2008), these skills most likely operate within a cognitive system that has been extensively studied in the context of text comprehension research.

Thus, we have identified a set of processes that have been deemed to be important by theory or have received attention in text comprehension research and have reflected upon how aspects of reading in the modern era might affect them. The questions we posed in the last section should be construed as starting points for the reader to develop specific research questions about these processes, rather than reflecting definitive questions that must be answered to understand the Modern Reader. Moreover, our discussion has focused on challenges created in the modern era, but it is possible that there are benefits to comprehension processes. It is beyond the scope of this chapter to speculate about what those might be.

The Modern Reader

In conclusion, Modern Readers face a complex, expanding wilderness of text-based information products. They engage in a variety of literacy practices that can differ dramatically depending on modality, accessibility, delivery system, and purpose for reading. In seeking to understand how the Modern Reader may be changing to adapt to this complex environment, we should begin by building our understanding through application of existing theory and research to inform our investigations of their literacy practices and how these practices are influenced by context. To develop an understanding of such readers, it is necessary to extend existing theories and models, or to develop new theories and models, to explain and predict the manner in which the Modern Reader comprehends and uses text. In this chapter, we provided what we consider to be fruitful questions to consider in such investigations.

References

Anmarkrud, Ø., Bråten, I., & Strømsø, H. I. (2014). Multiple-documents literacy: Strategic processing, source awareness, and argumentation when reading multiple conflicting documents. *Learning and Individual Differences, 30*, 64–76. http://dx.doi.org/10.1016/j.lindif.2013.01.007.

Baggett, P. (1979). Structurally equivalent stories in movie and text and the effect of medium on recall. *Journal of Verbal Learning and Verbal Behavior, 18*(3), 333–356.

Bazerman, C. (2004). Speech acts, genres, and activity systems. In C. Bazerman & P. A. Prior (Eds), *What Writing Does and How It Does It* (pp. 309–340). Mahwah, NJ: Lawrence Erlbaum Associates.

Bordwell, D. 1985. *Narration in the Fiction Film.* Madison, WI: University of Wisconsin Press.

Bråten, I., Ferguson, L. E., Anmarkrud, Ø., & Strømsø, H. I. (2013). Prediction of learning and comprehension when adolescents read multiple texts: The roles of word-level processing, strategic approach, and reading motivation. *Reading and Writing, 26*, 321–348.

Bråten, I., & Strømsø, H. I. (2010). Effects of task instruction and personal epistemology on the understanding of multiple texts about climate change. *Discourse Processes, 47*, 1–31.

Bråten, I., Strømsø, H. I., & Britt, M. A. (2009). Trust matters: Examining the role of source evaluation in students' construction of meaning within and across multiple texts. *Reading Research Quarterly, 44*, 6–28.

Britt, M. A., & Aglinskas, C. (2002). Improving students' ability to identify and use source information. *Cognition and Instruction, 20*(4), 485–522.

Britt, M. A., & Gabrys, G. (2000). Teaching advanced literacy skills for the World Wide Web. In C. Wolfe (Ed.), *Webs We Weave: Learning and Teaching on the World Wide Web* (pp. 73–90). New York, NY: Academic Press.

Britt, M. A., Perfetti, C. A., Sandak, R., & Rouet, J. F. (1999). Content integration and source separation in learning from multiple texts. In S. R. Goldman, A. C. Graesser, & P. van den Broek (Eds), *Narrative Comprehension, Causality, and Coherence: Essays in Honor of Tom Trabasso* (pp. 209–233). Mahwah, NJ: Lawrence Erlbaum Associates.

Britt, M. A., Richter, T., & Rouet, J.-F. (2014). Scientific literacy: The role of goal-directed reading and evaluation in understanding scientific information. *Educational Psychologist, 49*(2), 104–122.

Britt, M. A., & Rouet, J.-F. (2012). Learning with multiple documents: Component skills and their acquisition. In M. J. Lawson & J. R. Kirby (Eds), *The Quality of Learning* (pp. 276–314). Cambridge: Cambridge University Press.

Britt, M. A., Rouet, J.-F., & Braasch, J. L. G. (2013). Documents as entities: Extending the situation model theory of comprehension. In M. A. Britt, S. R. Goldman, & J.-F. Rouet (Eds), *Reading: From Words to Multiple Texts* (pp. 160–179). New York, NY: Routledge.

Claassen, E. (2012). *Author Representation in Literary Reading.* Utrecht, Netherlands: John Benjamins.

Coiro, J., Knobel, M., Lankshear, C., & Leu, D.J. (2008). *The Handbook of Research in New Literacies.* Mahwah, NJ: Lawrence Erlbaum Associates, Inc.

Cook, A. E., & O'Brien, E. J. (2014). Knowledge activation, integration, and validation during narrative text comprehension. *Discourse Processes, 51*, 26–49.

De Pereyra, G., Britt, M.A., Braasch, J. L. G, & Rouet, J.F. (2014). Reader's memory for information sources in simple news stories: Effects of text and task features. *Journal of Cognitive Psychology, 24*(2), 187–204. DOI: 10.1080/20445911.2013.879152.

357

Druckman, J. N. (2003). The power of television images: The Kennedy-Nixon debate revisited. *The Journal of Politics, 65*, 559–571.

Ekman, P. (1992). An argument for basic emotions. *Cognition and Emotion, 6*, 169–200.

Fabos, B. (2008). The price of information: Critical literacy education and today's Internet. In J. Coiro, M. Knobel, C. Lankshear, & D. Leu (Eds), *Handbook of Research on New Literacies* (pp. 839–870). New York, NY: Lawrence Erlbaum.

Fogg, B. J., & Tseng, H. (1999). The elements of computer credibility. *Proceedings of the SIGCHI Conference on Human Factors in Computing Systems*, 80–87. New York, NY: ACM. DOI: 10.1145/302979.303001.

Gee, J. P. (2001). *What Video Games Have to Teach Us about Learning and Literacy*. New York, NY: Palgrave Macmillan.

Gee, J. P. (2007). *Literacy and Education*. New York, NY: Routledge.

Gernsbacher, M. A. (2014). Internet-based communication. *Discourse Processes, 51*, 359–373. DOI: 10.1080/0163853X.2014.916174.

Gernsbacher, M. A., Varner, K. R., & Faust, M. E. (1990). Investigating differences in general comprehension skill. *Journal of Experimental Psychology: Learning, Memory, and Cognition, 16*(3), 430–445.

Godden, D. R., & Baddeley, A. D. (1975). Context-dependent memory in two naturalistic contexts: On land and underwater. *British Journal of Psychology, 66*, 325–331.

Goldman, S. R. (2004). Cognitive aspects of constructing meaning through and across multiple texts. In N. Shuart-Ferris & D. M. Bloome (Eds), *Uses of Intertextuality in Classroom and Educational Research* (pp. 313–347). Greenwich, CT: Information Age Publishing.

Goldman, S. R. (2011). Choosing and using multiple information sources: Some new findings and emergent issues. *Learning and Instruction, 21*, 238–242.

Goldman, S. R., Braasch, J. L. G., Wiley, J., & Brodowinska, K. (2012). Comprehending and learning from internet sources: Processing patterns of better and poorer learners. *Reading Research Quarterly, 47*, 356–381.

Goldman, S. R., & Scardamalia, M., (2013). Managing, understanding, applying, and creating knowledge in the information age: Next-generation challenges and opportunities. *Cognition and Instruction, 31*, 255–269.

Graesser, A. C., & Lehman, B. (2012). Questions drive comprehension of text and multimedia. In M. T. McCrudden, J. Magliano, & G. Schraw (Eds), *Text Relevance and Learning from Text* (pp. 53–74). Greenwich, CT: Information Age Publishing.

Graesser, A. C., Millis, K. K., & Zwaan, R. A. (1997). Discourse comprehension. In J. T. Spence, J. M. Darley, & D. J. Foss (Eds), *Annual Review of Psychology, Vol. 48*. Palo Alto, CA: Annual Reviews Inc.

Graesser, A. C., Singer, M., & Trabasso, T. (1994). Constructing inferences during narrative text comprehension. *Psychological Review, 101*, 371–395.

Graesser, A. C., Wiley, J., Goldman, S. R., O'Reilly, T., Joen, M., & McDaniel, B. (2007). SEEK Web tutor: Fostering a critical stance while exploring the causes of volcanic eruption. *Metacognition and Learning, 2*, 89–105.

Guthrie, J. T. (1988). Locating, information in documents: Examination of a cognitive model. *Reading Research Quarterly, 23*, 178–199.

Guthrie, J. T., & Kirsch, I. (1987). Distinctions between reading comprehension and locating information in text. *Journal of Educational Psychology, 79*, 210–228.

Just, M. A., & Carpenter, P. A. (1992). A capacity theory of comprehension: Individual differences in working memory. *Psychological Review, 99*, 122–149.

Keil, F. C., & Kominsky, J. F. (2013). Missing links in middle school: Developing use of disciplinary relatedness in evaluating internet search results. *PLOS ONE, 8*(6), e67777. DOI: 10.1371/journal. pone.0067777.

Kintsch, W. (1988). The role of knowledge in discourse comprehension: A construction–integration model. *Psychological Review, 95*(2), 163–182.

Kintsch, W. (1998). *Comprehension: A Paradigm for Cognition*. New York, NY: Cambridge University Press.

Kurby, C. A., Britt, M. A., & Magliano, J. P. (2005). The role of top-down and bottom-up processes in between-text integration. *Reading Psychology, 26*(4–5), 335–362.

Leu, D. J., Kinzer, C. K., Coiro, J., Castek, J., & Henry, L. A. (2013). New literacies and the new literacies of online reading comprehension: A dual level theory. In N. Unrau & D. Alvermann (Eds), *Theoretical Models and Process of Reading* (6th ed., pp. 1150–1181). Newark, DE: International Reading Association.

Leu, D. J., Zawilinski, L., Castek, J., Banerjee, M., Housand, B., Liu, Y., & O'Neil, M. (2007). What is new about the new literacies of online reading comprehension? In L. Rush, J. Eakle, & A. Berger (Eds), *Secondary School Literacy: What Research Reveals for Classroom Practice*. Chicago, IL: NCTE/NCRLL.

Lombardi, D., Sinatra, G., & Nussbaum, E. M. (2013). Plausibility reappraisals and shifts in middle school students' climate change conceptions. *Learning and Instruction, 27*, 50–62.

Long, D. L., & Lea, R. B. (2005). Have we been searching for meaning in all the wrong places: Defining the "search after meaning" principle in comprehension. *Discourse Processes, 39*, 279–298.

Macedo-Rouet, M., Rouet, J.-F., Epstein, I., & Fayard, P. (2003). Reading and understanding a science report through paper and hypertext: An experimental study. *Science Communication, 25*, 99–128.

Magliano, J. P., & Graesser, A. C. (1991). A three-pronged method for studying inference generation in literary text. *Poetics, 20*, 193–232.

Magliano, J. P., Kopp, K., McNerney, M. W., Radvansky, G. A., & Zacks, J. M. (2011). Aging and perceived event structure as a function of modality. *Aging, Neuropsychology, and Cognition, 19*, 264–282.

Magliano, J. P., Loschky, L., Clinton, J., & Larson, A. (2013). Differences and similarities in processing narratives across textual and visual media. In B. Miller, L. Cutting, & P. McCardle (Eds), *Unraveling the Behavioral, Neurobiological, and Genetic Components of Reading Comprehension* (pp. 78–90). Baltimore, MD: Paul Brookes Publishing.

Magliano, J. P., Trabasso, T., & Graesser, A. C. (1999). Strategic processes during comprehension. *Journal of Educational Psychology, 91*, 615–629.

Mangen, A., Walgermo, B. R., & Brønnick, K. (2013). Reading linear texts on paper versus computer screen: Effects on reading comprehension. *International Journal of Educational Research, 58*, 61–68.

Mayer, R. E. (2009). *Multimedia learning* (2nd ed.). New York, NY: Cambridge University Press.

Mayer, R. E. (2013). Fostering learning with visual displays. In G. Schraw, M. T. McCrudden, & D. Robinson (Eds), *Learning through Visual Displays* (pp. 47–73). Charlotte, NC: Information Age Publishing.

McCrudden, M. T., Magliano, J., & Schraw, G. (2010). Exploring how relevance instructions affect personal reading intentions, reading goals, and text processing: A mixed methods study. *Contemporary Educational Psychology, 35*(4), 229–241.

McCrudden, M. T., Magliano, J. P., & Schraw, G. (Eds). (2011). *Text Relevance and Learning from Text*. Greenwich, CT: Information Age Publishing.

McCrudden, M. T., & Rapp, D. N. (in press). How visual displays affect cognitive processing. *Educational Psychology Review*. DOI: 10.1007/s10648-015-9342-2.

McCrudden, M. T., & Schraw, G. (2007). Relevance and goal-focusing in text processing. *Educational Psychology Review, 19*, 113–139.

McCrudden, M. T., Stenseth, T., Bråten, I., & Strømsø, H. I. (2016). The effects of topic familiarity, author expertise, and content relevance on Norwegian students' document selection: A mixed methods study. *Journal of Educational Psychology, 108*(2), 147–162.

McKoon, G., & Ratcliff, R. (1998). Memory-based language processing: Psycholinguistic research in the 1990s. *Annual Review of Psychology, 49*, 25–42.

McNamara, D. S., & Magliano, J. P. (2009a). Self-explanation and metacognition: The dynamics of reading. In D. J. Hacker, J. Dunlosky, & A. C. Graesser (Eds), *Handbook of Metacognition in Education* (pp. 60–81). Mahwah, NJ: Lawrence Erlbaum and Associates.

McNamara, D. S., & Magliano, J. P. (2009b). Towards a comprehensive model of comprehension. In B. Ross (Ed), *The Psychology of Learning and Motivation*, vol. 51 (pp. 297–384). New York, NY: Elsevier Science.

Meyer, B. J. F. (1985). Prose analysis: Purposes, procedures, and problems. In B. K. Britton & J. Black (Eds), *Analyzing and Understanding Expository Text* (pp. 11–64, 269–304). Hillsdale, NJ: Erlbaum.

Meyer, B. J. F., & Freedle, R. O. (1984). Effect of discourse type on recall. *American Educational Research Journal, 21*, 121–143.

Myers, J. L., & O'Brien, E. J. (1998). Accessing the discourse representation during reading. *Discourse Processes, 26*, 131–157.

Naumann, J. (2015). A model of online reading engagement: Linking engagement, navigation, and performance in digital reading. *Computers in Human Behavior, 53*, 263–277. DOI: 10.1016/j.chb.2015.06.051.

New London Group. (1996) A pedagogy of multiliteracies: Designing social futures. *Harvard Educational Review, 66*(1), 60–92.

OECD. (2008). *PISA 2009 Assessment Framework: Key competencies in reading, mathematics and science*. Paris: OECD (retrieved August 5, 2010 from www.oecd.org).

OECD. (2011). *PISA 2009 Results: Students on line: Digital technologies and performance* (Volume VI). DOI: 10.1787/9789264112995-en.

Perfetti, C. A., Rouet, J.-F., & Britt, M. A. (1999). Towards a theory of documents representation. In H. van Oostendorp & S. Goldman (Eds), *The Construction of Mental Representations during Reading* (pp. 99–122). Mahwah, NJ: Erlbaum.

Richter, T., & Rapp, D. N. (2014). Comprehension and validation of text information: Introduction to the special issue. *Discourse Processes, 1–2*, 1–6.

Richter, T., Schroeder, S., & Wöhrmann, B. (2009). You don't have to believe everything you read: Background knowledge permits fast and efficient validation of information. *Journal of Personality and Social Psychology, 96*, 538–558. DOI: 10.1037/a0014038.

Rouet, J. F. (2006). *The Skills of Document Use: From Text Comprehension to Web-Based Learning*. Mahwah, NJ: Erlbaum.

Rouet, J. F., & Britt, M. A. (2011). Relevance processing in multiple document comprehension. In M. T. McCrudden, J. P. Magliano, & G. Schraw (Eds), *Text Relevance and Learning from Text* (pp. 19–52). Greenwich, CT: Information Age Publishing.

Rouet, J. F., Favart, M., Britt, M. A., & Perfetti, C. A. (1997). Studying and using multiple documents in history: Effects of discipline expertise. *Cognition and Instruction, 15*, 85–106.

Rouet, J. F., Ros, C., Goumi, A., Macedo-Rouet, M., & Dinet, J. (2011). The influences of surface and deep cues on primary and secondary school students' assessment of relevance in web menus. *Learning and Instruction, 21*, 205–219.

Rouet, J.-F., Vörös, Z., & Pléh, C. (2012). Incidental learning of links during navigation: The role of visuo-spatial capacity. *Behavior and Information Technology, 31*, 71–81.

Sabatini, J. P. (2005). What does it mean to comprehend or construct meaning in multimedia environments: Thoughts on cognitive and assessment construct development. In T. Trabasso, J. P. Sabatini, D. C. Massaro, & R. C. Calfee (Eds), *From Orthography to Pedagogy: Essays in Honor of Richard L. Venezky* (pp. 149–172). Mahwah, NJ: Lawrence Erlbaum.

Sanchez, C. A., Wiley, J., & Goldman, S. R. (2006). Teaching students to evaluate source reliability during internet research tasks. *Proceedings of the 7th International Conference of the Learning Sciences*. Bloomington, IN.

Santana, A. D., Livingstone, R. M., & Cho, Y. Y. (2013). Print readers recall more than do online readers. *Newspaper Research Journal, 34*, 78–92.

Scharrer, L., Bromme, R., Britt, M. A., & Stadtler, M. (2012). The seduction of easiness: How science depictions influence laypeople's reliance on their own evaluation of scientific information. *Learning and Instruction, 22*, 231–243.

Schraw, G., Wade, S. E., & Kardash, C. A. (1993). Interactive effects of text-based and task-based importance on learning from text. *Journal of Educational Psychology, 85*, 652–661.

Shanahan, T., & Shanahan, C. (2008). Teaching disciplinary literacy to adolescents: Rethinking content-area literacy. *Harvard Educational Review, 78*(1), 40–59.

Singer, M. (2006). Verification of text ideas during reading. *Journal of Memory and Language, 54*, 574–591.

Singer, M. (2013). Validation in reading comprehension. *Current Directions in Psychological Science, 22*, 361–366.

Singer, M., & Halldorson, M. (1996). Constructing and validating motive bridging inferences. *Cognitive Psychology, 30*, 1–38.

Smith, T. J. (2012). The attentional theory of cinematic continuity. *Projections, 6*, 1–27.

Snow, C. (2002). *Reading for Understanding: Toward an R&D Program in Reading Comprehension.* Santa Monica, CA: RAND.

Sperber, D., Clement, C., Heintz, C., Mascaro, O., Mercier, H., Origgi, G., & Wilson, D. (2010). Epistemic vigilance. *Mind & Language, 25,* 359–393.

Stadtler, M., Scharrer, L., Brummernhenrich, B., & Bromme, R. (2013). Dealing with uncertainty: Readers' memory for and use of conflicting information from science texts as function of presentation format and source expertise. *Cognition and Instruction, 31,* 130–150.

Stadtler, M., Scharrer, L., Skodzik, T., & Bromme, R. (2014). Comprehending multiple documents on scientific controversies: Effects of reading goals and signaling rhetorical relationships. *Discourse Processes, 51*(1–2), 93–116.

Steffens, B., Britt, M. A., Braasch, J. L., Strømsø, H., & Bråten, I. (2014). Memory for scientific arguments and their sources: Claim-evidence consistency matters. *Discourse Processes, 51*(1–2), 117–142.

Strømsø, H. I., & Bråten, I. (2002). Norwegian students' use of multiple sources while reading expository texts. *Reading Research Quarterly, 37,* 208–227.

Sundar, S. S., & Nass, C. (2001). Conceptualizing sources in online news. *Journal of Communication, 51,* 52–72. DOI: 10.1111/j.1460-2466.2001.tb02872.x.

Tewksbury, D., & Althaus, S.L. (2000). Differences in knowledge acquisition among readers of the paper and online versions of a national newspaper. *Journalism & Mass Communication, 77,* 457–479.

Toulmin, S. E. (1958). *The Uses of Argument.* Cambridge: Cambridge University Press.

Trabasso, T., & Magliano, J. P. (1996). Conscious understanding during text comprehension. *Discourse Processes, 21,* 255–288.

van den Broek, P., Bohn-Gettler, C. M., Kendeou, P., & Carlson, S. (2011). When a reader meets a text: The role of standards of coherence in reading comprehension. In M. T. McCrudden, J. Magliano, & G. Schraw (Eds), *Text Relevance and Learning from Text* (pp. 123–139). Greenwich, CT: Information Age Publishing.

van den Broek, P., Risden, K., & Husbye-Hartmann, E. (1995). The role of readers' standards of coherence in the generation of inferences during reading. In R. F. Lorch, Jr. & E. J. O'Brien (Eds), *Sources of Coherence in Text Comprehension* (pp. 353–373). Hillsdale, NJ: Erlbaum.

Voss, J. F., Fincher-Keifer, R., Wiley, J., & Silfies, L. (1993). On the processing of arguments. *Argumentation, 7,* 165–181.

Wallace, R. M., Kupperman, J., Krajcik, J., & Soloway, E. (2000). Science on the Web: Students online in a sixth-grade classroom. *The Journal of the Learning Sciences, 9*(1), 75–104.

White, S., Chen, J., & Forsyth, B. (2010). Reading-related literacy activities of American adults: Time spent, task types, and cognitive skills used. *Journal of Literacy Research, 42,* 276–307.

Wiley, J., & Voss, J. F. (1999). Constructing arguments from multiple sources: Tasks that promote understanding not just memory for text. *Journal of Educational Psychology, 91,* 301–311.

Wineburg, S. S. (1991). On the reading of historical texts: Notes on the breach between school and the academy. *American Educational Research Journal, 28,* 495–519.

Wittwer, J., & Ihme, N. (2014). Reading skill moderates the impact of semantic similarity and causal specificity on the coherence of explanations. *Discourse Processes, 51,* 143–166.

Wolfe, M. B., Magliano, J. P., & Larsen, B. (2005). Causal and semantic relatedness in discourse understanding and representation. *Discourse Processes, 39,* 165–187.

Zwaan, R. A., & Radvansky, G. A. (1998). Situation models in language comprehension and memory. *Psychological Bulletin, 123*(2), 162–185.

18

Toward an Integrated Perspective of Writing as a Discourse Process

Danielle S. McNamara

ARIZONA STATE UNIVERSITY

Laura K. Allen

MISSISSIPPI STATE UNIVERSITY

Toward an Integrated Perspective of Writing as a Discourse Process

Writing is perhaps the quintessential *discourse process*. From the simplest note we leave on the kitchen table (perhaps reminding a roommate to take out the trash), to the formulated message sent by email (again, as a polite reminder to take out the trash), to the short essay, and finally to the longer report that likely took months to compose—writers purposely plan, compose, erase, recompose, reread, reflect, and make conscious decisions about what to put on the page.

Like reading *comprehension*, text *production* processes center around the use of linguistic information to actively construct meaning. Indeed, writing incorporates many of the same processes inherent to reading, if only because we must read our own texts as we write. In addition, similar to *speech* production, writing involves the social act of constructing language, generally for the purpose of communicating information to a particular audience. Empirical accounts of this task are largely informed by a strict *cognitive* perspective of the writing process, with a large emphasis placed on the interplay of information storage, retrieval, and processing. Theoretical approaches, however, have also stemmed from *sociocultural* perspectives, emphasizing social factors such as audience, purpose, and medium. Although research from both perspectives has made significant contributions to our knowledge of writing, future progress in this field is likely to depend on a more integrated account of the writing process that considers both cognitive and sociocultural perspectives.

In this chapter, we argue that theoretical models and research that focus on writing as a discourse process can help to integrate these different perspectives. Research on discourse processes inherently focuses on the cognitive and social processes underlying communication within broad cultural contexts. Thus, writing serves as an exciting new avenue for research in this domain. Our perspectives of writing research are colored by two primary lenses. One is from the point of view of having conducted writing research over the past decade. Another is from the perspective of having conducted research on discourse comprehension for the past two decades. Unlike the majority of writing researchers, our foundations began from theoretical perspectives derived from comprehension research, rather than writing. These two lenses (writing and reading comprehension) necessarily color our views of writing theory and writing research. We must acknowledge this at the outset of this chapter. Our aim is to capitalize on these unique perspectives to critically analyze writing theory and to point toward research directions that have potential to further our understanding of writing.

There are inherent relations between reading and writing that are difficult to ignore; they are, for example, the primary forms of text-based communication. As researchers in both areas, however, we have observed few ties between the two communities of researchers. They attend different conferences and are often housed in different academic departments. There is also little overlap in terms of the theoretical accounts of reading and writing. Theories of comprehension and writing are quite different in nature. These differences in the literature open up exciting opportunities to broaden our empirical objectives as well as to potentially merge our theoretical notions of reading and writing.

In this chapter, we first provide a brief overview of writing theories along with research conducted to support those theories. We then present ideas on how approaches to the study of writing can be enhanced by looking to research conducted on text comprehension as a discourse process. In particular, we suggest that theoretical perspectives and research methodologies from the discourse processing community may provide a strong foundation on which to develop more robust theoretical models of the text production process. Ultimately, it is our hope that research in these two areas can be synthesized to support more thorough theoretical perspectives on literacy and text-based communication more broadly.

What Is Writing?

Writing is the transcription of sounds, concepts, thoughts, ideas, and images into a physical trace. This process is not limited by a specific medium or environment—indeed, writing can be achieved using rocks on sand, charcoal on rocks, ink on paper, or images on a computer monitor. Writing is the process of leaving a trace of our thoughts, and communicating ideas to others. Writing is the outcome of a deliberate action, with varying intentions and varying intended consequences.

Sumerians are credited with the invention of writing over 5,000 years ago, using wedge-shaped characters impressed on clay tablets to represent objects and ideas. Early writing is thought to have been primarily used as a means for record keeping, and few knew the art of writing. Today, writing is standardized and ubiquitous: Over 85% of the world's population can write (Central Intelligence Agency, 2015). Writing is used for any number of purposes, from record keeping, to the simple expression of ideas, to communication with others. Writing can involve information telling, storytelling, and knowledge transformation. We write notes to remind ourselves or others of tasks that need to be done or a list of items that we need. We send cryptic emails and more elaborate ones that spell out ideas that we wish to communicate to others. We write summaries of others' ideas, and we write papers that integrate multiple ideas and propose new ones. Writing provides external aids to memory, it provides a means to record our thoughts, and it provides a tool to build on our thoughts. Writing essentially involves all of the *discourse processes*: reading, comprehension, communication, dialogue, argumentation, and of course, language.

Current State of Writing in Education

Given the central importance of writing to our lives, it is not surprising that the ability to write high-quality texts is an important component of success in both the classroom and the workplace (Geiser & Studley, 2001; Light, 2001; Powell, 2009). However, many individuals struggle to develop this skill. According to the 2011 National Assessment of Educational Progress (NAEP) report, nearly a quarter (21%) of United States high school seniors were unable to meet the standards for basic proficiency in academic writing and only 3% of students performed well enough to be considered advanced writers. This situation is much the same internationally. Although a few countries (e.g., Singapore, Japan, South Korea, Finland) have achieved remarkable levels of literacy, the majority of the world suffers from writing deficiencies equivalent to or below those of the United States. These statistics reveal an extremely skewed distribution, with few students showing mastery of the writing process; and (at least in the United States) the picture is even grimmer for non-white students compared to white students (NAEP, 2011).

More time and more instruction are needed for students to learn how to write effectively. However, large class sizes have made it increasingly difficult for educators to provide students with adequate writing instruction (National Commission on Writing, 2003). Engaging in the writing process takes time for students. Grading the assignments and providing feedback takes time for teachers. Furthermore, many teachers are not provided with adequate training to teach writing and provide feedback to students. Recently, writing has received increased attention by researchers, educators, and policy makers. In the United States, the introduction of the Common Core State Standards (CCSS; National Governors Association & Council of Chief School Officers, 2010) has had a marked impact. The CCSS take a step toward aligning the diverse sets of standards and curricula currently used across the United States. Specifically, a unitary set of English Language Arts and Mathematics benchmarks have been established, which define the skills and knowledge that should be mastered at each grade level, beginning in Kindergarten and continuing through the 12th grade.

The CCSS for English Language Arts (which includes standards for writing) were developed to ensure that graduating seniors were prepared for the literacy demands at the college and career levels. The development of these standards drew information from a variety of sources, including empirical research studies, school systems, teachers, assessment developers, and other individuals involved in the education system. Unlike many educational standards and assessments in the past, the CCSS place a strong emphasis on students' ability to write proficiently. Accordingly, these expectations should increase pressure for researchers and educators alike to develop interventions aimed at solving the current writing problem.

Current State of Writing Research

Not only is writing sometimes neglected in the classroom, but compared to other fields, it has also received relatively little focus by researchers (Santangelo, Harris, & Graham, 2016). For instance, compared to other educational domains (e.g., reading comprehension, science, mathematics), little information is known about the writing process, including the range of individual differences that influence skilled and unskilled writers or the treatments that lead to the greatest improvement in students' writing performance (National Commission on Writing, 2003). Writing is difficult to study because of variations in how it is used, why it is used, and of course, when. It can also be a long process. Writing this paper, for example, took months (or years if you count the prior years of studying and conducting research on writing). Perhaps because of this complex nature of writing, we know relatively little about writing and how it develops over time (Shanahan, 2016).

What *Do* We Know about Writing?

Given the fragmentation between the cognitive and sociocultural approaches to writing, it is perhaps not surprising that relatively few comprehensive theories of writing have been developed, particularly in comparison to other constructs. In the field of text comprehension, for instance, researchers have developed a wide assortment of models and frameworks that address the many facets of the reading process. Indeed, in their review of the most prominent theories of comprehension, McNamara and Magliano (2009) looked at seven contemporary models. By contrast, there have been relatively few impactful theories of writing, and these theories have generally built upon each other, rather than approach the process from a new lens.

The most accepted, or widely cited, model of writing was proposed by Flower and Hayes (1981; Hayes, 1996, 2006; Hayes & Flower, 1980). The Flower and Hayes model differentiated the writing process as involving three independent processes: planning, translating, and reviewing. As shown in Figure 18.1a, *planning* processes include generating ideas as well as organizing ideas and setting goals for writing. *Translation* involves transforming ideas into written language. Finally, *reviewing* involves both the evaluation and the revision of a piece of writing, including both reading and editing processes. In contrast to its predecessors, the Flower and Hayes model viewed writing as an interweaved process, with the assumption that there were discrete phases of writing, but they were not as linear as previously described

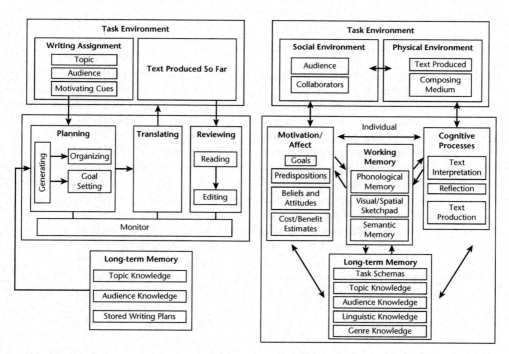

Figure 18.1 a–b Together these two figures illustrate that the three writing stages (planning, translating, and reviewing) were no longer specified in Hayes' *stage theory* model, and the primary additions were the addition of working memory, motivation, and affect. Figure 18.1a (on the left) is adapted from the Flower and Hayes (1981) model. Figure 18.1b (on the right) is based on the Hayes (1996) model.

(cf. Britton, Burgess, Martin, McLeod, & Rosen, 1975; Rohman, 1965). Writing was assumed by Flowers and Hayes to be a dynamic process, wherein writers can move from one stage to another and back again. While completing these processes, writers were assumed to monitor what they were doing, mindful of progressing toward their overall goal. In the Flower and Hayes model, monitoring served as a sort of homunculus, prompting decisions to switch from one stage of the writing process to another.

The Flower and Hayes (1981) model also acknowledged the impacts of both the task environment and the writer's long-term memory. The task environment included the writing assignment (i.e., topic, audience, motivating cues) and the body of text as it was being produced (i.e., the text so far). The long-term memory component, including knowledge of the topic, audience, and writing plans, was assumed to primarily influence planning processes (i.e., generating text, organizing, goal setting).

Later revisions of this model (see Figure 18.1b) included the additions of working memory, motivation, and affect (Hayes, 1996, 2006). The task environment was further delineated to include the social environment and the physical environment. The depiction of the model dropped the explicit specification of the three stages (planning, translating, and reviewing) and adopted a stage theory model, placing working memory as the centerpiece of the model. The construct of working memory was akin to that proposed within the Baddeley (1986) working memory model, including phonological memory, a visuospatial sketchpad, and semantic memory, and was assumed to draw upon and be influenced by motivation and affect, cognitive processes, and long-term memory.

Working Memory in Writing

The Flower and Hayes models (Flower & Hayes, 1981; Hayes, 1996) laid the foundation for writing research. Following this model, writing research from the cognitive perspective has placed a heavy focus on the role of working memory, and the notion that writers must *hold* information in working memory. Working memory was depicted implicitly in the Flower and Hayes model (Figure 18.1a) in the bottom right of the model, where the processes of planning, translating, and reviewing occurred, and explicitly in the center of the Hayes model (Figure 18.1b) which was driven by cognitive processes, motivation/affect, and long-term memory. According to these models, skilled writers can hold and process more information such as knowledge of the content and writing situation, language, and writing processes. There is little to no debate in the writing literature on the importance of working memory to writing, though some hold the strong position that working memory capacity constrains writing ability, and others hold that fluency in writing sub-skills helps to free up working memory resources while writing (e.g., McCutchen, 1996; McCutchen et al., 1994).

The importance of working memory in writing predominantly stems from this concept of fluency. Linguistic and text production processes during writing become increasingly fluent as writers develop (e.g., Alamargot & Fayol, 2009; Berninger et al., 2002; McCutchen, 1996, 2000; McCutchen, Covill, Hoyne, & Mildes, 1994), and thus, many writing researchers reason that lower-level linguistic processes demand less working memory capacity as writers develop. Accordingly, skilled writers can coordinate more ideas (e.g., Scardamalia, 1981) and devote more resources to higher-level aspects of writing such as rhetorical considerations of genre, audience, and goals. For example, in Kellogg's (1996, 2001) working memory model of writing, working memory capacity must be distributed among processes related to planning conceptual content, translating images and propositions into connected sentences, and reviewing the content and text produced.

One line of evidence considered in support of the role of working memory has focused on correlations between working memory span and writing performance (Berninger, Cartwright, Yates, Swanson, & Abbott, 1994; Jeffrey & Underwood, 1996; McCutchen, Covill, Hoyne, & Mildes, 1994). For example, McCutchen and colleagues (1994) found moderate correlations between writing quality and scores on working memory span tasks (i.e., reading span and speaking span) for elementary and middle school students, although the correlation was weak between reading span and writing scores for elementary-aged students. Similarly, Jeffrey and Underwood (1996) identified a significant correlation between elementary students' working memory capacity and their ability to coordinate ideas in a sentence; however, the correlation between working memory scores and text quality was not significant.

Few studies have considered the potential contributions of other skills to the correlations between writing quality and working memory (cf., Allen et al., 2014; Babayigit & Stainthorp, 2011; Hoskyn & Swanson, 2003; Ransdell & Levy, 1996). The correlation between writing quality (or some aspect of writing) and working memory is typically calculated absent from considerations of potential factors such as specific writing skills, reading skills, knowledge of writing, or domain knowledge (to name a few considerations). One exception is a study by Babayigit and Stainthorp (2011), which followed two groups of children (2nd and 4th grades) for one year (into the 3rd and 5th grades, respectively). They found that working memory scores (as measured by a modified version of the reading span task) were moderately related to both reading comprehension and writing at both time points; however, working memory capacity scores failed to make unique contributions when other measures, such as vocabulary, were considered. Similarly, Allen, Snow, Crossley, Jackson, and McNamara (2014) found that the working memory capacity (i.e., operation span scores) did not correlate with writing quality scores, whereas vocabulary knowledge showed a large ($r = .55$) correlation with the writing quality scores.

Nonetheless, a further source of evidence for the role of working memory in writing comes from aging research that shows that older adults produce shorter sentences with fewer embedded and subordinate clauses (Kemper, Kynette, Rash, O'Brien, & Sprott, 1989; Kemper, Rash, Kynette, & Norman, 1990) and maintain coherence less successfully (e.g., Kemper, 1990; McCutchen, 1986; Pratt, Boyes, Robins, & Manchester, 1989) compared to younger adults. For example, in a study of diary entries made by adults over a seven-decade period, Kemper found that as writers aged, they produced narratives with lower cohesion and simpler syntax (Kemper, 1990). These results are interpreted as indicating that elderly adults write with reduced syntactic complexity because of working memory limitations. Further, and perhaps most convincing in this regard, Hoskyn and Swanson (2003) found that working memory scores correlated with structural complexity[1] in writing across three age spans (15, 30, 77 years), and that this effect remained significant when performance on a short-term memory task (i.e., digit span), reading comprehension, word knowledge, spelling, and handwriting were included within a hierarchical analysis.

A good deal of research on writing from the working memory perspective has manipulated secondary cognitive loads during the writing process. The majority of this research has focused on the competition between lower-level processes of transcription and higher-level planning and evaluation processes. In these studies, researchers prompt participants to engage in a secondary task (e.g., maintaining a list of words in memory) to distract their executive attention from a cognitively demanding primary task. Results from these studies indicate that performance on primary writing tasks worsens when these secondary tasks are added. For example, Ransdell, Levy, and Kellogg (2002) found that increasing secondary load during text production negatively affected the length of sentences generated by students, although only if the load was extremely high. Nonetheless, many researchers interpret the results from these secondary task paradigms as providing convincing evidence for the central role of working memory during the writing process.

Despite the fact that working memory is (moderately) related to a large number of cognitive tasks, it is essential to note that individual differences in working memory are not predictive of performance on *all* cognitive tasks (Unsworth, Schrock, & Engle, 2004). In fact, high-working-memory-capacity participants typically only outperform low-working-memory-capacity participants on tasks that require them to control their attention; thus, working-memory-related performance differences are consistently absent during automatic processing tasks (Heitz & Engle, 2007; Unsworth, Schrock, & Engle, 2004). For instance, Unsworth and colleagues (2004) reported no differences between high and low span individuals on prosaccade (i.e., saccade toward a target) trials, compared to notable differences between participants on antisaccade (i.e., suppression of a rapid movement of the eye between fixation points) and mixed (i.e., antisaccade and prosaccade) trials.

Because of the limited capacity of a writer's working memory system, success on writing tasks requires individuals to coordinate the demands of the separate writing processes through two primary means: developing automaticity for certain tasks (e.g., typing, decoding) and using appropriate strategies, such as outlining or freewriting, for other tasks (McCutchen, 1996). Students can develop automaticity of certain processes through explicit instruction and deliberate practice, which should lead to a reduction in demands on the working memory system. Following this reasoning, if certain processes cannot be automatized (e.g., idea generation or organization), writing strategies should be effective. And indeed, writing strategies, such as planning and revising, allow students to focus their attention on a specific set of writing problems, reducing the difficulty of the writing process. In fact, Graham and Perin's (2007) meta-analysis of over 120 published studies of writing interventions and the results indicated that strategy instruction was the most successful form of writing instruction.

In sum, the central role of working memory in the Hayes (1996) writing model has led to a strong focus on working memory by writing researchers over the past two decades. A number of studies have demonstrated significant correlations between performance on working memory tasks and aspects of written texts (e.g., writing quality, sentence length), and studies employing dual-task paradigms have found that increasing working memory load can reduce writing performance. However, discrepancies between studies arise due to the type and number of indices included in the analyses. Correlations between working memory and writing ability vary, for instance, based on the measure of writing quality being used (e.g., holistic scores, sentence length, etc.). Further, when additional indices are controlled for in these analyses, the correlation between working memory and writing ability is often reduced or removed entirely, indicating that working memory may be less predictive when other skills and knowledge are considered.

Self-Regulation in Writing

In the Flower and Hayes (1981; Figure 18.1a) model, monitoring prompts decisions to switch from one stage of the writing process to another. In the Hayes (1996) model depicted in Figure 18.1b, monitoring was implicitly represented in terms of reflection, goal setting, and cost/benefit estimates. Given its tight link to monitoring, self-regulation has been considered intrinsic to theories of writing. Self-regulation is a metacognitive strategy that involves cognitive, behavioral, and motivational strategies that individuals use to set, assess progress on, and achieve goals (Graham & Harris, 2000; Zimmerman & Risemberg, 1997). More proficient writers are assumed to use a wider range of self-regulatory strategies than novice writers (Zimmerman & Risemberg, 1997). Self-regulatory strategies allow writers to manage and coordinate the complex processes required to successfully complete a written product. Self-regulation can include behaviors as simple as choosing a quiet environment for writing, and as complex as self-evaluation of progress.

Zimmerman and Risemberg (1997) particularly focused on the role of self-regulation in a *social cognitive model* of writing. This model included three forms of self-regulation: environmental, behavioral, and covert/personal. Writers are assumed to monitor and react to feedback on their self-regulatory strategies for controlling their actions, the writing environment, and their internal thoughts and processes.

Zimmerman and Risemberg (1997) further assumed that self-regulation was closely tied to self-efficacy. Self-efficacy is the self-judgment about the ability to complete a particular task, in contrast to an objective assessment of ability (Bandura, 1977; Pajares, 2002), and is assumed to motivate individuals to initiate and persist in completing tasks such as writing (Bandura, 1971, 1977). The relationship between writing performance and self-efficacy has been extensively studied (see Pajares, 2003, for a review), generally showing moderate correlations, and several models of writing have included self-efficacy for writing as well as self-efficacy for self-regulatory behaviors (Harris & Graham, 1992; Schunk & Zimmerman, 1994). Self-efficacy for self-regulatory behaviors has been found to correlate with both writing self-efficacy and writing performance (Schunk & Zimmerman, 1994; Zimmerman & Kitsantas, 1999). Notably, while writing apprehension might also be associated with self-efficacy, and many students experience fear and anxiety when faced with a writing task (Daly & Miller, 1975), writing apprehension is generally not predictive of writing performance (Pajares, 2003). This aligns with Bandura's (1986) assertion that anxiety is, to a large extent, the result of individuals' lack of confidence in their ability to complete the task.

Problem Solving in Writing

Problem solving is not an explicit focus of the Flower and Hayes models (Flower & Hayes, 1981; Hayes, 1996). However, according to many cognitive scientists, writing is a problem-solving activity that requires individuals to coordinate their linguistic knowledge, thoughts, and audience expectations for the purpose of developing a coherent text. During this process, writers often encounter a number of problems that they must solve, such as generating relevant ideas, organizing ideas into a coherent structure, generating grammatically correct and sophisticated sentences, establishing coherence, revising for errors, and establishing an appropriate tone and voice for a particular audience.

In light of this complexity, it is essential that writers engage in goal-oriented problem-solving activities to write at a proficient level. This perspective of writing as a problem-solving activity was first made explicit by Bereiter and Scardamalia (1987), who noted a number of key differences between the writing processes of novice and skilled writers. The model included two separate problem spaces, content and rhetorical, with problem translation processes linking the two. They proposed that one difference distinguishing novice and skilled writers was the degree to which they engage in *knowledge telling* versus *knowledge-transforming*. Specifically, novices tend to engage in a process known as *knowledge telling*, wherein they compose text through a simple memory retrieval process, allowing recovered information to prompt the generation of additional text. In this process, writers do not shape knowledge according to a specific audience; rather, they simply produce text based on the retrieved knowledge structures. By contrast, skilled writers are assumed to engage in knowledge-transforming, which includes a greater emphasis on the composition process as a problem (referred to as knowledge-transforming), with writers establishing goals and dynamically revising their writing to shape their knowledge according to their needs and the needs of their audience. The largest impact of the model was its greater focus on writing as a problem-solving task and on the impacts of prior knowledge. Nonetheless, however oft cited, empirical validation of the model has been unfortunately limited (MacArthur & Graham, 2016).

The Cognitive Approach versus the Sociocultural Approach

While there has been little controversy over *theories* of writing, there have been far greater contrasts drawn between two approaches that have emerged in the writing literature: the *cognitive* approach and the *sociocultural* approach. The cognitive approach to writing research places a strong emphasis on the interplay of information storage, retrieval, and processing during a given writing task. One major problem with the research conducted in this field, however, is the failure to address the needs of an increasingly diverse population of students in United States classrooms. A narrow view of literacy (i.e., one that only addresses a subset of a population) inherently lacks sensitivity to the social inequalities that exist within diverse populations. *Sociocultural* researchers, on the other hand, propose that it is impossible and irresponsible to separate literacy from the cultural, community, and familial influences of a person's environment. This inherently produces inequalities among students (Purcell-Gates & Tierney, 2009), particularly students from diverse backgrounds (Au, 2000). Importantly, both the cognitive and sociocultural approaches align with the Flower and Hayes (e.g., 1981) model of writing, but each emphasizes different aspects of the theory: the lower half (i.e., the individual) versus the upper half (i.e., the task) of Figure 18.1 a–b.

Cognitive Approaches to Writing Research

Researchers who have adopted the cognitive approach to writing have focused on writing from the individual's perspective, seeking to explain the impacts of the writer's cognitive processes on the writing process and the final product. Because much of the research has been prompted by the Flower and Hayes (e.g., 1981) models, research in this arena has focused on processes that were central to the models, such as planning, translating, and reviewing, and the impact of cognitive mechanisms such as self-regulation (monitoring), writing strategies, long-term memory, and especially, working memory.

Although specific components may vary, most contemporary cognitive models of the writing process are founded on the concept of a limited-capacity cognitive system. To illustrate this point, researchers have compared writers to computers that have too many programs running in the background (Torrance & Galbraith, 2006) or switchboard operators trying to juggle multiple phone calls (Flower & Hayes, 1980). A primary concern among cognitive writing researchers, therefore, is the wealth of processing demands that writing places on the limited-capacity working memory system (Kellogg, 2008). It is often assumed that the problem-solving, knowledge-transforming process can only take place when a writer can direct and control their attention throughout the writing process. Accordingly, cognitive interventions tend to focus on techniques that will alleviate demands on this system, such as consistent, deliberate practice (Kellogg & Raulerson, 2007), cognitive apprenticeship (Kellogg, 2008; Rogoff, 1990), and explicit instruction and practice of writing strategies (Graham & Perin, 2007; Roscoe & McNamara, 2013). Many writing researchers assume that these training tasks will lead to increased automaticity in certain skills and better regulation for other, more complex skills.

Researchers who adopt the cognitive framework commonly investigate typically developed (i.e., students with no learning disabilities) students in high school or college (e.g., Kellogg, 2001; Roscoe & McNamara, 2013). Although a number of cognitive *interventions* have been tested on students across a range of ages and skill levels (see Graham et al., 2013; Graham, MacArthur, & Fitzgerald, 2013; Graham, McKeown, Kiuhara, & Harris, 2012), most of the writing research studies have been conducted on middle-class students in their teens or early twenties who tend to come from mainstream backgrounds. Importantly, cognitive studies are rarely conducted on minority groups, such as non-native speakers or students from lower socioeconomic classes. Some interventions have been examined for students with learning disabilities (see Graham, Harris, & Larsen, 2001); however, it is still the case that cognitive studies have a relatively narrow range of participant demographics.

Sociocultural Approaches to Writing Research

The sociocultural approach to writing research is focused primarily on the top sections of the Flower and Hayes models (Flower & Hayes, 1981; Hayes, 1996)—the task environment. As such, researchers from this perspective point to one limitation of cognitive perspectives—their isolated examination of the writing task. That is, researchers from the cognitive perspective do little to consider the societal and environmental factors that may influence the skills and processes of student writers. From the sociocultural framework, literacy is unable to be separated from the environment in which it is intended; therefore, the social and cultural purposes for writing must be considered in any assessment of text. According to Faigley (1985), people learn specific forms of discourse that allow them to participate in certain communities; therefore, understanding literacy necessarily requires one to consider the surrounding environment of an individual.

The roots of the sociocultural approach lie in Vygotsky's (1978) socio-cognitive theories of language and learning. The primary premise of Vygotskian theory is that knowledge is constructed through social interactions. Along similar lines, Bakhtin (1981) proposed the notion of the dialogism, whereby the nature of learning relates to social discourse within classrooms and communities. An integral assumption is that discourse is influenced by social speech genres and practices. Speech production, communication, and social interactions are influenced by various factors such as pragmatics, grounding, context, and goals (Clark, 2004). Similarly, there are multiple differences in goals and criteria between writing within the classroom, outside the classroom, and in professional settings. The sociocultural perspective views writing as a social event involving the construction of that event and relationships with others. Accordingly, children are agentive beings whose thoughts and actions are inseparable from their interactions with others. As such, writing and the writing process are inseparable from the task environment (e.g., genre, objective, sources) and the social environment (e.g., peers, classroom, teachers, co-authors). Students' awareness of differences in rhetorical demands across writing contexts is crucial to the writing process. Individual factors such as skills and strategies are not necessarily denied, but they are not emphasized (and usually not examined) by sociocultural writing theorists.

Modern sociocultural theorists expand upon the work of Vygotsky to address a number of social and cultural factors related to communicative literacy (Prior, 2006). These theories typically share the idea that writing is *situated* within a realistic context, *improvised* (not just produced from templates), *mediated* by social conventions, and *acquired through socialization* with a particular community of individuals. According to the sociocultural framework, cultural practices within particular groups of people can drastically influence an individual's perceptions of literacy. Specifically, cultures differ in the writing tasks that they require, the format of writing that they value, and their perceptions and attitudes toward the audience. An additional component of the sociocultural framework is the idea that modes or genres of writing are context-specific. Specifically, these genres are conventional structures that reflect the given society within which they are used. To illustrate this point, a number of studies have shown that the characteristics of modes and genres develop in a way that directly reflects the historical changes and development within specific societies (Bazerman, 1988; Bazerman & Prior, 2005).

Overall, unlike the cognitive framework for writing, sociocultural perspectives suggest that writing is a purpose-driven process that is governed by expectations of a specific community. Therefore, writing is informed by a host of factors, including the purposes for engaging in writing, the expectations surrounding these purposes, the writer's knowledge of discourse, the available writing tools, and other cultural variables. Together, these influences interact to reflect the social context within which the writer is motivated to communicate through a writing activity.

New Literacies Approach

Integral to the sociocultural approach to writing has been research on differences in writing across time, in particular as a function of modern technological affordances such as computers and the internet. The internet has had a profound impact on society, including the nature of writing. The shift from paper to screen has instigated an area of research referred to as *new literacies* (e.g., Kist, 2005; Leu, Kinzer, Coiro, Castek, & Henry, 2013). Word processing programs afford more efficient editing processes during writing, such as deleting, copying and pasting, spell checking, and so on. The internet, in turn, facilitates searching for information, storing and searching for documents, and using multimedia elements (e.g., visual, sound, and animated elements) in writing. The process of writing is intrinsically non-linear—writers plan, draft, and revise in non-linear ways—and word processing technologies together with internet searching and storage have increased, and facilitated, non-linear, intertextual, multilayered, and multimodal writing.

The internet also engenders a broader range of social practices for writers, including greater communication between co-authors, increased ease in passing documents from one author to another, and online collaborative writing (Fernheimer, Litterio, & Hendler, 2011; Gross & Buehl, in press; McCarthy, Grabill, Hart-Davidson, & McLeod, 2011; Starke-Meyerring et al., 2011). Modern media increase the rapidity of the writing process: text messages are sent and received instantaneously; emails are exchanged in rapid succession; documents are shared and exchanged hourly. These exchanges are much speedier than earlier forms of writing dissemination, like sending a note or letter that might arrive days later, or typing a manuscript to receive feedback weeks or months later.

Research on new literacies seeks to discover common principles of internet use, including social practice and multimodality. New literacies researchers argue that modern technological affordances require new and different writing practices, skills, and strategies and raise new requirements and demands in collaboration while writing (Orlikowski & Yates, 2002). Student writers are required to learn how to write across a wider range of media and genres. New literacies researchers argue that technological changes call for a more complex research agenda, with a greater focus on the intrapersonal, institutional, and contextual demands that shape writing objectives (Driscoll & Wells, 2012; Leu, Slomp, Zawilinski, & Corrigan, 2016; Slomp, 2012).

New literacies also argue that the modern communication practices and the skills they call upon are not adequately considered among the constructs included in large-scale writing assessments (Slomp, Corrigan, & Sugimoto, 2014; Stagg, Peterson, McClay, & Main, 2011). There has been an increased focus in writing research on writing outside of school since the 1990s. Yet, current assessments are largely removed from the literacy practices of literate people in modern society (Stagg Peterson, McClay, & Main, 2011). Whereas many situated writing practices represent a blend of forms and sources of knowledge and skills, these factors are not considered within most modern assessments.

The arguments raised by researchers of new literacies are compelling. Indeed, some students excel at cognitive tasks outside of the school context but struggle in school (Hull & Schultz, 2002). Yet, compelling empirical evidence is not yet available. In particular, it is not clear the degree to which new literacies contribute to writing quality over and above other factors such as basic knowledge of writing processes and domain knowledge. While researchers in the area of new literacies stress the importance of factors relevant to the specific task and the environment, the basic processes in writing are often ignored. While those writing about new literacies expound on the importance of multiple genres of writing and skills relevant to real-world tasks, they themselves communicate these ideas using traditional academic writing, retaining the practice of having introductions, bodies, and conclusions, with claims and evidence. And so, while many of the researchers on new literacies deride the lack of alignment of traditional writing assessments with new writing practices, they also still value and engage in the very practices that are traditionally called upon within large-scale assessments.

Nonetheless, new literacies and their importance cannot be denied. From one perspective it is doubtful that writing tweets and emails will transfer to passing a writing exam. However, from another, students may learn to recognize the appropriateness of rhetorical styles across different genres and media and perhaps become more flexible in their use of discourse patterns. Capturing differences in writing as a function of genre and authoring modes may be crucial to a comprehensive model of writing. For example, within the genre of persuasive writing, skilled writers do not simply rely on a specific template for high-quality writing each time they produce a text. Rather, these writers are more flexible in their cohesion and rhetorical style across multiple essays (Allen, Snow, & McNamara, 2014, 2016). The recognition of a text's audience (along with their knowledge, beliefs, and other characteristics) is a critical component of writing skill and so students may become more adept at thinking about audience when they compose texts that are directed at a variety of audiences.

Relations between Reading and Writing

Research areas devoted to the study of reading and writing have largely developed in isolation from each other, and are often housed in different academic departments. However, given the (perhaps obvious) similarities between the tasks, small subsets of researchers have focused on the empirical examination of the similarities between these tasks. The majority of this research area consists of correlational studies, which test relations between performance on measures of knowledge and skills and measures of reading and writing ability. Additionally, research has been conducted to investigate the impact of writing (about a target text) on reading comprehension.

Correlations between Reading and Writing

Several perspectives within the writing literature, such as the rhetorical relations view (Tierney & Shanahan, 1991) and the shared-knowledge view (Fitzgerald & Shanahan, 2000), assume that reading and writing rely on common knowledge and processes. Hence, a number of studies have examined the potential overlap between processes associated with reading comprehension and writing (e.g., Allen et al., 2014; Galda, 1983; Shanahan, 1988; Stotsky, 1983; Tierney & Shanahan, 1991), generally substantiating early claims that poor readers are also poor writers (Loban, 1963, 1967). In a review of the literature, Tierney and Shanahan (1991) reported consistently moderate to strong correlations between various measures of reading and writing (though typically never exceeding r = .50). With a few exceptions (Abbott & Berninger, 1993; Juel et al., 1986; Loban, 1967), these studies have typically collected one measure of reading ability (e.g., holistic comprehension score, vocabulary knowledge) and one for writing (e.g., holistic writing score, organization, grammar), and interpreted the correlation between the two as further evidence for the overlap in the skills and knowledge bases required to read and write.

Although correlations between knowledge and skills related to reading and writing have been fairly consistent across age and text levels (Fitzgerald & Shanahan, 2000), these correlations have been found to falter somewhat when multiple measures are used to capture specific aspects of textual knowledge (e.g., vocabulary knowledge, text comprehension, and coherent text production). For instance, Juel et al. (1986) conducted a longitudinal study that followed students from 1st to 2nd grade and analyzed the reading–writing relationship at multiple levels of text, including spelling, word recognition, reading comprehension, and writing ability. They concluded that the lowest-level aspects of reading and writing (e.g., word recognition and spelling) relied upon similar knowledge bases, such as phonemic awareness and vocabulary knowledge, but the higher-level abilities (e.g., comprehension and production) relied upon different, yet somewhat overlapping, knowledge bases (e.g., discourse knowledge, strategic knowledge).

Additionally, Berninger et al. (2002) examined the relations between reading and writing as part of a larger research project comparing written language (i.e., reading and writing) to oral language (i.e., listening and speaking). For each construct, they assessed knowledge with multiple measures, yielding shared variances of up to 85% for word recognition and spelling, and up to 66% for surface-level text comprehension and production. Their results indicated that reading skills had a greater influence on writing skills than the reverse, but that both skills were strongly related across multiple grade levels. In a more recent study, Allen and colleagues (2014) investigated the role of higher-level cognitive skills in both reading comprehension and writing tasks. Specifically, they investigated how individual differences commonly related to reading comprehension ability overlapped and contributed to students' proficiency in writing. University students (n = 108) completed a battery of assessments related to their reading and writing skills, as well as their vocabulary knowledge, lower-level cognitive skills (i.e., working memory capacity), and higher-level skills (i.e., text memory, text inferencing, prior knowledge access, and knowledge integration). Their results indicated that reading comprehension was strongly related to both vocabulary knowledge and higher-level cognitive skills, whereas writing ability was moderately associated with a subset of these variables, namely vocabulary knowledge and prior knowledge access. Hence, few higher-level skills associated with reading were predictive of writing performance. The skills that seem to overlap most, and most consistently, are related to students' knowledge, their knowledge of words, and their ability to access knowledge.

How Writing Improves Reading

An additional line of research has focused on how writing improves reading comprehension. While the shared-knowledge view (Fitzgerald & Shanahan, 2000) of writing predicts that writing processes should enhance comprehension, research on this topic has been a greater focus of discourse processing researchers, primarily because many comprehension strategies instruct students on generating an external (coherent) representation of their comprehension of text. These strategies include self-explanation, extended writing, summarization, note taking, and asking or answering questions (see e.g., McNamara, 2007).

Self-explanation is the process of rewording the text in familiar terms and linking the current to prior content or knowledge to enhance understanding. Few readers self-explain effectively. However, practice in self-explanation combined with instruction in using comprehension strategies such as making bridging inferences and elaborating the text with outside information effectively improves self-explanation quality, comprehension ability, and course grades (Jackson & McNamara, 2013; McNamara, 2004, 2017).

Self-explanation is a comprehension strategy that is generally not considered from the writing perspective because writing per se is not intrinsic to self-explanation—it can be achieved orally or in writing (Muñoz, Magliano, Sheridan, & McNamara, 2006). For example, self-explanation was not included in a recent meta-analysis of 95 studies on *writing to read* by Graham and Herbert (2011). They examined the effects of writing about the material on text comprehension, the effects of writing skill instruction on students' (grades 1–12) reading skills, and the effects of extended writing on learning to read.

Graham and Herbert (2011) found that writing about the material improved reading comprehension in 94% of the studies reviewed, with an average weighted effect size of 0.37 on norm-referenced comprehension measures and 0.50 on researcher-created measures, with larger effects for less skilled readers and writers (ES 0.64). As a rule of thumb, effect sizes around 0.20 are considered small, effects around 0.50 are moderate, and effects above 0.80 are large. Extended writing, going beyond single statements or a summary (including nine studies), had the largest effect size (ES = 0.68). Summarization was also highly effective (including 19 studies), with an effect size of 0.54. From the perspective of comprehension, summarization helps readers to identify the main ideas and purpose within a text, putting less emphasis on content that is irrelevant or redundant (Brown, Campione, & Day, 1981). Summarizing also reinforces readers' mental representations of the content, enhancing not only retention of text material (Rinehart et al., 1986), but also conceptual understanding (Wade-Stein & Kintsch, 2004), particularly for lower-achieving students and those with learning disabilities (Gil, Bråten, Vidal-Abarca, & Strømsø, 2010).

Graham and Herbert (2011) further found that providing students with *writing instruction* (e.g., on sentence construction, writing processes, and spelling) had significant, positive effects on students' *comprehension* of texts. Notably, however, the largest effect sizes were reported for lower-level components of reading, such as reading fluency (average weighted ES = 0.66; n = 5 studies) and word reading (average weighted ES = 0.62; n = 6 studies). These findings align with studies showing that the greatest overlap in shared knowledge between reading and writing is in lower-level aspects of reading and writing such as phonemic awareness and vocabulary knowledge (e.g., Allen, Snow, Crossley, Jackson, & McNamara, 2014; Berninger et al., 2002; Juel et al., 1986).

Generally, studies that have examined the effects of writing on reading have focused on single-text comprehension. However, an important area of research in the discourse literature has focused on the processes involved in the evaluation and comprehension information using multiple text documents (Britt & Aglinskas, 2002; Rouet, Britt, Mason, & Perfetti, 1996; Wineburg, 1991). The aim of these studies has been to focus on a form of comprehension that is arguably more relevant to *real-world* learning tasks—that is, using the internet or a collection of library books to research a complex topic, rather than relying on only one text source. In these studies, researchers commonly use source-based writing tasks as a method for evaluating students' comprehension of the topics. The processes involved in generating these essays, however, are typically not considered by the researchers, and the writing of the essay is not *used* to enhance comprehension. Analyses of the writing have predominantly focused on the proximity of the content to the source materials or on students' selection of source materials (Britt & Aglinskas, 2002; Foltz, Britt, & Perfetti, 1996; Rouet, Britt, Mason, & Perfetti, 1996). Although some studies have evaluated the quality of these source-based essays, the researchers tend to place little emphasis on the writing itself and are predominantly focused on the source material present in the essays (e.g., Foltz, Britt, & Perfetti, 1996).

In addition, few studies have investigated the impact of instruction or training on students' ability to use source material in an essay (cf. Britt & Aglinskas, 2002; Foltz, Britt, & Perfetti, 1996). In these rare cases, however, the training is similarly focused only on the source material and does not emphasize other factors related to the writing process (Britt & Aglinskas, 2002; Foltz, Britt, & Perfetti, 1996; Rouet, Britt, Mason, & Perfetti, 1996).

Overall, the results of these (and other) studies suggest that the processes of comprehending and producing texts are somewhat similar tasks that draw on some overlapping knowledge sources and higher-level cognitive skills, but primarily in terms of word and world knowledge. Reading and writing also draw upon each other: reading draws upon writing in service of helping readers to consolidate their understanding of text, externalizing their understanding, and creating an externalized object that readers can work with and through. In turn, writing draws on reading by giving fodder to composition as many writing tasks call on writing about external sources. While we have a basic understanding of the relations between reading and writing, there is a good deal more that we do not know. And the few connections that have been identified between reading and writing skills leave vast gaps in how the two processes might be explained using similar theoretical frames.

The Impact of the Modal Model on Theories of Writing

Our view of writing theories, as we've mentioned, is naturally filtered through a lens shaded by experience working with comprehension frameworks. As such, it naturally struck us that many of the principle perspectives of writing research remain housed in stage theories grounded in the *modal model* (Healy & McNamara, 1996). These theories fundamentally assume that processes are serial and rely on separate working memory and long-term memory components (e.g., Hayes, 1996). The models depicted in Figure 18.1 a–b of this chapter, for instance, describe individual components and factors that influence writing, potentially recursively, but from one stage to another, from one mechanism to another. These models emerged in the 1980s (Flower & Hayes, 1981) when this type of model dominated our understanding of memory and cognition. Yet, since their onset, these models have placed strong constraints on the type of research and theories that have emerged from the field.

One principal limitation of modal models that has largely influenced writing research is their emphasis on task components rather than processes. This may seem contradictory to the fact that Flower and Hayes' model delineates three critical processes of writing.

As shown in Figure 18.1a, *planning* processes comprise the generation of ideas as well as the act of organizing ideas and setting goals for writing. *Translation* involves the act of transforming ideas into written language. *Reviewing* involves both the evaluation and the revision of a piece of writing, including both reading and editing processes. However, the mechanisms underlying these processes are underspecified. For example, how do writers activate and generate ideas during the planning phase of a writing task? How is one idea transformed into another? What forms of knowledge afford skillful evaluation of one's own writing? Current models of writing do not prompt explorations into these types of questions. Fine-grained depictions of the way in which writing processes unfold have yet to comprise a major focus of writing research.

The foci of stage theories are imposed by the constraints of the model: (a) serial processes are naturally constrained by working memory resources, and (b) some mechanism is necessary to move from one stage to another. Essentially, a central executive, or homunculus, is needed to guide transfer from one process to another, from one mechanism to another, from one memory store to another. Researchers in other fields have commonly cited this problem as the "degrees of freedom problem" (Turvey, 1990). According to this perspective, modular approaches to language and cognition more generally assume that there are an almost infinite number of ways in which our language processes can be manipulated over time. Each of these processes would, therefore, be working in isolation, without being connected to other, simultaneous processes. With some reflection, of course, this perspective cannot possibly account for the complexities of writing. This modular approach likely imposes an impossible "dead end" perspective on the writing process that obscures the complexity of the interacting linguistic processes. Writing consists of multiple, interacting processes that work together to produce *coherent* texts. Text-based communication, by its very nature, must involve a parallel integration of the component processes.

In sum, stage theories (or modal models) ignore basic concepts accepted in cognitive science (e.g., MacKay, 1998) such as spreading activation and parallel processing. Text comprehension theorists have more widely accepted the assumptions of basic connectionist models. For example, the Construction-Integration model of text comprehension assumes that information (represented as nodes) is activated during reading and this activation is spread throughout a network of activated concepts that includes both the present information and information available from prior knowledge (Kintsch, 1998). In this model, working memory is represented as the activation of information in the environment (e.g., text, discourse) and the information that is available from long-term memory. Hence, while some researchers have explored the role of working memory in reading (e.g., Carpenter, Miyake, & Just, 1994; Just & Carpenter, 1992), many theories of text and discourse comprehension do not hold the role of working memory as a central concept as do the principal theories of writing.

In sum, one effect of the stage theory approach in writing theories has been a focus on the memorial constraints of writing and on the monitoring mechanisms necessary to drive the writing process. Another effect of the modularity of these models has been a separation of research camps, with a divide between those who have focused on cognitive mechanisms (the lower halves of Figure 18.1 a–b) and sociocultural mechanisms (the upper halves of Figure 18.1 a–b). How can we begin to develop research that is sensitive to (and informative of) the complexities of writing, and at the same time consider both the cognitive factors as well as sociocultural factors? The current research in the field is largely constrained by research on product measures, as well as by correlational and intervention-based research. This methodological approach naturally follows and supports stage models.

377

Future Directions

The consideration of writing as a complex, contextualized, and dynamic system calls for a fundamentally different empirical approach. It calls for approaches that reveal the processes in writing within the context of more fine-grained, dynamic analyses. To this end, we outline three potential avenues for research that may open up doors for examining the multiple complexities of writing. We emphasize these avenues because they allow for empirical investigations of the writing process without sacrificing nuance and sensitivity to complexity.

The first is to capitalize on the emerging technologies that afford automated analyses of text features. With these technologies, discourse analyses that previously required hundreds of hours now take mere hours. Such analyses open up doors to understanding the nature of writing through close inspections of the fine-grained features of written text.

The second proposed avenue is to place a greater focus on the differentiated sub-processes involved in writing, and in particular on the temporal structure of these processes. Emerging research in cognitive science points to the importance of examining the temporal structure of behaviors to develop a comprehensive understanding of a phenomenon (e.g., Port & van Gelder, 1995; Spivey, 2007). Therefore, analyses of writing behaviors that are sensitive to time may go a long way in developing our theories of the writing process.

Finally, we propose that researchers should further examine the roles of prior knowledge and component skills in the production of text. A significant body of research suggests that prior knowledge, along with lower-level and higher-level cognitive skills, are important for the *comprehension* of texts (e.g., Kendeou & van den Broek, 2007; McKeown, Beck, Sinatra, & Loxterman, 1992; McNamara & Magliano, 2009). Therefore, similar investigations may prove fruitful in the analysis of text *production*.

Linguistics and Writing

One approach that may serve to further our understanding of writing relates to the linguistic properties of the texts that are either being read or written. Within the discourse processes community, for instance, there exists a wealth of information on the relations between text comprehension processes and performance and the linguistic properties of the texts being read, such as their cohesive devices or the complexity of their sentence structures (Britton & Gülgöz, 1991; Graesser, Cai, Louwerse, & Daniel, 2006; McNamara & Kintsch, 1996; McNamara, Kintsch, Songer, & Kintsch, 1996; O'Reilly & McNamara, 2007).

In many of these studies, natural language processing (NLP) techniques have been employed to automatically analyze the linguistic properties of texts (Graesser, McNamara, Louwerse, & Cai, 2004; McNamara, Graesser, McCarthy, & Cai, 2014). A number of tools have been used by discourse processes researchers to further examine the role of linguistic properties on text comprehension (Crossley, Allen, Kyle, & McNamara, 2014; Crossley, Kyle, & McNamara, in press; Kyle & Crossley, in press; McNamara, Graesser, McCarthy, & Cai, 2014). Together, this research area has served to provide important information about the interactions between linguistic features and the cognitive processes involved in text comprehension.

Beyond research on text readability, NLP techniques have commonly been used to analyze student writing. This research, however, has predominantly focused on the development of computational models for automatically scoring and providing feedback on essays (Allen, Jacovina, & McNamara, 2016; Deane, 2013; Dikli, 2006; McNamara, Crossley, Roscoe, Allen, & Dai, 2015; Shermis & Burstein, 2003, 2013). In particular, automated essay scoring (AES) engines have been developed to model essay scores assigned by expert human raters through calculations that rely on the extraction of linguistic features. Although, this research has not focused on advancing theories of writing, the development of these models has revealed important information about the linguistic properties of high-quality texts. For example, Crossley and McNamara (2011; Crossley & McNamara, 2014) found that high-quality essays contained more diverse and sophisticated word choices, as well as more complex sentence constructions.

More recently, researchers have begun to investigate how and whether individual differences among students can be modeled using the linguistic features captured with NLP (Allen & McNamara, 2015; Allen, Perret, & McNamara, in press; Allen, Snow, & McNamara, 2015). Allen and McNamara (2015), for example, used indices related to the lexical properties of students' essays to successfully model their scores on a vocabulary knowledge assessment. Similarly, Allen, Perret, and McNamara (in press) demonstrated that students' working memory capacity could be modeled using only the linguistic features of their essays, and moreover, that these effects were moderated by inferencing skills. Overall, these (and other) previous studies suggest that NLP techniques are an extremely powerful source of data and have strong potential to inform models and research on the writing process.

Temporal Analyses of Writing

An additional research area that can contribute to our understanding of the complexity of the writing process relates to the question of how writing behaviors unfold over time (i.e., *online* writing processes). In other words: *How do the temporal patterns of writing behaviors (e.g., pauses, bursts of writing) differ across different contexts and skill levels?* Reading researchers, for example, have relied heavily on reading times and eye tracking to provide information about participants' cognitive processes while reading texts (Just & Carpenter, 1980; McDonald, Carpenter, & Shillcock, 2005; Rayner, 1998; Yang & McConkie, 2001). Although researchers have made a significant effort to leverage these methodologies to better understand reading processes, there has been a significantly smaller amount of research conducted on students' online writing processes. Specifically, most of the previous research on writing has focused on students' finished writing products and not their moment-by-moment writing process (cf. Van Waes, Leijten, Lindgren, & Wengelin, 2016).

While eye tracking and reaction time methodologies have been fruitful in terms of better understanding text comprehension, these approaches may be less so for understanding text production, primarily because writing is more straightforward with respect to the text on the screen. A more beneficial methodology may instead lie in the temporal tracking of the handwriting or keystrokes produced by writers (e.g., Breetvelt, van den Bergh, & Rijlaarsdam, 1994; Rijlaarsdam & van den Bergh, 1996; van den Bergh & Rijlaarsdam, 2007; Van Waes, Leijten, Lindgren, & Wengelin, 2016). Writing analyses have generally focused on the words on the page, the interim or final products of writing. By contrast, keystroke analysis focuses on the writing process by examining the keys that are pressed while writing, and in particular, the timing of the keystrokes as well as the backspaces that are invisible within the final product.

Van Hell, Verhoeven, and van Beijsterveldt (2008), for instance, examined pause time patterns in writing and the relations between these pause times and linguistic characteristics of students' texts. In their study, 4th-grade children and adults each handwrote a narrative and an expository text on a tablet, which recorded their handwriting movements. Results of their analyses revealed that the duration of writers' pauses differed across genres (e.g., adult writers paused longer for expository texts compared to narrative texts) and varied according to syntactic location of the pause (e.g., longer pauses before coordinating than subordinating clauses). These results point to the importance of investigating the temporal structure of behavioral patterns during writing.

More recently, tools have been developed to facilitate recording the individual keystrokes pressed by individuals during writing (Allen et al., 2016; Bixler & D'Mello, 2013; Van Waes et al., 2016). These tools provide a unique means to study the processes associated with computer-based writing (Leijten & Van Waes, 2006; Sullivan & Lindgren, 2006), including investigations of L1 and L2 writers (see Sullivan & Lindgren, 2006, for a review) and studies relating keystroke patterns to the affective states observed during writing (Allen et al., 2016; Bixler & D'Mello, 2013).

To illustrate the importance of these keystroke analyses, consider how it feels to enter into a state of "flow" during writing (Csikszentmihalyi, 1997). Consider the process of generating a sentence, and then backspacing, and then pausing, reordering the words in the sentence. How might the patterns of your keystroke presses differ when you enter into a flow state compared to when you are bored or having a hard time generating ideas? Writers' affective states during writing may have significant impacts, but may not be apparent from the written products alone.

Bixler and D'Mello (2013) provided preliminary results supporting the promise of keystroke analyses in the detection of affective states. They found that a combination of keystroke and individual difference measures (i.e., scholastic aptitude, writing apprehension, and exposure to print) afforded the diagnosis of self-reported affective states (i.e., neutral, boredom, engagement) during writing with accuracies of 11% to 38% above baseline. Similarly, Allen et al. (in press) predicted engagement and boredom across multiple writing sessions using a combination of academic ability (e.g., scholastic aptitude), linguistic text properties, and keystroke indices. The combination of these indices achieved an accuracy of 77% in classifying high and low engagement and boredom in writing sessions.

These studies represent initial explorations of writing using online keystroke analyses. Many more questions on the contributions of various factors can be explored using this approach. Consider, perhaps as a more real-world example, pausing to search the internet for a word, a concept, or to check the correct syntax for a particular phrase. What are these processes and how can we use information about them to understand writing? How can an integration of technologies, such as keystroke logging and NLP inform writing theories? Our strong sense is that pursuing answers to these (and other) questions will help to inspire theories of the cognitive and sociocultural processes that drive writing performance.

Knowledge and Writing

Finally, a critical component of discourse processes research has focused on the role of prior knowledge. Writing theorists have examined knowledge of the writing process (e.g., rhetorical knowledge), as well as knowledge of writing strategies. However, research has placed less emphasis on world and domain knowledge, partly because many writing tasks are designed to tap into common knowledge, to level the playing field across students. The lack of focus on domain knowledge also stems from the theories that guide writing research—topic knowledge is named as a factor (in a box as in Figure 18.1b), but writing theories rarely seek to explain the role of this knowledge, nor of the higher-level processes that make use of this knowledge (e.g., integrating knowledge or generating inferences; cf. Bereiter & Scardamalia, 1987).

By contrast, the impact of world and domain knowledge has been a dominating focus of reading research. Although models diverge in their specific characteristics, a principal focus of many contemporary discourse comprehension models rests on the active construction of meaning using prior knowledge (e.g., Graesser, Singer, & Trabasso, 1994; Kintsch, 1998; Zwaan, Langston, & Graesser, 1995). This makes sense. Reading words activates either new or prior knowledge, which in turn activates (or fails to activate) related knowledge. This activation process (of knowledge) ultimately drives the coherence of the reader's mental representation of the text or discourse.

Following this perspective, text comprehension relies not only on the prior knowledge of the reader, but importantly, also on the processes needed to capitalize on this knowledge. This critical feature of text comprehension can potentially be applied to the process of text production. For example, during the writing process, individuals (at least, skilled writers) actively consider the perspectives and knowledge of their audience within the broader context of the writing assignment. They then strategically rely on their own prior knowledge (of the domain, language, and the world more broadly) to *construct* a coherent representation of a particular construct (or group of constructs) for this particular audience.

Writing is, in essence, the prompting of knowledge to spill out onto a page (or screen), followed by the revision of this knowledge to suit particular communicative goals. The entire process is the construction of meaning by combining knowledge about the world, the domain, and language, and to integrate that knowledge into a coherent structure that is appropriate for a given task and audience. Perhaps because the use of knowledge dominates the entire process, studying writing is studying knowledge, or its expression. Yet, this has not been a principal focus in the writing literature.

Conclusion

The purpose of this chapter was to provide a brief overview of writing theories and research, and to propose new areas of research in this field. Writing is an important topic: it is a pervasive activity in today's society and is a complex discourse process that calls for researchers' attention. We naturally consider writing theory, at least partially, from the vantage of reading comprehension theories. There are similarities: like reading comprehension, writing requires individuals to leverage their knowledge of the linguistic system to actively construct meaning for a particular audience. This overlap is supported by correlations between performance on comprehension and writing tasks. But, we are also struck by the differences between these tasks and the lack of significant correlations in many cases. A strong theoretical framework is needed to understand the sources of this variability. This presents a vast number of opportunities for discourse scientists to advance writing theory, potentially by considering the multiple roles of discourse in writing, and by considering alternative theoretical approaches to writing.

One necessary step is to go beyond the stage theory models that have largely constrained writing perspectives, and consider current perspectives that focus on characterizing emergent systems and interacting processes. To progress as a field, it behooves writing theorists to consider the complexities of the writing process in terms of the underlying cognitive and social processes (e.g., Newell, Beach, Smith, & Vanderheide, 2011), as well as the parallel interplay between the various factors that influence writing.

Our view is that writing research has, to date, typically adopted a *divide and conquer* problem-solving strategy, wherein individual communities of researchers take on one layer of the pie (e.g., the top or bottom halves of Figure 18.1 a–b), and usually one slice of the pie (e.g., the working memory box in Figure 18.1b). Such a reductionist approach is unlikely to provide a comprehensive understanding of writing. Characterizing the complexity of writing requires collecting information at multiple levels, using multiple streams of information: the keystrokes, the words, the linguistic features of the words, and information about the context, writer, and the task. These multiple sources of data provide the means to observe the writing construct from multiple angles, leading to a multidimensional picture. If we imagine that multiple factors may influence writing, such as the task, the situation, writing ability, speech planning and production processes, motivation, knowledge, and so on, then information about those constructs is likely to be available from multiple sources of information as well (e.g., keystroke patterns; linguistic features of the words). A potential mistake is to remain stuck in a paradigm wherein information about a process is available from only one source. These one-to-one mappings between data sources and constructs will lead to static, uni-dimensional models, rather than the big picture that we seek.

We come far short of offering an alternative to the Flower and Hayes models of writing. Writing theories are faced with explaining a highly complex process. Writing involves reading but it also involves complex processes associated with the production of not just one word, not just one sentence, but a coherent thread of thoughts. Ultimately, we envision a model of writing that is multidimensional and dynamic, affording multiple layers of influences from the text, the context, and the writer. It is impossible at this stage, however, to draw out this model, primarily because we know too little about writing processes.

In this chapter, we have pointed toward several directions that we consider particularly fruitful. However, any number of directions might be taken to establish a more comprehensive understanding of writing, For example, text production naturally emanates from speech production; they are both *discourse processes*. However, little (to no) research has examined the potential alignment between the planning and production processes of speech and writing. Likewise, there is much to learn about how writing differs across different registers (e.g., academic writing, literary writing, writing-in-a-diary, writing text messages to friends) and across different writing systems (e.g., character-based, alphabetic) and different languages. In these different contexts, writing is likely to have different literary styles and rhetorical norms (e.g., argument usually followed by evidence, or evidence followed by argument). Naturally, writing occurs in the context of a globalizing world; yet, there has been little research on the impact of the modern world on writing.

We have also made an explicit argument for the integration of writing research into the field of discourse processes. Research on the writing process has largely been conducted separately from discourse processes research. One objective here is to encourage researchers in the discourse processes community to extend their research to the study of writing, and to encourage writing researchers to draw on literature from the discourse processes community to help move writing research forward. We believe that such an approach is essential to integrating notions from the cognitive and sociocultural perspectives, to better understanding the potential impacts of new literacies on writing, and to developing an integrated theory of writing as a discourse process.

Acknowledgments

We are grateful to Cecile Perret for her help in preparing this manuscript. This research was supported in part by the Institute for Educational Sciences (IES R305A130124; R305A120707), the National Science Foundation (NSF REC0241144; IIS-0735682), and the Office of Naval Research (N00014-14–1-0343). Any opinions, findings, conclusions, or recommendations expressed in this material are those of the authors and do not necessarily reflect the views of the IES, NSF, or ONR.

Note

1 Structurally complex narratives have a hierarchical structure, with multiple embedded episodes that are causally connected.

References

Abbott, R., & Berninger, V. W. (1993). Structural equation modeling of relationships among developmental skills and writing skills in primary- and intermediate grade writers. *Journal of Educational Psychology, 85,* 478–508.

Alamargot, D., & Fayol, M. (2009). Modelling the development of written composition. In R. Beard, D. Myhill, J. Riley, & M. Nystrand (Eds), *The SAGE handbook of writing development* (pp. 23–47). Thousand Oaks, CA: SAGE.

Allen, L. K., Jacovina, M. E., & McNamara, D. S. (2016). Computer-based writing instruction. In C. A. MacArthur, S. Graham, & J. Fitzgerald (Eds), *Handbook of writing research* (2nd ed.) (pp. 316–329). New York, NY: The Guilford Press.

Allen, L. K., & McNamara, D. S. (2015). You are your words: Modeling students' vocabulary knowledge with natural language processing. In J. Boticario, O. Santos, C. Romero, & M. Pechenizkiy (Eds), *Proceedings of the 8th International Conference on Educational Data Mining (EDM 2015)* (pp. 258–265). Madrid, Spain.

Allen, L. K., Mills, C., Jacovina, M. E., Crossley, S. A., D'Mello, S. K., & McNamara, D. S. (2016). Investigating boredom and engagement during writing using multiple sources of information: The essay, the writer, and keystrokes. In D. Gašević, G. Lynch, S. Dawson, H. Drachsler, & C. P. Rosé (Eds), *Proceedings of the 6th International Learning Analytics and Knowledge Conference (LAK'16)* (pp. 114–123). New York, NY: ACM.

Allen, L. K., Perret, C. A., & McNamara, D. S. (in press). Linguistic signatures of cognitive processes during writing. *2016 Annual Meeting of the Cognitive Science Society.* Philadelphia, PA.

Allen, L. K., Snow, E. L., Crossley, S. A., Jackson, G. T., & McNamara, D. S. (2014). Reading comprehension components and their relation to the writing process. *L'année psychologique/Topics in Cognitive Psychology, 114,* 663–691.

Allen, L. K., Snow, E. L., & McNamara, D. S. (2014). The long and winding road: Investigating the differential writing patterns of high and low skilled writers. In J. Stamper, S. Pardos, M. Mavrikis, & B. M. McLaren (Eds), *Proceedings of the 7th International Conference on Educational Data Mining* (pp. 304–307). London, UK.

Allen, L. K., Snow, E. L., & McNamara, D. S. (2015). Are you reading my mind? Modeling students' reading comprehension skills with Natural Language Processing techniques. In J. Baron, G. Lynch, N. Maziarz, P. Blikstein, A. Merceron, & G. Siemens (Eds), *Proceedings of the 5th International Learning Analytics & Knowledge Conference (LAK'15)* (pp. 246–254). Poughkeepsie, NY.

Allen, L. K., Snow, E. L., & McNamara, D. S. (2016). The narrative waltz: The role of flexibility on writing performance. *Journal of Educational Psychology.* Advance online publication. doi: 10.1037/edu0000109.

Au, K. H. (2000). A multicultural perspective on policies for improving literacy achievement: Equity and excellence. In M. L. Kamil, P. B. Mosenthal, & P. D. Pearson (Eds), *Handbook of reading research (Vol. 3)* (pp. 835–851). Mahwah, NJ: Lawrence Erlbaum Associates.

Babayigit, S. & Stainthorp, R. (2011). Modeling the relationships between cognitive–linguistic skills and literacy skills: New insights from a transparent orthography. *Journal of Educational Psychology, 103*(1), 169–189.

Baddeley, A. D. (1986). *Working memory.* New York, NY: Oxford University Press.

Bakhtin, M. M. (1981). The dialogic imagination: Four essays by M. M. Bakhtin (M. Holquist, Ed.; C. Emerson & M. Holquist, Trans.). Austin, TX: University of Texas Press.

Bandura, A. (1971). Vicarious and self-reinforcement processes. In R. Glaser (Ed.), *The nature of reinforcement*. New York, NY: Academic Press.

Bandura, A. (1977). Self-efficacy: Toward a unifying theory of behavioral change. *Psychological Review, 84*(2), 191–215.

Bandura, A. (1986). *Social foundations of thought and action: A social-cognitive theory*. Englewood Cliffs, NJ: Prentice Hall.

Bazerman, C. (1988). *Shaping written knowledge: The genre and activity of the experimental article in science* (Vol. 356). Madison, WI: University of Wisconsin Press.

Bazerman, C., & Prior, P. (2005). Participating in emergent socio-literate worlds: Genre, disciplinarity, interdisciplinarity. *Multidisciplinary Perspectives on Literacy Research, 2*, 133–178.

Bereiter, C., & Scardamalia, M. (1987). *The psychology of written communication*. Hillsdale, NJ: Lawrence Erlbaum.

Berninger, V. W., Abbott, R. D., Abbott, S. P., Graham, S., & Richards, T. (2002). Writing and reading: Connections between language by hand and language by eye. *Journal of Learning Disabilities, 35*, 39–56.

Berninger, V. W., Cartwright, A. C., Yates, C. M., Swanson, L., & Abbott, R. D. (1994). Developmental skills related to writing and reading acquisition in the intermediate grades: Shared and unique functional systems. *Reading and Writing, 6*, 161–196.

Bixler, R., & D;Mello, S. (2013). Detecting boredom and engagement during writing with keystroke analysis, task appraisals, and stable traits. In *Proceedings of the 2013 International Conference on Intelligent User Interfaces* (pp. 225–234). New York, NY: ACM.

Branigan, H. P., Pickering, M. J., & Cleland, A. A. (2000). Syntactic co-ordination in dialogue. *Cognition, 75*(2), B13–B25.

Breetvelt, I., Van den Bergh, H., & Rijlaarsdam, G. (1994). Relations between writing processes and text quality: When and how? *Cognition and Instruction, 12*(2), 103–123.

Britt, M. A., & Aglinskas, C. (2002). Improving students' ability to identify and use source information. *Cognition and Instruction, 20*(4), 485–522.

Britton, B. K., & Gülgöz, S. (1991). Using Kintsch's computational model to improve instructional text: Effects of repairing inference calls on recall and cognitive structures. *Journal of Educational Psychology, 83*(3), 329–345.

Britton, J., Burgess, T., Martin, N., McLeod, A., & Rosen, H. (1975). The development of writing abilities. *Schools Council Research Studies*. London, UK: MacMillan.

Brown, A. L., Campione, J. C., & Day, J. D. (1981). Learning to learn: On training students to learn from texts. *Educational Researcher, 10*(2), 14–21.

Carpenter, P. A., Miyake, A., & Just, M. A. (1994). *Working memory constraints in comprehension: Evidence from individual differences, aphasia, and aging*. San Diego, CA: Academic Press.

Central Intelligence Agency. (2015). *The World Factbook*. Retrieved from www.cia.gov/library/publications/the-world-factbook/fields/2103.html.

Clark, H. H. (2004). Pragmatics of language performance. In L. R. Horn & G. Ward (Eds), *Handbook of pragmatics* (pp. 365–382). Oxford: Blackwell.

Crossley, S. A., Allen, L. K., Kyle, K., & McNamara, D. S. (2014). Analyzing discourse processing using a simple natural language processing tool (SiNLP). *Discourse Processes, 51*, 511–534.

Crossley, S. A., Kyle, K., & McNamara, D. S. (in press). The Tool for the Automatic Analysis of Text Cohesion (TAACO): Automatic assessment of local, global, and text cohesion. *Behavior Research Methods*.

Crossley, S. A., & McNamara, D.S. (2011). Text coherence and judgments of essay quality: Models of quality and coherence. In L. Carlson, C. Hoelscher, & T. F. Shipley (Eds), *Proceedings of the 33rd Annual Conference of the Cognitive Science Society* (pp. 1236–1231). Austin, TX: Cognitive Science Society.

Crossley, S. A., & McNamara, D. S. (2014). Does writing development equal writing quality? A computational investigation of syntactic complexity in L2 learners. *Journal of Second Language Writing, 26*, 66–79.

Csikszentmihalyi, M. (1997). *Finding flow: The psychology of engagement with everyday life*. New York, NY: Basic Books.

Daly, J. A., & Miller, M. D. (1975). Further studies on writing apprehension: SAT scores, success expectations, willingness to take advanced courses and sex differences. *Research in the Teaching of English, 9*(3), 250–256.

Deane, P. (2013). On the relation between automated essay scoring and modern views of the writing construct. *Assessing Writing, 18*, 7–24.

Dikli, S. (2006). An overview of automated scoring of essays. *Journal of Technology, Learning, and Assessment, 5*, 3–35.

Driscoll, D. L., & Wells, J. (2012). Beyond knowledge and skills: Writing transfer and the role of student dispositions in and beyond the writing classroom. *Composition Forum: Special Issue on Transfer of Learning, 26.*

Faigley, L. (1985). Nonacademic writing: The social perspective. In L. Odell & D. Goswami (Eds), *Writing in nonacademic settings* (pp. 231–248). New York, NY: Guilford Press.

Fernheimer, J. W., Litterio, L., & Hendler, J. (2011). Transdisciplinary texts and the future of web-scale collaboration. *Journal of Business and Technical Communication, 25*(3), 322–337.

Fitzgerald, J., & Shanahan, T. (2000). Reading and writing relations and their development. *Educational Psychologist, 35*(1), 39–50.

Flower, L. S., & Hayes, J. R. (1980). The dynamics of composing: Making plans and juggling constraints. In L. W. Gregg & E. R. Steinberg (Eds), *Cognitive processes in writing* (pp. 31–50). Hillsdale, NJ: Lawrence Erlbaum.

Flower, L. S., & Hayes, J. R. (1981). A cognitive process theory of writing. *College Composition and Communication, 32*, 365–387.

Foltz, P. W., Britt, M. A., & Perfetti, C. A. (1996). Reasoning from multiple texts: An automatic analysis of readers' situation models. In *Proceedings of the 18th Annual Cognitive Science Conference* (pp. 110–115). Hillsdale, NJ: Lawrence Erlbaum.

Galda, L. (1983). Research in response to literature. *Journal of Research and Development in Education, 16*, 1–7.

Garrod, S., & Pickering, M. J. (2004). Why is conversation so easy? *Trends in Cognitive Sciences, 8*(1), 8–11.

Geiser, S., & Studley, R. (2001). *UC and SAT: Predictive validity and differential impact of the SAT I and SAT II at the University of California.* Oakland, CA: University of California.

Gernsbacher, M. A. (1997). Coherence cues mapping during comprehension. In J. Costermans & M. Fayol (Eds), *Processing interclausal relationships in the production and comprehension of text* (pp. 3–21). Mahwah, NJ: Erlbaum.

Gil, L., Bråten, I., Vidal-Abarca, E., & Strømsø, H. I. (2010). Summary versus argument tasks when working with multiple documents: Which is better for whom? *Contemporary Educational Psychology, 35*(3), 157–173.

Graesser, A. C., Cai, Z., Louwerse, M., & Daniel, F. (2006). Question Understanding Aid (QUAID): A web facility that helps survey methodologists improve the comprehensibility of questions. *Public Opinion Quarterly, 70*, 3–22.

Graesser, A. C., McNamara, D. S., Louwerse, M., & Cai, Z. (2004). Coh-Metrix: Analysis of text on cohesion and language. *Behavior Research Methods, Instruments, & Computers, 36*, 193–202.

Graesser, A. C., Singer, M., & Trabasso, T. (1994). Constructing inferences during narrative text comprehension. *Psychological Review, 101*, 371–395.

Graham, S., & Harris, K. R. (2000). The role of self-regulation and transcription skills in writing and writing development. *Educational Psychologist, 35*(1), 3–12.

Graham, S., Harris, K. R., & Larsen, L. (2001). Prevention and intervention of writing difficulties for students with learning disabilities. *Learning Disabilities Research & Practice, 16*(2), 74–84.

Graham, S., Harris, K. R., McKeown, D., Swanson, H., Harris, K. R., & Graham, S. (2013). The writing of students with learning disabilities, meta-analysis of self-regulated strategy development writing intervention studies, and future directions: Redux. *Handbook of Learning Disabilities, 2*, 105–438.

Graham, S., Harris, K. R., & Santangelo, T. (2015). Research-based writing practices and the common core. *The Elementary School Journal, 115*(4), 498–522.

Graham, S., & Herbert, M. (2011). Writing to read: A meta-analysis of the impact of writing and writing instruction on reading. *Harvard Educational Review, 81*(4), 710–744.

Graham, S., MacArthur, C. A., & Fitzgerald, J. (Eds) (2013). *Best practices in writing instruction.* New York, NY: The Guilford Press.

Graham, S., McKeown, D., Kiuhara, S., & Harris, K. R. (2012). A meta-analysis of writing instruction for students in the elementary grades. *Journal of Educational Psychology, 104*(4), 879.

Graham, S., & Perin, D. (2007). A meta-analysis of writing instruction for adolescent students. *Journal of Educational Psychology, 99*, 445–476.

Gross, A. G., & J. Buehl (Eds) (in press). *Science and the Internet: Communicating knowledge in a digital age*. Amityville, NY: Baywood.

Harris, K. R., & Graham, S. (1992). Self-regulated strategy development: A part of the writing process. In M. Pressley, K. R. Harris, & J. T. Guthrie (Eds) *Promoting academic competence and literacy in school* (pp. 277–309). San Diego, CA: Academic Press.

Hayes, J. R. (1996). A new framework for understanding cognition and affect in writing. In C. M. Levy & S. Ransdell (Eds), *The science of writing: Theories, methods, individual differences, and applications* (pp. 1–27). Mahwah, NJ: Lawrence Erlbaum Associates.

Hayes, J. R. (2006). New directions in writing theory. In C. A. MacArthur, S. Graham, & J. Fitzgerald (Eds), *Handbook of writing research* (pp. 28–40). New York, NY: Guilford.

Hayes, J. R., & Flower, L. (1980). Identifying the organization of writing processes. In L. W. Gregg & E. R. Sternberg (Eds), *Cognitive processes in writing*. Hillsdale, NJ: Erlbaum.

Healy, A. F., & McNamara, D. S. (1996). Verbal learning and memory: Does the modal model still work? *Annual Review of Psychology, 47*, 143–172.

Heitz, R. P., & Engle, R. W. (2007). Focusing the spotlight: Individual differences in visual attention control. *Journal of Experimental Psychology: General, 136*(2), 217–240.

Hoskyn, M., & Swanson, H. L. (2003). The relationship between working memory and writing in younger and older adults. *Reading and Writing, 16*(8), 759–784.

Hull, G. A., & Schultz, K. (Eds) (2002). *School's out: Bridging out-of-school literacies with classroom practice* (Vol. 60). New York, NY: Teachers College Press.

Jackson, G. T., & McNamara, D. S. (2013). Motivation and performance in a game-based intelligent tutoring system. *Journal of Educational Psychology, 105*, 1036–1049.

Jeffrey, G. C., & Underwood, G. (1996). Writing as problem solving: The role of concrete and abstract knowledge in the production of written text. In G. Rijlaarsdam, H. van den Burgh, & M. Couzjin (Eds), *Current trends in writing research: What is writing? Theories, models and methodology* (pp. 61–86). Amsterdam: Amsterdam University Press.

Juel, C., Griffith, P., & Gough, P. (1986). A longitudinal study of the changing relationships of word recognition, spelling, reading comprehension, and writing from first to second grade. *Journal of Educational Research, 78*, 243–255.

Just, M. A., & Carpenter, P. A. (1980). A theory of reading: From eye fixations to comprehension. *Psychological Review, 87*, 329–354.

Just, M. A., & Carpenter, P. A. (1992). A capacity theory of comprehension: Individual differences in working memory. *Psychological Review, 98*, 122–149.

Kellogg, R. T. (1996). A model of working memory in writing. In M. C. Levy & S. E. Ransdell (Eds), *The science of writing: Theories, methods, individual differences and applications* (pp. 57–71). Hillsdale, NJ: Laurence Erlbaum Associates.

Kellogg, R. T. (2001). Long-term working memory in text production. *Memory & Cognition, 29*, 43–52.

Kellogg, R. T. (2008). Training writing skills: A cognitive developmental perspective. *Journal of Writing Research, 1*, 1–26.

Kellogg, R. T., & Raulerson, B. (2007). Improving the writing skills of college students. *Psychonomic Bulletin & Review, 14*, 237–242.

Kemper, S. (1990). Adults' diaries: Changes to written language across the life-span. *Discourse Processes, 13*, 207–224.

Kemper, S., Kynette, D., Rash, S., O'Brien, K., & Sprott, R. (1989). Life-span changes to adults' language: Effects of memory and genre. *Applied Psycholinguistics, 10*(01), 49–66.

Kemper, S., Rash, S., Kynette, D., & Norman, S. (1990). Telling stories: The structure of adults' narratives. *European Journal of Cognitive Psychology, 2*, 205–228.

Kendeou, P., & van den Broek, P. (2007). The effects of prior knowledge and text structure on comprehension processes during reading of scientific texts. *Memory and Cognition, 35*, 1567–1577.

Kintsch, W. (1998). *Comprehension: A paradigm for cognition*. Cambridge, UK: Cambridge University Press.

Kist, W. (2005). *New literacies in action: Teaching and learning in multiple media* (Vol. 75). New York, NY: Teachers College Press.

Kyle, K., & Crossley, S. A. (in press). Automatically assessing lexical sophistication: Indices, tools, findings, and application. *TESOL Quarterly*.

Leijten, M., & Van Waes, L. (2006). Inputlog: New perspectives on the logging of on-line writing processes in a Windows environment. *Studies in Writing, 18*, 73.

Leu, D. J., Kinzer, C. K., Coiro, J., Castek, J., & Henry, L. A. (2013). New literacies: A dual level theory of the changing nature of literacy, instruction, and assessment. In D. E. Alvermann, N. J. Unrau, & R. B. Ruddell (Eds), *Theoretical models and processes of reading* (6th ed.) (pp. 1150–1181). Newark, DE: International Reading Association.

Leu, D. J., Slomp, D., Zawilinski, L., & Corrigan, J. (2016). Writing research through a new literacies lens. In C. A. MacArthur, S. Graham, & J. Fitzgerald (Eds), *Handbook of writing research* (pp. 41–55). New York, NY: The Guilford Press.

Light, A. (2001). In-school work experience and the returns to schooling. *Journal of Labor Economics, 19*(1), 65–93.

Loban, W. D. (1963). *The language of elementary school children*. Urbana, IL: National Council of Teachers of English.

Loban, W. D. (1967). *Language ability: Grades 10, 11, and 12: Final report*. Urbana, IL: National Council of Teachers of English.

MacArthur, C., & Graham, S. (2016). Writing research from a cognitive perspective. In C. MacArthur, S. Graham, & J. Fitzgerald (Eds), *Handbook of writing research* (2nd ed.) (pp. 24–40). New York, NY: Guilford.

MacKay, D. G. (1998). Stage theories refuted. In W. Bechtel & G. Graham (Eds), *A companion to cognitive science* (pp. 671–678). Oxford: Blackwell.

McCarthy, J. E., Grabill, J. T., Hart-Davidson, W., & McLeod, M. (2011). Content management in the workplace: Community, context, and a new way to organize writing. *Journal of Business and Technical Communication*, 1050651911410943.

McCutchen, D. (1986). Domain knowledge and linguistic knowledge in the development of writing ability. *Journal of Memory and Language, 25*, 431–444.

McCutchen, D. (1996). A capacity theory of writing: Working memory in composition. *Educational Psychology Review, 8*, 299–325.

McCutchen, D. (2000). Knowledge, processing, and working memory: Implication for a theory of writing. *Educational Psychologist, 35*, 13–23. http://dx.doi.org/10.1207/S15326985EP3501_3.

McCutchen, D., Covill, A., Hoyne, S. H., & Mildes, K. (1994). Individual differences in writing: Implications of translating fluency. *Journal of Educational Psychology, 86*, 256.

McDonald, S. A., Carpenter, R., & Shillcock, R. (2005). An anatomically constrained, stochastic model of eye movement control in reading. *Psychological Review, 112*, 814–840.

McKeown, M. G., Beck, I. L., Sinatra, G. M., & Loxterman, J. A. (1992). The contribution of prior knowledge and coherent text to comprehension. *Reading Research Quarterly, 27*, 78–93.

McNamara, D. S. (2004). SERT: Self-explanation reading training. *Discourse Processes, 38*, 1–30.

McNamara, D. S. (2007). IIS: A marriage of computational linguistics, psychology, and educational technologies. In D. Wilson & G. Sutcliffe (Eds), *Proceedings of the 20th International Florida Artificial Intelligence Research Society Conference* (pp. 15–20). Menlo Park, CA: The AAAI Press.

McNamara, D. S. (2017). Self-explanation and reading strategy training (SERT) improves low-knowledge students' science course performance. *Discourse Processes*. http://dx.doi.org/10.108 0/0163853X.2015.1101328.

McNamara, D. S., Crossley, S. A., Roscoe, R. D., Allen, L. K., & Dai, J. (2015). Hierarchical classification approach to automated essay scoring. *Assessing Writing, 23*, 35–59.

McNamara, D. S., Graesser, A. C., McCarthy, P., & Cai, Z. (2014). *Automated evaluation of text and discourse with Coh-Metrix*. Cambridge: Cambridge University Press.

McNamara, D. S., & Kintsch, W. (1996). Learning from text: Effects of prior knowledge and text coherence. *Discourse Processes, 22*, 247–288.

McNamara, D. S., Kintsch, E., Songer, N. B., & Kintsch, W. (1996). Are good texts always better? Interactions of text coherence, background knowledge, and levels of understanding in learning from text. *Cognition and Instruction, 14*, 1–43.

McNamara, D. S., & Magliano, J. P. (2009). Towards a comprehensive model of comprehension. In B. Ross (Ed.), *The psychology of learning and motivation*. New York, NY: Elsevier Science.

Muñoz, B., Magliano, J. P., Sheridan, R., & McNamara, D. S. (2006). Typing versus thinking aloud when reading: Implications for computer-based assessment and training tools. *Behavior Research Methods, Instruments, & Computers, 38*, 211–217.

Myers, J. L., & O'Brien, E. J. (1998). Accessing the discourse representation during reading. *Discourse Processes, 26*, 131–157.

National Assessment of Educational Progress. (2011). *The Nation's Report Card: Writing 2011.* Retrieved from www.nces.ed.gov/nationsreportcard/writing.

National Commission on Writing. (2003). *The Neglected "R."* College Entrance Examination Board, New York.

National Governors Association & Council of Chief School Officers. (2010). *Common Core State Standards.* National Governors Association Center for Best Practices, Council of Chief State School Officers, Washington D.C.

Newell, G. E., Beach, R., Smith, J., & Van Der Heide, J. (2011). Teaching and learning argumentative reading and writing: A review of research. *Reading Research Quarterly, 46*(3), 273–304.

O'Reilly, T., & McNamara, D. S. (2007). The impact of science knowledge, reading skill, and reading strategy knowledge on more traditional "High-Stakes" measures of high school students' science achievement. *American Educational Research Journal, 44*, 161–196.

Orlikowski, W. J., & Yates, J. (2002). It's about time: Temporal structuring in organizations. *Organization Science, 13*(6), 684–700.

Pajares, F. (2002). Overview of social cognitive theory and of self-efficacy. Retrieved from www.emory.edu/EDUCATION/mfp/eff.html.

Pajares, F. (2003). Self-efficacy beliefs, motivation, and achievement in writing: A review of the literature. *Reading & Writing Quarterly, 19*(2), 139–158.

Port, R. F., & van Gelder, T. (1995). *Mind as motion: Explorations in the dynamics of cognition.* Cambridge, MA: MIT Press.

Powell, P. (2009). Retention and writing instruction: Implications for access and pedagogy. *College Composition and Communication, 66*, 664–682.

Pratt, M. W., Boyes, C., Robins, S., & Manchester, J. (1989). Telling tales: Aging, working memory, and the narrative cohesion of story retellings. *Developmental Psychology, 25*(4), 628.

Prior, P. (2006). A sociocultural theory of writing. In C. MacArthur, S. Graham, & J. Fitzgerald (Eds), *Handbook of writing research* (pp. 54–66). New York, NY: Guilford.

Purcell-Gates, V., & Tierney, R. (2009). *Increasing literacy levels of Canadian students. Public Policy Brief on Early Literacy*, University of British Columbia. Retrieved from http://cpls.educ.ubc.ca/content/pdfs/ LiteracyPolicyBrief.pdf.

Ransdell, S., & Levy, C. M. (1996). Working memory constraints on writing quality and fluency. In C. M. Levy & S. E. Ransdell (Eds), *The science of writing: Theories, methods, individual differences, and applications* (pp. 93–106). Mahwah, NJ: Lawrence Erlbaum Associates.

Ransdell, S., Levy, C. M., & Kellogg, R. T. (2002). The structure of writing processes as revealed by secondary task demands. *L1-Educational Studies in Language and Literature, 2*(2), 141–163.

Rayner, K. (1998). Eye movements in reading and information processing: 20 years of research. *Psychological Bulletin, 124*, 372–422.

Rijlaarsdam, G., & van den Bergh, H. (1996). The dynamics of composing – An agenda for research into an interactive compensatory model of writing: Many questions, some answers. In C. M. Levy & S. Ransdell (Eds), *The science of writing* (pp. 107–125). Mahwah, NJ: Lawrence Erlbaum.

Rinehart, S. D., Stahl, S. A., & Erickson, L. G. (1986). Some effects of summarization training on reading and studying. *Reading Research Quarterly*, 422–438.

Rogoff, B. (1990). *Apprenticeship in thinking: Cognitive development in social context.* New York, NY: Oxford University Press.

Rohman, D. G. (1965). Pre-writing: The stage of discovery in the writing process. *College Composition and Communication, 16*(2), 106–112.

Roscoe, R. D., & McNamara, D. S. (2013). Writing Pal: Feasibility of an intelligent writing strategy tutor in the high school classroom. *Journal of Educational Psychology, 105*(4), 1010–1025.

Rouet, J. F., Britt, M. A., Mason, R. A., & Perfetti, C. A. (1996). Using multiple sources of evidence to reason about history. *Journal of Educational Psychology, 88*(3), 478.

Santangelo, T., Harris, K. R., & Graham, S. (2016). Self-regulation and writing: An overview and meta-analysis. In C. MacArthur, S. Graham, & J. Fitzgerald (Eds), *Handbook of writing research* (2nd ed.) (pp. 174–193). New York, NY: Guilford.

Scardamalia, M. (1981). How children cope with the cognitive demands of writing. In R. J. Spiro, B. C. Bruce, & W. F. Brewer (Eds) *Writing: The nature, development, and teaching of written communication Vol 2: Writing: Process, development, and communication* (pp. 81–104). Hillsdale, NJ: Erlbaum.

Schunk, D. H., & Zimmerman, B. J. (1994). *Self-regulation of learning and performance: Issues and educational applications.* Hillsdale, NJ: Lawrence Erlbaum Associates.

Shanahan, T. (1988). The reading-writing relationships: Seven instructional principles. *The Reading Teacher, 41*, 636–647.

Shanahan, T. (2016). Relationships between reading and writing development. In C. MacArthur, S. Graham, & J. Fitzgerald (Eds), *Handbook of writing research* (2nd ed.) (pp. 194–207). New York, NY: Guilford.

Shermis, M., & Burstein, J. (Eds). (2003). *Automated essay scoring: A cross-disciplinary perspective.* Mahwah, NJ: Erlbaum.

Shermis, M. D., & Burstein, J. (Eds). (2013). *Handbook of automated essay evaluation: Current applications and future directions.* New York, NY: Routledge.

Slomp, D. H. (2012). Challenges in assessing the development of writing ability: Theories, constructs and methods. *Assessing Writing, 17*(2), 81–91.

Slomp, D. H., Corrigan, J. A., & Sugimoto, T. (2014). A framework for using consequential validity evidence in evaluating large-scale writing assessments: A Canadian study. *Research in the Teaching of English, 48*(3), 276.

Spivey, M. J. (2007). *The continuity of mind.* Oxford, UK: Oxford University Press.

Stagg Peterson, S., McClay, J., & Main, K. (2011). An analysis of large-scale writing assessments in Canada (grades 5–8). *Alberta Journal of Educational Research, 57*(4), 424–445.

Starke-Meyerring, D., Par, A., & Artemeva, N. (Eds) (2011). *Writing in knowledge societies.* Anderson, SC: Parlor Press.

Stotsky, S. (1983). Research on reading/writing relationships: A synthesis and suggested directions. *Language Arts, 60*, 627–642.

Sullivan, K. P. H., & Lindgren, E. (Eds) (2006). *Computer keystroke logging and writing: Methods and applications.* Oxford: Elsevier.

Tierney, R. J., & Shanahan, T. (1991). Research on the reading-writing relationship: Interactions, transactions, and outcomes. In R. Barr, M. L. Kamil, P. Mosenthal, & P. D. Pearson (Eds), *The handbook of reading research (Vol. 2)* (pp. 246–280). New York, NY: Longman.

Torrance, M., & Galbraith, D. (2006). The processing demands of writing. In C. A. MacArthur, S. Graham, & J. Fitzgerald (Eds), *Handbook of writing research* (pp. 67–80). New York, NY: Guilford.

Turvey, M. T. (1990). Coordination. *American Psychologist, 45*(8), 938.

Unsworth, N., Schrock, J. C., & Engle, R. W. (2004). Working memory capacity and the antisaccade task: Individual differences in voluntary saccade control. *Journal of Experimental Psychology: Learning, Memory, and Cognition, 30*(6), 1302.

van den Bergh, H., & Rijlaarsdam, G. (2007). The dynamics of idea generation during writing: An online study. *Studies in Writing, 20*, 125–150.

van Hell, J. G., Verhoeven, L., & van Beijsterveldt, L. M. (2008). Pause time patterns in writing narrative and expository texts by children and adults. *Discourse Processes, 45*, 406–427.

Van Waes, L., Leijten, M., Lindgren, E., & Wengelin, A. (2016). Keystroke logging in writing research: Analyzing online writing processes. In C. MacArthur, S. Graham, & J. Fitzgerald (Eds), *Handbook of writing research* (2nd ed.) (pp. 410–226). New York, NY: Guilford.

Vygotsky, L. S. (1978). *Mind in society: The development of higher psychological processes.* Cambridge, MA: Harvard University Press.

Wade-Stein, D., & Kintsch, E. (2004). Summary Street: Interactive computer support for writing. *Cognition and Instruction, 22*(3), 333–362.

Wineburg, S. S. (1991). Historical problem solving: A study of the cognitive processes used in the evaluation of documentary and pictorial evidence. *Journal of Educational Psychology, 83*(1), 73–87.

Yang, S. N., & McConkie, G. W. (2001). Eye movements during reading: A theory of saccade initiation times. *Vision Research, 41*, 3567–3585.

Zimmerman, B. J., & Kitsantas, A. (1999). Acquiring writing revision skill: Shifting from process to outcome self-regulatory goals. *Journal of Educational Psychology, 91*(2), 241–250.

Zimmerman, B. J., & Risemberg, R. (1997). Becoming a self-regulated writer: A social cognitive perspective. *Contemporary Educational Psychology, 22*(1), 73–101.

Zwaan, R. A., Langston, M. C., & Graesser, A. C. (1995). The construction of situation models in narrative comprehension: An event-indexing model. *Psychological Science*, 292–297.

Afterword
World-Wide Changes in Discourse and the Changing Field of Discourse Processes

Arthur C. Graesser

UNIVERSITY OF MEMPHIS

Morton Ann Gernsbacher

UNIVERSITY OF WISCONSIN-MADISON

Susan R. Goldman

UNIVERSITY OF ILLINOIS AT CHICAGO

The world is very different now than when the first *Handbook of Discourse Processes* was published in 2003. The differences can be traced to rapidly changing digital technologies. There is now a World Wide Web that involves nearly half of the children and adults throughout the globe. People can communicate with one or with hundreds of "friends" depending on the social media platforms they use and how broadly they designate the audience. Scanning emails, sending and receiving text messages, visiting chat rooms, and trawling Facebook are just a few of the options familiar to an older generation of non-digital natives. To digital natives, tweets, texts, Instagrams, and Snapchats are commonplace with little attention to email. Millions of people can and do publish web blogs that are available to anyone who can find them. Whereas "in the flesh" face-to-face meetings used to dominate commercial and professional interactions (e.g., meetings, seminars, and conferences), there has been a marked shift to digitally enabled virtual meetings and conferences (Skype, GoToMeeting, Google hangout, WebEx, telephone conference calls). "How should we communicate?" is a ubiquitous question we ask of our friends and colleagues.

Revolutionary changes in digital technology have had repercussions on many sectors of society. Billions of citizens routinely surf the Internet on topics of their choosing. As countries become technologically more advanced, employees are expected to acquire complex subject matter and to keep pace with new developments in their fields at a faster rate.

Doing so demands deeper comprehension and learning of content from technically complex text and discourse, using heuristics, strategies, skills, and knowledge that are rarely taught in school. These include selecting relevant information, integrating information from multiple documents, scrutinizing the quality of information, self-regulating learning, communicating through multiple representational and media forms, and collaborative problem solving. Communication throughout the globe is virtually instantaneous, so we are increasingly interacting with people from different nations and cultures as well as different languages. Quite clearly, discourse has changed throughout the world.

The field of discourse processes has nimbly and adaptively changed as well. In one dominant paradigm at the time of the 2003 *Handbook*, researchers investigated the cognitive processes that unfold when a person comprehends a printed text. The texts were often textoids constructed by experimental psychologists, but sometimes the texts were naturalistic stories, persuasive essays, and informational texts. The cognitive processes investigated included interpreting the semantic meaning of explicit text, constructing situation models, generating inferences, monitoring rhetorical structures, and other processes that were encapsulated within a single text. Researchers continue to investigate such texts and cognitive processes, but the texts and associated research questions have changed as we read the 2017 *Handbook*.

So how has the field of discourse processes changed? We have identified at least five major shifts in research.

Five Thematic Changes between 2003 and 2017 *Handbooks*

Importance of Metacognition

Modern readers run the risk of information pollution as they read documents on the Internet that might be factually incorrect, contradictory, and replete with opinions. Therefore, discourse researchers are investigating metacognitive strategies that scrutinize the quality of information and the authors' expertise. These strategies have not been sufficiently acquired by the majority of the citizens, even in the most powerful nations, so there is an uphill battle educating the public and establishing a sensible curriculum in our schools. Skilled modern readers read multiple documents when issues are controversial, inconsistent with their background knowledge, and contradictory. They attempt to construct an accurate and coherent mental model, to consider the evidence as well as different perspectives, and to ultimately take a sensible position. Unskilled modern readers are seduced by the peripheral route to persuasion where the discourse is littered with anecdotes, stories, outrageous claims, and emotional appeals. Unskilled modern readers are prisoners of their existing knowledge and belief systems. They accept the first text that comes along that sides with their own point of view and resist taking a critical stance that challenges their personal knowledge by reading the documents of their adversaries. Many citizens still fundamentally believe that whatever is said in print is true. But the world has changed and that is no longer true as we explore the available documents on the web, many of which are not edited by professionals. How might adults and children change these epistemological assumptions and acquire a more critical stance in their reading? These are some of the pressing issues in the *Handbook* of 2017 but not 2003.

Currency and Validity of Information

We remember the days when a salesman knocked on our door and tried to sell our parents an encyclopedia. These encyclopedias were the bastion of truth for decades in the latter half of the 20th century. Some of us remember that Encyclopedia Britannica was hard to read compared with the easier Colliers Encyclopedia that had more captivating pictures and shinier pages. It took boxes to deliver these encyclopedias, with volumes organized by letters. We worried when our encyclopedias were getting old. There was a trade-off between age of information and money because these encyclopedias were expensive. We bragged to our neighbors when we received the most recent encyclopedia, whether it be the status of Britannica or Colliers. "Is this still true?" was a question we often asked as we explored information in our 10-year-old encyclopedia set.

Alas, times have changed in the 21st century. We now have Wikipedia on the web. The content of each entry is dynamically changing by a social collaborative process that attempts to be current. Anyone in the world can nominate a change to a Wikipedia topic but that change may or may not survive the test of time. There is a community of "experts" who try to minimize information pollution, but that process is invisible to everyone except the passionate advocates of truth. Wikipedia is surprisingly accurate compared with encyclopedias that have been edited by experts, although some researchers question this claim. So we have an ideal situation, namely an encyclopedia on the web that is up-to-date, free, and reasonably accurate. This opens interesting doors to many research questions. How are these Wikipedia documents created and revised? How do people comprehend them? When do readers believe the information is high quality? To what extent do they search multiple documents strategically as they journey through the hyperspace of links?

Goal-Directed Reading

Citizens are increasingly goal-directed in their reading as they try to keep pace with the modern technology-driven world. People have always had a list of goals and worries to guide them through the days, weeks, months, and years. However, as the pace of information throughput increases, citizens need to be more selective in what they read and to retrieve relevant documents to help them achieve their goals. The skilled modern reader has strategies of self-regulation, with sensible metacognitive judgments, that drive that process: Is this information relevant to any goal I have? Is the writer competent? Are the claims supported by facts? Does a recommendation have problematic outcomes? Many of us wish we had more time to leisurely read a document out of mere curiosity, but a lot of our time is consumed by goals and tasks to complete in a digital world. Goal-directed reading was a theme in many of the 2017 *Handbook* chapters.

Learning from Complex, Specialized, Technical Text

Skilled modern readers are expected to read technical texts at deeper levels of comprehension. Deeper levels of comprehension require systems thinking, reasoning, inferences, and construction of causal mental models in addition to accurate interpretations of the explicit text. The high complexity of texts is undeniable when we read medical, legal, and government documents that are posted on web sites for citizens to read. The texts are too difficult for many if not most citizens to comprehend because of limitations in their language comprehension skills, background knowledge, and understanding of the institutions that serve them. There is a push in many countries for students to pursue professions in STEM (Science, Technology, Engineering, and Mathematics) areas with difficult content because high paying jobs are in those areas. However, most citizens will not pursue those fields. Moreover, STEM content is often extremely specialized and idiosyncratic so the mastery of one STEM area will not transfer to another. It is unrealistic to expect citizens to improve their reading of difficult material by increasing their background knowledge because the landscape of knowledge is much too large and most of the knowledge is acquired through print and oral discourse. Technical documents for the public need to be comprehensible to a broader distribution of readers who vary in comprehension abilities. One approach is to have multiple versions of a document that are scaled on reading difficulty and tailored to the reader's profile. For example, there is a Simple English Wikipedia version that is tailored for readers for whom English is a second language.

Attention to Discourse Diversity

One of the themes of the 2017 *Handbook* chapters is the diversity of people, genres, conversational registers, disciplines, institutions, cultures, and languages. This diversity is much more apparent in the 2017 *Handbook* than the 2003 *Handbook*. Discourse researchers need to consider differences among people across the life span, differences in genre (e.g., narrative, persuasion, vs informational texts), differences in conversational registers (e.g., doctor-patient, tutor-student, vs dinner talk among spouses), differences in the epistemological foundations of disciplines (history, literature, social studies, sciences, vs branches of science), differences in the pragmatic ground rules of discourse among institutions in a society, and differences among cultures and languages. The authors in a number of chapters express that it is unproductive to view this diversity as a static set of categories or traits when analyzing particular people, texts, conversations, and contexts. Instead, there is a dynamic process of discourse interaction that both define and transform the constructs of diversity. This clearly adds a level of challenge in doing our work in discourse processes if a theoretical analysis of discourse has fuzzy multicomponent categories, is a moving window over time, and is a dynamical system. However, such complex dynamical mechanisms are inherent in all mature sciences.

Methodological Approaches

Not surprisingly, the 2017 *Handbook* attends to a broader array of methodologies and explicitly includes short essays on the evolution of methods that were embedded in the various chapters in the 2003 edition. The advances in digital technologies that fueled much of the evolution of the field also figure prominently in the research methods that discourse researchers currently employ.

A core paradigm in discourse processes consists of qualitative analyses of conversations. There are rich interpretations of the speech acts, conversational turns, multiparty conversation patterns, intended meanings of both literal and nonliteral utterances, establishment of common ground, politeness norms, power differences, and ideological perspectives. These researchers typically ask multiple experts to make the theoretical qualitative judgments on discourse excerpts, and then compute inter-judge reliability scores on these judgments as well as inferential statistics so that the generality of findings can be assessed. Such qualitative analyses involved small samples of discourse when the 2003 *Handbook* was written. However, the sample sizes and scientific precision have increased substantially since that time with advances in digital technologies. Corpora of annotated texts have increased dramatically through the Linguistic Data Consortium, the shared tasks in the field of computational linguistics, and research centers throughout the world. The large and diverse samples of digitized discourse allow researchers to test theoretical claims about language features and discourse patterns in a small amount of time, measured in weeks, days, or even hours. Amazon's Mechanical Turk gives researchers the opportunity to collect data on hundreds of other people's ratings and annotations of discourse within a day. For many research projects, qualitative conversation analysts can complete a project in a week when the same project would have taken a decade 20 years ago. However, it is also important to acknowledge that it takes substantial expertise for a judge to annotate some theoretical categories and dimensions of discourse. Some aspects of discourse are out of reach of computers and novice judges to analyze.

Our introductory chapter in the 2003 *Handbook* projected a future evolution of corpus analyses and automated computer analyses of language and discourse. This projection has been confirmed, as a number of authors have expressed in this 2017 *Handbook*. In fact, big data is larger than any of us imagined in 2003. We can now analyze the entire Wikipedia in a couple of days to extract higher-dimensional spaces (such as latent semantic analysis), topic analyses, trigrams, and many other features of language and discourse. This can be accomplished for Wikipedia sites in multiple languages and cultures so the word representations, texts, and topics can be compared with respect to similarity in meaning. Google translations occur between multiple languages, primarily based on word correspondences. IBM Watson uses these large corpora to answer Jeopardy questions and to generate pro versus con arguments that are relevant to debates over controversial issues; these systems have the capacity to outperform the most accomplished humans. Speech recognition has improved because of large corpora collected by Siri; this was accomplished in spite of the long line of skeptics who said that speech recognition could never be accomplished reliably (at the time of the 2003 *Handbook*). Now it is possible to have speech-to-text discourse samples transcribed quickly and with surprisingly high accuracy. This allows researchers in computational linguistics and discourse to perform machine learning analyses that discover new discourse patterns and quickly test hypotheses about discourse in diverse contexts.

These advances in digital technologies allow discourse researchers to analyze conversations in different discourse registers. Both spoken interactions and computer mediated conversations can be analyzed and compared. There are also sensing technologies that analyze facial expressions, body posture, speech intonation, gesture, and other paralinguistic dimensions. At this point in history, we are just beginning to discover features and patterns within and between channels of communication in a temporally coordinated manner. One important direction for future research is to identify systematic mechanisms of multichannel communication and to test hypotheses about such interactions.

Social media and computer mediated conversation are much more prevalent now than when the 2003 *Handbook* was written. One consequence of this transformation is that it gives people the opportunity to generate more language and discourse in digital communication channels. This presumably taps the creative side of children and adults. They do not simply respond to educational and entertainment media, but actively interact with individuals, groups, and the public. We are seeing the evolution of new forms of iconic and semiotic symbols, if not entirely new languages. The next decade of research will undoubtedly be investigating the evolution of language and communication of new communication media.

In addition to advances in corpus analysis, automated computer analyses, big data, and qualitative analyses, progress continues to be made on the more conventional methods that are used in experimental psychology, such as the collection of ratings, memory data, think aloud protocols, answers to questions, reading time, and eye tracking. Our introductory chapter in the 2003 *Handbook* projected the use of neuroscience data as an important future direction. This projection has indeed been confirmed as reflected in two of the chapters in the 2017 *Handbook*, whereas there were no chapters with a neuroscience focus in the 2003 *Handbook*.

Following the rise of cognitive neuroscience methodology at the turn of the millennium, discourse researchers have taken these tools to understand how the brain gives rise to discourse comprehension and production. As reflected in the 2017 *Handbook*, contemporary neuroscience tools allow researchers to not only identify the brain regions involved in various discourses processes, but to also measure the activity of those brain regions and even selectively disrupt those processes. Never before have researchers been able to so fully watch the brain at work while discourse is being processed. However, the challenge remains on how to create the most natural settings for measuring brain activity during discourse processing, given the unnatural context of brain scanners, electrodes, and magnetic devices.

Contributions of Discourse Research to Education

Those in the education sectors of society are experiencing unsettling transformations as they attempt to cope with the changes in technology, culture, and the myriad new pedagogical practices of modern society. Teachers have not had opportunities to acquire the expertise needed to help their students benefit from many new types of learning experiences, including intelligent tutoring systems, MOOCs, games, simulations, mobile devices, and social media. At the same time, there is greater diversity among students in terms of cultures, languages, socioeconomic status, and life experiences.

Discourse researchers have used a variety of methodologies to build a rich knowledge base on classroom practices that support the learning recommended in the current "standards" documents. Some notable examples include the *Common Core State Standards in English Language Arts, History/Social Studies, and Science and Technical subjects*, the *Common Core State Standards in Mathematics*, the *Next Generation Science Standards*, and the social studies *C3 Framework for College, Career and Civic Life*. There are promising new methods of teachers' orchestrating productive discourse in the classroom, such as accountable talk, academic language, emphasis on authentic teacher and student questions, and teacher uptake of productive student contributions through revoicing. Discourse researchers can play a critical role in increasing the likelihood of teachers enacting these pedagogical techniques. Annotated corpora of classroom discourse, accessible via digital technologies, could serve as objects of study and critical analysis by teachers. Discourse researchers can contribute to developing methods for tracking classroom discourse automatically and providing informative feedback to teachers and students regarding participation, quality of contributions, and other dimensions of learning goals.

From Multidisciplinary to Interdisciplinary Research

Our introductory chapter in the 2003 *Handbook* recommended a shift from multidisciplinary research to interdisciplinary research. In multidisciplinary research there is a collection of researchers who investigate a particular phenomenon from the lens of their own discipline. In contrast, interdisciplinary research requires a deeper integration of the wisdom and methodologies of two or more disciplines. Interdisciplinary research is much more difficult because the researchers need to collaboratively solve problems by taking each other's perspective into account, negotiate decisions, and coordinate plans. That is very different than merely sitting in a room and listening to presentations in a research meeting, seminar, or conference.

There has been progress in conducting more interdisciplinary research in discourse processes, thanks to investments by funding agencies that target interdisciplinary research. In the United States, this includes the National Science Foundation, the National Institutes for Health, the Institute of Education Sciences, the Department of Defense, and foundations (Spencer, McDonnell). These organizations have funded hundreds of projects that integrate discourse processing with learning environments, medical applications, social media, and national defense. At the more global level there is the European Union and the Organization for Economic Co-operation and Development (OECD), the organization that funds PISA (Programme for International Student Assessment) and PIAAC (Programme for International Assessment of Adult Competencies). Discourse processing researchers have played leadership roles in the expert groups of PISA and PIAAC in assessments of literacy, science, and problem solving. Discourse researchers have also led and participated in large Center grants funded by the Institute for Education Sciences, such as the $100 million Reading for Understanding initiative and the $10 million Center for the Study of Adult Literacy. All of these initiatives are explicitly interdisciplinary and attempt to scale up research to have a larger impact on society.

In closing, as the world has changed, discourse has changed and thankfully the field of discourse processes has changed. In turn, the field of discourse processes has played some role in changing the world.

Index

Publisher's note: Our policy is that subject headings in the index refer to significant information relating to the topic, rather than including every occurrence of the term. Cited authors are indexed where their work is discussed in some detail, or where the context is significant; simple citations are not included in the index.

Abedin, M. 327
ABI-Model of trustworthiness 239
Abraham, A. *et al.* 279
accommodation 40
Adams, C. *et al.* 259
Adelman, J. 121
adjacency pairs 28–30, 37, 43
AES (automated essay scoring) engines 378–9
age effects *see* discourse processing through the adult lifespan
Aglinskas, C. 154
Albrecht, J. E. 125–6, 128, 167, 181
Alexander, P. A. 15
Allen, L. K. *et al.* 367, 374, 379
Alozie, N. M. *et al.* 330
Altmann, U. *et al.* 279
Anderson, A. A. *et al.* 152
Anderson, A. H. *et al.* 41, 197
Anderson, C. A. *et al.* 176, 304
Anderson, R. 326
Andreassen, R. 147
Anmarkrud, Ø. *et al.* 146
Appel, M. 308
argumentation 16
association 207
Astolfi, L. 286
audibility 25, 193
audience design 36, 112, 209
audience forms 209–11
Austin, J. L. 75
automated essay scoring (AES) engines 378–9

Babayigit, S. 367
Babiloni, F. 286
back-end processes 350, 354
Baddeley, A. D. 366
Bajzek, D. 233
Bakhtin, M. M. 371
Banarescu, L. *et al.* 119

Bandura, A. 369
Bangerter, A. *et al.* 34, 88, 199
Barasch, A. 54
Baretta, L. *et al.* 277
Barzilai, S. *et al.* 146, 149, 156
Bašnáková, J. *et al.* 284–5, 287
behavioral studies 281
Beier, S. 15–16
belief change 303; awareness of 305; backfire/ polarization effects 306; mediating factors 304–5; moderating factors 304; narrative texts 307–8; text factors 303–4; theories 306–7
beliefs and discourse processing 295, 297–8; attitudes 296; belief-basis 299–300, 310; belief change 303–8; belief-consistent/belief-inconsistent information 299–301; beliefs *vs.* empirical evidence 333–4; defining beliefs 296–7; discourse comprehension 297–8; file drawer problem 309; influence of worldview 309; knowledge 296; mental representation of belief-consistent/inconsistent information 301–2; mental representation of information 299; why study beliefs? 298–302; conclusions and future directions 308–10
Bellack, A. *et al.* 322
Bereiter, C. 369
Berger, J. 54
Berninger, V. W. *et al.* 374
Berns, G. S. *et al.* 287
Bernstein, M. S. *et al.* 210
Betsch, C. *et al.* 152
Bezdek, M. A. *et al.* 180
big data approaches 117–18, 394; "deep" semantic tools 120–1; discourse relations 121–2; surface-level NLP tools and databases 118–20; challenges and future directions 122
bilingualism 280–1
Bixler, R. 380
Blanc, N. *et al.* 181

397

Index

Blood, A. J. 283
blood oxygen level dependent signal (BOLD) 131–3
Bloom, B. S. 331
bodily gestures and institutionalizing communication 86–7
Bohn-Gettler, C. M. 16
Bohus, D. 203
Boje, D. M. 88
Boroditsky, L. 74
boyd, d. 53, 210
Boyd, M. P. 332
Braasch, J. L. G. *et al.* 148, 154, 157
brain imaging techniques *see* neuroscientific methods
Branigan, H. P. *et al.* 50, 51
Bransford, J. D. *et al.* 273
Bråten, I. *et al.* 146, 147, 148, 149
Brave, S. *et al.* 200
Brennan, S. E. 25, 38, 52, 193, 194, 206, 207, 208
bridging inferences 345, 354
Brigham Young Corpus Repository 119
Britt, M. A. *et al.* 143–4, 154, 302
Brock, T. C. 179, 308
Bromme, R. *et al.* 144, 148, 235, 238
Brown, P. 76, 237
Brown-Schmidt, S. 46, 51, 112
Buccino, G. *et al.* 134
Buchweitz, A. *et al.* 281
Buehl, M. M. *et al.* 304
Burkhardt, P. 182

CA *see* conversation analysis
CallHome American English Corpus 23–4, 28–9
Camblin, C. C. *et al.* 126–7
categorical perception 228
Causal Network model of reading comprehension 8, 9
Cavanaugh, J. C. 259
Cazden, C. 322
CCSS *see* Common Core State Standards
CDA (critical discourse analysis) 78
Chakraborty, R. *et al.* 158
Chapanis, A. *et al.* 195
Chapman, S. B. *et al.* 250
Chase, W. G. 227
Cheetham, M. *et al.* 282
Chen, X. *et al.* 87
Chi, M. T. H. 14, 177
Chin, J. *et al.* 255
Chiou, W.-B. 53–4
Chow, H. M. *et al.* 281
Christianson, K. *et al.* 255–6
Christianson, M. 83
CI *see* Construction-Integration model (CI) of reading comprehension
Clark, H. H. *et al.* 25, 34–5, 36, 37–8, 39, 46, 50, 52, 53, 70, 76, 77, 111, 193, 194, 206, 207, 208, 224, 230–2, 234, 240

classroom discourse: analytical and operational complexity 315–17; discourse formats 315–16
classroom discourse and instructional concerns 318; constant concerns 318–19; lecture/recitation 319–20; managing instruction within discourse formats 322; small-group discussion 321–2; whole-class discussion 320–1
classroom discourse: discussion 333; beliefs *vs.* empirical evidence 333–4; issues deserving further study 334–5; student opportunity to learn *vs.* teacher burnout 336; type, intensity, duration, frequency 335
classroom discourse: infrastructure 328; amount of talk by students *vs.* teacher 331–2; participant structures 328–30; participation frameworks 330–1; question type 332; summary 332–3
classroom discourse: research 322; lecture/recitation 322–3; small-group discussion 326–7; teacher's role 325–6; whole-class discussion 323–5; summary 327–8
clefting 257
Cleland, A. A. 41
Clemens, E. S. 80
Cobb, M. D. 304
cognition and communication 76–7
cognitive aging 248
cognitive dissonance theory 304
cognitive neuroscience of discourse 269, 395; advanced neuroimaging designs 286–7; conversation 284–6; embodied language effects 274–5; evolution and neurobiology 269–71; mechanisms and phenomena 271–6; new directions 276–88; populations 279–82; predictive processing 271–2; reader response 282–4; segmentation 272–3; situation model construction: dmPFC 273–4; texts 277–9; theory of mind (ToM) 275–6, *276*; conclusion 288
Cognitive Reconstruction of Knowledge Model (CRKM) 307
Coh-Metrix 74, 119
Cohen, E. G. 327
Collaborative Reasoning (CR) 326–7
collateral signals 34
Collins, H. 224
Common Core State Standards (CCSS) 317, 364, 395; English Language Arts and Literacy (CCSS/ELA) 13–14, 16, 364
common ground 35–6, 37, 38, 44, 45, 86, 87–8, 192–3, 223
common ground communication model 230–4; anticipation and adaptation 233; establishing common ground 231–2; hampering of expert knowledge 233–4; reciprocal understanding 230–1
communication: and cognition 76–7; fundamentals of successful communication 192–3
communicative constraints 24–5; co-presence, visibility, audibility 25, 193; cotemporality,

simultaneity, sequentiality 25, 193; reviewability, revisability 25–6, 193, 208

communicative literacy 371–2

communities and conventions 79

community co-membership 192

comprehension: defined 344–6; discourse comprehension 297–8

computational tools 74–5

computers *see* technology-mediated environments

conceptual change 177–8, 227

conceptual pacts 38

Conrad, F. G. *et al.* 204

Construction-Integration model (CI) of reading comprehension 8, 9, 168–9, 297, 377

Constructionist model of reading comprehension 8, 9, 11

content-source integration (CSI) model 144, 148

context collapse 210

conversation 284–6; and aging 258–9; in online technologies 51–4; *see also* language processing in conversation

conversation analysis (CA) 27–8, 54, 70–1, 76, 77, 99–105; adjacency pairs 28–30, 37, 43; applied uses 103–4; data gathering 100; data sessions 101; embodied interaction 88, 101–2, 103–4; epistemics 104; gesture and gaze 74, 87, 101–2, *102*, 112–13, 198–9, 269, 270; mixed methods research 102, 103; organization of sequences 28–30; quantification 32–3, 104–5; transcription 100–2; turn-taking 30–2, 49–50, 100, 103, 203; use 99–100

conversation and interactive discourse 22; communicative constraints 24–6; nature of conversation 23–7; participant roles 26–7; conclusion 54–5

conversation as collaboration 33–5; common ground 35–6, 37, 38, 44, 45; grounding 36–8, 50

conversation: cognitive processes 39; interactive alignment 39–41, 43; prediction-by-simulation 41–2; whither alignment? 42–3

conversation: current and future directions 48; multiparty interaction 49–51; neurocognitive correlates of communicative interaction 48–9; online technologies 51–4

conversational coordination 43–4; constraint-based models 45–6; integrative challenges 47; other cognitive constraints 46–7; perspective adjustment 44–5

conversational maxims 75

Cook, A. E. 128–9, 182, 183

cooperative principle 75, 76

Cooren, F. 75

Copeland, D. E. 252

Cornelissen, J. P. *et al.* 74, 87

corpora 31, 42, 100, 117, 118–20, 121, 393–4

cotemporality 25, 193

Coulthard, M. 322

count algorithms 119

CR (Collaborative Reasoning) 326–7

critical discourse analysis (CDA) 78

CRKM (Cognitive Reconstruction of Knowledge Model) 307

Crossley, S. A. *et al.* 119–20, 379

Crouch, C. H. *et al.* 330

CSI *see* content-source integration (CSI) model

Csikszentmihalyi, M. 380

D-ISC (Discrepancy-Induced Source Comprehension) 148

Dale, R. *et al.* 43

Danescu-Niculescu-Mizil, C. *et al.* 53

Davies, Mark 119

Davis, M. H. 282

De Fatima Oliveira, M. 90

De Pereyra, G. *et al.* 148

declarations 75

"deep" semantic tools 120–1

deeper comprehension 9–10

default mode network (DMN) 256

Dehghani, M. *et al.* 120

Derix, J. *et al.* 285–6

dialogism 371

Dickinson, D. K. 323

Diehl, D. 84–5

DiMaggio, P. 80

DiMicco, J. M. *et al.* 208

Disciplined Reading and Learning Research Laboratory (DRLRL) 15

discourse and institutions *see* institutional contexts; institutional contexts: encounters between traditions; institutional discourse

discourse and social action 71, *72*, 75–6; communication and cognition 76–7; communities and conventions 79; conversation analysis (CA) 77; critical discourse analysis (CDA) 78; discursive psychology 78; interacting with/through computers 78; interactive alignment and egocentric processing 77; workplace studies 78–9

discourse comprehension 297–8

discourse processing 248–50

discourse processing through the adult lifespan 247–8; aging, resource allocation, and engagement 255–7; change and stability 248–61; cognitive aging 248; conversation 258–9; discourse processing 248–50; effects of discourse processing on aging 261; effects of knowledge on discourse processing 253–5; memory and comprehension of discourse content 250; in new ecologies 259–61; understanding situations from discourse 250–2; use of discourse context in understanding 253

discourse production and comprehension 70, 71, *72*, 73, 76; computational tools 74–5; embodied cognition 74; situation models 73

discourse relations 121–2

399

discourse updating 167–8; Construction-
Integration model (CI) 168–9; contexts of
updating 180–4; integration, validation,
and updating 182–4; memory access
181–2; multiple levels of representation
168; relationship to basic memory processes
169–70; revision of established memories
through learning from text 175–80; situation
model updating during comprehension 170–4;
structure building 169; conclusion 184
Discrepancy-Induced Source Comprehension
(D-ISC) 148
discursive psychology 78
Ditto, P. H. 306
diversity 25, 28, 54, 393
D'Mello, S. 380
DMN (default mode network) 256
documents model framework (DMF) 143, 145,
146, 353, 354
Doherty, G. M. 79
Dole, J. A. 307
dorsal language comprehension stream 270
DRLRL (Disciplined Reading and Learning
Research Laboratory) 15
Duhaylongsod, L. 332
Duke, N. K. 153
Dumas, G. *et al.* 286
Dunham, P. J. 52

Eagly, A. H. *et al.* 301–2
Eastin, M. S. *et al.* 150
Ecker, U. K. H. *et al.* 176
editability 208
Edlund, J. 31
education 395
Edwards, K. 300
egocentric processing 77
Elaboration Likelihood Model (ELM) 142
electrocorticography (ECoG) 285–6
electroencephalography (EEG) 129, 271, 277, 286
electrophysiological and electromagnetic methods
129, 133–5, 285–6
email 52
embodied cognition 74
embodied language effects 274–5
embodied turn 88, 101–2, 103–4
embodiment 274, 275; sensemaking, and
institutions 86, 88
emotions 15–16
epistemic vigilance 184, 348, 355
epistemics 104
Ericsson, K. A. 12–13
ERP *see* ERP experiments; evoked response
potentials
ERP experiments 129, 133–4, 182
Eseth-Alkalai, Y. 149
Eshghi, A. 50

EST *see* event segmentation theory
ethnomethodology 27, 76
evaluation 298
Evans, R. 224
event horizon model 171, 172
event-indexing model of reading comprehension
8, 9, 272–3
event model of processing *see* surface form level
of processing
event-related potentials (ERP) *see* ERP
experiments
event segmentation theory (EST) 170–1, 172,
272, 273
evoked response potentials (ERP) 129, 271
evolving discourse processes 1–2
experimental psycholinguistics 70
experimental semiotics 79
expert–laypeople communication 222–4; division
of cognitive labor 224; establishing common
ground 231–2; establishing common ground
on technical concepts 235–6; expertise 224;
experts' cognitive frameworks 227–8; experts'
communication with laypeople 226; experts
defined 224–6; fallacies of adaptation 236;
frames of reference and politeness rules
236–7; hampering of expert knowledge
233–4; laypeople *vs.* novices 226; laypeople's
cognitive frameworks 228–30; psychology
of reciprocal understanding 230–4; research
240–1; specialized terminology 234–5; trust
and power 237–40; conclusions 240–1
eye-mind hypothesis 126
eye tracking 112–13, 126–8; and beliefs 300;
dual user eye-tracking 198–9, 201–2; and EEG
129; mobile eye-tracking systems 198, 201–2;
phrase-level measures 127; scan paths 128;
and text production 379; use of search engines
151; validation effects 182, 184; word-level
measures 126–7

face 237
face-to-face interaction 76
Faigley, L. 371
Fairhurst, G. T. 82
false beliefs 14
Fay, N. *et al.* 51
Fazio, L. K. *et al.* 178–9
Ferreira, V. S. 46
Ferretti, T. R. *et al.* 182
fictional character identification 282
Fiedler, K. 15–16
file drawer problem 309
Filik, R. 184
Fitzgerald, D. 329
Flower and Hayes model of writing *365*, 365–6,
368, 369, 370, 371, 376–7
Flower, L. S. *see* Flower and Hayes model of writing

fMRI (functional magnetic resonance imaging) 131–2, 180, 273, 278, 280, 283, 284, 285, 287
Fox Tree, J. F. *et al.* 52
frame analysis 76, 84
frames 84–5, 86
frames of reference 230–1; *see also* expert–laypeople communication
framing and institutional change 87–8
Frank, C. K. *et al.* 280
Fraundorf, S. H. *et al.* 257
Friesen, J. P. *et al.* 305
front-end processes 349–50, 354
Fusaroli, R. 43
Fussell, S. R. 231

Galantucci, B. 79
Garfinkel, H. 27, 76
Garrod, S. 39–40, 41–2, 43, 47, 49, 50, 77, 79
gaze 102, *102*, 112–13, 198–9, 201–2
gender 104, 280
Gergle, D. *et al. 196*
Gernsbacher, M. A. 171, 272
Gerrig, R. J. 46, 47, 178, 179, 278
gesture 74, 86–7, 101–2, 199, 269, 270
Gibbs, R. 87
Gilbert, D. T. *et al.* 176
Gilbert, E. 211
Giles, H. *et al.* 40
gist-based processing 248, 250
Glenberg, A.M. *et al.* 134
Global Integrated Scenario-Based Assessment (GISA) 15
goal-directed reading 344–5, 351–2, 392
Goffman, E. 26, 27, 76, 84, 85, 87
Goldman, S. 148, 238
Goldman, S. R. *et al.* 10, 146
Goodwin, M. H. 331
Gottlieb, E. 147, 149
Graesser, A. C. *et al.* 15, 90, 303
Graham, S. 368, 375
Grant, D. 88
Green, M. C. 179, 180, 308
Green, S. *et al.* 81
Grevet, C. 211
Grice, H. P. 75, 76
Griffin, T. D. 296–7, 299–300, 302
grounding 36–8, 50, 76, 84, 192
grounding in technologically mediated settings 193–4, 202; features of the task 194–5; features of the technology 195–6, *196*; task by technology interactions 196, 197
Grundmann, R. 225
Gylfe, P. *et al.* 88

Hallett, T. 82
Hamm, V. P. 256
Hancock, J. T. 52

handwriting analyses 379
Hanna, J. E. *et al.* 45–6
haptic feedback 199–200, *200*, *201*
Hasher, L. 256
HathiTrust Digital Library 117–19
Hauk, O. *et al.* 274
Hayes, J. *et al.* 304–5
Hayes, J. R. 233; *see also* Flower and Hayes model of writing
HCRC Map Task corpus 42
Healey, P. G. T. 50
Healy, A. F. 376
Heldner, M. 31
Heller, V. 331
Hendriks, F. *et al.* 239
Herbert, M. 375
Heritage, John *et al.* 102, 104
Heuristic-Systematic Model (HSM) 142
Hills, T. T. 121
Hinds, P. J. 233
Hoffman, E. T. A. 278
Horton, W. S. 46, 47, 259
Horvitz, E. 203
Hoskyn, M. 367
Howe, C. 327
Howell, K.L. 299
Hsiao, L. 324–5
HSM (Heuristic-Systematic Model) 142
Hsu, C. *et al.* 278, 279, 280–1
human–computer interaction 78
Hutchinson, S. 134
Hynd, C. R. 303
hyperscanning 49

Iding, M. K. *et al.* 150
illocutionary utterances 75
IM *see* instant messaging
inconsistency paradigm 126, 127
indirect speech acts 75, 76
inferences 345, 350, 354
inferential model of communication 76–7
information: mental representation 297–8, 299, 301–2; processing 297, 391–2
instant messaging (IM) 52, 205
institutional contexts 69–73; discourse and social action 70–1, *72*, 75–9; discourse production and comprehension 70, 71, *72*, 73–5, 76; institutional discourse 70, 71, *72*, 79–85; social change 69–70, 85, 89–90; conclusions 89–90
institutional contexts: encounters between traditions 85; bodily gestures and institutionalizing communication 86–7; embodiment, sensemaking, and institutions 86, 88; framing and institutional change 87–8; organizational storytelling 88–9
institutional discourse 70, 71, *72*, 79–80; discourse and institutional frames 84–5;

401

Index

discourse and institutional logics 83–4; discourse as constitutive of institutions 81–3; performative approaches 80–1; representational approaches 80; sensemaking and institutions 83
interaction order 76
interactive alignment 39–41, 43, 77
interdisciplinary research 90, 303, 395–6
Internet *see* sourcing in digital contexts; technology-mediated environments
Interpersonal Reactivity Index (IRI) 282
interpersonal synergies 43
Isaacs, E. A. *et al.* 205, 232, 240
Isberner, M.-B. 183

Jacovina, M. E. *et al.* 308
Jang, G. *et al.* 284, 285
Jefferson, G. 27, 77, 100–1
Jeffrey, G. C. 367
Jiang, J. *et al.* 49
Johnson, F. *et al.* 151
Johnson, H. M. 175–6
Johnson, M. 74
Johnson, M. K. *et al.* 144
Jones, C. *et al.* 80
Jucks, R. 235
Juel, C. *et al.* 374

Kalish, M. L. *et al.* 229
Kambe, G. *et al.* 129
Kammerer, Y. *et al.* 148, 157
Kardash, C. M. 299
Kellogg, R. T. 366
Kelter, S. 39, 109–10
Kemper, S. 367
Kendeou, P. *et al.* 14, 174, 306
Keysar, B. *et al.* 44–5, 46, 77, 240
keystroke analyses 379, 380
Kintsch, W. 12–13, 168–9, 181, 297
Kitcher, P. 224
Knobloch-Westerwick, S. *et al.* 152
Knoeferle, P. *et al.* 272
knowledge: acquisition 13–14; activation 346; and beliefs 296; of discourse processing 253–5; encapsulation 227; misconceived 14; mutual 37, 76, 77; partitioning 229; revision 13, 14; and writing 380–1
knowledge-based inferences 345, 354
Knowledge Revision Components (KReC) Framework 306–7
Kothiyal, A. *et al.* 329
Krauss, R. M. 231
Kraut, R. E. *et al.* 193
Krawietz, S. A. *et al.* 256–7
Krych, M. A. 36
Kuiper, E. *et al.* 153
Kuklinski, J. H. 304
Kunda, Z. 302

Küpers, W. *et al.* 88
Kurby, C. A. *et al.* 171, 172, 251, 259, 274, 354

Lakoff, G. 74
landscape model of reading comprehension 8, 9
language processing in conversation 109–10; experimental manipulations 111; eye-gaze measures of real-time comprehension 112–13; referential communication tasks *110*, 110–11, 112, 231–2, 258–9; challenges and promise for the future 113
Latent Dirichlet Allocation 121
Latent Semantic Analysis (LSA) 74, 120–1
laypeople's theories *see* expert–laypeople communication
Lea, R. B. 11
Leatherbarrow, M. 175
lecture/recitation 319–20, 322–3
Lee, C.-C. 53–4
Lehne, M. *et al.* 278
Leonardi, P. M. 207, 208
Leu, D. J. *et al.* 143
Lev-Ari , S. 240
Levelt, W. J. M. 39, 109–10
Levinson, S. 31, 70, 76, 237
lexical alignment 236
Liberman, M. 118
Lilienfeld, S. O. *et al.* 295
linguistic co-presence 192
Linguistic Data Consortium 119, 393
Linguistic Inquiry and Word Count (LIWC) 74, 119
linguistics and writing 378–9
Litt, E. 210
Liu, X. *et al.* 260
locutionary utterances 75
Lodge, M. 300
Loewenstein, J. *et al.* 80
Long, D. L. 11
long-term memory (LTM) 170, 171–2, 297
long-term working memories (LT-WM) 170, 172
Lord, C. G. *et al.* 306
Lotan, R. A. 327
Louwerse, M. 134
LSA *see* Latent Semantic Analysis

Ma, S. *et al.* 324, 327
McCrudden, M. T. *et al.* 147–8
McCutcheon, D. *et al.* 367
McElhone, D. 331
McFarland, D. A. 84–5
McNamara, D. S. 10, 13, 345, 365, 376, 379
McNeill, David 87
McNerney, M. W. *et al.* 15
McPherson, C. M. 82
MacWhinney, Brian 119
Madden, C. J. 174

Index

Magliano, J. *et al.* 10, 251
Magliano, J. P. *et al.* 345, 349–50, 365
magnetic resonance imaging (MRI) 286
magnetoencephalography (MEG) 133, 134, 197, 286
Maier, J. 149, 302
Maitlis, S. 83
Maïza, O. *et al.* 286–7
Majid, A. 33
mapping 171
Marsh, E. B. 254, 255, 256
Marsh, E. J. *et al.* 178, 179
Marshall, C. R. 35, 46
Martin, J. *et al.* 88
Marton, M. 271
Marwick, A. E. 53, 210
Mason, L. *et al.* 154–5
maxim of relevance 76–7, 284
Mayer, R. C. *et al.* 238, 239
Mayer, S. J. 325
MD-TRACE *see* Multiple-Document Task-based Relevance Assessment and Content Extraction
media choice 204
MEG *see* magnetoencephalography
Mehan, H. 322
MEM (multiple-entry modular memory system framework) 144
memory: access 181–2; and comprehension of discourse content 250; long-term memory (LTM) 170, 171–2, 297; working memory (WM) 12–13, 169–70, 172, 366–8
memory-based account 46–7
memory-based text processing 170
mental models 14, 73, 345–6, 350, 352–5; *see also* surface form level of processing
mental representation of information 297–8, 299, 301–2
mentalizing *see* theory of mind (ToM)
MEPs (motor-evoked potentials) 134
metacognition 391
metaphors 74
methodological approaches 393–4
Metzger M. J. *et al.* 151
Michaels, S. 329, 331
Miller, L. M. S. *et al.* 253
Mills, G. 43
mind-wandering 256–7, 284
misconceived knowledge 14
mixed methods research 102, 103
mobility 193–4
mobility cues 201
modal model 376
modalities 349–50
mode choice and mode switching 203–7
the Modern Reader 343–4, 346–7; comprehension defined 344–6; content devices 348–9; content producers 348; modalities 349–50; text

accessibility 347; using multiple texts in the moment 350–1; summary of implications 351
the Modern Reader: implications on comprehension and future research: implications for coherent mental models 352–5; implications for goal-directed reading 351–2; implications for validation 355; important research questions 355–6; conclusion 356–7
Montague, P. R. *et al.* 286
Moore, J. D. 42
Morek, M. 331
Morrow, D. G. *et al.* 254
Mortimer, E. 330
motor-evoked potentials (MEPs) 134
MRI (magnetic resonance imaging) 286
multidisciplinary research 2, 3, 90, 303, 395
multimodal communication 74, 197–203
multiparty interaction in conversation 49–51
Multiple-Document Task-based Relevance Assessment and Content Extraction (MD-TRACE) 143–4, 145, 146
multiple-entry modular memory system framework (MEM) 144
Munro, G. D. 305, 306
Murdock, J. *et al.* 121
Murphy, K. *et al.* 324, 331–2
Mutlu, B. *et al.* 202, *203*
mutual knowledge 37, 76, 77; *see also* common ground
Myers, J. L. 181

Nakashima, R. *et al.* 228
Nardi, B. A. *et al.* 205
narratives 84, 307–8
National Assessment of Educational Progress (NAEP) 364
natural language processing (NLP) 378–9; surface-level tools and databases 118–20
naturalistic texts 15
neuroaesthetics 283
neurobiology of language and discourse 269–71
neurocognitive correlates of communicative interaction 48–9
neuroimaging 131–3, 286–7
neuroscientific methods 131, 394–5; electrophysiological and electromagnetic methods 129, 133–5, 285–6; neuroimaging 131–3, 286–7
new literacies approach to writing 372–3
Newtson task 251
Nijhof, A. D. 283
NLP *see* natural language processing
Noh, S. R. 252
Nokes, J. *et al.* 154
Nozari, N. *et al.* 135
Nyhan, B. *et al.* 14, 304, 306

403

Index

Oakley, I. *et al.* 200
Obama, B. 172–3
O'Brien, E. J. *et al.* 14, 125–6, 128–9, 167, 174, 182, 183, 306
Ocasio, W. 83–4
O'Connor, C. *et al.* 324, 331
Ohlsson, S. 302
online measures of text processing 125, 297; eye tracking paradigm 126–8; as function of belief 299; probe reaction time paradigms 128–9; self-paced reading time paradigm 125–6; future directions: combining different methods 129
online technologies *see* technology-mediated environments
ontological categories 14
O'Reilly, T. 13
organizational storytelling 88–9
Orr, J. E. 88

Paideia Seminar 324
Papacharissi, Z. 90
paratextual information 279
Pascual-Marqui, R. D. 134
Patson, N. D. 182–3
Paus, E. 235
Peer Instruction (PI) 330
Perfetti, C. *et al.* 8, 353
performative utterances 75
Perin, D. 368
perlocutionary utterances 75
persistence 208
perspective adjustment 44–5
PET *see* positron emission tomography
Petty, R. E. *et al.* 142
Philips, S. U. 328–9
Philosophy for Children 324, 328, 331
physical co-presence 25, 192, 193
PI (Peer Instruction) 330
Pickering, M. J. 39–40, 41–2, 43, 47, 49, 50, 77
"piggyback prototyping" 211
Plato 296
politeness theory 237
Pomerantz, Anita 104
positron emission tomography (PET) 131, 132
Prasad, M. *et al.* 14
prediction-by-simulation 41–2
predictive processing 271–2
Prentice, D. A. 178
Price, J. M. 257
principle of optimal design 35–6
privileged information 233–4
probe reaction time paradigms 128–9
Purohit, H.*et al.* 53
Putnam, L. L. 82

quantification 32–3, 104–5
Quinn, R. 75–6, 83

Radvansky, G. A. *et al.* 172, 252
Ransdell, S. *et al.* 367–8
Rapp, D. N. *et al.* 16, 174, 176, 179
Ravasi, D. 86
reader response 282–4
reading and writing 373; correlations 374; writing improving reading 375–6
reading comprehension 344–6; complexity: cluster approach 11–13; comprehension defined 344–6; goal-directed reading 344–5, 351–2, 392; implications of complexity 14–16; mental models 345–6; nature of reading comprehension 7–8; passive to strategic processes 10–11, 381; prior knowledge: integral component 13–14, 381; self-explanation 375; theory 8–10; validation against relevant world knowledge 346; conclusions 16–17
reading disabilities: cluster approach 12
reading goals 344–5, 351–2, 392
Reading Inventory and Scholastic Evaluation (RISE) 15
reading time 15, 125–9, 171, 173–4, 181, 183, 251–2, 271, 299, 308
recipient design 36, 50
reciprocal understanding 230–1
referential communication tasks 37, *110*, 110–12, 231–2, 258–9
Regan, A. *et al.* 152
Reifler, J. 14
Reitter, D. 42
relevance 76–7, 284–5
repetitive transcranial magnetic stimulation (rTMS) 133, 134
research methods: big data approaches 117–22; conversation analysis (CA) 99–105; interdisciplinary research 90, 303, 395–6; language processing in conversation 109–13; mixed methods research 102, 103; multidisciplinary research 2, 3, 90, 303, 395; neuroscientific methods 131–5, 394–5; online measures of text processing 125–9, 297, 299
resonance model of reading comprehension 8, 9, 11, 47
reviewability 25–6, 193, 208
revisability 25–6, 193, 208
revision of established memories through learning from text 175; conceptual change 177–8; continued influence of misinformation 175–6; misinformation and belief change through narrative texts 178–80
Reznitskaya, A. 331
Richter, T. 149, 183, 302, 308
Rijkers, R. M. J. P. 227
Rikers, R. *et al.* 227
Rinck, M. *et al.* 127

RISE (Reading Inventory and Scholastic
Evaluation) 15
Risemberg, R. 369
Ritter, A. *et al.* 52
robotics 202–3, *203*
Ross, L. D. *et al.* 175
Rouet, J. F. *et al.* 143–4, 147
routinization 228
rTMS *see* repetitive transcranial magnetic
stimulation
Rubin, D. L. 332

Sabatini, J. *et al.* 15
Sacks, H. *et al.* 27, 31, 32, 36, 49–50, 77, 100
Sahami, A. *et al.* 200
Saito, D. N. *et al.* 286
Salas, C. R. 300, 302
Salmerón, L. *et al.* 152, 158
Sanford, A. J. 257
Sauder, M. 82
Scardamalia, M. 369
Schaefer, E. F. 37
Scharrer, L. *et al.* 240
Schegloff, E. A. 27, 30, 33, 50, 77
Schmälzle, R. *et al.* 285
Schmidt, H. G. 227
Schneiberg, M. 80
Schober, M. F. 50, 111
Scissors, L. E. *et al.* 205–6
Scott, P. 330
Searle, J. 75
segmentation 272–3, 297
Seifert, C. M. 175–6
self-efficacy 369
self-paced reading time paradigm 125–6
self-regulation 368–9, 392
semantic processing 120–1, 271
sensemaking 83, 86, 88
sequentiality 25, 193
Sewell, W. F. 84
Sfard, A. 328
Shake, M. C. 253
Shanahan, T. 374
Sharma, A. 88
shifting 171, 272
Short, J. *et al.* 195
Silbert, L. J. *et al.* 132, 285
Simon, H. A. 227
Simple View of Reading (SVR) 12
simultaneity 25, 193
Sinatra, G. M. 307
Sinclair, J. M. 322
Singer, M. *et al.* 346
situation model construction: dmPFC 273–4
situation model level of processing 249–50, 297
situation model updating during comprehension
170; constructing and shifting among

discourse structures 170–1; detecting discourse
inconsistency and situational updating 172–4;
structure building and memory updating 171–2
situation models 9–10, 73
sLORETA 134
Slusher, M. P. 304
small-group discussion 321–2, 326–7
Smallwood, J. *et al.* 284
Smith, E. E. 300
SMS text messaging 52
SNSs (social network sites) 207–8
social action *see* discourse and social action
social change 69–70, 85, 89–90
social cognitive model of writing 369
social computing technologies 209
social interaction 76
social media 53, 89–90, 120, 204, 207, 209, 210,
390, 394
social network sites (SNSs) 207–8
social networking 51–4
socio-cognitive theories 371
sourcing in digital contexts 135, 152–3; design
of web pages 151; digital reading as social
activity 151–2; particular challenges 149–50;
search engine delivery 151; web page authors'
expertise and intention 150
sourcing in discourse comprehension 141–2;
assessment of sourcing skills 155–7;
correlational evidence 146–7; developmental
roots 145; individual and contextual factors
147–9; sourcing in digital contexts 149–53;
sourcing interventions 153–5; students'
sourcing 145–6; theoretical frameworks 142–5;
future directions 157–9
sourcing interventions 153; elementary
school 153; later school years 154;
post-secondary education 154–5; what
works for whom? 155
sourcing skills: assessment 155; attention to
source information 155–6; source evaluation
156, 355; use of source information 156–7
spatial cues 200, 201
speech act theory 75
speech recognition 270, 394
Speer, N. K. *et al.* 273, 274
Sperber, D. *et al.* 76–7, 184, 348
Spiegelhalder, K. *et al.* 285, 286
Spieler, D. H. 259
Stadtler, M. *et al.* 144, 148, 154, 157
Stafura, J. 8
Stainthorp, R. 367
Staub, A. *et al.* 182
Stehr, N. 225
Stephens, G. J. *et al.* 48–9, 285
Stigliani, I. 86
Stine-Morrow, E. A. L. 252, 253
Stivers, T. 33

Index

stories and transportation 179–80, 278, 282, 283, 307–8
Strømsø, H. I. *et al.* 146, 147, 156
Stroop paradigm 183
structure building 8–9, 169, 170, 172, 272
style matching 40
Sullivan, M. E. *et al.* 227
surface form level of processing 118–20, 248–9
surface structure of text 297
SVR (Simple View of Reading) 12
Swanson, H. L. 367
Swett, K. *et al.* 277
Switchboard corpus 42
syntactic prediction 271–2
Szaflarski, J. P. *et al.* 286
Szirtes, J. 271

TAACO software 119
Taber, C. S. *et al.* 300
TACIT software 120, 121
tactile feedback 199–200, *200, 201*
talk move 331
tangibility 193
Tannen, D. 87
Taylor, J. R. 75
tDCS *see* transcranial direct-current stimulation
team mental models 73
technical text 226, 234–6, 392–3
technology-mediated environments 78, 191–2, 390–1, 394; accessibility of texts 347; content devices 348–9; content modalities 349–50; content producers 348; conversation 51–4; current trends and issues 197–211; fundamentals of successful communication 192–7; gaze and eye tracking 198–9, 201–2; gesture 199; grounding in technologically mediated settings 193–7, 202; human–computer interaction 78; keystroke analyses 379, 380; mobility and spatial cues 200–1; mode choice and mode switching 203–7; multimodality and mobility 74, 197–203; new audience forms 209–11; robotics 202–3, *203*; social and network-based affordances 207–9; tactile and haptic feedback 199–200, *200, 201*; task by technology interactions 196–7; summary and future directions 211–12; *see also* sourcing in digital contexts
terror management theory 304
text-based information products 346–7
text comprehension *see* reading comprehension
text processing, memory-based 170
text production *see* writing as a discourse process
text relevance 344–5
textbase level of processing 249, 297
textoids 15, 391
texts 277–9; accessibility 347; content producers 348

theories, defined 84
theory of mind (ToM) 48, 275–6, *276*
Think-Pair-Share (TPS) 329–30
Thom-Santelli, J. *et al.* 208
Thornton, P. H. *et al.* 83–4
Tierney, R. J. 374
topic models 121
Torreira, F. 31
trait empathy 282
transcranial direct-current stimulation (tDCS) 133, 135
transcranial magnetic stimulation (TMS) 133, 134
transcription 100–2
transportation 179–80, 278, 282, 283, 307–8
Treem, J. W. 207, 208
trust in expert–laypeople communication 237–8; trust as requirement as well as outcome 238–9; who is trustworthy? 239–40
turn-taking 30–2, 49–50, 100, 103, 203
Turvey, M. T. 377
Tylén, K. 43

Umanath, S. 254, 255, 256
Underwood, G. 367
Unsworth, N. *et al.* 368
updating *see* discourse updating

validation 182–4, 346, 355, 391–2
Van Berkum, J. J. A. *et al.* 271
Van den Broek, P. *et al.* 11
Van der Schoot, M. *et al.* 127
Van Dijk, T. A. 70
Van Hell, J. G. *et al.* 379–80
ventral language comprehension stream 270
video-mediated communication (VMC) 194, 195
visibility 25, 193, 208
visual word form area (VWFA) 270
visual word recognition 270
visual world paradigm 44
Vosniadou, S. 227
Voss, J. F. *et al.* 301
Vygotsky, L. S. 371

Wang, S. *et al.* 127
Wardlow, L. 46
Wardlow-Lane, L. 46
Warren, T. 182–3
Wehbe, L. *et al.* 287
Westerwick, A. 158
whole-class discussion 320–1, 323–5
Wiley, J. *et al.* 154
Wilkes, A. L. 175
Wilkes-Gibbs, D. 37–8, 50
Wilkinson, I. A. *et al.* 328, 334–5
Willems, R. M. 283
Williams, T. J. *et al.* 305
Wilson, D. 76–7

Windsor, L. *et al.* 74
Wineburg, S. 147
Wineburg, S. S. 146
Wolfe, M. B. *et al.* 299, 300, 302, 305, 345
working memory (WM) 12–13, 169–70; long-term working memories (LT-WM) 170, 172; in writing 366–8
workplace studies 78–9
world knowledge 346, 381
worldview 309
Worline, M. C. 75–6, 83
writing as a discourse process 362–3; affective states of writers 380; cognitive approaches to writing research 370–1; current state of writing in education 363–4; current state of writing research 364; handwriting analyses 379; impact of modal model 376–7; keystroke analyses 379, 380; knowledge and writing 380–1; linguistics and writing 378–9; models of writing *365*, 365–70; new literacies approach 372–3; problem-solving in writing 369–70; relations between reading and writing 373–6; self-regulation in writing 368–9; social cognitive model 369; sociocultural approaches to writing research 370, 371–2; temporal analyses 379–80; working memory in writing 366–8; writing defined 363; future directions 378–81; conclusion 381–2

Yarkoni, T. *et al.* 273, 274, 283
Yatani, K. *et al.* 200, *200, 201*
Yoon, S. O. 51, 112
Young, J. J. *et al.* 200

Zacks, J. M. *et al.* 171, 172, 251, 272, 273, 274
Zatorre, R. J. 283
Zeman, A. Z. J. *et al.* 277, 283
Zhang, S. 153
Zimmerman, B. J. 369
Zwaan, R. A. *et al.* 172, 174, 272, 274